INDIA'S
WAR

INDIA'S WAR

World War II and the Making of Modern South Asia

SRINATH RAGHAVAN

BASIC BOOKS

A Member of the Perseus Books Group
New York

A catalog record is available from the Library of Congress.
LCCN: 2016933273
ISBN: 978-0-465-03022-4 (hardcover)
ISBN: 978-0-465-09862-0 (e-book)

First published in 2016 by Allen Lane

Allen Lane is part of the Penguin Random House group of companies whose addresses can be found at global.penguinrandomhouse.com.

UK ISBN: 978-1-846-14541-4

10 9 8 7 6 5 4 3 2 1

For Sukanya Venkatachalam

Contents

CONTENTS

List of Figures

List of Maps

List of Tables

List of Illustrations

Acknowledgements

I should like to thank the staff at the following archives and libraries: National Archives of India; Nehru Memorial Museum & Library, New Delhi; The National Archives, Kew; British Library, London; Imperial War Museum, London; Liddell Hart Centre for Military Archives, King's College, London; School of Oriental and African Studies Library, London; University of Technology, Sydney; Van Pelt Library, University of Pennsylvania; and the Library of Congress, Washington D.C. My debt to the scholars upon whose work I have relied is recorded in the notes to this book. But I would like particularly to express my gratitude to the authors of the 25-volume Indian official history of the Second World War – an unfortunately neglected series of books that remains an indispensable mine of information.

In researching this book I had stellar assistance at various times from Sandeep Bhardwaj, Vipul Dutta, Sarah Khan and Swetha Murali. Several other friends and colleagues sent me materials that were difficult to access: Rakesh Ankit, Rohit Chandra, Alan Jeffreys, Madhav Khosla and Kaushik Roy. I am especially grateful to A. R. Venkatachalapathy and Heather Goodall for drawing my attention to sources of whose existence I was entirely unaware. Aditya Balasubramanian and Avinash Celestine not only shared their excellent, unpublished work on the economic history of the period but spent long hours discussing their ideas and mine.

I owe a huge debt to Pratap Bhanu Mehta and other colleagues at the Centre for Policy Research. They have not only encouraged my interest in the history of India's global engagements but have taught me fresh ways of thinking about the subject. It is a matter of deep regret that three remarkable senior colleagues – Ramaswami Iyer, K.

ACKNOWLEDGEMENTS

C. Sivaramakrishnan and B. G. Verghese – are no longer around to see this book. While writing this book, I was also affiliated with the India Institute at King's College, London. I am extremely grateful to Sunil Khilnani for his encouragement and support over the years.

Thanks are also due to Mahesh Rangarajan, Rudra Chaudhuri, Venu Madhav Govindu, Jahnavi Phalkey, Pallavi Raghavan and Pranay Sharma for indulging my interest in India's role in the Second World War. For opportunities to present the arguments of this book and receive useful feedback, I am grateful to: David Edgerton at the Sir Michael Howard Centre for the History of War, King's College, London; Devesh Kapur at the Center for Advanced Study of India, University of Pennsylvania; Karuna Mantena at the South Asia Studies Colloquium, Yale University.

The manuscript in draft was read by David Gilmour, Ramachandra Guha and Nandini Mehta. Their detailed and perceptive comments on substance and style immensely improved the book. The penultimate draft was read closely by Keshava Guha, and his suggestions were extremely useful in knocking the text into final shape. I am most grateful to all of them for taking the time out of their own projects to help me with this book.

My agent, Gill Coleridge, was instrumental in persuading me to embark on this work. Her tact, patience and advice have been indispensable during the course of writing it. Gill's colleague, Melanie Jackson, was very helpful in placing the book in North America. My thanks also go to Cara Jones of Rogers, Coleridge and White.

It was a huge privilege to work with my editors Simon Winder at Penguin Books and Lara Heimart at Basic Books. Their formidable knowledge of the Second World War helped me frame India's experience in a wide context and their suggestions were incredibly useful in thinking through and presenting my arguments. Meru Gokhale at Penguin Random House India came to the book in its later stages but with a burst of enthusiasm.

Richard Duguid was marvellously efficient in keeping the various parts of the book together. Charlotte Ridings did a superb job as copy-editor. Octavia Lamb was untiring in her research for the pictures. Jeff Edwards drew the maps. The index was compiled by Dave Cradduck. For their varied contributions to the making of this book, I am also grateful to Emma Bal and Maria Bedford at Penguin, and Leah Stecher and Alia Massoud at Basic.

As ever, this book could not have been written without the love and support of my family. My wife, Pritha, has been magnificently supportive of my obsession with yet another war. Our children, Kavya and Dhruv, have been cheerful despite my long absences. My parents, Geetha and K. S. Raghavan, provided much needed support at home during a crucial phase in the writing of this book. My mother-in-law, Sukanya Venkatachalam, has been a quiet source of encouragement for nearly fifteen years now. None of my books would have been written but for her solidarity, and this one is no exception. This book is for her – as a token of my gratitude and affection.

Prologue

A viceregal broadcast on a Sunday evening was rather unusual. Yet at 8.30 p.m. on 3 September 1939, the All India Radio stood by for a message from Lord Linlithgow. Speaking from his summer eyrie in Simla, the viceroy tersely announced that His Majesty's Government was at war with Germany – and so was India. 'I am confident', he solemnly declared, 'that India will make her contribution on the side of human freedom as against the rule of force.'[1] That was all. In taking this decision, the viceroy had consulted neither his Executive Council, nor the Central Legislative Assembly, nor yet any Indian leader. To him it was a foregone conclusion. And so began India's Second World War.

When the war ended six years later, India stood among the victors. Indian soldiers had fought in a stunning range of places: Hong Kong and Singapore; Malaya and Burma; Iraq, Iran and Syria; North and East Africa; Sicily and mainland Italy. The Indian army had raised, trained and deployed some 2.5 million men. Even at the time, this was recognized as the largest volunteer army in history. Nearly 90,000 of these men were killed or maimed. Many more millions of Indians were pulled into the vortex of the Second World War – as industrial, agricultural and military labour. India's material and financial contribution to the war was equally significant. India emerged as a major military-industrial and logistical base for Allied operations in South-East Asia and the Middle East, and the country was also among the largest wartime creditors of Britain. Such extraordinary economic mobilization was made possible only by imposing terrible privations on a population that barely skirted the edge of subsistence. The human toll on the Indian home front must be counted in millions.

And yet, the story of India's war is only dimly remembered.

Just over five decades after the end of the war, I joined the Officers Training Academy of the Indian army. Soon after our arrival, we were corralled in the drill square to be divided into training companies. As I awaited my turn, nervously sweltering in the late summer sun, the Subedar Major tipped his regimental cane towards me and said, 'Meiktila.' It took me a moment to realize that 'Meiktila' was the name of the company to which I was assigned. And it took me much longer to understand the significance of the name. The names of the other companies sounded equally strange. 'Jessami' rang no bell, while I knew 'Kohima' only as the capital of the Indian state of Nagaland. Back in our barracks, I found that my fellow cadets were quite as bemused. Those who had friends training in the Indian Military Academy trotted out names of some companies there: Keren and Cassino, Alamein and Sangro – almost all were unfamiliar to our ears.

I wrote off my ignorance to my training in the sciences and my unfamiliarity with anything more than high school history. And soon, I figured out that these were names of places where the Indian army had fought famous battles during the Second World War. Yet, even instructors in military history at the Academy were unable to tell me much more than that. Indeed, my instructors seemed to proceed on the premise that 'Indian' military history began on 25 October 1947 – with the outbreak of the First Kashmir War.

On completion of my training, I was commissioned into an infantry regiment: the Rajputana Rifles. In his welcome speech, the Colonel of the Regiment loftily reminded us that we were privileged to join the oldest and most decorated rifle regiment of the Indian army. On my first visit to the regimental officers' mess, I was struck to note from the banners that thirteen battalions of my regiment had fought in almost every theatre of the Second World War – from Malaya to Italy, including in such seemingly exotic countries as Eritrea and Tunisia. Skimming through the soporific regimental history, I picked up some basic details about which battalion fought where and who won the Victoria Cross. I was hooked. But subalterns in the Indian army rarely have the leisure to read history – never mind trying to write it. In the event, it was my interest in Indian military history that prompted me to abandon the seductive rigours of the army for the sheltered groves of academia.

Over the years, I have come to take a more charitable view of my ignorance as a cadet. There are two large and apparently uncontrollable bodies of work that are germane to anyone interested in India's Second World War. On the one hand, there is the unceasing outpouring of books on the war itself. In most of these, India is rarely assigned more than a walk-on part. Some aspects of the war relating to India – especially the Burma campaign – have received more sustained treatment. But these tend to be insulated from the wider context of India's contribution to the war. On the other hand, there is a mountain of monographs on Indian history in the decade preceding 1947. Almost all of these, however, treat the Second World War as little more than mood music in the drama of India's advance towards independence and partition. The plot and the acts are by now wearily familiar: the resignation of the Congress ministries at the outbreak of war; the Cripps Mission and the Quit India movement of 1942; the Cabinet Mission of 1946; Independence with Partition in August 1947.

To be sure, there are some fine specialized studies that throw important light on particular aspects of Indian involvement in the war: military, economic or social.[2] Yet there is no comprehensive account of India's war. Two books come close. Johannes Voigt's *Indien im Zweiten Weltkrieg* was published in 1978 – an English translation appeared almost a decade later. A model of scholarly thoroughness, the book offered an as yet unsurpassed account of Indian politics and military policy during the war. And in *Forgotten Armies*, Chris Bayly and Tim Harper presented a brilliantly fascinating social history of the war in the 'great crescent' arching from Bengal to Singapore. Yet the book is not – and does not claim to be – a history of India during the Second World War. More recently, we have had Yasmin Khan's *The Raj at War*, which offers an engaging 'people's history' of India's participation in the war. As with many studies of the 'home front' in various wars, however, the exclusion of the strategic and military dimensions results in a partial and puzzling picture. Still missing is the single volume that presents a rounded narrative, bringing in the manifold dimensions of the war.

The book in your hands attempts to provide such an integrated account. In so doing, I am interested not just in telling the story of India's war but in explaining the course of events and exploring their consequences. The narrative that follows has five intertwined strands.

First, there is the strategic dimension of the war. It is tempting to see India merely as an appendage of the British Empire. Didn't the viceroy unilaterally take India into the war? Of course, India was a cog in the imperial machinery. But India was also a significant power in its own right, with the Raj having a sub-imperial system of its own. India's sphere of influence and interference stretched from Hong Kong and Singapore to Malaya and Burma, Tibet and Xinjiang, Afghanistan and southern Iran, Iraq and the Persian Gulf states, Aden and East Africa. This 'empire of the Raj' – to use Robert Blyth's resonant phrase – was as variegated as the British Empire itself. Some of these territories had been directly governed by India, while others were dependencies where India's formal and informal writ continued to run. Others still were nominally independent states in which India discerned vital interests or which were seen as useful geopolitical 'buffers'.[3] Even before the war broke out in 1939, the Raj stood ready to defend its own empire.

In many ways, British India exercised greater freedom in its external relations than the Dominions of Australia, Canada and South Africa. As the viceroy of India observed in 1929, 'Though India, unlike the Self-Governing Dominions, does not formally enjoy an independent position in the sphere of foreign policy, she is possibly more continuously and practically concerned with foreign policy than any of them.'[4] India's peculiar situation as a colonial entity but also a regional power was recognized in the international system. India was a signatory to the Treaty of Versailles after the Great War. And it was a founding-member of the League of Nations – the only non-self-governing entity in the League.[5]

This brings us to the second theme running through the book: the international dimension of India's war. The Raj's security commitments remained manageable so long as East Asia was quiescent and no European power could credibly threaten an invasion of the Middle East. The belying of these expectations led to an enormous expansion of India's commitment during the war. India's war was strongly shaped by the actions and choices of several major powers apart from Britain: the United States and Japan, China and Germany, Italy and the Soviet Union.

The strategic and international contexts were closely related to a third thread in the story: domestic politics. In the two decades before the onset of the war, the British government had, in response to the rising tide of nationalism, been compelled to undertake political reforms. These were designed to increase the involvement of Indians in the administration, and apparently progress India towards self-government within the British Empire. Yet the British wished neither to hand the Indians any serious power nor to hasten self-government. As war loomed, the politics of India directly impinged on strategic matters. The viceroy's decision to join the war without consulting the Indians would considerably complicate politics during the war. And the widening political divide would also lead other great powers to intervene in the affairs of India.

Politics also had an impact on the fourth strand of our narrative: the economic and social dimensions of the war. The billowing demands on India would entail ever greater extraction of societal resources. Yet the wartime mobilization of India was contingent on securing popular support and participation, which in turn depended on co-opting Indian political parties and leaders. At the same time, the demands of war led the Raj to rely heavily on traditionally marginalized social groups, and so gave them greater political voice.

The story of the 'home front' can be fully understood only by relating it to the fifth concern threading through this book: the war front. After all, it was the demands of the war front that led to the wide-ranging mobilization and the ensuing transformations at home. Understanding why the military effort required such resources leads us to the terrain of military history. In focusing on the various theatres in which the Indian troops fought, I do not aim at providing a blow-by-blow – or hillock-by-hillock – account of battles. The really interesting story is the transformation of the Indian army, step by painful step, from a backward constabulary outfit into an effective and adaptable fighting force. In this story, such seemingly mundane matters as training and logistics, health and morale loom large.

Wars are ultimately waged, opposed and supported, won and lost by individuals. In the domain of 'high' politics and strategy there is a stellar cast of characters: Gandhi and Churchill, Nehru and Roosevelt, Jinnah and Linlithgow, Bose and Chiang Kai-shek, Wavell and Mountbatten, Auchinleck and Slim. But perspectives from 'below' are rarer. In particular, the voice of the Indian soldier has been rather difficult to recover. We have only slivers of letters exchanged between soldiers and their families, captured in censors' reports and other official documents. Few soldiers wrote down or orally recorded their memories. Nevertheless, I have tried to understand what the war meant for those who fought it on the fronts and those who supported it from home.

Finally, this book is not just about what India did for the war. I also look at what the war did to India. The South Asia of today is in very many ways the product of India's Second World War. The emergence of Pakistan and its protracted rivalry with India; the establishment of a constitutional democracy in India and the dominance of the military in Pakistan; the adoption of planning for economic development; the role of the state in the provision of social goods; the popular movements in the region fired by ideas of economic and social rights – none of these can be understood without accounting for the impact of the war. In the absence of a full reckoning with the war our understanding of modern South Asia remains deeply deficient. The Second World War is the one black hole in our historical imagination that exercises a deep gravitational pull on the region even today. By restoring the war to the centre-stage, this book challenges and revises our understanding of the making of modern South Asia.

The story of India's war is also central to understanding the country's rise on the world stage. India is now acknowledged to be an emerging global power – one that could buttress an open and liberal international order. Yet the rise of India was first foretold during the Second World War, when a desperately poor country mobilized to an astonishing degree and simultaneously fought for its own freedom and that of the world. As we ponder India's emerging role on a global canvas, the story of its Second World War provides the crucial starting point.

I

Politics of War

As the train pulled into New Delhi station, a large crowd surged towards it chanting 'We do not want any understanding.' Travelling in the train was Mohandas K. Gandhi, the unquestioned – if also uncrowned – leader of the Indian National Congress. Over the previous two decades, Gandhi had transformed the Congress from a party of the urban educated classes to a formidably organized nationalist outfit. In successive waves of countrywide mobilizations, the Congress had under Gandhi's leadership emerged as the foremost adversary of the British Raj. Now, in early September 1939, Gandhi was travelling to Simla at the invitation of the viceroy, Lord Linlithgow.

The viceroy's unilateral declaration of war had roiled political India right from the start. The Congress and its supporters were peeved at the manner in which their country was being dragged into a war without so much as a by-your-leave. The leadership of the party was pulled in different directions by equally pressing concerns. On one side was their opposition to Nazi aggression as well as the desire to stand by the Western democracies. On the other was the imperative of refusing to co-operate with the British Empire unless it was willing to pay the right political price to India. Throughout the war, the Congress never managed to reconcile these competing imperatives. In practice, its political stance on the war kept oscillating between one position and another.

From the outset, Linlithgow was determined to give no quarter to the Congress. In his three and a half years as viceroy, he had made little attempt to establish a working relationship with any Congressman. This was partly a matter of personality. Exceedingly tall and

7

well built, with a stern countenance caused by childhood polio, Linlithgow cut a distant and forbidding figure. The Indian nationalists mocked him as the 'Great Mogul'. In fact, there was a lighter side to the avid sportsman and hunter who targeted monkeys with a catapult from the bay windows of his bedroom in Simla. In his official dealings, however, Linlithgow was deliberate, ponderous and unimaginative.

The viceroy's attitude towards the nationalists also stemmed from the political context of the times. Linlithgow had been sent to India after the passage of the Government of India Act of 1935. This constitutional measure aimed at establishing in India a federation of the directly-ruled provinces and the indirectly-ruled princely states. Under the Act, Indian political parties could hold power only in the provinces – and not in the central government. Presented as a milestone on India's road towards eventual self-governance, the Act sought in fact to leash the most powerful of these parties, the Congress, firmly in the kennel of provincial politics.

The Congress had initially been divided on the question of making a bid for office in the provinces. Many of Gandhi's senior lieutenants wanted to seize the opportunities opened up by the Act of 1935. Others felt that embracing provincial power would spell the end of the Congress as an all-India force. In the event, the Congress contested the elections of 1936–37 and emerged victorious in eight of the eleven provinces. This stunning political outcome portended problems for the British when the shadow of war began lengthening over Europe. Among their principal concerns was the Congress's attitude towards India's strategic obligations. Throughout the inter-war years, nationalists of all stripes had been vociferous in calling for a reduction in India's overseas military commitments – if only because it would lead to a concomitant drop in the Raj's massive military expenditure.

In narrowly constitutional terms, Linlithgow was well within his rights in taking India to war. Yet the move was also spurred by strategic considerations, and especially the security of British India's own expansive zone of influence. The various parts of this sub-imperial system, extending from Hong Kong to East Africa, were tied to the Raj in different ways. Many of these places had initially been conquered by the Indian army and continued to be policed by Indian men. Indian capital and entrepreneurs were important players in the local economies of Singapore and Kuala Lumpur, Rangoon and Nairobi, among other commercial centres. The infrastructure and enterprises in large parts of South-East Asia and East Africa had been built and worked by migrant labour from India. Between 1834 and 1937, around 30 million Indians had left their homes to toil in other parts of the Raj's empire. The administrative set-up in many of these places mirrored that of British India. Architecture and ideas too radiated out of the sub-imperial centre.[1]

In the years after the First World War, this system had begun to fray. The Great Depression and the unravelling of pre-war economic globalization led to a backlash against Indian capital and labour. Indeed, the rising nationalism in many of these parts was directed as much against the Indians as the British.[2] Yet one form of dependence on India persisted right through: military security. During the 1914–18 war, the Indian army's main effort was focused on the Middle East and East Africa, and India's military involvement in the erstwhile Ottoman territories continued in the post-war period. The economic depression and the resultant tightening of financial belts led India periodically to review its military commitments. Yet, in the event of another global war, it seemed a foregone conclusion that India should secure its spheres of influence. Indeed, even before the British government had formally declared war in September 1939, India had despatched nearly 10,000 troops to Egypt, Aden, Singapore, Kenya and Iraq.[3]

At the same time, the viceroy was aware that his executive fiat would be resented by the Congress party. In response to the despatch of troops in August 1939, the Congress had already accused the government of undermining the Central Assembly and defying public opinion. The Congress provincial governments were also instructed to desist from war preparations. So, Linlithgow harboured no illusions about the response that his declaration would elicit from the Congress. However, he was confident of being able to secure its co-operation on his own terms.

This belief stemmed from his reading of the Congress party as a set of provincial interests penned in by the central leadership. The centrifugal forces in the party had apparently been accentuated by the assumption of office. The provincial leaders wanted to govern, while the central leadership struggled to maintain the façade of opposition. A month before the outbreak of war, Linlithgow had asserted that 'the theory that Congress Ministries were in office not to govern the country but to wreck the constitution from inside . . . [has been] given an unostentatious burial'.[4]

To be sure, there were differences in the attitudes of the Congress ministries and the party leadership. Nor was the viceroy's assumption about the willingness of these provincial governments to co-operate with the war effort wholly mistaken. Even so, Linlithgow underestimated the political machinery at the disposal of the Congress leadership as well as its willingness to crack the whip. Then again, the viceroy and his officials were inclined to think that the eclipse of the Congress ministries might be a blessing in disguise. The bureaucracy could then lead the war effort untrammelled by pesky Indian politicians.

In the event, the Congress's stance on the war was shaped not so much by tensions between central and provincial units as by the conflicting impulses of its top leadership and by the wider course of the world war.

On 4 September 1939, Gandhi arrived in Simla. Despite the demands from the rank-and-file of the party to desist from co-operation, Gandhi struck a conciliatory note with Linlithgow. His sympathies were with England and France: 'I could not contemplate without being stirred to the very depth the destruction of London.' Gandhi broke down as he pictured the destruction of the Houses of Parliament and Westminster Abbey. He insisted that he was not thinking of 'India's deliverance'. This would come in due course, but hopefully not through the ruination of England. The unyielding apostle of non-violence observed that 'it almost seems as if Herr Hitler knows no God but brute force' and that Indians would have collectively to decide 'what part India is to play in this terrible drama'.[5]

Over four intense days, starting on 10 September, the Congress Working Committee debated its stance on the war. The spectrum of opinion stretched from complete support to total opposition. Gandhi stood alone in advocating unconditional but non-violent support for the Raj. The country, he explained, was 'not ready for any kind of resistance'. British repression would be of the fiercest variety. Besides, no foreign power would be easier to deal with than the British. In any case, the war was bound to destroy imperialism. All things considered, 'the best policy would be to help and not hinder'.[6]

Among those who dissented from this view was Chakravarti Rajagopalachari, Gandhi's senior lieutenant and the premier of Madras. A perceptive and pragmatic politician, Rajagopalachari seldom shied away from speaking his mind – an attribute that had led Gandhi to call Rajagopalachari his 'conscience keeper'. Unlike his leader, Rajagopalachari was ready to provide 'wholehearted cooperation in the fight against gangsterism personified', even if it breached the norm of non-violence. The Congress, he felt, should demand that Britain announce a timetable for granting Dominion status to India and induct some Congressmen into the central government.

At the opposite end of the spectrum was Subhas Chandra Bose, who was specially invited to attend the meeting. The forty-two-year-old Bengali had lately metamorphosed from being the *enfant terrible* of the Congress to a charismatic leader capable of stirring the masses with his doughty opposition to the Raj and his ringing oratory. Unlike other senior Congressmen, Bose was fascinated by all things martial. At the annual Congress meeting of 1928 in Calcutta, Bose drilled a squad of volunteers, himself dressed in an ill-fitting khaki uniform complete with boots, breeches and a cane. Even as Gandhi looked askance at these military pretentions, Bose began making his own mark as a radical. After an obligatory spell in His Majesty's Prison, Bose made his way to Europe in 1933. There he met several statesmen including Italy's Benito Mussolini, who took a liking to the Indian.

During this period, Bose also began to spell out his own political philosophy, calling for a synthesis between fascism and communism. In these vacuous ideas, some of his colleagues in the Congress discerned a troubling fascination with authoritarian rule. Nevertheless, when Bose returned to India, Gandhi orchestrated his election as Congress President in 1938. Within a year, however, Gandhi was working to prevent Bose from standing for another term in office. Bose refused to bow to Gandhi's wishes and surprisingly managed to win the election. Gandhi and his followers worked thereafter to render Bose's position in the party utterly untenable, and he had no choice but to resign and form a new radical group within the Congress known as the 'Forward Bloc'. After the outbreak of war, Gandhi requested Bose to join the deliberations on the future course of the party. Bose argued against any co-operation and urged the Congress to launch a mass movement to wrest India's independence from Britain.[7]

In this welter of conflicting opinions, one voice proved particularly influential. Jawaharlal Nehru had for long been acknowledged as the most elegant communicator in the Congress. Born in 1889 into a family of well-off Kashmiri Brahmans, the Harrow- and Cambridge-educated Nehru had been pulled into the ruck of nationalist politics under the influence of Gandhi. Nehru also stood out among his colleagues for his ability to place India's nationalist struggle in a longer historical perspective and a wider international context. During the latter part of the 1920s, Nehru came in contact with anti-colonial activists from across the globe and began regarding himself as a socialist – albeit one closer to William Morris than Karl Marx. During the next decade, he staunchly opposed European fascism and Japanese militarism, and advocated a tough stance on a range of international crises: Manchuria and Abyssinia, Spain and Czechoslovakia. Over the same period, he also emerged as leading figure in the Congress – his growing ideological differences with Gandhi being subordinated to their personal affection.

On the eve of war, Nehru had been travelling in China at the invitation of Chiang Kai-shek, the Nationalist leader resisting the Japanese. No sooner had Linlithgow announced India's participation in the war than Nehru had flown back to India via Burma. He had no doubt in his mind that the Nazi aggression had to be opposed. At the same time, he did not trust the British to do the right thing by India. So, he felt that the Congress must test the waters before making any further moves.

Following Nehru's lead, the resolution of the Working Committee condemned the Nazi attack on Poland. Yet it also insisted that India could not participate in a war for freedom and democracy when that freedom had been denied to it. If Britain was truly fighting for democracy then it should logically forsake its own empire and introduce full democracy in India. If the war was to defend the status quo then India would have no truck with it. The operative paragraph of the resolution called on the British government to 'declare in unequivocal terms what their war aims are in regard to democracy and imperialism . . . in particular, how these aims are going to apply to India and to be given effect to in the present'.[8]

By tossing the ball back into the British court, the resolution sought to bridge a fundamental divide in the Working Committee. Those in favour of co-operation could hope that Britain would respond creatively; those opposed to co-operation could hope that a rejection by the Raj would then sway the Congress in their direction. Gandhi commended the resolution, despite its apparent dilution of the commitment to non-violence. 'Will Great Britain have an unwilling India dragged into the war', he asked, 'or a willing ally co-operating with her in the prosecution of a defence of true democracy?'[9]

Prior to the Working Committee's meeting, Linlithgow believed that the Congress provincial ministries were 'ready and even anxious to remain in office and to give reasonable cooperation'.[10] Indeed, some Congressmen in office were even willing to give the lead to British officials. Rajagopalachari, for instance, was eager to detain all German nationals on the outbreak of hostilities and seize their bank balances. When the governor of Madras disagreed, he muttered that the English wanted 'to wage war according to High Court rules'.[11] Even as the viceroy hoped for the Congress's co-operation, he was clear that it would have to be on terms of his choosing. He informed the secretary of state for India, Lord Zetland, that the government should pull up the drawbridge and prepare for the resignation of Congress ministries. In fact, it was better to face this situation early 'rather than at a later stage of the War when we may be engaged in an extensive campaign in the Middle East'.[12] The Congress's demand thus fell on stony ground.

Linlithgow, however, knew that simply digging in his heels would not suffice. From the outset, he sought to encourage countervailing forces to the Congress. If the Congress played for high stakes, the viceroy even contemplated convening an all-party conference, 'at which the hollowness of the Congress claim to speak for India would very soon be exposed'.[13] Though he did not act on this idea, Linlith-gow did invite to Delhi a stream of non-Congress political leaders.

The viceroy drew his staunchest support from the traditional, conservative elite of India: the princes. A week before hostilities commenced, several princes, led by the nizam of Hyderabad, the nawab of Rampur and the maharajas of Travancore and Kapurthala, offered their services to the king emperor.[14] As in the First World War, the princes discerned an opportunity both to demonstrate their loyalty to the crown and to advance their own political interests. The latter were particularly salient in the context of 1939. Although the princes had accepted the idea of federation, they had grown con-cerned about their powers being usurped by the federal authority. Their disenchantment deepened when they realized that the feder-ation would not bring any financial gain, and eventually the outbreak of Congress-inspired mass movements in the princely states set the rulers firmly against both the idea of federation and the Congress. By contributing to the war effort, the princes hoped somehow to extri-cate themselves from this tight political corner.

No sooner had the war begun than they were handed a reprieve. 'The federal offer', Zetland observed, 'is now in cold storage.'[15] He was confident, however, that 'the States will not fall short in the pre-sent war on the notable contribution made by them in the last War to the Allied cause'.[16] The princes were as good as their word. They opened their coffers to the viceroy's War Purpose Fund. By mid-October 1939, the jam sahib of Nawanagar had pledged to contribute one-tenth of his state's annual revenue to war expenses. The nizam of Hyderabad contributed £100,000, and promised to meet the cost of maintaining a regiment of state cavalry and a battalion of state infan-try with the British forces in India. Six months into the war, the princes had already contributed £377,000 in donations and pledged a further £225,000 for the War Purpose Fund. By the end of the war, the princes had given grants of cash to the tune of £13.5 million. In addition, they provided war materials worth £5 million: Hyderabad alone paid for three squadrons of military aircraft. In addition, over 300,000 men enlisted from the princely states to serve in the war.[17]

In political terms, though, the states could help only to a limited extent in neutralizing the Congress. With the federation in abeyance, the princes could not actively help the viceroy puncture the Congress's pretensions to hegemony. Of greater significance on this score was an array of smaller political outfits that sought to challenge the dominance of the Congress. The viceroy's announcement on 11 September of the suspension of federation created the requisite room for manoeuvre for the leaders of these parties.

Prominent among these was the leader of the so-called depressed classes – the 'untouchables' at the bottom of the Indian caste system – B. R. Ambedkar. A brilliantly incisive thinker and sharp polemicist, Ambedkar had been a prominent opponent of Gandhi for several years. He held that the Congress was a curious combination of the exploiters and the exploited. The party might be necessary to achieve political freedom, but its upper-caste leadership was hardly a force for social reconstruction. Ambedkar was also opposed to the federal scheme on the grounds that it was a misshapen plan that would simultaneously impede the attainment of independence and democracy.

At the outbreak of war, Ambedkar issued a statement condemning the German attack on Poland, but also criticizing the latter for its treatment of Jews. He disagreed, however, that Britain's danger was India's opportunity: India needed no new masters. He maintained that it was unfair that India should have no say in the declaration of war, nonetheless, India should remain within the British Commonwealth and aim for equal partnership. Ambedkar asked the government to prepare the Indians for the defence of their country and urged it to raise a regiment of soldiers from the depressed classes. He also asked Britain to assure India of its status within the Empire at the end of the war.[18]

The viceroy regarded Ambedkar as an 'impressive figure' and over the course of a long meeting sought his views on the political situation. Ambedkar said that the depressed classes were suffering grievously at the hands of the Congress. There was a concerted attempt to drive his community into the Congress camp. He also assured the viceroy that he was '100 per cent opposed to self-government at the Centre and would resist it in any possible way'.[19] Linlithgow was even more impressed when Ambedkar signed a joint statement with seven other leaders, including prominent liberals such as Sir Chimanlal Setalvad, declaring that the Congress's claim to represent all Indians was fascist and that it would spell the end of Indian democracy.

Among the signatories was a man of vastly different ideological and political persuasion from Ambedkar: Vinayak Damodar Savarkar. Savarkar's political career had begun almost three decades previously, when as a student in London he was involved with anti-colonial revolutionary groups. Arrested and sentenced to two life-terms in 1910, Savarkar spent eleven years in the infamous cellular jail of the Andaman Islands, designed on the same lines as Bentham's 'Panopticon'. During these years, he came into his own as an ideologue of Hindu nationalism and superiority. Released on the promise of renouncing revolutionary activity, Savarkar soon emerged as a prominent leader of a Hindu nationalist and chauvinist outfit, the Hindu Mahasabha, and an outspoken critic of the avowedly secular Congress.

Savarkar saw the war in Europe through the lens of realpolitik. None of the belligerent powers, he held, were driven by 'any moral or human principle' such as freedom, democracy or justice. Yet he was clear that the Mahasabha must continue with its policy of 'responsive co-operation'. They should reiterate this stance and demand more recruitment of Hindus in the army. Savarkar preferred to watch the Congress's moves before issuing any statement on the war. Senior colleagues such as M. R. Jayakar, however, felt that time was of the essence and that Savarkar must register his presence with the viceroy.[20]

A few weeks on, Savarkar received an invitation for a meeting from Linlithgow. The tall, stooping marquess found his guest 'a not very attractive type of little man', but interesting all the same. The former revolutionary observed that the interests of the Hindus and the British were now closely bound together: 'the old antagonism was no longer necessary'. He urged the importance of military training for the Hindus and increased recruitment in the army, adding that the Hindu Mahasabha wanted an 'unambiguous undertaking of Dominion Status at the end of the War'. As an immediate step, he sought the introduction of responsible and popular government at the centre. Savarkar also challenged the Congress's claim 'to represent anything but themselves' and requested the viceroy 'not to inflate Congress too much'.[21]

Interestingly, the Hindu nationalist's stance was mirrored by that of the Muslim League led by Mohammed Ali Jinnah. A successful lawyer and a shrewd politician, Jinnah had been prominent in the Congress even before Gandhi came on the stage – not least owing to his efforts to forge a political compromise between the Hindus and the Muslims during the First World War. Following the advent of Gandhian mass nationalism, however, Jinnah found his brand of elite politics increasingly marginal to the programme and direction of the Congress. In consequence, he became more active in leading the Muslim League.

The elections of 1936–37 had come as a rude shock to Jinnah and the League. While the Congress failed to win in the Punjab, Bengal and Sindh – all provinces where Muslims were a majority – the League too fared poorly in them. All three provinces came under the control of strong regional players, who at best paid token obeisance to the League and Jinnah. Further, despite having an electoral system where seats were reserved for Muslim candidates, to be elected by Muslim voters alone, the League's performance in the provinces where Muslims were a minority was lacklustre. By contrast, the Congress swept the Hindu electorate and made some dents in the Muslim seats as well. In short, the outcome of the elections threatened to consign the Muslim League to political oblivion.

After the elections, Jinnah had turned decisively against the federation plan, although the League's poor showing had left him with a feeble hand. By April 1939, Zetland was 'almost certain' that the Muslims would refuse to work the federal scheme. The viceroy had a more realistic appreciation of the Muslim League's predicament. He was confident that Jinnah and his associates would accept the federation if it was 'imposed on them' and did 'not expect any serious trouble' from the League.[22] As the war approached, though, Linlithgow executed a swift volte-face. Given his desire either to secure the Congress's unconditional co-operation or to cut it down to size, the viceroy turned to Jinnah and the Muslim League.

On 4 September Linlithgow met Jinnah and informed him that the federal provision of the 1935 Act stood suspended until the end of hostilities. Jinnah was doubly delighted. For starters, the viceroy had openly invited him on a par with Gandhi. Indeed, Jinnah was 'wonderstruck why all of a sudden I was promoted and given a place side by side with Mr. Gandhi'.[23] What was more, the government had thrown the Muslim League a vital political lifeline. For the suspension of the federation gave Jinnah another opportunity to return to the high table of politics.

The Congress resolution of 14 September allowed Jinnah to make his first moves. Four days later, the Muslim League adopted its own resolution asking the British government to abandon the federation and 'to review and revise the entire problem of India's future constitution *de novo*'. It also sought a guarantee that no plan of constitutional reform would be decided without the League's approval. Condemning Nazi aggression, the resolution stated that to secure the co-operation of Muslims the government must ensure justice was done to them.

This slotted in smoothly with the viceroy's desire to undercut the Congress's claims to speak for all of India.[24] Meeting Jinnah, Linlithgow generously acknowledged his 'very valuable help by standing firm against Congress claims'. Had Jinnah 'supported the Congress in their demand for a declaration and confronted me with a joint demand, the strain upon me and upon His Majesty's Government would have been very great indeed.'[25] Jinnah, in turn, thanked the viceroy 'with much graciousness for what I [Linlithgow] had done to assist him keep his party together and expressed gratitude for this'.[26]

Meanwhile, the viceroy had also managed to secure the co-operation of the key Muslim-majority provinces: Punjab, which was the principal reservoir for recruitment to the Indian army; and Bengal, which housed a significant chunk of Indian industry. Neither of these provinces was under Jinnah's thumb. In fact, the League's resolution had been carefully worded to avoid a breach with those who wanted to support the war effort. Fazlul Haq, the premier of Bengal, wrote to Linlithgow that the Congress's stance was 'absolutely unjustified and baseless'.[27] The premier of Punjab, Sikandar Hayat Khan, assured the viceroy of his total support. He called for a 'Defence Liaison Group' composed of Indians, whether or not the Congress was prepared to co-operate.[28] His colleague in the Punjab Unionist Party, Chhotu Ram, insisted that the declaration of British war aims ought not to be 'a prerequisite of our cooperation and support'.[29] Subsequently, the Punjab Legislative Assembly adopted a resolution tabled by the Unionist Party offering unconditional support to Britain.

The viceroy's confabulations with this diverse array of Indian leaders not only bolstered his position against the Congress but also shaped the decision-making in London. In his exchanges with Whitehall, Linlithgow firmly argued against caving in to any demand from the Congress. 'Nothing could be more foolish', he insisted, than 'to commit ourselves to a series of objectives which may at the moment appear reasonable, but which might as the war goes on call for very substantial revision.'[30] The furthest he was willing to go was to involve 'non-official' Indian leaders in a defence liaison committee with consultative functions.

The viceroy's views were considered by the war cabinet in London over three sittings. The first meeting, on 27 September, set the tone for all that followed. The cabinet stoutly opposed the viceroy's modest proposal. Providing war-related information to Indians and securing advice from them 'opened up dangerous possibilities'. In particular, 'it would be fatal to allow the Congress Party . . . to have a majority on the new body'. Instead of bringing in politicians, it may be more useful to have several advisory panels comprising industrialists and provincial notables. Such an arrangement would have the 'advantage of preventing too much attention from being directed to questions of Defence' – an area of policy that was and should remain exclusively under British control. As far as constitutional changes were concerned, the cabinet agreed that it was 'undesirable' to make any commitment. It was pointed out that 'it seemed unlikely that for many years there would be any diminution of the feud between Hindus and Moslems'. This, of itself, would be enough to prevent 'a sufficient basis of agreement'.[31]

This last observation was evidently made by the first lord of the Admiralty, Winston Churchill. Churchill's views on India and the beneficence of British rule were formed during his ten-month stint in the country as a subaltern in 1896, and they remained unchanged for the rest of his life. So strong were his feelings about India that, for much the 1930s, Churchill chained himself to the Conservative back-benches owing to his opposition to any political reform in India. An after-dinner joke of his was that Gandhi should be bound hand and foot at the gates of Delhi and trampled on by a huge elephant ridden by the viceroy.[32] In the war cabinet, though, Churchill was not wholly inflexible. It was at his suggestion that the idea of an advisory committee was conceded to India. Yet on matters of constitutional and political import, he would give no ground.

Churchill's advocacy in the cabinet at once drew support from and strengthened Linlithgow's stance. Zetland was anxious not to adopt so rigid a stance as to result in a complete break with the Congress. This, he told the cabinet, would lead to a 'difficult situation'. If the Congress ministries resigned, the provincial governors would 'face grave problems' in maintaining order. Churchill and Linlithgow demurred. The viceroy agreed with governors such as Erskine of Madras, who held that 'we should not enter into any bargain, for if Congress do go out it will be their funeral not ours'.[33]

The officials' intransigence towards the Congress was reinforced by a resolution of the All-India Congress Committee, adopted on 10 October. This resolution incorporated the previous one of 14 September and added that 'India must be declared an independent nation and present application must be given to their status to the largest extent possible.'[34] The qualifier at the end underlined the Congress's desire to leave ajar the door to co-operation. But New Delhi and London used the main demand to shut it in the party's face.

On 17 October 1939, the viceroy issued his long-awaited statement. Stressing differences among the Indian political parties, Linlithgow claimed that no precise definition of war aims – apart from resisting aggression – was possible. On India's future, he merely recited a litany of old promises. Significantly, he stressed that the terms of future constitutional advance would take into account the minorities' views and interests. It was 'unthinkable' to proceed without taking counsel of 'representatives of all parties and all interests'. The only concession held out by the viceroy was the establishment of a 'consultative group' for 'association of public opinion in India with the conduct of the war and with questions relating to war activities'.[35]

The Congress's response was predictably harsh. 'The Congress asked for bread', said Gandhi, 'and it has got a stone.' Nehru scathingly called the viceroy's statement 'a complete repudiation of all that India

stands for nationally and internationally . . . it has absolutely no relation to reality'.[36] Rajagopalachari, the champion of full co-operation,
felt that an excellent opportunity had been simply thrown away.
Bose, on the other hand, claimed that it was the strongest vindication
of his stance of opposition to the war effort.[37] On 22 October, the
Congress Working Committee adopted a resolution condemning the
viceregal statement as 'an unequivocal reiteration of the old imperial-
istic policy'. In these circumstances, the Congress could not possibly
give any support to Britain. The resolution called on all Congress
ministries to tender their resignations. At the same time, it cautioned
Congressmen against taking 'any hasty action in the shape of civil
disobedience, political strikes and the like'.[38]

The warning against precipitate popular action stemmed from the
Working Committee's concerns about radicals in their own camp.
Gandhi insisted that there was 'no question of civil disobedience for
there is no atmosphere for it'.[39] But this claim was contested from
several quarters within the baggy organization of the Congress.

Furthest to the left were the members of the Communist Party of
India (CPI). The CPI, noted the Intelligence Bureau in late 1939, 'has
no more than a few hundred members. But its influence is to be measured not so much by its size as by its ability to guide other groups and
organizations.'[40] This was certainly true of the party's objectives over
the previous four years. The Comintern's decision in mid-1935 to
form anti-fascist popular fronts had dramatically changed the context for communist parties all over the world. As usual, it was left to
the Communist Party of Great Britain to explain the new 'line' to
their Indian comrades. A note prepared by Ben Bradley and Rajni
Palme Dutt of the mother party – and ferried to India by the young
historian Victor Kiernan – advocated a united front in the struggle
for national independence under the Congress's umbrella.[41]

Following Stalin's pact with Hitler in August 1939, the CPI was
ordered to re-calibrate its stance. The party's initial statement urged
the Congress to show the lead by resigning from the ministries and
commencing mass action. 'A mass struggle at such a time', noted the
party's organ, 'cannot but open up new possibilities for us to win the
final battle for independence.'[42] The CPI also circulated secret, 'pro-
lix instructions', calling on its cells and front organizations to mix

anti-war propaganda with demands for a 25 per cent increase in wages for labour and for remission of rent for the peasantry.[43] In these circumstances, the Congress leadership was anxious not to allow the radicals to bring matters to the boil. They need not have worried much. The radicals' inability to pull together considerably curbed their clout.

Some of their differences were ideological – as for instance between the CPI and the League of Radical Congressmen led by the maverick Marxist, sometime international revolutionary and founder of the Mexican Communist Party, M. N. Roy.[44] As opposed to the CPI's new 'imperialist war' line, Roy persisted with an anti-fascist stance. 'So long as the war is against Hitlerism', he wrote, 'no matter whatever may be the motive of British Imperialism, we cannot have any objection to India participating in it. Indeed, it is the duty of all socialists and communists to help such a war.'[45] Naturally this did not go down well with the CPI.

Ideological conflicts were overlaid with past political ones. Only a few months before, the CPI had attacked Roy's call for alternative leadership in the Congress as 'ultra-leftist antics' and 'Inverted Rightism'. Roy initially agreed to work with the Forward Bloc, but later criticized Bose for his 'opportunism'. And the CPI condemned Bose for his 'blind negative anti-Rightism'.[46] Although the onset of war helped paper over some of these cracks, the splintered radical groups were unable to mount a serious challenge to the Congress's policy. Worse, the changing course of the war would compel the radicals to make major departures from their original positions.

As the Congress ministries prepared to step down, Lord Zetland drew the cabinet's attention to the unfavourable impression this would cause in neutral countries, especially the United States, as well as the propaganda opportunity it would create for Britain's enemies. To limit the damage, the cabinet clutched at a proposal floated by Sir Zafrullah Khan – law member of the viceroy's Executive Council – suggesting an increase in Indian representation on the Council. Zafrullah had argued that the three key portfolios of finance, home affairs and defence should be held by Indians who had significant experience of government service.[47]

The prime minister was sympathetic to the idea. Neville Chamberlain felt that it was quite natural for Indians to play a part in a war into which their country had been pulled without choice. A refusal to concede this desire might touch off a bitter conflict. He was clear, however, that the defence portfolio should remain with the commander-in-chief of India. While most cabinet members were open to this idea, Churchill was forceful in his opposition. He considered the proposal 'dangerous' because it might spur the Congress to demand more. Yet he was open to considering it – if the viceroy's supremacy remained unimpaired, if there were no dilution of British control over military and strategic matters, and if the British Parliament refrained for the duration of the war from making any changes to the constitutional position of India. The cabinet felt that the prime minister's suggestion met these criteria and decided to authorize the viceroy to commence negotiations. They soon realized, however, that neither the Congress nor the Muslim League was interested in such a proposal.[48]

Zetland remained anxious at the prospect of an impending collision with the Congress. He was unconvinced by the arguments floating around him: that India's heart was with Britain in the struggle against Germany; that the demands of war would bring prosperity to the Indian peasant and disincline him from joining any prolonged agitation; and that the edge of the Congress's opposition would be blunted. This picture, he believed, was 'unduly optimistic'. As the date of the Congress ministries' exit neared, Zetland was inclined to believe that the Congress would be prepared to co-operate, if Britain 'substantially' met its demands by promising independence immediately after the war, with the right to frame its own constitution via an elected constituent assembly. In the meantime, Indians should be encouraged into responsible participation in the conduct of the war. The cabinet shot down the proposal. It was felt that these conditions would impede the military conduct of war. Most importantly, the Muslim League would certainly oppose such a scheme.[49] In the event, the Congress ministries left office on 10 November 1939.

The League had welcomed the viceroy's statement of 17 October. Its Working Committee read the statement both as rejecting the Congress's claim to speak for all of India and as recognizing that 'the All-India Muslim League alone truly represents the Mussulmans of

India and can speak on their behalf'. Linlithgow had not gone quite as far, yet by making constitutional advance contingent on an agreement between Congress and the Muslims, he had effectively handed a veto to anyone who could claim to speak for all Muslims.[50]

The Congress was virulently opposed to conceding the League's claims: as a secular party it claimed to represent all religious communities. As Rajendra Prasad put it, if the Congress accepted the League's stance it would be 'denying its own past, falsifying its history, and betraying its future'.[51] In order to counter the League's claims and demands, the Congress elaborated its own idea of an elected constituent assembly to frame the constitution of an independent India. This was mooted by Nehru and adopted by the Congress in its resolutions.

Gandhi was initially sceptical. 'I reconciled myself to it', he quipped, 'because of my belief in his [Nehru's] superior knowledge of the technicalities of democracy.' Soon, however, he came to regard it as the only way to slice the Gordian knot of the communal problem and arrive at a 'just solution'. He called for a constituent assembly elected by 'unadulterated adult franchise' for both men and women – 'Illiteracy does not worry me' – including the existing system of separate Muslim electorates.[52] In the last week of November 1939, the Congress Working Committee published a resolution stating that the proposed constituent assembly would be elected on adult suffrage. Minorities would be represented by members elected by separate electorates and their rights in the constitution would be 'protected to their satisfaction'. Any details that could not be settled by negotiations would be submitted to arbitration.[53]

Meanwhile, in exchanges and meetings with Jinnah, Gandhi and Nehru sought to assure the Muslim League that the constituent assembly would be widely representative and would provide full protection for the rights and interests of all minorities. For a fleeting moment it seemed as though an agreement might be clinched. Linlithgow confided to Zetland that he had 'one or two rather anxious moments during the period when he [Jinnah], Jawaharlal and Gandhi were discussing the situation together'.[54] The viceroy needn't have worried. Chastened by the experience of the 1936–37 elections, Jinnah was clear that any representative mechanism, including a constituent assembly, that pigeon-holed the Muslims as a 'minority' would fail to secure their interests. Excoriating the proposed assembly as 'a packed body manoeuvred and managed by the Congress caucus', he called on Gandhi to apply himself seriously to the Hindu–Muslim problem.[55]

Jinnah also called on all Muslims to observe Friday, 22 December 'as the day of deliverance and thanksgiving as a mark of relief that the Congress Governments have at last ceased to function'.[56] He was joined by Ambedkar, who declared that he 'felt ashamed to have allowed him [Jinnah] to steal a march over me and rob me of the language and the sentiment which I, more than Mr. Jinnah, was entitled to use'.[57] The Justice Party in Madras also stood by Jinnah in marking the day. Its leader, E. V. Ramasamy 'Periyar', was opposed in equal measure to Brahmans, north Indians, the Hindi language and – to him the embodiment of all three – the Congress party. His party had come out in support of the war and contested the Congress claim to represent the minorities and stand for the unitary nation. 'I have no inclination to be troubled with India,' said a colleague of Naicker. 'I care for my own country – and that is Dravida Land.'[58] More interestingly, there were reports that Savarkar was soon to meet Jinnah. A broad anti-Congress front seemed to be coalescing. Gandhi himself congratulated Jinnah for 'lifting the Muslim League out of the communal rut and giving it a national character'.[59] He was prescient, if for the wrong reasons. At any rate, the political impasse precipitated by the war was amply clear.

Surveying the scene at the end of the year, Linlithgow observed that the 'political quarrel' had entered a new phase. Yet the 'tranquillity' across the country was 'remarkable'. There was 'no sign' of any move towards civil disobedience. The viceroy concluded on a note of satisfaction:

> In spite of the political crisis, India has not wavered in denunciation of the enemy in Europe, and has not failed to render all help needed in the prosecution of the war. The men required as recruits for the Army are forthcoming: assistance in money from Princes and other continues to be offered: a great extension of India's effort in the field of supply is proceeding apace.[60]

*

The new year got off to a splendid start. On 10 January 1940, the Orient Club of Bombay threw a lavish luncheon. As he rose to make a short speech, the towering guest of honour could see the waves of the Arabian Sea crashing on the beach. In his remarks Linlithgow sought to strike a conciliatory note. He began by expressing 'deep regret' at the suspension of the federal plan and went on to reiterate the British commitment to India's attainment of 'Dominion Status of Westminster variety'. The government was ready to reopen the federal scheme 'as soon as practicable after the war with the aid of Indian opinion'. Meanwhile, he was prepared to expand his Executive Council by including 'a small number of political leaders'. The political problem in India, he reminded his audience, was not susceptible of easy solution. There were the 'insistent claims of minorities' – especially the Muslims and the depressed classes – whose position had to be safeguarded. He was ready 'to consider any practical suggestion' and would 'spare no effort' to hasten India along the road to Dominion status.[61]

Indians in the audience may have been tempted to think that the viceroy had been softened by the setting. In fact, his remarks were premeditated. And they stemmed from wider strategic considerations.

The backcloth to the speech was provided by the Soviet Union's attack on Finland – underway since the end of November 1939. The war cabinet in London had been actively considering the possibility of launching with France a diversionary campaign in support of the Finns. At the same time, the British and French also discussed the option of an attack on the soft underbelly of the Soviet Union, including air strikes on the oilfields of Baku and the opening of a front in the Caucasus. Any of these moves would trigger a war with the Soviet Union – and hold grim implications for Afghanistan and India. It was important therefore to soothe Indian tempers and preclude any lurch towards civil disobedience.

From the war's outset, the cabinet had been alive to the possibility of a Russian threat to India. A Russian incursion into Afghanistan could have a deleterious impact on India's restive north-west frontier. The problem was that India had adopted 'a strictly defensive policy on the frontier even against the minor menace, i.e. an incursion by Afghan forces similar to that of 1919'.[62] A land invasion by the

Russians was deemed unlikely, but the possibility of 'long range air action' against targets in India could not be ruled out. In the event of any attack, no further reinforcements could be drawn for other fronts from India. On the contrary, there might be calls from India itself for land and air reinforcements.[63] These concerns were heightened by the onset of the Russo-Finnish war.

In this context, Zetland yet again pressed for a positive policy towards the Congress. In a memorandum to the cabinet on 31 January, he proposed granting India Dominion status and self-government. Further, he suggested that Indian parties should be encouraged to arrive at a constitutional settlement without British involvement. He also proposed an arrangement whereby Britain's defence and economic interests in India could be protected. Linlithgow, however, urged that 'we ought to go very slow'. He was not convinced that the Congress's shoulders were 'broad enough to carry the burden which we shall relinquish'. Further, the experience of recent months had shown that India's contribution to the war remained unimpaired. Finally, the viceroy felt that it was better to have a showdown with the Congress now rather than later. He preferred conflict to a compromise of little durability or utility to Britain.[64] Zetland pointedly disagreed. In a cabinet meeting on 2 February, he argued that there was 'no chance' of the viceroy's approach succeeding unless it was 'substantially modified'. If 'substantial progress' could be made in securing agreement with the Congress, then the party might resume office in the provinces. If not, the 'recurrence of civil disobedience must be anticipated'.[65]

The secretary of state's remarks set off a heated debate in the cabinet. Churchill said that similar problems were envisaged just before the Congress ministries had resigned, but the government had stood firmly by the viceroy. 'What had been the result?' he asked. 'India had enjoyed a period of perfect tranquillity.' Nor was he in favour of making any effort to promote unity between Hindus and Muslims. 'Such unity was, in fact, almost out of the realm of practical politics, while, if it were to be brought about, the immediate result would be that the united communities would join in showing us the door.' The Hindu–Muslim problem, Churchill added, was 'a bulwark of British rule in India'.

Sir Samuel Hoare, lord privy seal and a former secretary of state for India, contested Churchill's arguments. All available evidence suggested that a complete breach with the Congress would be 'a calamity'. Nehru and the 'extremists' in Congress would carry the day and the government would have to deal with a 'period of civil disobedience, if not of terrorism'. Was the cabinet prepared, he asked, 'to contemplate that possibility at a time when we might be involved in operations on the Western Front and with Russia?' If the viceroy's proposals were unacceptable to Indians, it would be much better to proceed as suggested by Zetland. 'Our position in the world', Hoare insisted, 'would be greatly strengthened if we were able to negotiate a treaty with Indian politicians.'

Eventually the prime minister intervened and said that the viceroy should be asked to begin preliminary talks with Gandhi – but at his own pace. If there was any progress, the cabinet could consider the next steps.

Gandhi was intrigued by the viceroy's Bombay speech. Ever the sharp lawyer, he felt that the Dominion status in terms of the Statute of Westminster was equivalent to independence. So, although he had reservations about the references to minorities, Gandhi wrote to the viceroy seeking clarification.[66] Unsurprisingly, nothing came of this and on 6 February, Gandhi announced that the negotiations had failed. 'The vital difference between the Congress demand and the Viceregal offer,' he said, 'consists in the fact that Viceroy's offer contemplates the final determination of India's destiny by the British Government, whereas the Congress contemplates the opposite.'[67]

Nehru too felt that the way ahead was unclear. While there was no question of compromising, the Congress had no appetite for a showdown either. Not expecting anything much to happen, he took to travelling on slow trains as a diversion and contemplated a trip to Switzerland to meet his daughter. 'There is no need to worry overmuch either about our personal affairs or national affairs', he wrote to a friend. In the run up to a Congress Working Committee meeting on 1 March 1940, Nehru prepared a draft resolution reaffirming that nothing short of independence – never mind Dominion status – and a constituent assembly was acceptable. He also mentioned exercising the option of restricted or mass civil disobedience, although this idea was dropped from the final text that he sent on to his colleagues.[68]

In subsequent discussions of the Working Committee, Nehru and Maulana Abul Kalam Azad – the prominent Muslim leader of the Congress who had taken over as party president in January 1940 – argued for an early, if not immediate, launch of some form of civil disobedience. Azad remonstrated with Gandhi that his attempt to restrain mass action was demoralizing party workers. Gandhi shrugged off such criticism. If civil disobedience was commenced, he insisted, '"disobedience" will remain and "civil" will disappear'. Given his abiding commitment to non-violence, Gandhi could not bring himself to contemplate launching such a movement.[69] Cracks in the Congress were evidently surfacing in this political cul-de-sac. This was obvious from Gandhi's speech at the Ramgarh session of Congress, where he stated that, 'Your General finds that you are not ready, that you are not real soldiers and that if we proceed on the lines suggested by you, we are bound to be defeated.'[70]

The radicals in the Congress, however, continued to press for a mass movement. In parallel to the Congress session in Ramgarh, Bose presided over an 'All-India Anti-Compromise Conference'. Bose charged the Congress leadership with simultaneously passing red-hot resolutions and issuing emollient statements towards the Raj. The latest Working Committee resolution, he argued, continued this approach. Declaring that 'our leaders are wobbling', he called on all leftists to come together to wage an uncompromising war against imperialism.[71]

The Communist Party of India also demanded an 'unconditional call to mass civil disobedience, national strikes, no-rent, no-tax campaigns to destroy the rule of robbers and war-mongers'.[72] The politburo issued a secret policy statement titled 'Proletarian Path', exhorting India to make 'revolutionary use of the war crisis to achieve her own independence'. Among other things, the CPI advocated a general labour strike with a countrywide 'no-rent and no-tax' action. To smash the Raj's machinery and to win over the rank-and-file of the army, the movement would have to develop into a 'nationwide armed insurrection'. As a first step, 150,000 textile workers of Bombay were persuaded to go on a forty-day strike. The Raj responded by arresting nearly five hundred Communist Party members, including the entire top leadership. The communists were forced to cool their heels in prison – until another twist in the global conflict turned them into supporters of India's war.

Far more concerning to the Congress was a resolution adopted by the Muslim League on 23 March 1940. This resolution was the outcome not only of thinking within the League, but also of viceregal prodding – for some time now, Linlithgow had been asking Jinnah to come up with 'a constructive policy'.[73] Merely stonewalling the Congress's call for a constituent assembly would not take the League very far. In February 1940, the League's Working Committee tasked a constitutional sub-committee with drafting a statement. Several options were considered before a text was prepared in time for the League's session at Lahore. The Lahore declaration called for the creation of 'Independent States' in the north-western and eastern zones of India where Muslims were a majority. These states would be 'autonomous and sovereign'.[74] The vagueness of the resolution and its contradictions were remarked upon at the time of its publication and subsequently.

Much ink has been spilt debating whether Jinnah actually wanted to partition India, or merely sought to use the demand for partition as a bargaining counter, and if so to what end. Strenuous efforts have been made to know the mind of a man who always kept his own counsel. Yet it is not clear if at this point Jinnah knew his own mind. The war had injected such uncertainties into Indian politics that none of the leading players could claim clarity of objectives as well as strategy. The only thing that he could have known at this stage was that he could expect British support during the war – support that he must leverage to the Muslim League's advantage. The only strategy he could deploy was to deny that the Muslims were a minority and insist that they were a separate 'nation' on a par with the Hindus.

These developments strengthened Linlithgow's position in the debates in London. He wrote to Zetland that the Congress Working Committee's latest resolution had stated its claims 'in a more extreme, fashion than hitherto employed and one which denies the possibility of treating Dominion Status as consistent with India's freedom or independence'. A settlement with the Congress, he claimed, 'would be unlikely materially to improve our contributions in terms of either men or of supply'. Besides, they had to consider the position of Muslims who would be 'submerge[d]' and of the princes who were to be 'steam-rolled' under the Congress's proposals. All this reinforced his earlier views: 'I am ... strongly in favour of taking no action, and of lying back.'[75] The viceroy revealingly added: 'I am not too keen to start talking about a period after which British rule will have ceased in India. I suspect that day is very remote and I feel the least we say about it in all probability the better.'[76] So much for all the unctuous assurances about progressing India towards self-rule.

On the League's resolution, Linlithgow feigned surprise. Jinnah, he wrote, may have put forward this scheme to 'dispose of the reproach that Muslims have no constructive scheme of their own'. He himself saw the statement as 'very largely in the nature of bargaining' and rife with inconsistencies. Yet the declaration had raised 'to a remarkable degree Jinnah's prestige' and cemented his claims to being the spokesman for all Muslims. More importantly, it had 'offset extreme Congress claims to independence' and its demands for a constituent assembly.[77] Linlithgow argued that he was personally not in favour of assuaging Jinnah to the extent of recognizing the claim for partition of India. But in view of the Congress's attitude, the League's demand should be given sympathetic consideration. In particular, a 'specific reference' should be made in Parliament – and it should be bluntly stated – that 'we cannot possibly ignore the views of 80 to 90 million Mussulmans in India'.[78]

Zetland continued to differ from the viceroy on policy towards the Congress. 'I cannot conceive', he told the cabinet, 'that a policy of "lying back" will serve us for very long, even if there should be no early resort to civil disobedience.' He urged the need for a 'constructive plan of action'. Such a plan should bridge the gap between the Congress's demands and those of the minorities and princes. Zetland suggested announcing that after the war an all-India body would be set up to prepare a constitution for India as a member of the British Commonwealth. This body must include minorities and the princely states and its composition must be determined by an agreement between the Indians themselves.[79]

The League's Lahore Resolution threw these discussions off kilter and Zetland conceded the need for further reflection before making any fresh move in India. On 12 April, the cabinet endorsed Linlithgow's assessments and decided that 'it would be inexpedient . . . to take any action which might be interpreted as a change of policy or a concession to the demands of the Congress'.[80] Zetland continued to insist that inaction would not help. 'When the time is ripe', he told the cabinet, 'a solution on the lines I have advocated will require serious consideration.'[81] Four weeks later, Zetland was out of office, along with Prime Minister Neville Chamberlain.

2

Defence of India

At the outbreak of war, India's defence policy and plans were splayed all over the strategic map. From the standpoint of India's defence, the war came at a most inopportune time. The strategic debates and dilemmas that had exercised defence planners in New Delhi and London in the preceding years had hardly been settled. And the Indian army was barely prepared to face the ruthless tribunal of modern warfare. Yet until the fall of France in June 1940, it seemed as if India's role in the war might correspond with the plans that had proliferated in the years between the world wars. This was not entirely an illusion, though by clinging to them strategists in India and Britain made subsequent adaptation all the more painful.

In September 1939, the 200,000-strong Indian army was subject to three competing claims: those of internal security, external defence and imperial duties. This had been the case for nearly half a century. Since the Rebellion of 1857, internal security had been a central concern of military policy in India. In 1881, the government of India claimed that 'the Indian Army is required to maintain internal tranquillity rather than for employment against external foes'.[1] As late as 1912, an Army in India committee led by Field Marshal Nicholson had identified the principal mission of the army as 'maintaining internal security and tranquillity'.[2] Although internal security took a back seat during the First World War, it soon returned to the fore. The Kuki-Chin (1917–19) and Saya San (1930–32) rebellions in Burma; chronic unrest in Punjab and the north-west frontier; the Mappila rebellion of 1921 in Malabar; the rise of mass nationalism; the escalation of communal riots – all ensured that internal security remained a top priority in the inter-war years. Only a few months before the

Second World War began, the Indian army was busy stamping out the embers of revolt on the north-west frontier fanned by charismatic leaders such as the Faqir of Ipi and the Shami Pir.[3]

For much of this period, the only serious external threat to India envisaged by military planners was from the north-west. From the late 1870s, the Raj was transfixed by the spectre of Russia, whose swelling boundaries were coming to be coterminous with Afghanistan. This threat was, for the most part, a fantasy, yet military organizations do need enemies for their own survival. So, from Kitchener onwards, successive commanders-in-chief conjured up the threat of a Russian attack – with or without the connivance of Afghanistan – against India's north-west frontier and advocated focus on external defence. This expectation held even after the Russo-British alliance of 1907 and in the early years of the Bolshevik revolution when Russia lay prostrate. Defence planners in India and London diverted themselves by drawing up a variety of plans – Blue, Pink, Interim – that designed armed advances to meet the enemy at Kabul and Kandahar.[4] But this assumption of a threat from Russia now acquired a fresh lease of life with the Nazi-Soviet pact of August 1939.

The imperial commitments of the Indian army were altogether more contentious. In the nineteenth century, India was the central strategic reservoir of the British Empire and was crucial to securing imperial interests throughout Asia and large patches of Africa. As popular parodists put it,

> We don't want to fight; but, by Jingo, if we do
> We won't go to the front ourselves, but we'll send the mild Hindoo.[5]

During the First World War, India's imperial commitments bloated enormously. The Raj supplied almost 1.5 million troops, nearly three-quarters of whom served in the Middle East. In 1920, Indian troops were still stationed in Iraq and Egypt, Palestine and the Persian Gulf, Aden and Cyprus, Burma and Malaya, North China and Hong Kong.

India's subsequent unwillingness to provide troops on tap has led some historians to conclude that the government of India was not solicitous of imperial interests in the inter-war years.[6] This is misleading, for it overlooks the fact that the Raj discerned a range of interests of its own – not least strategic – in most of these parts. After all, they constituted the informal 'empire of the Raj'. The central concern of the managers of this sub-imperial system mirrored that of the larger empire: how to work their system on the cheap.

The wrangling between India and Britain over the question of financing the external ventures of the Indian army had been carried on since the 1870s. In 1902, the Indian government had accepted the suggestion of a Royal Commission that it should bear financial responsibility for areas which contained its 'direct and substantial interests'. These included the Suez Canal, Persia, the Persian Gulf and Afghanistan. During the 1914–18 war India not only bore a substantial cost in raising and deploying troops, but also made a generous gift to Britain by taking over some of its war debts, worth £100 million. India, as the viceroy put it, was bled 'absolutely white' by the war.[7]

After a short-lived economic recovery in 1919–20, Indian trade followed the worldwide slump of 1920–22. During this period, the exchange rate of the rupee underwent violent fluctuations, so the economy was unable to recover wartime credits.[8] The fiscal crisis extended well into the decade after the war and was prolonged by the Great Depression.[9] It was in this context that India began to assert its unwillingness to assume wider commitments. Even so, India's aversion was not so much to sending troops on occasion as necessary as to providing permanent garrisons across the Empire. Thus, in the late 1920s India accepted contingency plans for sending troops to Iraq, the Persian oilfields, Singapore and Shanghai, on the understanding that London would share the bill.

In fending off London's importunate demands, the Indian government had a handy excuse. Under the Montagu–Chelmsford reforms of 1919, a Central Legislative Assembly of elected Indian members had been created. Although the assembly had no powers to vote on defence, it could on taxation. More importantly, Indian nationalists – even of the moderate and mendicant variety – had long criticized the army's external forays as well as the Indian government's financing of them.[10] During the inter-war years, the government routinely invoked 'Indian opinion' to fob off demands from London that it thought unnecessary.

In 1921, when the Esher Committee recommended placing the Indian army directly under the control of the British government, the viceroy commended to London a resolution passed by the Assembly stating that the Indian army should not be used outside India. In August 1938, when London pressed New Delhi to provide an Imperial Reserve Division at its own cost, the Treasury was told:

> Whatever the legal position might be, we are under a moral obligation to consult the Legislature . . . in the event of a situation arising which rendered desirable the despatch of troops from India to some other theatre of operations, and anyone who thought otherwise was living in a wholly unreal world.[11]

Just a year later, the viceroy took India to war without even a sidelong glance at the legislature.

By 1935, however, it was becoming clear that India could not duck its imperial commitments. Japan's deepening penetration into China as well as its more belligerent external posture in Asia portended problems for Britain. As early as 1932, the chiefs of staff warned the Committee of Imperial Defence that a war with Japan would imperil all Britain's possessions in the Far East – Hong Kong and Singapore were practically undefended – and would threaten the coastline of India as well. Soon after, the cabinet approved the fortification of the Singapore base. The Singapore strategy rested on the hope that the main fleet of the Royal Navy would be free of commitments in Europe. This was belied by Mussolini's attack on Abyssinia and Hitler's reoccupation of the Rhineland, and buried by Germany's agreements with Italy and Japan in 1936.[12]

All this drastically and rapidly changed the context in which India's imperial role was considered. Italy could threaten imperial communications through the Mediterranean and the Red Sea, while Japan could menace imperial interests in the Far East and endanger India's coastline and shipping in the Indian Ocean. In consequence, the scope of India's external defence expanded to include the area stretching from Suez, Aden and the Persian Gulf in the west to Singapore in the east. An Expert Committee under Admiral Chatfield stamped its approval on this: 'India should acknowledge that her responsibility cannot on her own interest be safely limited to the local defence of her land frontiers and coasts.'[13] The exhortation was gratuitous. Even before the committee stated its view, officials in India had come round to it. This was hardly surprising, for the arc of India's security had long been regarded as encompassing these parts of Asia and the Indian Ocean. In February 1938, New Delhi told London that in light of the evolving strategic scenario, 'It is impossible to ignore the fact that India is likely, in the future, to be called upon to accept wider overseas commitments.'[14]

In 1939, then, the defence of India continued to encompass the tripartite demands of internal security, frontier defence against the Soviet Union, and external defence in West and East Asia. Despite all the hand-wringing and shadow-boxing with London, New Delhi embarked on war with ever greater demands on the Indian army. The only snag was that the Indian army was hopelessly unprepared. For one thing, attempts at modernization had been wrecked by the parsimony of the treasuries in New Delhi and London. For another, the expanded internal security role in the inter-war years – using the army as essentially an armed constabulary – had militated against the introduction of new technologies and the related organizational reforms. Finally, the general staff in India had remained wedded to outdated concepts of warfare and resisted change.

An inter-departmental committee tasked by the British government in 1938 to look into the modernization of the Indian army recommended several measures, including the creation of a fully modernized imperial reserve division, which would be financially supported by London.[15] Modernizers in the Indian army chimed in at this point. A group of younger staff officers, led by Lieutenant General Claude Auchinleck, the deputy chief of the general staff, were increasingly concerned at the lack of preparation of the Army in India for a future conflict. They were provided with an opportunity to voice their opinions when the commander-in-chief appointed an in-house modernization committee. The findings of this group fed into the recommendations of the Chatfield committee, of which Auchinleck was also a member.[16]

The Chatfield committee recommended that London pick up part of the tab for the expanded commitments of the Indian army, and entirely subsidize the modernization of an imperial reserve division.

For the programme to be affordable, however, modernization would have to be accompanied by a downsizing of the Indian army. The committee also called for a programme to modernize the military-industrial base in India. The Chatfield committee was right in assuming that India and its army were not yet ready for a modern, industrial war. But it was wrong in assuming that they had until 1944 to implement these changes.

Even before Britain had formally declared war on 3 September 1939, the Raj had made the first moves to help secure its sphere of influence. In keeping with the Chatfield recommendations, India sent out a division-worth of troops – almost 10,000 men – to Egypt, Singapore, Aden, Kenya and Iraq.[17]

Three days after the war began, New Delhi proactively informed London that it was 'anxious to take timely steps to render further aid to His Majesty's Government'. As a first step, India had arranged to increase the output of its munitions factories, not just to meet its own requirements but also to cater for wider needs. Further, it proposed to raise two additional brigade groups: one for reinforcing the defences of Burma and the other for the protection of Anglo-Iranian oilfields or similar duties in the Middle East. It also intended to raise two more brigade groups of around 7,000 men each to replace the ones that would be sent out of India. All these measures, which went well beyond the Chatfield recommendations, would be met from India's own resources. Although New Delhi was 'extremely reluctant' to flag the financial issue at this point, it hoped that an equitable arrangement would soon be worked out.[18]

In the early months of the war, however, Britain did not draw on any additional Indian resources. London as well as New Delhi remained fixated on the traditional threat to India from Russia via Afghanistan. It was believed that with Britain locked in a long conflict on the continent, 'it would only be logical for Kremlin to give a free rein to expansionist tendencies inherent in the character of the Soviet state' – especially in areas of its traditional interest such as Afghanistan.[19]

The government of Afghanistan was even more apprehensive on this score. For several years, it had hankered after a British guarantee against the threat of aggression from Russia. The Afghan prime minister had even visited London in 1937 to press for such a guarantee – to no avail. Although desultory talks had been carried on until the eve of war, London had been leery of any binding commitment. Britain did not want to tie itself down in advance in a fluid international situation. Moreover, it was well understood that the Indian army – the chief instrument for executing any guarantee – was in the throes of reorganization and consequently was in no shape to assist Afghanistan. The Anglo-French guarantee to Poland raised Afghanistan's hopes, but London was prepared to offer no more than a treaty of goodwill, non-aggression and mutual consultations. The proposed agreement expressly avoided any military commitment, at the insistence of India. By the time Kabul was informed, the Nazi-Soviet pact had been signed and the idea of such an empty Anglo-Afghan treaty of goodwill was dead on arrival.[20]

After the war broke out, the Foreign Office and the India Office in London returned to the question of Afghanistan. The preservation of an independent Afghanistan as a buffer state, they asserted, was essential to the defence of India and the Empire. Until very recently there had been no reason to expect Russia to adopt an aggressive policy towards Afghanistan. With the Nazi-Soviet pact, though, that assumption could 'no longer be safely relied on'. The flip-side of this was the need to keep Afghanistan 'on our side'. Kabul already had a large contingent of German technicians working on various projects, who might pull it closer to Berlin. It was suggested that the proposed treaty must be coupled with oral assurances that in the event of a crisis Britain and India would go beyond consultation and look at concerted measures for assistance, though these might not involve the despatch of Indian or British forces. As a token of their sincerity, India would immediately send a military mission to Kabul to assess Afghan requirements, provide training for Afghan air force officers in India, and lend technical advisers to the Afghan forces.[21]

When these proposals were placed before Kabul, the Afghan prime minister took a cautious tack. His overriding concern now was to avoid antagonizing Russia, which did not seem to be bent on an imminent act of aggression. So Kabul procrastinated. The Soviet attack on Finland at the end of November, however, shocked the

Afghans. The director of military operations, Brigadier G. N. Moles-worth, was sent from India to quietly confer with the Afghans on their military requirements. He quickly realized that the Afghans had no contingency plans – military or diplomatic – on the basis of which assistance could be discussed. Overnight, after their first meeting, the Afghans drew up a 'stupendous and fantastic list' of desired war material worth several million pounds. When Molesworth suggested more practical measures of training, the Afghan premier turned eva-sive, claiming that it would take time for Afghan soldiers to get used to the idea of British training.[22]

London and New Delhi were increasingly concerned not so much about a ground invasion, which would be rather difficult to mount, as about air attacks on north-west India. The Indian government had at its disposal all of one anti-aircraft battery, consisting of eight 3-inch guns – and not a single fighter aircraft. Apart from any mater-ial damage, Soviet air raids would shatter the morale of the defenceless population and dent the prestige of the Raj.[23]

The war cabinet felt that while any large-scale air attacks were unlikely, 'even a light scale would make the internal security problem acute'. Even without such attacks, Russia could create trouble for India. The annexation of northern parts of Afghanistan by Russia was considered a 'feasible proposition' – one that might topple the Afghan government and spread unrest to the Indian frontier. In turn, Bolshevik propaganda would heighten the internal security problem of India. 'We may be faced with a civil disobedience campaign in India in the near future', the chiefs of staff grimly noted, 'possibly supported and financed by Russia.' The Indian reservoir of troops might dry up and Britain might even have to send reinforcements to India.[24]

These concerns took more definite shape in the context of Britain's own plans for a diversionary attack in aid of Finland. On 6 December 1939, the Foreign Office circulated a memorandum arguing that Rus-sia was well poised for an expansionist policy towards Afghanistan. Such a move would 'clearly enjoy the full support of Germany'. Mos-cow could aim to grab parts of northern Afghanistan either by an outright military attack or by a combination of military pressure, political intrigue and propaganda. The Red Army had shown itself quite capable of occupying territory against an 'enemy unprovided with modern means of defence'. While an attack on India was still seen as improbable, Soviet penetration into Afghanistan would be a 'definite advance in this direction' and would deal a 'grave blow' to Britain's prestige.[25] Days before the Finnish surrender, the chiefs of staff insisted that 'Germany and the Soviet Union have for the moment common interests in achieving the disruption of the British Empire' – important parts of which could be attacked from Russia. Germany would be willing to provide such assistance as the Russians would be willing to accept.[26]

But Kabul continued to play cat-and-mouse with New Delhi and London. In March 1940, the Afghan prime minister asked the British government for a 'clear definition' of its 'attitude and action' in the event of a Russian attack on Afghanistan. After a careful triangular consideration of views between London, New Delhi and the legation in Kabul, the war cabinet decided in early April to convey an assurance to Afghanistan: in the event of a Soviet attack the British would give 'all assistance in their power', including some immediate land and air assistance from India. At the same time, however, Britain could not take up any obligation for the defence of the northern frontier of Afghanistan.[27]

This assurance was conveyed to the Afghan premier on 1 May. Another visit to Kabul by Brigadier Molesworth was also proposed. The Afghans yet again shrank from embracing the British offer. The Wehrmacht's spectacular successes in the Low Countries had caused a 'considerable setback in Afghan opinion'. The younger members of the government in particular wondered if this was the right time to tilt towards Britain. Indeed, three weeks passed before Kabul formally replied to London. The Afghans felt that in the prevailing circumstances, they could not risk offending Russia by openly receiving an Indian military delegation. Instead they proposed sending their own senior officers to India.[28]

The fall of France dealt a further setback to the efforts to woo Afghanistan. The Afghans were amazed to hear that 'the countries of Western Europe were falling like nine-pins before the German advance'. By the end of June 1940, they were forced to reckon with the fact that Britain was on the ropes. The Afghan prime minister politely declined an offer of 5,000 rifles and supplies of ammunition from India until Britain was able to cater to his country's major requirements. The arrival of a small consignment would only 'give a bad impression'. And now that arms were off the table, what was the point in sending a military delegation to India?[29] It was evident that Kabul now sought to defuse the Russian threat by other means. The first indication of this was the signing of a trade agreement with the Soviet Union towards the end of July 1940. Over the next few months, the threat of a Soviet invasion of Afghanistan visibly receded.

Despite Kabul's desire to eschew a strategic embrace, the viceroy felt it imperative to avoid giving any impression that India would not come to the aid of Afghanistan against a Soviet threat. This would have 'serious and damaging repercussions in Muslim India, on the North-West Frontier and in the Indian Army'. The rub lay in making good on these assurances in the event of a crisis.[30]

India knew full well that it would have to shoulder this hefty load. But its own military resources were already overstretched and it would need considerable aid from Britain to implement any plan of assistance to Afghanistan. In consequence, the Indian general staff had suggested focusing their plans on supporting Afghan forces in the southern parts of the country – the Kandahar–Gereshk area. However, the British chiefs of staff maintained that there had to be at least a token presence in Kabul. These differences had been subtly manipulated by London telling the Afghan government that it could expect no assistance for the defence of its northern frontier. In early May, Molesworth had observed despairingly that London's attitude was that 'We will take all and give nothing. But you must implement our new policy which we have already announced to the Afghan Government.'[31]

The Indian general staff were set against sending even token forces to Kabul. At a conference chaired by Linlithgow, it was decided that they should draw up a full plan for effective assistance of Afghanistan and then confront the British government with the magnitude of the problem. Accordingly, on 15 May 1940, the defence department had conveyed to the India Office a fleshed-out plan for assisting

Afghanistan. This envisaged a two-pronged advance into Afghanistan: a northern line aimed at reinforcing Kabul and a southern line to forestall a Soviet advance towards Helmand and to stabilize the Kandahar area.[32]

The implementation of the plan would require no fewer than sixteen infantry brigades, three mobile brigades, eight field artillery regiments, three anti-aircraft regiments and twenty-one air force squadrons. India now had six RAF squadrons and one squadron of the Royal Indian Air Force, so the remaining fourteen squadrons would have to be provided by London. Besides, all the anti-aircraft units would have to come from British resources. New Delhi, for its part, undertook to embark on a major of plan of expanding the Indian army by eighteen infantry battalions, three field artillery regiments, and all support and logistics units for a total of six divisions. These additional forces would be raised, trained and ready for deployment by April 1941.[33]

The chiefs of staff's reaction was wholly predictable. They saw 'no prospect' of giving the commander-in-chief any of the additional resources he had demanded. India would have to make do with what it had and 'accept the risks involved in operations undertaken with relative[ly] small forces, and without air support'.[34] India was accordingly asked to prepare a watered-down interim plan for Afghanistan. The general staff went back to the drawing board and concocted a limited plan towards the end of June 1940. This plan sought only to prevent Soviet forces from reaching the north-west frontier by a forward deployment of Indian troops to Jalalabad in the east of Afghanistan and, if possible, to Kandahar in the south. By the time it was drawn up, however, the general staff knew that the Russian threat to Afghanistan had 'largely receded' and the problem was more of containing hostile propaganda and clandestine activity aimed at overthrowing the government in Kabul.[35]

The chiefs of staff concurred with this assessment. They were also delighted at the Indian government's initiative in expanding the Indian army. The more so, since India had indicated that if Afghanistan remained quiescent, these troops could be used elsewhere. Thus, even after the Russian hobgoblin had conjured itself away, the threat to Afghanistan continued to be invoked to justify a major expansion of the Indian army. New Delhi and London knew that the Raj would be called upon to make a major contribution to the defence of countries that traditionally fell under its sphere of influence. And the Middle East loomed large in the minds of strategic planners in India as well as Britain.

Up to June 1940 the main threat to British interests in the Middle East was perceived to be from Russia. From the outset, the chiefs of staff believed that the penetration of northern Iran would be an 'easy matter' for Russia. This could subsequently develop into a threat to the Anglo-Iranian oilfields in the south of the country. What was more, Russian incursion into Iran could unsettle Iraq and threaten the land communications linking the Persian Gulf with Egypt. Only India would be able to provide forces to safeguard these interests.[36] India, of course, was of its own volition willing to send troops to protect the oilfields in Iran.

In December 1939, the Foreign Office felt that alongside Afghanistan, Iran would be a prime target for Soviet expansion with the connivance – if not direct assistance – of Germany. The chiefs of staff were clear that at the first sign of a Russian move on Iran, they would have to cater for the internal security and air defence of the Anglo-Iranian oilfields and the port of Basra. While this might not initially entail a large commitment, if the Russian advance continued then they would have to prepare for the defence of Iraq as well as the oilfields.[37] Within a month, the British generals came to a grimmer view of the problem. They now believed that 'considerable forces' might be required to protect vital interests in the Middle East. Although no troops were immediately sent, logistical preparations were set afoot to support future force deployments. In mid-January 1940, London also took up India's offer to send an army division to protect the Anglo-Iranian oilfields.[38] In the event, however, the threat to the Middle East materialized not from Russia but from the Axis powers.

Well before the onset of the war, the British government was aware that a hostile Italy could pose a serious danger to imperial interests and communications in the Middle East and North Africa. The Chamberlain government was relieved when the country did not throw in its lot with Germany immediately after war broke out. The war cabinet was abuzz with ideas to appease Italy into continued neutrality, including one for naval détente in the Mediterranean and mutual withdrawal of land and air forces from North-East Africa. Although the chiefs of staff opposed schemes that sought to surrender their military positions, they initially believed that 'the danger of Italian hostility seems to be receding'. They also recognized, however, that reversals in Europe could draw Italy into the fray alongside Germany. So, they advocated preparing to fight Italy in North-East Africa.[39]

The nightmare of British planners was the scenario in which both Russia and Italy turned aggressively against Britain's interests in the Middle East and North Africa. Towards the end of April 1940, when the Wehrmacht was racing across the European continent, London grew desperate to keep Italy from entering the war. The war cabinet approved Foreign Secretary Halifax's proposal to make further attempts to reach an economic agreement with Italy.[40] The Anglo-French supreme war council also decided that no action should be taken that could precipitate conflict with Italy before the Allies had concentrated their forces in the eastern Mediterranean. The chiefs of staff, however, suggested making a series of minor military deployments in North and East Africa as well as the Middle East. As one of these moves, London accepted India's offer to send a battalion to reinforce Aden. In early June, India was asked to despatch another battalion to Aden.[41] By the time these troops were in place, however, Italy was already at war.

Italy's entry hugely inflated India's commitment to the war. The turning of the strategic spotlight on North-East Africa and the Middle East inevitably downgraded the importance of the Far East. This was ironic, for only a few months earlier the chiefs of staff had emphatically stated:

> Our interests in the Middle East, as important as they are, are not as important as the security of France and Britain or Singapore. Steps to increase our forces in the Middle East must therefore not be taken at the expense of our essential requirements in the West or our ability to defend Singapore.[42]

Moreover, the chiefs of staff conceded that the idea of concentrating the main fleet at Singapore was a chimera; the bulk of the Royal Navy had to give priority to the northern Atlantic and Mediterranean. They could only draw comfort from the small steps being taken for reinforcing fortress Singapore, and thereby 'extending the period' for which it could notionally hold out against a Japanese attack.[43]

Yet, in mid-March 1940, the chiefs of staff pulled out two medium bomber squadrons from the meagre defences of Singapore. These were sent to India and thence to the Middle East to prepare for the possibility of a Russian threat to the region. The bomber squadrons had originally been sent to Singapore from India as 'insurance' against a Japanese attack. 'Since then the situation has changed materially,' the chiefs argued, 'in that risk of war with Japan has considerably receded while that of war with Russia has increased.'[44] Though the latter part of this assumption was belied, the entry of Italy into the war did activate the Middle Eastern and African theatres of the conflict. Until December 1941, the balance of India's external priorities remained tilted towards the west.

3

Competing Offers

The German *Blitzkrieg* in the spring of 1940 stunned India. As the Wehrmacht punched its way through to the Channel coast and Paris, a spasm of fear coursed through many parts of the country. After the fall of France, the viceroy sought information on the impact of German successes on the Indian public. These reports spoke of 'general bewilderment and some depression and nervousness as to the nearing possibility that India may actually be subject to attack'. In some places, there was evidence of panic as well. There had been 'unusually heavy withdrawals from the Post Office Savings Bank' – a key indication of alarm in rural and small-town India. In cities too there were substantial drawings from bank accounts, though there was no 'run on the Banks'.[1]

So widespread was the panic that even Gandhi felt impelled to issue a public statement urging the people not to hastily withdraw their deposits or turn their promisory notes into hard cash. 'Your metal buried underground or in your treasure chests', he wrote, 'need not be considered safer than in banks or in paper if anarchy overtakes us.' He counselled his readers not to lose their nerve or imagine that 'tomorrow there will be no Government'.[2] Gandhi's thoughts on the panic were prompted by the letters that he received during this period. But he too felt the tremors of the Nazi occupation of Western Europe. Gandhi himself observed that if Britain and France failed, 'the history of Europe and the history of the world will be written in a manner no one can foresee'.[3]

As the Germans cut through the Low Countries, Gandhi's senior colleagues grew concerned. Rajendra Prasad, the devout Gandhian from Bihar, was 'deeply distressed'. He felt that Hitler was

47

determined to wipe weaker nations off the map. His anger against the British for not reaching out to the Congress was somewhat assuaged and he now felt that it was 'our duty to help the British in defeating Germany and help stop the rot'. Prasad was so overwhelmed by these thoughts that he issued a press statement to this effect.[4] He was not alone. Asaf Ali, another member of the Congress Working Committee, publicly called for the immediate formation of a national coalition government to steer the war effort.

Nehru was irked by these statements.[5] 'Hitler may win this war', he conceded, 'but Hitler will not dominate the world. He will fall as Napoleon fell.' More than the invasion of Western Europe, he was struck by the 'singular obtuseness' of the British government. Even the hammer-blows of war and disaster had failed to dent their imperialist outlook or change their approach to India. Worse, even the Labour Party's stance mirrored these attitudes. While it would be wrong at this moment to rush at Britain's throat, Nehru was clear that the Congress must not change its stance in the slightest. He was convinced that the British Empire had had its day: 'It will go to pieces and not all the king's horses and all the king's men will be able to put it together again.'[6]

The Congress leadership decided – 'as a demonstration of coolness' – not to call for an emergency meeting of the Working Committee.[7] Eventually it was convened in Wardha towards the end of June 1940. Although Gandhi sympathized with Britain's plight, he was preoccupied not with the political but the moral question. He asked the Working Committee to demonstrate its faith in nonviolence by proclaiming at this critical juncture that an independent India would not maintain armed forces for defence against external aggression or internal disorder. Others baulked at this suggestion. Given the realities of politics and human nature it seemed simply impractical to rule out the last resort of force. Yet the debate on principles had political undercurrents – not least because of the immediate crisis.

Leading the dissent against Gandhi's position yet again was Rajagopalachari. The former premier of Madras had reluctantly given up office the previous year. In the fall of France, he discerned an opportunity. A deal could be struck with the Raj, for Britain might want to get as an ally 'a free India when she has lost France'.[8] Rajagopalachari set about convincing his colleagues of the merits of his proposal. The Congress president, Azad, was the first convert, but his 'greatest prize', as Gandhi put it, was Vallabhbhai Patel. This stalwart Gandhian from Gujarat, who exercised formidable influence on the Congress machinery, felt unable to rule out the utility of force. Moreover, he too wanted to see the Congress party back in power. Yet a break with his master seemed inconceivable.

'If you order me,' Patel told Gandhi, 'I will shut my eyes and obey you.'

'Don't,' replied Gandhi.[9]

Gandhi insisted, however, that the Working Committee must absolve him of the responsibility for the Congress's policy and allow him to chart his own course. What was more, he wanted this to be made public. On 21 June, the Working Committee published a resolution stating as much.

This public acknowledgement of a breach with Gandhi sent tremors through the rank-and-file of the Congress party. So, the Working Committee resumed its deliberations on 3 July; but these only served to widen the rift. At this meeting, Rajagopalachari tabled a resolution reiterating India's demand for independence. The crux of the resolution, though, was an offer to withdraw non-cooperation – if the entire field of central government, including defence, was immediately placed under the charge of a national government.[10] Gandhi said that he was not afraid of power: 'Some day or the other we will have to take it.' But it was important, he insisted, to find out if Rajagopalachari's thinking reflected the wishes of most Congressmen. He asked the Working Committee not to publish any resolution, but to go to the provinces and quietly ascertain opinion there.[11]

Nehru was opposed to the assumption of political office. Real power, he argued, was the Congress's hold on the people, and this would be diluted by 'office power'. A drastic shift from the stance staked out previously would be disastrous for the Congress. Yet, with Patel and Azad backing Rajagopalachari, Nehru reluctantly fell into line. The final text went even further than Rajagopalachari's draft. The resolution proclaimed that if its suggestion were taken up by the government, the Congress would 'throw in its full weight in the efforts for effective organization of the Defence of the country'.[12] Commending the resolution to the All-India Congress Committee in Poona, Nehru said: 'It may be that the dancing star of independence may emerge out of chaos, but it may also be that nothing but black clouds may emerge out of chaos.'[13]

The final note of scepticism in Nehru's speech stemmed from his awareness of the new prime minister's record on India. Nehru had welcomed the eclipse of Chamberlain and the ascension of the 'far abler and more virile Mr. Churchill'. He observed that 'England now speaks with a different and a sterner voice so far as her defence is concerned ... But in other matters has there been any change?'[14] Nehru also took a dim view of the new secretary of state for India, Leo Amery. When Amery took over on 10 May 1940, Nehru wrote a short note on his past support for Japanese imperialism in Manchuria. In a speech in the Commons in 1933, Nehru recalled, Amery had said: 'Our whole policy in India ... stands condemned, if we condemn Japan.'[15]

Amery had actually been born in India and lived there till the age of four. A contemporary of Churchill's at Harrow, he was elected a fellow of All Souls College in Oxford. Thereafter, he served as a correspondent for *The Times* during the Boer War and entered politics as a Conservative. Like many of his colleagues at All Souls, he was a Christian imperialist who held that 'The empire is not external to any of the British nation. It is something like the kingdom of heaven within ourselves.'[16] After a stint as colonial secretary between 1924 and 1929, Amery found himself in the political backwaters. From the mid-1930s, however, he joined Churchill as a ferocious critic of the appeasement of Germany and a fervent advocate of rearmament. When war broke out, Amery was outspoken in his disapproval of Prime Minister Chamberlain's wartime leadership. After a series of debacles in early 1940, he attacked the government famously quoting Oliver Cromwell: 'You have sat too long here for any good you have been doing. Depart, I say, and let us have done with you. In the name of God, go!'

As secretary of state for India, Amery's policies continued to be shaped by his views about the divinity of the British Empire. While he did not share Churchill's views about the need to sustain a Hindu–Muslim divide in India, Amery too believed that religious divisions in India were age-old and deep-seated. So, the future of India had to be decided on the basis of an agreement between Hindus and Muslims.

In his first statement to Parliament, Amery reaffirmed that his government wanted India to attain Dominion status and that it was for Indians to devise the best constitution. The difficulty at the moment was an acute divide in Indian opinion on fundamental issues. Yet he refused to 'regard the cleavage as unbridgeable'. Amery also expressed appreciation for Nehru's statement that 'he would not take advantage of our difficulties'.[17]

A week later, Amery wrote to Linlithgow: 'I suppose there is no chance of enlisting Nehru as recruiter-in-chief?'[18] Considering Britain's strategic isolation, as well as the expressions of sympathy – if not support – from leading Congressmen, Amery wondered if the viceroy could take some initiative. Indeed, he discerned 'an opportunity which might not recur'. Amery proposed an informal conference with leaders of the Indian parties, the current and former premiers of the provinces and princes' representatives to consider constitutional developments after the war. Such an idea would turn the tables on their critics and meet the demands for a constitution devised by Indians. Above all, 'while the Committee was prosecuting its useful studies India could get on with the war'.[19]

Amery's scheme of gainful employment for Indian politicians was received icily by the viceroy. Warning Amery 'not to take a false step', Linlithgow pointed out that these were matters of 'real delicacy'. Despite the Congress's opposition, Britain had every reason to feel satisfied about India's contribution to the war. The viceroy argued against any attempt to mollify the Congress, especially in view of the demand for Pakistan – an 'admirable rallying cry' – advanced by Jinnah. Besides, there were the Hindu Mahasabha, the depressed classes, the princes: all of whom contested the Congress's claims to speak for India. Linlithgow was certain that 'we should continue as before and make no move until circumstances are more propitious for one'.[20] The viceroy was not oblivious to the softening of the Congress's stance; he merely believed that the premier Indian party needed to soften itself into surrender.

Replying to Linlithgow's patronizing advice, Amery wrote that they would incur a 'grave responsibility' if they failed to use the opportunity opened by the spontaneous response in India to the European crisis. Amery urged upon him 'most strongly the reconsideration of your position, but on the basis of a revised plan'. This plan would involve a British declaration offering India Dominion status at a future date; the freedom to decide its own constitution; the setting up of a constituent body immediately after the war and after the Indians had reached an agreement among themselves; and an undertaking to accept this constitution provided British security, financial and commercial interests were safeguarded. Meantime, the Indians could form an informal committee to examine constitutional questions.[21]

Linlithgow remained unpersuaded by Amery's proposal. However, in the light of the French collapse and its dangerous portents, he invited Gandhi and Jinnah for further discussions. At their meeting on 29 June, the viceroy held out his old ideas of eventual Dominion status and an expansion of his Executive Council by roping in a few Indians. He added, however, that Dominion status would be granted within a year of the war's end – provided there were prior agreement among the Indians. Gandhi promptly said that the Congress would never approve of it and strongly advised the viceroy against proposing it in public. He sought 'nothing short of immediate unequivocal declaration of independence'.[22]

Jinnah told the viceroy that the Congress's call for a national government – with a 'composite cabinet' – was not acceptable unless the government associated the Muslim leadership as equal partners in Government both at the Centre and in all the provinces.[23] By this time, Linlithgow needed no convincing that Muslim leadership was vested with the League. Jinnah's demand for parity not only helped scuttle the Congress's offer of co-operation, but allowed Linlithgow to tell Amery that his scheme was unworkable.

The viceroy had not reckoned with Amery's tenacity, however. Unfazed by Linlithgow's pessimism, he placed before the war cabinet a draft declaration for India. The persistence of the current political deadlock in India, Amery argued, could not be seen coolly. It was essential to go beyond the 'vague generalities of previous declarations' and put out a statement that was 'far-reaching and precise'.

Such a declaration would at once take the sting out of the critics and enable the viceroy to begin useful discussions with Indian leaders. The declaration would state that India would attain the status of 'an equal partner member' of the British Commonwealth at the 'earliest practicable moment after the war'. It would recognize the right of the Indians to frame their own constitution subject to prior agreement among themselves, though the government would not abdicate its responsibility towards 'large and powerful elements' in India. The viceroy would invite representatives of most parties and groups to join his Executive Council as well as a wider 'War Council'. And the governors of provinces would stand ready for the resumption of office by Indian political leaders.[24]

Linlithgow reluctantly agreed, and suggested the announcement of Dominion status within a year of the end of the war. But he also claimed that the Congress was unlikely to at all modify its position. Indeed, the more Linlithgow examined the draft declaration, the less he liked it. He grumbled that the declaration was 'arbitrarily urged upon me' and stoutly protested against the 'insistent pressure' from Amery: 'There can be no question of dictation from one or the other.' Having flashed his ire, the viceroy agreed to go along with the draft, subject to some modifications.[25]

Linlithgow also asked Amery to place their exchange before the cabinet. The prime minister now joined the debate. Churchill pointedly asked Linlithgow why he had abandoned his earlier stance that 'in view of the attitude of Congress and the widening rift between the Moslem League and Congress, the right course was to lie back and make no further gesture or pronouncement'. The prime minister saw great difficulties in agreeing to any such declaration at a time 'when invasion appears imminent, when the life of the Mother-country is obviously at stake'.

Sensing the opportunity to claw back some lost ground, Linlithgow replied that he had cautioned Amery against 'any premature move' and had only agreed to his draft on the misapprehension that the cabinet backed the idea. Left to himself, Linlithgow wanted to announce only the expansion of the Executive Council with 'some reference to the general constitutional position'. Even the ideas recently discussed with Gandhi had to be taken up with others: the Muslim

League, the Mahasabha and the Chamber of Princes as well as his own officials.[26]

On 25 July, the cabinet considered a draft sent by the viceroy that was centred on his recent proposals to Gandhi. Churchill felt that even such a declaration was 'full of danger'. If they went ahead with it, 'opinion in the United States might well take the line that, having gone so far, we had better give Indians all that they asked for and have done with it'. Besides, any such declaration would stoke 'acute controversy' in India. They should say no more than what Amery had earlier told Parliament. All this met with the agreement of the war cabinet, including the leader of Labour Party, Clement Attlee. The prime minister took it upon himself to prepare a draft of the viceroy's statement announcing the expansion of his Executive Council and the creation of a War Advisory Council.[27] Amery's draft declaration lay dead in the water.

On 8 August 1940, Linlithgow announced that he had been authorized to invite some 'representative Indians' to his Executive Council and to establish a War Advisory Council. As for India's constitutional future, he made only two points. First, the British government could not contemplate transferring power to any Indian government whose authority was 'directly denied by large and powerful elements in India's national life'. Nor would they sit back and allow those elements to be coerced. Second, they would agree to set up after the war a representative body of Indians to craft the framework of the new constitution. Meanwhile, they invited Indian leaders to confer among themselves on the post-war representative body as well as the principles of the constitution.[28]

The Congress lambasted the so-called 'August offer'. This was hardly surprising. The statement was merely a diluted version of the ideas put by the viceroy to Gandhi – ideas that had been explicitly rebuffed by the latter as unacceptable. Moreover, even the specific time-frame – a year after the war ended – for constitutional reform suggested by Linlithgow had been airbrushed out of the statement. Above all, the statement handed an unambiguous veto to the Muslim League and the princes on the future political development of India. Coming in the wake of an explicit offer of co-operation – in the teeth of Gandhi's opposition – the government's offer was intensely galling to the Congress.

Gandhi was vindicated, of course. His senior colleagues who had steered the 'Poona offer' were left seething. Nehru declared the idea of Dominion status 'dead as a doornail'.[29] He sneered at the suggestion that India's right to self-determination would be exercised by

> a noble company of bejewelled Maharajahs, belted knights, European industrial and commercial magnates, big landlords and taluqdars, Indian industrialists, representatives of the imperial services, and a few commoner mortals, all sitting together, possibly under the presidentship of the Viceroy himself.

It was strange to be told that the British government did not approve of coercion: 'What else does it do in India?' Nehru declared that 'the whole thing is fantastic and absurd, and has not even the merit of decent phraseology about it' – an observation that would surely have stung the prose stylist in Churchill.[30]

Patel declared that the government was sowing discord among the Indian people. India's problems were for Indians to solve. 'It is as if a watchman were to say to his employer, "What will happen to you if I leave?" The answer will be: "You go your way. We shall either engage another watchman or learn to keep watch ourselves."'[31] The leader of the rebels, Rajagopalachari, was disillusioned and disappointed. 'I am angry,' he said in a public meeting: 'I want you also to feel angry.'[32]

The sole effect of the viceroy's statement on the Congress was to reunite the party under the leadership of Gandhi. The break with their leader was already gnawing at the Working Committee, and Gandhi too was upset. So there was palpable relief among senior Congressmen at the brusque rejection of their offer of co-operation by the Raj. Nehru publicly stated that the 'Poona offer' of the Congress was 'dead and gone, past all resurrection ... Many of us who did not fancy it may well feel relief at this escape from its dangerous implications.' The Congress was back to the position adopted in the March 1940 resolution at Ramgarh. The only difference was that the resolution – which had called for civil disobedience *at an appropriate time* – had to be given immediate effect.[33]

On 22 August 1940, the Congress Working Committee expressed

'deep pain and indignation' at the viceroy's statement. Not only did it deny India its right to freedom, but it turned the issue of minorities into 'an insuperable barrier' to progress.[34] Three weeks later, the All-India Congress Committee adopted a resolution tabled by Gandhi. It observed that the 'Poona offer' was rejected by the British government in a manner that left 'no doubt that they had no intention to recognize India's independence, and would, if they could, continue to hold this country indefinitely in bondage'. The Congress's offer of co-operation no longer applied: 'It has lapsed.' Gandhi continued, however, to flinch from the prospect of launching mass civil disobedience. Thus the resolution noted that the Congress had no desire at the moment to undertake non-violent resistance, except to preserve civil liberties.[35] The inflexible master conceded that his colleagues may debate pros and cons with him; but eventually 'my judgement should prevail because I am both author of *satyagraha* [non-violent resistance] and general in *satyagraha* action'. They could only skirt his judgement by absolving him of leadership.[36] This course of action his associates had forsworn. As Patel told Gandhi, 'It shall never happen again in our lifetime.'[37]

Even Rajagopalachari acquiesced in the new party line. The Poona offer, he wrote to Gandhi, had been aimed at making Congress's participation in the war effort 'consistent with self-respect and fruitful'. But the proposal was swept aside by the British government. The Congress was now 'entitled to refuse to participate in the war'.[38] Nevertheless, Rajagopalachari was concerned that the viceroy's statement 'justified Ulsterism'. To undercut the British claim to exclusive solicitude for Indian minorities, he advanced a proposal to the Raj and the Muslim League:

> Let me make a sporting offer. If HMG will agree to a provisional national government being formed at once, I undertake to persuade my colleagues in the Congress to agree to the Muslim League being invited to nominate a Prime Minister and let him form the national government as he would consider best.[39]

Neither His Majesty's Government nor Jinnah deigned to take notice. The Muslim League had welcomed the viceroy's statement and noted with satisfaction that the government had met its demand for a veto. Yet Jinnah continued to raise the stakes. So, even while expressing its satisfaction, the League claimed to find it 'very difficult' to deal with the offer because the details of the expansion of the Executive Council were unclear. The League also called on the government to take it as 'equal partners in charge of the reins of the Government'.[40] The viceroy held out only two seats to the Muslim League. Claiming that this did not give 'any real and substantive share' in the government, Jinnah turned down the 'August offer'.[41]

The Muslim League's position influenced that of the Hindu Mahasabha. Savarkar had welcomed Linlithgow's speech of 10 January 1940 as a 'clear and definite' promise of Dominion status. In May, the Mahasabha Working Committee had reiterated that it was prepared to accept Dominion status as an immediate step towards full independence. The grant of Dominion status should not, however, be conditional on any Hindu–Muslim pact. Mirroring the League's stance, the Mahasabha had insisted that the Congress could not claim to speak for all Hindus.[42]

Savarkar welcomed the viceroy's August offer. After two meetings with Linlithgow, he even sent a list of Mahasabha members who could be nominated to the Executive Council and the War Advisory Council. Declaring the League's demand for Indian partition to be unacceptable, he warned that the Muslims had to deal not with 'colourless Congressites or their Pseudo-Nationalistic innuendos but with the organic racial forces of genuine Hindudom for whom India, this Hindusthan, constitutes not only an indivisible Father Land but an Indivisible Holy Land too'.[43] Although Linlithgow was inclined to offer no more than one seat on the Council, Savarkar was ready to co-operate. He urged Linlithgow not to abandon the plan for the expansion of the Executive Council.[44]

The viceroy, however, asked the cabinet to place the proposal on ice.[45] The only firm offer of 'unconditional cooperation' he had received was from the Independent Labour Party, whose leader, Ambedkar, had agreed to serve on the Executive Council.[46] In any case, rejection by both the Congress and the Muslim League gave the Raj the perfect excuse to cling to the status quo during the war.

*

Faced with this impasse and yet disinclined to launch full-fledged civil disobedience, Gandhi desperately cast about for a solution. The Congress leadership realized that torpidity was no longer an option: it would sap the morale of Congressmen and could unhinge the party's organizational framework. At the same time, they wished to refrain from embarrassing Britain when it was being bombed by the Luftwaffe. Gandhi's mind harked back to the idea of individual civil disobedience which he had used in the past, and which was now advocated by Patel. Gradually, he came round to the idea that such a campaign should be fought on the grounds of civil liberties.

Meeting the viceroy towards the end of September 1940, Gandhi demanded that Indians should be able to air to their views about the war, as long as such expression was not violent. Linlithgow pointed out that in Britain conscientious objectors were exempt from conscription and were allowed to profess their views in public, but they were not permitted to persuade others – soldiers or civilian workers – to discontinue their efforts. Gandhi insisted that under India's condition of servitude, the Indian objector should be untrammelled in the expression of his views. The viceroy cautioned him that this would be tantamount to the 'inhibition of India's war effort'. Gandhi replied that while India did not want to embarrass Britain, it was 'impossible for the Congress to make of the policy a fetish by denying its creed'.[47]

Two weeks later, Gandhi presented his plan of individual civil disobedience, starting with just one volunteer, to the Working Committee. The discussion, by Gandhi's own account, was tempestuous; there was 'stubborn dissent' from at least two of the members.[48] But Gandhi carried the meeting. After the recent rapprochement, there was not much appetite among the Congressmen for another wrenching debate with Gandhi. Moreover, the radicals in Congress were effectively neutralized. Bose's Forward Bloc had already launched a civil disobedience campaign, which had been supported by Congressmen in Bengal. But Bose himself had been taken into custody on 3 July 1940, and the leaders of the CPI were cooped up in a prison compound near the princely state of Kota.

Ironically, the radicals who were still free to criticize Gandhi's moves now called for complete co-operation with the British war effort. The

Marxist-humanist M. N. Roy had, since late 1939, advocated that the Congress adopt a neutral stance. By so doing, he sought to square his anti-fascist outlook with opposition to the Raj's rigid posture. Roy's political judgement was capsized by the fall of France. He was now convinced that the forward march of fascism could only be thwarted by global mass mobilization in a 'genuine anti-Fascist struggle'. India should actively participate in this struggle, for its own freedom was bound up with the larger fight for human freedom. What was more, this participation 'cannot be made conditional upon any declaration of Indian independence to be made by the British Government'.[49]

This was indeed a radical departure from the Congress's stance. Even Roy's colleagues in the League of Radical Congressmen were dubious. Roy retorted that they underestimated the dangers of fascism, 'the old saying, that adversity brings strange bed fellows, is not altogether meaningless'. Then he played his trump card: if the Soviet Union could align itself with Nazi Germany, why should India not stand with Britain?[50] When the Congress decided to offer civil resistance, Roy observed that it 'will only please Berlin and Rome'. He called on 'more realist politicians' to form coalition ministries and assist the war effort. For his temerity, Roy was stripped of the Congress's primary membership for a year.[51]

Gandhi's choice for flagging off the civil disobedience campaign was a little known but devout follower: Vinoba Bhave. Following Gandhi's death in 1948, Bhave would rise to prominence as the spiritual heir to the Mahatma. Later still, he would disgrace himself in the eyes of many as a supporter of the high-handed daughter of the Mahatma's political heir: Indira Gandhi. On 21 October 1940, Bhave stated in public the seditious sentence: 'It is wrong to help the British war effort with men or money.' He was promptly arrested. Nehru offered himself as the next volunteer, but was taken into custody before he uttered the unlawful phrase – the Raj judged that he had already made seditious statements aplenty and sentenced him to four years. Others followed: Patel and Rajagopalachari; Azad and Prasad. Gandhi alone refrained from offering civil resistance, for it was felt that his imprisonment would cause more embarrassment to the government than anything done by the Congress. By the end of the year almost seven hundred Congressmen had courted arrest.

The Raj was more than ready to come down on the Congress. In the summer of 1940, the government had finalized a Revolutionary Movement Ordinance (RMO), which was to be proclaimed with a statement accusing the Congress of seeking to overthrow the government. Reginald Maxwell, the home member and author of the ordinance, was clear that they must aim not merely to reduce the party to submission, but to 'crush the Congress finally as a political organization'. The RMO not only gave the government sweeping powers of arrest and seizure, but declared the Congress as a whole an unlawful organization. On 8 August 1940 – the same day that he made the August offer – Linlithgow wrote to the provincial governors: 'I feel very strongly that the only possible answer to a "declaration of war" by any section of Congress in present circumstances must be a declared determination to crush the organization as a whole.'[52]

On 17 November 1940, Linlithgow cabled Secretary of State Amery that they were swiftly reaching the point when the RMO would have to be proclaimed. The viceroy added that he must be free to take decisions without reference to London. Amery refused to be hustled. Discussing this at the war cabinet, Amery said that he was unable to understand how the situation could have deteriorated so rapidly. The almost leisurely course of the Congress's campaign did not suggest an impending crisis. Indeed, the resolution adopted by the Congress was 'colourless'. Was it essential, he asked, to proclaim the Congress illegal, thus making 'every member of the Congress party in India guilty of an offence?' Would it not suffice merely to arrest members of the Working Committee? Amery's colleagues were inclined to agree with him. Even the usually obdurate Churchill conceded that he did not expect any serious trouble. He thought that the Congress was probably trying to 'keep itself alive by a demonstration'. Churchill instructed that the viceroy should be told that there would be 'an infinity of trouble' if the Congress as a whole were banned, and asked for any new facts that justified anything more than the arrest of the Working Committee.[53]

In the event, the RMO was substantially whittled down. Instead of banning the Congress as a whole, only specific parts of the organization would be targeted. The text of the announcement was also edited to remove incendiary phrases such as 'total extinction' of the

Congress. To top it all, the viceroy was denied blanket prior approval to issue the ordinance. Amery insisted that the RMO was suitable only for dealing with a 'sustained emergency' and that they had to be mindful of 'public opinion'.[54] The Congress, for its part, carefully refused to hand the Raj a pretext to announce its oblivion. And the political stalemate persisted until the end of 1941.

By the end of May 1941, Linlithgow had decided both to enlarge the Executive Council, by inducting non-political Indians, and to create a War Advisory Council – moves that had been suspended owing to the opposition of both the Congress and the Muslim League. The viceroy was clear that this was 'well within the four walls of the declaration of August [1940]'. Nor was he under any illusion that they amounted to 'even a temporary solution of the political problem'.[55]

The decision was underpinned by three considerations. Owing to the expansion of the war, the Raj was digging ever deeper into India's manpower and resources. In consequence, the government was subject to competing imperatives. While efficiency required experienced officials at the helm, the increasing extraction of societal resources underscored the need for greater Indian presence in, and association with, the government. Further, much as Linlithgow wished to perpetuate the status quo, he was aware of a rising 'muted resentment' in India – even among moderates who had been supportive of the war – because of the prolonged and complete gridlock in politics. Lastly, following the launch of the civil disobedience campaign, developments in India were under increased scrutiny abroad. Public opinion in the United States as well as Britain had to be placated.[56]

The prime minister doggedly opposed the idea. Churchill believed that it was very important not to antagonize Jinnah and Sikandar Hayat Khan, the premier of the Punjab. The support of Muslims and, more broadly, of the Punjab was too important for the war effort. In any case, Gandhi and the Congress would denounce the move – and so spark a debate on India at a most undesirable time. The expansion of the war, Churchill believed, might bring the Wehrmacht to the gates of India. Only then would it be essential to draw in all political forces. Meanwhile, they should continue with the policy of doing nothing and count every quiet month in India as a notable success.[57]

When Amery pointed out that the viceroy's plan was the least they could do to parry criticism of the government's India policy in the Commons, Churchill reluctantly gave in. The war cabinet gave its go-ahead on 9 June.[58]

On 21 July 1941, the viceroy announced the implementation of these steps. Of the twelve members of the expanded Executive Council, eight were Indians. But the key portfolios of defence, finance, home and communications remained safely in British hands. The appointment only of non-political figures drew the ire of Indian political parties that had supported the war. Ambedkar charged, for instance, that the exclusion of any representative from the depressed classes was 'an outrage and a breach of faith' – not least because the Muslims were almost on a par with the Hindus in the Council. 'Adding one [member] cannot hurt', he cabled Amery.[59]

Ironically it was the less significant National Defence Council (NDC) – as the putative War Advisory Council was now named – that created most trouble for the viceroy. The council numbered thirty, with representatives of the princely states and the provinces, industry and labour, commerce and agriculture garnished with members of political parties. Its functioning was intended to be entirely innocuous. Each meeting would open with a review of the war, then of the supply situation, and finally of civil defence measures such as air raid precautions. The problem arose from Linlithgow's keenness to include the premiers of Punjab, Bengal and Assam – all Muslim Leaguers – in the council. By this time, the Indian army had a sizeable presence in the Middle East and in North and East Africa, and the viceroy was eager to secure the loyalties of the Muslim-majority provinces. Linlithgow deliberately chose not to consult Jinnah. He assumed that Jinnah would 'climb down' and allow the premiers to serve. If he didn't, the low Muslim representation in the NDC could be blamed on the League.[60]

Jinnah, however, was in no mood to allow the Raj to undermine his control over the provincial Muslim Leagues. At his direction, the League Working Committee passed a resolution demanding, on the threat of punishment, the resignation of the Muslim League premiers from the NDC. Sikandar complied with the diktat, mainly to keep Jinnah from interfering in the war effort in the Punjab. Premier

Fazlul Haq of Bengal was more truculent. Despite facing a rebellion in the ranks, he denounced Jinnah's 'arbitrary use of powers' and stayed in office by stitching up – with the governor of Bengal's help – a coalition with the Hindu Mahasabha.[61]

Meanwhile, the Raj had some respite on the Congress front. The individual civil disobedience campaign was spluttering to a halt. By mid-March 1941 over 7,000 individuals had been convicted and 4,400 were serving sentences. Six months later, the numbers in prison stood at 5,000; most of them were from United Provinces and Madras.[62] Gandhi met the viceroy many times during these months. Although Linlithgow was all along unyielding, Gandhi refused to sanction a mass civil disobedience movement. Moreover, he was importuned by senior Congressmen who had served their sentences – especially Rajagopalachari – to reconsider his strategy.

Simultaneously, the viceroy was being petitioned by the Indian members of his Executive Council to release the Congressmen held in prison. Their unanimous stance forced the viceroy's hand. Linlithgow wrote to Amery that if their demand were spurned, it might become 'extremely difficult, if not impossible', to keep the Council together. Amery himself favoured a 'contemptuous act of clemency'. Churchill thought that Amery was 'overpersuaded' and argued that they would be ill-advised to take an immediate decision.[63] It took a week and two more meetings for the cabinet to wring out of Churchill his reluctant consent. On 3 December 1941, the Raj announced the immediate release of all Congressmen, including Azad and Nehru.

Four days later, Japanese planes struck Pearl Harbor.

4

Mobilizing India

In March 1943, the chief of the general staff of the Indian army wrote a candid letter to the army commanders. Prior to the war, he observed, the Indian army was a 'mercenary army with its morale and loyalty based on four factors'. First, recruitment was confined to 'classes with long-standing martial and professional traditions which have long been centred on loyalty to the "Sarkar" and to the King Emperor'. Second, the army was officered all but exclusively by 'experienced British officers' who could command the 'respect and affection' of these classes. Third, pay and conditions of service contrasted favourably with opportunities in civilian employment. Finally, the size of the army was small enough to ensure competition for vacancies. In almost all these respects, he noted, the situation had now 'radically changed'.

These radical changes, he might have added, had been thrust upon a conservative military top brass by the exigencies of the war. In October 1939, the total size of the Indian army was 194,373 troops. At the end of the war, in August 1945, the army stood at 2,065,554. Over the same period, the Indian air force was transformed from a miniscule entity of barely one squadron, with 285 officers and men, to one of nine squadrons with 29,201 officers and men. And the Royal Indian Navy had risen from 1,846 men to 30,748, along with a considerable increase in kind and quality of vessels.[1] Such an enormous expansion, especially the ten-fold increase in the size of the army, was only achieved by setting aside some of the cherished principles that underpinned military policy in the past. Even so, the Raj sought to manage the expansion in ways that would not entirely undermine the foundational features of the Indian army.

*

The wartime growth of the Indian army fell into three distinct phases, though not by design. In the first eight months of the war expansion was slow. Only some 50,000 troops were added to the pre-war number – and this included Indian territorial battalions raised for internal security duties. This sluggish start stemmed partly from the absence of a previously agreed plan for expansion. A plan had, in fact, been hastily drawn up as war approached but it had never been formally adopted. This was perhaps just as well – the proposed plan envisaged expansion on an even smaller scale and slower pace. The idea of raising only one division every six months was risible in the light of the subsequent events. Part of the problem was also that, even after the war began, there was no directive from the British government on possible troop demands from India. Only one thing was clear: the timetable of modernization drawn up by the Chatfield committee would have to be binned.

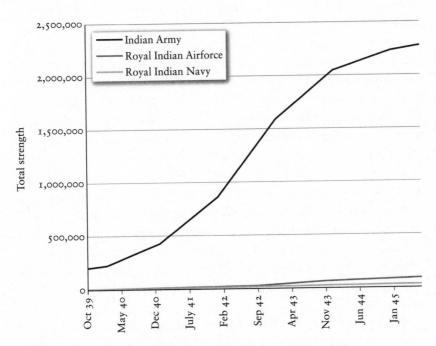

Source: Sri Nandan Prasad, *Expansion of the Armed Forces and Defence Organization, 1939–45* (New Delhi, Ministry of Defence, Government of India, 2012), Appendix I

Figure 1. Expansion of Indian armed forces

After idling many months away, the general staff in India proposed a major plan of expansion in May 1940. This marked the beginning of the second stage of wartime enlargement. The plan had been advanced in the light of London's desire to offer a guarantee to Afghanistan against a Russian attack (see Chapter 2). Although the general staff knew that their operational plan would not be approved by the British chiefs of staff – on account of the demands it would place on British forces – it was felt that the time was propitious for undertaking an expansion of the army. For one thing, the general staff believed that India would be called upon at some point to contribute to the defence of the Middle East. For another, the fall of the Low Countries and the invasion of France had made Indian opinion more sympathetic to the Allied cause than at any time since the start of the war. Even the Congress was expressing its willingness to co-operate in the war effort. In this context, the Indian government felt that the 'Russian menace and India's apprehensions regarding it . . . provide a most favourable opportunity for initiating these efforts with minimum political opposition'.[2]

The general staff proposed augmenting the army by raising eighteen infantry battalions and three field artillery regiments, as well as supporting services such as engineers and signals, organizational and logistical units for six army divisions. These divisions would be available for deployment elsewhere, if the situation in Afghanistan remained quiescent. Simultaneously, India would raise an equal number of units to replace the ones that might be sent out of the country. Whitehall's permission was sought to immediately embark on this plan. Implementing these measures, the general staff emphasized, would absorb their 'entire energies' for at least a year and would be the 'maximum' that India could contribute to the war effort.[3] The secretary of state for India was naturally keen to give the go ahead. The plan, he advised the war cabinet, was 'a valuable step forward towards enabling India to pull her weight yet more fully in the present struggle'.[4]

Weeks after the plan was approved in London, Italy entered the war. Linlithgow promptly offered to despatch to the Middle East eight infantry brigades (three with mechanized transport), one motorized cavalry brigade and one field artillery regiment as well as supporting units – in all nearly 90,000 men. These troops would be sent out in phases from July 1940 to April 1941. The chiefs of staff welcomed the viceroy's offer, but pointedly added that these forces from India should not be 'regarded as the total which will eventually be required from her'.[5] Indeed, India would thenceforth have to stand ready to meet an insatiable demand for troops.

In August 1940, New Delhi offered to prepare four infantry divisions and one armoured division for overseas deployment – if the British government agreed to equip these forces. On 26 September, London accepted the offer and agreed to deploy one of these divisions in Malaya and three in Iraq. However, instead of an armoured division, India was asked to send out an armoured cavalry brigade and an additional infantry division. In the event, it was agreed that India would raise four new infantry divisions by December 1941 and a fifth by mid-1942.[6]

Although the Soviet threat to Afghanistan had ebbed by the end of 1940, the general staff continued to plan for the defence of India's north-west frontier. The Japanese encroachment in French Indo-China also stoked their concerns about the security of eastern India, though, as before, the threat perceived was of air strikes on the Indian coast. Towards the end of March 1941, the general staff came up with the '1941 Defence of India Plan'. The plan was divided into two phases. The first would entail purely defensive operations along the north-west frontier, and the second an advance into Afghanistan, including the reinforcement of Kabul. The general staff were clear that the second phase could be undertaken only if there were considerable additional support from Britain. In short, the plan mainly envisaged only defensive operations on the Indo-Afghan frontier. Even this was projected to require five infantry divisions, two armoured divisions and a heavy armoured brigade.[7]

Beyond this, new units were needed for guard duties and lines of communication in India and abroad. For instance, fourteen garrison battalions were required simply for guarding Italian prisoners of war. Besides, there was the large requirement of troops for internal security: no fewer than twenty-nine infantry battalions and thirty-five garrison companies. In 1941, the general staff calculated, India would need to raise fifty new infantry battalions and an armoured division – apart from other arms and services.[8]

Between April 1940 and December 1941, the Indian army swelled to almost 900,000 troops. At its peak, monthly recruitment exceeded 50,000. Recruitment of technical personnel, which was non-existent before the war, touched 9,000 a month. Forces from princely Indian states were also pressed into service. They were not only used to release units of the regular army for overseas duties but were themselves deployed abroad. By August 1941, seventeen units of princely state forces were serving in Egypt and East Africa, Iraq and Malaya. The maharaja of Nepal also loaned eight battalions of his army for duties in India.[9]

Meanwhile, the changing course of the war necessitated further commitments. On 22 June 1941, Germany attacked the Soviet Union. With Russia now on the Allied side, the spectre of a Soviet threat to Afghanistan was finally exorcised, though New Delhi and London remained concerned about German and Italian subversive activity in and around Kabul.[10] The German drive towards the Caucasus would draw India deeply into Iraq and Iran. In early 1942, 264,000 Indian troops were serving overseas, including 91,000 in Iraq, 20,000 in the Middle East, 56,000 in Malaya and 20,000 in Burma.

Some six weeks before the German attack on Russia, the Indian government had been pondering its expansion plans for 1942. New Delhi informed London that if its demands for equipment and personnel were met, India would be ready by the latter half of 1942 to provide for overseas deployment four more infantry divisions and one armoured division – troops that were currently deployed for India's own defence. As earlier, these would be made available only if India could plan for their prompt replacement.[11] Not until August 1941 did London approve of the expansion plan for 1942. The raising of five divisions, including an armoured division, with the full complement of supporting units entailed the recruitment of another 600,000 men. Japan's entry into the war in December 1941 threw the plan slightly off-balance and necessitated some improvisation. Nevertheless, at the end of 1942, the Indian army stood at almost 1.55 million. The Indian states forces and British units in India added up to another 170,000 men.[12]

By December 1941, New Delhi was already preparing its expansion plans for 1943. The general staff catered for a further infantry division, a parachute division and a heavy armoured brigade. In addition, they aimed to raise five field artillery regiments, seven anti-tank regiments and ten anti-aircraft regiments as well as an array of new administrative and logistics units. All in all, the plan for 1943 proposed increasing the Indian army's size by 240,000 men. Yet by 1943 it was becoming clear that quality manpower, and especially technical aptitude, was now at a premium in India. Further, the performance of Indian units on the front line underscored various deficiencies in training. In the summer of 1943 two infantry divisions were converted into training divisions – an unprecedented experiment for the Indian army. Although another 280,000 men were recruited in 1943, it was evident to the Indian government that the peak of recruitment had passed.

The third stage of the wartime enlargement lasted from January 1944 to September 1945. By early 1944, it was obvious that the fortunes of war were turning. Axis forces had been routed in Africa; Italy was under Allied invasion and occupation; the Red Army was steadily grinding down the German forces in eastern Europe; and Allied forces were gearing up for a landing on the French coast. In January 1944, Churchill went so far as to suggest an actual reduction in the size of the Indian army by 500,000 troops. The Indian general staff, however, refused to contemplate any downsizing of allocations for frontier defence or internal security, pointing out that slimming the army at this point would inevitably blunt its combat edge.[13] At the same time, though, the general staff sought no further increases than those envisaged for the replacement of combat casualties: the 'war wastage ratio' in military jargon. In 1944–45, the focus was on maintaining the Indian army at its 'maximum strength in maximum efficiency'.[14] Training and modernization rather than recruitment were now foremost in the minds of military planners in India.

Throughout the war, the problem of equipment and modernization dominated the discussions between New Delhi and London. From the outset, India's offer of troops was coupled with demands for the provision of equipment by Britain. From the British perspective, this was not simply a question of giving equipment that India could not produce, but also of forking out the money. While the chiefs of staff were thrilled at the prospect of Indian troops being earmarked for the Middle East, the Treasury was more circumspect. As one mandarin trenchantly put it, 'if we pay everything, India's offer simply means that employment is given to a considerable number of Punjabis entirely at our expense'.[15]

Even after a financial settlement had been hammered out, India's requirement of equipment remained a potentially fatal flaw in its plans for expansion. The exclusive dependence on Britain was particularly problematic. In June 1940, Amery conceded that Indian forces 'though considerable are extremely weak in artillery, and the infantry and cavalry units would only have 20 and 35 automatic weapons respectively and probably no mortars and anti-tank rifles'.[16] Yet in discussing the expansion plan of 1940, he told the Indian government that 'while everything possible is being done to obtain your equipment, immediate prospects are not good'. New Delhi shot back: 'our offers of troops are worthless and misleading unless His Majesty's Government can produce the equipment'. In October 1940, the deputy chief of the general staff, Major General Thomas Hutton, was sent to London to smooth over the problem. Hutton proposed that the war cabinet earmark for India a monthly quota of arms and equipment produced in Britain. After much wrangling at both ends, London agreed to set, in principle, a monthly allocation of 10 per cent of its equipment production. In practice, though, the flow of the pipeline was contingent on several factors, ranging from production levels to the impact of enemy air raids.[17]

As a consequence, the forces raised in India and sent abroad were chronically under-equipped and reliant on all manner of patchwork solutions. In particular, there were serious problems with supplies of anti-tank and anti-aircraft weapons, armoured fighting vehicles and artillery guns – all of which were excluded from the monthly equipment quota for India. Thus, the 4th and 5th Indian Divisions deployed in the Middle East – tank country par excellence – did not have the requisite complement of anti-tank regiments. In discussions with London over the plans for 1942, India insisted upfront that its monthly allocation be substantially increased as well as enlarged to encompass hitherto excluded items.[18] Faced with continued stonewalling by Whitehall, New Delhi sternly wrote in September 1941:

'We are not justified in sending Indian divisions to theatres of war where they may meet tanks unless they can be provided with anti-tank regiments.'[19]

The commander-in-chief of India, General Archibald Wavell, sent a stern note on 'Indian Military Problems' to the chiefs of staff. While India was making a 'very large contribution to the Imperial war effort', he observed, it was 'receiving an extremely small supply of essential equipment for her own defence'. Wavell listed a devastating catalogue of deficiencies:

> There is not a single fighter aircraft in India at present capable of taking the air against modern German or Japanese machines; India has not at present a single modern tank or armoured car; has only eighteen light and twelve heavy anti-aircraft guns; and only twenty 2-pdr [sic] anti-tank guns . . . The absolute minimum of anti-aircraft guns required for even a moderate defence in India is approximately 300 heavy and 200 light anti-aircraft guns.[20]

Amery, too, informed the cabinet that in preparing under-equipped formations for overseas deployment, India had 'overcome most serious handicaps and accepted grave risks'.[21]

In the event, India's inclusion in the American Lend-Lease programme threw a lifeline to the general staff. From 1942 onwards, problems with the supply of equipment gradually eased. The bottleneck was no longer the availability of equipment but shipping. The onset of the Battle of the Atlantic exacerbated the problems for India. In September 1942, for instance, New Delhi wrote to London that 'Diversion of tanks to Mideast, heavy losses at sea, the delays in shipping tanks from U.S.A., now aggravated by proposed cut in shipping, have seriously affected rate at which Armoured Formations in India can be trained and equipped.'[22]

Indeed, the raising of tank units was very much a seat-of-the-pants undertaking. Consider the case of the 8th Light Cavalry Regiment. In October 1940, the regiment received orders for conversion from horsed cavalry into an armoured car regiment. In September 1941, the regiment got some Chevrolet armoured cars and Vickers Mk VII light tanks. These were insufficient even for training, which was consequently carried out in borrowed civilian trucks. Eighteen months later, the regiment was issued some armoured cars from South Africa and a few Mk IV Humbers. And finally in December 1943, the regiment took over Daimler tanks from another regiment.[23]

In the last two years of the war, however, the situation changed considerably. In early 1943, it was decided that India would be given 125,000 tons of stores every month. Despite some fluctuations this target held and the results were striking. In September 1943 India had 1,040 2-pounder anti-tank guns – up from twenty two years earlier – and by April 1944 their number had increased to 2,149. Similarly, in early 1943 the light divisions – the 7th, 25th and 34th Indian Divisions – had only one artillery regiment apiece. By mid-1944, each had the full complement of three artillery regiments. As a general staff memorandum observed, the Indian army could now be 'compared not unfavourably with other well found and up to date forces'.[24]

More striking by the end of the war was the altered composition of the Indian army. Wartime expansion wrought important changes to traditional recruitment policies and patterns. The magnitude of these changes, however, tends to mask both the reluctance with which they were undertaken and the continuity with older trends in some key areas. That said, the changing complexion of the Indian army did pose several challenges to the conservative military and political establishments.

The cornerstone of the Indian army's composition had been the idea of 'martial races'. This was at once ideological and instrumental. To be sure, the notion that certain groups were more warlike than others was neither exclusive to colonial India nor indeed to the British Empire. Yet the idea of martial races acquired an impressive grip on the imagination of the Raj by the late nineteenth century. It was part of a larger ideological shift – in the aftermath of the Rebellion of 1857 – in British views of Indian society.[25] The ethnographic literature produced for official use buttressed and perpetuated the ideology of martial races. As late as 1937, *Caste Handbooks* of the Indian army traded in its tropes. For example, groups like the Jats, Gujars and Ahirs were described as 'thick headed and manly . . . yeomen cultivators . . . eminently adapted to the profession of arms'. Never mind that Gujars were also 'surly in disposition'.[26]

Then too, the recruitment of martial races was seen as imperative to secure the loyalty of the Indian army. From the early 1880s, the army was predominantly recruited from the Muslim and Sikh peasantry of the Punjab, the Pathans of the North-West Frontier Province (NWFP), and the Dogras, Jats and Rajputs, Marathas and Garhwalis. In addition, there was a sizeable number of Gurkhas from Nepal. This resulted in a finely tuned balance of region, religion and caste in the Indian army's overall make-up. The soldiers were recruited predominantly from north-west India – a region that was supposedly immune to the currents of anti-British feeling that might flow elsewhere. The crucial province of Punjab was specially inoculated by several schemes for soldiering families, including land grants, irrigation and other welfare measures.[27] Muslims, although a minority in the population of India, were represented there in slightly larger numbers than the Hindus and Sikhs taken together. And even among the Hindus, only certain sub-castes from the higher castes – excluding the Brahmans – were tapped for recruitment. The ensuing 'class composition' – the official euphemism for caste – was deemed crucial to ensuring that the Indian army remained the reliable sword-arm of the Raj.

This policy had been strained to the point of breaking during the First World War. Regiments that had recruited seventy-five men a year were suddenly called upon to deliver a hundred a month for the devouring front line. The army authorities responded by drawing more intensely on the favoured martial classes through a mix of coercion and inducements. Even so, the army was forced to look elsewhere for volunteers, especially for non-combatant roles. So, the social base of the army did widen during the Great War. However, the magnitude of the change was not large. By November 1918, the Punjab had provided nearly 360,000 men – half of the total combatant recruitment during the war. The post-war retrenchment restored the *status quo ante bellum* of the Indian army: the non-martial classes being the first to be axed. What is more, the discourse of martial races was revitalized in the inter-war context of racial ideologies. The publication in 1932 of Lieutenant General Sir George MacMunn's *The Martial Races of India* underscored the continuing pull of the idea.[28]

Prior to the outbreak of war in 1939, the Punjab accounted for

43.72 per cent of the army and the NWFP for 4.67 per cent, although together they accounted for just about 7 per cent of India's total population. Muslims from the Punjab, the NWFP and other parts of north India made up 34.06 per cent of the army, while Muslims as a whole were 23.5 per cent of India's population; Sikhs provided 17.51 per cent of the army, though they numbered less than 1.4 per cent of the population. And all the non-martial Hindu castes cumulatively amounted to a miniscule 3.7 per cent of the army.[29]

During the Second World War the social mosaic of the army was transformed. Of the little over 2.5 million soldiers recruited during the war, Punjab provided 18.33 per cent and the NWFP another 2.7 per cent. By contrast southern India, which accounted for just 3 per cent of the pre-war army, provided 17.87 per cent of the total recruits during the war. The geographic base of recruitment stretched to include eastern and central India as well. Bengal, for instance, had had no representation in the army prior to 1939. But during the war it provided 3.7 per cent of new recruits. In terms of religion, Muslim recruits accounted for 25.5 per cent of total recruitment and Sikhs for 4.57 per cent, while Hindus (excluding Nepalese Gurkhas) catered for 28.8 per cent. Equally interesting was the rise in the recruitment of Christians and of the 'miscellaneous classes' that were located at or beyond the edges of the Indian caste system.[30]

These seemingly dramatic changes, however, have to be read more closely. For example, while recruitment from south India saw a whopping increase, the martial-class provinces of Punjab and NWFP proportionately continued to supply more soldiers. This becomes clear when we consider total recruitment from these provinces as a proportion of the total recruitable males identified by the army. During the war, recruits from Punjab and NWFP were 32.82 and 53.51 per cent respectively of the total recruitable men from these provinces. By contrast, recruits from south India were only 15.94 per cent of the total recruitable male population in these parts. In short, the traditional bastion of the north-west continued to be mined intensively for military manpower.

Similarly, while the absolute numbers of Hindu recruits did rise, proportionately the Muslims of India continued to supply more soldiers. Thus Hindu recruits were 12.43 per cent of the total recruitable

Hindu males, while Muslim recruits made up 21.16 per cent of recruitable Muslim males. Further, the overall numbers of Hindu recruits mask the fact that the rise in proportional contribution was due to the larger presence of the depressed classes: the Mahars and Chamars, the Kumhars and Kabirpanthis, the Lodhis and Minas, among others. These castes amounted to nearly 60 per cent of the Hindu recruits. Two factors accounted for this. Some of these groups, such as the Mahars, had served in the Great War and had been stripped of their uniforms afterwards. As such, they remained keenly aware of the benefits of military service. Secondly, the so-called untouchable castes had no truck with the Congress party and its qualms about supporting the war. Their stalwart leader, Ambedkar, had from the outset spoken out in favour of the war. In 1942, he was appointed as labour member in the viceroy's Executive Council; thereafter, he was instrumental in galvanizing the depressed classes into the war effort.

Among these communities, the contribution of lower-caste Sikhs was particularly striking. The Mazhabi and Ramdasia Sikh recruits accounted for 97.6 per cent of their total recruitable population. Put differently, almost every recruitable lower-caste Sikh served during the war. Alongside the depressed classes, the army also drew in tribal groups that stood at the margins of Indian society. The Hos and Mundas, Oraons and Santhals, Coorgs and Assamese tribal peoples: all were sucked into the military dragnet. All this was undoubtedly intended to check the possibility of the army being dominated by upper-caste Hindus – groups that were regarded as the mainstay of the Congress party.

However, the army's fondness for the martial classes was in no way diminished by these changes. The rub was that the demands of war far outstripped the supply from these communities. When army expansion began in earnest from mid-1940, the commanders initially sought to do no more than to beef-up martial-class regiments with recruits from other classes. Soon it became apparent that this would be unsustainable. So, the recruitment net began to be cast wider. Following Japan's entry into the war, the army was forced to restrict the raising of new units to non-martial classes, especially the 'Madrassis' of south India.[31] 'The pre-war classes are becoming exhausted', noted the adjutant general, 'and further expansion of them is only possible to a very minor degree, and then at the expense of maintaining existing units.'[32]

The solution lit upon by the top brass was to retain the martial classes on the front line and relegate the new class soldiers as far as possible to support, logistics and administrative functions. Indeed, only 30,000 recruits from the new classes were employed in infantry battalions. At the end of the war, the infantry units raised from non-martial classes amounted to less than 5 per cent of the total strength of infantry in the Indian army. The armoured corps was almost entirely composed of the martial classes. Artillery and air defence regiments recruited from other classes, but only those manned by the martial classes were deployed in the front line of battle.[33]

In September 1943, the former director of military operations, the now promoted Major General Molesworth, ruefully noted that they had managed to get through the Great War by 'exhaust[ing] Fortnum and Mason, without tapping Marks and Spencers or Woolworths to any great extent'.[34] The Indian army could not avoid this lowering fate during the Second World War, but its leaders certainly sought to limit the perceived damage.

The government's policy was not the only determinant of the expansion of the Indian army. It was, after all, a volunteer force. Why were Indians willing to sign up? Men from the martial classes were well aware of the benefits that flowed from military service. They were also drawn by traditional notions of service and loyalty – ideas that were transmitted from one generation of soldiers in a family to the next. 'You should continue to discharge your duties faithfully and to the satisfaction of your officers,' advised a father from the NWFP. 'To do so is the virtuous tradition of a Rajput.' The father of another soldier urged him from Waziristan not to worry about home: 'Forget everybody for the present and work whole heartedly for King and Country.'[35] Loyalty to the king emperor ran particularly deep among the traditional soldiering families. Following the 4th Indian Division's victorious run in Tunisia, a soldier wrote home: 'our beloved King (God save him) has conquered this country'.[36] Another senior soldier was ecstatic at having seen the king in Egypt: 'You have seen His

Majesty in the pictures, whereas I have seen in person with my beloved eyes and purified my thoughts and soul.'[37]

Recruits from the non-martial classes who swarmed to the army had more prosaic reasons. 'I joined the Army', confessed a south Indian soldier, 'in order that I may get rid of this accursed devil of unemployment so very prevalent in India.'[38] Beyond the mere opportunity of employment was the belief that the army looked after its own. A restaurant manager wrote to a friend that 'While the poor suffer on account of high prices and food shortage, Govt. has made elaborate arrangements for tea and other refreshments for its Sepoys at Railway Stations. Every Sepoy gets a very good supply of tea, cold drinks and food.'[39] In the past, the army's doors were firmly shut for Indians from such backgrounds. Now it was desperately looking for recruitable men. 'Advise Ram Singh to join the Indian Army', wrote a soldier from the states forces. 'He will surely be selected. At present training period is not more than 3 months. We are in need of every type of soldiers.'[40] Particularly attractive was the opportunity to serve in technical and logistical services such as Signals, Electrical and Mechanical Engineers, the Supply and Ordnance Corps. 'Earning while learning' enabled recruits to pick up skills that would stand them in good stead in the civilian job market after the war.[41]

Even as Japanese planes buzzed over Indian skies, few lining up to join the army seemed to be driven purely by patriotism. Recruiting officers realized that volunteers were keener on knowing the scope for personal gain. The authorities agreed that it was best not to use emotional appeals to patriotism, especially in 'politically advanced areas'; best to 'rely on the solid practical advantages of joining the army'.[42] A job offering decent pay, a pension or good post-war employment prospects was the bottom line for the army as well as the recruits.

Yet, the ballooning demand for troops forced the government to rely on a range of techniques for recruitment. In the first two years of the war, recruitment had been undertaken solely by the army without any involvement of civilian and local authorities. This had limited the army's ability to carry out propaganda for recruitment. The ignorance among the villagers, noted a civil servant from the Moradabad district of United Provinces in December 1941, was 'appalling': 'I asked one chap, if he had ever heard of Hitler Budmash [unscrupulous] and he said he supposed it must be the new Patwari [village accountant].[43]

By early 1942, the army realized that it could do with some help. Joint military and civil conferences were held to consider policies that would offer greater incentives for recruitment. One proposal adopted was to name the new regiments and battalions after the classes that comprised them. Another was to offer financial incentives, honours and recognition to civilians who helped with the recruitment drive.[44]

A third was to adopt the techniques of modern marketing to attract potential recruits. A sizeable recruitment advertising financial grant was sanctioned in 1942 and increased every subsequent year. This was used to mount a press campaign as well as to produce posters and booklets. Carefully designed advertisements were placed in a number of vernacular newspapers. Large colour posters with details of the pay and perks on offer were put up on prominent sites in catchment areas. These posters typically had a photograph of a soldier on duty and exhorted young men to sign up or their parents to allow them to join. Around forty pocket-sized booklets were published with colour photographs and attractive descriptions of life in the army. A popular booklet published in 1943, *Mutu Joins Up*, was designed as a pictorial record of the transformation of a young recruit in the 3rd Madras Regiment into a strapping *jawan* (soldier). Copies were circulated via the families of recruits in villages across south India. So keen was the interest that the booklet was republished several times.[45]

A range of other marketing tools were adapted for the army's purposes: static and mobile information kiosks, models and clothing displays, advertisements on radio and in the theatres. Several short recruitment films were specially shot and screened by mobile cinema units. Their titles often left little to the imagination: *Taraqqi* (Progress), *Future Leaders of India*, *Soldiers of the South*, *Johnny Gurkha*, and so forth. In 1941–42, a defence services exhibition train displaying the equipment and tools used by soldiers was sent on a 1,500-mile journey through recruitment grounds in central and southern India, often chugging deep into the hinterland.[46]

Despite its best efforts, the army continually struggled to meet its targets. Several factors were at play. First, there was competition with the civilian labour market. The onset of war provided an economic boost to the middle and upper strata of the Indian peasantry. After a decade of depressed agricultural prices, the demands of war led to a boom. This trickled down to tenants, farm labourers and artisans as well. In consequence, there was a marked reluctance even among the martial classes to leave the land.[47]

The governor of Punjab was told, for instance, that Jat Sikh recruits were unwilling to come forward in numbers because the boom had 'brought them such prosperity that the economic argument for enlistment has no longer much force'.[48] 'In the more prosperous Provinces and Districts', New Delhi informed London in early 1944, 'the high wages being paid for civil labour and the favourable prices obtainable by Zamindars [landlords] for grains have reduced the economic urge to enlist, particularly for low-paid non-technical categories.'[49] A survey conducted in the Lahore and Amritsar districts of Punjab asked: 'What keeps the young man from joining the Army?' The crisp response: 'Hearty meals at home.'[50]

Similarly, by 1943 war-related industrial activity in India had gathered pace. This opened avenues of employment, especially for men with technical aptitude. As the central army commander observed, 'the pay of the Indian rank, particularly in the infantry, no longer compares favourably with that of the civilian labour'.[51]

Second, the physical quality of the men joining up was appalling. Even recruits from north-west India were found to be 'under-weight and anaemic and often exhibited frank signs of deficiency. Their dietary intake before enlistment was far from being satisfactory.'[52] The widespread incidence of famine and hunger in 1943–44 led to severe under-nourishment and placed large numbers of young men beyond the pale of recruitment. Indeed, monthly recruitment figures for 1944–45 show an unremitting decline.[53]

Third, a considerable percentage of the intake into the army was lost due to desertion and discharges for unsuitability. In December 1941, monthly desertions touched a high-water mark of 2,161 – up from 1,858 in October 1941. The bulk of these were recruits and young soldiers and the main reasons for desertion were believed to be 'homesickness, change of environment and family difficulties'.[54]

There was also the curious phenomenon of the 'professional deserter': men who 'enrolled in unit after unit with the deliberate intention of deserting with the proceeds'. A man from the Gujrat district of Punjab had successfully deserted from nine different units. The army authorities were particularly miffed that men from the 'newly enlisted classes . . . do not comprehend the gravity of the offence'.[55]

Tribal recruits like the Santals seemed resistant to the straitjacket of military life. Groups of up to two hundred recruits were apt to leave their lines and head to the nearest town for entertainment. There was more than a dash of Orientalism in the army's treatment of these groups:

> The Santal loves his individual independence and is liable for this reason to break away from authority, but he is loyal to his village councils and has a strong communal feeling. He has little or no idea of the value of money, and as a normal good wage will enable him to live in comparative comfort for a week on the earning of two or three days he is liable to expect only part-time work and to get into trouble if he has money in his pocket.[56]

The last factor, and perhaps most worrying for the Raj, was the impact of politics on recruitment. Officials tended to be concerned about the anti-war propaganda of the Congress. In the United Provinces and Central Provinces, the Congress machinery was active. Visits by recruiting officers to various districts were often preceded by teams of Congressmen seeking to dissuade men from signing up. The authorities felt that it was 'difficult to get any response from areas where large numbers used to come forward'.[57] Although the government tended to overstate the Congress's influence, one theme of the latter's propaganda certainly resonated with potential recruits. This was the disparity in pay between Indian and British soldiers serving in the Army in India. As Recruit Behari Prasad put it to his company commander in the 17th Dogra Regimental Centre: 'In the eyes of Mahatma Gandhi all are equal, but you pay a British soldier Rs. 75/- and to an Indian soldier you pay Rs. 18/- only?'[58]

Yet the party that had the most adverse political impact on recruitment was not the Congress but the Muslim League. And the impact was not on the new groups being brought in but on the army's favourite martial class: the Jat Sikhs of Punjab. The umbrella organization of the Sikhs, the Shiromani Akali Dal (SAD), was divided in its attitude towards the war. The nationalist factions of the SAD were loath to support an 'imperialist' war, while others argued that the Sikhs stood to gain much by supporting the Raj. Besides, there was the propaganda of radical, communist-influenced Sikh organizations like the Kirti Kisan that caused unrest among the ranks of Sikhs in the army. The increasing numbers of deserters led the government to conclude that 'all was not well in the Sikh community'.[59]

Adding to the disharmony was the Muslim League's 'Pakistan' declaration of March 1940. Fearing that they would end up in a Muslim state, the Sikhs staunchly opposed handing over Punjab to the Muslim League. Relations between Muslims and Sikhs slid rapidly down the communal slope. The latter's fears were aggravated by the Cripps Mission in 1942, which conceded the essence of the Muslim League's demand. The governor of Punjab warned the viceroy that this would 'seriously affect recruitment as all communities will wish to keep their young men at home to defend their interests'.[60] This was prescient with respect to the Sikhs. In the aftermath of the Cripps Mission, the Sikhs began focusing on the defence of their own community and there was a steep decline in Jat Sikh recruitment. Indeed, of all the martial classes it was the Jat Sikhs who proportionately contributed the least to wartime recruitment: only 27.67 per cent of their recruitable men signed up, compared to 35.18 per cent from Punjabi Muslims and 53.51 per cent from Pashtuns.[61]

How did the experiment with recruiting diverse castes and communities work out for the Indian army? It would be hasty to link the army's performance directly with its social composition. For one, this would mirror the martial races fallacy. For another, fighting efficiency depends more on training, leadership and morale than on ethnicity. Yet the coming together of so many diverse groups of Indians made the army an interesting social laboratory.

The barriers of caste and religion proved far less insuperable than imagined by the army leadership. The British commander of an Indian field engineering company was 'surprised at the depth of feeling against the caste system'. His troops appeared to realize that 'the caste system is holding back progress and unity in India'. The pre-war non-commissioned officers (NCOs) and viceroy commissioned officers (VCOs – the equivalent of warrant officers) tended to be strict in enforcing the caste divide, owing to 'a "diehard" sense that the Corps has always been run that way and any change was contrary to "Standing Orders"'. The 'time was ripe', he felt, to break down even single-caste companies in mixed battalions. Religious barriers, too, seemed to be thinning on the war front:

> Already we have some Xtians [Christians] as cookhouse orderlies with no ill feeling at all . . . Mussulmans, I think, would forgo their Halal if given a lead – but it is a bit of a wrench for them. All Coys. [Companies] once ate New Zealand frozen mutton – faute de mieux. The position seems to me that established corps customs are in retard of contemporary feeling and restricting any progress.[62]

The expansion of the Indian army also resulted in far-reaching changes to the officer corps. Until the First World War, Indians were not allowed to hold the King's Commission. The best they could hope for was a Viceroy's Commission – granted only to senior soldiers who had risen from the ranks. From 1917, however, ten places at the Royal Military Academy at Sandhurst were reserved every year for Indians. These King's Commissioned Indian Officers (KCIOs) were carefully selected: most of them hailed from the martial classes that had fought in the war.

Following the political reforms of 1919, Indians in the new Central Legislative Assembly (CLA) began to take a keen interest in the 'Indianization' of the army. In response to the Esher Committee report of 1921, a set of resolutions was tabled in the CLA by P. S. Sivaswamy Aiyer, a leading liberal from Madras. These included demands for setting aside 25 per cent of the places at Sandhurst for Indian cadets and for the provision of preparatory training in India.[63]

The commander-in-chief of India, as well as the India Office, rebuffed the resolutions, arguing that their provisions would dilute the efficacy of the Indian army and that no British officer would deign to serve under an Indian. Even a plan drawn up by the commander-in-chief in 1923, proposing complete Indianization in forty-two years, was swatted aside in London. The summary rejection of even so conservative a plan riled the Indians. Speaking at the next budget session of the CLA, Jinnah noted that the Indian army had 2,078 British officers. At the going rate, he asked, 'how many centuries will it take to Indianise the Army?'[64] Concerned about a nationalist backlash, the viceroy, Lord Reading, protested to London. This resulted in a plan to 'Indianize' eight units (six infantry battalions and two cavalry regiments). Thenceforth the KCIOs would be posted only to these segregated units.[65]

The Indians saw the establishment of a military college in India – along the lines of Sandhurst – as the fastest way to Indianize the officer corps. After several resolutions were tabled in the CLA, the government constituted the Indian Sandhurst Committee under the chief of the general staff. The Indian component of the committee included Jinnah and Motilal Nehru (the father of Jawaharlal). The committee proposed a large-scale increase in Indianization, including the immediate doubling of places for Indians at Sandhurst; the setting up of an Indian academy by 1933 with an intake of three hundred cadets for a three-year course; and the abolition of the eight-unit scheme in favour of unrestricted induction of Indian officers.

The government was taken aback. After being placed on ice for over a year, the report was rejected on the grounds that it had exceeded its remit. But realizing the need to mollify the Indians, the government held out minor concessions, such as increasing the number of places for Indians at Sandhurst from ten to twenty-five. The nationalists were left cold. Motilal Nehru asserted that the term Indianization was a misnomer: 'The Army is ours; we have to officer our own Army; there is no question of Indianizing there. What we want is to get rid of the Europeanization of the Army.'[66] The constitutional report prepared by the Congress under his leadership in 1928 also called for accelerated Indianization.

By 1930, seventy-seven KCIOs had been commissioned into the army. So, in April 1931, the viceroy announced the extension of Indianization from eight units to a full combat division of fifteen units. An Indian Military College Committee, chaired by the commander-in-chief, submitted its report later that summer. The committee recommended the establishment of an Indian Military College, with an annual intake of sixty cadets for a three-year programme. On passing out, they would be called Indian Commissioned Officers (ICOs). The Royal Indian Military Academy was opened in Dehradun in October 1932. But it had an annual intake of only forty cadets. Less than half of these would be selected by open competition; the remainder were reserved for VCOs and the princely states' troops.

Through the rest of the decade, Indianization proceeded at a leisurely pace. As war clouds gathered, the CLA passed a resolution in September 1938 calling for a committee to recommend ways of increasing Indianization. The government responded by appointing one led by the chief of the general staff, Auchinleck, to examine the issue. After interviewing several KCIOs and ICOs, Auchinleck was inclined towards the Indians' viewpoint, but before he could set down his recommendations, war broke out in Europe.[67]

The commander-in-chief, General Robert Cassels, was prominent among the conservatives, however. In March 1940, a study commissioned by him to assess the requirements of the expanding army recommended that Indian officers should not be sent to units officered solely by the British. This would have an undesirable impact 'not only on the efficiency of such units but might be likely to prejudice the future requirement of British officers'. Clearly, old assumptions died hard. Nor did the study recommend the Indianization of more units. It merely suggested that the Indians now being given Emergency Commissions could be absorbed in garrison and administrative units.[68]

Cassels produced a plan that he hoped would mitigate the challenge posed by the growing number of Indian officers. His solution was to fix a high ratio of British to Indian officers in the army and plan accordingly for recruitment. Any further acceleration of Indianization, he warned the viceroy, would 'inevitably result in ruining the Indian Army as an instrument of war'.[69] The upshot of this was that the average number of officers in units had dropped to desperately low levels by 1941. Only after Cassels' departure from office and the appointment of Auchinleck as commander-in-chief did the army adopt a rational policy towards Indian officers. From January 1942, there was marked upturn in the number of Indian officers – right through to the end of the war. During the same period, the ratio of British to Indian officers fell sharply.

Indianization during the War

Date	Indian Officers	Ratio of British to Indian Officers
1 October 1939	396	10.1:1
1 January 1940	415	9.7:1
1 January 1941	596	12:1
1 January 1942	1,667	8.3:1
1 January 1943	3,676	6.9:1
1 January 1944	6,566	4.5:1
1 January 1945	7,546	4.2:1
1 September 1945	8,340	4.1:1

Source: Gautam Sharma, Nationalisation of the Indian Army 1885–1947 (New Delhi: Allied Publishers, 1996), p. 184.

The recruitment of officers was a two-stage process. Initially the volunteers were screened by their local Provincial Selection Board. Those who got past this were then interviewed by the Central Selection Board of the General Headquarters. Initially, the army used rather informal techniques for officer recruitment. K. V. Krishna Rao – future chief of the Indian army – was among the youngsters who made it to the second stage. There he was quizzed on general questions about the war and at greater length about his passion for cricket: 'how a leg-break was bowled, what a late cut was, what position was known as gully and so on'. Satisfied with his replies, the chairman of the board remarked: 'Well, Mr. Rao, I hope you will get to play plenty of cricket in the Army.'[70] A successful Jewish volunteer, J. F. R. 'Jake' Jacob, was asked in his interview in mid-1941: 'Do you shoot games?' Jacob replied, 'No sir, I don't shoot games, I shoot goals.' There were peals of laughter round the table and no further questions.[71]

The officers so recruited went through a five-month crash course at Dehradun or the new officer training schools at Belgaum and Mhow. By 1943, the rapid Indianization of the officer corps began to raise questions about the quality of the volunteers. This led to the adoption of a more 'scientific' system based on applied psychology – one that aimed at selecting men fitted by temperament and character for the duties of an officer. To attract suitable candidates, the army offered such incentives as the reservation of a percentage of appointments in government services for retired officers. Age and educational qualifications were relaxed. Propaganda was stepped up in schools and colleges. Teams of officers travelled around showing films depicting the life of an officer and interviewing potential candidates prior to the formal selection process. Yet, 50 to 65 per cent of the volunteers were weeded out by the Provincial Selection Boards. Of the rest, almost 75 per cent were rejected by the GHQ Central Selection Board.[72]

The army, in short, was unable to attract the best talent. Most of those who signed up saw it simply as an avenue of employment. As one Indian officer cheerfully confessed, 'Hats off to the University for granting me the degree but I think a degree of the Punjab University is not worth much.'[73] There were only a few officers like A. M. Bose – nephew of the distinguished scientist J. C. Bose – who joined the army because they 'wanted to do my bit to fight the Nazis'.[74] Why did the best men not volunteer in adequate numbers? While there may have been a variety of reasons at the individual level, collectively high school and college students were strongly drawn to the nationalist movement. As Krishna Rao recalled, 'Whenever a great leader such as Mahatma Gandhi visited, most of the students used to cut classes and attend the public meetings, as volunteers'.[75] Indeed, students were in most places the backbone of the Quit India revolt in 1942 and went to prison in droves. Given the political deadlock during the war, the best and brightest seem to have chosen not to volunteer.

For all its problems, recruiting men was the easier part of mobilizing India. Rather more difficult was gearing up the Indian economy for the exigencies of war. Very simply, India was a desperately poor country. Between 1900 and 1939, per capita income in India grew by a mere 0.42 per cent. And during the inter-war period, per capita income was actually stagnant.[76] The dismal economic performance between the wars stemmed from a combination of a sharp increase in population growth and the stagnation of the largest sector (accounting for almost half) of the Indian economy, agriculture. The latter, in turn, occurred for various reasons: lack of an increase in cultivated areas; an inability to improve productivity per acre; and, above all, the slump in global demand for agricultural products, particularly during the Great Depression. The Indian government's refusal to devalue the rupee, especially after Britain abandoned the gold standard in 1931, made economic recovery extremely slow, halting and painful.[77]

At the same time, India was also a significant industrial power outside the Western world, not incomparable in scale with Japan and the Soviet Union. During the previous century, India – very like other colonized tropical countries – lacked well-developed capital and labour markets or the capacity to achieve a technological revolution. The colonial connection, however, did help India surmount these obstacles to industrialization by drawing on British capital, investment and trading networks. The principal beneficiaries of this were those industries, pre-eminently textiles, where India had a relatively strong resource cost advantage. Capital industries like machine tools and chemicals failed to take off since they needed much higher levels of capital and technology than, say, textile or steel mills.[78]

The First World War underscored both the utility of India as a manufacturing base and its limitations. Although the Indian government was granted some leeway to pursue an industrial policy, especially on tariffs, London also sought to protect British goods in the Indian market. In consequence, Indian industry grew more by expansion than diversification. Additional factories in cotton and jute textiles, iron and steel, cement and sugar, paper and matches sprang up across India, especially outside the traditional industrial cities of Calcutta and Bombay. During the inter-war years, while the economy as a whole stagnated, manufacturing output grew annually by almost 4.7 per cent.[79] Nevertheless, the squeezing of rural India's purchasing power during this period left industry facing a vicious cycle of high costs, low prices and insufficient effective demand. All told, by 1939 Indian industry had limited capability to contribute to the manifold requirements of modern war.

Unsurprisingly, India's arms industry was rather rudimentary. The government had only six ordnance factories, which by 1938 produced barely enough military equipment to meet the needs of a peacetime force for internal security duties. In 1936–37, India imported arms worth Rs. 100.5 million – the bulk of them from Britain. There was no private arms industry. Nor did the configuration of Indian industries allow the government to expand the indigenous production of armaments. Although India produced 1.55 million tons of steel in 1936–37, it still had to import an additional 6 per cent of its own production level to meet the overall demand. India relied even more heavily on imports of aluminium. Worse, there was no production of aluminium in ingots and finished forms. Further, India had no domestic automobile manufacturing capability – almost 82 per cent of its cars were imported from Britain, the United States and Canada – never mind any aircraft industry.[80]

The Indian and British governments were aware of these problems prior to the outbreak of war. Even as India was called on to defend its traditional sphere of influence, strategic planners in India sounded a note of caution. A modernization committee led by Auchinleck submitted its report on 10 November 1938. The committee bluntly observed that India had 'neither private armament firms nor those basic industries, such as chemical and optical industries, which are essential to the production of armaments'. The burden would, therefore, have to fall on the government's ordnance factories. Yet the government could not, with its 'strictly limited financial resources', afford to invest adequately to attain self-sufficiency – not least because the peacetime requirement and output would be rather low. Even if it did so, India would be heavily reliant on imports of raw materials as well as a range of components, especially for automobiles and aircraft. Despite these grim conclusions, the committee recommended expanding the ordnance factories to produce more light machine guns, field artillery and ammunition. Key ingredients such as cordite, trinitrotoluene (TNT) and amatol must also be manufactured in the ordnance factories. In addition, these factories should develop the capacity for the maintenance and replacement of certain types of equipment – heavy artillery guns and ammunition, aeroplane bombs – that would otherwise have to be imported from Britain. This programme of modernization was envisaged over a five-year period.[81]

The Chatfield committee, which submitted its report on 30 January 1939, echoed these suggestions. It held that India ought to become 'in all major respects self-sufficient in munitions in time of war'. This self-sufficiency, however, 'cannot be complete, and it is not proposed to provide for the manufacture of those types of warlike stores . . . where the article is of so complicated a character as to make the installation of the necessary plant disproportionately uneconomical'. The Chatfield committee also ruled out the possibility of enlisting private, indigenous enterprise. Even with the Tata Steel Works – the largest producer of steel in India – it felt that there was 'little chance of satisfactory arrangements being made . . . for the installation of special plant for meeting possible military requirements in war'. The best course was to augment the capacity of the ordnance factories.[82]

The Chatfield report's description of the state of Indian industry was reasonably accurate. Not so its assumptions about the limits of industrial potential and the role of private enterprise in armaments production. The course of events from 1940 onwards – and especially the entry of Italy and Japan into the war – would gradually compel the Indian government to cast aside these assumptions. Yet the initial conservatism proved immensely frustrating for Indian businessmen.

After the years of depression, Indian business naturally welcomed the prospect of expansion and the opportunities to profit by the war. Until the outbreak of war, many major Indian industries were faced with excess capacity: over 40 per cent of the total production of sugar and cement lay unsold. The textile industry, for instance, had hit a plateau by the late 1930s. Of the 389 equipped cotton mills, 22 were idle by August 1939. Not a single new mill started production in the western Indian hub of Ahmedabad after 1932.[83] Going by the experience of the Great War, Indian industry expected an immediate boom triggered by government purchases of a range of commodities. They proved prescient – up to a point.

In the last quarter of 1939, for instance, many textile mills were able to clear their accumulated stocks. The Delhi Cloth Mills (DCM), owned by Sir Shri Ram, sold all its stock of 4.83 million lbs by the end of the year. In early 1940, however, the situation was abruptly reversed. With the fall of the Low Countries and France, Indian agricultural exports to Europe suddenly dwindled. This, in turn, severely curtailed the purchasing power of rural India, resulting in a slump in agricultural prices that lasted till the end of 1941.[84] Industry was affected not only by the ensuing drop in demand, but also by the fact that some players had accumulated stocks of raw materials that were now cheaper. Big players like DCM found themselves having to compete with new mills that could purchase cotton at lower prices. Indeed, in 1939–40, Shri Ram could make a net profit only 4.9 per cent higher than the previous year.[85]

These problems were compounded by developments on the political front. The resignation of the Congress ministries and the ensuing stand-off with the government put the industrialists in an awkward spot. On the one hand, they wanted to make the most of the opportunities opened up by the war. A group of businessmen in Calcutta – including the future magnate Kailash Chandra (K. C.) Mahindra – pondered ways to ensure 'closer cooperation' with the government and to convince it of the 'potentialities of India particularly in relation to Bengal's engineering capacity'.[86] Their concerns were typical of the entire Indian business community. On the other hand, a powerful section of industry vocally supported the nationalist movement, especially the Congress.

The Federation of Indian Chambers of Commerce and Industry (FICCI) was set up as a pan-Indian body in 1927 by the leading lights of Indian capitalism: Ghanshyam Das (G. D.) Birla of Calcutta, Sir Purshottamdas Thakurdas of Bombay and Shri Ram of Delhi. FICCI reflected the aspiration of the dominant Indian business communities to create an autonomous national arena of capital accumulation. This ambition arose from the fact that in the post-war period the imperial connection – which had hitherto provided an integrated international market for capital, commodities and labour – was not advancing their interests any longer. In the following years, these men worked closely with the top leadership of the Congress, adopting a shrewd anti-colonial posture without forsaking their commercial interests.

Following the onset of war, the industrialists sought to reconcile the imperatives of co-operating with the government and supporting the Congress. Initially, it seemed easy. As soon as war broke out, Birla cabled Churchill that the 'sympathies of most of us who belong to the Gandhi school of thought are whole-heartedly with Britain'. The Congress ministries' resignation and the subsequent deadlock caught him off guard. For the best part of the next two years, Birla cast about for ways to bridge the gap between the positions of the Congress and the viceroy.[87]

Thakurdas similarly believed that India's interests would be best served by backing Britain and its allies. He too sought to close the gulf between the government and the Congress. At a public meeting organized by the governor of Bombay in July 1940, he said that the

> Congress, though not actively cooperating with the government in the manner it would have liked to, has done nothing in any way to obstruct or slacken the pace or nature of help that India can give . . . The commercial community in India strongly feel that this attitude of Mahatma Gandhi and the Congress should not only not be under-valued but be appreciated at its correct worth.[88]

Shri Ram wanted to go further and impress upon the viceroy the need to constitute a national government with the major political parties.[89] In a statement prepared in June 1940, FICCI 'emphatically urge[d] the Government to utilise the present opportunity for establishing such key industries as those for manufacturing aircraft, ships and automobiles under Indian ownership, control and management'. The statement went on to warn the government that any such plan would be 'frustrated, unless the policy and administration of defence are under a popular Minister'.[90]

The government was unwilling to countenance both the economic and political stances of Indian businessmen. Worse, it suspected leading industrialists like Birla of covertly financing the Congress's civil disobedience campaign. Be that as it may, the course of the war also forced to the government to reconsider its economic ideas. Italy's entry into the war compelled the British government to look for alternative sources of supply – especially those that did not deplete its dollar and gold reserves.

In September 1940, a Supply Mission was sent from London to advise India on expanding its industrial capacity for war production. Led by Sir Alexander Roger, chairman of the Tank Production Board, the mission consisted of six members and fourteen technical advisers. Over the next six months, the mission prepared no fewer than twenty-five reports on various dimensions of Indian industry. The nub of the problem, the mission argued, was that the engineering industry in India had been organized on a jobbing basis – mainly to maintain other industries and not for actual production. This underlying feature of Indian industry had to be changed if its production potential were to increase. The mission recommended a capital expenditure plan of £14.5 million and the procurement of certain machine tools and equipment from Britain and other countries. Among other things, the plan entailed creating five new ordnance factories, the expansion of the existing ones, and the conversion of three railway workshops for munition production. After protracted discussion, the Indian and London governments agreed on a watered-down version of the plan that would cost £9 million and would be carried out by 1943. More significantly, the mission's calls for dispensing with the old system of tenders and establishing close and direct relations with various industries went unheeded.[91]

The business community's frustrations throughout this period were exemplified in the efforts of Walchand Hirachand. A leading industrial magnate and nationalist sympathizer, Walchand controlled the Scindia Steam Navigation Company. As a mandarin in the India Office observed,

> he has been for twenty years a thorn in the side of British shipping interests . . . His methods in the last year or two have been a suitable combination of a professed desire to help the war effort, an ambition to promote the industrialisation of India and the prosecution of his own interests.[92]

Walchand had long dreamed of building ships in India – an industry that had been monopolized by British firms. After the war began, he lobbied for a site in Calcutta, but his efforts were thwarted by the Calcutta Port Trust authorities. In January 1940, he broached the idea of constructing a shipyard in the eastern Indian port of Vizag. Walchand's proposal was examined by the government in June 1940 – only for him to be told that the site had already been earmarked for the Royal Indian Navy. Another six months passed before the navy could be convinced to waive its claim over the site.

After leasing the location, however, Walchand found the government unwilling to support his efforts to import the requisite equipment. Although he promised to place every vessel built in the yard at the government's disposal, his request was rebuffed: 'Government does not consider it to be a part of the War effort, and therefore no direct assistance can be given.' Walchand went ahead just the same. In June 1941, the foundation stone of the yard was laid by the Congress president, Rajendra Prasad. Yet the delays in procuring equipment, especially railway wagons, ensured that the yard was not functional before the Japanese turned on Britain's Asian empire. Subsequent Japanese air raids on Vizag put paid to Walchand's plans.[93]

Walchand's attempt to manufacture automobiles in India fared no better. The idea was originally floated in 1934 by the engineer, statesman and diwan of the princely state of Mysore, M. Visvesvaraya. Walchand worked with him on the business plan and managed to persuade the Congress government of Bombay to support the industry. Thereafter, he travelled to the United States to explore the possibility of collaboration with an American car manufacturer. Negotiations with Ford Motor Company fell through owing to the latter's insistence on having a majority interest in the venture, but Walchand managed to stitch up a more favourable agreement with Chrysler Corporation.[94] By this time, however, the Congress ministries had resigned. Walchand's plans now received a double blow. The governor of Bombay was opposed to honouring the commitment made by the Congress ministry. More damagingly, the government refused to declare his proposed automobile factory as essential for the war effort – and so deprived him of critical imports and capital.[95] Walchand's Premier Automobile would not roll out its first car until after the war.

Yet more dogged were Walchand's attempts to manufacture aircraft in India.[96] A chance meeting with the chairman of an American aircraft conglomerate in October 1939 set him on this tortuous road. After discussions with his American interlocutors, Walchand cabled the commander-in-chief of India offering to build military aircraft according to their specifications. He promised to hand over the first aircraft nine months after starting production. In the tenth month he would produce ten planes; thereafter, twenty a month. The government's response was tinged with scepticism and lethargy. Not until the summer of 1940 was Walchand summoned to Simla for discussions. The trigger, of course, was the fall of France. However, the viceroy and the commander-in-chief were impressed by Walchand's plans and gave him the go-ahead.

The stumbling block proved to be the British government. The minister of aircraft production, Lord Beaverbrook, argued that India's demands would detract from Britain's own requirements of the United States. Eventually, it was agreed that Walchand could set up his factory but not import materials from Britain or America. Raising the requisite capital also proved tricky. Walchand turned to the state of Mysore, which agreed to provide land near Bangalore as well as other concessions, including finance. On 23 December 1940, the Hindustan Aircraft Company came into existence. The government placed orders for seventy-four long-range bombers, forty-eight fighters and thirty trainers. At end the end of August 1941, the first trainer was handed over. Other aircraft too began to be turned out on schedule.

It was Japan's entry into the war that derailed the project. For one thing, the government was concerned that Japanese planes could easily target the factory. For another, while the company had begun receiving supplies from America on a Lend-Lease plan, the US government insisted that these should not be used in a profit-making venture. The Indian government decided, therefore, to take control of the factory. In early 1942, Walchand and the Mysore state were strong-armed into divesting their stakes. So cut up was Walchand with the whole affair that he told an American journalist that he might be better off under Japanese rule: 'What do I care about losing my property? Look at me now, am I a free man? No, I am just a slave!'[97] Nevertheless, the mobilization of the economy would begin in earnest after the Japanese onslaught.

5

Into Africa

General Archibald Wavell was enjoying his golf at the Gezira Club in
Cairo. About half way through the eighteen holes, the game was
interrupted by his senior intelligence officer. The brigadier bore grave
news: France had surrendered. Wavell paused and then moved on. 'I
thought for a moment if there was anything I could do about it,' he
later recalled. 'There wasn't. So I went on with the game and was
rather pleased that I did the next two holes in three and four.'[1] This
was entirely in character. The commander-in-chief of the Middle
East was a man who measured every move. His detached and taci-
turn demeanour masked a meticulous and imperturbable mind.
Wavell's punctiliousness tended, however, to shade into ponderous-
ness. Fortunately, his initial adversary in the Middle East was gripped
by caution and indecisiveness. Unfortunately, his own political
master itched for action.

Wavell had taken over his post only a month before the war began
in Europe. The Middle East Command (MEC) lay spread-eagled
from the shores of the Persian Gulf, through Iraq and Transjordan to
Palestine, and from Cyprus through Egypt and Sudan to Somaliland.
The multifarious strategic challenges of the command were matched
by the range of political problems in almost every country that came
under it. Nevertheless, MEC was tasked with securing interests that
became irreducible for Britain after the fall of France. The eastern
Mediterranean – including the Suez Canal – was the windpipe of the
British imperial communications system. And its defence dictated
the need to dominate the sprawling region assigned to the command.
The Mediterranean became an important theatre for yet another reason. In the summer of 1940, it was the only place where Britain could

directly fight the Axis forces. This was as important to maintain morale as to attract American aid and inveigle the French back into the war.[2]

Yet this was a prospect that Britain had striven to avoid. Not only had the Chamberlain government been keen on Italy continuing its 'non-belligerence', but it forbade Wavell from making any move that might impair ties with Italy – such as running intelligence networks in the Italian territories of North and East Africa. Nor had the chiefs of staff formulated any strategic plans for this theatre. Italy was an equally reluctant entrant into the Mediterranean campaign. The dissolution of the Anglo-French defences in May–June 1940 alarmed Mussolini, who was all too aware of the inadequacy of his own armed forces. He sought both to avoid all-out war and to prevent Germany from pocketing all the gains. In the event, the Duce decided on a 'parallel war' aimed at boosting Italy's prestige and share of the spoils. The only problem was that he had made no preparations for such a campaign. Indeed, he had not even informed his military chiefs that he intended to fight. Worse still, Mussolini refused to accept Hitler's offer of German mechanized forces to fight alongside the Italian army.[3]

Wavell had used the previous year methodically to come to grips with the diverse tasks of his command, to ponder operational plans, and to initiate the preparation of a large administrative and logistics base in the Middle East. Following the Italian declaration of war on 10 June 1940, the forces under his command began raids and ambushes on Italian positions along the Egypt–Libya frontier in the Western Desert. Wavell could do no more because his command was numerically and materially inferior to the Italian forces in North Africa. MEC had a little over 85,000 men, against the 415,000 Italians in the theatre. Further, not a single unit or formation under Wavell's command had its full complement of equipment. There was a serious shortage of anti-aircraft and anti-tank guns as well as artillery. The Italian air force was vastly bigger than the RAF, though the latter had better aircraft and pilots.

Not surprisingly, Wavell chose to remain on the strategic defensive until his forces were increased. 'We cannot continue indefinitely to fight this war without proper equipment,' he informed London at the end of July 1940, 'and I hope that Middle East requirements will be delayed no longer.'[4] Churchill, however, felt that Wavell was devoid of imagination and initiative. Standing at the nadir of Britain's military fortunes, the prime minister craved for a victory. But Wavell was not the flamboyant buccaneer for whom Churchill longed. In turn, Churchill's relentless probing and prodding pushed Wavell to the end of his tether. He would later observe that Churchill 'never realized the necessity for full equipment before committing troops to battle'.[5] Their meetings in August 1940 only served to reinforce these impressions, and their relationship never really recovered from these early encounters.

Meanwhile, the Italians equivocated. In Libya, Marshal Rodolfo Graziani, the chief of staff of the Italian army, had assumed direct command of the forces. By sending him to Libya, Mussolini had evidently hoped to inject vigour and flourish into the lacklustre performance of the Italians in North Africa so far. Graziani was undoubtedly his most distinguished soldier – a veteran and hero of the Senussi War of 1931 and the conquest of Abyssinia in 1935–36. As chief of staff, Graziani had directed the commander in Libya to seize the initiative with an offensive against British forces in Egypt. Now in Libya himself, though, the marshal grew rather circumspect. He observed that his forces were not sufficiently mobile for fighting in the Western Desert and demanded ever more equipment. Nor were the terrain and temperature conducive to an offensive.[6]

Eventually, after much nudging and cajoling by Rome, Graziani's 10th Army commenced an advance into Egypt on 13 September 1940. The marshal had originally planned to turn the British flank in the desert in a daring manoeuvre, but the leading brigade lost its way and the plan had to be aborted. Singed by this unpropitious start, Graziani turned ever more cautious. So, the advance of 13 September was a languid affair, led by carefully positioned divisions. A British officer quipped that it resembled nothing so much as 'a birthday party in the Long Valley at Aldershot'. Having trudged through 65 miles of desert, the elephantine column came to a halt at Sidi Barrani, a small fishing village on the coast, where Graziani's forces erected a monument to mark their glorious advance and dug themselves in in a semi-circle of defensive camps. Italian propaganda went into overdrive, claiming

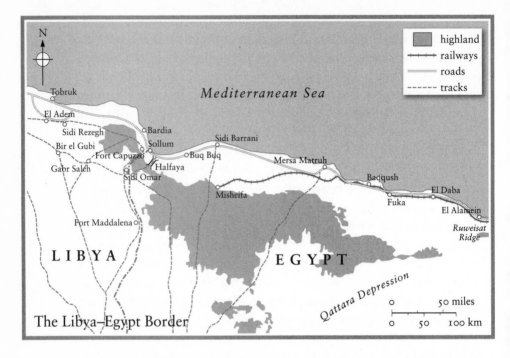

The Libya–Egypt Border

that 'British resistance has been smashed'. A British commander observed that Sidi Barrani, comprising a 'solitary mosque, police post, and a few mud huts had achieved an unexpected rise to a big city'. Back home, the Italians bragged to the Germans that once Graziani reached the Nile Delta the Arab world would rise in revolt.[7]

In fact, the Italians had suffered nearly 2,000 casualties to delaying action by small groups of British forces. More importantly, Sidi Barrani was over 80 miles from Mersa Matruh, where Wavell's forces were concentrated. Had the Italians continued their advance they may well have inflicted substantial damage on them. But Graziani's decision to stop at Sidi Barrani provided a reprieve and passed the initiative to Wavell.

Against Graziani's six divisions, Wavell and his subordinate commander of the Western Desert Force, Major General Richard O'Connor, had a paltry force of two insufficiently equipped divisions. The 7th Armoured Division consisted of two brigades, only one of which was fully equipped. The 4th Indian Division had two infantry brigades – the

5th and 11th – each of which had two Indian and one British infantry battalions. The 4th Division had received its armoured regiment, the Central India Horse, only five weeks before the Italian offensive had begun.

The 4th Indian Division was the first formation of the Indian army to serve on the frontline of the war. The Indian government had earmarked troops for despatch to the Middle East even before the outbreak of hostilities. On 22 July 1939, the secretary of state for India, Zetland, had requested Linlithgow to send them out immediately. The 11th Indian Infantry Brigade, with an artillery regiment, had sailed from India and reached Suez in mid-August. Three weeks into the war, the 5th Indian Infantry Brigade with a force headquarters embarked for Suez. In Egypt, these units were amalgamated into the 4th Indian Division, which was then placed under the Middle East Command.

Shortage of equipment apart, the units forming the 4th Indian Division had been seriously underprepared for desert warfare. As their official historian wryly observes, 'Neither the officers nor the men had ever handled an anti-tank rifle or a mortar. They had no motor vehicles or trained drivers.'[8] Although the mechanization of the Indian army had been approved some time back, the new equipment had not yet reached India. So, these units had at once to be equipped and trained. Prior to the Italian declaration of war, the division spent much of its time training to fight in its new fully motorized organization. The division also trained for mobile warfare alongside the 7th (British) Armoured Division, with which it enjoyed a close working relationship. Training continued even after Italy entered the war: as late as October 1940, troops from the division were being trained in anti-tank warfare by a New Zealand anti-tank battery. O'Connor knew that he was badly outnumbered and placed a premium on realistic training and careful rehearsals. In a letter to the two divisions under his command, he insisted that 'All troops taking part must be trained to such a pitch that their action is almost automatic.'[9] Thus, by the time the 4th Indian Division encountered the Italians it was very well trained. As a staff officer of the 11th Infantry Brigade recalled, 'We were sent out into the desert . . . and since our training for desert warfare had been hard and continuous, we were fit, we were tough and we were ready for battle.'[10]

Indeed, the morale of the troops remained high despite the devastating reverses suffered by Anglo-French forces in Europe. An Indian soldier wrote home from Egypt: 'We do not hope to come back soon; not before the death of Hitler. We are determined to finish him off this year.' With Italy's entry into the war, the military censors noted, the Indian troops 'appreciate the possible chance of fighting and increase in work relieves monotony'.[11] However, the induction of the Central India Horse (CIH) into the division introduced an element of uncertainty.

When the regiment was preparing for embarkation from Bombay in July 1940, 108 Sikh soldiers – equivalent to one squadron – had refused to proceed on overseas service. This was an early indication of the various concerns that were gradually enveloping the Jat Sikh peasantry of the Punjab, including the demand for 'Pakistan' by the Muslim League and the anti-war propaganda by radical Sikh outfits such as the Kirti Kisan. Despite attempts by officers and VCOs to cajole them, they persisted in their disobedience. The men had apparently been prepared to resist attempts at coercion and had even talked of shooting the officers and deserting with arms. Thanks to some tactful handling, the situation had not escalated into anything more than a refusal to serve abroad. But the eventual British response had been calculated to set an example. The men had been disarmed, arrested, charged with mutiny and served stiff sentences – sixteen soldiers were executed.[12]

By the time the regiment joined the 4th Indian Division on 6 August, things were under control. The same day, there was a change in the divisional leadership, with Major General Noel Beresford-Peirse taking command. Once the new commander was satisfied of the combat readiness of the CIH, the division stood ready to be deployed for the first time to a forward position in the Western Desert. On 19 August, the division moved to Nagamish – just short of Mersa Matruh. The following month the division received its third brigade, the 7th Indian Infantry Brigade, which was deployed on garrison duties at Matruh.

With the onset of the Italian offensive, the division was ordered immediately to pull back to another position at Baqqush. Faced with the Italians' numerical superiority, Wavell was cautious enough to feel the need for a prepared position further to the rear of Nagamish.

Yet Graziani surprised him by staying firmly put in Sidi Barrani and refusing to oblige by advancing on Matruh. O'Connor recalled 'a real disappointment at the time, as complete plans had been prepared to destroy his [Graziani's] whole force had he made the attempt'.[13]

In consequence, the 4th Indian Division was ordered back to Nagamish on 10 October. Towards the end of the month, it had its first land engagement with the Italians in a small raid on an Italian camp. The Italians responded by bombing the Nagamish divisional area with fifteen aircraft, losing nine of them to the RAF fighters. Ajit Singh Mann, a medical orderly from Punjab, recalled that the enemy also dropped explosives 'camouflaged as pens, pencils, watches and dolls. Indian troops used to pick [them] up and these used to blow up.'[14]

By this time, the long-awaited reinforcements – especially tanks – had reached Suez. Churchill used the opportunity to ascertain why Wavell persisted with his dilatory approach. The secretary of state for war, Anthony Eden, was sent on a fact-finding mission to Egypt in mid-October. Mindful of Churchill's 'desire to have at least one finger in any military pie', Wavell cagily revealed to Eden his evolving plan to attack the Italians at Sidi Barrani. On learning of the proposed offensive – 'Operation Compass' – Churchill by his own account 'purred like six cats'. The prime minister was rapturous, believing that Britain was at last going 'to throw off the intolerable shackles of the defensive'. In mid-November, Churchill cabled Wavell that Germany was unlikely to leave its ally unsupported for long: 'now is the time to take risks and strike the Italians'. Wavell refused to be hustled into action. The operation was under preparation, he replied, but 'not possible to execute this month as originally hoped'.[15]

At Nagamish, the Indian units were engaged in further training. The exercises were conducted in full sight of the Italians – the idea being that when necessary, training moves could be used to mask actual moves for an offensive. The divisional armoured regiment, the CIH, moved out of Nagamish and trained with the 7th Armoured Division to maintain a harassing contact with the Italians. An Indian infantry battalion was also moved up to establish logistics dumps for the division in the forward area. Petrol and ammunition, food and water were systematically stored in a dumping area of 6 square miles.

In the last week of November, the entire Indian division took part in a massive training manoeuvre organized by the Western Desert Force.[16]

The overall plan for Compass sought to exploit a key flaw in Graziani's defences. The Italian positions at Sidi Barrani were a chain of fortified camps running south for about 40 miles. Strangely, the Italians had constructed them in two clusters, with a 15-mile gap between Nibeiwa, the last camp of the northern lot, and Sofafi, the first camp of the southern group. The gap apart, the minefields ringing Nibeiwa were left open at the rear to enable the passage of supplies. The British plan tasked the 4th Indian Division with punching through this gap and attacking Nibeiwa from the rear. Thereafter the division would head north for the camps of Tummar East and West and thence to Sidi Barrani. The 7th Armoured Division would protect the flank of the 4th Indian Division from an attack from Sofafi and subsequently would turn on the southern camps. A small mixed force from Matruh would work with the Royal Navy to thwart Italian reinforcements from the north. The RAF would attack various Italian airfields in Libya to prevent the Italian air force from intervening. In short, the plan was to box in the Italians and attack them in an enclosed area.[17]

The 4th Indian Division was beefed up with a third (British) brigade as well as the recently arrived 7th Royal Tank Regiment. The regiment had forty-eight 'I' (Infantry) or 'Matilda' tanks. Fitted with a 40mm gun and a thick plating of armour, the Matildas were the spearhead of the 4th Indian Division. They would lead the strike on Nibeiwa supported by the 11th Indian Infantry Brigade, and would subsequently attack Tummar with the 5th Indian Infantry Brigade.

On 7 December, the RAF began its bombardment of the Italian airfields. The next night, the Desert Force moved its formations to within 15 miles of the Nibeiwa gap. At 0700 on 9 December the artillery units began registering their targets. Fifteen minutes later, the seventy-two guns with the 4th Indian Division sent shells raining down on the Italian defences. At 0735, the Matildas reached the Nibeiwa perimeter and made short work of the Italian MII tanks that were lined up unmanned in parade-ground formation. As the Matildas pushed into the camp, the Italians fired all weapons at their disposal – only to realize that none of their ammunition could pierce the skin of the British tanks. The 11th Indian Infantry Brigade followed closely behind and stubbed out all pockets of resistance. Within an hour from the start, the Indian brigade was in control of Nibeiwa.

Tummar West fell in a similar fashion. Emboldened by these quick successes, the divisional commander ordered an immediate attack on Tummar East. The Italians were coincidentally setting out from that position for a counter-attack and were mowed down by the machine guns of the 5th Indian Infantry Brigade. Even before Tummar East was mopped up by the brigade, Beresford-Peirse ordered the third, British, brigade to cut the road from Sidi Barrani to Buq Buq. By early afternoon on 10 December, the division had encircled Sidi Barrani. The commander decided to press on with an attack on the Italian camp near the village. Thirty-six hours after it began, the battle of Sidi Barrani was at an end;[18] 38,000 Italian troops were captured as well as 73 medium and light tanks, 237 guns, over 1,000 vehicles and large quantities of ammunition and stores. The British force sustained 624 casualties, the majority of them only wounded.

At 1630 hours on 10 December, as Beresford-Peirse watched one of his battalions leaving the start line for the final assault on the village, a liaison officer arrived from Cairo in a staff car. He carried orders that the 4th Indian Division was to be replaced at the soonest by the 6th Australian Division and was to move to the Sudan. 'This was at that moment a singularly unpalatable order for the Indian Division', Beresford-Peirse would note later, 'involved as they were in winning the first big success of the war.' He did not pass on the order until the Italians had finally surrendered on 11 December 1940.[19]

The decision to pull out the 4th Indian Division was controversial. The commander of the Western Desert Force was not alone in thinking that it impeded the subsequent pursuit of Italian forces along the coast of North Africa. 'There is no doubt', O'Connor later insisted, 'that the loss of the 4th Ind. Div. lost us three weeks or more, since 6 Aus. Div. was not ready . . . for a full month.' And he added: 'what a lot we could have done with the 4 Ind. Div. & a fleeing enemy'.[20] The division was indeed well trained, fully equipped and battle tested. As such its replacement with a new division was deeply problematic. The switching of the divisions may well have been decisive in preventing the British from capturing Tripoli before Rommel arrived with German reinforcements. More generally, the pulling out of the 4th Indian Division inaugurated a trend whereby well-prepared and battle-hardened Indian units would frequently find themselves tossed around between various fronts and theatres. That said, Wavell had his own reasons and compulsions. To be sure, he had not foreseen the extent to which Operation Compass would succeed and the possibilities it would throw open. Nevertheless, the decision was primarily taken in response to a combination of political pressure and a deteriorating operational situation in East Africa.

In July 1940, the Italians based in Abyssinia (Ethiopia) and Eritrea had attacked and captured the border towns of Kassala and Gallabat in the Sudan. The following month, they had overrun British Somaliland. The withdrawal of the small British force from Somaliland with minimal casualties had enraged Churchill. It felt like an African Dunkirk – only worse for the troops having been turfed out by the Italians. 'What you need out there is a court martial and a firing squad', he growled: 'Wavell has 300,000 men.'[21] Although Wavell disagreed, observing that 'a big butcher's bill was not necessarily evidence of good tactics', he was thereafter on the back foot in East Africa.

Wavell, for his part, was well aware of the importance of East Africa. With the closing of the Mediterranean, the Red Sea provided the only route for his command to receive supplies from Britain and India. He was anxious for the defence of Port Sudan and Djibouti, but perceived the principal danger as the presence of eight Italian submarines and seven fleet destroyers in the Eritrean port of Massawa.

During his visit to Egypt in October 1940, Eden flew down to Khartoum with Wavell and conferred with the local military commander as well as with General Jan Smuts of South Africa. General Platt, the commander in the Sudan, said that he was planning offensives to retake Gallabat and Kassala; Smuts insisted that these offensives be co-ordinated with military operations in Kenya to capture Kismayo – and eventually attack Ethiopia. Eden concurred with this view. It was agreed that offensive operations towards these ends must

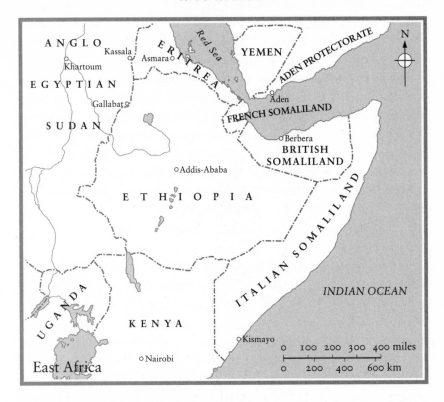

East Africa

begin as early as possible.[22] Churchill, of course, was raring for an offensive.

Sudan initially had only three British battalions. A squadron of tanks was despatched from Egypt in early September 1940. Later that month, the 5th Indian Division began arriving from India. Formed in 1939, the division was badly trained and worse equipped for combat in East Africa. An Indian staff officer recalled that they were 'grossly overloaded with extraneous material, both personal and military, presumably to meet any contingency including social ones'.[23] The division also had an unquiet passage to Africa. En route to embarkation, it was abuzz with rumours about a ship being sunk off the coast of Bombay by a German U-boat. This led to desertions in some units. Sardara Singh, a young soldier with the transport company, was handcuffed with his comrades and placed under British guard. In Bombay, his unit was put on board HMS *Talamba*. The ship was then taken some miles out to sea to anchor. 'The British officer then removed the handcuffs and told us that we were now free. From here it was impossible to desert.' Sardara felt that the British had been 'over cautious'. Some of his comrades had panicked only because they had 'hardly been given any worthwhile briefing for the war'.[24] But German intelligence and propaganda were busy as well – not least because of appalling operational secrecy in the Indian army. An Indian officer noted that 'though our destination was supposed to be secret, everyone from canteen contractors to the General knew it was Port Sudan'.[25] William Joyce, the Irish-American admirer of Hitler known as 'Lord Haw-Haw', broadcast to India the precise details of the 5th Indian Division's shipping arrangements, adding for good measure that 'none of them will arrive at their destination which is Port Sudan'.[26]

The voyage also set the men on edge. Second Lieutenant Prem Bhagat wrote to his girlfriend that 'a sea journey does get a bit exacting when there is a ship full of men with nothing to do'.[27] As the ships approached Port Sudan, there was another surprise for the Indians. An enemy plane flew overhead, scattering leaflets in Punjabi, Hindi and English with warnings to the effect: 'We will come two hours later and sink the ship, so better run away but we will not attack soldiers running away.'[28] This briefly rattled the British as well as the Indian troops.

On reaching Sudan the division was reorganized. It originally had two brigades with three Indian battalions each. The existing units in the Sudan were placed under its command bringing it up to its full strength. The 5th Indian Division now had three infantry brigades – the 9th, 10th and 29th – each of which had two Indian and one British battalion, and two regiments of artillery and two companies of engineers. In addition, a mobile unit called 'Gazelle Force' was formed around the divisional armoured regiment, the Skinner's Horse.

The 5th Indian Division's main task was the defence of Khartoum and it was deployed in the vicinity of Kassala. However, the divisional commander, Major General Lewis 'Piggy' Heath, was determined to undertake local offensives against the Italians. In early November 1940, Gazelle Force engaged Italian forces 25 miles north-east of Kassala. After ten days of skirmishing, the force was tasked with attacking Big Hill, an imposing mile-long feature immediately to the north of the Italian position. The plan was based on dubious intelligence about the strength and morale of the Italian troops – it was believed that the majority of the Italians would surrender at the first opportunity. In the event, they put up a tenacious defence and no headway could be made. The attack failed and Gazelle Force had to pull back.[29]

This early engagement suggested that the Italian troops in East Africa were better prepared, led and motivated than Graziani's forces in North Africa. These facts, as well as British weaknesses, were amply underscored by another abortive offensive in the first week of November. On Wavell's instructions, Heath prepared a plan to capture the forts of Gallabat and Metemma. The attack was to be carried out by the 10th Indian Infantry Brigade with a British armoured squadron of twelve tanks.

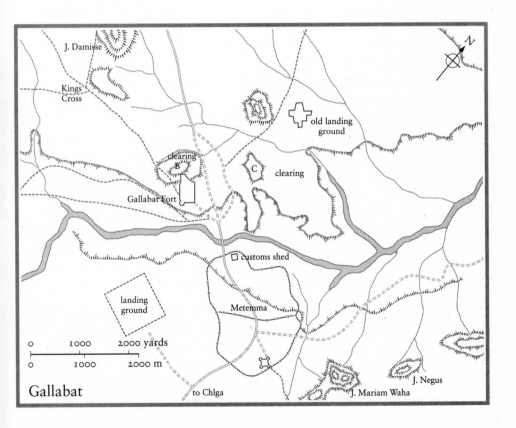

The brigade was led by an officer who would, by the end of the war, be recognized as one of the outstanding Allied commanders: Brigadier William Slim. Originally commissioned into the British army during the First World War, 'Bill' Slim was transferred to the Indian army in 1919. Between the wars, he shinned up the professional ladder, serving as an instructor in staff colleges in India and Britain as well as commanding his battalion, the 2/7th Gurkha Rifles. Of humble origins, Slim commanded universal respect, from British and Indian soldiers alike, for his down-to-earth style and his twinkling sense of humour. His ability to quickly grasp the human angle to any situation was obvious to anyone who read the novels, short stories and hilarious essays that he penned under the pseudonym of Anthony Mills. Captain J. N. Chaudhuri, who served with Slim in Sudan and later became chief of the Indian army, was 'impressed by his calmness in any situation and his inherent powers of leadership which were immediately apparent. There was no guile about the man. He meant what he said and he said it pleasantly.'[30]

On reaching the Sudan, though, Slim was peeved with the set-up. In particular, he was unhappy with Heath's decision to reshuffle his troops by replacing an Indian battalion, the 3/2nd Punjab, with the 1st Battalion of the Essex Regiment. He thought that this smacked of an old belief that the presence of white troops would stiffen the natives. Slim protested but was overruled. His brigade went into action with the 4/10th Baluch and the 3/18th Royal Garhwal Rifles as well as the 1st Essex. The plan was first to capture Gallabat and then move on to Metemma. On the evening of 5 November, the 10th Indian Brigade advanced to forward positions a mile and half from the Gallabat fort. Preparations were made with perfect secrecy. From his command post on a nearby hillock, Slim looked on with a measure of satisfaction.

> Our plans were made, the attacking troops had reached their start lines, and guns and tanks were ready with their crews sleeping beside them. I felt as I lay down and pulled a blanket over me that while like other mortals we could not command success, we had done all we could to deserve it.[31]

Slim was up before dawn and anxiously awaited the first wave of air strikes by the RAF. At 0530 hours the artillery and air bombardment began. The fort was shrouded in dust as shells rained down on it. For a while it became all but invisible to Slim, who was peering through his binoculars. As the guns fell silent, the tanks roared up to the fort with the Garhwalis in tow. The Italians had carefully laid down their defences and Slim's troops initially found the going tough. By 0730, however, the fort was overrun and captured, but of the ten tanks that led the attack only one remained serviceable. The tank commander informed Slim that a truck loaded with spares was on its way but it would take several hours before the tanks could be fixed. The Italians sensed that the attack was sputtering and launched a counter-attack on the positions now occupied by the Indians. Although the counter-attack was repulsed, Slim decided to postpone the attack on Metemma and consolidate the Garhwal and Essex battalions at Gallabat.

At this point, the Italians gained the upper hand in the air. Italian Caproni bombers escorted by a squadron of CR42 fighters bombed Gallabat. Five British Gladiator fighters sought to engage them and were promptly shot down. Prem Bhagat was in Gallabat fort with his company of sappers: 'in 40 minutes some 14 planes just littered the place with bombs. I lay flat on the ground and after the bombing was over I was covered with earth, two bombs having dropped just five yards away.'[32] Worse still, the bombing began minutes after the 1st Essex entered the fort. The British troops scrambled for cover as shrapnel and rocks whizzed around them. The explosion of an ammunition truck unhinged a few of them, who fled and implored the others to join them. Waves of panic swept through the battalion and before the officers could get a grip on the situation, several men had seized two trucks and bolted out of the fort. The morale of the battalion was seriously shaken. Italian bombers returned that night and the next morning without any interference from British aircraft. After consulting his senior officers, Slim reluctantly ordered a withdrawal.[33] Although the attack had gone awry, Slim was lucky enough to come out of the East African theatre professionally unscathed – ironically, because he was strafed by an Italian aeroplane a few days later.

The failure at Gallabat underscored Italian strengths as well as British weaknesses in the East African theatre. The Italian defences

were well prepared, with extensive use of obstacles, mutually supporting firing positions and carefully stationed reserves. Italian aircraft
and artillery were capable of supporting the infantry formations and
the men fought in terrain with which they were familiar and were
strong on the defensive. British forces, on the other hand, were
grouped into brigades that had not trained, let alone fought, together.
Although the Indian units had some experience of fighting in similar
conditions at the north-west frontier, their skills were rusty. For several months, the units had been preparing to operate as a mechanized
force. Slim's brigade, for instance, had spent considerable time learning to drive motorized vehicles and fighting mobile wars. But their
ability to operate alongside tanks was clearly of little use in a terrain
most unsuited to tank warfare. Further, the Indian formations were
ill-prepared to cope with Italian air superiority: they had no anti-
aircraft guns. The inability to protect forward troops against air
attack was a major shortcoming.

After the setback at Gallabat, Wavell reverted to his cautious self.
He now decided to postpone the larger operation to capture Kismayo
until after the rains in May 1941. On 23 November, Wavell informed
the chiefs of staff of his thinking. In the war cabinet, Churchill
strongly criticized Wavell's procrastination and asked the chiefs to
obtain a full explanation. Against this backdrop, Wavell chaired a
conference in Cairo on 2 December to consider the strategy in East
Africa. The South Africans pressed the case for an offensive on Kismayo, but the others agreed with Wavell that this would be premature.
It was decided that preparations were to be made for recapturing
Kassala in early February 1941 – provided reinforcements could be
sent from Egypt. And Wavell planned to send the 4th Indian Division
to the Sudan if the attack on Sidi Barrani went well.[34]

At this point, Wavell 'did not intend . . . a large scale invasion either
from Kassala towards Asmara and Massawa, or from Kismayu to the
north'. These offensives were merely designed to secure the flanks
while the main effort would be to support by irregular operations a
brewing indigenous, 'Patriot', revolt against the Italians in Ethiopia –
operations that were co-ordinated by Lieutenant Colonel Orde
Wingate. In fact, after the capture of Kassala and Kismayo, Wavell
intended to 'withdraw as many troops as possible from the Sudan

and East Africa for the theatres further north'.[35] The plan for East Africa was thus carefully circumscribed. It was designed to stave off political pressure and prevent further deterioration of the British military position. As in North Africa, it was the Italians who would hand the initiative to Wavell.

The 4th Indian Division began disengaging from the Italians near Sidi Barrani on 12 December 1940. Sixteen days later, the division's 7th Indian Infantry Brigade – the garrison force at Matruh – embarked on the short voyage to Port Sudan. The 11th Indian Infantry Brigade followed on New Year's Day 1941, while the 5th Indian Infantry Brigade was moved overland by rail and by Nile steamer. The redeployment was nearly flawless – the only glitch being an Italian air attack on the train carrying the 3/14th Punjab battalion, which resulted in some losses. By the end of January 1941, the entire division was concentrated in the Sudan. The 7th Indian Brigade was deployed to defend Port Sudan and its lines of communication; the rest of the division headed for the Kassala sector, where it was joined by the Gazelle Force. The 5th Indian Division stayed put in the Gallabat sector and engaged in an elaborate deception to divert the Italians' attention from the coming offensive on Kassala.

Yet again, however, it was the Italians who surprised their adversary. From early January there were indications that the Italian forces might be preparing to withdraw from Kassala. The British commanders hesitated to pre-empt this move, fearing that a hasty attack launched with inadequate forces might prove disastrous. The Italian intention to pull back became clearer by the day, so an operation was planned to prevent the Italian forces from getting away intact. The attack was to be launched by a mixed force of the 4th and 5th Indian Divisions on 19 January. The night before, the Italians gave them the slip. The Indian divisions were ordered immediately to commence a pursuit.[36] The Italian withdrawal lifted the threat to the Sudan and pulled the Indian forces into Eritrea.[37]

The Indian forces pursued the retreating Italians on two axes. In the north, the 4th Indian Division, led by the Gazelle Force, advanced from Kassala to Wachai and thence to Keru and Agordat. The 5th Indian Division took a southerly route from Kassala to Aicota

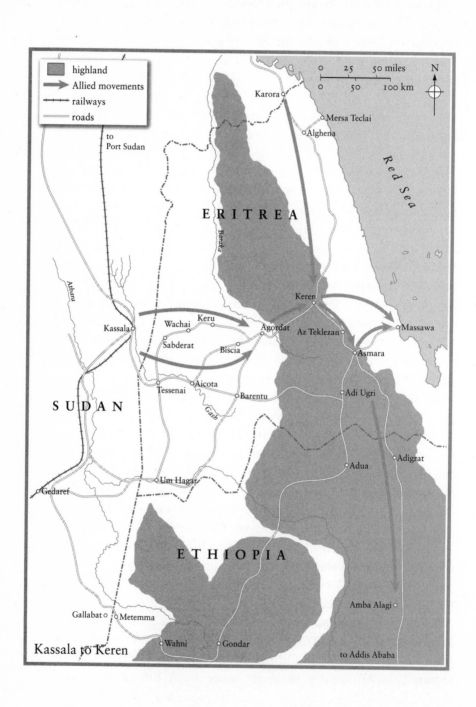

Kassala to Keren

and thence to Barentu and Agordat. The Italians staged a fighting retreat. They had prepared delaying positions on tactically important hills and mined the key approaches. In particular, they offered considerable resistance at Keru and Barentu. The terrain, too, was not suited to a rapid chase by the Indians. The country around Kassala was a desert plain with knee-high scrub and the odd hillock, but to the east of Kassala the hills rose high and the valleys were rocky. And these posed a formidable challenge to the passage of mechanical transport.

A few days after their withdrawal from Kassala, the Italians pulled out of Gallabat as well. The Italian retreat here was less hasty, for they had heavily mined the area. Bhagat's sappers worked ahead of the 9th Indian Infantry Brigade in clearing this route. 'The last ten days have been a bit trying,' he wrote on 10 February 1941, 'especially as I have had three narrow escapes. Luckily the only damage done is that I have now got a deaf ear.' Bhagat had been on the road for ninety-six hours, sweeping fifteen minefields over a 55-mile stretch, despite being blown off his vehicle twice and ambushed by the Italians – an astonishing display of courage under fire for which he had just been awarded the Victoria Cross. But he found little glorious about the pursuit of the Italians: 'The last ten days have been quite a revelation to me of war. Dead bodies lying on the road, some mangled and no one taking any notice of them. To think the same body had life and enjoyed himself a few hours before is preposterous.'[38]

Near Agordat the Italian forces put up a tenacious defence, counter-attacking positions taken by the Indians and bringing to bear accurate artillery fire on the Indian forward positions. Eventually, they broke contact with the Indian forces and retreated further. Agordat was the first town in Eritrea to be captured by the Indians, and its fall prodded Wavell into perceiving greater opportunities in Eritrea. He now favoured a major operation aimed at capturing Asmara itself. He realized that this would thwart his earlier plan of sending forces back to Egypt, but felt that the operations in the Western Desert were 'going very well . . . there was no immediate need of additional troops in Egypt'. Wavell instructed General Platt to 'continue his pursuit and press on towards Asmara'.[39] But the road to Asmara ran through Keren.

The town of Keren stood on a plateau at a height of over 4,300 feet.
The region around Keren, the British realized, was 'a wild immensity
of peaks, knife-edge ridges, precipices, gorges and narrow defiles'.[40]
The road from Agordat ran in a north-easterly direction up the
narrow Ascidira Valley towards a range of imposing hills that stood
guard around the Keren plateau. As the road hugged the lower reaches
of these hills, it passed through a narrow cleft – nowhere wider than
300 yards – called the Dongolaas Gorge. Along the eastern wall of
the gorge, the road wound its way up to Keren. On either side of the
gorge stretched a series of tangled ridges and massifs. To the east lay
mounts Dologorodoc and Zeban, Falestoh and Zelale. In the west
were the even more formidable mounts Sanchil and Samanna. The
Italians had long realized the strategic importance of Keren for the
defence of Asmara and had deployed the bulk of their troops there
in defensive positions that dominated the high ground and key
approaches in the area.

The first assault on the defences of Keren was undertaken by the 4th
Indian Division. In the afternoon of 3 February, the 2nd Cameron
Highlanders of the 11th Indian Brigade attacked and captured a ridge
just south of Sanchil. The feature was promptly dubbed Cameron
Ridge. Thereafter, the going was tough. The 3/14th Punjab attacked a
peak on Sanchil but were unable to hold it against Italian counter-
attacks supported by artillery and machine-gun fire. The 1/6th
Rajputana Rifles secured a position to the west of Cameron Ridge, but
were eventually dislodged by successive waves of counter-attacks. By
the night of 6 February, the Indians were left with only a tenuous toe-
hold at Cameron Ridge. This too was under attack from the Italians.[41]
'In the ding-dong battle', Babu Singh of the 3/1st Punjab was injured
at around 6 p.m. on 10 February. 'By then heavy casualties had taken
place. Our Colonel . . . who was also injured, announced that there
was no arrangement to evacuate the dead and injured, and called
upon each man to fend for himself and retreat.'[42]

General Platt now realized that the 'storming of Keren position
was no light task . . . Gaining surprise was unlikely. The forcing of
Keren was bound to mean hard fighting and casualties which would
be difficult to replace.'[43] Finding a way around the road and the main
Italian defences was evidently desirable. Between Falestoh and Zelale

lay a low-slung ridge called Acqua Gap, over which ran a secondary track to Keren. The 5th Indian Brigade of the 4th Division was tasked to capture this gap on the night of 7 February. The brigade was reinforced by a troop of four Matilda tanks. 'The hope of gaining surprise was very strong and the low morale of the Italian forces was expected to be of considerable help.'[44] It did not work out like that. The 4/6th Rajputana Rifles came under intense fire and sustained heavy losses on the approach to Acqua Gap. Although the battalion managed to capture parts of the ridge, it position was precarious at daybreak. The entire area and all lines of approach were dominated by Italian positions. The brigade commander decided against deploying his reserves and ordered a withdrawal at dusk.[45]

Beresford-Peirse thereafter decided on a co-ordinated divisional operation for the capture of Keren. In the first phase, the 11th Indian Brigade would capture a peak on Sanchil. In the next, the Gazelle Force with two battalions would take Acqua Gap. The 5th Indian Brigade would then break through to Keren. It was an unimaginative plan that unsurprisingly ended up reinforcing the earlier failures and totting up casualties. By the morning of 14 February, when the operation was finally called off, the Indians held nothing more than Cameron Ridge.[46]

The inability of the 4th Indian Division to crack the Keren defences stemmed from several factors. To begin with, the division suffered from a combination of over-confidence and under-preparation. Flush with success in North Africa, the division believed that it was up against Italian soldiers of the same poor quality and morale as it had earlier encountered. At the same time, it had – even more than the 5th Indian Division – unlearnt its previous skills of operating in such terrain. What is more, not all its troops had been bloodied in the battles of North Africa. A British officer recalled his experience of being shelled by the Italians in Keren: 'It was the first time I had been under fire and I was quite surprised at first – rather feeling that the enemy was cheating using live rounds on manoeuvres.'[47]

Attacks tended to peter out as the troops neared the enemy positions above them and the artillery fire was lifted. The lack of training was also evident in the inability of troops to hold the features they captured. Most often the defences of these positions were not reoriented fast enough to stave off counter-attacks by the Italians, or indeed to protect against air and artillery strikes. Commanders tended to shy away from night attacks, too; these called for greater levels of training and preparation but also carried greater possibilities of surprise.

Further, all the battalions of the division were organized for mechanical transport, but the terrain rendered movement by vehicles impossible. In consequence, the battalions had to employ one company entirely for porterage. Supplies of water, rations and ammunition had to be dumped ahead of offensives. All arms and ammunition had to be carried by the soldiers up steep hills during attacks. Worse, this had to be done in hot weather – the approach marches tended to sap the strength out of the troops even before an assault commenced. A related problem was the futility of employing tanks in this terrain. Even the light tanks broke down whenever deployed. Hence, regiments like Skinner's Horse were used as infantry, providing fire support during attacks – a role for which they had no training or experience.

As the 4th Indian Division pondered the lessons of the failed offensives, Wavell informed London of the lack of progress: 'the enemy has been counter-attacking fiercely and repeatedly shows no immediate signs of cracking'. Ever eager for a victory, Churchill shot back: 'I presume you have considered whether there are any reinforcements which can be sent to give you mastery at Keren.' There were none. Wavell was also concerned about the possibility of a German offensive in Libya to bail out the Italians and was worried that the stalemate in Keren would obviate the possibility of moving troops out of East Africa.

After the failure of the 4th Indian Division's attacks to the east and west of the Dongolaas Gorge, General Platt realized that 'any further assault on the Keren position would be a major operation'.[48] Both the 4th and 5th Divisions would have to be hurled against the resolute Italians. Logistically, however, it was impossible simultaneously to maintain both divisions in the Keren area and to prepare dumps of supplies for an attack by two divisions. Hence, the 5th Indian Division was pulled back to positions behind Agordat, where it could be supported from the railhead at Kassala.

This turned out to be doubly advantageous. First, it enabled the division to carry out intense training in mountain warfare. Brigadier

Frank Messervy, acting commander of the 9th Indian Brigade, issued training instructions stating that 'It is the problem of the last 400 yards when our men are tired, when our fire support problem becomes more difficult, and when the enemy will put in everything he can to stop us, which has to be satisfactorily solved.'[49] Tactics were studied and practised; the men were knocked into high levels of physical fitness. Second, the division could be brought forward to Keren at the last moment. This kept the Italians guessing both about the date and size of the attack, and so secured a measure of surprise at the outset.

As the logistical build-up proceeded apace, the 4th Division had a tough time holding on to Cameron Ridge. The division took almost twenty-five casualties a day and its commander grew anxious about remaining for much longer. Pulling out, however, would have rendered a further attack all the more difficult. So, the 4th Division stayed put. In retrospect, this hiatus was useful for the division to acquaint itself with the terrain and brush up its tactics.

The outline plan for the renewed operation was drawn up by Platt on 1 March 1941, in consultation with the divisional commanders: Major General Beresford-Peirse of the 4th Division and Major General Heath of the 5th Division. The 4th Division would attack features to the north and west of the road – Sanchil and beyond. The 5th Division would operate east of the road, though its objectives were initially undefined. After detailed reconnaissance, it was decided that this division would capture mounts Dologorodoc and Zeban. These were formidable objectives with well-prepared defences. But they held certain advantages for the attacker. For one, the reverse slopes of these hills were relatively gentle and Italian targets on the other side of the crest could be hit by artillery. This would be most useful in repelling the inevitable counter-attacks. For another, these objectives – unlike the Acqua Gap – were close to the 4th Division's axis of attack. The combined artillery fire of the divisions could therefore be trained initially to support the 4th Division and then easily switched to support the 5th Division.[50] For a third, bypassing these strongholds would have been the easier tack to take: the 4th Division had already attempted this twice. The Italians naturally expected the enemy to persist with these attempts.

At 0700 hours on 15 March 1941, the battle for Keren began again. Unlike earlier, the 4th Division could now deploy all three brigades to capture objectives east of the road. By 0945, the situation on this front seemed sufficiently satisfactory to allow the 5th Division to commence its attack. But as the men of the 4th Division crawled up the mountains they came under heavy and accurate fire. The battalions that managed to rush the Italian defences were so drained by casualties that they could not hold these positions for long. The 1/6th Rajputana Rifles and the 2/5th Mahratta Light Infantry lost upwards of 50 per cent of their strength; all barring one officer of the 3/18th Garhwal Rifles became casualties.[51] By the night of 18 March, several positions captured initially had to be abandoned.

The 5th Division's attack on Dologorodoc began on the morning of 15 March with a single battalion, the 2nd Highland Infantry. It was an oppressively hot day and the Highlanders' failure to make any headway was as much due to fatigue as enemy fire. The commander of the 9th Indian Brigade, Brigadier Mosley Mayne, sensibly decided to renew the attack with two fresh battalions, the 3/12th Frontier Force and the 3/5th Mahrattas. More importantly, he launched the attack after dusk. The decision to risk a night attack paid off and the two battalions managed to capture sub-features of Dologorodoc. Although Mayne lost touch with them, he sent forward his third battalion. The 2nd West Yorkshire established contact with the other battalions at midnight and occupied a wedge between them. When the Italians counter-attacked at first light, they came up against the entire brigade. And they were swiftly trapped in a field of fire between the positions of the 9th Brigade and their own fort, which was now under accurate artillery fire. As the Italians fled, the 9th Brigade moved ahead and occupied Fort Dologorodoc.

The 5th Division's plan was for the 29th Indian Infantry Brigade to pass through the positions of the 9th Brigade and make for Zeban. On the night of 16/17 March, the 29th Brigade began its attack. However, the Italians put up a stern defence and prevented the brigade from advancing more than 800 yards beyond the Fort. The brigade was not only pinned down but also faced a serious logistical problem. The next day, food and ammunition had to be dropped to the troops by RAF planes. The divisional commander had no option but to reel in the brigade and consolidate his hold on Fort Dologorodoc.

Over the next week, the Italians launched no fewer than eight counter-attacks – all of which were beaten back with heavy casualties. The haemorrhaging of Italian fighting power in these attacks proved decisive to the course of the campaign. On 25 March, the 5th Division renewed its offensive. By this time, Italian air power had been completely neutralized. Between them the one fighter and three bomber squadrons of the RAF in the theatre had chased the Italian aircraft out of the skies and destroyed them on the ground. The last Italian air-attack on the Indian divisions came on 26 March. Thereafter, the RAF had complete air superiority.[52]

Early next morning, there were indications that the Italians might be withdrawing. When the 29th Brigade captured Zeban, there was no opposition. The Italians had evacuated Keren. The Indians were swift in pursuit and at 10 a.m. on 27 March 1941, a mobile force from the brigade entered Keren. Throughout that morning, white flags popped up from Italian positions, especially those to the east and north of Dongolaas Gorge that had put up a staunch fight against the 4th Division.

Keren was captured at the cost of 500 killed and 3,000 wounded. This was a high price, but it amounted to just 5 per cent of the Italian casualties and prisoners. 'I must say the Italians fought very well', wrote Prem Bhagat, 'but could not stick to it as long as us. We had literal hell for a month or so, but I think it was worth it. The danger to India from this quarter is over.'[53] Indeed, with the capture of Keren, the road to Asmara and beyond lay wide open. Although the Italians staged a planned withdrawal from Keren, taking with them about 60 per cent of their artillery and all their anti-aircraft guns, their morale was battered. As the Italians pulled out, their wounded and stragglers were left behind. Sardara Singh saw a young Italian lying by the road just outside Keren.

Stopping my truck, I got down and unseen slowly moved to the spot. With my gun ready I suddenly came upon him. He closed his eyes on seeing me. I saw him bleed profusely. I tied a bandage tightly on his thigh and folded his pants up. He had no water in his water bottle. So I put some water from my water bottle. I took out his identity card and a photograph of a girl. I looked at his young, handsome almost teenaged face.

I carefully put back his papers. Young men had a common bond. My thought was clear. I had no enemies, so I helped him and moved away.[54]

The 5th Division, now under the command of the newly promoted Major General Mayne following General Heath's transfer to Malaya to command the Indian 3rd Corps, undertook a hot pursuit. Bhagat was out with his sappers one night: 'it was raining and fairly cold with a cutting wind. To make matters worse the enemy were mortaring (shelling) heavily. I contrived to find a place behind a rock and actually went to sleep.'[55] Nevertheless, the advance was inexorable. At first light on 1 April, an Italian convoy with white flags streamed out of Asmara and surrendered to the advancing troops. The 5th Division pressed onwards to Massawa, which fell on 8 April.

The Italians did considerable damage to the town and port of Massawa before the 5th Division took control. Asmara was in better shape but posed a trickier problem. Of the 80,000 residents of Asmara, almost half were Italians. The African population included soldiers and conscripts for local defence. Disarming and administering Asmara taxed the resources the 5th Division, but fortunately the locals were somewhat awed at the sight of the Indian, especially Sikh, soldiers. The owner of a photo studio made so bold as to walk up to Sardara Singh:

> he asked me about my turban and wanted to know what was hidden beneath. I explained to him the meaning of a turban for a Sikh. He offered a cigarette which I declined. He was again surprised . . . eventually asked me to show what lay below the turban. They held their breath as I took off my turban and showed my hair. They were amazed.

The Indians, for their part, found Asmara 'a cool place'. Coffee was a novelty that they encountered there, though they did not take to its aroma.[56]

Meantime, units of the 5th Division moved from Massawa to Amba Alagi in Ethiopia, where they joined up with African forces that had advanced from Western Abyssinia. At noon on 19 May 1941, the Duke of Aosta, the Italian commander-in-chief in East Africa, formally surrendered to General Mayne, effectively ending the East African campaign. Wavell wrote to London that the 'ultimate pattern of the conquest was a pincer movement on the largest scale'. With characteristic candour, he admitted that 'this result was not foreseen in the original plan but arose gradually through the development of events. It was in fact an improvisation after the British fashion of war rather than a set piece in the German manner.'[57]

Well before Amba Alagi fell, Wavell's attention had turned again to North Africa, where the long-feared German intervention had resulted in Rommel's forces rolling back the Western Desert Force. On 29 March, two days after the capture of Keren, the 4th Indian Division had been ordered to move to Port Sudan for embarkation to North Africa. The division would, however, leave one brigade behind. Thus, for the second time in four months, the 4th Division was pulled out of theatre at the moment of victory.

Historians continue to wonder if it was wise on Wavell's part to have taken the 4th Division out of North Africa in the first place. The East African campaign is at best seen as a sideshow, if not an irrelevant diversion. From India's vantage point, however, the campaign was essential for the security of its sub-imperial sphere of influence. By clearing Axis forces from the Arabian and Red Seas, India's connectivity with the Mediterranean and Britain was preserved. Moreover, for the Indian army, East Africa was a significant theatre of war. Officers and soldiers gained valuable tactical, operational and logistical experience, and the learning acquired at Keren would shape the army's performance in other theatres. Indeed, it is striking that officers from the two divisions in Eritrea went on to hold so many important command positions: Brigadier Slim of the 10th Indian Brigade commanded the Fourteenth Army in Burma; Major General Heath of the 5th Indian Division commanded the 3rd Corps in Malaya; while Brigadier Messervy of the Gazelle Force and the 9th Indian Brigade commanded the 4th Corps in Burma. Seven other officers rose to become divisional commanders in the Middle East, Burma and Italy.[58] More important was the moral and psychological effect of the victory in East Africa. Babu Singh of the 3/1st Punjab conceded that 'Many soldiers died or were wounded in the brief span of time. Village families lost their young hopes and young soldiers were to carry the scars and incapacities for the rest of their lives.' Yet, 'the bloody battle sent a signal to the enemy. The Hindustani soldier was not a pushover.'[59]

6

The Oil Campaigns

The commander-in-chief of India was not enthusiastic about the move. General Claude Auchinleck had taken over barely three months before and now, in April 1941, his Army Headquarters – recently renamed the General Headquarters (GHQ) – had to shift to Simla. The move was part of the annual migration of the government of India to the hills to escape the torrid Delhi summer, a tradition that continued despite the ongoing war. Auchinleck was already perturbed at the persistence of such pre-war practices and mores in his headquarters. The war had not touched India's frontiers and the Indian army was mostly deployed in distant theatres. Still, he was alert to the possibility that the Indian security glacis might be imperilled in the not-so-distant future. The war, he felt, was gradually encroaching on the Raj's sphere of influence and yet there was a general obliviousness to this within the Raj – summed up by the almost absurd inefficiency of the move to Simla. Although he was not unaware of the potential threat to the east, Auchinleck's immediate concern was in the west – where a crisis was brewing in Iraq.

An erstwhile province of the Ottoman Empire, Iraq had been occupied by Britain during the First World War. The Indian army had played an important role in its conquest: nearly 675,000 Indian troops had been deployed in Iraq, and although the Indian army had suffered a humiliating defeat, at Kut in 1916, it had gone on to occupy the country. After the war, Iraq was administered by Britain as a League of Nations mandated territory. The outbreak of a major rebellion in 1920 had led London to turn again to India for troops. Eventually the country was granted independence under the Anglo-Iraqi treaty of 1930 and British troops departed in 1937. Under the terms of the treaty, however, Britain retained the right to use Iraqi facilities in the event of war. In turn, Britain supplied equipment and advisers to the Iraqi armed forces.

Iraq was of considerable strategic importance to Britain. For one thing, there was oil. Pumped from the British-controlled fields in Mosul and Kirkuk, Iraqi oil flowed through pipelines to the ports of Haifa in Palestine and Tripoli in Syria. Moreover, the Iraqi port of Basra was the principal outlet for the main Iranian oilfields – owned by the Anglo-Iranian Oil Company – just across the frontier at Abadan. The Middle East accounted for only 5 per cent of world oil production in 1941: the United States produced 83 per cent.[1] Yet American neutrality and German ability to interdict supplies crossing the Atlantic lent great importance to the cheap oil coming out of the Middle East. By the same token, if these oilfields fell under German domination, let alone control, it would deal a huge blow to Britain.[2]

Moreover, Iraq was an important link in imperial communications. It provided a land-bridge from the Mediterranean to India – a route that would be of great value in sustaining British forces in Egypt, if the Suez and Red Sea routes were closed. British airbases in Iraq, especially Habbaniya near Baghdad and Shaiba near Basra, were important stops on the air route to India, the Far East and Australia.

From the standpoint of India, Iraq was important on two more counts. First, it was an integral part of the external defence strategy of India. Not only did Iraq border Iran, but controlling the mouth of the Persian Gulf at Basra was regarded as indispensable to the wider security of India. As the chiefs of staff put it, 'if Iraq and Iran became subservient to the Axis powers our enemies would be at the gates of India'.[3] Second, developments in Iraq would inevitably impact on the Arab littoral states and on Saudi Arabia, which all fell under the Raj's sphere of influence. In particular, India's ability to use the area from Bahrain to Kuwait depended on a friendly regime in Iraq.

At the outbreak of war, Iraq was ruled by a pro-British regent and an equally well-disposed government. Prime Minister Nuri as-Said promptly accepted British demands to sever diplomatic ties with Germany and provide assistance to Britain. The alacrity with which he acted gave a handle to his opponents. Britain's role in the affairs of an

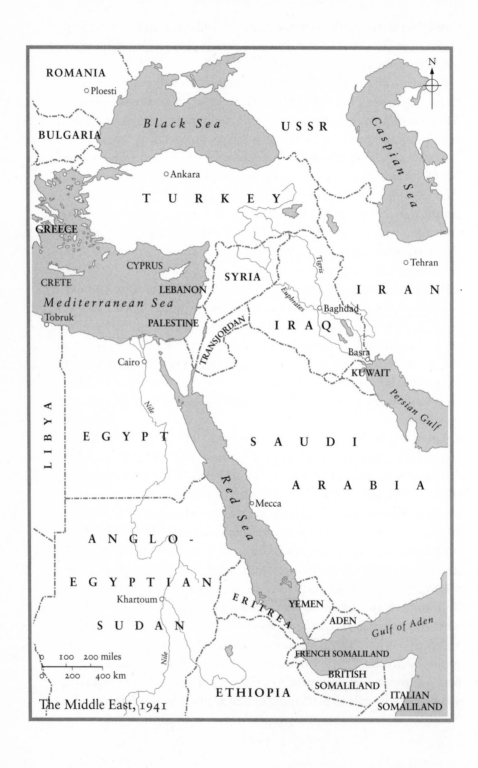

The Middle East, 1941

ostensibly independent Iraq was already a rallying point for the opposition; the Palestinian problem provided another. The presence in Baghdad of the exiled mufti of Jerusalem, Amin al-Husseini, further fuelled anti-British and anti-Jewish politics. The opposition included a group of four senior colonels of the Iraqi army, known popularly as the Golden Square, who were fired by the vision of a pan-Arab state and harboured pro-Axis sympathies.

Nuri as-Said initially tried to balance his pro-British policy with pan-Arab politics. Unsurprisingly he failed, and he was replaced as prime minister by Rashid Ali el-Gailani in March 1940. A former lawyer and judge, Rashid Ali had opposed the government's unconditional support for Britain's war effort. The subsequent course of the war seemingly confirmed his belief that Britain's hegemony in the Middle East was on the wane. In June 1940, when Italy entered the war, he refused to break ties with Rome. Rashid Ali was also reluctant to acquiesce in Britain's demand to allow its troops to pass through Basra to Palestine. Most importantly, he opened a secret channel of communication with the Axis powers.

In shaping Axis policy in the area, Germany allowed Italy to take the lead while reserving the right to take its share of Middle Eastern oil. The Italians were eager to supplant the British in the region and had no interest in the independence of the Arab states. The pan-Arab, pro-Axis politicians in Iraq had to satisfy themselves with a joint declaration by Berlin and Rome in October 1940 which merely expressed 'full sympathy' for the Arab cause. The German Foreign Office felt that the Arabs were a 'tremendously important power factor', but that their utility should not be overestimated. 'We have no reason at all to be sentimental about these people who are basically anti-European and torn by religious, family and tribal differences.'[4]

The British began leaning on the regent to rid them of Rashid Ali. But the attempt to prise him out of power went awry, leading to a bloodless military coup by the Golden Square on 31 March 1941. Rashid Ali was reinstated as prime minister and the regent took refuge in the American Legation in Baghdad.

The Indian government watched the tangled web of Iraqi politics with mounting concern. Plans for intervention in the Middle East had been discussed from the beginning of the war. Until the summer of 1940, London and Delhi had planned on the assumption of an incursion by the Soviet Union. In early March 1940, the chiefs of staff had ordered the Middle East Command under General Wavell to plan for a force of three divisions to be maintained in the area of Iraq and Iran. At a subsequent conference it was agreed that India would, in the first instance, provide a force consisting of one infantry division and ancillary units for operations in the area of Basra–Abadan. In July 1940, the chiefs had sent a fresh directive to India, defining the role of this force as not just confined to Basra–Abadan, but also as strengthening the morale of the friendly government in Iraq and deterring hostile Iraqi forces from disrupting lines of communication to Palestine. By the end of the year, the chiefs defined the role of the three divisions (Force Sabine) as checking an Axis attack on Iraq through Syria or Turkey and preventing internal disturbances in Iraq and the Anglo-Iranian oilfields.[5]

The drastic expansion of the task of Force Sabine naturally necessitated a reconsideration of the Indian contribution. Auchinleck wrote to Wavell on 8 February 1941 that 'the situation in Iraq looks none too pleasant'. He was 'not at all happy' about the plans for Sabine, either operationally or administratively. He wanted to 'clear the air on the major problems', so that his staff could get down to detailed planning. The nub of the matter was operational control of the force. Since India would be responsible for the bulk of the operations, Auchinleck felt that the responsibility – especially for the occupation of Basra – should be vested entirely with GHQ India. However, he was prepared thereafter to place the force under Middle East Command, if necessary.[6] Auchinleck was not merely battling for turf. The division of responsibilities hithero envisaged between India and MEC was a recipe for confusion, not to say chaos. India would despatch men and materials, but they would be under MEC's control from the moment they sailed; India would provide the supplies, but MEC would decide the requirements; India would plan the administrative base, while MEC would approve it.

Wavell took a month to respond, but accepted Auchinleck's suggestion that operations in Iraq would initially be under the control of India. Wavell's dilatory attitude underscored his aversion to launching any operation in Iraq. This stemmed from a couple of sources. In the first place, Wavell felt that he was fast running out of resources. His command was already fighting the enemy in North Africa, East Africa and Greece. He had little time and fewer troops for an intervention in Iraq. In the second place, Wavell allowed himself to be persuaded by the argument – prevalent among the Arabists in the Foreign Office – that they should eschew any move, military or political, which could kindle the wrath of Arab opinion. Ultimately Wavell felt it best to placate Arab politicians and keep the crisis from bubbling over.

By contrast, Auchinleck was quick off the blocks. By 21 February 1941, the Indian general staff had drawn up a detailed appreciation. The central aim of Sabine was to deny air or land bases in Iraq to any hostile power. The plan would be implemented in three stages: the landing of a force and the creation of a bridgehead and a base at Basra; the establishment of forces in the Baghdad–Habbaniya area; and deployment of troops in northern Iraq and towards Syria. The operation would be planned, led and controlled (at least initially) by India. MEC would be responsible only for the provision of air power.[7] The plan had been sent to London as well as Wavell on 21 February. By 10 March Auchinleck had even identified a commander for Force Sabine.

Auchinleck's urgency rose not just from his reading of the political situation in Iraq, but from the logistical demands of a large-scale intervention. Moving a division from Karachi to Basra would need about thirty-six ships – not counting those for base units – and the round trip would take three weeks. Sufficient shipping was simply unavailable to move an entire division and base units at one go – and to ensure that it would be self-supporting in active operations for five weeks. Stocking a temporary base in Basra would take between three to five months, while a permanent base would need six to nine months. The enormity of the task impelled Auchinleck to take a proactive stance on the unfolding crisis.

The commander-in-chief's activism met with the approval of Leo Amery. The secretary of state for India wrote to him in mid-March: 'it may well be that sooner or later you may have to face the necessity of sending troops to Basra'. Auchinleck promptly replied: 'I feel more and more certain that it will not be long before we shall have to send troops to Iraq . . . we are preparing for that contingency and planning has now started in earnest.'[8] Despite his distaste for the venture, Wavell agreed that the plans for Sabine had to be dusted off and updated. He also informed London that the detailed planning should be done in India and that the operational command should initially be with India. The chiefs of staff agreed.

Towards the end of March 1941, Wavell convened a meeting in Cairo. India was represented by the chief of the general staff, Lieutenant General Thomas Hutton. Prior to his departure from Delhi, Auchinleck had emphasized to Hutton that he was 'most anxious to gain a foothold in Iraq. The sooner we begin to get control, militarily, in Iraq, the better.'[9] The consensus at the conference, however, departed sharply from the appreciation prepared by India. It was thought that instead of despatching a large force from India to establish a bridgehead at Basra, it would be better to have a smaller strike force located in Palestine. Such a force could threaten Baghdad more quickly and effectively. And a threat against Baghdad would be infinitely more credible than any against Basra. Wavell's own predilections were also in play. Thus it was concluded that tying up any force in Iraq, unless absolutely necessary, would be a grave error. If Britain could attain its objectives without any commitment of troops, so much the better.

Confronted with the 'considered and unanimous opinion of all those authorities', Hutton executed a volte-face. He now cabled Auchinleck that India should undertake to provide troops for the strike force as well as Sabine. Auchinleck replied that he was 'disturbed by this tendency to depart from the object which was decided after careful consideration'. Wavell's proposals entailed a considerable expansion in India's commitments, and these could not be met unless London supplied equipment and trained personnel. More importantly, he felt that the occupation of Basra was of fundamental importance because it would enable operations to be carried out in both Iraq and Iran. Clearly, there was a yawning gulf between the approaches advocated by Auchinleck and Wavell. Auchinleck asked Hutton to return to Delhi to discuss this 'changed strategic conception'. By this time, Rashid Ali had staged his coup in Baghdad.

*

The regime change in Iraq came as rude shock to London. The British ambassador in Baghdad, Sir Kinahan Cornwallis, laid out three options for his government: reinstate the regent by armed action; publicly reject the new government, hoping thereby to shake its standing; or recognize the regime and reach a *modus vivendi*. Cornwallis himself held that if Britain failed to stand up for the deposed regent, its standing in Iraq, as well as in the wider Arab world, would be gravely impaired. Churchill stood for a robust response and for the non-recognition of Rashid Ali's new government. So did Linlithgow and Auchinleck. But Wavell had other ideas.

On 3 April 1941, the chiefs of staff asked Wavell what troops he could provide for a military intervention in Iraq. Two days later, intercepts of Italian cables from Tehran indicated that Germany was planning on sending arms to Iraq via Vichy-controlled Syria. And yet Wavell insisted that all he could spare was one British battalion based in Palestine: 'any other action is impossible with existing resources'. The only alternative was to cow Rashid Ali's clique by strong diplomatic action and an aerial 'demonstration' by the RAF units stationed in Iraq.[10]

On 8 April, Churchill wrote to Amery: 'The situation in Iraq has turned sour. We must make sure of Basra . . . I am telling the Chiefs of Staff that you will look into these possibilities. General Auchinleck also had ideas that an additional force could be spared.' Amery sent a personal cable to Linlithgow, explaining that it was imperative to demonstrate support to the regent – even if it was only to hold Basra and Shaiba. Prodded by Auchinleck, the viceroy promptly offered to divert to Basra a force – consisting of one infantry brigade and one artillery regiment – that was embarking for Malaya. He also proposed to airlift to Shaiba four companies of infantry with twelve light machine guns, six Vickers guns and two anti-tank rifles. The viceroy further suggested that the force in Basra should be reinforced at the soonest by two more infantry brigades and base units, bringing it up to a full division. As for Wavell's plan of sending troops to Palestine, these could only be considered after a division was built up at Basra. Amery approved of these moves on 10 April.[11]

As the 10th Indian Infantry Division led by Major General William Fraser prepared to sail from Karachi on 12 April, London muddied the waters. Churchill and the chiefs insisted that while the 10th Division in Basra would be under the command of Auchinleck, northern Iraq including Baghdad would fall under Wavell's operational sphere. Wavell had, in fact, persisted with his reluctance: 'I am fully committed in Cyrenaica [Libya] and can spare nothing for Iraq.'[12] In the teeth of Wavell's protestations, the chiefs ordered him to send a sizeable force from Palestine to Habbaniya and take operational charge of northern Iraq.

What's more, London wobbled on the despatch of the Indian force. On 11 April, Rashid Ali solemnly assured the Iraqi senate of his commitment to abide by the Anglo-Iraq treaty. This disingenuous statement led Ambassador Cornwallis to suggest to Whitehall that Rashid Ali be given the time to prove his bona fides and that the arrival of the Indian troops be delayed. By landing the force at Basra, they may actually strengthen Rashid Ali's standing; for he could then rally the Iraqis by claiming that they were the victims of unprovoked aggression. And he could use this as an excuse to invite German intervention.

Auchinleck expressed 'gravest misgivings' about London's proposal to 'temporize and compromise'. He strongly felt that the ambassador's advice 'may very well result in our never getting to Basra at all'. Possession of a base in Basra would make all the difference to Britain's prospects in the Middle East. Auchinleck argued that the 'time for diplomatic parleying has passed'. Rashid Ali would use the reprieve not only to bolster his position, but to invoke German aid. The viceroy backed his commander-in-chief. Linlithgow wrote to Amery that the failure to secure Basra would at once imperil India's security and undermine its influence in other Gulf and Arab states. 'I have no doubt', he emphasized, 'that we must be prepared to take a strong line now.'[13]

On 13 April 1941, London finally decided that the force for Basra should proceed as planned. By this time, the convoy carrying the leading 20th Indian Infantry Brigade of the 10th Division was already at sea. The troops were not told of the change of mission from Malaya to Iraq until they had set sail. Lieutenant Satyen Basu, a medical officer, was on board one of the eight ships:

The officers gathered the men and gave them topographical lectures with map and diagram of the Middle East with Basra boldly marked on the black-board. We must be going to Basra then. But why was the ship going south-west? But was it? It had suddenly changed its course, and was now going north-west heading straight for the Persian Gulf.

The passage through the Arabian Sea was rough, but the troops were comfortable: 'there was table rice and Indian curry at lunch daily and a delicious mango at the end'. The men were given lectures on hygiene and sanitation as well as tactics. The artillery at the stern boomed occasionally as the gunners warmed up for the campaign. On the morning of 17 April, Abadan swam into view: 'a beautiful city with clean asphalt roads and nice buildings. There were hundreds of Aluminium painted cylindrical reservoirs which contained petrol.' Four hours later, they touched the port of Basra.[14]

During the voyage, it was unclear if Rashid Ali would honour the terms of the treaty and allow the troops to land. The commander of the 20th Indian Brigade, Brigadier Donald Powell, prepared plans to land his troops in the face of opposition from Iraqi forces. Cornwallis was minded to give Rashid Ali advance notice of the arrival of the force and attempt to secure a peaceful landing. Delhi insisted that the warning should not be so early as to allow the Iraqis to effectively oppose the landing. So, Cornwallis informed Rashid Ali only on the evening of 16 April. The prime minister was surprised, but slickly offered to abide by the treaty. The British military mission in Baghdad simultaneously sounded out the Iraqi general staff and obtained their concurrence. The Indian force landed unopposed the next morning. At the same time, the first of the four infantry companies landed in Shaiba, having been airlifted from Karachi via Sharjah and Bahrain.[15]

The BBC immediately announced the landing, claiming for good measure that 'a warm welcome had been given to the Imperial troops by the local population'.[16] Yet Rashid Ali insisted that the terms of the treaty called on Iraq only to allow safe passage for troops through its territory. He asked Cornwallis to move the forces immediately to Palestine: 'at no time should there be any large concentration of British troops in the country'. The ambassador was open to making some concessions to meet this legitimate demand. He proposed retaining just enough troops in Iraq to secure Basra and strengthen Habbaniya, and sending the rest of Force Sabine to Palestine.[17]

The Indian government scotched the idea. New Delhi informed London that it was preparing to send a second brigade in mid-May for deployment in the Baghdad–Habbaniya area and a third in mid-June to act as a reserve. India was intent on securing its hold on Iraq – not on opening the lines of communication to Palestine. Churchill endorsed India's stance. He asked the foreign secretary to instruct Cornwallis that 'Our position at Basra . . . does not rest solely on the treaty but also a new event arising out of the war.' They owed Rashid Ali no undertakings or explanations. As ever, once Churchill's attention was fixed his impatience waxed. Mid-May seemed rather too late for the arrival of further reinforcements in Iraq. The prime minister urged the chiefs of staff to nudge the Indian government and expedite the departure of the rest of the 10th Indian Division. His wishes were anticipated by Auchinleck. On 29 April, a second convoy landed in Basra. The following day, the last part of the division decamped from India.[18]

Meanwhile, Rashid Ali was preparing for a showdown. On 19 April, two days after the first Indian units landed in Basra, he received a joint German and Italian message assuring him of their 'greatest sympathy', advising 'armed resistance against England', and asking him to spell out his requirements.[19] Rashid Ali asked the Italian envoy if the Iraqi army could count on 'support from the air force of the Axis powers' and on 'receiving rifles and ammunition by air transports'. When no reply was forthcoming, he told the Italians on 26 April that he intended to move shortly against the British forces. He now requested a loan to the tune of £1 million as well as ten squadrons of aircraft and fifty light tanks.[20]

By now, Germany had taken charge of the Axis policy towards the Middle East; Italy's disastrous performance in the Mediterranean had pricked its pretensions to regional hegemony and several agencies of the Nazi regime had grown eager for active involvement in the region. The *Abwehr* (military intelligence) was already in touch with the mufti of Jerusalem and was keen to expand covert operations in Iraq. The German navy and generals such as Rommel also felt that the time was propitious for exploiting Arab nationalism in parallel with a military intervention in the Mediterranean.

On 3 May 1941, Foreign Minister Ribbentrop wrote to Hitler that 'Germany had a big chance to build up in Iraq a centre of resistance for our fight against the British . . . an Arab revolt will spread out and thus be of greatest assistance to our decisive advance into Egypt.' Hitler agreed that the 'Arab Freedom movement is our natural ally against England in the Middle East. In this connection the rising in Iraq is particularly important.' The Führer, however, was focused on the coming attack on the Soviet Union. Any large-scale intervention, he decreed, 'to break the British position between the Mediterranean and the Persian Gulf is a question which will be decided only *after BARBAROSSA*'. Axis support for the Iraqi nationalists was thus restricted to two German and one Italian squadron of fighter planes.[21] On 13 May, the first of these flew in through Syria and landed at Mosul.

Rashid Ali's revolt against Britain was already underway. In the early hours of 30 April, two brigades of the Iraqi army had surrounded the RAF base at Habbaniya and a third occupied the nearby towns of Fallujah and Ramadi. Simultaneously, Iraqi troops had taken control of the oilfields at Mosul, shutting down the pipeline to Haifa and reactivating the connection to Syrian Tripoli. By so doing, Rashid Ali apparently sought to pressure the British to a negotiated settlement.

When the crisis erupted, the division of command and responsibility between India and MEC had not yet been sorted out. Auchinleck was all too aware of Wavell's reluctance to embark on any substantial military campaign in Iraq. But the chiefs had not reckoned on the scale of Wavell's recalcitrance. For one, he threw up his hands at their demand for a force to relieve Habbaniya: 'My forces are stretched to the limit everywhere.' Moreover, he would not accept responsibility for the force at Basra: 'this must be controlled from India'. Above all, Wavell was set against escalating the conflict in Iraq and advised 'negotiations with Iraqis on the basis of liquidation of a regrettable incident by mutual arrangement'. The chiefs bore down on him, insisting that a commitment to Iraq was 'inevitable' and operational responsibility 'cannot be divided'.

Under pressure, Wavell scratched together a brigade-sized force that would move from Palestine towards Habbaniya. Yet he remained reluctant to despatch the 'Habforce', warning London 'in gravest possible terms that . . . prolongation of fighting in Iraq will seriously endanger defence of Palestine and Egypt'. The same day, 5 May 1941, he sent a more conciliatory personal cable to the chief of the imperial general staff (CIGS): 'Nice baby you have handed me on my fifty-eighth birthday. I hate babies and Iraqis, but will do my best for the little blighter.' Churchill was 'deeply disturbed' by Wavell's stance and felt that he was 'tired out'. Wavell was told that there was no scope for negotiations and that there was 'an excellent chance of restoring the situation by bold action if it is not delayed'.[22]

Auchinleck followed these exchanges with mounting disquiet. He felt that the strategy advocated by London too did not go far enough. On 9 May, he cabled the CIGS that 'success or failure in Iraq [is] vital to the safety of India'. There was 'only one policy' that could prevent Axis penetration into Iraq and other parts of the region: 'This policy is to establish ourselves with minimum delay in sufficient force at Baghdad and other key points such as Mosul and Kirkuk . . . and this must in our opinion lead from Basra.' The viceroy agreed and informed Amery that 'an immediate and bold movement of troops from Basra might well prove highly successful'.[23]

Wavell continued to disagree. On 7 May, the siege of Habbaniya was lifted by RAF action, and an advance column from Habforce began moving towards the base. Wavell was averse to further escalation. 'Forces from India can secure Basra', he wrote to Churchill the next day, 'but cannot . . . advance northwards unless the co-operation of the local population and tribes is fully secured.'[24] The appearance of German planes over Iraq lent credence and urgency to India's approach, but the command was with Wavell. Moreover, General Quinan, who had taken over Force Sabine, felt that his first task was to secure the base at Basra. Any premature advance to the north would be dangerous. Quinan's stance strengthened Wavell's hand. And the triangular argument between Cairo, Delhi and London stretched on inconclusively.

The cycle of indecision and inaction was not broken until Wavell and Auchinleck met in Basra on 27 May 1941. The two commanders recognized that they saw Iraq from very different vantage points. Wavell felt that his main task of defending Egypt and Palestine would 'not be greatly jeopardized by hostile control of Iraq'. Auchinleck regarded Iraq as an 'absolutely vital outpost of their [India's] defence . . . hostile Iraq would mean hostile Iran and Afghanistan and compromise whole defence of Indian Empire'. After much discussion, it was agreed that the 4,000-strong Habforce, which was now advancing towards Baghdad, should be allowed to occupy the capital. Further, the 10th Indian Division under Quinan's command should move up from Basra towards Habbaniya. Finally, in light of India's 'greater interest and greater stake' in Iraq, Delhi should resume control as soon as possible. Auchinleck insisted to London that 'we must take and keep Baghdad . . . and having got it, we must . . . then secure key points in the north such as Mosul, Kirkuk, Erbil . . . this can be done by bluff and boldness . . . if we act now'. To support these operations, he was not only prepared to send more troops but also recall two Blenheim bomber squadrons lent by India to the Far Eastern Command: 'the Iraqi demand is more urgent than the Malayan, for the moment'.[25]

The day after the Basra conference, Quinan ordered the commander of the 10th Indian Division to move up the Euphrates road to Baghdad. The division was now commanded by the recently promoted Major General William Slim. After being injured in the Eritrean theatre, Slim had been posted as director of military operations at the GHQ. When Force Sabine was being prepared, Auchinleck decided to appoint Slim as the senior staff officer for operations. He wrote to Quinan that Slim's 'recent war experience ought to be of great value to you'. No sooner had the 10th Division landed in Basra than General Fraser had requested to be relieved of his command. Auchinleck immediately appointed Slim to the job. 'I have every reason to expect', he informed the viceroy, 'that Slim's energy, determination and force of character will prove equal to the task.'[26]

In the event, Slim's troops faced barely any resistance as they headed north towards Baghdad. By 30 May, Habforce also stood at the outskirts of Baghdad. The RAF had destroyed the Axis planes on Iraqi territory. Rashid Ali, the Golden Square and the mufti of Jerusalem fled the country, while the Iraqi army sued for an armistice. On 1 June 1941, the regent returned to Baghdad and installed another pro-British regime.

After the fall of Baghdad and the opening up of communications from Basra, GHQ India took command of Iraq. The 10th Division was deployed in and around Baghdad and Mosul, while the freshly landed 8th Indian Division took control of southern Iraq. By 20 June 1941, the occupation of Iraq was completed. It was a victory, but not a glorious one. As Lieutenant Basu's unit passed through Baghdad, he was struck by 'how averse the Iraqis were to the presence of British and Indian troops there. Street urchins jeered at us and people were spitting on the ground at the sight of us.'[27] Indian soldiers would remain in Iraq until the end of the war.

Even as the invasion of Iraq was underway, Britain's sights were trained on Syria. The proximate cause of concern was the use of Syrian airfields by German and Italian planes while transiting to Iraq. Yet London's aversion to the French regime in Syria ran altogether deeper. Days after the fall of France, the cabinet's Middle East Committee had concluded that 'the whole British position in the Middle East, including Egypt and Arabia, will probably be untenable unless Syria and Lebanon are under friendly control or failing that British control'.[28] Britain initially sought to woo the French colonial government in Syria, but the latter accepted the armistice with Germany and fell in with Marshal Pétain's Vichy regime back home.

Although Vichy Syria was ostensibly neutral in the war, its relations with Britain were fraught. Churchill's decision to destroy the French fleet in North Africa had at once frightened and angered the French in Damascus. It stiffened the spine of the local Vichy authorities, who had at their disposal some 35,000 troops. London was clear that the regime in Syria 'should be prevented from taking action hostile to our interests'. But a military occupation was deemed a measure of the last resort – only to be used if the Axis forces sought to advance through Syria into the Middle East. Short of this, there were several options to shape the regime's behaviour. For one thing, economic and financial pressure could be used 'to show that Syria is dependent on our goodwill'. For another, anti-Vichy officers in Syria could be encouraged 'in the hope of an early coup d'etat'.[29]

As with Iraq, Wavell was opposed to any pre-emptive move on Syria. All he wanted was 'a stable and neutral Syria on my northern flank, in view of my general weakness'. Wavell was even averse to making any moves that 'might result in disorder in Syria, which I did not want'.[30] Of greater concern to him than the Vichy Syrian regime were the clamorous demands of the Free French forces under General Charles de Gaulle, who deplored Britain's coddling of the Syrian government and insisted on securing the Levant for the Free French. The Gaullists hectically lobbied London and Cairo for the launching of an offensive on Syria. While de Gaulle sought Britain's military support, he also harboured a deep suspicion that the British sought to dismantle the French empire and sully the glory of France. This schizophrenic stance jangled on London's nerves. Wavell, for his part, remained unwavering in his opposition to any military venture in the Levant.

In early April 1941 de Gaulle landed in Cairo, intending to bring matters to a head. At a meeting with Wavell on 15 April, de Gaulle's Middle East envoy, General Catroux, insisted on nothing less than an immediate Anglo-French invasion of Lebanon and Syria aimed at capturing Beirut and Damascus. Catroux also demanded that MEC contribute two full divisions for the operation. Nothing could be better calculated to draw Wavell's ire. His antipathy to opening another front apart, Wavell had been working to prevent a collapse of the Syrian regime and the ensuing instability by relaxing the economic embargo and concluding a trade agreement. So he dismissed the Free French plan out of hand.[31]

De Gaulle's demands, however, fell on sympathetic ears in London. By the end of April 1941, the crisis in Iraq was bubbling up, and signals intelligence gleaned by British codebreakers revealed that Germany and Italy planned to use Syrian territory to support Rashid Ali's revolt. Also, the Syrian government was apparently providing direct military aid to the Iraqis. Churchill wrote to President Franklin Roosevelt that 'If the German air force and troop carrier planes get installed in Syria they will soon penetrate and poison both Iraq and Iran and threaten Palestine.'[32] As hostilities broke out in Iraq, London leaned on Wavell to consider options for Syria. The general reluctantly convened a conference in Cairo on 5 May. Catroux held on to his earlier demands, impervious to the fact that Wavell had just suffered defeat in Greece and had Iraq on his hands as well. An exasperated Wavell shot back that 'the loss of Syria would be better than the risk of . . . intervening with inadequate forces'.[33]

Churchill did not take kindly to Wavell's resistance. 'A supreme effort must be made', he instructed the chiefs, 'to prevent the Germans getting a footing in Syria.' If Wavell did not have resources to spare, he should provide transport and air support to the Free French forces and allow them to go ahead with an invasion.[34] Wavell was unpersuaded. On 17 May 1941, he wrote to the CIGS that the only force he had in Palestine had been sent to Iraq. 'I feel strongly', he added, 'that Free French without British support would be ineffective and likely to aggravate situation.'[35] This was not an unreasonable opinion, given that the Free French forces stood at barely two brigades, a little over 5,000 men.

Churchill, however, insisted that the Free French should be allowed to proceed with their plans, and ordered Wavell to give them as much military and air support as possible. Wavell curtly asked the chiefs of staff to either trust his judgement or relieve him of his command; the chiefs felt that they should stand by Wavell. Opinion in the cabinet swung towards Churchill's stance, however; the foreign secretary Anthony Eden noted that 'if the Free French are prepared to chance their arm . . . we are in favour of letting them have a shot, *faute de mieux*'.[36]

The prime minister was already vexed at Wavell's dragging his feet over Iraq and had thought aloud more than once about sacking him. He now came down heavily on Wavell. On 21 May, he wrote to his commander: 'Our view is that if Germans can pick up Syria and Iraq with petty forces, tourists and local revolts we must not shrink from running equal small-scale military risks and facing the possible aggravation of political dangers from failure.' Churchill took full responsibility for the decision. If Wavell could not implement it, he would be relieved of his command. Wavell beat a hasty retreat and ordered the 7th Australian Division, less a brigade, to move to Palestine and prepare for an advance into Syria.[37]

The force that assembled in Palestine included a Free French division and the 5th Indian Infantry Brigade. The brigade was part of the 4th Indian Division and had fought at Sidi Barrani and Keren. Led by

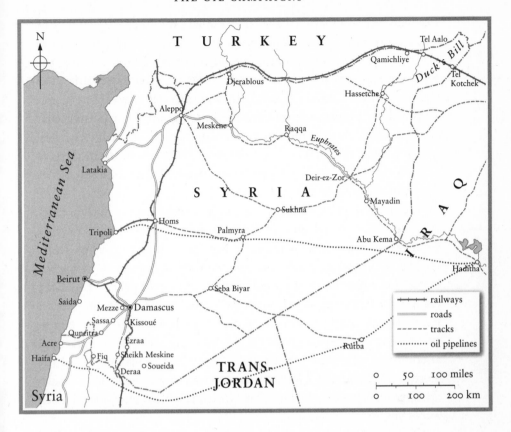

Brigadier Wilfred Lewis Lloyd, it included the 4/6th Rajputana Rifles, the 3/1st Punjab and the 1st Royal Fusiliers. The operation began at 0200 hours on 8 June 1941. The initial advance was smooth and by the following morning the brigade had entered the town of Deraa, which was evacuated by the Vichy troops. At the next objective, Sheikh Meskine, the Rajputana Rifles encountered stiff resistance. The Vichy forces made effective use of artillery, machine-gun nests and armoured cars to hold the Indians at bay for over twelve hours. When the battalion launched a final assault, it found that the Vichy troops had evacuated under the cover of darkness.[38]

The botched operation at Sheikh Meskine portended the challenges that the 5th Brigade would confront during the attack on the village of Mezze, on the outskirts of Damascus, ten days later. The brigade began the attack on the night of 18 June with the Punjabis in the lead.

The advance company of the 3/1st Punjab was met with a hail of machine-gun fire. The Indian troops immediately took to the ground and dispersed widely. Although the firing stopped after a while, the battalion found it difficult to regroup the scattered companies and platoons. In the ensuing melee, the Rajputana Rifles went ahead and captured the village. By the time the Punjabis got their act together and assaulted the fortified positions adjoining Mezze, mortar and artillery shells rained down on them from Vichy positions to the rear of the village. The attack on the forts failed and the Rajputana Rifles were isolated in Mezze.

At 0900 the next morning, as the Indians were setting up road-blocks around the village, the Vichy troops counter-attacked with a number of tanks. Several Indian troops were taken prisoner, while the rest pulled back to a two-storey building in the village. Over the next twenty-four hours, they put up a doughty fight against the Vichy forces that had entirely surrounded their position, but at 1430 on 20 June, after the Vichy troops brought in their heavy artillery, the Indians had to surrender. Brigadier Lloyd made several unsuccessful attempts to relieve his beleaguered forces, but it was not until the morning of 21 June that Mezze was retaken and secured by the brigade, opening up the road to Damascus. At 1430 on 21 June, Free French forces entered Damascus.[39]

As the initial attack on Mezze faltered, Wavell was forced to deploy additional troops in Syria. He now ordered up another brigade and an artillery regiment from Egypt. Troops from Iraq were also diverted to Syria. Habforce was asked to advance to Palmyra. On 19 June, Auchinleck told General Quinan that the operations in Syria were of greater importance than securing southern Iraq. In consequence, the 10th Indian Division under Slim was asked to concentrate a force at Haditha and advance up the Euphrates River to Aleppo. The major objective for the division was identified as Deir-ez-Zor, the capital of eastern Syria, a hundred miles or so inside the border with Iraq.

The first major problem confronting Slim was logistical. Despite using 'native boats on the Euphrates, hiring all available civilian lorries from Baghdad and even the village donkeys', it took days before the division reached Haditha.[40] By this time, Damascus had fallen.

Nevertheless, the Vichy forces continued to resist and control the bulk of the country. More importantly, the logistical problems would become all the more acute from Haditha onwards. Slim realized that only one brigade of the division could be deployed for battle so far ahead of the bases near Baghdad. And so the 21st Indian Infantry Brigade was beefed up with supporting units and provided with all available mechanical transport. The commander of the brigade group, Brigadier Weld, drew up a plan for the attack on Deir-ez-Zor which was approved by Slim on 29 June. The plan envisaged moving the force of nearly 800 vehicles over a distance of 200 miles in two days and enveloping the target in a two-pronged attack.

The second problem was the weather. When the brigade group commenced its advance, the mercury was soaring in the desert summer. Captain John Masters of the 2/4th Gurkhas was in the convoy:

> The earth shimmered and heaved, at first only in the distance, then closer and closer until sometimes the trucks in front of me took on distorted shapes of animals or vanished altogether. I felt heatstroke closing in on me. The dust billowed up now and I began to choke.[41]

Only part of the route had been reconnoitred by the Indians. No sooner had they crossed this stretch than a dust storm kicked up. Satyen Basu's vehicle lost contact with the unit to which he was attached: 'at one place where the road bifurcated immediately after a turn, I went the wrong way. When I realised my mistake, I turned back and searched for another hour to find the unit in vain.' Basu's travails did not end even after he caught up with the convoy. 'Dust and smoke had made visibility extremely poor . . . My only duty was to follow the vehicle in front of me. We had eaten very little in the last few days and had nothing to drink in the last 24 hours.'[42]

Under these conditions, the brigade group struggled to keep together. The armoured cars in the front and flanks lost touch with the main body. The vehicles were forced to move in a low gear, so consuming large quantities of petrol. The sandstorm also scrambled the wireless network and severed communications between the brigade headquarters and the units. By the time the brigade group was to have formed up for attack, the commander had no option but to call it off. Worse still, Vichy aircraft dived in at dawn, carpeting with bombs the Indian positions in the desert. Masters hurled himself into a trench as he sighted the Martin Maryland bombers: 'Suddenly the ground jumped. A huge force lifted and shook me and the trench and the whole earth in which the trench had been dug, moving everything bodily upwards and sideways. Thick yellow earth clogged my mouth and nostrils.'[43]

Slim was in a quandary. He had lost the advantage of surprise; his stocks of petrol were running dangerously low; and his troops had no anti-aircraft guns to counter Vichy bombardment. Yet he resolved on a bold plan. He decided to send one column to probe the main defences of Deir-ez-Zor, while another would move out wide, round the southern flank of the Vichy positions, take the Aleppo Road and swing at Deir-ez-Zor from the north. The plan carried both the promise of surprising the enemy from a direction he was unprepared to defend and the danger of the column losing its way and being destroyed piecemeal. Slim's gamble paid off. On the morning of 3 July Deir-ez-Zor fell to Indian troops.

As the Indians moved into the town, they were struck at the sight of large numbers of Syrian troops peeling off their uniforms and melting into the population. The prisoners of war taken by the Indians were almost entirely French. Equally striking was the attitude of the local populace, which was sharply at variance with that of the Iraqis. As Basu entered the city, 'the inhabitants were waving welcome to us and the constable at a road corner saluted as our car passed by'. Slim found the streets 'full of men milling round, Indian sepoys, native civilians, and, judging by their undress, some of our friends the Syrian soldiers . . . the bank holiday atmosphere pervading the scene did not fit in at all with my idea of the serious business of capturing a city by assault'.[44]

Yet the Syrian campaign was no walk in the park. When the armistice was finally signed on 13 July, the Allies counted 4,600 dead and wounded. The Levantine flank of the Middle East had been secured, but the Persian Gulf still seemed dangerously exposed.

Iran had long been a fixture in British imperial strategy. Since the mid-nineteenth century, Britain and India saw it as an important buffer state that held an expansionist Russia at a secure distance from the frontiers of the Raj. Controlling the Persian Gulf was also deemed critical to securing the sea lanes to India and ensuring that the Indian Ocean remained a British lake. The treaty of 1907 ushered in a détente between Britain and Russia and divided Iran into two informal spheres of influence: Russian to the north and British-Indian to the south. The country was accordingly occupied by the two powers during the Great War. Following the Bolshevik revolution, however, Russia and Iran concluded a separate treaty in 1921. That accord allowed Russian forces to enter northern Iran if any other power sent its troops to the southern part of the country. Thereafter, British and Indian policies were geared towards ensuring that no pretext was provided to Russia to send its forces into Iran.

In the inter-war years, Britain's interests in Iran had centred on oil. The Anglo-Iranian Oil Company pumped out most of the oil in the Middle East. Securing these fields and the refinery at Abadan figured prominently in military planning and eventually shaped the decision to occupy Basra. From India's standpoint, Iran's importance was also strategic. Not only did India share a border with Iran, but it was believed that a hostile Iran would threaten the stability of Afghanistan and the tribal areas of Balochistan and the North-West Frontier Province. It would also endanger the sea and air routes of communication between India and the Arab states of the Persian Gulf littoral.[45]

At the outbreak of the Second World War, Iran had declared its neutrality. The country had been ruled since 1925 by Reza Shah Pahlavi. An authoritarian modernizer, the shah sought both to leverage economic assistance from all corners and to shield the sovereignty of Iran.[46] Apart from granting oil concessions to the British, the shah brokered trade relations with the United States, the Soviet Union and, above all, Germany. Indeed, he gratefully accepted Nazi Germany's generous offers of financial and technical assistance for the industrialization of Iran. At the same time, the shah refused to hitch his wagon to any of the great powers. Thus, when Berlin pressurized him to support Rashid Ali's regime in Iraq, the shah remained unyieldingly aloof. If anything, he looked askance at the Iraqi putsch, and even toyed with the idea of sending his own forces to tame the rebellion.[47]

The British government was initially keen to respect the neutrality of Iran. The chiefs of staff did not consider 'a Russian land advance through Iran as likely'. If war broke out with Russia, they would set in motion the existing plans to secure Basra and the Anglo-Iranian oilfields against 'internal disturbance and air attack'. If these contingencies did not occur, then it would be best to avoid sending troops into Iran: 'in order to preserve Iranian neutrality until such time as we needed Iranian co-operation for offensive operations against Russia'.[48] When Force Sabine was preparing to sail from Karachi, the commander was instructed not to infringe the neutrality of Iran. However, in the wake of the crises in Iraq and Syria, London's attitude towards Iran began to change.

The shift in Britain's stance was initially spurred by two problems. Eight German and Italian ships had been stranded since September 1939 at the Iranian port of Bandar Shahpur. If these vessels were scuttled in the channel that led to the Shatt al-Arab waterway, they could prevent the passage of oil-bearing ships through the Persian Gulf. The Royal Navy could easily stop this happening, but it would involve taking steps that would impinge on Iranian neutrality. Further, and more important, was the presence of German nationals in Iran. Up to three thousand Germans were working in Iran on a range of technical and commercial ventures, and intelligence intercepts showed that the German Legation in Tehran had played an important role in supporting Rashid Ali's coup. London concluded that all Germans in Iran 'may be counted as fifth-columnists'.

With the launch of Operation Barbarossa on 22 June 1941, Britain's concerns about Iran were greatly magnified. The German invasion of the Soviet Union threw out all the assumptions underpinning British military plans for Iran. As German forces made stunning thrusts into Soviet territory, the British feared that in the months – if not weeks – ahead, the Wehrmacht would strike through the Caucasus and reach the northern frontiers of Iran. As the director of military operations put it, 'If the Germans were to appear in force in Iran by way of Russia, our whole position in Iraq would be threatened and our communications in the Persian Gulf might be cut.'[49]

As soon as Germany supplanted Russia as the threat to the Persian Gulf, Britain and Russia began shuffling towards a strategic embrace. And Iran proved to be an area where their interests closely coincided. Towards the end of June, both Britain and the Soviet Union delivered communiqués to Iran, warning that the presence of German nationals pointed towards an imminent coup.[50] On 1 July 1941, the British envoy in Tehran, Sir Reader Bullard, met the Iranian prime minister and asked that the Axis ships in Bandar Shahpur be immobilized, either by removing their crews or by stripping them of essential machinery. Bullard also demanded that 80 per cent of the Germans in Iran be immediately expelled.

The Iranians took a cautious tack. Their prime minister informed Bullard on 27 July that Britain's demands amounted to abridging Iranian sovereignty. The Iranian government was alive to the need for vigilance and was taking some steps to reduce the number of Germans. They had also posted a gunboat at Bandar Shahpur to ensure that the Axis ships could not move out. Bullard felt that these steps were inadequate and pressed his demands again.

Meanwhile, the Indian government had watched the developments in Iran with a premonition of disaster. Linlithgow urged London to take a tough stance with Tehran. On 9 July, he wrote to Amery: 'In our view positive policy to secure elimination of enemy centres in Iran is a matter of most vital importance.' He staunchly opposed the sale of military aircraft to Iran, which could make that country 'considerably better equipped in air than India herself which at present has no fighters at all'. A week later, the viceroy wrote again 'to protest in strongest terms' against London's lassitude on Iran – 'a country where we are most directly interested, and from which most dangerous threat to India's security may well develop'. On 20 July, Linlithgow advocated the imposition of an economic blockade. The Iranians should be made 'to understand that restoration of supplies depended solely on expulsion of German technicians and tourists'.[51]

More surprising was the stance taken by the new commander-in-chief of India. Wavell had recently swapped commands with Auchinleck. From his perch in New Delhi, the problem of the Persian Gulf now looked very different to Wavell – bearing out the dictum that where one stands depends on where one sits. Thus he wrote to the CIGS on 17 July:

> The complaisant attitude it is proposed to adopt over Iran appears to me incomprehensible. It is essential to the defence of India that the Germans should be cleared out of Iran now, repeat now. Failure to do so will lead to a repetition of events which in Iraq were only just countered in time. It is essential we should join hands with Russia through Iran and if the present Government is not willing to facilitate this it must be made to give way to one which will.

India's activism chimed with the prime minister's desire for a firm policy towards Iran. But the cabinet was initially divided. Amery voiced India's views in calling for a joint strategy with the Soviets to coerce Iran. If the threat of force failed to work, he argued, a joint military invasion of Iran should be considered. Eden felt, however, that the threat of force should be invoked only if 'forces are available to give effect to that threat'. The perennial problem of insufficient troops once again presented itself, although the boot was now on the other foot. Churchill explained to Wavell that troops for a massive invasion of Iran could only come from Iraq and the latter would have to be replaced from the overburdened Middle East. Nevertheless, Eden informed the Soviet envoy in London that they might have to consider joint military action against Iran – if the shah refused to accede to their demands.[52]

Wavell promptly instructed General Quinan in Iraq to stand ready to secure the oil refinery at Abadan and to occupy the oilfields at Naft-i-Shah and Khuzestan in south-west Iran. Two days later, on 24 July 1941, the war cabinet approved the plan to exert Anglo-Soviet diplomatic pressure backed by a show of force. A joint communiqué would be presented to Iran on 12 August. In the meantime, Quinan would complete the preliminary concentration of a strike force near the Iranian border in the Basra area.

Bullard was unhappy with these developments. He felt the presence of Germans in Iran was not an adequate *casus belli* and that military action against Iran would violate all principles of neutrality. On 11 August, he cabled London that the Germans were now being watched very closely by the Iranians: 'I do not think they could give serious

trouble.' Writing to Amery the next day, Linlithgow let fly. The Iranians seemed to 'have Bullard in their pocket'. The viceroy hoped that
'local complacency will not be permitted to divert H.M.G. from
pressing home their demands on Persia'.[53]

He need not have worried. Opinion in the British government had
turned in favour of intervention. Despite Eden's misgivings, the Foreign Office felt that Britain's principal objective was to prevent the
Anglo-Iranian oilfields from falling to German forces, if the Russians
lost control of the Caucasus. This would 'not be accomplished simply
by the removal of the Germans from Iran . . . it will at some stage be
necessary for us to take over the protection of the oil fields'.[54]

The case for violating Iran's neutrality became stronger owing to
yet another development. With the Red Army on the ropes, the
importance and urgency of supplying materiel to the Soviet Union
was starkly clear to Britain and the United States. In late July 1941,
President Roosevelt had sent his envoy, Harry Hopkins, to assure the
Soviets of American readiness to help and to find out their requirements. On his way back, Hopkins informed Churchill that Stalin had
suggested sending American supplies through Iran. This fit snugly
with London's evolving thinking on Iran. At this point, US assistance
to the Soviet Union was not covered under the Lend-Lease Act. The
Roosevelt administration was also keen to keep this under wraps
owing to concerns about anti-Soviet sentiments in American public
opinion. The materiel for Russia would, therefore, be delivered via
Britain.[55] Thus, British control of southern Iran became something of
an imperative for the United States as well. Meeting Roosevelt on 11
August in Placentia Bay off the coast of Newfoundland, Churchill
informed him of the plan for intervention in Iran.

The presence of German nationals in Iran remained the pretext
on which the intervention was undertaken. On 17 August, Bullard
handed a missive to the Iranian government reiterating the demand
for the expulsion of German nationals – by 31 August 1941. The
Russians simultaneously gave a similar note to the Iranians. The
next day, the Iranian foreign minister told Bullard that his
government was acting on the demand – 'but in accordance with
our own programme'. On 21 August, Bullard received a formal
reply, stating that the Iranian government was 'ready to carry out

any plan that they might consider necessary for safety of their country ... but they could not accept any proposal which was contrary to their policy of neutrality, or to their rights of sovereignty'. On the morning of 25 August, the British and Russian envoys jointly presented notes to the Iranian premier stating that they were resorting to 'other measures to safeguard their essential interests'. Soon, they were summoned for a meeting with the shah. 'The Shah looked old and rather feeble', noted Bullard. He politely asked 'whether Great Britain and Russia were at war with Iran'.[56] They were. Early that morning, the Anglo-Russian invasion of Iran had begun.

The Russians moved in from the north-west with nearly 100,000 troops and 1,000 tanks towards Kazvin. The British advanced from Iraq in two separate directions. In the south-west, the 8th Indian

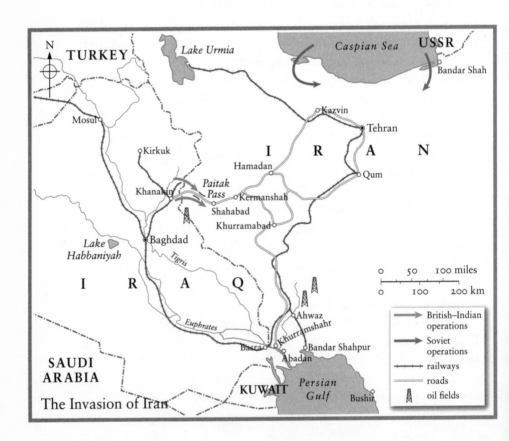

The Invasion of Iran

Division, led by Major General Charles Harvey, was tasked with capturing the oilfields of Khuzestan and dislodging the Iranian forces deployed near the Gulf. Harvey launched simultaneous operations on three axes. The 24th Indian Infantry Brigade crept up along the Gulf coast in a variety of vessels and captured the ports and towns of Abadan and Bandar Shahpur. The 18th Indian Infantry Brigade attacked the river town of Khurramshahr, while the 25th Indian Infantry Brigade took the fort at Qasr Shaikh. All these objectives were under the division's control by the evening of 26 August.

Further north, the 21st Indian Infantry Brigade of the 10th Indian Division crossed the frontier near Khanakin and captured the oilfields near Naft-i-Shah. Apart from the brigade group, the force under Slim comprised two ostensibly mechanized formations: the 2nd Indian Armoured Brigade and Habforce, now renamed the 9th Armoured Brigade. The 9th Armoured Brigade had in practice no armour: 'it was made up of dismounted cavalry carried in 30-cwt. trucks'. And the 2nd Indian Armoured Brigade had one regiment, 14/20th Hussars, with 'gallant but decrepit and slightly ridiculous old Mark VII tanks, whose only armament was a single Vickers machine-gun apiece and whose armour almost anything could pierce'.[57] Having taken the oilfields the force was to advance through the formidable Paitak Pass. Fortunately, it encountered little resistance. At 1000 hours on 28 August, the town of Kermanshah surrendered to Slim.

Later that day, the shah ordered all his troops to cease resistance. After parleying for terms with the British and the Russians, he succumbed and abdicated in favour of his pliant son, Mohammad Reza Pahlavi, on 16 September 1941. The British operations conducted by the Indian divisions had lasted barely a hundred hours.

The Indian government's official account rightly observes that the 'campaign in Iran cannot strictly be called a war or a military operation'.[58] Indeed, it was more in the nature of an imperial expedition – the last one undertaken by the Raj in its own empire. With the invasion and occupation of Iran, India's army had completed the task of securing its western flank.

7

Fox Hunting

On 11 January 1941, Adolf Hitler issued Directive 22. It came in the wake of Italian debacles in North Africa and committed Germany to helping its ally by sending a small armoured 'blocking force'. Speaking to the Wehrmacht and Luftwaffe High Command in early February, Hitler observed that while Libya had no military significance, if the Italians were shovelled out of it Mussolini's grip on power might be shaken. Moreover, British forces might then be freed up for operations against southern France or in the Balkans. In consequence, the 5th Light Division – put together from elements of the 3rd Panzer Division – would be sent to Italy and would subsequently be reinforced by another full Panzer Division. The Luftwaffe would operate from its bases in Sicily and secure safe passage for the German forces.[1]

Even as Hitler outlined his plan for an intervention, the Western Desert Force was nipping at the heels of the Italian army. After the defeat at Sidi Barrani, Marshal Graziani had begun a strategic withdrawal into Libya, based on the defensive strongholds of Bardia and Tobruk. The 6th Australian Division, which had replaced the 4th Indian Division, took Bardia on 5 January. Three days later, Tobruk had fallen and the retreating Italians were pursued along the coast of Libya by the Australians. Simultaneously, the 7th Armoured Division raced through the desert plateau from El Adem to Mechili, eventually cutting off the Italians at Beda Fomm on 7 February 1941. Over 130,000 Italians were taken prisoner, along with hundreds of tanks, guns and vehicles. The commander of the Western Desert Force, General O'Connor, signalled to Wavell: 'Fox killed in the open.' The road to Tripoli now beckoned.[2]

Wavell rightly refused to permit an advance beyond El Agheila on the coast. The Western Desert Force was already 900 miles ahead of its base in Egypt. Moving another 500 miles to Tripoli would have crippled its supply chain and made it vulnerable to a counter-offensive. The Italians retained numerical superiority in the air and at sea: the British forces were unable to use the port of Benghazi, never mind Tripoli. Moreover, Wavell was faced with a new front in Greece, which inevitably called on the resources of the Middle East Command. Churchill – never one to spurn a chance for a victory – agreed and allowed Wavell to halt O'Connor's offensive on 11 February.[3]

The first German units of what would become the Deutsches Afrika Korps took up positions near El Agheila on 7 February 1941. The day after the British offensive was halted, the commander of the German force landed in Tripoli. General Erwin Rommel was Hitler's own choice for commanding this theatre. An infantry officer with a reputation for drive and boldness from the Great War, Rommel had led Hitler's bodyguard battalion. In February 1940, he was promoted to General and given command of the 7th Panzer Division – a formation that he led with great panache during the invasion of Western Europe and soon became the toast of Germany. Yet Rommel's tactical acuity and audacity were not adequately tempered by a grasp of the strategic picture or by an appreciation of logistical constraints. All these qualities and limitations would be on full display in North Africa.

No sooner had Rommel reached Tripoli than he began contemplating an offensive. He did not regard the task of his force as merely blocking the British advance. Rather, he sought to bundle the enemy out of Egypt and set the stage for a German conquest of the Middle East. Hitler, however, turned down his request to launch an offensive into Cyrenaica (eastern Libya), insisting that he limit offensive operations to securing Tripolitania (western Libya). In the event, Rommel's advance into Cyrenaica was triggered by intelligence reports of British withdrawal from El Agheila.

Wavell, on the other hand, received intelligence – including decoded intercepts from Bletchley Park (known as 'Ultra intelligence') – indicating that Rommel would not be in a position to go on the offensive before May 1941 at the earliest.[4] So, in March 1941, he dismantled

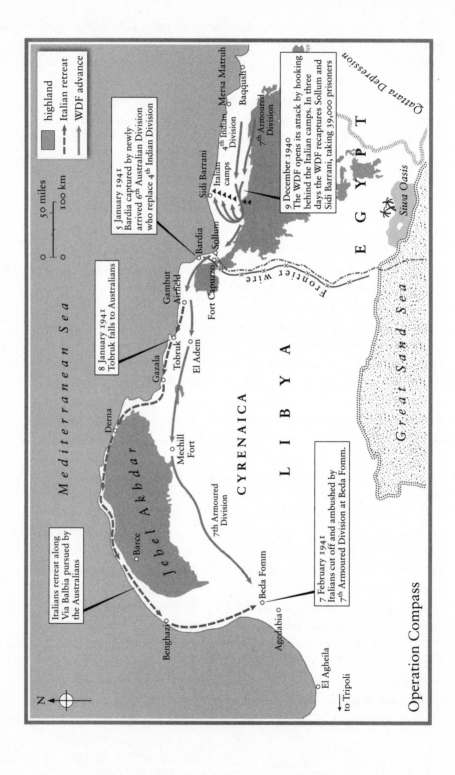

Operation Compass

highland
Italian retreat
WDF advance

50 miles
100 km

Mediterranean Sea

5 January 1941
Bardia captured by newly-arrived 6th Australian Division who replace 4th Indian Division

8 January 1941
Tobruk falls to Australians

9 December 1940
The WDF opens its attack by hooking behind the Italian camps. In three days the WDF recaptures Sollum and Sidi Barrani, taking 39,000 prisoners

Italians retreat along Via Balbia pursued by the Australians

7 February 1941
Italians cut off and ambushed by 7th Armoured Division at Beda Fomm.

Mersa Matruh
Baqqush
4th Indian Division
7th Armoured Division
Sidi Barrani
Italian camps
Sollum
Bardia
Fort Capuzzo
Gambut Airfield
Gazala
Tobruk
El Adem
Derna
Mechill Fort
Barce
Jebel Akhdar
Benghazi
Beda Fomm
Agedabia
El Agheila
to Tripoli

Frontier wire

C Y R E N A I C A

L I B Y A

E G Y P T

Great Sand Sea

Siwa Oasis

Qattara Depression

7th Armoured Division

N

the Western Desert Force, sending the exhausted 7th Armoured Division for a full overhaul and the 6th Australian Division to Greece. These experienced divisions were replaced by the 3rd Armoured Brigade of the 2nd (British) Armoured Division and the 9th Australian Division. These newly arrived, poorly equipped and inadequately trained formations joined the 3rd Indian Motor Brigade in defending the gains in Cyrenaica. In the last week of March, these forces under Lieutenant General Philip Neame – previously commander of the 4th Indian Division and now of the Cyrenaica Command – were tasked with delaying an Axis advance, over the 150 miles from El Agheila to Benghazi, for a period of two months during which no reinforcements would be available. The armoured brigade was accordingly deployed north of El Agheila. A brigade of the 9th Australian Division stretched out to the east of Benghazi – the second brigade was stuck in Tobruk, while the third was yet to assemble in Libya. And the 3rd Indian Motor Brigade stood at El Adem, ready to move to Mechili.

The thinning of the British forces at El Agheila gave Rommel his opportunity. On 31 March, he struck. At this point, Rommel had only one Panzer regiment of the 5th Light Division at his disposal: the Italians refused to part with any motorized units. Not only did Rommel hurl these towards El Agheila, but he also latched on to an ambiguous message from the Führer and assumed de facto command of all forces on the front lines.[5] Rommel's opening punch landed on the 3rd Armoured Brigade. The retreating British tanks were outmanoeuvred and outgunned by the Panzers. By 2 April, the brigade was mangled and Rommel's scanty armour assumed substantial superiority.

The same day, Wavell flew to the tactical headquarters of the Cyrenaica Command. The commander-in-chief wanted immediately to sack Neame for his poor tactical deployment of troops and to replace him with O'Connor. Although the latter arrived from Cairo the following day, he dissuaded Wavell from dismissing Neame and agreed to stay on as an adviser. As it turned out, Neame had a better instinct for the unfolding course of the Axis offensive. He wished to pull the remainder of the armoured forces to the east of the Benghazi road – a position from which they could support the Australian brigade as well as deny the desert routes to Rommel's forces. Wavell was adamant that they should remain on the road – in order to defend

Benghazi. But the defence of Benghazi was neither essential nor feasible. Eventually, it had to be evacuated on the night of 3 April. At O'Connor's suggestion, the Australian units were moved across Jebel Akhdar to Derna and the remainder of the armoured brigade sent to Mechili. Together these forces would hold a line from Derna to Mechili.[6]

Meanwhile, Rommel had split his forces into four columns. The first, consisting mainly of a motorized Italian division, chased the British forces along the coast. The other three ripped through the desert plateau and converged at Mechili. Rommel had planned thereafter to drive towards the coast and cut off the British forces between Derna and Tobruk.

The 3rd Indian Motor Brigade moved from El Adem and reached Mechili on the afternoon of 4 April. The brigade was tasked with holding Mechili until the arrival of the remnants of 2nd Armoured Division – after which it would pass under the division's command. The headquarters of the armoured division turned up on the night of 6 April, but there was no sign of its principal fighting formation, the 3rd Armoured Brigade. Nor were the Australians moving down from Derna towards Mechili. Neither of these units would reach Mechili. It transpired that the armoured brigade was out of petrol and hence diverted to Derna. The Australian units took a severe beating from the pursuing Axis column and eventually retired to Tobruk. The 3rd Indian Motor Brigade was thus isolated at Mechili.[7]

The brigade had been formed in India on 1 July 1940. It epitomized the problems faced by the expanding Indian army and highlighted its lack of preparation for modern warfare. The brigade was made up of three cavalry regiments: the 2nd Royal Lancers, the 18th Cavalry and the 11th Cavalry (Frontier Force). But these units did not come together until the brigade was mobilized for overseas deployment in December 1940. As late as October 1940, two of its regiments, the 2nd and the 18th, were still undergoing conversion from horsed to mechanized cavalry. Having no tanks or armoured cars at all, they trained for mechanized warfare with Morris six-wheeler trucks. Even as the men made their acquaintance with these machines, the better trained among them were sent out to form new cavalry regiments and to serve as instructors at the new Indian cavalry training centre. The 11th Cavalry was slightly better placed. Being employed for frontier duties, it initially had some light tanks and two armoured cars. But this regiment, too, was 'milked' of men and material – an entire squadron being sent to Central India Horse. At the time of embarkation towards the end of January 1941, the 11th Cavalry had no tanks; only 3 anti-tank rifles (against a planned 126); few wireless sets and even fewer trained signallers.[8]

The brigade sailed from Bombay and berthed at Suez on 6 February 1941. Two days later it arrived at the camp in El Tahag and stayed there till the end of the month, trying to complete its basic training and assemble its equipment. On 8 March, the brigade moved to Mersa Matruh and started training for desert warfare. Only two days before the Axis offensive began, the brigade reached El Adem. In advancing to Mechili, it left behind the 18th Cavalry to protect the airfield at El Adem. Apart from the 2nd Lancers and 11th Cavalry, the brigade was bolstered by an Australian anti-tank regiment and a wireless link for calling in close air support. Such was the state of the 3rd Indian Motor Brigade, commanded by Brigadier E. W. D. Vaughan and tasked with delaying Rommel at Mechili.

As it waited for the armoured units and the Australians, the brigade took up all-round defence centred on the fort. Soon after, on the morning of 6 April, the advance elements of Rommel's force reached Mechili and began shelling the fort's defences. That evening, a German staff officer crossed no-man's-land with a white flag and was taken to the brigade commander. The officer told Vaughan that Mechili was surrounded by German forces and further resistance was futile. He demanded an immediate capitulation. Vaughan flatly refused, sending the German back blindfolded. Over the next twenty-four hours, the Germans sent two more messengers, including one bearing a letter from Rommel himself, demanding surrender. Vaughan responded slowly, hoping to delay the inevitable German attack. In the meantime, attempts by the Australian anti-tank regiment to take on the German guns proved a failure. Vaughan had no more success with his requests for artillery reinforcements and air strikes.[9]

At 2130 on 7 April, General Neame ordered the brigade to

withdraw the next morning to El Adem. The move was to be carried out by deploying the brigade in a 'box', which would be capable of defending itself against tank attacks on its northern and southern flanks. This was an ambitious plan. The brigade had little training to pull off such a fighting withdrawal. Moreover, the plan could only succeed if substantial numbers of Axis guns were silenced before daybreak. But Vaughan had limited artillery and no air power. The only reinforcement he had received at Mechili was a mechanized squadron of 18th Cavalry from El Adem. So his only option was to rush the guns with the squadron firing on the move.

Unsurprisingly, the withdrawal did not work to plan. The formation of the box was delayed and withdrawal could only commence fifteen minutes after first light, and the squadron of 18th Cavalry that was to spearhead the breakthrough was unable to silence the enemy's guns. In consequence, the brigade had hardly moved when it came under intensive artillery and machine-gun fire. Soon the German tanks began attacking from both sides. After attempting for a while to inch ahead, Vaughan and the armoured division commander decided that the withdrawal was impracticable and held out a white flag.[10]

The headquarters as well as the supporting units were taken captive. The ill-starred Indian regiments put up a brave show. The breakthrough squadron of 18th Cavalry eventually fought its way past the Axis guns, suffering some 25 per cent casualties. The 11th Cavalry – covering the two flanks of the box – appears to have lost over 65 per cent of its troops. The 2nd Lancers, which formed the rearguard, came off worst. Only parts of two squadrons – led by Major M. K. Rajendrasinhji, a cousin of the famous cricketer Ranjitsinhji ('Ranji') and a future chief of the Indian army – managed to fight their way out. The rest were either killed or taken prisoner.

The 3rd Indian Brigade was badly mauled. So high was the rate of attrition that when the survivors of the 2nd Lancers joined those of the 11th Cavalry at El Adem, they were grouped together as just one squadron. After moving from one location in the rear to the next, these troops would eventually join the 4th Indian Division in the summer of 1941. The third regiment of the brigade, the 18th Cavalry, pulled back from El Adem to Tobruk – where it was joined by the retreating 9th Australian Division.

Looking back at these events, Brigadier Vaughan would recall the 'staunch courage with which the Indian ranks, young and inexperienced, lacking full equipment and training, standing firm when others retired ... Where much else failed, their spirit did not.'[11] The Indian official history makes an altogether grander claim, that the stand of the brigade at Mechili 'started a chain of events which ended with Allied victory in Africa and the invasion of Italy'.[12] Discounting regimental and national loyalties, it is clear that the Indian troops were pummelled by the Germans. The main achievement of the 3rd Indian Motor Brigade was to hold up – if only by bluff – Rommel's forces at Mechili for forty-eight hours, so preventing the Australians from being cut off before they reached Tobruk.

On 11 April, German and Italian forces stood at the gates of Tobruk. Although his pursuit of British forces had not worked out as planned, Rommel had managed to roll back the Allied gains in Libya and into the bargain had captured Wavell's top commanders, including Neame and O'Connor. Having reached Tobruk, Rommel was determined to take it. Successive attacks launched against the hastily cobbled-together defences were beaten back by the Australians. Faced with Rommel's incessant demand for troops, the German High Command sent Lieutenant General Friedrich Paulus to take stock of the situation. Paulus reported in early May that 'the crux of the problem in North Africa is not Tobruk or Sollum, but the organization of supplies'. The Royal Navy was interdicting Axis cargo and troop ships to Benghazi, and the Axis lacked the requisite transport to open a supply channel across the 1,100-mile land route from Tripoli. At best, they could cater for a third of Rommel's requirements – sufficient only for his troops to survive near Tobruk. Rommel was stuck: he could neither advance nor retreat.[13]

The British learnt of Paulus' appreciation through Ultra intelligence. Bruised by the defeats in Greece and Cyrenaica, Churchill was raring to have a crack at Rommel's forces before their logistical situation improved. He immediately ordered the shipment of 300 tanks through the Mediterranean to Egypt. Churchill cabled Wavell that it was 'important not to allow fighting round Tobruk to die down, but to compel the enemy to fire his ammunition and use up his strength by counter-attack'. He asked Wavell to consider reinforcing Tobruk and harrying Rommel's forces near the frontier with Egypt.[14]

Halfaya and Sollum were two key passes that had fallen under Rommel's control. Wavell was keen to retake these before making any move to throw the Axis forces back west of Tobruk. Operation Brevity was launched with three brigade groups on 15 May. It was an unalloyed failure. Within twenty-four hours, the British forces were driven back to their side of the Egyptian frontier. By the time the operation was launched, the 4th Indian Division had returned from East Africa. The division was deployed over a stretch of 130 miles from Sidi Barrani to El Daba, protecting 14 landing grounds. More importantly, having fought in the mountains for over three months, the troops were training yet again for desert warfare – and now against a formidable enemy.[15] The 4th Division was assigned a dual role for Brevity: as a reserve striking force and as a shield against attempts by Axis forces to bypass British thrusts. In the event, the division did nothing more onerous than passing on the wounded and prisoners to rear areas.

The 4th Indian Division played a more prominent role in another offensive, launched in mid-June 1941. Operation Battleaxe was a more exacting gambit aimed at clearing the frontier area of all Axis forces and at pushing Rommel's troops back to the west of Tobruk. Yet Wavell was also aware of the fate of Operation Brevity and wished to proceed cautiously. Churchill disagreed. Having sent his tanks, the prime minister wanted his offensive; Wavell reluctantly complied. The plan was to attack in three columns. Advancing along the coast, the eponymous Coast Force – made up of one brigade from the 4th Division – would attack and secure the Halfaya Pass and Sollum. The Escarpment Force – the rest of 4th Division with additional infantry, artillery and armour – would advance atop the escarpment and expel the Axis forces from Halfaya, Bir Musaid and Capuzzo. The (now rested) 7th Armoured Division would move parallel to the Escarpment Force and protect its left flank. Further, the division would draw Axis armour into battle and destroy it. Thereafter, the two divisions would move towards Tobruk.

To keep Rommel guessing about the direction of the main attack, the concentration of forces for Battleaxe took place in dribs and drabs over a week. A little after midnight on 15 June, the approach march was completed. The attack began at dawn. First off the blocks was the Coast Force, which aimed to capture the lower Halfaya Pass. The Coast Force was drawn from the 11th Indian Infantry Brigade, along with six Matilda tanks of the 4th Royal Tank Regiment. Supporting the Coast Force was the so-called Halfaya Group – a battalion, the 2nd Cameron, of the 11th Brigade and a squadron of the Royal Tank Regiment (RTR) with twelve Matildas – which attacked the pass from atop the escarpment.

The Halfaya Group's advance towards the pass was initially smooth. The Matildas raced ahead with the Camerons following in motor vehicles. As the tanks drew close to the objective, two 88mm anti-aircraft guns opened up at close range and made short work of the entire squadron of the RTR. Shorn of their armour and wireless links to their artillery guns down below, the Camerons tried to advance on their own – only to be attacked by Axis tanks, and forced to withdraw by noon. The Coast Force, moving up the slopes of the escarpment towards the Halfaya Pass, met with a similar fate. The six tanks of the RTR ran into a minefield and only two managed to limp ahead. Simultaneously, the leading infantry battalion, the 2nd Mahrattas, came under heavy artillery and machine-gun fire from close quarters resulting in several casualties. Soon, it became evident that the attempt to wrest the Halfaya Pass from the Axis forces had failed.[16]

The Escarpment Force fared only a bit better. The advance brigade of the 7th Armoured Division faced a curtain of fire brought down by Axis guns from well-entrenched positions. Only later that afternoon did the tanks manage to take control of Capuzzo–Bir Weir. By the time infantry units had arrived, consolidated the position and prepared to clear Axis forces near Bir Musaid and Sollum, it was reported that a hundred Axis tanks were massing for a counter-attack on Capuzzo. In consequence, the planned operations were halted.[17]

On the morning of 16 June, as both sides' armour engaged in skirmishes, the Coast Force made another attempt at taking the Halfaya Pass. The 2nd Mahrattas and the 1st Rajputana Rifles made for the pass, while the Camerons were held in reserve. Both the battalions had barely crept up when they came under sustained fire. When they had managed to reach to within 500 yards of the road leading to the Halfaya Pass, the Camerons were called up from the rear. The Rajputana Rifles, however, came under a barrage of artillery fire – losing their commanding officer and almost two rifle companies. As night fell, the coast Force was pulled back.[18]

Another attack was planned for the next day, but it never went in. The British commanders had hoped to entice Rommel's Panzers into a main battle and destroy them. As it turned out British armour was no match for that of the Axis forces. By the morning of 17 June, the 7th Armoured Division had to beat a hasty and unseemly retreat in the face of an Axis threat to envelop all the British forces. The commander of the 4th Indian Division followed suit, undertaking a 'record withdrawal', as he later observed. In three days, the British had sustained heavy casualties: 122 officers and men killed, together with almost 850 wounded and missing. More telling were tank losses. The British lost ninety-one tanks, while the Germans lost only twelve. Later that morning, Wavell cabled the CIGS: 'Regret to report failure of Battleaxe.'[19]

The performance of the Indian units showcased some of the key problems that led to the defeat. The Matildas were designed to fight in support of infantry. As such they had much armour and little speed. Moving at a maximum of 15 miles per hour, they were sitting ducks, from both near and afar, for the 88mm anti-aircraft guns of the Axis. In turn, the Matildas' own 2-pounder gun was little more than a souped-up pea-shooter. More importantly, the British forces suffered from a flawed – not to say missing – doctrine. Unlike the Germans, they had no conception of combined-arms warfare. Training for infantry–armour co-ordination was inadequate. Nor was there any attempt to integrate the operations of anti-tank units with advancing armour supported by infantry and artillery.[20]

The failure of Operation Battleaxe reinforced Churchill's doubts about Wavell's abilities as a commander. Not only had he presided over the defeats in Greece and Crete, but even the successes in Iraq and Syria had been secured in the teeth of Wavell's resistance. Churchill concluded that 'Wavell was a tired man'.[21] This was more than a trifle unfair to Wavell, for Churchill's insatiable demands had also contributed to the outcome of Battleaxe. Wavell had, in fact, made clear the problem posed by his slow armour and had yielded to polit-ical pressure against his better judgement. That said, Wavell's grip over operations, from the latter stages of Operation Compass through to Battleaxe, had been less than sure. And the prime minister was not wrong in thinking that a change in leadership was essential. Having been impressed by General Auchinleck's initiative in the campaign in Iraq, Churchill now decided to swap his command with that of Wavell. In July 1941, Auchinleck took over Middle East Command, while Wavell went to India as commander-in-chief.

Auchinleck set about preparing his forces for a more deliberate offen-sive aimed at relieving Tobruk. He took his time. Despite Churchill's carping, Auchinleck spent four months reorganizing, re-equipping and training his troops. Lieutenant General Alan Cunningham was given the command of the newly created Eighth Army, consisting of two corps, the 13th and the 30th. Immense quantities of materiel began flowing into the Middle East. The armoured force of the Eighth Army was upgraded by gradually replacing the discredited Matildas and hastily produced Crusaders with the superior American-built Stuart and Grant tanks. And the formation in October 1941 of the Desert Air Force ensured better support for ground operations and overall air superiority in the theatre.[22] Auchinleck also gave much attention to training. A Training Memorandum issued by Middle East Com-mand headquarters soon after Operation Battleaxe noted: 'A war of movement such as this one requires troops to be trained to a consider-ably higher standard.'[23] Particularly emphasized was the movement in the desert of mechanized columns by day and night. An entire brigade of the 4th Indian Division was also sent for a full course at the Combined Training Centre at Kabrit.[24]

The Eighth Army's plan for the offensive – Operation Crusader – aimed at encircling Rommel's forces in a two-pronged attack. The 30th Corps, which contained the main armoured forces, would outflank from the south the Axis defences near Sollum and would turn north-west as if to relieve Tobruk. This would smoke out Rommel's armour, which could be destroyed near Gabr Saleh. Having taken the battle to the Panzers, the infantry-heavy 13th Corps would swing around the Sollum front, push north to the coast and thence west to Tobruk.

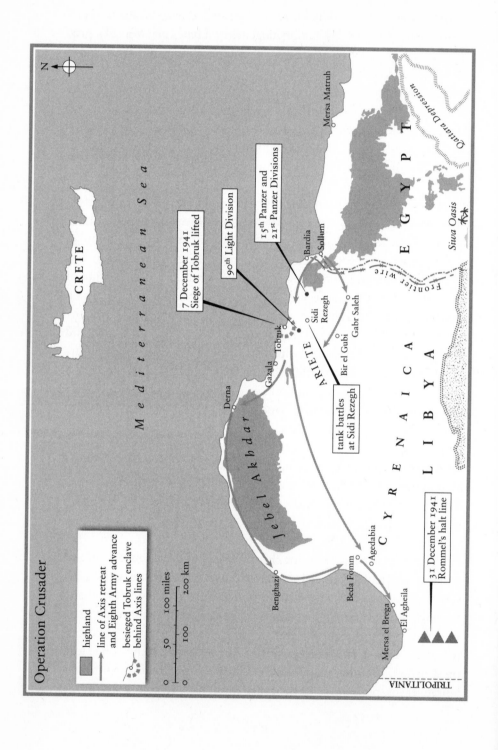

Operation Crusader

Legend:
- highland
- line of Axis retreat and Eighth Army advance
- besieged Tobruk enclave behind Axis lines

Scale:
- 50 · 100 miles
- 100 · 200 km

Mediterranean Sea

CRETE

N

EGYPT

Mersa Matruh

Siwa Oasis

Qattara Depression

15th Panzer and 21st Panzer Divisions

90th Light Division

7 December 1941 Siege of Tobruk lifted

Bardia

Sollum

Frontier wire

Sidi Rezegh

Gabr Saleh

Bir el Gubi

ARIETE

tank battles at Sidi Rezegh

Tobruk

Gazala

Derna

Jebel Akhdar

CYRENAICA

LIBYA

Benghazi

Beda Fomm

Agedabia

Mersa el Brega

El Agheila

TRIPOLITANIA

31 December 1941 Rommel's halt line

After several false starts, Operation Crusader was launched on 18 November 1941. The 30th Corps was soon bogged down in a series of tangled and whirling armoured battles around Sidi Rezegh. A week into the offensive, Auchinleck had to replace Cunningham with Major General Neil Ritchie. However, the latter also struggled to impose his design on the churning battlefield. Rommel characteristically sought to up the ante and threw all he had into these engagements. But he too was unable to master the confusion. As a British officer put it, 'Apparently nobody, not even the enemy, knew what the hell was going on anywhere.'[25]

Meanwhile, the 13th Corps marked time waiting for orders to kick-start its operations. These were originally planned to begin only after the 30th Corps had substantially degraded the Axis armoured formations. As it happened, Cunningham gave the 13th Corps the green light on 21 November, harbouring a misapprehension about the scale of enemy tank losses. Given the course of the tank battles near Sidi Rezegh, this was just as well.

The 13th Corps consisted of the 4th Indian Division, the New Zealand Division and the 1st Army Tank Brigade. The 4th Division's initial task was to attack with forty-five tanks and capture the two main defended areas along the frontier: the Omar Nuovo and the Libyan Omar. These attacks laid bare the problems that continued to plague the Indian forces as well as the Eighth Army.

In the first place, the division was widely dispersed and could bring only one brigade into battle. The 5th Infantry Brigade had returned from Syria barely a month before and was short of both equipment and transport. In consequence, it was employed in the rear areas to secure communications and key facilities. Of the remaining two, the 11th Brigade was deployed in a holding role to prevent Axis forces from sloping down the escarpment towards the sea. The 7th Brigade was pressed into action. In fact, it was the only brigade of the 4th Division that had had collective training and that held its full complement of motor vehicles.[26]

Secondly, the standard of training was still below scratch. During the attack on Omar Nuovo, for instance, the forty-five tanks supporting the leading battalion were supposed be in position two minutes after the artillery fire was lifted, but arrived only after twenty minutes – so squandering the effect of the preparatory shelling. Furthermore, the British commanders bafflingly continued to under-estimate the role played by the 88mm guns of the Axis. At Omar Nuovo, these guns stopped the tanks squarely in their tracks and almost derailed the attack; the infantry had to fix bayonets and rush the gun nests. At the Libyan Omar, too, the 88mm guns inflicted con-siderable losses on British tanks. In the event, these positions were taken only after several days and at a substantial cost.[27]

The confusion in the 30th Corps area had a knock-on effect on the 4th Division. On the afternoon of 24 November, a young staff officer at the division headquarters noticed

a great column of vehicles of every size and description, which turned out to be most of XXX Corps supply column, with a few other odd detachments which had joined up. The whole column went through the Div. HQ [sic] at a good speed and in a great cloud of dust . . . we stopped one or two lorries and asked what it was all about. No one apparently knew what was really happening but the general idea seemed to be that a column of tanks was somewhere behind them and they were getting out of it quick.[28]

Given the possibility of Axis tanks attacking British lines of com-munication, it was decided to pull back the division behind the Omars. The fear was not unfounded, for Rommel was dashing ahead on a raid towards the Egyptian frontier.

By this time, the rest of the 13th Corps was headed towards Tobruk. The new army commander, General Ritchie, also abandoned plans for Sidi Rezegh and instead sought to capture El Adem. This would provide the British tanks with a better location in which to fight the Axis forces. On 3 December, the 4th Indian Division with all its bri-gades – 5th, 7th and 11th – was ordered up from the frontier to the 30th Corps area south of Tobruk.

As a prelude to the attack on El Adem, the 11th Indian Brigade was tasked with capturing Bir el Gubi. The attack began at 0700 on 4 December 1941, but the Italian troops made good use of artillery and anti-tank guns as well as armour to keep the Indians at bay. By the following day, all three battalions of the brigade had been committed to the attack – but to little effect. Not only did the Italians inflict considerable casualties, but they counter-attacked and dislodged the brigade from the positions it had captured. Two companies of the 2nd Mahrattas were completely overrun and the 2nd Camerons suffered heavily too. The next day, the brigade was reinforced by tanks. But it turned out that the Axis forces were thinning out from their positions.[29]

The Axis withdrawal was precipitated by Rommel's over-extension. His push towards the Egypt frontier had been repulsed. What's more, the New Zealand Division had linked up with the garrison in Tobruk. In consequence, Rommel made a few probes around Tobruk and on 4 December decided to pull back to its west. Three days later, he was told by Berlin and Rome not to expect any reinforcements. So Rommel withdrew to Ain el Gazala, around 50 miles west of Tobruk.

The Eighth Army quickly reorganized for pursuit. Since its supply chain was rather inadequate to support two corps, Ritchie decided that the 30th Corps should consolidate on the frontier, while the 13th Corps chased the Axis forces in Cyrenaica. The 13th Corps had under its command the 4th Indian Division, the 7th Armoured Division and the 5th New Zealand Brigade. The logistical constraints of the Eighth Army were replicated in the 4th Division. Hence the divisional commander, Major General Frank Messervy, decided to advance with only two brigades – the 5th and 7th – leaving behind the bulk of the third – 11th Brigade – at Tobruk. The division's plan was to skirt from the south the Axis defences at Gazala, take a few strongholds behind them and push north towards Derna.

In the afternoon of 11 December, the 4th Division commenced its advance. Bypassing the defences at Gazala, however, proved difficult. Rommel's forces were strung out in a long line of strongpoints and defensive localities stretching south-west from the coast. As long as these were held, there was no question of outflanking Gazala and moving to objectives behind it. So it was decided to force the line of defences with brigade-sized punches at two key points. The attacks by the 5th and 7th Brigades on 13 December met with stern resistance. Rommel also threw in a tank column supported by motorized infantry and artillery at the 4th Division's artillery guns. Soon, waves of German Stukas droned above the battlefield and began dive-bombing.

The next afternoon, as the attack got bogged down, the division was reinforced by thirty assorted tanks. The 7th Armoured Division was also brought into the fray – tasked with moving south of the Axis line and supporting the 4th Division's attacks. Co-ordination between armour and infantry continued to prove elusive; the leading brigade of the 7th Armoured Division reached its destination four hours behind schedule, leaving the 5th Indian Brigade with little choice but to attack with a handful of Matildas. They were easy meat for the defenders. Even where the Indian brigades managed to obtain a finger-hold, they were unable to stave off counter-attacks.[30]

The fate of the 1st Buffs of the 5th Brigade – overrun by a mobile all-arms Axis column – highlighted several shortcomings of the Eighth Army as a whole. For one thing, the battalion had not dug proper gun emplacements soon after capturing the enemy's position. For another, the infantry and tanks were too widely dispersed to assist the field artillery against enemy attacks. Finally, the British tanks sought to engage the Axis tanks by firing from extreme ranges. As a result, by the time they closed in with the enemy, they were almost out of ammunition.[31] Put simply, despite improvements in technology, the 4th Division suffered from flawed tactics and insufficient training for combined-arms warfare.

Having failed to pierce the Axis defences, the 4th Division fell back for reinforcements and prepared to resume its offensive on 17 December. That morning Messervy received a message from the Corps headquarters, informing him that the bulk of the Axis forces were pulling out of the Gazala defences and withdrawing to the west. Inside the hour, the division set out on pursuit. Messervy kept his units going at a good clip, exploiting opportunities to bypass lightly defended positions and moving by night. By 21 December, the division was well on its way to clearing the Jebel Akhdar. As the brigades entered populated areas evacuated by the Axis forces, they had to curb the local Arabs who went on a rampage against any remaining Italian settlers, so slowing down their advance. As the infantry battalions fanned out to the west, the Central India Horse with some armoured cars and anti-tank guns moved down the coast road, pressing hard on the retreating Italians.

As the division raced ahead, its logistical line stretched taut and thin. The motor transport of almost an entire brigade had to be withdrawn for repairs. The petrol allocation was considerably scaled down. By 23 December, it was evident that the Axis forces were preparing to evacuate Benghazi. The 4th Division and the 7th Armoured Division were tasked with preventing them from getting away intact. But the Indian division was practically at a standstill; Messervy managed to get just enough petrol to rush forward the CIH in support of the armoured division. By the time the regiment reached Benghazi on Christmas Eve, the town and the port had been evacuated by the Axis forces. Four days later, the division headquarters reached Benghazi. General Messervy, having been selected to command the 1st British Armoured Division, handed over to Major General Francis Tuker.

Meanwhile, the Axis forces had withdrawn initially to Agedabia and then to El Agheila, where they decided to make a final stand. The 4th Division's long journey from Matruh had cost it 2,633 casualties, including 150 British officers and 28 Indian officers. The Eighth Army commander was generous in his assessment. 'The 4th Division have really done the most magnificent work', Ritchie wrote to Auchinleck. 'No praise can be high enough for these achievements.'[32] Holding on to these gains, however, turned out to be rather more difficult.

The Eighth Army could not secure its hold on Cyrenaica so long as the Axis forces held the area around El Agheila. Unless Rommel was forced to retreat further west back into Tripolitania, there was the danger of a counter-offensive. This, as earlier, would compel the British forces into a futile retreat all the way back to the Egyptian frontier. Auchinleck was aware of this all-or-nothing operational predicament. Yet, he also knew that El Agheila was a highly defensible locality and that currently he could himself barely support one corps in the forward area. A serious build-up of troops and materiel was imperative before taking on the Axis forces near El Agheila. Auchinleck erred, however, in thinking that he had until mid-February 1942 to complete his preparations. He believed that Rommel – with some 35,000 troops and 70 tanks – would not risk an offensive until he had received reinforcements.[33]

Very like Wavell, Auchinleck underestimated the sheer chutzpah

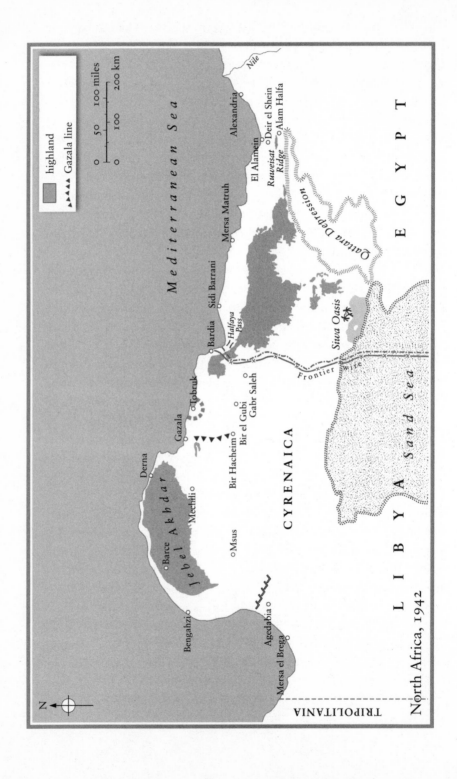

North Africa, 1942

of his adversary. Rommel launched his attack on 21 January 1942 – a month earlier than expected. The forward troops of the 1st Armoured Division were too weak and scattered, and after five days of combat, the division lost 100 tanks with nearly 1,000 troops taken prisoner. On 27 January, Rommel's forces stood at Msus – a tactically important location from which they could advance on Mechili and render Jebel Akhdar untenable for British forces.

The 4th Indian Division was as unprepared for an attack as the 1st Armoured Division. Its forces were equally scattered: the brigades being located at Benghazi, Barce and Tobruk. Worse still, it was immobile. The division had initially been ordered to hold a position south of Benghazi both to prevent the Axis forces from moving north along the coastal road and to deny them east–west routes to Jebel Akhdar. But the Axis advance towards Msus had threatened to cut-off the division at Benghazi. This resulted in much confusion. The division was twice ordered to pull out of Benghazi – only to be then told to stand firm.[34]

On the morning of 26 January, a staff officer arrived from the Eighth Army headquarters with instructions from on high for Tuker. Auchinleck believed that Rommel's advance was only a show of force and that an offensive defence would thwart his drive. Tuker was asked therefore to take the maximum risk and engage the Axis forces in his area with as many mobile columns as he could muster. Tuker thought otherwise. He disagreed with this assessment of Rommel's intent. Nor did he regard the proposed plan as at all feasible. His division had only one brigade – the 7th – in fighting trim. The other two were tied down with duties elsewhere and lacked transportation besides. Above all, Benghazi was not a particularly defensible position. Accordingly Tuker urged the army commander to consider withdrawing the division back to Derna, whence a counter-offensive could be deliberately prepared and launched. Ritchie was convinced, however, that the 4th Division should take the fight to the enemy. Following a meeting in Benghazi on 27 January, he agreed to Tuker's alternative suggestion for a co-ordinated attack on Msus by the 4th Indian Division and the remnants of the 1st Armoured Division.[35]

As the hour of attack neared, General Ritchie learnt the extent of the damage done to the armoured division. Realizing the seriousness of Rommel's offensive, he asked the armoured units to pull back towards Mechili – the direction in which Rommel seemed to be heading. This was, in fact, a feint. As British tanks pulled away from the Msus area, Rommel's forces swung west towards Benghazi. As Axis columns closed in on Benghazi, Tuker had no option but to request permission to evacuate. On the afternoon of 28 January, the divisional headquarters began pulling out of Benghazi after demolishing key installations and stores. The 7th Indian Brigade was to follow after dusk. However, a strong Axis column had looped across Benghazi and snipped the main road at one point. The brigade commander decided to split his forces into three columns – each of which would independently fight its way out of Benghazi towards the east. The plan did not work out smoothly, but the brigade did manage to regroup at Mechili with most of its troops and guns on 31 January 1942.

Auchinleck wanted the Eighth Army to stabilize along a line running south from Jebel Akhdar to the desert, regroup, and go on the offensive. The line was little more than a series of positions overlooking the nodal points of the roads and tracks that scored the face of Cyrenaica. Over the next four days, the 4th Indian Division took up and abandoned ten such lines, hoping at each point to delay the Axis advance, eventually falling back on the line running from Gazala on the coast to Bir Hacheim in the desert.[36]

The Gazala–Bir Hacheim Line was intended to shield Tobruk, which in turn would act as a forward supply base for the resumption of the counter-offensive. When the Eighth Army reached Gazala, the line was more notional than real. Ritchie quickly set about erecting fortified strongpoints in the triangular area of Tobruk, Gazala and Bir Hacheim. The Gazala Line evolved not as a continuous chain of defences but as a series of more than half a dozen 'boxes' – all-round defensive perimeters shielded by a 40-mile-long minefield. The gaps between the boxes were patrolled by tanks; the latter would also assist any of the boxes that came under particularly heavy attack.

On 12 February, two brigades of the 4th Division stood at the Gazala Line while the third, 7th Brigade, was deployed on the Egyptian side of the frontier. In early April 1942, however, the division was dispersed widely: the 7th Brigade was sent to Cyprus, the 5th

Brigade to Palestine for garrison duties, and the 11th Brigade to train for combined operations. The division's artillery and anti-aircraft assets were also parcelled out. And the divisional armoured regiment, the CIH, was posted to an armoured formation for training. The division as a whole was replaced in the North African desert by the 5th Indian Division.[37]

Rommel halted his forces ahead of Gazala owing to the now familiar shortages of tanks and supplies. Over the next four months both sides prepared themselves to go on the offensive. By early May 1942, the Eighth Army held the Gazala Line with 100,000 men, 849 tanks and 604 aircraft. Rommel, on the other hand, had built up 90,000 troops with 561 tanks (half of which were inferior Italian machines) and 542 aircraft. At last, the British enjoyed qualitative as well as quantitative superiority. Many of their armoured regiments held American-made Grant tanks, which were more than a match for the Axis tanks. British forces had also begun to receive the new 6-pounder anti-tank guns. Furthermore, the British knew from Ultra intelligence that Rommel planned to attack the Gazala Line towards the end of May.[38]

Rommel's attack came on 27 May – a week before Auchinleck's own offensive was to have been launched. Among the points at which his forces fell on the Gazala Line was the 'box' near Bir Hacheim. Deployed 30 miles east of the box was the 29th Indian Infantry Brigade of the 5th Division. Closer still – just 4 miles south-east of Bir Hacheim – was the 3rd Indian Motor Brigade.

This brigade had held up Axis forces at Mechili just over a year previously, and had been decimated during that action. Not until early May 1942 was it fully reconstituted and trained. The training took place at a camp 20 miles north of Cairo and was focused on static and mobile defence as a box. The latter proved particularly tricky to master. After one practice manoeuvre at night that ended in utter confusion, the brigade commander prophetically remarked, 'If this had happened during a move whilst in contact with the enemy the brigade would be wiped out in half an hour.'[39]

The brigade was initially moved to Mersa Matruh. On 22 May, it was ordered forward from Matruh. As the units drove along the

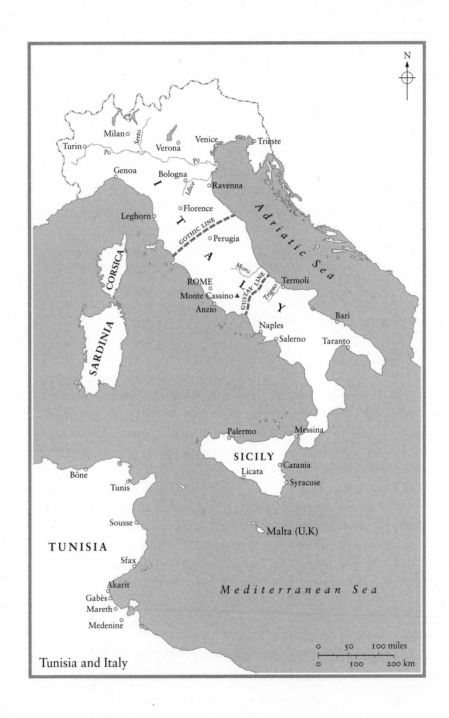

N

Milan
Serio
Turin
Po
Verona
Venice
Trieste
Po
Genoa
Bologna
Ravenna
Idice
Leghorn
Florence
GOTHIC LINE
Perugia

I   T   A   L   Y

Adriatic Sea

CORSICA

SARDINIA

ROME
Monte Cassino ▲
Anzio
Moro
GUSTAV LINE
Trigno
Termoli
Bari
Naples
Salerno
Taranto

Palermo
Messina
SICILY
Licata
Catania
Syracuse

Bône
Tunis

TUNISIA

Sousse

Malta (U.K)

Sfax
Akarit
Gabès
Mareth
Medenine

Mediterranean   Sea

Tunisia and Italy

	50	100 miles

0   50   100 miles
0   100   200 km

coast road, they were strafed by the odd enemy aircraft. More serious were the duststorms that kicked up as the brigade turned inland. 'Sand got into every nook and cranny of the body', recalled an Indian artillery officer in the brigade. 'It was everywhere, in the food, the eyes and ears and was the biggest nuisance to one's ease and comfort.'[40]

The brigade was deployed in Bir Hacheim just in time for the Axis offensive. It had only thirty anti-tanks guns – less than half of what it was supposed to hold; no tanks; and only a fraction of its carriers. Nor did it have much time to emplace its guns. Shortcomings in materiel were matched by those of men. The veterans of 1941 had all been sent back to India as instructors in the new cavalry training centres. The reconstituted brigade, then, had little real experience of fighting in the theatre.

By the evening of 26 May, the brigade had taken up position in a defensive box facing west, with two regiments ahead, the third covering the flanks and rear, and the artillery regiment in the centre. A little later, the men were served a hot meal and the officers went to the field mess for a drink and dinner. 'Every one was in good spirits that at long last we had made it to the front line of confrontation with the enemy.'[41] That night an advance column of the Axis forces tried to skirt the Bir Hacheim box and ran into the 3rd Motor Brigade. At first light, the brigade opened up with its artillery and targeted the soft-skinned vehicles of the Axis troops. By 0730 the Panzers counter-attacked and overran the brigade in thirty minutes. The commander refused to surrender and ordered all his troops to fight their way out to a rallying point 4 miles to the east. In attempting this, the brigade paid heavily: 41 officers, including 3 commanding officers, were killed or wounded, and about 600 soldiers were taken prisoner.[42]

The British fared little better in the other battles. Although the Axis forces were bogged down by the dense minefields, Ritchie was unable to think ahead of the fluid battle and squandered the opportunity to defeat Rommel. By the time he decided to hurl the 7th Armoured Division and the 5th Indian Division (less one brigade) on the Axis bridgehead, it was too late. The counter-offensive was an unleavened disaster. The usual problem of infantry–tank co-operation was exacerbated in this instance by the fact that the armoured division was under the command of 13th Corps while the infantry was under the 30th Corps. The two-pronged attack by the infantry and armour converged at the wrong place. The Axis counter-attack was savagely effective: fifty of the seventy British tanks were knocked out. The Axis tanks then took the infantry in their cross-hairs and pinned an entire brigade down by fire. The limited gains made by the other infantry brigade were swiftly liquidated by the enemy's counter-attacks.

With the fall of Bir Hacheim on 8 June, the wind was in Rommel's sails. Auchinleck reluctantly decided to pull back the Eighth Army from the Gazala Line and concentrate on the defence of Tobruk. Among the formations allocated for this was the 11th Indian Infantry Brigade of the 4th Indian Division. From 6 June onwards, the brigade set about repairing the defences of Tobruk and training on anti-tank guns and mortars. The withdrawal of other formations, including the 20th Indian Brigade, through Tobruk undoubtedly hit the morale of the men.[43] Over the following days, the brigade was reinforced by a battalion of the 29th Indian Brigade, which trickled in after the fall of El Adem. All along, the 11th Brigade kept up an active routine of patrolling every night.

The attack on Tobruk began on the morning of 20 June. The 11th Brigade took the brunt of the first thrusts. The 2/5th Mahrattas gave a good account of themselves for nearly three hours before being overrun by the German tanks. The 2/7th Gurkhas were isolated in one pocket of the garrison, but refused to surrender: they had to be rooted out platoon by platoon. By the afternoon the brigade head-quarters also caved in. The 22,000-strong garrison surrendered early the next morning.

The fall of Tobruk sent shockwaves rippling far out of North Africa. It came as a heavy blow to Churchill, who was then in Washington. The troops in the theatre were also badly shaken. Lieutenant Basu was with his unit some 50 miles from Tobruk when he heard the news of the surrender on the radio:

> The fall of Tobruk shook us. That complacent feeling that all was going well with our army was gone. More than that, it had taken our confidence away. Worse still, many got panicky and rumours that

Germans had been seen near the camp were whispered with all seriousness and awe even by responsible officers. We were always ready
for any eventuality. The trucks were kept ready to move out at half
an hour's notice. And then one night we were told to move back to
Sollum box.[44]

The retreating Eighth Army now fell back behind the Egyptian frontier. From his tactical headquarters at Sollum, Ritchie hoped to rebuild
his army, the remnants of which were limping towards Mersa Matruh.
However, his superiors knew that he had lost his hold on the situation.
Nor could they overlook the fact that Rommel's forces were not paus-
ing at the frontier but pursuing the British. On 25 June, Auchinleck
took personal command of the Eighth Army. And he ordered a withdrawal to the defences of El Alamein.

8

Collapsing Dominoes

The commander-in-chief of India landed in Calcutta on the morning of 7 December 1941. Later that day Wavell made a speech at the National Defence and Savings Week, calling on 'the second city of the Empire' to contribute to the war effort. 'In view of the threatening Japanese attitude at present', he told the audience, 'you may like to know that when I recently visited Burma and Malaya I was impressed by the strength of the defences which any attackers are likely to meet. And these defences by land, sea and air are constantly being reinforced.' Wavell was not striking a confident note merely to drum up support for the war. He genuinely believed that an attack on Malaya was not on the cards. As he wrote to Auchinleck a month earlier, 'the Jap has a very poor chance of successfully attacking Malaya and I don't think myself, that there is much prospect of his trying'.[1] Hours after Wavell's speech in Calcutta, the Japanese struck Malaya, Thailand and Hong Kong as well as Pearl Harbor. India was caught out not so much by Japanese deception as by self-deception.

The fall of France in June 1940 had catalysed the entry of Italy into the war, and so drawn India to the defence of its western bastions. The impact of these events on India's eastern sphere of interest was similar – albeit slower. The possibility of conquering South-East Asia and upending the European empires was no longer a glint in the eyes of Japan. It was an unprecedented opportunity. In mid-July 1940, a new government led by Prince Konoye Fumimaro took office. Tokyo was keen to attain self-sufficiency by seizing South-East Asia and promoting a new order in East Asia. Konoye's foreign minister, Matsuoka Yosuke, coined the phrase 'Greater East Asia Co-Prosperity Sphere' to designate Japan's own *Lebensraum*. The core of it would consist of China and Manchuria as well as the European colonies in South-East Asia.[2]

This was not a new idea. Notions of self-sufficiency had been prominent in Japanese thinking since the end of the Great War. Ironically, it was the advocates of self-sufficiency who sounded a note of caution in the summer of 1940.[3] They were acutely cognizant of Japan's material weakness for a venture in South-East Asia that would not only involve conflict with Britain but possibly the United States. Moreover, the southern expansion would have to be undertaken at a time when Japan was already waging an inconclusive war in China and when the old enemy, the Soviet Union, lurked in the wings. Tokyo was on the horns of this strategic trilemma for almost a year. Hitler's attack on the Soviet Union in June 1941 galvanized the planners in Tokyo, however, and hastened them along the road to Pearl Harbor.[4] If the Germans were able to defeat the Soviet Union and subsequently Britain, as seemed likely in the summer of 1941, then all of Japan's European enemies would be prostrate and their Asian empires helpless to prevent an enormous accretion of Japan's power – a moment of destiny comparable to that of Britain itself in the aftermath of the Napoleonic Wars. This, as it proved, woeful miscalculation was to result in three ruinous years of devastation for much of Asia.

The escalation of Japanese strategic aims from mid-1940 portended a conflict with India. To be sure, Tokyo did not plan an invasion of India. Nor was India regarded as an essential part of the Co-Prosperity Sphere. Nevertheless, numerous blueprints drawn up in Tokyo – including some by the luridly named Total War Research Institute – stretched the conception of the sphere to include India. This was hardly surprising given India's importance for Japanese trade. For the bulk of the inter-war period, India was the leading supplier of raw cotton to Japan. From 1928 to 1934, India on average accounted for 40 per cent of raw cotton imports into Japan. If we set aside the anomalous years of 1932–33, the figure is almost 46 per cent. Conversely, India emerged as the single largest market for Japanese textile goods – the most important of Japan's export items. From 1922 to 1935 India took on average 36 per cent of Japan's total exports of cotton piece-goods.[5]

The surge in textile imports from Japan not only came at the expense of Britain but threatened to crowd out India's own fledgling textile industry. In a rare joining of hands, the Indian industry and the Lancashire textile lobby combined to decry Japanese 'dumping' into India. Following the Imperial Economic Conference of 1932, India cancelled the trade agreement of 1904 with Japan and raised import duties for non-British goods to 75 per cent, up from 15 per cent in 1930. The Japanese retaliated by slashing imports of raw cotton from India. An attempt was made to settle the so-called Indo-Japanese 'cotton war' by a fresh agreement in 1934, which set the ceiling of Indian import duties on Japanese cotton piece-goods at 50 per cent and fixed quotas of Indian exports and Japanese imports to protect both sides' interests. When the agreement came up for renewal three years later, the Indian government remained dissatisfied with its working. It believed that a weak yen was allowing Japanese exports to flourish. In fact, Japanese industry on the whole was rather competitive – as evidenced by the rise in exports to India of articles ranging from bicycles and paints to chemicals and electrical appliances.[6] The Indian government sought to wriggle out of the agreement, but the Japanese stood firm. So the agreement was renewed for another three years. The friction with India over cotton was important in shaping Japanese thinking about self-sufficiency.

Indian influence was also prominent in the ideology underpinning the notion of a Co-Prosperity Sphere. Since the turn of the century, Japanese ideas of pan-Asianism had accorded a central place to India. The extended engagement between the Indian poet and Nobel Laureate Rabindranath Tagore and the Japanese aesthete and curator Okakura Tenshin nurtured one strand of pan-Asianism in Japan. Another strand stemmed from Indian nationalists' fascination with Japan in the wake of its military triumph over Russia in 1905. Thereafter, Tokyo became a refuge for revolutionaries against the Raj. Japanese ideologues unsurprisingly saw themselves as the leaders of an Asia released from the European harness.[7] The ruthlessness of the policy that sprang from the ideology of pan-Asianism should not obscure its importance. Indeed, ideological and economic considerations fused together in shaping Japanese attitudes and policy. India was no exception to this. A Japanese play staged at the height of the 'cotton war' closes with the leader of the trade delegation from Tokyo saying: 'Behold, the sun is setting: it will rise again. Fare-well people of India. We await the time when we can join hands for the peace of the world.'[8] These attitudes would shape Japan's policy towards India after December 1941.

Irrespective of India's location in Japanese ideas of a Co-Prosperity Sphere, Tokyo's strategic moves in South-East Asia were bound to collide with India's conception of its own security. Prior to the outbreak of war in Europe, India had drawn up no plans at all for the defence of its eastern land and maritime borders. It was assumed that any potential threat would develop from the north-west frontier of India. Nevertheless, Indian military planners regarded Singapore, Hong Kong and Rangoon as the outer ramparts to the east – on the defence of which rested India's own security. And the Indian army stood ready to send troops to secure these places.

This appeared to fit well with the wider imperial strategy for the Far East. In the aftermath of the First World War, policy-makers in London had planned for a major naval base at Singapore to which the main fleet of the Royal Navy would be sent in the event of a conflagration in the Far East. Both the assumptions underpinning the Singapore strategy – the availability of the base and the main fleet – were flaky. Financial constraints ensured that the Singapore base was a papier-mâché fortress, capable at best of berthing a peacetime fleet. This was perhaps just as well; for by the mid-1930s it was obvious to British planners that the international context would not permit sending the main fleet to Singapore.

The fragility of the situation in the Far East was driven home to the British government soon after the surrender of France. Tokyo demanded the closure of the Burma–China border and the Hong Kong frontier, as well as the withdrawal of British forces from mainland China. The Japanese interest in the Burma–China border was centred on the road connecting Lashio in northern Burma with Kunming in south-west China – a major supply artery for Chiang Kai-shek's forces battling the Japanese in China.

The war cabinet initially thought that the Japanese were bluffing. The chiefs of staff took a different view. The British garrisons in China, they held, were strategically useless and tactically unviable.

Nor was Hong Kong a vital interest: the garrison could not stave off a Japanese attack, in any case. Most importantly, given the threat posed by the German and Italian navies, there was now no question of sending the main fleet to Singapore. In this situation, the defence of Singapore would turn on the defence of the Malayan Peninsula from an attack via Thailand or Indo-China. Since neither India nor Britain could spare additional troops for Malaya, the chiefs advised beefing-up the air force in Malaya, ultimately from 8 obsolescent squadrons to 22 squadrons with 336 first-line aircraft. To begin with, two fighter squadrons would be sent to Malaya by the end of 1940. Meanwhile, it was imperative to avoid a war with Japan. The chiefs advocated the immediate closure of the Burma Road and a general settlement with the Japanese. The cabinet agreed that the military situation did not warrant risking war with Japan. Accordingly, it was decided to close the road for three months.[9]

Soon after, Konoye came to power in Tokyo and Japan's relations with Britain deteriorated further. A number of British nationals were imprisoned in Japan, leading to retaliatory measures. On 23 September 1941, Japanese forces entered northern Indo-China. Churchill was confident, however, that Japan would not go to war unless Germany successfully invaded Britain. He told the chiefs of staff that the Japanese threat to Singapore was remote. Nor did he agree with their views on Malaya. 'The defence of whole of Malaya', he wrote, 'cannot be entertained.' The defence of Singapore should be based on a strong local garrison and the 'general potentialities of sea power'. He also opposed the build-up of a large air force in the Far East. Instead Churchill urged the United States to take a tough line against Japanese encroachments on French and Dutch possessions in South-East Asia. He wrote to President Roosevelt: 'Everything that you can do to inspire the Japanese with the fear of a double war may avert the danger.' Following Germany's attack on the Soviet Union in June 1941, Churchill's reading of the situation turned upbeat. 'I cannot believe', he wrote, 'the Japanese will face the combination now developing around them. We may therefore regard the situation not only as more favourable but as less tense.'[10]

The government of India was only a bit more responsive to reality.

Following Tokyo's demand for the closure of the Burma Road, the general staff argued that even if Japan did not embark on aggression it might make unreasonable demands that would ultimately force it into a war with the British Empire. French Indo-China seemed a low-hanging fruit for the Japanese to pluck.

> Should Japan take this step our strategic position not only in Malaya and Singapore but also Burma and India will have to be reconsidered . . . it is perfectly obvious that Japanese control of Indo-China may be a first and very large step towards extending her influence to India in furtherance of the aims of her ultimate Asiatic policy.[11]

While the general staff were prepared to contemplate Japanese attacks on Hong Kong, Singapore, Malaya and even Thailand, a land attack on Burma was not deemed likely or feasible. They did allow, though, for the possibility of air attacks on Burma, Assam and eastern Bengal, as well as a naval thrust into the Indian Ocean. Accordingly, the defence plan of 1941 called for no more than the location of fighter squadrons near the industrial areas of Bengal and Assam.

Until Japan's entry into the war, writes the Indian official historian, 'the General Staff in India were suffering from a peculiar complacency, which prevented them from adopting effective measures to counteract any possible Japanese threat against Eastern India or her coastline'.[12] This was partly because of their preoccupation with the Middle East and North Africa, and partly because Japan did seem a distant threat, with no twentieth-century precedent for such a colossal strategic leap. But it also reflected the fact that India shared London's faith in bluff and bluster as substitutes for ends and means in strategy.

In mid-February 1941, Leo Amery – secretary of state for India – wrote to General Auchinleck – the newly appointed commander-in-chief of India – that 'the Japanese definitely mean mischief . . . I have a feeling things may well come to a head between them and us by May.' However weak the British position in the Far East, they must demonstrate resolve in the face of Japanese moves. 'As long as a cat arches her back, spits and faces the dog in front of her, he will hesitate and sometimes go away: the moment she turns tail she is done for.'[13]

Such were the zoological assumptions on which the defence of the Far East rested. Little wonder, it failed to survive contact with the enemy.

When Tokyo finally struck in December 1941, the first domino to fall was Hong Kong. No one expected to hold Hong Kong. Back in 1937 it was decided that the colony was an important but not vital outpost; it should be defended for as long as possible without being unnecessarily fortified with troops. These views were reiterated by the chiefs in the summer of 1940. Indeed, they held that the British position in the Far East would have been stronger without the unsatisfactory commitment to Hong Kong.[14] Churchill agreed with them. When the commander-in-chief of the Far East, Air Marshal Robert Brooke-Popham, suggested reinforcing Hong Kong with two more battalions, the prime minister wrote: 'We must avoid frittering away our resources on untenable positions ... I wish we had fewer troops there, but to move any would be noticeable and dangerous.'[15]

There was more at stake in Hong Kong than the reputation of the British Empire. The island was valuable to the Chinese forces as a port of access. An estimated 60 per cent of China's arms were imported through Hong Kong. Chiang Kai-shek was naturally anxious about its fate. At one point, he even offered ten divisions of trained soldiers to defend Hong Kong – if the British could equip them. London understandably turned down the proposal.[16] By the end of 1940, Hong Kong was defended by two battalions each from Britain, Canada and India. There was limited artillery and practically no air power available to the defenders.

Technically a British Dependent Territory, Hong Kong had long been regarded as an outpost of the Raj. It had been conquered by Indian troops and had done rather well out of the Indian opium trade. Hong Kong also housed a large community of expatriate Indians, who 'ate *tiffin* at midday and stored their merchandise in *godowns* and drained away their rainwater through *nullahs*; and the ladies did their light shopping at Kayamally's dry goods emporium and similar enterprises run by the small but prosperous band of Sindhi and Parsee merchants'.[17] Sikhs and Punjabi Muslims were sent from India to serve as auxiliaries in Hong Kong's police force. By a special arrangement with the Indian army headquarters, they were also recruited for the Hong Kong and Singapore Royal Artillery (HKSRA).

In the run up to the Japanese invasion, Indian troops in Hong Kong were rumbling with discontent. The source of disaffection seemed innocuous. Sikh soldiers in the HKSRA refused to wear the recently issued steel helmets. To use the helmets they would have to cut their hair – an act that would violate their ritual vows as baptized members of the Sikh community. The problem had also touched other Sikh units of the Indian army and was a source of consternation in the Punjab.[18] The authorities later attributed the problem to anti-British propaganda by Japanese fifth-columnists. The Sikhs, being the best educated of the martial races, were held to be more politically aware, and susceptible to seditious propaganda. However, the political problem that was of foremost concern to the Sikhs was the Muslim League's 'Pakistan' Resolution of March 1940. This sowed doubts in the minds of the Sikhs about the Raj's continued reliability in securing their interests. Such concerns had also led to the mutiny in the Central India Horse. Moreover, it led to a discernible fall in Jat Sikh enlistment in the Indian army.

The unhappy mood of the Sikhs in the HKSRA also influenced the Sikh company of 2/14th Punjab. By the end of 1940, there was a marked reluctance on the part of Sikh soldiers to moving crates of army stores – owing to the fear that these might contain steel helmets. This prompted the commander in Hong Kong, Major General Arthur Grasett, to issue an order that steel helmets would be worn by all ranks – British, Chinese or Indian. The Sikh battery of the 12th HKSRA bluntly refused to obey the instruction. Blandishments by the commanding officer and exhortations to their *izzat* or honour did not work either. In consequence, eighty-five Sikh soldiers were detained under guard. This triggered a rash of insubordinate acts in other Sikh units in Hong Kong, leading Grasett to fear a mutiny by the 800 Sikhs under his command. In the event, his fears proved unfounded. The arrested soldiers were court-martialled in January 1941. Stiff sentences were handed out – only to be remitted for all but eleven men. Grasett could hardly afford to lose an entire battery from the meagre defences of Hong Kong.[19]

The morale of the Indian troops, then, was at best middling. Even if it had been high, it was unlikely to have made much of a difference to the doomed defence of Hong Kong. Japanese planes attacked early on the morning of 8 December. Ten days later, their troops were assaulting the island. Hong Kong held out until Christmas evening, when the governor formally surrendered to the Japanese commander. Both the Indian battalions, the 2/14th Punjab and 5/7th Rajput, faced the brunt of the initial Japanese attack on the mainland and were the last units to pull back into the island. The fighting withdrawal took a heavy toll. The Rajputs suffered more casualties than any other unit in Hong Kong – one of its companies lost all its officers and 65 per cent of its men. The battalion practically disintegrated before the surrender. Some soldiers abandoned the front and armed deserters sought refuge in air-raid shelters. Others went across to the Japanese holding aloft propaganda leaflets that had been dropped on them by the Japanese air force.[20] The defence of Hong Kong was a gallant affair, but it also prefigured the problems that would confront the Indian army in South-East Asia.

The attack on Malaya began a few hours before the bombing of Hong Kong on 8 December 1941. The convoy carrying the invading force had set out from Hainan Island four days earlier. Lieutenant General Yamashita Tomoyuki's Twenty-Fifth Army, comprising some 17,000 combat troops, moved in serene waters screened by a slew of destroyers and cruisers. A professional soldier of common origins, Yamashita had steadily worked his way up the chain of command, embracing with equal eagerness the principles of *Bushido* and *Blitzkrieg*. Indeed, as head of the Japanese military mission to Germany in late 1940, he had closely studied the German advance into Western Europe and grasped the psychological impact of rapid and powerful movements combining armour, artillery and air power. Although Yamashita's main force would land in Thailand, he chose not to waste any time in fortifying its positions and aimed to strike south immediately.

Two regiments of the 5th Division would land on the south-eastern coast of Thailand at Singora and Patani and dash into the Kedah province of Malaya. A third regiment, from the 18th Division, would land at Kota Bharu and push its way into Kelantan. On both axes of advance, the first objectives were the British airfields. Yamashita

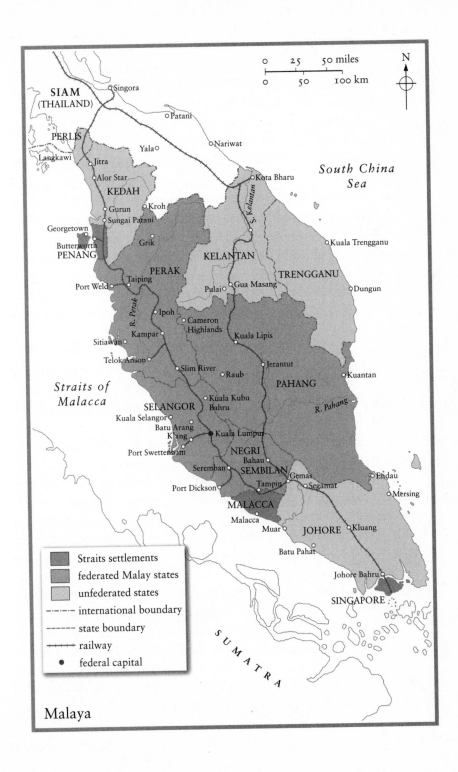

Malaya

knew that his force was smaller in numbers and his logistical links slender. Yet he was encouraged both by intelligence reports that the bulk of the British forces in Malaya were poorly trained and by his own dismissive assessment of the fighting prowess of the Indian units.[21] Notwithstanding the racial stereotyping, Yamashita's assessment and plans were not off-beam.

British plans for the defence of Malaya were mired in wishful thinking. Given Churchill's reluctance to commit enough troops for the defence of the entire peninsula, the default plan was to rely on air power. The chiefs of staff as well as the commander-in-chief of the Far East, Brooke-Popham, knew that the RAF did not have adequate aircraft. Yet the construction of airbases proceeded apace and continually outstripped RAF resources. By the autumn of 1941, eleven airfields were available – but only nine were occupied by the eve of war. What's more, the sprinkling of airbases across Malaya resulted in ground forces being deployed for their protection in places that were thoroughly unsuitable from an operational standpoint. For instance, the aerodrome in Alor Star compelled the deployment of troops at Jitra, while a far better defensive position was available further south at Gurun. Similarly, the airbases near Kota Bharu were plonked on the east coast and vulnerable to an attack from the sea.[22] In any event, the effort to build up airfields was rendered futile by London's refusal to send top-of-the-range fighters, resulting in the air defence of Malaya being entrusted to obsolete, painfully vulnerable planes.

The ground plan for the defence of Malaya was equally muddled. For the best part of 1941, British planners toyed with the idea of a pre-emptive strike into southern Thailand, aimed at forestalling a Japanese attack on that country. The origins of Operation Matador stretched back to 1937 when the idea of 'forward defence' was first mooted. In August 1940, the chiefs of staff set the ball rolling by agreeing to consider the military advantages of a move into Thailand. Six months passed before Brooke-Popham sent them a sketchy plan indicating various lines up to which British forces could advance. If they went all the way up to Jumbhom, they could seize and deny to the enemy all six airfields in southern Thailand. At a minimum, they should capture the major port of Singora and annihilate the Japanese forces as they sought to land on the beaches.

This seemingly sensible plan was dogged by a couple of problems. For a start, the Malaya Command did not have enough troops. It needed at least two more brigades to undertake the advance into Thailand as well as hold the defensive positions in Malaya. More importantly, a pre-emptive strike would entail the violation of Thailand's neutrality. London was unwilling to oblige on either count. Although the chiefs of staff underscored the strategic advantages of Operation Matador, the prime minister wanted to stay in step with the Americans and avoid complicating their negotiations with Japan. This was not surprising. Churchill had shown a similar sensitivity to American views on violating the neutrality of Iran – an area where the United States had no direct interests in play. This effectively ruled out Matador, though the chain of command from London to Malaya persuaded itself that the plan could still be set in motion *after* Japan's aggressive designs became as clear as daylight.[23]

The strategic dithering over Matador impinged on tactical plans as well. To prevent the defensive positions in Kedah from being outflanked, the Malaya Command was keen to cut the road linking Patani in Thailand with Kroh in Malaya. The idea was to pre-emptively occupy a position – the Ledge – about 23 miles north of Kroh. Since London and Brooke-Popham refused to rule out Matador, the commanders down the chain continued to plan on sending a column – Krohcol – to capture the Ledge. They were entirely oblivious of the fact that this too would violate Thai neutrality. Unsurprisingly, when the Japanese struck, the plans for Krohcol and Matador remained stapled in the files of the Malaya Command. And no other plans existed which would have allowed for anything more than an inert, passive defence, leaving the initiative to Japan.

The fact that such unreal assumptions underpinning the defence of Malaya went unchallenged attested to the weaknesses in the British chain of command. The sixty-three-year-old Brooke-Popham had been governor of Kenya for three years before being recalled to service as commander-in-chief of Far East Command in November 1940. There was a significant gap between his grand title and his actual powers: neither the Royal Navy nor the civilian bureaucracy was under his control. The General Officer Commanding-in-Chief Malaya, Lieutenant General Arthur Percival, had taken over only in

April 1941. 'General Percival is a nice, good man who began life as a school-master', noted the visiting minister of state, Duff Cooper. 'I am sometimes tempted to wish he had remained one.'[24] This was at once incorrect and unfair. Percival had never been a school-master, though he had taught at staff colleges. More pertinently, he was sharp, diligent and experienced. Percival's principal flaws were his inability to assert himself and his tendency to shy away from confrontation.

These were compounded by his fraught relationship with the commander of the 3rd Indian Corps, Lieutenant General Heath. Percival had never commanded a corps and had spent most of his career as a staff officer. Heath was not only senior to him in service, but had led the 5th Indian Division to victory in East Africa and had recently been knighted. While Heath resented serving under a junior and less distinguished officer, Percival wheeled around the trolley of prejudices held by British officers towards their colleagues in the Indian army. If it was any consolation, Percival's relations with the commander of the 8th Australian Division were no better.

Heath had under his command the 9th and 11th Indian Infantry Divisions. Both were peppered with difficulties – problems that underlay the disastrous performance of the Indian units in the face of a Japanese attack. To begin with, there was a serious shortage of experienced soldiers. The massive expansion of the Indian army, while impressive on paper, resulted in a substantial dilution of skills and standards. The pre-war regular units were milked of their trained officers and VCOs, NCOs and soldiers, who went on to form the nuclei of the new units. The latter in turn were milked to raise yet more units. In consequence, the new units rolled out by the Indian army had few seasoned officers or soldiers and were packed with raw recruits and green officers. The war diary of 5/11th Sikh noted, for example, that the unit had joined the 9th Division in August 1941 'having been thoroughly milked, 450 recruits and 6 BOs [British officers] unable to speak Urdu having joined a few weeks prior to embarkation'. Then too, the battalion lost another thirty experienced men to a newly formed machine-gun unit.[25]

Second, as with Indian forces elsewhere, the units sent out to Malaya were woefully under-equipped. This stemmed from the fact that the rate of expansion of the Indian army was not matched by the provision of weapons and equipment by Britain. Indeed, most units deployed in Malaya did not receive their full equipment until November 1941. For instance, the 1/13th Frontier Force Rifles of the 9th Division received the standard light machine gun only weeks before fighting broke out and had little time to get used to the new weapon. Similarly, most artillery regiments did not get their main 25-pounder field gun until very late in the day. The Malaya Command's helpful advice to units facing serious shortages was that they 'must constantly agitate until they get them'.[26]

Third, and related to the above, was the lack of training. In the absence of equipment, training naturally took a back seat. But the divisional, corps and Malaya commands also bore responsibility for the neglect of training. Even in 1941 the Malaya Command hardly functioned as a wartime formation. John Baptist Crasta, an NCO from southern India, reached Malaya in April 1941 and was pleasantly surprised at the conditions in the garrison.

> Life for the troops in Malaya left nothing to be desired. Electrified huts were provided for accommodation. There was plenty of water and good scenery. Food was ample and wholesome. Beer and liquor were available in moderate quantities in canteens, and other amusements such as camp cinemas and picnics were arranged. Discipline was not too exacting.
>
> Even in the topmost circles, war was not expected in Malaya.[27]

Commanders and staffs at various levels made little effort to study the conditions under which their troops would confront the enemy. This was especially problematic because whatever little the Indian troops had picked up pertained to fighting in the desert. They were entirely untrained to fight in the jungle or countryside thick with cultivated rubber plantations but linked by roads.

The only formation which had any clue of these conditions was the 12th Indian Infantry Brigade. The brigade had been shipped out of India in August 1939 and stationed in Singapore. The officer commanding one of the battalions of the brigade – 2nd Battalion Argyll and Sutherland Highlanders – Lieutenant Colonel Ian Stewart, took the lead in training his battalion in Johore. In a series of exercises held in 1939–40, the Argylls familiarized themselves with the sights, sounds and smells of the jungle. They taught themselves the tactical actions best suited to this environment: all-round defence, aggressive patrolling, flanking moves. These methods trickled into the rest of the 12th Indian Brigade – but no further.

The brigade was attached directly to the Malaya Command and did not operate with the other Indian formations. Further, the Malaya Command had scant interest in Stewart's attempts. Not until autumn 1940 did the Malaya Command prepare the *Tactical Notes for Malaya 1940*. Although it drew on the 12th Indian Brigade's experience, the pamphlet was amateurish. It did more harm than good by giving currency to myths about Japanese tactical weaknesses and encouraging wrong notions about ease of operations such as withdrawal. GHQ India also prepared a training pamphlet titled *Notes on Forest Warfare* which was sent to Indian units in Malaya from early 1941. None of this was of much use, owing to the lassitude of Malaya Command in drawing up a serious programme of individual and collective training for its units and formations – let alone creating a theatre-level training school. Even the limited training envisaged for the Indian units was scuppered by the need to prepare defensive positions and other tasks at hand.[28]

Indian troops in Malaya were thus inexperienced, under-equipped and ill-trained. The upshot was a series of debacles in the face of a determined Japanese onslaught.

At 2100 hours on the night of 7 December 1941, Brooke-Popham was informed that RAF aircraft had sighted the Japanese force at sea and had been shot at. It was too late to launch Operation Matador and make for Singora. However, instead of launching the Krohcol to secure the Ledge, Brooke-Popham ordered Percival only to postpone Matador. The Japanese, he felt, had not yet committed a 'definite act of hostility'. He wanted an aerial reconnaissance the next morning to confirm Japanese intentions. Just before midnight, the Japanese task force anchored off Kota Bharu. Two hours later, the assault began.[29]

As the Japanese waded their way through heavy surf, the pillboxes on the beach crackled into life. The 8th Indian Brigade (9th Division) pinned the attackers down with heavy fire. The Japanese commander,

Tsuji Masanobu, reported that 'our men lying on the beach, half in and half out of water, could not raise their heads'. By daybreak, the attackers – 'creeping forward like moles' – managed to inch their way towards the defences.

> Suddenly one of our men covered a loophole with his body and a group of moles sprang to their feet in a spurt of sand and rushed into the enemy's fortified position. Hand grenades flew and bayonets flashed, amid the sound of war cries and calls of distress, in a cloud of black smoke the enemy's frontline was captured.[30]

Having punched a hole in the defences, the Japanese found the going easier. The 8th Brigade was stretched thin on the ground. Two of its battalions were deployed behind to protect the airbases near the coastline. The other two battalions manned a long line of pillboxes strung along the beach with machine-gun nests deployed on a line to the rear. The Japanese infiltrated these lines in small groups, isolated and attacked the pillboxes, and quickly headed inland to capture the airbases.

At nightfall, the divisional commander, Major General Barstow, ordered the brigade to pull back if threatened with destruction. The withdrawal through the swampy terrain and in heavy rain proved confused, arduous and hazardous. The Japanese, having taken the airfields, sought to block and cut down the retreating Indian forces. A battalion of Hyderabad State Infantry practically disintegrated: its commanding officer was apparently killed by his own troops when he tried to restore a modicum of order. Confusion was compounded by fear and panic. Rumours coursed through the countryside that the brigade commander had been captured. As the Japanese pressed hard in pursuit, the Indian units had no option but to head south with the minimum loss of men, materiel and morale. By 12 December 1941, Kelantan was almost entirely in Japanese hands. The movement of Indian forces thereafter was 'analogous to that of a man walking back step by step while still facing the tiger with a sword in hand'.[31]

The fate of Malaya, however, turned on the defenders at Kedah. The Japanese landed unopposed at Singora and Patani and swiftly made their way south. Brooke-Popham learnt of the landing by 0930 hours on 8 December. By the time he made up his mind to launch the

Krohcol and the order filtered down to the unit, it was 1500 hours. No sooner had the Krohcol crossed the border than it was engaged by the Thai police, who astonishingly managed to block its advance. Another twenty-four hours passed before the column neared the Ledge – only to be shot at by Japanese tanks that had beaten them to the goal. Even as the Krohcol fell back, the rest of the 11th Division scampered to take up defensive positions.

The abortion of Operation Matador had unhinged the division and dented its morale. The torrential rain did little to cheer the troops. In these circumstances, the division was ordered to hold hastily prepared defensive positions at Jitra. Poorly planned and sited, these defences stretched over a 12-mile front covering jungle, paddy fields and plantations. The defensive dug-outs were sited too far apart to support each other by fire. Worse, the defences were shallow – incapable of absorbing a major blow and bouncing back with a punch. Nowhere did the line have a depth of more than a mile and a half.

A Japanese reconnaissance detachment of about 500 men and a dozen tanks moved south to probe the British defences. Joined by Tsuji, the detachment was ambushed by a screening force of the 11th Division. But when the Japanese regrouped the screening troops fell back. Although the defenders blew up bridges to delay the Japanese, they seemed most reluctant to stand and fight. 'We now understood the fighting capacity of the enemy', noted Tsuji. 'The only things we had to fear were the quantity of munitions he had and the thoroughness of his demolitions.' Tsuji conveyed his impressions to Yamashita and got the go-ahead for a 'driving charge' on the defences of Jitra.[32]

The 11th Division's commander, Major General Murray-Lyon, deployed two battalions – the 1/14th Punjab and the 2/1st Gurkha Rifles – north of the main line of defences. On the afternoon of 11 December, the Japanese tanks, followed by infantry in trucks, tore through the Punjabis. Most of the troops had never even seen a tank before and the Japanese charge shattered the battalion. As Captain Mohan Singh, a company commander, recalled: 'Men were running helter skelter. The Japanese tanks had broken in and had created havoc, ammunition trucks were on fire, bombardment was heavy . . . The Battalion had dispersed, in utter confusion. It was a case of – "Everyone for himself".'[33] Unfortunately, it was neither the first nor the last battalion to suffer this fate. In any event, the Japanese infantry now began infiltrating the Gurkhas' position. The forward companies of the Gurkhas fought literally to the knife, but were cut off from the rest of the battalion and attacked by the tanks. By the end of the day, two battalions of the 11th Division had ceased to exist.[34]

Later that evening, Japanese patrols picked out gaps in the main defensive position at Jitra. Around midnight, their infantry and tanks fell on the division, infiltrating the gaps, outflanking the positions and attacking isolated sections of the defences. Unnerved by the speed of the Japanese thrusts and the scale of his own losses, Murray-Lyon was minded to withdraw the entire division by the following noon. On Percival's orders, he stuck it out for a few more hours before disengaging from the advancing enemy and falling back to Gurun. The retreat turned into a rout as the Japanese snipped the communications between various units and used roadblocks and ambushes to devastating effect. The 2/9th Jat was caught in one such ambush just before dawn on 12 December. 'In the melee which ensued in the darkness', the brigade war diary noted, 'the battalion became disintegrated among the buildings, drains and slit trenches of the camp and a *sauve qui peut* ensued'. The stragglers had not got very far when the men's nerves began to tell: they began 'seeing things' and the cry 'Dushman' (enemy) led to the further disintegration of the survivors.[35]

Jitra was the decisive battle in Malaya. And the 11th Indian Division suffered a bloody defeat. By mid-December, the division's 15th Indian Infantry Brigade was reduced to a quarter of its original size, the 28th Brigade to a third, and the 6th Brigade to about half. During the retreat the division also lost the bulk of its motor transport and equipment, ammunition and supplies.[36] For weeks afterwards, the Japanese enjoyed the 'Churchill rations'. More importantly, they now had air superiority in northern Malaya and naval superiority around the Malayan Peninsula and Singapore. Over the next fortnight, the Japanese used the same tactics – spiked with improvisations like the use of bicycles – in a three-pronged advance to push the defenders out of Kedah and Kelantan. Crasta saw lorries and motorcycles moving at top speed, conveying defeated men, both Indian and British, retreating. They had apparently abandoned their armies. Groups of soldiers were retreating on foot, their faces aghast with fear, their clothes and boots tattered and torn. They appeared badly shaken. They had only a few words to say, words like: Oh, the Japanese are terrible. We are gone. There is no hope.[37]

By 23 December, the 11th Division was forced to fall back behind the Perak River. Two of its truncated brigades were clubbed together to form a new 6/15th Brigade. Murray-Lyon was also replaced as commander by Major General Archie Paris. However, the lack of experience and the deficiencies in training continued to tell on the troops' performance. When the Japanese crossed the Perak River, the 6/15th Brigade put up a determined fight, but was forced eventually to withdraw south of the Slim River. General Percival sent a note on tactics to the 3rd Corps: 'The enemy is trying to dislodge us from our positions by flanking and encircling movements and by attacks on our communications . . . We must play the enemy at his own game.' These were academic instructions. As Colonel Stewart of the Argylls put it, 'new techniques cannot be learnt in the middle of a battle'.[38]

As Indian and Australian formations retreated into Central Malaya, they began receiving reinforcements from home. When the 6/14th Punjab sailed into Singapore, it was immediately strafed and bombed by Japanese planes. 'We were advised to immediately disembark', recalled Sepoy Gurdial Singh. The troops left the ship with only their personal weapons: 'there was no time to unload anything else'. A dozen Japanese planes dived in over the next hour and a half and destroyed the ships. The battalion lost all its stores and possessions. Gurdial found it 'annoying [that] not a single British aircraft came to challenge the enemy'. Even the British troops around him were muttering 'bloody Churchill' under their breath. Realizing the adverse impact on morale, the British officers assured them: 'Our aircraft are also coming.' None did. When the unit reached the front line in Malaya, they were merely instructed to 'follow the fighting tactics of the British troops already engaged in battle'. Gurdial felt it was 'a peculiar situation, rumour mongering was rife. Many soldiers said why die in these far off lands and for what purpose.' An NCO claimed that 'internally arrangement had been reached with the Japanese', that is, a tacit agreement had been struck that the Japanese would not harm the Indian soldiers. 'Even Indian officers were in two minds.'[39]

The parlous state of morale and training resulted in a major fiasco at Slim River on the night of 6/7 January 1942. Two Indian brigades were wrecked by around a thousand Japanese troops supported by thirty tanks. The next day, the new supreme commander of the South-West Pacific Command arrived in Singapore. The hapless Wavell had yet again been given a sprawling command – worse for being multinational – in a seemingly impossible situation. After a debriefing at the 3rd Corps headquarters, he mumbled: 'Well, I have never listened to a more garbled account of an operation.' His ADC wrote in his diary: 'I have never seen men look so tired.' Wavell cabled London about his decision to pull out 3rd Corps from a fighting withdrawal. 'Retreat does not bring out best qualities of Indian troops and men are utterly weary and completely bewildered by Japanese rapid encircling tactics, by enemy air bombing . . . and by lack of our own air support.'[40]

The plan was to make a 'strategic retreat' to northern Johore. It was in fact the beginning of the end. The 9th Indian Division was deployed in depth along the trunk road. The newly arrived 45th Indian Brigade (originally part of the 17th Indian Division) was also thrown into operations. The brigade had been equipped and trained for desert warfare and had been earmarked for Iraq before being diverted to Malaya. The troops found themselves fighting along the Muar River in northern Johore, and took a nasty beating at the hands of the Japanese. 'The young Indian recruits were helpless', wrote Percival. 'They did not even know how to take cover and there were not enough officers to control them.'[41] This was true enough, although the British and Australian troops were afflicted by the same set of problems – training, leadership, morale – as the Indians.

In subsequent operations, the remaining Indian brigades suffered further losses. By the time the withdrawal into Singapore was carried out on 30 January, it was clear that the Indian formations were no longer capable of resisting the enemy. Wavell wanted the Malaya Command to continue fighting for two months. The defence lasted for barely two weeks. When Singapore surrendered on 15 February 1942, the Japanese took around 55,000 Indian prisoners of war.

The fall of Singapore was a crushing blow to the prestige of the British Empire. For India, however, the disaster in Burma overshadowed the debacle in Malaya. India's war would now have to be fought on its own frontiers. Worse still, it would have to be waged on a frontier that had been accorded the least priority in strategic plans and preparation. The sole consolation for New Delhi was that its army had not been entirely rounded-up by the Japanese and considerable numbers had survived to fight another day. Still, in many ways, the calamitous defeat in Burma mirrored the rout in Malaya.

To begin with, India's complacency about an overland invasion of Burma matched that of the British leadership on Malaya. Even after the Japanese began encroaching in South-East Asia, the Raj had all but written off the possibility of a Japanese ground attack on Burma and had made scant preparation for such an eventuality. The commander of the Burma Army had insisted since 1939 that 'on the Siamese [Thai] border there is not much scope for a larger force [than raiding parties] to attack Burma by land . . . I do not regard the land threat very seriously – air attack by Japan from Siamese aerodromes is the bigger danger.'[42] The governor-general of Burma, Sir Reginald Dorman-Smith, believed that if the Japanese invaded his territory, the Burmese people would rise up in resistance. After a visit to Rangoon in October 1941, Wavell was persuaded by these judgements. He went so far as to believe that if the Japanese did risk an invasion of Burma, they would 'get it in the neck'.[43]

Given the sheer size and topography of Burma, this was not an unreasonable supposition. Still, as in Malaya, weaknesses in the chain of command precluded the tough-minded testing of assumptions and clear apportioning of responsibility. Since late 1940, India had been pestering London to place Burma under its operational control rather than that of the Far East Command. Wavell personally took it up with the chiefs during a trip to London in September 1941 and continued to send a stream of cables on this matter. The cabinet, however, was solicitous of the constitutional status of Burma. Moreover, given the American interest in the Burma–China road it did not wish to complicate matters by bringing India into the frame.

Only four days after the Japanese attack on Malaya did the prime minister agree to place Burma under GHQ India's control. 'You must now look east', Churchill cabled Wavell. 'Burma is now placed under your command. You must resist the Japanese advance towards Burma and India.' 'We will do our best', replied Wavell, '. . . in spite of nakedness of our air and anti-aircraft defences.' Wavell remained fixated on the air defence of Burma. While Brooke-Popham agreed to transfer his air force in Burma to India's command, he insisted that they should be available on call to him. Much thought and energy was also expended in copious telegrams between London, New Delhi and Rangoon, trying to work out the constitutional relations between the governor-general of Burma and the commander-in-chief of India.[44]

Wavell appointed Lieutenant General Thomas Hutton as commander-in-chief in Burma. When Hutton took over, he had at his disposal the 1st Burma Division. Formed only in July 1941 and commanded by Major General James Bruce Scott, this division was made up of the 13th Indian Infantry Brigade and the 1st and 2nd Burma Brigades. The 1st Burma Division was headquartered at Toungoo and tasked with the defence of the Shan States in north-east Burma. The 16th Indian Infantry Brigade arrived in Burma in early December 1941. By early January 1942, two more Indian brigades – the 46th and 48th – along with the headquarters of the 17th Indian Division had reached Burma. These three brigades as well as the 2nd Burma Brigade – amounting to around 22,000 troops – formed the nucleus of the 17th Indian Division, tasked with the defence of the southern, Tenasserim region and commanded by Major General John Smyth.

The army in Burma was impressive only on paper. If anything, it was even worse prepared than the Malaya Command to fight the Japanese. The Burmese units had undergone considerable expansion since 1939. The Burma Rifles had doubled from four to eight battalions; new Frontier Force and Military Police units had also been raised. Traditionally, British officers from the British or Indian army were seconded to Burma for fixed tenures of four years. However, after 1939 the supply of officers could not keep up with the expansion of the Burmese units. Emergency Commissions were offered to

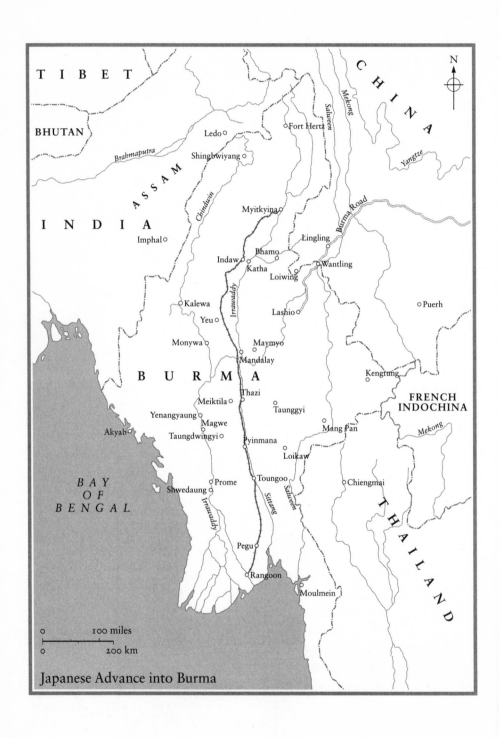

N

TIBET

CHINA

BHUTAN

Ledo

Fort Hertz

Mekong

Brahmaputra

Shingbwiyang

Yangtze

ASSAM

Chindwin

Myitkyina

Burma Road

INDIA

Imphal

Lingling

Indaw

Bhamo

Bhamo

Katha

Wantling

Loiwing

Kalewa

Irrawaddy

Lashio

Puerh

Yeu

Monywa

Maymyo

Mandalay

BURMA

Thazi

Kengtung

Meiktila

Taunggyi

FRENCH
INDOCHINA

Yenangyaung

Magwe

Mang Pan

Mekong

Akyab

Taungdwingyi

Pyinmana

Loikaw

BAY
OF
BENGAL

Shwedaung

Prome

Toungoo

Chiengmai

Irrawaddy

Sittang

Salween

Pegu

THAILAND

Rangoon

Moulmein

100 miles

200 km

Japanese Advance into Burma

British civilians already employed in Burma. While their knowledge of the language and terrain was excellent, the lack of military experience could not be masked.[45]

The condition of the Indian formations was wearily familiar. The 13th Indian Brigade had reached Rangoon in April 1941, milked heavily of experienced soldiers and officers, stripped of artillery and other supporting units. The brigade had done little training for jungle warfare in either India or Burma. Indeed, the 1st Burma Division did no collective training at all. GHQ India's training pamphlet *Forest Warfare* was duly sent to Burma – only to be treated as 'bumf'. As in Malaya, Hutton's command headquarters showed little interest in organized training. A few commanding officers took the initiative to conduct unit-level exercises, but most battalions got no further than a jaunt around the local golf course. The 16th Infantry Brigade and other formations that arrived after December 1941 were equally inexperienced and ill-equipped. Of course, they had no time to train and were thrown on to the front immediately. General Smyth rightly observed that 'this heterogeneous new 17th Division was a Division only in name'.[46]

Nevertheless, the 17th Division had to hold a 400-mile front of mountainous jungles in Tenasserim. Its lines of communication varied between execrable and non-existent. Yet this region was deemed vital to the defence of Rangoon and the Burma Road – and it was to be held until further reinforcements flowed in from India. Having set up his headquarters at Moulmein, Smyth trekked up the Pagoda-dotted ridge that overlooked the town. No sooner had he reached the top than he felt: 'What an impossible place to defend with a small force! And what an even more impossible place from which to withdraw, as the only line of withdrawal was by river steamer across a broad expanse of water.'[47] The thought would be echoed by many a commander in the weeks and months ahead.

Burma had not initially been prominent in the Japanese military plans for South-East Asia. The rapidity with which the defences of Malaya collapsed, though, led the Japanese to sense a similar opportunity in Burma. By capturing the country they hoped at once to seal the western periphery of the planned Co-Prosperity Sphere and to cut the Burma Road, which was being used by the

Allies to supply the Chinese forces under Chiang Kai-shek. In retrospect it was clearly a grievous mistake to go for Burma. The country could have been a useful military buffer – one that would have forced the British rather than the Japanese to experience the horrors of extended logistical lines. But the maelstrom of war sucked the Japanese almost inexorably into Burma.

The much-awaited Japanese offensive, with a little over 25,000 troops, began on 20 January 1942. The 55th Division crossed the Thai border and struck towards Moulmein, while the 33rd Division advanced further north along the jungle tracks to the Salween River. The 16th Indian Brigade was badly knocked in an encounter at Kawkareik ahead of Moulmein. The Japanese typically sought to infiltrate and outflank the Indian defences. The brigade commander panicked and sought permission to withdraw. Although the brigade managed to demolish important roads and bridges, the withdrawal turned into a confused melee. As the official history notes: 'The junior officers were quite panicky and the panic spread to the lower ranks also. They were all new to jungle fighting and the first day's experience had shattered their nerves.' Rumours travelled faster than the enemy: it was reported, for instance, that the Japanese were using gas.[48]

The withdrawal left the brigade in tatters. All transport and equipment, including the entire signals unit, was lost. Orders had also been given to destroy arms: soldiers even discarded their rifles. The morale of the troops was steeply depressed. Hutton sent a stirring Order of the Day to his forces on 27 January: 'There must be no question of further withdrawal . . . All troops must understand that they must on no account give ground because the enemy have penetrated to their rear; these parties will be dealt with by other troops disposed in depth.' It was too late. Three days later, the Japanese turned on Moulmein. Although some units performed creditably, others – especially the Burma Rifles – were diluted by large-scale desertions.[49] Smyth knew that not only was morale low but Indian and Burmese soldiers mistrusted each other. In any case, he was always inclined to pull back from Moulmein to fight on the ground of his own choosing. Hutton reluctantly acquiesced in Smyth's request to reel-in behind the Salween River.[50]

'Take back all you have lost', thundered Wavell when he reached the front line. Hutton placated him by promising to hold Martaban, on the north side of the river.[51] The 17th Division was reinforced on this line by its 46th Indian Brigade. But the Japanese were able to ford the Salween rather easily. On 8 February they crossed the river, cut-off Martaban by a roadblock and captured the town the next day. Further north, the Japanese crossed the river unopposed near Pa-an. On the night of 11 February they attacked the 7/10th Baluch.

This newly raised battalion had reached Rangoon on 16 January. As with most Indian units, it was totally unready for fighting in the jungle. When the commanding officer inquired about training, a senior staff officer shot back: 'Training – you can't do any training because it is all bloody jungle.' On reaching the operational area, the Baluchis sent out patrols to familiarize troops with the terrain. These were clumsy affairs: the patrols were too large and unwieldy, and the men hacked their way through the jungle, at once tiring themselves out and intimating their presence to the enemy.[52] The Japanese attack began with shelling and airstrikes on the Baluch position. When the main attack came, the Baluchis found themselves surrounded by the infiltrating Japanese. The battalion put up a stern defence. Charlie Company, led by Captain Srikant Korla, was particularly tenacious in its resistance. But once the Baluchis decided to pull out, the Japanese made short work of them. When the battalion regrouped at the brigade headquarters the next morning, it counted five officers, three VCOs and sixty-five soldiers; 7/10th Baluch had more or less ceased to exist.[53]

Smyth now tried to regroup his division behind the Bilin River. But the river was no more than a ditch – hardly a suitable defensive position. The troops at his disposal included the 48th Indian Brigade, which had the most experienced Indian units in Burma: all three Gurkha battalions pre-dated the war. Inevitably, there were inexperienced units as well. The 5/17th Dogra, a new unit, was battered by the Japanese in an attack on 17 February. The battalion disintegrated and dispersed in confusion, losing most of its equipment and transport, and carrying with it the unnerved 8th Burma Rifles. Hutton realized that 'if this battle should go badly enemy might penetrate the line of River Sittang without much difficulty and evacuation of Rangoon would become imminent possibility'. Hence, he ordered Smyth to fight it out at Bilin by launching counter-attacks. The Indian forces were hardly up to the task and were easily repelled. On the morning of 19 February, Hutton permitted Smyth to pull his troops back behind the Sittang.[54]

That night the 17th Division disengaged and withdrew along a narrow track towards the Sittang River. The Japanese were more enterprising in pursuit. As ever, they abandoned the road and struck out through the jungle in small parties. Their boldness paid off. On 22 February, they caught the 17th Division on the hop as it sought to cross the Sittang bridge. Smyth was forced to order a premature demolition of the bridge, even though the bulk of his troops were on the wrong bank. Those trapped on the far side had little option but to surrender or swim across the fast-flowing, quarter-mile-wide river. Just about 3,500 officers and men made it with little more than their personal weapons. The 17th Division effectively ceased to be a fighting force. And the road to Rangoon was wide open.

On 27 February, Dorman-Smith, the governor-general, cabled Linlithgow: 'This is the last message I will send from Rangoon until we have recaptured it . . . nothing short of a seasoned army could retrieve the Sittang situation. Our troops have fought very well but they are worn out . . . Rangoon will have to be evacuated tomorrow.'[55] Wavell thought otherwise. He flew to Burma the next day and met Dorman-Smith and Hutton. He was beside himself with anger. He stormed at Hutton for his alleged defeatism and ordered him to hold Rangoon for as long as possible. Hutton felt that if Wavell had his way, the Japanese would trap the entire Burma Army in Rangoon. But he chose to stay quiet. Meanwhile, Smyth sent a request to withdraw his forces to Pegu. So enraged was Wavell that he drove down the country track to Smyth's headquarters and personally relieved him of his command. His deputy, David 'Punch' Cowan, was asked to take over the division.[56]

Four days later, Hutton was replaced as commander-in-chief of Burma by General Harold Alexander, whose principal assets were that he was imperturbable and in favour with the prime minister. Bolstered by the arrival of the battle-hardened 7th Armoured Brigade and the 63rd Indian Infantry Brigade, Alexander lost no time in ordering a counter-attack at Pegu. The 63rd Brigade had barely landed in

Rangoon when it was launched into battle. Like most Indian units in Malaya and Burma, it had a large proportion of new officers, fresh recruits and unsuitable equipment. The brigade lost almost all its senior officers in the opening encounter. The counter-attack was very nearly a disaster. The Japanese hit back and threatened to box in and destroy the troops at Pegu. On hearing the news, Alexander immediately ordered the evacuation of Rangoon. His own headquarters as well as that of the 17th Division narrowly missed being trapped by the Japanese, retreating north towards Tharrawaddy. As the Japanese approached Rangoon, the sky was lit up by columns of fire. The retreating troops had blown up the installations of Burmah Oil Company – an act that led to two decades of litigation after the war.[57]

The fall of Rangoon enabled a rapid build-up of Japanese forces in Burma. The Fifteenth Army was reinforced by sea with two well-trained divisions and tanks, heavy artillery and aircraft. The Japanese wasted no time in destroying the RAF in Burma. On 21–22 March, Japanese aircraft launched five devastating strikes on the airbase at Magwe and crippled British air power for the rest of the campaign. Wavell refrained from making good these losses. The tiny air force in India was held back for the defence of Calcutta and other eastern towns. In consequence, the Japanese enjoyed unchallenged control of the air over Burma.[58]

As the 17th Division retreated north towards Prome, the 1st Burma Division provided a screen behind which additional troops were being deployed at Toungoo in the Sittang valley. The troops were not Indian or British – but Chinese. Since December 1941, Generalissimo Chiang Kai-shek had been gravely worried at the prospect of the Burma Road being severed by the Japanese. The closure of the road for three months in 1940 had given him a taste of things to come and he was desperate to keep alive this supply artery – not least because American Lend-Lease supplies to China were routed through Rangoon. On 10 December, Chiang sent a long telegram to the British government, expressing his willingness to fully collaborate in any concerted military plan adopted by the Allies. On receiving a copy of this cable, Wavell flew to Lashio and met Chiang on 22 December. Wavell thought that the Generalissimo was 'not a particularly

impressive figure at first sight: he speaks no English, but makes cluck-
ing noises like a friendly hen when greeting one'. Nor did Wavell
think much of Chinese military prowess. Thus, when Chiang offered
the Chinese Fifth and Sixth Armies (each the equivalent of an Indian
division in size) for the defence of Burma, Wavell turned them down.
He would later claim to have advanced 'a very qualified acceptance of
one Army'. Wavell's qualms apparently stemmed from Chiang's
demand for a separate supply channel for Chinese troops – a logistical impossibility under the prevailing conditions in Burma.[59]

This was at best a half-truth. Both Wavell and Dorman-Smith were
loath to use Chinese troops for the defence of Burma. As Wavell
explained to Churchill, 'It was obviously better to defend Burma
with Imperial troops than with Chinese and the Governor particularly asked me not to accept more Chinese for Burma than was
absolutely necessary.'[60] In any event, Chiang was miffed by the British response. The United States, however, was keen to placate the
Chinese leader. President Roosevelt was worried that his 'Europe
first' policy might lead a disenchanted Chiang to conclude a separate
peace with Japan, so freeing up Japanese forces for use elsewhere. In
a bid to stiffen Chiang's resolve, the Americans leaned on the British
to accept his offer of troops for Burma. Further, they sent Lieutenant
General Joseph Stilwell as chief of staff to the Generalissimo.

The acerbic Stilwell was aptly called 'Vinegar Joe' – a title that he
embraced with relish. Although his grasp of Chinese affairs was less
than sure, Stilwell more than made up for it by his tenacity and tough-
ness. He was not particularly suited, though, to the politic needs of
coalition warfare. Stilwell quickly developed a degree of contempt
both for the British – 'Limeys' – and for Chiang, whom he dubbed
'Peanut'. Prior to flying out to India, Stilwell read the cables on the
state of Sino-Indian relations. 'Archie misled Peanut at Lashio', he
concluded, 'and now they are both sore each thinking the other
ducked out on him.' By the end of January, Stilwell was gloomy: 'Will
the Chinese play ball? Or will they sit back and let us do it? Will the
Limeys cooperate? Will we arrive to find Rangoon gone?'[61] His apprehensions were not unfounded.

Under pressure from the Americans, Wavell had already invited the
Chinese to take up the defence of the Shan States on Burma's

north-eastern border. Yet, owing to the scarcity of transport, the Chinese troop movements were excruciatingly slow. The three divisions (equivalent to Indian brigades) of the Chinese Sixth Army – the 49th, 55th and 93rd – were in place only by early March. Around the same time, the Chinese Fifth Army also began moving into Burma. By this time, Rangoon had fallen.

Chiang believed that the best strategy in Burma was to hold an east–west line at Mandalay. Stilwell wanted to resist the Japanese at Toungoo as a prelude to a counter-offensive on Rangoon. Chiang, however, was opposed to a premature attack that might denude his army of its best troops and formations. Stilwell professed to agree, but his plans were unchanged: 'to work toward the recapture of Rangoon; and only if this failed to fall back on Mandalay'.[62]

Another point of contention was the chain of command in Burma. On 15 March, Stilwell was informed by Washington that he and his forces would operate under the overall command of Wavell. Chiang, however, was smarting from Wavell's earlier rebuff and objected to British command in Burma. The British, for their part, were not pleased with Stilwell's presence in Burma. Not only did Alexander expect to command the Chinese forces, he also held that Stilwell had neither staff nor understanding of the situation on the ground. A compromise was struck whereby Stilwell was only nominally under Alexander's command. More problematic for Stilwell was his own uncertain position vis-à-vis the Chinese forces ostensibly under him.[63]

Meanwhile, another layer of command sprouted up. On 19 March, the newly arrived Burma Corps Headquarters assumed control of ground operations under the Indian army's most experienced senior commander, Lieutenant General William Slim. Operating with a shoe-string staff, Slim quickly got down to assessing the situation. He concluded that there were many reasons for the dismal performance of the British troops: a complacent grand strategy; poor intelligence; an apathetic, if not hostile, civilian populace; loss of men and morale; and lack of equipment and training for jungle warfare. The British forces had to learn 'how to move on a light scale, to become accustomed to the jungle, to do so without much transport, to improve our warnings of hostile movements, and above all to seize the initiative from the enemy'.[64]

The deficiencies in training could hardly be improved on a retreat. So, Slim set himself the task of tying down and delaying the Japanese for as long as possible, while maintaining contact with the Chinese. The plan was to strike at the Japanese with mobile forces from well-defended positions. Although some of these actions went well, the fighting power of the Burma Corps was dwindling. The morale and discipline of the Indian troops remained a matter of concern. Besides, the Indian units suffered from limited mobility. The complete lack of air support added to their casualties and lowered their spirits further.

Against this backdrop, the Japanese attacked Toungoo on 19 March. The 200th Division of the Chinese Fifth Army put up a stern resistance but by 25 March, the Japanese had surrounded the town. Stilwell, however, refused to allow the division to pull out. What's more, he was still intent on sending two divisions down south to attack the Japanese at Pyinmana and Pyawnbwe. Ultimately, on 30 March, Chiang personally ordered the divisional commander to break out of Toungoo. Stilwell claimed that 'Through stupidity, fear and defensive attitude we have lost a grand chance to slap the Japs back at Toungoo. The basic reason is Chiang Kai-shek's meddling.' Chiang, in turn, rightly felt that his fears about Stilwell's impetuosity were proving true.[65]

The battle at Toungoo proved a further major setback to the Burma Corps. A counter-attack by the 17th Indian Division to relieve the Chinese was repulsed with heavy losses. Slim reported that the morale of troops 'left a great deal to be desired'. Moreover, the capture of Toungoo rendered infeasible the planned defence of Prome and necessitated a northwards withdrawal towards Yenangyaung.[66] As the British sought to escape Japanese encirclement, the retreating Chinese made their position more precarious by failing to demolish a bridge on the upper reaches of the Sittang River, so allowing the Japanese to make a rapid thrust into the Shan States.

On 3 April, the 17th Division and 1st Burma Division attempted to take up another line of defences at Yenangyaung and to stay in touch with the Chinese Fifth Army. The defensive position was hastily improvised, extremely lengthy and insufficiently deep. A week later, the Japanese 33rd Division moved up the banks of the Irrawaddy,

infiltrated on a broad front and threatened the oilfields at Yenangyaung. The 48th Indian Brigade gave a good account of itself against
an advancing Japanese division. But the 1st Burma Division fared
poorly and escaped annihilation only thanks to the assistance of a
Chinese division. On 15 April, Slim gave the signal for the demolitions to commence. Towers of flame leapt up into the sky as millions
of gallons of oil began to burn. Stilwell was stunned: *British destroying the oil fields.* GOOD GOD. What are we fighting for?'[67]

The short answer was: nothing more than survival. With the loss
of Yenangyaung the momentum was now with the Japanese. The
grievous shortages of supplies and fuel, the sinking morale, the
increasing incidence of disease and indiscipline, the utter exhaustion
of troops: all convinced Alexander that the defence of northern
Burma was a forlorn hope. As he wrote to Wavell on 29 April:

> it is not an exaggeration to say that as a fighting Force it has reached
> the end of its tether. When it can be done they must be relieved . . .
> rested, reorganized and equipped. And more important still – they
> must be *trained*. They DO NOT know their job as well as the Jap,
> and there's the end to it.[68]

Alexander ordered a withdrawal across the Irrawaddy to India.

Moving ahead of the retreating columns of the Burma Corps were
hundreds of thousands of Indians living in Burma. Relations between
the Indians and the Burmese had been strained for the better part of
the past decade. During the years of the Great Depression, the Indian
mercantile community's role in the economy of Burma came to be
deeply resented. Indeed, emergent Burmese nationalism was deeply
tinctured by anti-India sentiment. Indian businesses were boycotted
and Indian shops picketed. Tense stand-offs often escalated into violent attacks.[69] As the Japanese advanced towards Rangoon, the Indian
as well as British civilians sought to flee. Prior to the city's fall, some
70,000 Indians were evacuated to India by sea. Another 4,800 followed by air. The bulk of the exodus – the numbers may have been as
high as 450,000 – took place overland: either via the Arakan into
Chittagong or by the much more arduous route through the Chindwin valley into Manipur. The absence of basic amenities along the

land routes fuelled charges of British racism even in rout and retreat. As many as 50,000 Indians may have perished in the attempt to reach India and safety.[70] This massive influx of refugees would have important social and political consequences for India.

Helping the passage of the Indians along the Manipur route were the elephants of the Burmese forest department. In February 1942, orders had gone out for all elephants to be pulled out of timber extraction and put to work in building roads and bridges along the route to India. The elephants and their riders worked under the supervision of J. H. Williams, a senior forest department official. 'Elephant Bill' managed to bring to India several hundred elephants over several treks across the Chindwin. His final effort to get a further 200 out of Burma had to be aborted: 'if I had carried on with my plan I should have congested the one remaining walking-track for the wretched Indians, and so have caused even greater hardship and loss of life'.[71] Williams would go on to become 'Elephant Adviser' to the Fourteenth Army commander with the rank of Lieutenant Colonel. This huge provision of elephants was to have a significant impact later in the war. Indeed, the Burma campaign would be the last occasion in the long history of warfare in Asia when elephants were employed on the battlefield.[72]

Meantime, two Chinese divisions and fragments of three others were also pulling out of Burma towards India. As the Burma Corps snaked its way up the valleys and mountains towards the Indian frontier, the Japanese nipped hard at its heels. The onset of the monsoon came as a boon to the retreating force. The rag-tag remnants of the army in Burma arrived in Manipur in mid-May 1942. On the last day of the 900-mile retreat, Slim stood on a bank beside the road watching the last of his men trickle into India:

> All of them, British, Indian and Gurkha, were gaunt and ragged as scarecrows. Yet, as they trudged behind their surviving officers in groups pitifully small, they still carried their arms and kept their ranks, they were still recognizable as fighting units. They might look like scarecrows but they looked like soldiers too.[73]

9

Coils of War

Speaking in Bombay before his incarceration in October 1940, Jawaharlal Nehru noted: 'the coils of war increasingly strangle the world . . . What happens in Europe is of great consequence to America, to India, to China. What happens in India and China is of equal importance to America and Europe. War is indivisible now.'[1] Nehru's prescience was borne out by the time he got out of prison in early December 1941. India now stood at the intersection of the two major theatres of war: the Mediterranean, North Africa and the Indian Ocean on the one side; and South-East Asia, China and the Pacific on the other. The defence of India was no longer the preserve of the British, but became a focal point of Allied grand strategy. By the same token, Indian politics could not be insulated from wider pressures emanating from Britain's key wartime allies.

On their release from prison, senior Congressmen recognized the dramatic changes following the entry into the war of the Soviet Union as well as the United States and Japan. The stakes for India were much higher. Although Gandhi was unwilling to call off the individual civil disobedience campaign, his colleagues thought that it had run into sand. The Congress would have to consider its stance anew – especially in the light of the turns taken by the war. As before, Rajagopalachari advocated conditional co-operation with the Raj. India, he argued, should work with the British in the war to 'facilitate the transfer of power'.

Nehru agreed that the world had changed a great deal over the past year, but felt that Britain's attitude had made it 'almost impossible for us to do anything but offer resolute opposition'. He 'entirely' disagreed with Rajagopalachari's approach, which he felt was a 'dangerous policy ... even from the narrowest viewpoint of national self-interest'. To Britain, he paraphrased Leo Amery's own words to Prime Minister Chamberlain in the Commons: 'We have had enough of you. Get out.'[2]

These differences reached a head during the Congress Working Committee meeting in Bardoli. In the last week of December 1941, the Committee deliberated on the future course of action. Gandhi insisted that he could not forsake the path of non-violence. His colleagues, he found, fell into three groups. A small minority followed him in advocating non-participation in the war on the grounds of non-violence. Others, including Nehru, advocated non-participation for political reasons. The third group, led by Rajagopalachari, believed that the Congress should not allow its commitment to non-violence to preclude participation under all circumstances. The last group eventually carried the day. A draft statement prepared by Nehru was amended to read that the Congress took full consideration of the 'new world situation' created by the Japanese attacks on South-East Asia and Pearl Harbor, but only a free and independent India could undertake the defence of the country and support the wider war.

The final declaration, however, muddled the issue by stating that the Congress also stood by the Bombay resolution of September 1940. This resolution had, of course, been the ostensible basis for the individual *satyagraha* campaign. Gandhi insisted, however, that there was no question of co-operating with the British war effort: 'the door is barred altogether against Congress participation'. Owing to these differences with his colleagues, he once again requested them to absolve him of the responsibility to guide the campaign. The Congress had come full circle from the 'Poona offer' of July 1940.[3]

Nehru hoped that by the time the All-India Congress Committee met a 'satisfactory way out' would be found. Yet at the meeting, Gandhi himself urged the adoption of the Working Committee's resolution. The document, he observed, was a compromise between various views. Like the Indian dish *khichri*, 'it contains pulses, rice, salt, chilli and spices'. Gandhi conceded that after the Bardoli conclave, he had thought of putting the resolution to a vote. After all, senior colleagues like Patel and Prasad were unhappy with it. Now he wanted the Congress to adopt it unanimously and relieve him of his leadership. His colleagues, Gandhi believed, should have the courage of their convictions. Speaking at the same session, Rajagopalachari declared, 'Our co-operation is available if the British do the right thing.'[4]

The British, however, were willing to do nothing. 'If . . . Rajago-palachari and friends were able to stifle me in their close embrace', Linlithgow wrote to Amery, 'I feel quite sure that the Mahatma would emerge once again upon the stage to give the *coup de grâce* to British influence in India.'[5] Given the evident strains within the Congress, the British government felt it was best to carry on with magisterial inactivity.

In the wake of British reversals in South-East Asia, Nehru realized that Britain was 'already a second class power'. And his eyes turned towards the country that seemed destined to shape the future of the world: the United States. At the onset of the war, he wrote in the American magazine *Fortune*, Indians had hoped 'to be able to play an effective role in the world drama': 'Our sympathies were all on one side, our interests coincided with these.' Britain's response made it clear that it 'clings to the past'. Nehru called on the United States to declare that every country was entitled to its freedom, that India was also entitled to frame its own constitution, and that 'all races and peoples' must be treated equal.[6] The article's chief merit was its timing. For the United States was now alive to the importance of India.

Before the Second World War began, the United States showed no strategic interest in India. To most Americans, India was a land of fantasy and faith. Popular perceptions of India were shaped by the adventure tales of Rudyard Kipling and exotic Hollywood productions featuring regal maharajas and stern colonial officials. Among the cognoscenti, it was religion that served as a vestibule to India. In the middle of the nineteenth century, Emerson, Thoreau and other Transcendentalists held up Indian spirituality as a refreshing contrast to the materialism of the West. At the Parliament of Religions, held in Chicago in 1893, Swami Vivekananda of India shot to prominence. His fellow Bengali, the poet Rabindranath Tagore, held out his own version of Indian spiritualism to enthusiastic American audiences during his visits between 1912 and 1930.[7]

Religion was also the conduit for the transmission of negative images of India. American missionaries, active in India since the early nineteenth century, were appalled at practices such as self-mutilation and torture, the immolation of widows and female infanticide. The influence of such perceptions lingered in popular imagination well into the next century. Helen Bannerman's *Story of Little Black Sambo*, for instance, was rife with racist clichés yet a popular book for children. The most notorious case was of Katherine Mayo's *Mother India*. Published in 1927, the book presented a sensational picture of the most degenerate aspects of Hindu society and advanced the case for continued British rule in India. Famously dismissed by Gandhi as a 'drain inspector's report', the book sold an astonishing 256,697 copies, making it the biggest best-seller on India, though it also sparked a fiery public debate in ways that were not anticipated by its author.[8]

By this time, however, some progressive activists – including prominent figures such as the founder of the American Civil Liberties Union, Roger Baldwin – and African-American leaders were keenly following the nationalist movement in India and Gandhi's experiments with non-violent civil disobedience. In 1921, an American, Samuel 'Satyanand' Stokes, was even appointed to the All-India Congress Committee.[9] Nevertheless, for most Americans Gandhi remained an inscrutable figure and his country a collage of conflicting and remote impressions.

The indifference towards India was reflected in official relations as well. Although George Washington had appointed Benjamin Joy as consul in Calcutta as far back as 1792, the United States saw little need to expand official ties. The Raj moved its capital to New Delhi in 1931, but the American consul stayed put in Calcutta. Commercial exchanges, too, were meagre. American investment in India in the late 1930s amounted to less than $50 million, with over half of this accounted for in missionary schools, hospitals and other non-commercial activities.[10]

All this changed as war loomed on the horizon. By late 1938, American officials in India were expressing doubts about the loyalty of the Indian army to the Raj and the susceptibility of nationalist sentiment to German or Japanese propaganda. No sooner had war broken out than officials in the State Department began insisting that 'the Indian attitude towards the War is of great importance'. Assistant secretary of state, Adolf Berle, Jr, head of the Near Eastern Division, dealing with India, was told that there were 'large American interests in India'. Meanwhile, American officials in India took a sympathetic stance towards the Congress's demands. The British, they reported, were following a policy of divide-and-rule by deliberately jilting the Congress in favour of the Muslims – a policy that they believed was also underpinned by British military interests in the Middle East. The viceroy's 'August offer' was deemed inadequate; his unwillingness to accept the Congress's offer of co-operation short-sighted. The beginning of the individual civil disobedience campaign sufficiently alarmed the State Department to demand more frequent reports from India. By May 1941, the US consul general, Thomas Wilson, had concluded that the situation in India was 'very serious indeed'. The viceroy was a man of 'small vision' and too hidebound to manage the crisis. Amery was described as 'unimaginative' and unwilling to take 'a realistic view' of the problem.[11]

The American press reflected these views. The 'August offer' was criticized as insufficient by such prominent magazines as *The New Republic*, *The Nation* and *Time*. Editorials in traditionally pro-British papers like the *New York Times* and *Christian Science Monitor*, as well as others like the *Los Angeles Times*, were sceptical of the British stance. Even the conservative *Reader's Digest* carried a favourable profile of Nehru, written by John and Frances Gunther. American journals also opened up their columns for supporters of Indian nationalism to expound their views: Nehru used these opportunities to present the Congress's case at strategic points in April 1940 in the *Atlantic*, and in November 1940 in the *Asia*.[12]

Even before sections of the American press grew censorious, the British cabinet was alert to American opinion on India. Indeed, hardly any major decision on India was taken without reference to its impact on public opinion in the United States. Zetland's criticism of Linlithgow's 'do nothing' policy; Amery's demand for a fresh declaration in July 1940; Churchill's rejection of it; Amery's call for implementing the 'August offer': all were influenced by this concern. With a view to keeping a closer tab on American opinion, as well as shaping it, the British government proposed to the State Department in April 1941 the appointment of a senior Indian official to its embassy in Washington. The State Department expressed no objection to the proposed 'Agent-General' of India, but sought and obtained the reciprocal appointment of its own 'Commissioner' in New Delhi.[13]

The State Department's demand reflected its growing realization of the strategic importance of India. The country had recently become a member of the Lend-Lease system, which was approved by the US Congress in March 1941. The Roosevelt administration was well aware of India's contribution to the war effort. India, the US Treasury noted in May 1941, had already raised over 300,000 men and could 'greatly increase' the number. India had sent 'important forces' to fight in North and East Africa and supplied garrison troops for the Far East. The Allied operations in Iraq and the Persian Gulf were entirely based on India. Further, from the beginning of the war, India had made a 'most important contribution' to war supplies. Indeed, for the past year, the Allies had 'wholly relied' on India to supply all their forces in Africa and the Middle East. Both for logistical and strategic reasons, they had accepted India as the centre of the Eastern Supply Group, which aimed at supplying half a million men and substantial naval requirements besides. If India were to fully mobilize its 'enormous basic internal resources', it needed to be able to 'import finished and semi-finished manufactures and certain materials' for which the United States was the sole source.[14]

Simultaneously, the State Department was concerned about the situation in the Middle East. And this brought to the fore the political problem of India. Berle believed that if the political impasse were not resolved, India could become an 'active danger' to the war effort in that region. The British seemed to be doing 'nothing' about it. Berle recommended sending a formal note to the British government, underlining India's 'vast influence' on the Middle East and the need to convert India into an 'active, rather than a passive, partner' in the war. They should ask Britain to 'promptly explore' the possibility of granting India equal membership in the British Commonwealth. Berle conceded that this may seem 'sensational', but added that 'this is no time for half measures'.[15]

At his suggestion, Secretary of State Cordell Hull met the British ambassador, Lord Halifax. In an earlier incarnation, as Lord Irwin,

Halifax had been viceroy of India from 1925 to 1931. Widely regarded as a liberal viceroy, he had announced the goal of Dominion status for India, had parleyed with Gandhi, and had been famously denounced by Churchill for 'drinking tea with treason'.[16] Later in the 1930s Halifax had, as foreign secretary, been prominent among the appeasers. When Hull questioned him about the possibility of further 'liberalizing' moves towards India, Halifax claimed that conditions in India were 'really very good'. Indians had self-government in the provinces and had been offered berths in the viceroy's council. Despite Gandhi's opposition, support for Britain was very strong. Halifax concluded that his government did not think it 'feasible or even necessary now to make further liberalizing concessions'.[17]

There the matter rested – until three months later when the Americans were worried by Japanese strategic moves in the Far East. The US ambassador in London, John Winant, felt that India had a 'large' role to play in securing the Far East, and that in the rapidly evolving context, it might be wise for the United States to raise the question of India with Britain. The British, he observed, had emphasized the minority problem as the main obstacle towards a settlement. Winant, however, believed that the absence of such a settlement 'handicaps the support of war in India itself'. It might be possible, he argued, at least to get the British to announce Dominion status for India within a stated period after the end of the war. Among other advantages, such a move would have 'a sobering effect upon the Japanese'.[18]

Berle supported Winant. He suggested to Under Secretary of State Sumner Welles that they point out to the British government that this was a 'more opportune time' than ever for such a declaration. It would be 'very helpful' from the standpoint of American public opinion. Besides, India could become the 'nucleus of a Far Eastern alliance', which included China, Australia and New Zealand, and which could hold its own against Japan or possibly even Germany. Welles disagreed. He wrote to Secretary Hull that in his judgement the United States was 'not warranted' in suggesting a status for India to Britain. But if the president was inclined to take up the matter, he might wish to discuss it 'in a very personal and confidential way directly with Mr. Churchill'.[19]

Three days later Franklin Roosevelt and Winston Churchill met secretly off the coast of Newfoundland. While the principal objective of the meeting was to weld the Anglo-American alliance and discuss grand strategy, a statement of war aims – the Atlantic Charter – attracted attention the world over. In fact, the Charter had emerged without much deliberation.[20] Over dinner on 9 August, Churchill and Roosevelt talked about the possibility of a joint statement. The next morning the British advanced the draft of a five-point declaration. The third point originally read: 'they respect the right of all peoples to choose the form of government under which they will live; they are concerned only to defend the rights of freedom of speech and of thought without which such choosing must be illusory'. Welles, however, was dubious of the American Congress and public support for such a sweeping pledge to defend human rights – rights that had been abolished by the Axis countries. Roosevelt accordingly suggested removing the second clause and substituting it with: 'and they hope that self-government may be restored to those from whom it has been forcibly removed'. Churchill agreed, only suggesting adding 'sovereign-rights and' before 'self-government'. Obviously all this was in the context of European countries under enemy occupation.

The Atlantic Charter took on a life of its own and sent ripples of excitement through the colonial world. The Burmese premier asked if it applied to his country, and dashed off to London to obtain an answer. Savarkar of the Hindu Mahasabha wrote to Roosevelt urging him to state whether or not the Atlantic Charter applied to India and whether the United States guaranteed freedom to India within a year of the war's end. If the United States failed to affirmatively respond, 'India cannot but construe this as another stunt like the War aims of the last Anglo-German war'.[21] Indeed, the response to the Atlantic Charter was comparable in enthusiasm to that evoked among colonial subjects by Woodrow Wilson's famous Fourteen Points after the First World War.[22]

Amery informed the war cabinet that the third point of the Charter had 'excited wide-spread interest' and that an authoritative statement was expected from the British government spelling out its implications for India.[23] Amery himself loathed the Charter. He wrote to Linlithgow of its 'meaningless platitudes and dangerous ambiguities'.

Article three, he blithely claimed, had been inserted as a 'reassurance' that the Allies were not out to 'democratise countries that prefer a different form of government' and that it had already given 'substantial comfort' to Salazar in Portugal as well as 'friendly dictators elsewhere'.[24] The lord privy seal and leader of the Labour Party, Clement Attlee, however, stated that the Charter had universal applicability. Churchill scotched any such suggestion. On 9 September, he told the Commons that article three applied only to countries under Nazi occupation and that it did 'not qualify in any way' the various statements made about India from time to time.

In India, the reaction to Churchill's comment was uniformly critical. Even such loyalists as the Punjab premier, Sikandar Hayat Khan, termed it the strongest rebuff ever received by India. Sir N. N. Sircar, a leading light among the liberals, said that Churchill had offered India 'hot ice'. The Central Legislative Assembly passed a resolution demanding the application of the Atlantic Charter to India. The Council of State adopted a resolution that the non-applicability of the Charter would 'prejudice the war effort' of India.[25] Gandhi was typically witty and incisive in his comments:

> What is the Atlantic Charter? It went down the ocean as soon as it was born! I do not understand it. Mr. Amery denies that India is fit for democracy, while Mr. Churchill states the Charter could not apply to India. Force of circumstances will falsify their declarations.[26]

Consul General Wilson cabled the State Department that Churchill's statement was a 'most unfortunate pronouncement', one that went 'far toward banishing perhaps forever' any goodwill towards him in India. As for the British Government of India, he wrote dyspeptically, there was 'no leadership worthy of the name anywhere to be found'.[27]

Churchill had, in fact, shared in advance the text of his speech with Ambassador Winant, especially since it had referred to a statement issued jointly with the United States. Winant felt that Churchill's references to the inapplicability of article three to countries like India was unwise. It ran 'counter to the general public interpretation' of the article. It would intensify charges of imperialism and leave Britain with 'a do nothing policy' towards India. Minutes before Churchill left for the Commons, Winant urged him to omit the offending paragraph in his speech. The prime minister was determined to go ahead, however. He told Winant that this position was approved by the cabinet and was, in any case, a matter of internal British politics.[28]

On learning of this, officials at the State Department urged that the matter be brought to the president's notice. Since Churchill had offered an interpretation of the joint declaration, it was an opportune moment to raise with the British government the question of Indian politics and do so along the lines suggested earlier by Winant. The political situation in India, it was felt, was 'deteriorating rapidly' owing to the stalemate between the government and the nationalists. This was in turn preventing India from doing its best to help win the war. Welles yet again threw a wet blanket on the idea. Interestingly, he now held that if article three had 'any real meaning, it should be regarded as all-inclusive' and in consequence applicable to India. Yet the United States, at least for the present, was 'facing a question of expediency'. He had been told by Halifax – the 'most liberal viceroy that India has ever had' – that British officials were unanimous that an immediate grant of Dominion status would trigger 'internal dissension in India on a very wide scale' and render it thoroughly useless for the war effort. US officials were not familiar with the problems of India. Nor did the issue mean 'very much to public opinion' at home. Above all, Churchill would feel that the administration was taking advantage of British dependence on America to force its hand against its considered judgement.[29]

In the wake of Pearl Harbor, thinking within the administration underwent important changes. Apart from advocates in the State Department, intelligence assessments by the Office of the Coordinator of Information argued that the United States had to help arrest the downward political slide in India.[30] Thus when Churchill arrived in Washington two weeks after Pearl Harbor, Roosevelt gingerly broached the question of India. The only available account of this meeting is in Churchill's memoir. The prime minister claimed to have 'reacted so strongly and at such length that he [Roosevelt] never raised it verbally again'. Towards the end of his trip, Churchill confidently informed his colleagues that they would not have 'any trouble with American opinion'.[31] This judgement was premature. For Churchill underestimated American leverage on India.

On 11 November 1941, President Roosevelt had decided that the defence of India was of vital importance to the United States and hence India could directly receive Lend-Lease supplies from America. While welcoming the decision, British officials realized that it was pregnant with difficulties for them. The American proposal to negotiate Lend-Lease supplies directly with the British-Indian mission in Washington was seen as 'something of a bombshell', for it threatened to displace Britain's economic pre-eminence in India. The United States' economic importance for India was already growing. Indian imports from the US had increased from 9 per cent in 1939–40 to 20 per cent in 1940–41, while over the same period imports from Britain had fallen to 21.2 per cent from 25.2 per cent. Similarly, Indian exports to the US had risen from 12 per cent to 19.6 per cent during these years, while exports to Britain had fallen to 32.3 per cent from 35.5 per cent.[32]

British officials were also aware of the Americans' proclivity for driving a hard commercial bargain. Earlier in the year, while negotiating a treaty of commerce and navigation with the Indian government, the Roosevelt administration had insisted on the inclusion of 'most-favoured nation' treatment for exploration of oil and mineral resources (particularly in Balochistan). The Americans also demanded that 'most-favoured nation' should be defined to include the United Kingdom. The Indian government pointed out that this would contravene the system of preferential tariffs – lower tariffs for imports – that operated within the British Empire, a system also known as imperial preferences. In the event, the Roosevelt administration forbore from pressing its demand in light of the 'unsettled world conditions'.[33]

With the onset of Lend-Lease, British officials grew concerned that this might become the key with which to open up the system of imperial preferences. These concerns were heightened during the negotiations between Washington and London on a 'Mutual Aid Agreement' or 'Master Agreement' of Lend-Lease supplies, when the Americans demanded a clause eliminating preferential tariffs. In so doing, Leo Amery believed, the Roosevelt administration demanded nothing less than Britain's abandonment of the economic unity of its empire as well as assured markets for its exports. London had little option but to cave in and the agreement was concluded in February 1942. Later in the year, when negotiations began for a similar agreement between Washington and India, the Americans pressed for the inclusion of a similar clause. On this occasion, it was the Indian member for commerce in the viceroy's Executive Council who objected, arguing strenuously that it would be detrimental to India's fledgling industries. The Roosevelt administration would not relent, however, and the negotiations had to be shelved – though the United States reluctantly agreed to continue with existing arrangements.[34]

The fact, however, remained that India's plans for the expansion of its war effort were heavily reliant on American economic assistance. Indeed by 1944–45, the United States would account for 25.7 per cent of India's total imports, while Britain would lag behind at 19.8 per cent. None realized this more clearly than the Indian agent-general in Washington, Sir Girja Shankar Bajpai. A senior official of the Indian Civil Service, Bajpai had previously served at the League of Nations and had been a member of the viceroy's Executive Council until 1940. Although he epitomized the 'Steel Frame' of the Raj, Bajpai – by his own account – did not regard India under British rule as 'the best of possible worlds'. Indeed, in private conversations with US officials Bajpai forthrightly disagreed with the stance espoused by Halifax.[35] At the same time, he was keen to leverage American assistance for India's war.

Soon after Pearl Harbor, Bajpai shared with Berle a report on India's war effort. The report observed that while India had 'modernized and expanded' its ordnance factories, it would continue to rely on Britain and the United States for 'some key items of supply'. What was more, despite the increased flow of more modern equipment from Britain, 'the releases have never been and cannot be equalled to India's needs'. Indeed, these could only be met by a 'generous flow of help' from the United States. India was similarly dependent on America for general engineering equipment, especially power generation sets, motor and machine tools, as well as motor vehicles which were entirely procured from the United States. The report also stated that

India planned to raise 124 Indian infantry battalions, taking the total strength of the Indian army to 1.5 million.

Following the meeting with Bajpai, Berle felt that for a considerable time the transportation of cargo from the United States to the Far East would be 'limited, difficult and dangerous'. In consequence, it was in America's interest to promote production in the region rather than shipping it from home. In this scheme, India loomed large. If, by providing 'technical assistance' alongside supplies, the Indian army could be strengthened, then the United States would achieve 'considerable economy' in the war effort, would make 'more effective use' of India's manpower, and would be building up 'defensive and offensive striking power in a region where it is vitally necessary'. Berle recommended sending to India a suitable representative to survey the possibility of increasing India's war effort.[36]

When nothing happened for a month, Bajpai met Berle and conveyed to him the gravity of the situation in the Far East. While China had put up a splendid resistance, India was more accessible to the Allies and had a highly developed system of internal communications. Underlining India's potential, Bajpai trotted out a series of figures: 64,000 miles of railways; steel production capacity of over a million tons a year; an industrial base that already produced 85 per cent of the 60,000 items required for the war; and 'almost unlimited manpower' for the army, which had already proved its mettle in modern warfare. When Japanese submarines closed the port of Rangoon, Bajpai yet again pressed Berle to consider India's needs with 'very great speed'. He also wrote to the viceroy recommending an American technical mission to assess India's potential and requirements. Berle was sufficiently impressed to write directly to the president, urging him to send a technical mission to India. Should things 'go badly in Singapore and Burma', he added, India's role might be of 'crucial importance'. On 2 February, President Roosevelt gave his go ahead.[37]

Meanwhile, the American mission in New Delhi was reporting the recent Congress resolutions. It was felt that while the Congress leadership – with the exception of Gandhi – was once again open to co-operation, the meaning and significance of the resolutions were difficult to gauge. The fall of Singapore alarmed the State

Department. Above all, it brought to the fore the latent yet lingering concerns about the political situation in India. Berle argued that they must 'immediately get to work' and the 'first item on the list ought to be to tackle the Indian problem in a large way'. The technical mission had already been approved by the president, but India's war effort would not go very far 'unless the political situation is handled with extreme vigor'. He called for a joint Anglo-American announcement that India would be brought in 'as a full partner in the United Nations'. In other words, the Atlantic Charter would apply to India. Not only should Churchill make such an announcement, but the viceroy should be directed to convene a 'constitutional conference' in India. Even if the Congress did not come in at this stage, its stance would determine whether India co-operated in waging the war, or whether there was 'more or less passive resistance', which would be exploited by Japan 'to the limit'.[38]

Interestingly, Berle noted that President Roosevelt had 'indicated his sympathy' for the view that Britain must promptly recognize India's aspiration to 'a freer existence and a full membership in the British family of nations'. For a host of reasons, the president's sentiment would be strengthened in the days ahead. To begin with, the American press turned sharply critical of Britain. Renowned columnists such as Walter Lippmann and John Thompson, as well as editorials in a series of newspapers and journals, argued that Britain's imperial policy must change. The New York Times witheringly observed that countries like India were no longer 'suppliants at the white man's door. Not all the faded trappings of imperialism, not all the pomp of viceroys . . . has much meaning for them now.'[39]

These feelings were reflected in political debates. The US Senate's Foreign Relations Committee commenced hearings on the situation in the Far East. There was a 'serious undercurrent of anti-British feeling' among the senators, who argued that having done 'so much' for Britain by Lend-Lease, the United States was well positioned to 'dictate to England' political changes in the British Empire. One senator went so far as to declare that 'Gandhi's leadership in India became part of America's military equipment'. India's contribution could only be secured by accepting 'Gandhi's political objective'.[40]

The president's views also seem to have been sharpened by a

gloomy letter written to Eleanor Roosevelt by the writer and Nobel Laureate Pearl S. Buck, which the first lady shared with her husband. The letter expressed deep concern at the prospect of the Allies planning a stand against Japan in India. Buck argued that there was a serious rift between Hindus and Muslims in India – 'fostered by the British divide-and-rule policy'. Jinnah, in particular, was 'a demagogue of the most dangerous type'. He had no love for his country and was the 'perfect tool for the Axis'. It was a 'fallacy' to think that Indians could defend their country as the Chinese had done. They were 'so filled with bitterness' towards the British that there would be 'revengeful massacres' on a large scale – massacres in which American soldiers might well be caught up.[41]

Finally, the president's thinking was influenced by intelligence and strategic assessments. The Office of the Coordinator of Information now believed that India 'might well be the decisive element in the war in southeast Asia'. Arguing that India 'lights a gleam in the eye of the German and the Japanese', the assessment concluded that the 'Allied cause *requires* that India should now cooperate more vigorously in the war than heretofore'.[42]

A worried Roosevelt ordered a detailed report on the military situation from the combined chiefs of staff. On 25 February, the president himself drafted a tough missive to Churchill. After commenting generally on Britain's attitude towards its colonies – out of date by a decade or two – and contrasting it with America's enlightened record in the Philippines, Roosevelt wrote that the Indians felt that 'delay follows delay and therefore that there is no real desire in Britain to recognize a world change which has taken deep root in India as well as in other countries'. There was, he concluded, 'too much suspicion and dissatisfaction' in India. In consequence, the resistance to Japan was not whole-hearted.[43]

Roosevelt turned the letter over in his mind until late that night. He hesitated to send it because he felt that 'in a strict sense, it is not our business'. At the same time, India was of 'great interest' from the standpoint of conducting the war. Eventually, the president decided against sending the letter to Churchill. Instead he asked his representatives in London, John Winant and Averell Harriman, to send him an assessment of Churchill's thoughts on India.[44] The next morning, the president received a cable on India from an unexpected quarter: President Chiang Kai-shek of China.

Of all Allied leaders, Chiang Kai-shek had the longest record of resistance to the Japanese. Chiang's government had been at war with Japan for over two years before the war had erupted in Europe. The Western Allies, however, tended to treat China with condescension, not to say contempt. Chiang's requests for a seat on Allied committees were serially rebuffed. Yet, by early 1942, Britain and the United States realized that if Chinese resistance collapsed, the over 600,000 Japanese troops currently engaged in China could be deployed to other theatres of the war. At the very least, therefore, they were determined to keep China in the war.[45]

Following Japan's lightning thrusts into South-East Asia, India became vital to the prospects of China's survival. The Burma Road was a key logistical artery for China. Chiang had already sampled the crippling effect of its closure when the British government had shut it for three months in the summer of 1940 in response to Japanese pressure. In its absence, war materiel had to be airlifted into China over the Himalayan 'hump'. As Japanese forces were poised to overrun South-East Asia, Chiang – in a curious symmetry of concern – grew anxious to keep India in the war.

Towards the end of January 1942, Chiang sounded out the British envoy to China, Sir Archibald Clark Kerr, if he and his wife could visit Burma and India. In India, he wanted to meet not just the viceroy but Gandhi and Nehru as well. Nehru, in particular, was his friend – and he wished to impress upon the Indian leaders the 'essential wisdom of cooperating fully' in the war. Chiang had also wanted his visit to be kept secret, but Linlithgow dismissed this as impractical. The viceroy was keen that Chiang also met Jinnah to avoid creating 'any impression' that India's co-operation depended only on the Congress. For the rest, Linlithgow was sure that he could handle Chiang well and send him home 'as pleased as Punch'.[46]

Churchill, however, was not keen on the visit. 'We cannot possibly agree', he cabled Linlithgow, to Chiang acting as an 'impartial arbiter' between the government and the Congress. In particular, there was no question of his meeting Nehru: 'nothing would be more likely to spread pan-Asiatic *malaise* through all the bazaars of India'. Churchill sent a personal message for Chiang stating that his idea of meeting Gandhi and Nehru, who were in a 'state at least of passive disobedience to the King Emperor', required 'very grave consideration'. In any case, if he saw leaders of the Congress, he would also have to meet Jinnah, who spoke for 80 million Muslims, as well as representatives of the depressed classes and the princes. The Congress, he emphasized, 'in no way represents the martial races of India who are fighting so well'. When Chiang landed in Calcutta, Clark Kerr, who was accompanying him, informed the viceroy's office that the Generalissimo's 'principal object' in visiting India was to meet Nehru and Gandhi. He advised against passing on Churchill's message to Chiang. Any attempt to persuade Chiang otherwise was 'unlikely to succeed' and if he was prevented he would feel 'tricked'. The prime minister could not fathom why, having invited himself over, Chiang should feel 'tricked'. But he trusted the viceroy to do the needful.[47]

Linlithgow found his guests interesting. The viceroy thought that Chiang was 'an able and determined man' but 'entirely Chinese in his mental furniture'. He also depended a great deal on his wife, Soong Mei-ling. Expressing all the condescension of his class, Linlithgow noted that she was 'a typical product of the American "Co-ed" system, complete with lipstick and "blue-stocking"!' In the upper reaches of her mind, he suspected, she was 'a typical American liberal whose enthusiasms are unimpaired by any restraining considerations of a practical kind'. They were an interesting act, noted the viceroy. 'When they are on a big job she starts with the family trousers firmly fixed on her limbs, but by the final stage of any venture the Generalissimo is invariably discovered to have transferred the pants to his own person.'[48]

The viceroy also found that neither Chiang nor his wife had the 'least notion' of Indian politics. In fact, Chiang admitted as much and told his host that he was anxious to help. Linlithgow held forth on the various cleavages in Indian politics, and especially the importance of Muslims to India's war. He 'exploded the myth' about India having been dragged kicking and screaming into the war. Chiang was shrewder than Linlithgow assumed. Drawing on his own experience, he told the viceroy that in modern war, 'the army alone could not produce success': it was necessary to have a civilian populace 'willing to endure sacrifices'. Chiang said that if he were the British government, 'he would offer India a firm promise of Dominion Status'; while if an Indian, he would ask for no more.[49]

The Generalissimo had ample opportunity to ply this line with his friend Jawaharlal Nehru. Soon after their arrival, Nehru had made his way to Delhi, and Chiang and his wife spent long evenings with him and his sister, Vijayalakshmi Pandit. Linlithgow cattily remarked that Soong Mei-ling had a 'kittenish weakness for Nehru's eyelashes'.[50] Since his trip to China in 1939, Nehru had remained in contact with Chiang and Soong Mei-ling. He was particularly touched by the gifts he had received from them while in prison. More generally, Nehru was convinced that the fortunes of India and China were braided together by the war and that their futures would also be intertwined.[51]

Nehru, however, refused to be swayed by Chiang's views on Indian politics. After their first meeting, he publicly stated that there would be no change in the Congress's stance owing to Chiang's visit. The Generalissimo was 'one of the topmost leaders of the world' and the Congress was trying to make him understand its position.[52] Chiang came away from the meetings surprised at the 'extreme nature of their attitude' and conceded to Linlithgow that he had 'done his best to persuade Nehru to play up but had failed'.[53] Nehru wrote a gracious letter to Chiang that his visit was 'a very great event for all of us, an event which may well have historic consequences'. He regretted, however, that Chiang had not so far been able to meet Gandhi.[54]

Churchill had actively dissuaded the Chinese leader from travelling to Wardha to meet Gandhi. On 12 February, he sent a message for Chiang that such a visit would 'impede' their efforts to rally all of India for the war against Japan. It might also have the 'unintended effect' of emphasizing 'communal differences'. His colleagues were not so sure. Foreign Secretary Anthony Eden wrote that it was 'of the utmost importance' not to cause Chiang offence at this 'critical juncture'. If things went wrong in Burma, it would be 'most difficult' to keep China in the war and Chiang would be their 'only hope'.[55]

In the meantime, Chiang had received a message from Gandhi

expressing 'greatest grief' that he could not travel to Wardha. Chiang was moved. 'I have to meet Gandhi', he told Clark Kerr. Eventually it was arranged that they would meet at Santiniketan, the university established by Tagore near Calcutta. Prior to seeing Gandhi, Chiang managed to meet Jinnah who also happened to be in Calcutta. He found Jinnah 'dishonest': 'the British make use of people like this – but it's not true that Hindus and Muslims can't get on'.[56]

On the evening of 18 February Chiang met Gandhi. With Soong Mei-ling translating, they spoke for some five hours. Gandhi expressed sympathy for China and vowed not to obstruct British aid to the country. He explained his idea of *satyagraha*, his 'weapon of war' – a weapon that 'makes no noise, which does not kill, but which, if anything, gives life'. All the while Gandhi worked his spinning-wheel. 'You will have to teach me this', said Soong Mei-ling. Come to my ashram, replied Gandhi. 'Let the Generalissimo leave you here as his ambassador, and I adopt you as my daughter.' Soong was charmed, but Chiang could not persuade Gandhi to change his stance towards the war. 'These foes', said Chiang, 'may not listen to active civil resistance, and may even make the preaching of non-violence impossible.' Gandhi responded that in the event of a Japanese invasion he would, as always, look to God for guidance.[57]

Chiang was disappointed. 'My expectations', he wrote in his diary, 'were too great.' Gandhi, he concluded, 'knows and loves only India, and doesn't care about other places and people'.[58] 'What about the Sheikh of China?' quipped Patel to Gandhi's secretary. Gandhi replied that Chiang came 'empty handed and left empty handed. He amused himself and entertained me. But I cannot say that I learnt anything.' Gandhi was cold to Chiang's call: 'Help the British anyhow. They are better than the others and will improve further hereafter.'[59]

Before flying out of Calcutta, Chiang addressed the people of India in a speech broadcast in English by Soong Mei-ling. Reminding his listeners about the Nanjing Massacre, he warned them not to place their hopes on Japan's anti-imperialist pretensions. Like Nehru, he also linked China's freedom with that of India and called on the British to devolve power to India.

On returning to China, Chiang sent a message to Roosevelt from Kunming. If the Indian problem was not 'immediately and urgently solved, the danger will be daily increasing'. If the British government waited until the Japanese bombed India and Indian morale collapsed, or if it waited until the Japanese army invaded India, 'it will certainly be too late'. The danger was 'extreme'. If Britain did not 'fundamentally change' its policy towards India, it would amount to 'presenting India to the enemy and inviting them to quickly occupy' the country.[60]

Even as Roosevelt read Chiang's cable, his representative in London, Harriman, was meeting Churchill. The prime minister emphasized to Harriman the need to avoid taking any political step that would antagonize the Muslims of India. Around 75 per cent of the Indian troops were Muslims, he claimed. (This was a gross exaggeration: the figure was closer to 34 per cent.) There was in India, he assured Harriman, 'ample manpower willing to fight'. Nevertheless, his cabinet was actively considering the next move towards India, and he would keep the president informed.[61]

The war cabinet was indeed seized of the matter. Days after America entered the war, Attlee had chaired a cabinet meeting in Churchill's absence. The minister of labour – the senior Labour politician Ernest Bevin – flagged the prevalent anxiety in Britain about the position of India from the standpoint of both defence and politics. Was British policy, he asked, 'calculated to get the fullest war effort from India?'[62] Although the cabinet agreed to consider this question at the earliest opportunity, Churchill was set against it. He wrote to Attlee from Washington, warning him of the danger of raising this issue – never mind making any moves – when the 'enemy is upon the frontier'. The prime minister conveniently elided the fact that he himself had previously noted that the time for action would be when the enemy stood at the gate. He now argued that they could not 'get more out of India' by bringing in the Congress. If anything it would 'paralyse action'. Besides, Indian troops owed their allegiance to the king emperor: 'the rule of the Congress and Hindoo Priesthood machine would never be tolerated by a fighting race'.[63]

When a group of Indian liberals led by Sir Tej Bahadur Sapru petitioned the prime minister in January 1942 to consider some 'bold stroke [of] far-sighted statesmanship', Linlithgow and Amery stood

by Churchill. The viceroy had 'no doubt' about the 'wisdom of standing firm'. Admittedly, he would not have an easy hand to play, but he
could hold his own: 'Vital thing is that people should stand firm at
home.' Amery agreed that there was 'nothing to be done at this
moment'.[64]

The lord privy seal disagreed with them. Attlee found the viceroy's
stance 'distinctly disturbing' and 'defeatist'. Congress leaders, he felt,
were looking for a 'way out of the impasse of their own creation'.
Expressing concern about Linlithgow's judgement, he wondered if
someone should not be sent on a political mission to India to bring its
leaders together. Attlee pointed out to Amery that this feeling was
shared on the Conservative as well as Labour benches in Parliament.[65]
The viceroy dug in his heels, however, arguing that India had no
'natural association' with the Empire: it had been conquered and held
by force.

In a memorandum to the cabinet on 2 February, Attlee pulled no
punches. He excoriated Amery for thinking that they could weather
the storm: 'Such a hand-to-mouth policy is not statesmanship.' The
viceroy's 'crude imperialism' was 'short-sighted and suicidal'. It was
dangerous, Attlee argued, to ignore the current situation. For one
thing, there was the possibility of a 'Pan-Asiatic movement led by
Japan'. For another, the Allies had accepted China as an equal. An
Indian would wonder why 'he, too, cannot be master in his own
house'. Taking a dig at Churchill, he added that Indians would not
forget their 'large contribution in blood, tears and sweat'. Finally, the
United States was leaning 'strongly to the idea of Indian freedom'.
Lord Durham, he reminded his colleagues, had in the nineteenth cen-
tury saved Canada for the British Empire. 'We need a man to do in
India what Durham did in Canada.'[66]

Members of the cabinet agreed with Attlee that it was dangerous to
perpetuate the present deadlock. Yet it was also difficult to conceive
of an interim step that would not prejudice the ultimate outcome
after the war ended. Amery was asked to prepare a draft statement.
Facing flak from his Labour colleagues, Churchill hit upon an
idea. The National Defence Council could be enlarged to a body of
100 members representing the provincial assemblies and the
princes. Not only would this body discuss the war effort, but after

the war it would proceed to frame a constitution for India. In the meantime, the viceroy's Executive Council would continue with business as usual.

Amery felt that the idea had 'some characteristic strokes of Winston's genius'. On 11 February, he wrote to Linlithgow: 'Please take strongest peg you can before continuing.' And he went on to outline the scheme which the prime minister proposed to broadcast. Linlithgow was astounded. Churchill's plan, he replied, was based on 'a complete failure to comprehend' the problem in India. By conflating the war effort and constitutional functions it created a hopeless muddle. Besides, neither the Congress nor the Muslim League would be amenable to the idea.[67] Amery and Churchill beat a hasty retreat.

A week later, Churchill was forced by the failures in Malaya and Burma to reconstitute the war cabinet. Attlee was designated deputy prime minister and Stafford Cripps, erstwhile ambassador to the Soviet Union, took over Attlee's old portfolio as well as becoming leader of the Commons. The deck was now stacked against the 'do nothing' stance of Churchill and Amery.

By the time Churchill met Harriman on 26 February, the cabinet was considering a new draft of a declaration for India produced by Amery. Soon Cripps pitched in with his own version. After several sittings, the newly formed India Committee of the war cabinet produced an almost final draft on 3 March. The salient points of the declaration were, first, that the objective was to make India an equal Dominion with the right to secede from the British Commonwealth. Second, immediately after the war ended a constitution-making body would be elected. The princely states would also join this body. Third, and most significant, any province that did not accept the new constitution could effectively secede from India. During the war, the British government would have to shoulder the full responsibility for India's defence, but it invited the immediate and effective participation of the main Indian leaders in the war effort.[68] In short, the declaration tried to bridge the Congress's demand for a constituent assembly with the Muslim League's demand for 'Pakistan', and held out the prospect of office to all.

Churchill had serious misgivings. Informing Roosevelt of the proposal, he added that he did 'not want to throw India into chaos on the eve of invasion'.[69] The draft was considered by the full cabinet on 5 March. In presenting it, Churchill made clear his own bias against the document. There was much confusion among cabinet members about its import. However, Churchill and Amery had an eye on America. Two days later, the prime minister informed Roosevelt that they were 'still persevering to find some conciliatory and inspiring process'.[70] Meanwhile the draft was assailed from several directions: by Conservative members of cabinet, the viceroy, the commander-in-chief of India, and even the governor of the Punjab. Despite multiple amendments, the draft did not satisfy everyone in London, let alone India. In a bid to save the process, Cripps offered to go to India and ascertain the willingness of Indian leaders to accept the proposal. On 9 March, the war cabinet assented to Cripps' offer with evident relief.[71]

In the meantime, Linlithgow threatened to resign in protest. He was persuaded by Churchill to stay and Amery sought to assuage the viceroy's concerns about the proposal. It was in essence 'fairly conservative'. The Congress's horns would come out the minute it realized that 'the nest contains the Pakistan cuckoo's egg'. In any case, Cripps would not 'go outside his brief' and try to commit New Delhi and London to 'really dangerous courses'. In explaining the decision, Amery stressed the 'pressure [from] outside, upon Winston from Roosevelt' as a prime factor.[72]

The Cripps Mission was clearly intended to head-off further American intrusion into Indian affairs. It was impeccably timed. Hours after the mission was approved, the Roosevelt administration announced the appointment of an American advisory mission to assist the war effort in India. The head of the mission, Louis Johnson, was appointed as the president's special representative.[73]

The next day Roosevelt wrote directly to Churchill. Expressing 'much diffidence', he suggested for India lessons from the history of the United States. Between 1783 and 1789, the Thirteen States had formed a 'stop-gap government' by joining in the Articles of Confederation – an arrangement that was replaced by the union under the US constitution. Roosevelt suggested setting up a 'temporary Dominion Government' in India, headed by 'a small representative group, covering different castes, occupations, religions and geographies'. This government would have executive and administrative powers over finances, railways, telegraph and other 'public services'. It could also be charged with setting up a body to consider a more permanent government for India. Having put forth these radical ideas, Roosevelt wrote: 'For the love of Heaven don't bring me into this, though I do want to be of help. It is, strictly speaking, none of my business, except insofar as it is a part and parcel of the successful fight that you and I are making.'[74]

The studied phrasing of the president's closing lines would not have been lost on Churchill. India was the United States' business.

1. Viceroy at bay: Lord Linlithgow

2. Gandhi arrives in Delhi with Rajendra Prasad (*left foreground*) and Vallabhbhai Patel (*far right*), October 1939

3. Nehru, Song Meiling and Chiang Kai-shek, September 1939

4. Generals Auchinleck and Wavell

5. Marching to war: Indian students in Lahore, *c.* 1940

6. Preparing for modern war: Indian infantrymen, *c.* 1940

7. Clearing a village in Eritrea, 1941

8. An Indian armoured division in Iraq, 1941

9. Securing an oil refinery in Iran, September 1941

10. 4th Indian Division in Tunisia, April 1943

11. Raising of the Free Indian Legion in Berlin, 1942

12. Subhas Bose and Tojo taking the salute in Shonan, 1944

13. General Stilwell inspecting Chinese troops in India, 1942

14. Quit India: protestors being teargassed in Bombay, 1942

15. Manufacturing armoured vehicles in an Indian railway workshop

16. Machines and Men

17. Building a US Army Air Force Base in Assam, *c.* 1943

18. A war artist's potrayal of Indian soldiers in the Arakan campaign of 1943

19. A cartoon by Shankar commenting on the neglected famine in Travancore

20. Gearing up for Burma, 1944

JOSH WILL STOP THE JAP RAT WHO TRIES TO GNAW AT INDIA.

21. Japanese rat trapped in India: cartoon from a Josh newsletter, April 1944

22. Fighting malaria

23. Indian soldiers in Rome, 1944

24. Into Burma, 1944

25 & 26. Commanders and Men: General Slim (*top*) and Lord Mounbatten (*bottom*) chatting with Indian troops, 1945

27. Road to Meiktila, 1945

28. On to Rangoon, 1945

29. Closing in on the Japanese in Burma, 1945

30. Towards Partition: Cabinet Mission members Pethick-Lawrence (*left*) and Cripps (*right*) with Jinnah, 1946

10

Declarations for India

'The most important event this week', the BBC's Indian listeners were told in mid-March 1942, 'is not military but political.' It was the appointment of Stafford Cripps to go to India and place before its leaders a scheme worked out by the British government. The broadcaster, George Orwell, admitted that little was known about the details of the scheme, but insisted that 'no one now alive in Britain is more suited to conduct the negotiations'. The terms of his praise made Cripps sound almost like a British Gandhi: 'a man of great personal austerity, a vegetarian, a teetotaller and a devout practising Christian'. Cripps' outstanding quality, Orwell added, was his 'utter unwillingness to compromise his political principles'. A friend of India, he had served 'brilliantly' in Moscow as Britain's wartime ambassador. Everyone in Britain, Orwell concluded, was delighted to see this mission undertaken by a 'gifted, trustworthy and self-sacrificing' man.[1]

The failure of Cripps' mission a month later deflated the hopes raised by his appointment and dealt a severe blow to all who desired India's full participation in the war. No sooner had Cripps returned to London than the first accounts of his mission began to be published. Scores more would be published in the months and years ahead. Indeed, no aspect of India's war has been more closely examined than the intricacies of Cripps' negotiations. The broad outlines of the story are worth recalling, however.[2]

Cripps reached India on 22 March 1942 and was soon engaged in a staggering number of meetings with Indian leaders of all persuasions. In his very first meeting with Congress President Abul Kalam Azad, it became clear that the Congress's main interest lay in his

233

proposals about immediate arrangements. The declaration, an official observed, was merely 'the wrapper round a pound of tea': the control of the government of India. Cripps said that the new Executive Council – except for the commander-in-chief – would consist entirely of Indians chosen by the viceroy from lists provided by the different Indian parties. Although the system of government would not be changed, the viceroy would function as a 'constitutional head like the King in the United Kingdom'. Azad took this to mean that the viceroy's special powers and veto would be rescinded. And here lay a major misunderstanding that would curdle into distrust. Much of their discussion, however, centred on Azad's demand for an Indian defence minister and its implications for the position and role of the commander-in-chief.

Jinnah, too, proved receptive to Cripps' idea. Surprised that his demand for 'Pakistan' was so readily conceded, he expressed willingness to help mobilize India for its own defence. Furthermore, Jinnah saw no great difficulty in changing the Executive Council, so long as the viceroy consulted him and treated the Council as a cabinet. The problem of securing the co-operation of the two main political parties seemed to have been solved. Gandhi, however, struck a discordant note. 'If this is your entire proposal to India', he told Cripps, 'I would advise you to take the next plane home.'[3] Unlike Azad, he paid more attention to the plans for the future of India, and he saw these as portending the Balkanization of the country. Gandhi urged the Congress Working Committee to reject the 'post-dated cheque' – a crafty journalist would add 'on a crashing bank' – though he left it to Nehru to discuss the proposals with Rajagopalachari and others.

Subsequent meetings with Rajagopalachari and Nehru turned on the question of the defence portfolio. At a press conference on 29 March, Cripps made public the declaration for India. The paragraph on defence arrangements had been reworded to affirm that the task of organizing India's defence must be the responsibility of the government of India, with the co-operation of the peoples of India. Linlithgow now intervened and insisted that defence functions assigned to an Indian member of the Executive Committee should in no way impinge on the functions of the commander-in-chief. By 1 April, it seemed as if the mission had failed. Linlithgow's own observation was: 'Goodbye Mr. Cripps!' Churchill sent a consolatory telegram praising Cripps for his efforts, and significantly adding: 'the effect of our proposals has been most beneficial in the United States and in large circles here'.

Cripps persisted and sought to work within the remit of the vice-regal proviso, which had been approved by the cabinet on the understanding that defence would not be held by a Congressman. Nehru and Azad conveyed the Congress Working Committee's opposition to this idea but continued the negotiations all the same. Tortuous talks followed on slicing and dicing the functions of defence between the member and the commander-in-chief. The dominant factor in the Working Committee's mind, Nehru observed, was the 'imminent peril to India' and their desire to throw their weight behind the war effort. Towards this end, they were prepared to swallow 'many a bitter pill'.[4] Meanwhile, the viceroy initiated direct communication with the prime minister and tossed a new point into the mix. His Executive Council could not, under any circumstances, function like a cabinet, where majority decisions were decisive.

Cripps had a reprieve by way of the arrival in Delhi of Louis Johnson, President Roosevelt's special representative. In his first cable home, Johnson requested the president to intercede with Churchill to prevent the failure of Cripps' mission. Although Roosevelt refused to intervene, he wished to be kept informed of developments. Thereafter, Johnson worked hard with Cripps and Nehru to try and carve out an arrangement whereby the division of labour on defence could be satisfactory to both sides. Eventually, it was not just on defence but also on the functioning of the Executive Council that Cripps' mission foundered. The Congress was clear that in a 'National Government' the Council had to function as a cabinet and the viceroy could not overrule it. Cripps thought that this was a question of devising procedural conventions, but Churchill dived in at this juncture and forbade Cripps from offering any further elaborations on the proposal. The Congress Working Committee's rejection swiftly followed. On 10 April, the Cripps Mission was at an end.

Churchill and his Conservative colleagues were relieved at the outcome. Amery wondered if there wasn't 'a shade of truth' in the Congress's claim that Cripps had led them up the garden path. Even so, he felt 'like someone who has proposed for family or financial reasons to a particularly unprepossessing damsel and finds himself lucky enough to be rejected'.[5] The outcome of the Cripps Mission was not quite as benign. The failure led to considerable acrimony between Cripps and the Congress leadership. Cripps put the blame on Gandhi's baleful influence on his colleagues, and subsequently claimed that the communal problem was an insuperable barrier. Nehru held that Cripps had been constrained by Churchill and had dishonourably gone back on his original offer.

The reasons for the failure continue to be debated by historians. Some argue that it was a 'Churchill–Linlithgow' axis that cut Cripps down to size. Others contend that neither the British government nor the Congress trusted each other: Cripps disappeared into the crevasse opened up by their mutual mistrust. Historians, however, have been less interested in the wider fallout of the Cripps Mission, especially its international ramifications. This is surprising considering Cripps was sent to India with more than one eye towards public opinion, particularly in the United States. The aftermath of his mission was arguably more important in the context of the war than the endlessly fascinating finer points of his negotiations.

The first consequence of the failure was a breach in relations between British socialists, both within and outside the Labour Party, and their Indian comrades within and outside the Congress. This gravely weakened, if not entirely undermined, the support for a saner policy towards India in Britain. Indian socialists differed from Nehru in their assessment of the reasons for Cripps' failure. Ram Manohar Lohia, a young turk of the Congress Socialist Party, wrote a scathing pamphlet, *The Mystery of Sir Stafford Cripps*, blaming Cripps himself for the outcome. Cripps' 'abuse of the Congress', he wrote, was 'clear and definite'. Cripps might have been 'part robot' in the hands of Churchill, but he was also 'part advocate'. 'He advocated the old imperialist plea of communal differences in India rather too well to be a machine.' Cripps, Lohia observed, was a *European* socialist and not a 'world citizen'. He belonged to 'the more modest, the less blood-and-iron, and the more arguing species of imperialists'. Hadn't he refused to take sides on Mussolini's invasion of Ethiopia, arguing that it was a 'struggle between Italian capitalism and Ethiopian feudalism'? In any event, wrote Lohia, there could be no more 'post-dated cheques'. Unless Gandhi's colleagues pulled him back from a complete showdown with the Raj, he may 'soon succeed in providing India with a full cash settlement'.[6]

Lohia's assessment of the mission, especially his *ad hominem* attack on Cripps, wounded British socialists. More cutting perhaps was the criticism from closer quarters. In June 1942, the Indian writer Mulk Raj Anand published a piece on the Cripps Mission in the *Fortnightly* magazine. Apart from being an acclaimed writer and protégé of the Bloomsbury group, Anand was well known among the British Left for his anti-fascist activism – including a mandatory stint in Spain – as well as his work for the India Independence League in London. Following the onset of the war, Anand had distanced himself from his colleagues in the League, who echoed the Congress's position. 'He is genuinely anti-fascist', Orwell noted in his diary, 'and has done violence to his feelings, and probably to his reputation, backing Britain up because he recognizes that Britain is objectively on the anti-fascist side.'[7]

The failure of the Cripps Mission breached the dykes of Anand's restraint. Written as a letter to a British working-class friend, Anand's article regurgitated Gandhi's criticism of the offer as a 'post-dated cheque' – one that promised the 'Ulsterization' and 'Balkanization' of India. Furthermore, the British government was 'not willing to concede any real power' to an Indian defence minister. 'The patent absurdity of expecting an Indian Defence Minister, one of whose chief functions was to organize canteens, to inspire people to fight for their motherland is obvious.' No 'self-respecting' Indian leader could take up such an 'abject and humiliating position'. Those who sought to defend Cripps and the war cabinet were indulging in nothing more than 'the sanctimonious humbug of bad propaganda'. Cripps himself was talking 'almost like Amery'. India was facing Japan with its hands tied to its back. 'Such is the invidious position', Anand concluded, 'to which Nationalist India has been forced by a recalcitrant government.'[8]

This letter, along with others denouncing various aspects of the Raj and demanding independence for India, was published by Anand in September 1942 as *Letters on India*. Leonard Woolf, the distinguished Bloomsbury of socialist and anti-imperialist bent, offered to write a preface to the book being published by the Labour Book Service. Woolf's preface took the form of a letter to Anand. It curiously criticized the 'dangerously biased' politics of Anand's pro-Congress case and the starkness of his portrait of British rule in India. Anand was taken aback. He thought Woolf had gone 'to the Amery extreme' and denied having sought a preface from him. Anand insisted that his publisher carry his own rejoinder to Woolf at the beginning of the book.[9]

The book caused a flutter in the socialist dovecotes of London. Among those who took exception to it was Orwell. Following the collapse of Cripps' mission, Orwell had assured the (mainly American) readers of the *Partisan Review* that while Cripps' standing might have been damaged in India, it remained intact in Britain. The negotiations had been opposed by the 'pro-Japanese faction in the Indian Congress party' and 'right-wing Tories' in Britain.[10] In reviewing Anand's book, Orwell disclaimed any 'serious disagreement'. He even took a dig at Woolf for being offended at the impression conveyed by Anand that 'Indian nationalism is a force actually *hostile* to Britain and not merely a pleasant little game of blimp-baiting'. Yet Orwell held that Indian nationalism was racist and xenophobic. 'Most Indians who are politically conscious hate Britain so much', Orwell patronizingly claimed, 'that they have ceased to bother about the consequences of an Axis victory.'[11]

Orwell's own ideas for India were seemingly more radical, but in fact were even more limited than the Cripps offer. India, he wrote to fellow socialist Tom Wintringham, should be 'declared independent immediately' and an 'interim national government' formed on a 'proportional basis'. All political parties would be required to co-operate fully in the war effort, but the 'existing administration to be disturbed as little as possible during the war period'.[12] The failure of Cripps' mission, in fact, brought out Orwell's submerged prejudices. He noted with approval Wintringham's observation that 'in practice the majority of Indians *are* inferior to Europeans, and one can't help feeling this and, after a while, acting accordingly'.[13] The gulf between British and Indian socialists – the Orwells and the Lohias – would remain unbridged for the rest of the war. In the absence of any moderating influence from the Left, the British government pursued a rock-ribbed policy towards Indian nationalists for much of the remainder of the war.

Even Orwell realized, however, that rather more than opinion in Britain, it was public opinion in America that counted. As he glumly wrote in his diary after Cripps had returned, 'American opinion will soon swing back and begin putting all the blame for the Indian situation on the British'.[14]

Churchill was all along concerned about influencing American opinion. As soon as he received Cripps' cable claiming that the Congress had rejected his proposals on the 'widest grounds', Churchill passed it on to Roosevelt. The prime minister also sent a copy of his cable to Cripps, wherein he observed that the effect of the mission on Britain and the United States was 'wholly favourable'. However, Louis Johnson had already written to the president that the Congress's rejection was 'a masterpiece and will appeal to free men everywhere'. Johnson pinned the blame squarely on Churchill. Cripps and Nehru could overcome the problem 'in 5 minutes if Cripps had any freedom or authority'. London, he wrote, 'wanted a Congress refusal'.[15]

On the afternoon of 11 April, Roosevelt sent a private message to Churchill urging him to postpone Cripps' departure from India and ask him to make 'a final effort'. The president observed that Churchill had misread the mood in America. 'The feeling is almost universally held here' that Britain was unwilling to go the distance despite concessions by the Congress party. Roosevelt warned that if the negotiations were allowed to collapse and India was invaded by Japan, 'the prejudicial reaction on American public opinion can hardly be over-estimated'. Cripps was already on his way home. Churchill sent an emollient reply to Roosevelt: 'Anything like a serious difference between you and me would break my heart and surely deeply injure both our countries at the height of this terrible struggle.'[16]

Although Roosevelt did not lean any further on Churchill, the prime minister took note of his warning about public perception in America. And the British embassy in Washington swung into action.

Even while Cripps was in India, Britain's ambassador, Lord Halifax, had argued in a nationally broadcast speech that the Congress party was not prepared to assume responsibility for defending India, nor indeed for maintaining law and order. After Cripps had conceded failure, the British embassy persisted with this line of propaganda, adding that the communal divisions in India were another reason for the failure. These arguments were faithfully reflected in prominent pro-British newspapers such as the *New York Times* and *Washington Post* in the immediate aftermath of the mission.[17] American newspapers also picked up on statements by Amery and Cripps in the House of Commons, which pointed to the Congress and the communal problem for the failure of the mission.

Cripps himself facilitated the next salvoes in the propaganda in the United States. Towards the end of April 1942, a Canadian member of Cripps' team, Graham Spry, was sent to the United States to expound the official version. Spry toured America for ten weeks and briefed more than a hundred groups on the 'true' story of the Cripps Mission.[18] In his talks with US officials, Spry set himself two tasks: to dispel the notion that Churchill had in any way scuttled the mission; and to attribute the blame 'almost entirely' to Gandhi's hold over his colleagues as well as their 'unwillingness to accept political responsibility during wartime'. In a bid to thwart any American move, Spry observed that there was 'little likelihood or possibility of a solution' in India.[19]

The climax of Spry's trip was the half an hour he spent with Roosevelt. Jabbing periodically into a Hitler pin-cushion on his table, the president explained the relevance of the Thirteen States' experience to India. Roosevelt came to the point: 'Some people believe that the mission would have been successful if the instructions had not been changed during the later stages of the negotiations. Can you tell me if there is anything to that – were there any restrictions placed on Cripps' instructions?' Spry recited the disingenuous lines in a cable from Cripps, asking him to assure the president that he been 'loyally supported' by all his colleagues in London and India.[20]

Meanwhile, Cripps had enlisted a well-known historian as a handmaiden for propaganda in America. Sir Reginald Coupland had been in Delhi writing a report on Indian constitutional problems when

Cripps had landed. He became part of the 'Crippery' and maintained a meticulous diary and notes. Cripps had initially wanted Coupland to write an article for *Life* magazine. Coupland did better.[21] In June 1942, he published under the Oxford University Press imprint a sixty-page pamphlet, *The Cripps Mission*, lauding Cripps' offer as a 'Declaration of Indian Independence' and sharply criticizing the Congress for spurning it. Coupland's central argument was fabricated. The Congress, he claimed, had rejected an offer of a cabinet government in which the viceroy would 'make it a custom to deal with his Council *as far as possible as if it were a Cabinet*'.[22] No such offer had been made by Cripps to the Congress, but coming from the Beit Professor of Colonial History at Oxford, it naturally carried credibility. By the summer of 1942, propagandists of the British government were chuffed by their campaign: 'The Cripps negotiations did a successful propaganda job . . . we were able to exploit the situation.'[23]

The Congress, in turn, struggled to get its version of events heard in America. At Louis Johnson's urging, Nehru had written directly to Roosevelt, expressing the Congress's continued eagerness 'to do our utmost for the defence of India and to associate ourselves for the larger causes of freedom and democracy'.[24] Following his exchange with Churchill, Roosevelt did not reply to Nehru. Matters were made worse by Gandhi's *obiter dicta* on the United States. In May 1942, he told the press that the United States should have stayed out of the war. Criticizing racial policies in the US, he added that Americans were 'worshipers of Mammon'. The following month, he called the presence of American soldiers in India a 'bad job' and the country itself a 'partner in Britain's guilt'.[25] Gandhi's subsequent calls for Britain to leave India were spun by the British embassy in Washington as indicative of his alleged sympathy for Japan.

In this contest over American hearts and minds, the Congress eventually found some useful allies: American journalists, who had descended on India in the summer of 1942. To be sure, not all of them were sympathetic to the Congress's stance, but at least two influential voices weighed in on their behalf. Louis Fischer of *The Nation* landed in India just as Cripps was leaving. Fischer had spent long years in Moscow, during which time he had got to know Cripps.

He had also met Nehru a few times in Europe in the 1930s. Fischer had returned to the US in 1941 and had plunged into a lecture tour where he made the case for a post-war world without imperialism. India naturally featured large in his arguments. Fischer knew senior State Department officials, including Cordell Hull and Sumner Welles. His trip to India had, in fact, been facilitated by Welles.[26]

In Delhi, Fischer met Nehru and requested him to facilitate an interview with Gandhi. Nehru wrote to Gandhi's secretary, who in turn promptly welcomed Fischer to Gandhi's ashram in Wardha. On the night of 3 June 1942, Fischer reached Wardha after a long, hot and dusty journey by train. He spent a full week with Gandhi, conversing with him on a range of subjects and sampling the ashram's austere regime. Cripps came up in their first meeting. Gandhi explained the reasons for his dissatisfaction with the proposal. Interestingly, he also made a cogent case for a civilian defence member. In war there must be 'civilian control of the military'. For instance, 'If the British in Burma wish to destroy the golden pagoda because it is a beacon to Japanese airplanes, then I say you cannot destroy it.' The British, said Gandhi with a touch of exaggeration, 'offered us wartime tasks like the running of canteens and the printing of stationery, which are of minor significance'. During his stay in Wardha, Fischer also met other leaders of the Congress Working Committee, and in particular Azad and Nehru, who briefed him on their understanding of what Cripps had and, importantly, had not offered. Azad specifically confirmed that the Congress had not – contrary to Cripps' claims – envisioned being a majority on the Executive Council.[27]

Fischer's stint in India overlapped with that of another influential journalist, Edgar Snow. Although junior to Fischer by a decade, Snow too had spent many years outside the United States – in his case in China, where he made a name for himself with his book *Red Star over China*, published in 1937. Unlike Fischer, though, Snow had been to India previously, in 1931, when he covered Gandhi's civil disobedience movement. On returning to America in 1941, Snow began to take a keener interest in India. Like many anti-colonial Americans, he drew an unfavourable contrast between the British Empire and the United States' own record in the Philippines. Soon he had an offer to go to India as a war correspondent for the *Saturday Evening Post*. In February 1942, he met President Roosevelt and discussed whether India 'might soon become an American problem'. Roosevelt asked him to write from India if he learnt of anything interesting and to report to him on returning home. The president also asked Snow to tell Nehru to write to him.[28]

Snow reached India in late April 1942. The mood among Indians was sombre in the wake of the Cripps Mission. 'Despondency was more widespread than before his [Cripps'] arrival', he noted. Among senior British officials, however, he found a 'curious sense of relief'. On 1 May, Snow travelled with a US diplomat to Allahabad, where the All-India Congress Committee had convened. There he met Nehru and Rajagopalachari. 'Cripps is a terrible diplomat, simply terrible!' said Nehru. Cripps' ideas about a reformed Executive Council would have left Indians as 'mere puppets'. Yet he did not blame Cripps for the failure: 'this combination of Churchill, Amery and Linlithgow is the worst we've had to face for many years'. Snow also met the viceroy, who candidly said that he had foreseen the outcome. 'Democracy?' said Linlithgow. 'This country will break up when we leave. There won't be a united democratic India for another hundred years.' Snow then travelled to Wardha. Sevagram ashram, he thought, was 'a cross between a third-rate dude ranch and a refugee camp'. Gandhi explained to him his ideas on non-violence and his plans for the coming showdown with the Raj.[29]

On returning home, Fischer and Snow wrote important articles drawing on numerous conversations with Indian and British leaders. These articles at once punched holes in British propaganda about the Cripps Mission and presented a sympathetic account of the Congress's predicament. Fischer published a two-part article, 'Why Cripps Failed', in *The Nation* in September 1942. His forensic pieces were laced with polemical verve. His case rested on two key arguments: Cripps had exceeded his brief, and he was 'bitched in the back' by Linlithgow and Churchill. Fischer also shredded the claim that the communal divide had exacerbated Cripps' difficulty. The Congress and the Muslim League, he rightly pointed out, were more or less on the same page. More damagingly, he quoted Jinnah's second-in-command, Liaquat Ali Khan, as stating that since the option of secession was conceded, the League was not only ready to join a 'national' government but 'after discussion we might decide we did not want to divide India'. The Congress, Fischer wrote, was 'ready to cooperate in the present'.[30] Cripps was sufficiently alarmed by this attack to get Spry to respond on his behalf.[31]

Snow focused on the consequences of the failure of Cripps' mission. His article, 'Must Britain Give up India?', appeared in the *Saturday Evening Post* a week before Fischer's first piece was published. Cripps' failure, Snow wrote, had increased the considerable mistrust of the British government harboured by Indians. Friends of Cripps were deeply disappointed. Snow quoted Nehru as saying that 'Cripps did Britain more harm in India than any Englishman sent out here in the past fifty years'. Even moderate liberals like Tej Bahadur Sapru were disillusioned by the outcome. Taking a broader view, Snow added that the humiliating defeat and withdrawal of British forces from Malaya, Singapore and Burma had punctured the standing of the Raj. India, he concluded, was the Allies' last bastion. If it fell, China and the Middle East would be endangered.[32]

These views were echoed elsewhere in the American press. The well-known *Washington Post* columnist Ernest Lindley wrote that the Roosevelt administration would be 'remiss in its duty' if it failed to 'assert its influence on behalf of the treatment of the Indian problem which will best serve to win the war'. Halifax was perturbed at this turn of opinion. Unless they did something to reverse this trend, he advised London, the American press would 'rapidly and perhaps completely change its attitude much to the detriment of Anglo-American relations'. The problem was not just the press. Top officials, including the president's close adviser Harry Hopkins, had spoken to him about the 'strong pressure now being exerted on the President from both official and unofficial quarters to do something'.[33]

Halifax would have been still more alarmed had he known of the attempt by Gandhi to reach out to Roosevelt. Prior to Fischer's departure from Wardha, Gandhi had asked him to carry a letter as well as a verbal message to President Roosevelt. 'I hate all war', wrote Gandhi. But he also knew that his countrymen did not share his abiding faith in non-violence in the midst of the raging conflict. Gandhi made a straightforward suggestion. India should be declared independent and the Allies should sign a treaty with the free government of India which would allow their troops to stay on in India 'preventing Japanese aggression and defending China'.[34]

On returning to America in early August 1942, Fischer sought a meeting with the president to share a message from Gandhi as well as his impressions of the situation in India. Roosevelt was tied up, so Fischer was asked to brief the secretary of state, Cordell Hull. Fischer, however, wrote again to Roosevelt, emphasizing that the Congress might lurch towards civil disobedience. 'A terrible disaster may be impending in India.' Gandhi had explicitly said to him: 'Tell your president that I wish to be dissuaded [from civil disobedience].' The viceroy, Fischer added, was hardly inclined to do so.[35]

By this time, however, the Roosevelt administration was not open to intervening on India. On 25 July, Chiang Kai-shek had written again to Roosevelt on the need to secure India's full participation in the war. The 'wisest course and the most enlightened policy for Britain' would be to grant complete freedom to India. Chiang asked Roosevelt to advise both Britain and India to seek a 'reasonable and satisfactory' solution. Senior officials like Sumner Welles felt that it was time for the United States and China to act as 'friendly intermediaries' and forge a settlement between Britain and India. However, the president sent Chiang's message to Churchill and sought his advice.[36] Churchill immediately replied that he disagreed with Chiang's assessment of the situation in India. The 'military classes . . . are thoroughly loyal'. If anything, their loyalty would be 'gravely impaired by handing over the Government of India to Congress control'. Implying that he might resign – 'I cannot accept responsibility for making further proposals' – Churchill asked Roosevelt to dissuade Chiang from 'his completely misinformed activities' and to lend 'no countenance to putting pressure upon His Majesty's Government'.[37]

Roosevelt had no desire to break with Churchill, especially when the Congress seemed set on civil disobedience. A few weeks later, Hull pointed out to the president that they had expressed to Britain their 'unequivocal attitude' about the need for change in India on the basis of agreement between the government and the Congress. 'Our attitude', he added, 'has not been one of partisanship toward either contender.' It was not clear that they could do more.[38] The president agreed. This was not surprising: the 'Quit India' revolt had just begun.

The battle of Indian opinion exercised not just the Allies but the Axis powers as well. Even as Cripps unfolded his plan in India, Germany, Italy and Japan were considering the possibility of issuing their own joint declaration for India. In fact, an Axis declaration was on the anvil for months before Cripps came onto the stage. The prime mover behind the idea was Subhas Chandra Bose.

By the time he had been sent to prison in July 1940, Bose knew that he had failed to turn the Congress towards uncompromising opposition to the war. His attempts to forge a radical front centring on his Forward Bloc movement were coming apart at the seams. Yet the course of the war seemed to open up other possibilities. When the Wehrmacht ripped through Western Europe, Bose was awed by Germany's military prowess. As the Nazis entered Paris, he wrote: 'A miracle in military warfare has happened, as it were, before our eyes, and for an analogy one has to turn to the Napoleonic wars or to the catastrophe at Sedan.' Britain, he realized, was ranged against a formidable set of enemies. Germany, Italy and the Soviet Union, he argued, were likely to have 'a plan of carving up the British Empire. In this task they may invite Japanese help and cooperation.'[39] Bose had no illusions about the Nazi regime, but believed that its power could be bent to the cause of Indian independence. 'Germany may be a fascist or an imperialist, ruthless or cruel,' he observed, 'but one cannot help admiring these [military] qualities of hers . . . Could not these qualities be utilized for promoting a nobler cause?'[40]

During his six-month stint in prison, these thoughts crowded Bose's mind. Towards the end of November 1940, he began a fast unto death. Soon after, the Bengal government shifted him home to ensure that he did not die in prison. In the early hours of 17 January 1941, Bose gave the slip to the policemen who kept him under surveillance and made his way to the town of Peshawar in the North-West Frontier Province. Two weeks later, he arrived incognito in Kabul. There he established contact with the German and Italian embassies. As the British secret service began closing in on him, Bose was spirited out of Kabul to Moscow. On 2 April, 'Orlando Mazzotta', armed with an Italian passport, landed in Berlin.

Bose's arrival was impeccably timed. Germany was then at the zenith of its power. Its forces controlled everything between the Arctic and the Pyrenees, the Atlantic and the Black Sea. Days after Bose's arrival, the Wehrmacht rammed its way into Yugoslavia and Greece. At the same time, Rommel was dealing a powerful blow to British forces in the deserts of North Africa. Bose was eager to make the most of this strategic situation.

Prior to leaving Kabul he told the Italian envoy that a 'Government of Free India' – along the lines of the various exile governments in London – should be constituted in Europe. Italy, Germany and Japan should 'promise, recognise and guarantee' the independence of India to this government. India, he argued, was 'ripe for the revolution': 'if 50,000 men, Italian, German or Japanese could reach the frontiers of India, the Indian army would desert, the masses would uprise and the end of English domination could be achieved in a very short time'.[41] Bose might have exaggerated for effect, but he firmly believed in the practicability of these ideas. A day after reaching Berlin, he met Under-Secretary Ernst Woerman of the German Foreign Office and floated the same ideas. Woerman was taken aback at Bose's suggestion of sending 100,000 German troops to invade India, but remained non-committal.[42]

A week later, Bose sent a lengthy memorandum to the German Foreign Office titled 'A Plan for Cooperation between Axis Powers and India'. The memorandum suggested setting up a Free India Government in Berlin and concluding a treaty between this government and the Axis powers promising freedom to India. It also outlined a plan for propaganda and subversion in Afghanistan and the tribal areas of the north-west frontier as well as in the rest of India. Bose insisted that only the British component of the army, numbering 70,000, and perhaps the Punjabi Muslims were actually loyal to the Raj. The rest of the ranks could be made to rise up in revolt. If at that moment some military assistance – 50,000 men with modern equipment – was available from abroad, 'British power in India can be completely wiped out'. A Japanese advance into South-East Asia would be most useful in the final stages of this plan. A defeat of the

British navy, especially the 'smashing up of the Singapore base', would lead to a crumbling of British prestige and military strength in India. Conversely, if Britain were allowed to retain its grip on India, it could recoup its strength and challenge the Nazi 'New Order'. 'And with this New Order', wrote Bose, 'the question of India is inseparably connected.'[43]

Bose's memorandum was a compound of some shrewd observations and wishful thinking. His approach, however, rested on a set of flawed assumptions. For one thing, it took for granted the continuation of the Nazi–Soviet pact. Without this any plan to foment an uprising in – let alone an invasion of – Afghanistan and north-west India would be chimerical. For another, Bose underestimated Germany's desire to come to terms with Britain. Establishing an Indian government-in-exile or promising freedom to India would constrain Berlin's future options in dealing with London. For a third, Bose assumed that the Germans would regard him as a strategic asset in the struggle against Britain. But Berlin merely saw him as a propaganda tool.

Thus when he met Foreign Minister Ribbentrop on 29 April 1941, the latter was cool to most of his suggestions. Bose emphasized the importance of a declaration of independence to 'win over the Indian masses completely'. Ribbentrop merely observed that he was 'quite sure' that India would attain its 'freedom in the course of this war'. He urged Bose to move 'step by step and not too hurriedly'. Ribbentrop, for his part, offered a clandestine radio station that Bose could use for broadcasting propaganda to the Indian people. Bose insisted, however, that propaganda would only be useful in conjunction with a declaration for India by the Axis powers.[44]

Despite the disappointing meeting, Bose persisted with his efforts. On 3 May, he sent another note to the foreign ministry, observing that the recent German victories in Yugoslavia, Greece and North Africa had 'created a profound impression in all Oriental countries', especially India, Egypt, Iraq and Palestine. This was the 'psychological moment' to capture their imagination by 'an early pronouncement . . . regarding the freedom of India and of the Arab countries'. The Axis powers, he argued, should now 'concentrate on attacking the heart of the British Empire, that is, British rule in India'.

As a prelude, the pro-British government in Afghanistan must be toppled and military aid given to Iraq to resist Britain.[45]

The strategic context did seem propitious for such a move. Even as Bose sent his memorandum, Ribbentrop was urging Hitler to assist Iraq and seize the initiative in the Middle East. The German High Command advised Hitler on similar lines. Soon, Hitler issued a directive stating that the Arab freedom movement was Germany's 'natural ally' against Britain and that Iraq would be given military assistance. Bose's request thus fell on receptive ears. On 10 May 1941, the German Foreign Office was told that the Führer had agreed to publish a declaration on India in the next eight to ten days. Meeting Mussolini on 13 May, Ribbentrop secured his immediate assent that Italy and Germany should 'stand up for the liberation of all peoples under British oppression'. Bose was elated. He submitted a detailed plan of work, underscoring the importance of a declaration. Interestingly, Bose now dropped the demand for a Free India Government. Instead he proposed the creation of a Free India Centre that would be the 'brain of the Indian revolution'.[46]

Bose also drafted a 'Free India Declaration' that was adopted almost in its entirety by the Foreign Office. The declaration affirmed the 'inalienable right of the Indian people to have full and complete independence'. The New Order that Germany had set out to establish envisaged 'a free and independent India'. Indians would also be free to decide the form of government they wished to adopt and the mechanism – 'constituent assembly or some other machinery' – by which they would frame a national constitution, though Germany would like free India to remain united. Bose was confident that the declaration would be issued 'within a fortnight' and was preparing to launch a propaganda offensive immediately afterwards.[47]

These hopes were soon deflated. The failure of the revolt in Iraq, the rapid assertion of British control, and the British advance into Vichy Syria led the Germans to back off from the declaration. The Italians agreed that while Bose should be supported, a declaration would be premature. Bose initially hoped that this was a postponement and not a cancellation. This, too, was belied by the launch of Operation Barbarossa on 22 June.[48]

The Nazi attack on the Soviet Union threatened to unravel all of

Bose's plans. Meeting Woerman almost a month later, Bose spoke at length about the deleterious impact on Indian opinion of the attack on Russia. He noted that the sympathies of the Indian people were 'clearly with Russia' and they felt 'definitely that Germany was the aggressor'. Bose expected the British government to propose some political reforms in India in order to secure the nationalists' participation in the war. When Woerman observed that Germany had its own declaration at hand, Bose demanded that Ribbentrop must be asked to issue it immediately. There was 'no reason to postpone this proclamation'. Woerman insisted that the declaration had to be issued keeping the overall context in mind. Bose had no option but to acquiesce.[49]

The proclamation of the Atlantic Charter goaded Bose into action. In mid-August 1941, he wrote to Ribbentrop that opinion in India was rapidly turning against the Axis. The war with the Soviet Union had given a propaganda coup to the Allies. The joint declaration by Roosevelt and Churchill portended a 'compromise between Gandhi and the British government' brokered by the Americans. Unless Germany issued a declaration on Indian independence, '*The march of the German troops towards the East will be regarded as the approach not of a friend, but of an enemy.*'[50]

Hitler, however, instructed Ribbentrop to hold off on the declaration. He was concerned that it would hand the British a pretext to march on Afghanistan and reinforce their position in the Middle East. Following the serial setbacks in Iraq, Syria and Iran, Hitler was not minded to risk another British victory. Further, the Germans believed that attention should be shifted to India only after the impending collapse of the Soviet Union. This was expected to help knock sense into British heads. The hope of a settlement with London continued to shape Berlin's policy – as late as 13 November 1941, Ribbentrop wrote to Hitler that the 'moment for such a declaration . . . will only come when it is clearly discernible that England does not manifest any willingness to make peace even after the final collapse of Russia'.[51]

Bose's consternation with his hosts' tardiness was compounded by the British revelation that he was living in Berlin – a fact that had so far been kept secret by the Germans. As a barrage of Anglo-American propaganda descended on him, Bose met Ribbentrop at the end of

November. Although he did not raise the question of the declaration, Bose asked Ribbentrop to initiate effective counter-measures. Moreover, he noted that Hitler's *Mein Kampf* – with its contemptuous references to Indians – was becoming a staple of the Raj's propaganda. Ribbentrop replied that the time for a declaration would only arrive when German troops were beyond the Caucasus and at the Suez Canal. 'The Axis could speak only when the military had a firm basis in the Near East, for otherwise any propaganda effect would come to nought. It was a guiding principle of German policy not to promise anything that could not be carried out later.'[52] Just as the German door to a declaration seemed to be shutting, however, Japan's entry into the war changed everything.

Even before Japan embarked on full-scale war, it had begun to sound out Germany and Italy about policy towards India. But it was the strike on Pearl Harbor that lifted the Axis powers out of their torpor. Hours after the attack, Berlin and Rome hastily convened a two-day conference on India with the Japanese. Bose was part of the German delegation and called for an immediate tripartite declaration on India. In the days ahead, he was stunned by the speed of the Japanese advance. On 17 December, he urged both the German Foreign Office and the Japanese envoy in Berlin to issue a declaration without delay. Bose was concerned that the Japanese military moves would outpace tripartite diplomacy. If Japanese forces reached the eastern frontiers of India before a declaration was issued, it would give a strong handle to British propaganda.[53]

Ribbentrop was persuaded. The Japanese were eager. Even the Italians showed a sense of urgency. But the Führer had not given up on the hope of an accommodation with Britain. When the Japanese ambassador broached the topic with him, Hitler abruptly said: 'If England loses India then a world will collapse.' 'There is no Englishman who does not constantly think of India now,' Hitler told a gathering of officials. 'If they had a choice to leave the continent to Germany and keep India instead, 99 out of 100 Englishmen would choose India.' Evidently, he continued to believe that a declaration of Indian independence would constrain his ability to force Britain to sue for terms. Besides, he continued to admire the Raj and doubt the

Indians' capacity to rule themselves. The Indians, he observed with a tinge of regret, 'do not waste a thought on the chaotic conditions that will prevail when the British go, all they want is freedom'.[54]

The fall of Singapore evoked mixed emotions in the Führer. Goebbels observed that while Hitler was 'full of admiration for the Japanese Army', he 'naturally views the strong ascendancy of the Japanese in Eastern Asia and the recession of the white man with certain misgivings'. The German diplomat Ulrich von Hassell confided to his diary that Hitler would 'gladly send the British twenty divisions to help throw back the yellow men'. As the Japanese advanced towards India, Hitler grew more opposed to granting India any autonomy, never mind freedom: 'If the English give India back her liberty,' he observed, 'within twenty years India will have lost her liberty again.'[55]

Oblivious of these feelings, Bose began a series of broadcasts to India over the 'Azad Hind Radio' (Free India Radio). His very first broadcast, on 19 February 1942, sent a frisson through India and created an international sensation. The announcement of the Cripps Mission spurred Bose's propaganda efforts. His message was clear and consistent. The tripartite pact spelled the end of the British Empire. Japan, Germany and Italy were well disposed towards India; those who claimed otherwise were either dupes or propagandists of the Allies. As for the Congress, its half-hearted measures had only encouraged Britain to persist with its old policy.

Bose had nothing but contempt for the Cripps Mission. 'No sane Indian', he declared even before Cripps reached India, 'can be pleased with this latest British offer.' So concerned was Cripps about the impact of Bose that he specifically asked the BBC to counter the German propaganda – a request that led to Orwell's broadcasts.[56] After the announcement of the Cripps offer, Bose sent out another blast of propaganda. Sir Stafford, he observed, was servicing the old imperial agenda of divide-and-rule. His proposals made it clear that 'the real intention of the British Government is to split India into a number of states'. In his next broadcast, Bose read out an open letter to Cripps, accusing him of abandoning his principles and convictions, and of advancing the cause of the most reactionary and imperialist government in Britain.[57]

In substantive terms Bose's rejection of the Cripps offer was entirely consonant with the views of Gandhi and the Indian socialists. Where he stood apart from everyone else was in his espousal of the Axis 'New Order' as the vehicle for Indian freedom. Bose also called on Indians to differentiate between internal and external policies: 'it would be a grievous mistake to be carried away by ideological considerations alone. The internal politics of Germany or Italy or Japan do not concern us – they are the concern of the people of those countries.'[58] Bose's amoral approach opened a cavern between him and his former colleagues. After several weeks of Bose's broadcasts, Nehru bluntly declared: 'Hitler and Japan must go to hell. I shall fight them to the end and this is my policy. I shall also fight Mr. Subhas Chandra Bose and his party along with Japan if he comes to India.'[59]

Bose's propaganda from Berlin, however, slotted in perfectly with that of Japan. On 6 April 1942, as Japanese aircraft bombed the east coast of India, Premier Tojo announced that 'The Japanese Empire has no wish to do anything to harm the four hundred million people of India.' Indeed, this was 'an excellent opportunity for the Indian people to do their utmost to establish an Indian's India'. To avoid being engulfed in war, Indians should 'break off your ties with Britain'.[60] Bose responded with a broadcast the same day, assuring Tojo that 'India will not miss this golden opportunity': 'it will be an honour and privilege for India to co-operate intimately with Japan in the noble task of creating a great Asia'.[61]

Yet the Japanese did not make any move towards issuing a formal declaration until after the failure of the Cripps Mission. At the liaison conference on 11 April, the Japanese circulated a draft tripartite declaration for India and the Arab countries. It did not contain an explicit guarantee of independence, but simply stated that the tripartite powers 'do not have the ulterior motive to replace Great Britain in India and the Arab countries'. The German Foreign Office opined that the draft was 'too journalistic and little concrete'. While the Germans were editing the text, Mussolini welcomed the initiative and urged Berlin to promptly support the declaration despite its shortcomings.[62]

The challenge, of course, was to convince Hitler. On 16 April, Ribbentrop sent a long note to the Führer addressing his reservations. The Japanese declaration would not 'ultimately rule out an understanding [with Britain] at the price of India'. On the contrary, Japan's refusal to step into British shoes 'could even be of advantage for an agreement with England'. 'I am of the opinion', Ribbentrop insisted, 'that it can only have a favourable effect on the preparedness of English circles for peace, if now in these circles we point out once more the danger threatening India.'[63] Hitler was unimpressed. He saw 'no point in adhering to such a declaration just when the Japanese want it'. He only agreed to discuss the matter with Mussolini at the end of the month. Hitler, however, readily accepted Bose's request to be sent to Tokyo. Clearly, the Führer had little use for India and even less for the Indian.

The Japanese were impatient. On 23 April, Tokyo urged the German ambassador to secure a quick decision from his government on the declaration. This served to further annoy Hitler. The Führer and the Duce met on 29 April in the Klessheim Castle near Salzburg. The diary kept by the Italian foreign minister, Count Ciano, captured the atmosphere of the meeting: 'Hitler talks, talks, talks. Mussolini suffers.' Hitler said that he was opposed to a declaration because it would strengthen Britain's resistance. During the Great War, he claimed, Germany could have had a special peace agreement with Tsarist Russia had she not declared Poland to be a separate kingdom. Further, he was averse to a 'platonic declaration to grant freedom to peoples as long as the military situation does not allow the enforcement of this guarantee'. In these circumstances, if they went ahead with a declaration, India would either fail to respond or if there was an uprising, the British would destroy all opposition.

While Mussolini and Ciano sat passively, Ribbentrop argued that if they abstained from the declaration Japan might construe it as part of an attempt to seek a separate peace with Britain. Mussolini mumbled that Japan should be allowed to issue a declaration on its own. Hitler maintained that the Japanese ought to be patient. In the event, the Japanese were told that the Führer and the Duce were agreeable in principle but did not consider the time suitable for a declaration.[64]

This decision was conveyed to Bose in Rome by Ciano. Bose was dismayed but not deterred, and he sought a meeting with Mussolini. The Duce had always been impressed by the Indian. On this occasion, Bose marshalled all his persuasive powers. Ciano noted that

'Mussolini allowed himself to be persuaded by the arguments produced by Bose to obtain a tripartite declaration in favor of Indian independence.' Mussolini cabled Hitler that they should, contrary to their earlier decision, proceed at once with the declaration. 'I feel that Hitler will not agree to it very willingly', wrote Ciano in his diary.[65]

In fact, it was Ribbentrop who nixed the idea. He was keen not to give Japan an impression of vacillating German policy. On the morning of 27 May 1942, Ribbentrop met Bose and explained why Germany could not issue a declaration for the time being. The foreign minister also told Bose that he could meet the Führer that afternoon.

Bose had waited many months for an audience with Hitler. When he finally met him, he greeted the Führer as an 'old revolutionary' and sought his advice. Hitler promptly obliged with a lengthy monologue. Describing himself as a soldier rather than a propagandist, Hitler observed that the military situation was not yet conducive to the issuing of a declaration. The road to India would have to run over the 'corpse of Russia'. And this could take up to two years. The Japanese already stood closer to India. Hitler conceded that he was unaware of Japanese plans, but advised Bose to 'bank on the Japanese to project the revolutionary war'. He even offered a German submarine to take Bose safely to Japan.

When Bose raised the issue of clarifying Hitler's remarks on India in *Mein Kampf,* the Führer said that they were rooted in the past. To Bose's request for continued German assistance to India after the war, he responded by promising economic aid. 'Bose should not forget that the power of a country could only be exercised within the range of its sword.' In closing, Hitler presented Bose with a fancy cigar case and wished him luck in his efforts to liberate India.[66]

The tripartite declaration had reached a dead end. Bose realized that the action was no longer in Europe but in South-East Asia. The political situation in India also took an unexpected turn. 'In view of the internal developments in India', he wrote to Ribbentrop on 23 July 1942, 'I would like to be in the Far East in the first week of August, if possible.'[67] The timing was just right. The revolt against the Raj was ready to begin.

11

Rumour and Revolt

The 'Quit India' revolt of 1942 was the final convulsion in India's year of upheaval. Indeed, it is difficult to understand the outbreak of the revolt without relating it to the waves of anxiety, fear and hope that washed through India in the preceding period. Then again, it is tempting to assume that the 'shiver of 1942' was a sudden reaction to Japan's stunning military advance through South-East Asia to the ramparts of India.[1] Contrary to appearances, however, subterranean eddies of anxiety and discontent were swirling earlier still. The Japanese victories cracked the edifice of the Raj and left large parts of India cowering at the prospect of war.

This was the cumulative effect of several factors. In the first place, the progress of the war was carefully followed in India. English and vernacular broadsheets and magazines were packed with news of the conflict. Regular radio broadcasts further ensured an unremitting diet of war news. The government of India encouraged the propagation of news and information on the war as this was believed to be important in securing India's own contribution. At the same time, the government could not – despite a tight regime of censorship – entirely mould the public understanding of the course of the war. A difficult task in the best of times, this proved impossible when faced with the chain of disasters that were steadily undermining the British Empire.

The fall of France in June 1940 had rattled India. 'The people have become afraid of the consequences of the failure of the British', wrote one correspondent to Gandhi. 'They apprehend civil war, communal riots, looting, arson, plunder and goondaism [thuggery].' 'You sitting lonely in Sevagram can have no notion', wrote another with a hint of reproach, 'of the talks and whispers going on in the busy cities. Panic has seized them.'[2] Such concerns ebbed and flowed with the shifting tides of war.

The British withdrawal from Libya in April 1941, for instance, told on nerves in India. The governor of Bihar observed in his province a 'feeling that danger is coming nearer and nearer home every day'. A British officer in charge of a district in the eastern United Provinces wrote: 'the brutal efficiency of the Germans is regarded with a kind of masochistic horror which promotes no desire to oppose'. An Indian officer from a western district of the same province added, 'the educated sections are inclined to an attitude of resignation, to prepare themselves for the worst eventuality of the fate confronting the smaller states of the Middle East overtaking them as well'. The Allied withdrawal from Greece triggered another bout of anxiety. As a district officer in Bihar put it, 'the apprehension that the War Demon will soon be moving towards Asia is spreading'.[3] Vendors in the streets of Calcutta warned their customers: 'Take what is available now, in a couple of months' time we shall all have stopped bringing supplies to Calcutta on account of the impending air-raid.'[4]

Japanese moves later in the year lent credibility to these concerns. More alarming to the authorities was the sullen attitude of parts of the population. A survey of public opinion conducted in Assam in August 1941 showed that 'a majority of the younger generation are only favourable to the British cause for the sake of Russia'. Worse still, there was 'a considerable body of opinion in various social spheres that it would be in the fitness of things for Britain to lose the war'.[5]

The government naturally sought to counter such opinions. A number of innovations were attempted. 'Reading circles' were formed in villages. These groups were led by a suitably identified, educated individual who would read and convey 'accurate' news of the war to his fellow villagers. The reading circles were periodically supplied with 'lantern slides' to enlighten rural India about the state of the war. The membership of some of these groups was as large as three hundred. 'Propaganda vans' were also supplied to provincial and local governments. These vans toured deep into the countryside, carrying pictures and news of British and Indian exploits in arms.

Another innovation was the use of aircraft to drop propaganda leaflets on urban population concentrations. This was first tried in the city of Madras in the spring of 1941 and subsequently extended to several other places.[6]

Although the government was satisfied at the progress of these efforts, they eventually proved counter-productive. News of crumbling British defences in South-East Asia came as a thunder-clap to India. And it swiftly showed up the government's propaganda for what it was.

Bad news from the war front was amplified by the influx of Indian refugees from South-East Asia who were fleeing ahead of the Japanese forces. This too was not unprecedented. The arrival in May 1941 of evacuees from Iraq had 'created considerable interest' among the people of Sind and Bombay.[7] But the scale of the inflow from South-East Asia was incomparably higher. The eastern Indian provinces of Bengal and Assam were faced with a cascade of refugees. In the first fifteen days of March 1942, over 9,000 refugees from Burma and Malaya landed in Calcutta, while a considerable number also reached the port city of Chittagong.[8] By May, an estimated 300,000 had arrived in Bengal, from where they headed back to their homes in other parts of India. By this time, Madras was housing well over 15,000 returnees. Bombay too had a sizeable number of Bohra and Muslim emigrants who had returned home. Eastern United Provinces and Bihar also saw the return of migrant workers from the paddy fields of Burma. By the end of 1942, the Gorakhpur district of the United Provinces counted no fewer than 30,000 returnees.[9]

The refugees carried with them harrowing accounts of their experiences. In consequence, there was much consternation in the areas to which they returned. By mid-February 1942, there was 'a feeling bordering on panic' in Bombay. The evacuees from Rangoon, the authorities held, were 'principally responsible for this feeling by spreading tragic tales of their sufferings'. What was more, there were 'exaggerated reports of Japanese prowess put into circulation by refugees from Burma and Malaya.'[10] A few weeks later, the governor of the United Provinces was rather worried about the deterioration of public morale. This was not so much due to such developments as the fall of the Andaman Islands to the Japanese as to the 'arrival of large number of refugees from Burma'. There were now 'very few people in the towns who believe that the Allied forces can win the war'. Moreover, the idea had taken hold that 'the only hope of doing so [winning] is to take help from the Congress on any terms'. Similar feelings were abroad in Bihar, where general levels of apprehension had been 'increased by the influx of refugees from Burma and elsewhere who are spreading alarming stories of the mutilation caused by Japanese bombs'.[11]

Such concerns were heightened by the sight of injured Indian and British soldiers being evacuated from Burma to district hospitals in eastern India. The passage of troops through Assam led the people to fear 'an imminent attack on the Province'. In Bengal, the anxiety caused by the refugees was 'further accentuated by casualties from Rangoon passing through Calcutta and Howrah'. The passage through the United Provinces and Bihar of trainloads of injured soldiers left another dent in public morale. Military intelligence reported from hospitals that the soldiers 'though battered about . . . were all very cheerful'. Heading home on sick leave, though, some of them seem to have painted a different picture. By the end of July 1942, the government knew that there was an 'undercurrent of uneasiness and discontent' in the country – not least because of the 'exaggerated and alarmist accounts given by both civilian and military evacuees from Burma'.[12]

Alongside news and stories of the war front circulated a variety of rumours. Even before the striking advances of the Japanese forces, parts of India were abuzz with rumours about the war. Following the Allied withdrawal from Greece, for instance, Bihar reported that 'fantastic rumours are afloat'. In particular, there was much hubbub over an 'astrological prediction that the 26th April [1941] was a time of great calamity for humanity in general'. In May 1941, it was rumoured in Bengal that Indians were already being evacuated from Burma. The next month, the military situation in the Middle East led to rumours in Bihar about an impending attack on India, especially the bombing of coastal towns. This 'created panic and led to an exodus' from Jamshedpur and other cities of Bihar. In the event, the intervention of the local police helped stanch the fear.[13]

Nevertheless, from January 1942 onwards the number and variety of rumours rose enormously. The intelligence summaries prepared for the government began to include a separate section on rumours. At one level, this spurt can be explained by the fact that the intensity of a rumour is directly proportional to the importance of the news. With the war knocking on India's doors, rumours were bound to increase. As an Air Raid Precautions (ARP) ditty went: 'R is for rumour, someone told me at noon / that a Japanese army has invaded the moon.'[14] At another level, though, rumours were not merely mistaken distortions of 'real' news. As the historian Marc Bloch noted, through rumours people unconsciously give expression to their fears, their hatreds and all their strong emotional desires. The spread of rumours is possible only because minds are already tending in certain directions, because imaginations are already brewing and because emotions are already being distilled.[15]

Despite their booming, buzzing profusion, the rumours in early 1942 fell into certain discernible categories. First, there were rumours about the shifting of government offices owing to the fear of Japanese attacks. In early January, following Japanese air raids on Rangoon, Bombay was humming with rumours that the government had plans to shift its offices and the law courts to Surat in the event of air raids on Bombay. Around the same time, there was commotion in parts of northern Bihar owing to rumours about the move of the subdivisional headquarters to a safer location. The senior civil servant had to address a crowd of 5,000 people to allay their fears. Yet there were strong rumours in the Ranchi district that 'His Excellency the Governor would soon go back to Patna, that Eastern Command headquarters would move westwards from Ranchi to a safer place'. In Madras, it was rumoured that aircraft were standing by to evacuate European officials and their families from the city. This had currency in Calcutta too – with the added twist that the government had 'done nothing for Indians'.[16]

A second set of rumours pertained to the Raj's preparation – or lack thereof – to meet the invading Japanese. Some of these speculations were about the possible demolition of key infrastructure – as part of a 'scorched earth' policy – in anticipation of a Japanese invasion. By early March 1942, it was widely held in Calcutta that plans had been made to blow up the two main railway stations in the city: Howrah and Sealdah. Soon rumours gathered steam that all industrial units would be presently shut down for 'the laying of demolition charges'.[17]

Related to these were rumours about pusillanimous military plans. Assam was rife with tales about strategic towns like Chittagong being defended by 'dummy anti-aircraft guns'. A variant on this was that anti-aircraft defences in Indian cities were oriented to protect only the British-inhabited areas. In Bihar it was believed that the British were adopting a policy of 'placing Indian troops in the front while British and Australians are kept to the rear of the fighting'. Closer home, British troops were apparently evacuated from Fort William in Calcutta and replaced with Indian troops – in keeping with 'the general policy of placing Indian soldiers in the forefront whenever serious fighting has to be done'.[18]

Indian soldiers, for their part, were rumoured to be deeply discontented. Indeed, one of the most persistent rumours was that Indian troops in Malaya had mutinied. British as well as Indian troops were said to be reluctant to go on active service. The flip side to this was the widespread concern that Indians would be forcibly recruited for the war. In Calcutta, a rumour was flying that 'universal conscription of labour is under consideration' and that 'control will be almost immediately taken by the military'. In the western city of Ahmedabad, it was thought that 'men were being forcibly recruited for military purposes'. The district magistrate personally addressed a large gathering of mill-owners and workers to deny this. In the United Provinces, too, labour was unsettled. Factories found it difficult to get casual labour owing to the rumour that 'some military lorries that recently passed through had come with the intention of "press-ganging" men for the army'. In Gorakhpur, large numbers of workers fled owing to the fear that they would soon be prevented from leaving the town.[19]

All this added up to the feeling that the Raj had no stomach for a fight against the Japanese. The rumour that most succinctly captured it was that 'India has been leased out to the Americans under the Lease and Lend arrangement'.[20] By contrast Japanese military prowess made a deep impression on the Indian people. Having taken Burma, it was believed, the Japanese would simultaneously attack

Chittagong, Calcutta and Madras. The Japanese were also expected to attack India via Tibet, eastern Assam and Burma. The operational plans were envisioned in some detail: 'The Japs will attack Dehra Dun from the air, and in addition to bombing, parachutists and arms will be dropped into the cages of prisoners of war and enemy internees. The latter with their assistance will overcome the guards and occupy the town.'[21]

By early April, there was in Bengal a 'widespread conviction that Britain cannot win the war and that a Japanese invasion of India is inevitable'. Madras was fizzing with the rumour that 'The Japs have issued an ultimatum to the Viceroy that they will invade India unless India is granted freedom.' In parts of Bihar, a rumour was afloat that 'Japan is reluctant to invade India and that she will try to negotiate some sort of settlement with India as soon as she achieves independence.' Set against this was the idea that the Japanese would come into India 'without causing any damage to the lives and properties of the people of this country'.[22]

Rumours also set up an invidious contrast between the racial attitudes of the British and the Japanese. They stressed the 'discriminatory treatment by Japan in favour of Asiatics in the areas they have overrun'. 'Rangoon was damaged more by the British than the Japanese,' ran another rumour, 'the latter gave financial help to those who suffered during the attack.' British airmen in Rangoon were even held to have 'machine gunned people sheltering in Buddhist temples who had been spared by the Japanese raiders'. A poster found pasted outside the Victoria Terminus in Bombay read: 'After all the Japs. are Asiatics: Let them in.' Notions of the mighty yet kind Japanese were neatly captured in the rumours about a Japanese soldier who had apparently dropped into a festive gathering by parachute, addressed the crowd in their own language, and flown out on his parachute.[23] Indeed, it would not be too reductive to say that the rumours collectively produced a picture of the Raj retreating with its tail between its legs when confronted with the brave yet benevolent Japanese.

It is impossible to measure the importance of such rumours. But the crisis of early 1942 was by any standards a turning point in the history of the Raj – a period during which many millions of Indians became vividly aware of British weakness and failure. With India now vulnerable to attack by an enemy who had so recently been so far away, a drastic political and cultural reorientation took place from which the British could never recover.

Apart from news, refugees and rumours, the government's own preparations added to the chaos. From the outset, the central and provincial authorities spent considerable time, energy and expenditure on air raid precautions.[24] While acquainting the populace with ARP procedures was important, it also carried the risk of unnerving them. This was the case well before Japanese aircraft presented any threat to India. In the hill station of Shillong, for instance, the preparations for ARP in April 1941 led people to believe that the town would be targeted. Hence, the influx of workers in spring from other parts of Assam was 'less than usual despite the large number of temporary visitors'.[25] A call for volunteers for ARP in Cawnpore led to an exodus of 4,000 people in one week. Similarly, efforts to recruit Air Raid Wardens in Agra and Jhansi resulted in the 'timid' relocating their families to the country. By contrast, those who grasped the import of these preparations condemned them for their inadequacy. The *Amrita Bazar Patrika* of Calcutta dismissed ARP shelters in the city as little more than 'slushy pools' during the monsoon. 'Where concrete shelters are proving useless are these holes in the ground going to protect the populace?'[26]

Other measures relating to the ARP caused disquiet as well. From May 1941, lighting restrictions were imposed on all towns with populations exceeding 20,000 that lay within 10 miles of the coastline.[27] In eastern and southern India the clock was advanced by an hour so that labourers and white-collar workers could get back to their homes before the blackout. This change in time proved deeply disorienting – not least because people had to eat by the clock rather than waiting for the sun to reach high noon.[28]

The Japanese raids on Calcutta, starting in mid-December 1941, as well as those on Madras, Vizag and Cocanada in early April 1942, lent a measure of urgency and seriousness to the ARP. Yet these precautionary steps continued to cause a stir among the people. There was widespread concern that those who volunteered simply as ARP wardens would then be despatched to the battle front. Measures such as bricking in factory windows and the construction of baffle walls were seen as attempts to prevent the workers from escaping. Slit trenches dug for protection during raids were referred to as 'burial grounds'.[29] Air-raid sirens told on people's nerves. 'I can hear something' was a common refrain in Madras, observed the great Tamil modernist writer Pudhumaipithan. Neighbourhood conversations during an air raid, he wrote, typically ran this way:

> 'I saw it,' insisted a voice.
> 'Only thereafter was the siren sounded,' added another.
> 'What aircraft? I didn't see a thing,' hissed a third.
> 'Then we are off tomorrow,' replied the second.
> 'Wait till it is dawn, darling!' snapped yet another.

The cumulative impact of news and rumour, refugees and raids led to 'palpitation in the people's nerves': 'As with a person suffering from the fever of typhoid, worry and tension dipped, rose and dipped again.'[30] One measure of this palpitation was a tendency to withdraw money from banks and post office accounts. This was in evidence even before the appearance of a Japanese threat to India. After the fall of France, there had been heavy withdrawals from banks and post offices. Similarly, when Japan began encroaching on South-East Asia, there was a trend towards withdrawing cash in eastern India. This accelerated from early 1942 onwards. As the Bengali poet Sukanta Bhattacharya told his friend, 'I wonder whether the postal department is going to function for long.'[31]

Concerned that the British Empire would not come through the war, millions of Indians evidently preferred to stash their savings under their mattresses. From 1939–40 to 1942–43 withdrawals consistently exceeded deposits. More tellingly, the number of post office savings bank accounts fell from 4.2 million in 1938–39 to 2.8 million in 1943–44.[32] After the fall of Singapore, there was a scramble to cash-in Defence Savings Certificates. Such was the rush to encash these certificates in Barrackpore that the police had to be brought in to control the crowds. There was also a reluctance to continue paying for insurance policies – a sign of the growing 'lack of confidence', as the managers of the Raj realized.[33] There was a spike in purchases of land and buildings owing to the fear that the currency might soon not be worth all that much. Equally significant was the tendency to hoard precious metals like silver and gold as well as foodstuffs. The stock markets and commodity exchanges in Bombay and Ahmedabad experienced extraordinary volatility.[34]

The fear, panic and depleting confidence in the government were evident in the large exodus from several cities. This was not a peculiarly Indian phenomenon during the Second World War. There had been similar mass exoduses in Belgium and France in 1940 owing to the terror of approaching armies. Given its proximity to Burma, it is not surprising that Calcutta had the largest outflow. People began fleeing the city even before the first bombs were dropped by Japanese planes on 19 December. Although the bombing was not heavy – about 160 bombs were dropped over five air raids in December 1941 – and the casualties limited, Calcutta witnessed a swift diminution in its population. Of the 2.1 million people living in the city, around 700,000–800,000 had left by the end of December 1941.[35]

The government had hastily to organize special trains to facilitate this unprecedented movement of people. Among those fleeing the city were a large number of Marwari traders and other 'up-country' folks living there. A few schools and training institutions shifted out of Calcutta to nearby towns like Krishnanagar and Bolpur. The working poor, however, accounted for the bulk of the numbers. The factories of Calcutta had drawn workers from the villages of Bengal as well as Bihar, Orissa and the Central Provinces. Fearing an imminent invasion of eastern India and the impending collapse of the government, these workers rushed to join their families back home. The population of the industrial zone of Howrah, for instance, dropped from 292,000 on 1 December 1941 to 219,000 by 31 December 1942. Industrial labour apart, those fleeing the city included dock workers and contract 'coolie' labour, members of the lowest ranks of the police and civil administration, cooks and household servants.[36]

The renowned Calcutta sociologist Benoy Kumar Sarkar observed that with 'the war at India's door 'interhuman relations are undergoing a swift transformation'. Indeed, the threat of war had led to social churning in Bengal of a kind that generations of social reformers had failed to achieve. With the departure of their servants, 'metropolitan residents are compelled to do cooking and cleaning'. This in turn had led to the 'breakdown of distinctions between superiors and inferiors'.[37] Sarkar was undoubtedly overstating his case, but his observations about the social impact of the threat of war were not far off the mark.

This massive outflow of people not only led to severe labour shortages but also affected the property markets. House rents plummeted in Calcutta and shot up in nearby small towns to which people fled. Most of these towns were also ill-equipped to provide civic amenities to such large numbers of incoming people, resulting in an outbreak of cholera.

Similar developments were observable in the western metropolis of Bombay. This is all the more striking because Bombay was not so much as grazed by a Japanese bomb. Yet starting from early January 1942, large numbers of residents began fleeing the city. Middle-class families hailing from western India – Gujaratis and Marwaris, Cutchies and Kathiawaries – despatched their women and children to the safety of their native towns and villages. Industrial workers, mostly mill-hands, left in droves after collecting their wages for the month. At the height of the panic in early April 1942, over 55,000 workers – almost 25 per cent of the total industrial workforce in Bombay – were reported absent. No fewer than six special trains were running every day to cope with this exodus. Steamers and ferries out of Bombay were packed with people fleeing the city. Special buses with extra rations of petrol were stationed at various places to facilitate the movement of people. Merchants began moving their stocks out of Bombay to safer storehouses in the countryside. As in Calcutta, house rents became cheaper in Bombay. By contrast, small towns like Baroda, which received a large influx, faced a serious shortfall of accommodation and a corresponding spike in rents. With the evacuation of families and servants, people also 'complained of difficulty in cooking their own food'.[38]

The coastal town of Vizag saw periodic outflows of people corresponding to alarms about Japanese air raids. A practice air raid towards the end of March touched off a huge wave of panic. On hearing the siren, an Indian magistrate closed his court and informed the senior judge that Japanese aircraft were approaching. Soon, all courts were closed and 'alarmist stories of bombing began to spread'. Despite efforts by the police to reassure people, a large exodus began. People cited the closure of courts as 'proof of the truth of the rumours of impending attack'.[39] When Japanese planes actually struck on 5 April 1942, there was massive confusion. The scope and scale of the attack were limited; only the port was targeted – and that by ten planes, which dropped twenty bombs. The ensuing chaos was well captured in the governor's report to New Delhi:

> The railways were practically paralysed and all the subordinate staff and labour fled from the place . . . All provision shops were closed and practically everyone fled the town. The port employees fled, as did the coolies employed on the construction of the new aerodrome. There was an acute food shortage and the DM [district magistrate] had to order the police to forcibly open and run some of the provision stores.[40]

Deeper inland, the industrial town of Jamshedpur – home to the famous Tata steel plant among others – was whirring with rumours about 'scorched earth' policies and fear of the approaching war. Industrial labour as well as casual workers and assorted service providers fled the town. By early February 1942, 63,000 people – nearly 40 per cent of the population – had left the town by rail, by bus and on foot. Workers in the cloth mills of Ahmedabad also fled the city.[41]

All these trends and more were at work in the other major coastal city: Madras. An exodus from the city to inland towns and villages began in late December 1941. Within a month almost 30 per cent of the population of 700,000 had left. At this stage, the bulk of those leaving the city were women and children. The Madras government's dithering approach added to the confusion. In mid-February 1942, after the fall of Singapore, the government issued a press communiqué informing the people of Madras that there was no need to leave the city. The communiqué, however, muddied the waters by noting that those who had no business in Madras and who wished to leave should do so as soon as convenient in order to avoid rush and confusion. Far from reassuring the people, it sparked another bout of panic. There was a heavy exodus from the city: schools and colleges had to be closed.[42]

Following the Japanese capture of the Andaman Islands and the bombing of Vizag, Cocanada and Colombo, the Madras government was told by the local military command that they expected a Japanese 'invasion in force' along the east coast – somewhere south of Masulipatnam. Lieutenant Gul Hassan Khan's battalion of the 9th Frontier Force had been deployed to Madras in early 1942. Tasked with defending the Madras coast against a Japanese landing, the battalion's nerves were frayed. One morning, the young officer saw a large plane flying out to sea. The air-raid siren was sounded: 'The alarm galvanized us into frenzied digging because the trenches we occupied during the alarm were only ankle deep.' It turned out that the plane was a British Catalina on a reconnaissance mission.[43] Given the military's nervousness, the government issued another communiqué asking people whose presence was not essential to leave the city at the soonest opportunity. More importantly, all government offices in Madras were moved to towns in the interior of the province. Essential staff relocated to the nearby towns of Chittoor and Madanapalle. The high court shifted to Coimbatore, the inspector general of police to Vellore, the board of revenue to Salem, and other departments to various inland districts' headquarters. The bulk of the secretariat moved to the hill station of Ooty in the Nilgiris. Only the governor, along with the chief secretary and other senior officials, stayed on with a skeleton staff in the government seat of Fort St George.

'The effect of the Government's decision to move offices', the governor baldly reported, 'did far more than the advice in their communiqué.' Between 8 and 14 April, about 200,000 people fled the city.[44] Perhaps the most unfortunate outcome of the pell-mell confusion caused by the move of the government was the shooting of 'all the lions, tigers, panthers, Polar bears and such dangerous animals in the zoo'. The police commissioner apparently feared that the animals might break loose if the Japanese attacked the city. The gory job was done by a platoon of the Malabar police.[45]

By this time, people of all classes who could leave the city were doing so. 'Railway stations became gateways to heaven for the city-folk', wrote Pudhumaipithan. All available modes of transport were pressed into service: coal-fired buses and bullock carts were departing the city as packed as the trains. The working poor fled to their villages or nearby towns. Rickshaw-pullers abandoned Madras for adjacent towns like Kanjeevaram, Dindivanam and Vellore. Even the ubiquitous beggars disappeared. As the writer A. K. Chettiar mordantly observed, 'Beggars can survive only if there are people in the city.'[46]

Buzzing commercial areas like the Flower Market, the Round Tana and the China Bazar were entirely deserted. Firms with offices and warehouses near the port shifted into ostensibly safer parts of the inner city. The university library and printing presses were moved out of Madras. As elsewhere, houses emptied in the city and drove down the rents. And they soared so high in the interior districts that the government had to warn house owners against charging exploitative rents.

A distinctive feature of Madras was the 'mess': an establishment that offered cheap accommodation and food to migrant workers. Many of these messes emptied out during the panic. Those who stayed on in them suffered from serious shortages of milk and food. An intriguing development during this period was the opening of Chinese restaurants in the city. Many Chinese who were formerly engaged in the sale of silk, lace and other products from China and Burma found themselves without supplies and a vanishing clientele. In an enterprising move, they opened several restaurants serving Chinese food – restaurants that continued to function when others shut down, and so turned a tidy profit. This is all the more interesting because Chinese restaurants were mushrooming in other parts of India too: Bombay, Delhi, Lahore, Jubbulpore, as well as most other major civilian and military stations.[47] Another lasting culinary consequence of the war was the *rava idli* – a variant of the staple south Indian breakfast that substituted semolina for the increasingly scarce rice.[48]

As official restrictions encroached on everyday life, evacuated Madras acquired its own zing. A. K. Chettiar nicely captured it:

> Hundreds of tanks came out in procession. Thousands of small explosions occurred. Bomb trenches were dug. Visiting the beach after 6 pm was prohibited. Wild animals in the Zoo were shot. Chinese restaurants opened. Dancing halls proliferated. Talcum powder became costlier . . . Use of electricity was restricted.[49]

By May 1942, as the Japanese threat receded, government departments returned to Madras. Gradually, the people came back too.

Schools and colleges opened as usual after the summer vacation. This was observable elsewhere too. Workers slowly returned to their factories, as did traders to their bourses. Families came back to the cities they had fled some months ago. A semblance of normality was in the air. But the political atmosphere was crackling with tension.

Throughout the summer of 1942, Gandhi and the Congress were casting about for ways to regain the political initiative. To a meeting of the Working Committee in late April, Gandhi sent a draft resolution stressing the 'eternal conflict between Indian and British interests' and stating that India bore 'no enmity either towards Japan or towards any other nation'. Gandhi, in fact, had no illusions about the Japanese. 'It is a folly to suppose that aggressors can ever be benefactors', he wrote in his newspaper. 'The Japanese may free India from the British yoke, but only to put in their own instead . . . I have no enmity against the Japanese, but I cannot contemplate with equanimity their designs on India.'[50] Unlike Nehru, who openly advocated preparing for a guerrilla war in the event of a Japanese invasion, Gandhi called for non-violent non-cooperation. Eventually, the Working Committee adopted Nehru's draft with its language of uncompromising anti-fascism.

After the meeting, while Nehru left for a break in the hills of Kullu, Gandhi stayed on in Bombay for a few weeks. There he saw for himself the stifling wartime atmosphere of fear and anxiety. Rajendra Prasad and Rajagopalachari kept him informed of the flight of population in eastern and southern in India. Although he was initially exercised about the American troops pouring into India, Gandhi came round to the view that they should be welcomed if India was declared independent and the Allies signed a treaty with the independent government to fight Japanese aggression against India and China. This was his message to President Roosevelt too.

Meeting in Wardha from 6 July to 14 July 1942, the Working Committee discussed a resolution demanding the termination of British rule in India. If the demand were not met, a civil disobedience movement would be launched. The following days found Gandhi in an unusually militant mood. He was certain that the 'Allies are in for defeat this time if they do not do this initial act of justice [granting

India freedom]'. 'We are betraying a woeful cowardice,' he declared. 'I do not mind the blood-bath in which Europe is plunged.'[51] This did not mean he endorsed violence, though. Nor did it imply any softening of his stance towards Japanese aggression. 'India as an independent Power', he insisted, 'wants to play . . . a decisive part in favour of the Allies.'[52] All the same, 'some form of conflict was inevitable to bring home the truth to the British mind'.[53]

The All-India Congress Committee met in Bombay on 7 August to consider the Wardha resolution. After two intense days of discussion, the 'Quit India' resolution was adopted by an overwhelming majority. Gandhi announced to the Committee that he would not settle for anything short of complete freedom for India. He offered the Congressmen a mantra: 'Do or Die'. At the same time, he said that 'If the Government keep me free, I will spare you the trouble of filling the jails. I will not put on the government the strain of maintaining a large number of prisoners at a time when it is in trouble.'[54] Gandhi evidently did not intend to force an immediate showdown.

The Raj, however, was rattled by the slogan of 'Quit India'. The government's response to a possible mass movement was under discussion throughout the summer. At a security conference held in June 1942 with civil and military officials, the consensus was to crush the Congress even before any campaign could be launched. The home member, Sir Reginald Maxwell, insisted that time was ripe for a final reckoning with the Congress. Amery, the secretary of state for India, was prepared to grant considerable leeway to the viceroy in advance. After the Wardha meetings of the Congress, he felt that the Indian government should not be placed in the impossible position of the apocryphal railway authorities in Calcutta: 'Tiger on platform eating station master. Please wire instructions.' The war cabinet held back for some weeks. Eventually on 9 August, the entire leadership of the Congress was swooped into custody. Amery had originally wanted to send Gandhi to Uganda, to join another sub-continental prisoner – former premier U Saw of Burma. Concerns about Gandhi's health, however, led to him being held in the Aga Khan Palace in Poona.[55]

The arrest of Gandhi and the other Congressmen triggered the most serious popular uprising in India since the Rebellion of 1857. The connected arc of revolt stretched from east to west via north

India. Although the unrest began in urban centres, it soon spread to the countryside. Local and regional particularities apart, the intensity of the Quit India revolt essentially stemmed from the combination of two factors: the levels of panic experienced earlier in the year and the strength of the local Congress organization. Thus the movement was strongest in Bombay, United Provinces, Bihar, Bengal and Assam. In Madras, however, the provincial Congress committee, led by Rajagopalachari, was opposed to the Quit India resolution. Hence, the protests in this province paled in comparison to the uprising elsewhere.

Although the revolt claimed the imprimatur of Gandhi, it rapidly escalated into a major violent confrontation with the Raj. Government offices and installations were attacked. Networks of communication – telegraph, railway lines, bridges – were systematically disrupted. The scale of the rebellion in parts of eastern India approached that of a fully fledged insurgency. The rebels in these areas deliberately targeted the lines of supply for the Allied troops. As a popular ditty in eastern United Provinces went: '*Hol-land khatam, Po-land khatam, / Eng-land ki aayil baari na?*' – 'Holland's gone, Poland's gone, / Isn't it England's turn anon?'[56] The government estimated that the rebels had fully or partially destroyed 208 police stations, 749 government buildings, 332 railway stations, and 945 post and telegraph offices. They had also derailed 66 trains, sabotaged railway lines in 411 places and severed 12,000 telephone lines.[57]

Despite its intensity, the Quit India movement was limited in many ways. Not only was it confined to specific – if crucial – regions of India, but it drew on a limited social and political base. With prominent Congress leaders in jail, the leadership of the movement passed, in the first instance, to students. The fact that many of them came from rural families facilitated the spread of the revolt to the countryside. The students as well as the peasants that participated in the uprising typically belonged to upper-caste landholding families or the dominant peasant communities that had swung behind the Congress in the past decade. Groups on the margins of Hindu society, especially the depressed classes and the tribal peoples, appear to have stayed almost entirely aloof. Leaders of these groups, especially Ambedkar, wanted to leverage the war effort to advance their own interests – just as the Raj sought to attract these groups for the expanding war effort.

The participation of Muslims was also conspicuously limited. Jinnah had denounced the Quit India resolution as

> the culminating point in the policy and programme of Mr. Gandhi and his Hindu Congress of blackmailing the British and coercing them to concede a system of Government and transfer of power to that Government which would establish a Hindu raj immediately under the aegis of the British bayonet.[58]

The Communist Party of India, too, condemned the uprising as a grave error. Following the German attack on the Soviet Union, the CPI had shifted yet again to an anti-fascist 'line' in support of the war. Realizing the importance of taking in any ally, however far-removed politically, the British cabinet had allowed New Delhi to lift the ban on the CPI only weeks before August 1942.[59]

The Quit India movement turned the political fortunes of the Congress. The party leadership was forced to cool its heels in prison for the remainder of the war, leaving the field open for anti-Congress forces to build and mobilize their own bases of support. None did this better than Jinnah and the Muslim League. The death in December 1942 of the powerful premier of Punjab, Sikandar Hayat Khan, greatly strengthened Jinnah's hand. Thenceforth, he was able steadily to tighten his grip on the Muslim majority provinces and so bolster his claim to speak for all Muslims of India, as well as his demand for 'Pakistan'. The Raj naturally welcomed the flourishing of these countervailing forces to the Congress.

More immediately, New Delhi was pleased with the performance of the Indian army during the Quit India revolt. In dealing with the uprising, the Indian army jettisoned many of the tenets of action in 'aid to the civil power' that had been adopted over the previous two decades: deterrence, limited force, no use of heavy weapons or other technology, civilian and legal control over the actual use of force.[60] In late 1942, at the moment of the Raj's greatest peril, the army was allowed to do away with these restrictions on using force against the people. Aircraft were used to machine-gun large crowds; mortars and gas were employed against rebels and mobs. The government introduced the Armed Forces (Special Powers) Ordinance, which allowed orders for the use of force to kill to be given by an officer of the rank of captain or above. The requirement of authorization to fire from a civilian magistrate was practically done away with.

In his novel *The Jewel in the Crown*, Paul Scott would sketch a memorable scene of the army being deployed to disperse a crowd: banners of warning held aloft; magistrate in tow; troops aiming below the knee. Scott was not in India during the Quit India revolt and he seems to have gone by the written doctrine in the army. The reality in late 1942 was very different. As a young British officer wrote:

> We were in one of the worst areas of the whole country . . . The damage done to communications and govt. property was enormous and our job was to get the damage repaired and communications going again by doing extensive road and railway patrols . . . we were given a free hand, pretty well, to use force where necessary without the usual rigmarole of getting a magistrate's sanction written or otherwise.[61]

The army noted with satisfaction that even new Indian units, such as troops of the 1st Battalion of the Mahar Regiment raised from the depressed classes, did not flinch at firing on their countrymen – and indeed were 'very effective'.[62]

Military intelligence picked up sporadic attempts by Congress sympathizers to undermine the loyalty of the Indian troops. Soon after the revolt broke out, it seemed to evoke little interest among the Indian soldiers. According to one intelligence report, the reactions of Indian troops in the fighting units fell into three groups. The first, and by far the largest, group appeared to be uninterested. The second, a smaller group, felt that a successful or even partially successful Congress campaign could create problems back home. As one NCO put it, 'I do not know what harm this wicked destruction is doing to the Sirkar; I do know that it is causing much misery to my family.' The third, and smallest group, was 'looking ahead to the period after the war, and wonders how the interests of Indian soldiers were going to be protected'. Even the more politically conscious recruits in technical and supporting services did not indicate much interest in the Congress's call.[63]

As the rebellion progressed over the following weeks, the army grew more concerned about its impact on the troops. There was a spike in the number of recruits failing to turn up at regimental centres for training. Soldiers travelling on leave reported that they were accosted by civilians and forced to strip off their uniforms. Troops in an Indian artillery battery conspired to desert en masse – only to be checked in time and court-martialled. By early October 1942, military intelligence felt that 'the cumulative influence of the present political ferment in India must consciously, or unconsciously, affect the army in general, and the ICO [Indian Commissioned Officer] in particular, to an increasing extent'.[64]

Nevertheless, the fact remained that the Indian army had held during the crucial weeks of the revolt. Churchill was understandably smug when he told the Commons in September 1942: 'It is fortunate, indeed, that the Congress Party has no influence whatever with the martial races . . . So far as matters have gone up to the present, they have revealed the impotence of the Congress Party either to seduce or even sway the Indian Army.'[65]

He was right. Attempts at suborning the loyalties of the Indian army would come from elsewhere.

12

Indian National Armies

The most serious attempt at turning the sword-arm of the Raj against it was mounted by Subhas Bose. The story of his Indian National Army that fought alongside the Japanese has become the stuff of legend. Yet the army that Bose raised in Malaya and Singapore was neither his first such attempt, nor indeed was it the first Indian National Army (INA).

The idea of using Indian soldiers against Britain was initially floated by Bose in his meeting with Ribbentrop on 1 May 1941. He suggested recruiting Indian prisoners of war who had surrendered to the Axis forces in North Africa, claiming that these soldiers would be promptly ready to fight against England. The presence of an Indian unit on the German side would have an extremely strong propaganda impact on the rest of the Indian army. The British, in turn, would lose confidence in these forces and would not be able to deploy them without reservation.[1]

In his detailed plan of work submitted to the German Foreign Office later that month, Bose proposed to organize a 'Free Indian Legion'. Made up of volunteers from prisoners of war, the Indian Legion would eventually join an Axis expeditionary corps to be sent to India. Bose planned to prepare a 'big military campaign in the independent Tribal Territory between Afghanistan and India'. Here a military and propaganda centre would be established for the penetration of India. Bose envisaged building an airfield and a logistics network with the help of European advisers. A training centre would also be established to prepare Indian officers and men for the future army of liberation.[2]

Bose's military plans may have been wishful thinking, but his move to set up an Indian Legion was well timed. In his opening offensive in North Africa, Rommel had netted part of an Indian motorized brigade at Mechili in Libya. The Indian prisoners of war were treated in accordance with the Geneva Convention. At the end of April 1941, a group of 1,000 Indian soldiers and 37 officers were interrogated by the German SS in their Italian prisoner-of-war camp at Derna in Cyrenaica. The Germans thought that they could detect a strong anti-British attitude among the Indians, which stemmed from the Indians' belief that they were being unfairly treated by British officers in the distribution of food in the camp. An officer with nationalist leanings would recall that 'the discriminatory attitude of the British undermined whatever of the Indian loyalty to the crown was left by those days'. An Indian VCO had allegedly gone so far as to write a letter to Mussolini, offering to organize Indian soldiers in captivity to fight with the Axis forces.[3]

In any event, the SS discerned an opportunity and sought the transfer of these soldiers to Germany in order to use them for anti-British propaganda. The Italians, however, refused to hand them over, hoping to exploit the Indian soldiers for their own propaganda purposes. Meanwhile, Bose's proposal wafted its way through the German government. The High Command was averse to hastily drafting prisoners of war and deploying them as envisaged by Bose; it insisted on a careful programme of screening and training. Organizing an effective military force, the High Command held, would take time and effort. Bose reluctantly fell in with these views.[4]

The first step was to arrange for the transfer of Indian soldiers in Italian custody. Rome had its own policy towards India and the central figure in the Italian machinations was Muhammad Iqbal Shedai. A near contemporary of Subhas Bose, Shedai had been in Moscow with M. N. Roy in the 1920s. Thereafter he moved to Europe and gradually established himself as the leading adviser on Indian affairs for the Italian government. Well before Bose, Shedai was broadcasting to India and Afghanistan over Radio Himalaya. He was also adroit in persuading the Italian government to set up an India Centre and create its own Indian Legion. Unsurprisingly, Bose and Shedai were at loggerheads. They disagreed on Indian politics – as a Punjabi

Muslim, Shedai was sympathetic to the demand for Pakistan – and they also disagreed on the nature of an Axis declaration for India. Above all, they wrangled over Indian prisoners of war.

Under pressure from Berlin, Rome transferred to Germany some Indian soldiers in the summer of 1941. To induce the Italians to co-operate further, the German Foreign Office invited Shedai to Berlin for discussions. They also arranged for him to visit a camp housing Indian prisoners of war near Annaburg. Shedai found the Indians doused in discontent, complaining about food and conditions in the camp. The Germans, he thought, had frittered away the goodwill aroused in the Indian soldiers while in Italian captivity. In particular, they had erred in allowing the Indian soldiers to mix with Indian officers and NCOs. This affected the soldiers' morale, as the officers had told them that Germany did not intend to free India but only to supplant Britain as the colonizer. Shedai claimed that the Indian soldiers had told him that 'they would prefer to remain under the British than to change masters'. What's more, he blamed Bose for this situation. Shedai informed Rome that Bose did 'not care a bit for these poor devils' and that he had 'committed the biggest crime by bringing them over to Germany'.[5] The subtext, of course, was that Italy should focus on its own Indian Legion under Shedai's leadership.

Two months passed before the Germans stirred themselves into activity. In mid-October 1941, Ribbentrop enquired about the 'range of possibilities of bringing into action Indian prisoners of war who had fallen into our hands'. He asked the High Command for the exact number of Indian prisoners of war in Germany, and whether they could be deployed in the Middle East against units of the Indian army.[6] Nevertheless, the Germans did not get their act together until the Japanese attack on Pearl Harbor.

In the co-ordination conference held on 8–9 December, it was agreed that a Free Indian Legion would be formed by recruiting prisoners of war. The Italians accepted that the raising of the Legion would be entirely under the control of the German High Command. Bose and Shedai joined the conference on the second day and agreed to this plan. It was decided that the Legion would be trained as a regular German motorized infantry battalion. During the first three months, it would be led entirely by German officers and NCOs.

Subsequently, suitable Indians could be brought in. Bose sought and obtained agreement on the conditions for deploying this force. The Indian Legion would not be merged with any German military unit, though it would be subordinated to the Wehrmacht's chain of command. Further, the Legion would be sent to fight only in India and not elsewhere.[7]

Towards the end of December 1941, Bose visited the Annaburg camp to kick-off the recruitment drive. He began by addressing the Indian officers. The atmosphere in the hall, one of Bose's associates recalled, was 'not very enthusiastic; it was rather reserved and cold'. Colder still was the reception of Bose's speech about the imperative of fighting for India's independence. At one point, some officers began coughing loudly while others scraped their boots to drown out his voice. The German officials were dismayed.[8] The camp commandant warned the soldiers, whom Bose was to address the next day, that if they showed signs of indiscipline or disrespect towards the visitor they would be shot. Unsurprisingly, Bose's interaction with the soldiers went well.[9]

After further engagement with the soldiers, Bose and his hand-picked Indian émigré colleagues short-listed 200 of the 1,300 prisoners of war at Annaburg as suitable for recruitment. The German officers pruned this list to sixty-eight. These men were then sent to the Legion's base at Frankenberg, which already had fifteen civilian volunteers. Thereafter, Bose's associates from the 'Free India Centre' worked on these men, explaining to them the cause for which they should enlist and the conditions under which they would serve. Of the sixty-eight soldiers that reached Frankenberg, though, only twenty-one finally volunteered to serve in the Indian Legion. The remainder were sent back to Annaburg.

Over the following year, as the number of Indian prisoners of war in Axis custody rose, the India Legion too grew in size. By November 1942, the Legion had 1,300 soldiers in two battalions. And by February 1943, it counted 2,000 men in arms. The increase in recruitment was mainly due to two factors. Once Bose came out into the open and began his broadcasts over Azad Hind Radio, the Indian prisoners realized his political stature and influence in India. Thereafter, his message of liberating India by waging war on the Raj had more resonance among Indian soldiers. Further, once a critical mass of soldiers had volunteered for the Legion, they were able to recruit others far more efficiently than Bose's civilian team. Ironically, while Bose envisaged the Legion as a national army, where distinctions of religion, caste and region would be dissolved, the recruitment process tapped directly into these very identities. Rates of recruitment were highest, a German officer of the Legion noted in February 1943,

> when the propagandists were allocated to their own racial groups. Muslims cannot be won over by the Hindus, Gurkhas follow Gurkhas more easily and Sikhs follow Sikhs, particularly since it is usually the different languages that bind these groups. Family connections or coming from the same region also play an important role, as does having served in the same unit of the Indian army.[10]

Then, too, the decision to disavow the Indian army was not an easy one for the volunteers. This was especially true of men from the martial classes whose allegiances had been tied to the Raj by long-running family traditions of military service, by generous schemes of welfare and pension, and by an abstract sense of loyalty to the king emperor. Thus Labh Chand Chopra, a twenty-two-year-old Punjabi trooper of the 2nd Royal Lancers from the 3rd Motorized Brigade, closeted himself 'in a room for 24 hours discussing with myself the pros and cons of breaking my oath to the King of England. It was indeed a very difficult task to decide, but inner sentimental, emotional and patriotic feelings prevailed and I finally chose the uniform of the Indian Legion.'[11]

It is not surprising, therefore, that of the 15,000 Indian soldiers in Axis captivity by early 1943 just over 2,000 volunteered for the Legion.[12] More significant was the fact that only one VCO joined the Legion, while not a single Indian officer signed up. Part of the problem lay in Bose's insistence that volunteers should not be enlisted with their previous ranks and should start from the bottom. Although some volunteers were quickly promoted to their earlier ranks, this deterred VCOs and many NCOs from coming forward. While VCOs might also have been more apolitical in their outlook, the Indian officers were not. They were simply unpersuaded that Germany wanted to help India attain its freedom. William 'Lord

Haw-Haw' Joyce, spoke to a group of Indian officers assuring them of Hitler's commitment to Indian independence and appealing to them to join the Legion. The officers were unmoved. The senior-most among them stood up and denounced Joyce as a traitor. The British government, he observed, had committed itself to India's freedom after the war and this was bound to come about.[13]

In consequence, the Legion was largely officered by Germans. Among those who joined it was a young recruit, Leopold Fischer. Born into a Viennese German middle-class family, Fischer had developed a keen interest in India after attending a performance by Uday Shankar and his troupe of singers and dancers. He joined the Indian Club in Vienna, picked up some Sanskrit and Hindi, and resolved on a career in Indology. Fischer even met Jawaharlal Nehru during the latter's visit to Vienna in 1938 and impressed the Indian leader by his command of Hindustani. On his sixteenth birthday, only months before the Second World War began, Fischer pledged to fight for India's freedom. Three years later, he was invited by an Indian friend to meet 'Signor Mazzotta' – the pseudonym of Subhas Bose. Later that year, when he was called up for military service, Fischer volunteered for the Indian Legion.[14] After the war, Fischer would go to India and eventually take the vows of a Hindu monk of the Dashanami Order. As Agehananda Bharati, he would become professor of anthropology at Syracuse University and a major exponent of Hindu philosophy.

By the time the Legion was recruited and trained, Bose was already preparing to leave for Japan. Prior to his departure, he reiterated his demand that the Legion should not be used for the campaigns in Russia or Libya. 'It would be best to use it in Iran or Iraq on the way to Afghanistan . . . The legionaries should feel that they are fighting for the freedom of India, and every theatre of war in which they fight should have some relation to India.'[15] Bose's secret departure from Germany in February 1943, however, dealt a blow to the Legion. For one thing, the legionnaires were not informed of Bose's whereabouts. Rumours and speculation led to a lowering of morale and an increase in disciplinary problems. For another, the Germans decided to use the Legion for policing functions in the Netherlands and subsequently along the Atlantic Wall. Although the Legion never saw active service, most of its soldiers ended up in Allied captivity after the opening of the second front in Normandy in 1944.

By the time Bose left Germany, he no longer pinned hopes on the Indian Legion. Japan's remarkable successes had opened up new possibilities of an armed liberation of India from its eastern frontiers. More importantly, the Japanese had already been rather more successful than Bose in raising an Indian National Army.

Even before the Tokyo typhoon struck South-East Asia, the Japanese had established contact with Indian anti-colonial activists in the region. On 18 September 1941, the Japanese army set up a small mission in Bangkok that enabled the forging of these links. A young, idealistic army intelligence officer, Major Fujiwara Iwaichi, was sent there to contact the Indian Independence League, the premier nationalist organization of expatriate Indians. Fujiwara was given a broad assignment: 'to consider future Indo-Japanese relations from the standpoint of establishing the Greater East Asia Co-Prosperity Sphere'. He fancied himself as a 'Japanese Lawrence of Arabia' – an epithet he would later quote with approval in his memoirs – and briskly set about realizing his mandate through his intelligence outfit, Fujiwara Kikan or F Kikan. The most significant contact made by Fujiwara was with the Sikh leader of the Indian Independence League in Bangkok, Giani Pritam Singh, who convinced him of the susceptibility of Indian troops in Malaya to anti-British propaganda.[16]

Days after the Japanese offensive on Malaya, Fujiwara made a crucial breakthrough. On 11 December, a battalion of the Indian army – 1/14th Punjab – was routed in a surprise attack with tanks near Jitra in north-west Malaya and rapidly surrendered to the Japanese forces. Fujiwara and Pritam Singh met a Sikh officer of the battalion, Captain Mohan Singh. An ICO who had risen from the ranks, Mohan Singh had been commissioned in 1934 and had rejoined his old battalion a year later. Fujiwara took him to the town of Alor Star and sought to convince him that the Japanese did not wish to hold Indians as prisoners of war, but rather wanted to help form an Indian Independence Army to liberate India.[17]

After several days of discussion, Mohan Singh became amenable to the idea. After the war, he would tell his British interrogators that he was

> Greatly agitated by British war aims ... Even at the most critical period of her [Britain's] history, when she was utilizing India to fight for her own freedom, she refused to consider the question of India's freedom. Instead, she ordered the arrest of Indian leaders, because they were guilty of asking freedom for India.[18]

Mohan Singh initially insisted that the force should be deployed not in Malaya but India – and on an equal footing with the Japanese army. It was agreed that the force would be called the Indian National Army (INA). But the limits of his ability to bargain with the Japanese soon became clear. When 229 soldiers of 1/14th Punjab volunteered, they had to join the Japanese advance to Singapore.[19]

The surrender at Singapore swelled the ranks of the INA. Indian soldiers were separated from the British and handed over to the Japanese. On 17 February, around 45,000 Indian soldiers were assembled in Farrer Park. A British officer, Colonel J. C. Hunt, made perfunctory remarks to the effect that the Indians were now prisoners of war and that they should abide by Japanese orders. Fujiwara then delivered a carefully crafted speech, which was simultaneously translated into English for the officers and Hindustani for the men. 'The Japanese Army will not treat you as POWs', he proclaimed, 'but as friends.' Explaining Tokyo's aims for associating the liberated peoples of Asia in a co-prosperity sphere, he announced that Japan stood ready to provide all assistance for the liberation of India and exhorted his audience to join the INA. Fujiwara recalled a tumult of excitement rising out the park on the announcement of the INA.[20]

Indeed, of the 65,000 Indian soldiers and officers who surrendered at Singapore, around 20,000 chose the join the INA.[21] Several battalions went over almost entirely intact. Why was the INA so much more successful in attracting volunteers than the Indian Legion? The contrast is particularly stark in the case of officers: 400 Indian officers joined the INA while only one VCO volunteered for the Indian Legion. To be sure, about 250 of these officers came from the medical corps and many of them volunteered to help treat their fellow soldiers. The remaining 150 included around 100 VCOs.[22] Even so, the differences are striking.

Several factors accounted for the disparity between the Indian Legion and the INA. In the first place, the expansion of the Indian army had resulted in a significant increase in the ICO component of the officer class. Between May 1940 and September 1941, 1,400 Indians were recruited as officers. In 1942, the annual intake was increased from 900 to 2,000.[23] More importantly, there were many more ICOs in the Malayan theatre than in North Africa. The general staff had initially attached higher priority to the Middle East and had avoided sending the Indianizing units to that theatre. Besides, there was an unstated assumption that the Indianizing units would be more than capable of tackling the inferior Japanese troops.

The ICOs were more politically attuned than the older King's Commissioned Indian Officers. This was particularly true of the younger ICOs – later designated as Emergency Commissioned Indian Officers (ECIOs) – who had joined after the outbreak of war. Military intelligence was concerned about the political attitude of these officers 'who are entering the Indian Army in increasing numbers': 'It is certain that the majority are Nationalist in outlook, and that many regard Gandhi with veneration.'[24] An Indian officer commissioned during the war and posted in Malaya until January 1942 observed that of Indian officers 'about 60% are "Nationalists" and desire an early independence for India. The remaining 40% are in a general way dissatisfied with British rule in India but hold no strong political views.'[25] A KCIO who had escaped from Japanese captivity similarly held that 'Every Indian (soldier included) desires a higher political status for India. The difference is only in degree. The extremists want complete independence – the moderates Dominion status and the last group will be satisfied with something approaching Dominion status.'[26]

The ICOs also felt that they were being discriminated against. Not only did they receive less pay and fewer perks than the British ECOs, but they were paid less than the KCIOs as well. 'ICOs do not understand', military intelligence noted, 'why they should be paid less than the British officers, sometimes possessing less experience, who are performing similar duties.' What's more, they felt that this was 'an example of racial discrimination'. An Indian officer, for example, compared his social status and military background with those of some British 'shopkeepers' who were obtaining commissions with higher salaries.[27]

The Indian officers felt the racial edge of discrimination in other ways too. 'I never once saw', recalled D. K. Palit, 'an Indian officer ever share a table with a British officer.' A. O. Mitha, who was commissioned into a Grenadier battalion in mid-1942, had a similar experience in his mess: 'They [British officers] talked among themselves, completely ignoring me, and when I tried to converse with them I either got no reply or only a grunt.'[28] The British ECOs, many of them from middle-class families with little exposure to the Empire, exhibited less racial prejudice than the old KCOs. Indeed, many young British ECOs held radical political views and were sympathetic to the cause of Indian independence. P. W. Kingsford – the future social historian – travelled to India to take up his commission as an ECO, carrying with him Lenin's *Imperialism*, Rajni Palme Dutt's *India Today* and E. M. Forster's *Passage to India*. 'How could I understand', he would later write, 'the absurdity of the situation that here I was travelling to India to help run a system of government which could only strangle any Indian opposition to fascism.' On reaching Bombay, he quickly established contacts with the Communist Party of India and began clandestinely meeting its leading lights such as P. C. Joshi and B. T. Ranadive. The principal challenge, he believed, was to get 'British troops to understand the Indians and the Indians to know the British soldiers, traditionally their oppressors, but now many, if not most of them, trade unionists and socialists of different sorts'.[29]

While British ECOs did not carry the hidebound prejudices of the older officers, they were mostly unable to bridge the social and cultural barriers with their Indian counterparts. As the Southern Army Commander observed, they 'were not good mixers and seemed to look down on their Indian brethren'. More galling was the promotion in the Malayan theatre of newly arrived British ECOs superseding more senior ICOs. Harbaksh Singh, a company commander in 5/11th Sikh deployed with the 22nd Brigade in Malaya, felt that his commanding officer had no confidence in his Indian officers. Several officers who had thus been passed over rose to command positions in the INA.[30] In the prevailing political climate, old KCOs could be rabidly racist. The British commanding officer of a field artillery unit that had several Indian officers wrote to his wife:

> Do you remember that chap in the regiment that looked like a buck nigger? By name . . . . . . ? Well, he went a bit politically minded at one time, chiefly because he wasn't thought fit for promotion. His line was that the majority of India would prefer Jap's rule to ours. I have just got rid of him! But can you beat it and that's a chap serving in the Indian army. I've only got one Indian left . . . I think he'll probably behave himself.[31]

The ICOs also reported discrimination between British and Indian officers in trains and other public transportation in Malaya. The European plantocracy in Malaya denied the Indians entry into clubs and swimming pools. This caused 'a good deal of bitterness among the officers'. One officer was heard saying that 'they had been sent all the way from India to defend the ---- Europeans and he was damned if he was going to lift a little finger to do it if and when the time came'. The officer rose to prominence in the INA.[32]

The VCOs were a different story. Most of them had served long years in the army and had benefited from its cradle-to-grave welfare system. Besides, a majority of them had little interest in politics. When asked about the prospect of a Japanese invasion of India, a subedar from Rawalpindi replied that 'he did not care whether the British or the Japanese ruled India so long as he went on receiving his pension'.[33] Nevertheless, about 100 VCOs joined the INA. This was partly because the VCOs believed that their standing in the Indian army was not recognized by the new British ECOs. Despite the authorities issuing numerous directives that 'their "izzat" [honour] should be respected', the VCOs frequently complained of the lack of consideration and respect.[34] By contrast, the INA offered them a higher standing and better terms than the Indian army – let alone what they would have received as Japanese prisoners of war. Thus VCOs, who served as platoon commanders in the Indian army, were offered command of companies with the rank of a commissioned officer and the prospect of further promotion. The INA, of course, adopted this policy owing to the shortage of commissioned officers. Yet the VCOs who signed up stood to benefit from it.

Then again, some of the VCOs *were* politically aware. The rank-and-file soldier also took 'a very lively interest in what is going on around him . . . he is aware the political developments will affect him and his future, and is watching them closely'. A KCIO observed that the soldiers fell into three groups. A 'small minority' was strongly anti-British and even pro-Japanese. Another 'small group' was strongly pro-British. The 'largest group' was indifferent and capable of 'adjusting to the Japanese masters if circumstances shape that way'. 'Loyalty is not as general as is believed by Senior Brit Officers', he emphasized. 'A number of people are loyal but they will only remain so as long as it suits them.'[35]

Further, the VCOs and the other ranks were not immune to the discontent rumbling among the Indian officers. Take the case of 4/19th Hyderabad, an Indianizing battalion sent to Singapore in August 1939. In April 1940, the military censor intercepted a letter written by an ICO of the unit – Lieutenant Mohammed Zahir-ud-Din – who wrote to an English lady in India that he hoped 'the present war might last for ten years, so that the British Empire . . . [will] be so exhausted that . . . [we] Indians . . . [will] be able to turn the British out of [the] country'. The British commanding officer of the battalion already took a dim view of his Indian officers and constantly carped about their performance of duties. His bile rose at Zahir-ud-Din's seditious letter. The officer was promptly suspended and despatched to India for a court martial. The Ahir Company of 4/19th Hyderabad, to which the officer belonged, rose in protest. The commanding officer had the company disarmed and replaced on duty by men from a British battalion. Fearing a full-blown mutiny, he finally took his Indian officers into his confidence and with their intervention the situation was controlled. K. S. Thimayya, a KCIO in the unit and later chief of the Indian army, recalled that 'the sympathy of the Indian officers was with the mutineers . . . The subaltern hotheads and the VCOs supported the mutiny . . . Fortunately we older officers were able to keep them in line.' After the fall of Singapore, 4/19th Hyderabad was among the battalions that volunteered, almost entirely, to join the INA.[36]

Ties between Indian officers and their men ran the other way as well. Some ICOs joined the INA in order to shield Indian prisoners of war from the Japanese and secure better conditions for them. As one ICO put it, he had joined the INA to 'protect Indian soldiers from Jap treatment'.[37]

Nationalist sympathies and racial discrimination, professional incentives and affinity among Indians do not by themselves explain why so many soldiers enrolled in the INA. Nor do they entirely account for the disparity in recruitment between the INA and the Indian Legion. A crucial factor was the dissolution of military cohesion, like a clump of earth thrown into a flowing river, when faced with the Japanese onslaught. The experience of Mohan Singh's battalion, 1/14th Punjab, was not unrepresentative. The battalion had been shattered in the battle of Jitra on 11 December 1941, leaving every man to fend for himself. The Indian soldiers joining his INA, he observed, 'had lost their sense of discipline and were demoralized. Some of them appeared to be completely shocked at what had happened. Practically, all of them were exhausted, not only bodily but also mentally.'[38]

The surrender at Farrer Park in Singapore reinforced the sense that the organizational scaffolding of the Indian army was crumbling. Shahnawaz Khan, an ICO who would subsequently join the INA, felt that he and his men had been 'handed over like cattle by the British to the Japs'. Another officer, Mohammad Zaman Kiani, also thought that the Indian soldiers were given to the Japanese 'like a herd of cattle'. It is significant that of the nearly fifty ICOs present at Farrer Park, about thirty-five elected to join the INA. These, the general staff later conceded, included 'many with distinguished records of service . . . whose loyalty before the fall of Singapore was never in question'.[39]

John Crasta, a south Indian soldier who refused to enrol, recalled 'several faces becoming sad'. One soldier sighed: 'What will become of my family? Oh God.' Crasta perceptively observed 'how the privations of a one-sided campaign, defections, despair, discouragement, and a sense of helplessness overcome a soldier'.[40] The breakdown of institutional cohesion made it easier for them to overcome their doubts about loyalty and oaths.

This breakdown also helps explain why the largest numbers of volunteers for the INA came from the martial classes – the classes whose loyalty the Raj had so assiduously cultivated and about which Churchill had so confidently boasted. Indeed, it was the martial-class battalions that defected almost intact to the INA. As the commander-in-chief, Archibald Wavell, wrote, 'the bulk of the active INA personnel are representatives of the classes (Sikhs and PMs [Punjabi Muslims] in particular) which formed the backbone of the prewar Indian Army'. Indeed, the Punjab alone accounted for 75 per cent of the volunteers to the INA.[41]

The Indian army did confront a tough enemy in North Africa, especially after the Afrika Korps came into its own, and suffered several reverses, not least the disaster in Tobruk. But there was no collapse of organizational cohesion comparable to that in South-East Asia. For instance, the logistical chain supporting the Indian units in Burma, Malaya and Singapore shrivelled to the point of non-existence by late 1941. By contrast, the supply system of the 4th Indian Division in North Africa during 1941–42 functioned reasonably well – even under adverse military circumstances.[42] Retreats and reverses in this theatre were undoubtedly demoralizing, but they did not feel like routs.

That said, it is important not to lose sight of the fact that around 45,000 Indian soldiers in the Far East refrained from joining the INA. The pull of military loyalty and discipline was substantially undermined, but not wholly neutralized. There were other factors at work as well. For one thing, there was considerable reluctance among captured soldiers to return to combat duties under anyone's command. For another, there was an undercurrent of communal feeling among the Indian prisoners of war. Some Muslim soldiers believed that 'not a single Sikh, young or old, was left out of the INA'. They feared that the Sikhs and Hindus were cosying up to the Japanese to perpetuate their domination over the Muslims of India. Even those who were not particularly sympathetic to the Muslim League disapproved of the 'framed pictures of Mahatma Gandhi' in the INA camps or the pro-Congress slogans raised by some Hindu and Sikh soldiers.[43]

Those who refused to switch allegiance underwent extraordinary privations. From December 1942, they were transported via transit camps in Jakarta and Surabaya to New Guinea, New Britain and Bougainville in the Pacific. Up to 2,000 men were crammed into small cargo vessels that afforded barely 3 square feet for each prisoner. There was little air, less water and even less food. Lieutenant Patel of the medical corps watched helplessly as almost 80 per cent of his comrades died on the fifty-six-day voyage from Singapore to Rabaul. On reaching their destinations, the Indians were treated by the Japanese as 'a race of coolies and barbarians'. When the officers demanded better treatment for their men, they were told to join the INA. On one occasion, the Japanese sought to impose rank badges on Indian prisoners of the 5/11th Sikh. The officers protested: 'We are Indian Army prisoners of war and according to the law we are not allowed to wear any rank badges except those worn in that Army.' They were beaten senseless for their defiance. Torture and summary execution were routine occurrences. The Indian prisoners may well have suffered an even worse fate than the European and American captives of the Japanese.[44]

The INA got off to a flying start under the command of 'General' Mohan Singh. Recruitment began in earnest in April 1942 and received a fillip with the onset of the Quit India campaign later in the year. By 1 September 1942, a full division with 16,000 men was formally raised. It comprised three brigades, named Gandhi, Nehru and Azad. The division paraded in Singapore on 2 October – Gandhi's birthday – and Mohan Singh proclaimed that it was ready for war.

However, Mohan Singh's relationship with the Japanese was steadily deteriorating during this period. There were two axes of tension. The first stemmed from the politics of the Indian Independence League (IIL). The IIL was an umbrella organization that brought together the numerous expatriate Indian associations in Malaya, Singapore and Thailand. It had been formed at the outbreak of war by Pritam Singh and Rash Behari Bose. A revolutionary in exile, Bose had lived since 1915 in Tokyo – a city that provided a haven for many Indian firebrands.[45] He had married a Japanese woman and had close links with the intelligence agencies in Tokyo. But Bose had an ambivalent relationship with the Indian expatriate leaders in

South-East Asia. On the one hand, they realized the practical import-ance of his Japanese connections. On the other, they were worried about the nature of the IIL's relations with Japan and the role of Japanese officials in its functioning. Mohan Singh shared their misgivings.

The second axis of tension ran between Mohan Singh and the Jap-anese army. Fujiwara and his F Kikan were replaced by Tokyo with a larger organization, led by Colonel Iwakuro Hideo. The Iwakuro Kikan began setting up several propaganda projects, such as the Swaraj Institute in Penang, under the lawyer N. Raghavan, which trained Indians in intelligence and espionage. Unlike Fujiwara, how-ever, Iwakuro had little interest in Indian independence. Moreover, he was apt to ride roughshod over the Indians and deploy their resources on his own volition. The thorough-going nationalist in Mohan Singh could not abide Iwakuro. The two men also had differ-ent plans for the INA. The 'general' wanted an army of two divisions, while the colonel believed that one would suffice. Iwakuro saw it largely as a propaganda force, while Mohan Singh was determined that his soldiers would spearhead the invasion of India. Mohan Singh wanted to retain those who had not volunteered for the INA as a potential reserve; Iwakuro wanted to use them as a labour unit.

These lines of tension crossed at the IIL's conference in Bangkok in June 1942. Mohan Singh felt that Rash Behari Bose was 'quite a weak person' and that 'Bose and his colleagues from Japan were not abso-lutely free in their actions'.[46] So, while Bose was declared leader of the IIL, a separate 'Council of Action' was created – apparently to cut him down to size. Dissatisfaction with Bose was also evident in the resolution adopted by the conference requesting Tokyo to arrange for the move of Subhas Bose from Germany to the Far East. The resolu-tion further called on Japan to protect Indians in the territories under its control and not treat them as enemy nationals. The INA was declared the military wing of the IIL and Tokyo was asked to recog-nize it as an equal allied army.

The last demand was obviously aimed at securing the autonomy of the INA. Not surprisingly, Iwakuro was unenthusiastic. The Imper-ial General Headquarters in Tokyo felt that Fujiwara had pampered the Indians and declined to respond to the Bangkok resolution.

Iwakuro sought to use Rash Behari Bose as an intermediary in dealing with Mohan Singh. Bose promptly arrived in Singapore and set up shop in the Park View Hotel. He could not, however, convince Mohan Singh of Tokyo's supposed sympathy for the Bangkok resolution. The divide between them sharpened. Bose felt that the INA was getting in the way of his efforts to find the best spot for Indians under the Japanese sun. Mohan Singh suspected that Bose saw the INA as a propaganda appendage to the IIL. Fujiwara flew down to Singapore of his own accord to break the impasse, but it was too late.[47]

By this time, Mohan Singh had grown paranoid about the Japanese. The attempts to deploy INA intelligence units in the field led to a sharp stand-off. Mohan Singh's autocratic and increasingly erratic style of command was also alienating officers of the INA as well as the civilian leadership of the IIL. On 9 December, Mohan resigned from the Council of Action. On 29 December 1942, Iwakuro called Mohan Singh to his headquarters and asked him to co-operate with the Japanese. He refused and was arrested with the concurrence of Bose. As a parting shot, the 'general' announced the dissolution of the INA. For the rest of the war, he was kept in Japanese confinement. Rash Behari Bose made some feeble attempts at holding the INA together before departing for Tokyo. The Japanese too were keen to keep it intact, if only for its propaganda value. In the event, the INA's revival had to await the arrival of the other Bose.

Six months passed before Subhas Bose reached Singapore, in a twin-engined Japanese aircraft. After travelling by submarine from Europe to the coast of Sumatra, Bose had flown to Tokyo on 16 May 1943. In his meeting with the Japanese premier on 12 June, Bose asked if Japan would offer 'unconditional support' to the Indian struggle. Tojo readily agreed. He was less forthcoming on Bose's request to authorize an offensive into India from Burma – an attack in which the INA would operate alongside the Japanese army. On 16 June, Bose sat as a special guest in the Imperial Diet and heard Tojo declare that Japan would do 'everything possible' to help India attain its independence.[48]

Accompanying Subhas to Singapore was the elder Bose. At a packed meeting in the Cathay Theatre on 4 July, Rash Behari Bose passed on the baton to his younger colleague. Subhas Bose received a guard of honour from the INA as well as a tumultuous welcome in Singapore. His political standing received a further boost when Tojo himself took the salute at an INA parade on 6 July 1943. In the months ahead, Bose addressed massive gatherings of civilians and soldiers, who were enthralled by his stirring speeches and transfixed by his charisma.

Subhas Bose's appeal was crucial to the resuscitation of the INA. Not only was he able to weld the force together, but he managed to draw in soldiers who had hitherto been sceptical of the INA. Captain Shahnawaz Khan had refused to join the INA under Mohan Singh's command. The 'general', he believed, lacked the requisite capacity for leadership. This was partly the disdain of the regular officer for a colleague who had risen from the ranks. And it was partly his concern that Mohan Singh would not be able to 'cope with Japanese intrigue' and that the INA would be 'exploited by the Japanese purely for their personal ends'. Khan initially worked with other officers in trying to convince the men not to switch sides. In June 1942, when the INA had attracted a critical mass of soldiers, he decided to join up. But his motives were mixed. 'I decided in the interests of my men to volunteer for the INA with the full determination that I would do everything possible to break it or sabotage it from within the moment I felt it would submit to Japanese exploitation.' Khan's meetings with Bose dispelled any lingering doubts. He confessed that 'from the moment I came into personal contact with him he exercised a strange influence over me . . . I knew in his hands, India's honour was safe, he would never barter it for anything in the world.'[49]

Bose did not confine himself to Indian prisoners of war and tapped into a wider pool of recruitment. Malaya had a large population of south Indians, mainly Tamils, who had come from India since the 1860s to work in the rubber plantations. The majority of them worked as tappers – lowest in the hierarchy of labour on the plantations. As the Japanese had advanced into Malaya, the British planters had fled. In the ensuing chaos, work on the plantations ground to a halt and many tappers left for nearby towns in search of employment. And they ended up volunteering in large numbers for the INA.[50] The expansion of the INA curiously mirrored that of the Indian army, where the old martial classes were being supplemented by large numbers of south Indians. Bose also formed a unit of women volunteers, called the Rani of Jhansi Regiment.[51] The regiment went on to acquire mythical status, but it was not as daring an innovation as the legend suggests. Most of the women were employed not in combat but in the stereotypical duties of nursing and welfare.

Bose had grand designs to raise the strength of the INA to 50,000 men and women under arms. This was unrealistic given the paucity of officers. But Bose was confident that 'When I land in Bengal everyone will revolt. Wavell's whole army will join me.' In any case, the Japanese agreed to train and equip no more than 30,000 soldiers, formed into three divisions. On the purposes of the INA, too, the earlier differences persisted. Field Marshal Terauchi Hisaichi, the commander of Japanese forces in South-East Asia, wanted the INA to be used as field propaganda units. Bose, however, insisted that the INA would lead the offensive on India. 'Any liberation of India secured through Japanese sacrifices', he maintained, 'is worse than slavery.' Terauchi eventually agreed to deploy one INA brigade in the front line to test its mettle and morale.[52]

On 21 October 1943, Bose announced the formation of the Provisional Government of Azad Hind ('Free India'). As head of state, he held the foreign affairs and war portfolios. Eleven other colleagues, including eight INA officers, were sworn in as members of the cabinet. Three days later, the Provisional Government declared war on Britain and the United States. By declaring the United States an enemy, Bose was not only underlining his intent to take on the American troops on Indian soil but also reaching out to Japan and the Axis powers. Nine states, including Japan and Germany, granted diplomatic recognition to the Provisional Government.

In his dealings with Japan as head of the Provisional Government, Bose sought to display considerable independence. Thus, when the Japanese Foreign Office sent a junior civilian official, Kakitsubo Masayoshi, as diplomatic representative to the Provisional Government, Bose refused to officially recognize him as such.[53] In early November, Bose travelled to Tokyo and negotiated on equal terms with Tojo. He asked Japan to hand over the Indian territory of the Andaman and Nicobar Islands in the Bay of Bengal to the Provisional Government. And he wanted to deploy a full division of the INA in combat. Bose also attended the Great East Asia Conference on 5–6 November, but only as an 'observer'. The Japanese Foreign Office observed that this was because 'he was of the opinion that India would not join the Greater East Asia Co-Prosperity Sphere'.[54]

Tojo indulged Bose's pretensions to independence. The propaganda value of the man was worth more to the Japanese than all the divisions of the INA. So, after Bose's speech at the Tokyo Conference, Tojo responded by reiterating Japan's support for Indian independence. He also announced that the Andaman and Nicobar Islands would soon be transferred to the Provisional Government of Azad Hind. Bose's idea of turning the Indian army against the Raj was now in the realm of possibility.

13

Allies at War

The assignment in the Arakan was a welcome respite for Frank Moraes. The war had seen the departure of most of his British colleagues on the *Times of India* and Moraes had found himself chained to an editorial desk. In January 1943, he was nominated by his former deputy editor – now director of public relations – Brigadier Ivor Jehu, to cover the forthcoming campaign against the Japanese in the Arakan. The freshly accredited war correspondent stopped on his way in Calcutta. There he came across Americans en masse for the first time. '[A]ccustomed to seeing India through Hollywood's cameras as a fabulous land peopled by Maharajas and elephants,' he would recall, the Americans 'were appalled and sickened by the stink and poverty of the place.' They were also censorious of the Raj. As they saw the hungry poor huddled on the streets of Calcutta and peering at the shops, a GI growled to Moraes: 'If I were they, I'd smash those glass windows and help myself to all that's there.'[1]

British troops, for their part, saw the Americans as lavish in their style and loutish in their sensibilities. As a British officer in India observed, 'They [Americans] seem to be heartily disliked by all our boys.' Part of the problem was the disparity in salaries and hence social standing: 'how on earth can a British Sgt [Sergeant] be pally with an American of the same rank when the Yank is drawing 1200/- a month, and flings money around? . . . pinching people's servants for four or five times the salary we are able to pay them.' British soldiers also found the Americans' behaviour boorish. A typical complaint was: 'The Yanks came down to the institute and got drunk and wanted to create trouble.' The American soldier's libido seemed equally out of control. A British soldier wrote from Calcutta:

The Americans are making themselves a nuisance over here, the other day they raped two girls, and sometime back a girl was found unconscious in one of the boy's rooms at the Grand Hotel. They are also causing a lot of fights amongst the English lads, and I think there will be bloodshed soon over here by the way things are going ... The sooner the Yanks get out of here, the better, they are such a wild crowd.[2]

Officers on both sides made 'determined efforts ... to improve relations between BORs [British Other Ranks] and American enlisted men'.[3] Yet their own relationships were far from easy. American officers took a dim view of the pomp and circumstance of the Raj. New Delhi seemed rather unlike a wartime capital. The social calendar underwent only minor changes during the war, such as the dropping of the Delhi Horse Show Week from the winter of 1942. The daughter of a British officer from the Rajputana Rifles recalled:

Dances every night at several places to the music of Glen Miller, Benny Goodman and all the other favourites of the time. There was the Imperial Hotel, or Wengers Ballroom, or the IDG Club, and there was a marvellous place a little outside Delhi called the Roshanara Club, which was mainly rich Indians, we danced out of doors there on a drugget with a background of fireflies ... One night at the Imperial, Noel Coward turned up ... The IDG club had a lovely swimming pool, and a regimental band played on the lawn on Sunday mornings, there were picnics, cinemas and supper parties.[4]

Some of this was undoubtedly enforced gaiety to take minds off the war. Yet the Americans felt that 'It was hard to take our main work seriously in that atmosphere ... Life in the evening was a rather hectic round of social festivity.'[5]

British officials, in turn, arched their eyebrows at such American practices as the segregation of Blacks in military units. Not only did African-Americans serve in separate units, but their social life in India was segregated too. In Calcutta, for instance, Black soldiers only frequented places like the Cosmos Club, managed by Black women from the Red Cross, or the Grand Hotel where Black pianist Teddy Wetherford performed with an Indian band. The US army sought to muffle criticism by producing a propaganda film – shot in Karachi and edited in Bombay – of 'coloured troops, their activities, recreational facilities and mode of living in India'. The African-American soldiers' experience in India was mixed. On the one hand, many Indians – especially of the upper classes and castes – displayed a 'marked attitude of aloofness' and a 'superiority complex' towards Black GIs.[6] On the other hand, they seem to have got on fine with at least some segments of local society. As the American military authorities noted, 'Negroes frequently are invited to attend native civilian parties to which white troops are not invited. Many Negro soldiers attempt to adopt civilian children as "mascots".'[7]

Friction between soldiers and officers was replicated in the ties between the commanders. Differences at the top, though, turned on the question of the strategy to be adopted in Burma and the resources to be devoted to it. These strategic, operational and logistical discussions were overlaid by sharp political differences. As earlier, the Americans were disinclined to shore up British rule in India or elsewhere, while the British, led by Churchill, were determined to restore the prestige of the Empire. Papering over these cracks proved almost as taxing as preparing to take on the Japanese.

The loss of Burma heightened American concerns about China's continued determination to resist the Japanese. The War Department's policy paper was tellingly titled 'Keeping China in the War'. Tangible support would have to be offered to Chiang Kai-shek in order to buttress his position. It was imperative to reopen the Burma Road, for airlifts alone could not deliver enough supplies over the Himalayan 'Hump' to China. The strategic responsibility for an offensive into Burma had to rest with Britain and India – supported by the American Tenth Air Force and Lend-Lease supplies.[8] General Stilwell initially called for the deployment of American divisions to retake Burma. 'I feel certain a serious mistake is being made in not sending American combat units into this theatre', he cabled Washington on 25 May 1942.[9] When General Marshall, the army chief of staff, and Roosevelt shot down this proposal, Stilwell turned his attention to two other pressing problems: training the Chinese troops, and securing Chiang's assent to using them for an offensive on Burma.

Around 10,000 Chinese soldiers had escaped overland to India from Burma. Most of them were in terrible physical shape, having had little access to food, water or medicines during the 200-mile trek. The Indian government decided to host them at a capacious camp in the town of Ramgarh in Bihar. The location was originally a prisoner-of-war camp, with several thousand German and Italian internees from North Africa. From early June 1942, Stilwell designated it the Ramgarh Training Center. Soon American supplies and trainers trickled into the camp. In July, the first trainload of Chinese troops arrived, followed by the rest over the next couple of months.

The Americans found Ramgarh reprehensible: 'hot, dusty, itchy, far from anything green or pleasant. The food was bad and the barracks cramped. The movies were old and Red Cross hamburger parlors and recreation rooms mocked rather than relieved the loneliness and exhaustion of the GIs.'[10] The Chinese, however, had seen nothing like it. There was ample food and meat for everyone: on average the emaciated Chinese soldier put on 20 pounds. The hospital treated them for everything from ulcers to malaria. Above all, they were paid – albeit in Indian rupees.

Stilwell and his subordinates drew up a serious programme of basic, advanced and special training. Chinese soldiers were paired with American instructors who taught them everything from fixing truck tyres to firing artillery guns. The Chinese were also put through an eight-day course in jungle warfare. Five days were devoted to learning the craft of surviving and fighting in the jungle; the remainder were spent on a continuous field exercise.[11] Although there was considerable friction, not least owing to the language barrier, the Chinese proved quick on the uptake. 'Thank God we don't speak Chinese and don't have enough interpreters,' said an American officer. 'We demonstrate and they copy. They are the greatest mimics in the world and are learning very, very fast.' When Stilwell showed Chiang photographs of Ramgarh in September 1942, the Generalissimo was pleased. 'Why shouldn't he be, the little jackass?' Stilwell noted in his diary. 'We are doing our damnedest to help him and he makes his approval look like a tremendous concession.'[12]

Chiang promptly agreed to fly more troops to India for training. Stilwell initially proposed to bring in an additional 8,000 soldiers. Soon he raised the number to 13,000, bringing the total at Ramgarh to 23,000. The Indian government, however, baulked at the prospect of having more Chinese soldiers on its territory. The viceroy felt Chiang had more than an eye on the future. The larger the Chinese participation in an attack on Burma, the greater their influence in deciding its future after the war. Further, Linlithgow was wary of Chiang's dalliance with the Congress leadership and felt that the presence of large numbers of Chinese forces in Ramgarh might allow Chiang to meddle in Indian politics.[13]

'So they are determined to bitch it', thought Stilwell in early October. '"Can't have the dirty Chinks"; Long-range policy: fear of Chinese-Indian co-operation; fear of independent operation; or what not.' 'Limeys getting nasty about Ramgarh', he noted a few days later:

> How many [Chinese] troops, and what for. WHAT FOR? My God! I told them to help our allies retake Burma. They are making it difficult; they don't want to be beholden to the Chinese for anything. Same old stuff, like closing the Burma Road and refusing troops. They appear to learn nothing.[14]

Wavell was inclined to accept the request, but sought to cap the numbers at Ramgarh at 20,000. Yet Linlithgow wrote to Amery outlining his concerns, and Amery agreed with them. Accordingly, London requested Washington to withdraw the proposal. It was argued that there was no immediate military advantage in training such large numbers of Chinese in India. Besides, there were considerable administrative and logistical difficulties in hosting them.

The Americans not only persisted with their demand but increased the numbers. General Marshall said that they envisaged bringing the Chinese force in India up to anywhere between 30,000 and 40,000 troops. Even as New Delhi and London engaged in another round of deliberations, President Roosevelt floated a figure of 45,000. Wavell thought this absurd; but it was clear that further stonewalling would not work. Eventually, Wavell and Stilwell struck a bargain at 30,000 troops: a corps with two divisions. Stilwell confirmed this – only to

ask for an additional 4,000. Delhi and London had little choice but
to acquiesce.

In February 1943, Chiang and Stilwell wanted to send another
division's worth of troops to train in India. Linlithgow protested yet
again:

> The presence of Chinese troops may cause the Chinese government to
> meddle in Indian politics. They have already shown an embarrassing
> tendency in that direction . . . There may even be a danger of Chinese
> troops assisting the Congress Party . . . in the event of really serious
> civil disorders breaking out in India . . . [And] the greater the part
> which Chinese troops play in the reconquest or subsequent garrison-
> ing of Burma, the greater the voice China will expect to have in the
> settlement of Burma's future.[15]

The viceroy, however, gave in to London on the assurance that the
number of Chinese troops was firmly and finally fixed at 42,000.
Four months later, Stilwell returned with a demand to allow more
Chinese troops: he wanted a total of 100,000. The additional 58,000,
he informed Delhi, would arrive between August and December
1943.

The Americans, Wavell wrote to the chiefs of staff, had been 'tire-
some' on this matter. They were continually asking for more, insisting
each time that this was their last requirement: 'it is rather like Hitler's
last territorial demand'. There was no question of accommodating
100,000 Chinese troops. Administratively, it would impose an enormous burden – not least in having to find another location apart from
Ramgarh. Strategically, it was not possible to employ and support so
many soldiers in Assam for operations into Burma. Politically, the
issue was 'even more complicated'. The Indian government was
staunchly opposed to taking in more Chinese troops: 'there are obvious objections to a large Chinese force in India or to the Chinese
being able to claim that they played a preponderant part in the recapture of Burma'. Moreover, an increase in Chinese troops 'undoubtedly
means an increase of American influence and of American claims to
run the campaign from Assam'. Ultimately, Wavell and Stilwell
settled on 15,000 more troops from China.[16]

*

An agreement on the strategy for Burma proved rather more elusive. For one thing, Stilwell found it difficult to pin down Chiang Kai-shek on this matter. Following the debacle in Burma, Chiang had little confidence in Stilwell's strategic acumen. Nor was he eager to throw his best-trained troops into battle with only half-baked preparation. However, Chiang did place a high premium on American power, believing that it could be deployed to good effect in the China theatre. At the end of June 1942, he was incensed when informed by Stilwell that the American B-29 heavy bombers located in India for operations in China were being moved to the Middle East for the ongoing battle with the Afrika Korps. The Generalissimo advanced three demands as a condition for continued co-operation with the United States: three American divisions should be despatched to India by September; 500 American planes should operate in the China theatre; and the monthly air supplies should be raised to 5,000 tons. Only in October did Roosevelt formally agree to two of Chiang's demands. As before, there was no question of sending American divisions.[17]

Meanwhile, Stilwell sought to placate the Generalissimo and offer him a 'face saving' solution to the impasse. He suggested that if Chiang agreed to participate in an offensive on Burma, the United States would have no option but to accede to his demands. 'If the Chinese and American units are ready to move', he wrote, 'the British could hardly fail to act to regain their own territory.' Stilwell drew up a plan that envisaged a two-pronged attack, with China contributing twenty divisions for the land offensive while British would regain naval superiority in the Indian Ocean by retaking the Andaman Islands and landing in Rangoon. Chiang accepted the idea, but shrewdly insisted 'that the attitude of Great Britain in this case should first be ascertained and that she be urged to act'.[18]

Stilwell's staff felt that the British 'have no intention of attempting to retake Burma in the foreseeable future'. This stance stemmed from

a British conviction that no Asiatic possession is worth any appreciable diversion of strength from the British Isles; that the war will be won in Europe; and that lost possessions will at the Peace Conference revert with clear title to the British if those colonies remain upon termination of hostilities under enemy occupation, whereas if those possessions are reoccupied with Chinese and American assistance British title may be compromised.[19]

This was a shrewd assessment of some of the impulses behind the British attitude towards Burma. Yet the Americans were wrong in believing that in the summer of 1942 the British had no desire to take back Burma.

Even before the evacuation from Burma, Wavell had been thinking of its reconquest. As early as 16 April 1942, he informed the chiefs of his intention 'to begin as soon as possible consideration of an offensive to reoccupy Burma'. He was aware that this was 'a long-term project' but felt that it must get off the ground right away. First it was essential to establish air superiority over Burma from airbases in north-east India. Since this would take time – not least because of the paucity of long-range bombers – Wavell began thinking about limited operations to secure part of upper Burma, north of Mandalay, during the dry season from December 1942 to May 1943. The plan, he wrote to Churchill in early June, was to advance on Myitkyina from Ledo and Kalewa, exploiting any success by moving towards the Irrawaddy, and supporting the operation with diversionary attacks elsewhere. The logistical problems confronting him were formidable. Roads and railway links between India and Assam, as well as in Assam itself, were 'extremely poor'. There were practically no roads in upper Burma. 'Troops will require much training . . . in bush warfare and animal transport.' Above all, airbases would have to be constructed; and long-range bombers and fighters urgently acquired.[20]

Meanwhile, news came of the serious reverses suffered by the Japanese navy in the battles of Midway and the Coral Sea. This considerably diminished the prospect of a Japanese seaborne invasion of the east coast of India or Ceylon. The Japanese threat to India was likely to be confined to the Assam frontier, Arakan and the east Bengal coast. Churchill replied to Wavell that the proposed operations were 'very nice and useful nibbling', but his real interest lay in the recapture of Rangoon and Moulmein, followed by an advance on Bangkok.

Following their recent losses, the Japanese navy would be cautious; so Wavell should plan to strike across the Bay of Bengal into southern Burma and thence Malaya. Wavell accordingly instructed his commanders and staff to undertake detailed planning for the limited operations in north Burma and to consider the question of launching a major offensive with Rangoon as its objective. The latter was given the code name 'Anakim'.[21]

Wavell had initially hoped to start the offensive in early October 1942. But the outbreak of the Quit India revolt necessitated the diversion of troops for internal security. More importantly, as planning proceeded apace, Wavell and his subordinate commanders realized that the administrative and logistical challenges were daunting. The monsoon heavily hindered efforts at road and rail construction. Malaria laid low large numbers of troops, and equipment and aircraft destined for India were diverted to the more urgent battlefields of Egypt. In consequence, the planned advance on north Burma was put off for at least six months. The major operation, Operation Anakim, was postponed by a year. Wavell, however, was keen to regain the initiative and so decided to embark on a more limited offensive on the Arakan.

Nevertheless, when in mid-October Stilwell proposed an offensive on Burma with Chinese support, Wavell agreed. Stilwell's plan also envisaged simultaneous naval operations, with a strong Anglo-American fleet to take control of the Bay of Bengal and enable landings on Rangoon. Chiang Kai-shek had insisted that this was essential to support land operations in northern Burma. Wavell disagreed with the naval component of the plan, pointing out that the six to eight aircraft carriers and numerous submarines needed were nowhere in sight. Yet there was enough common ground to get down to planning. It was agreed that the Chinese forces would advance from Ledo to the Hukawng Valley in north Burma and open the backdoor to Rangoon. Preliminary logistical details for Operation Anakim were also sketched out. Stilwell secured Chiang's tentative agreement to these plans on 3 November: the Generalissimo insisted that Britain should have the upper hand in the air and on sea. Wavell felt, however, that the necessary preparations – training of troops, dumping of supplies, achieving air and naval superiority – could not be completed by the proposed date of 1 March 1943. His staff also carped to the Americans about Chiang's conditional agreement.[22]

In early December, Roosevelt approved of Operation Anakim and directed that the requisite resources be placed at Stilwell's disposal. But Wavell's doubts about the enterprise were deepening. A major offensive on Burma in spring 1943 was out of the question. Even limited operations in north Burma could not be undertaken then. The problem was not getting troops into the area but maintaining them there during the monsoon of 1943. As Wavell put it to the chiefs of staff, 'I am determined not to get troops into position of last May when we had to withdraw through inability to maintain ourselves.' The chiefs backed Wavell, insisting that Burma was a British theatre of war and India was operationally responsible.[23] Stilwell was livid at India's dragging of its feet: 'Peanut and I are on a raft, with one sandwich between us, and the rescue ship is heading away from the scene.'[24]

On 7 December 1942, Wavell formally told Stilwell that Anakim would have to wait until the autumn or winter of 1943. Operations in upper Burma in the spring of 1943 would also be premature.[25] In subsequent meetings, Wavell elaborated on the enormous logistical and operational challenges and requested Stilwell to convey his views to Chiang. Stilwell could barely conceal his rage.

> 'Are you satisfied that this operation is not feasible?' asked Wavell.
> 'Yes, I am,' replied Stilwell.
> 'Are you satisfied on purely military grounds?' persisted Wavell.
> 'Yes, I am,' nodded Stilwell.
> 'What will you say to Chiang Kai-shek?' asked Wavell.
> 'I shall tell him the bloody British won't fight.'[26]

On 28 December, Chiang cabled Roosevelt that the British had reneged on their promises. Not only were they unable to assure naval superiority in the Bay of Bengal, but they had earmarked only three divisions for the Burma offensive. Roosevelt sent a strong reply in the new year, insisting that opening the Burma Road by operations in the north was more important than capturing all of Burma. The Americans also leaned on the British: 'Means must be found to give the

Generalissimo the necessary assurance that will enable the attack to jump off.' The British emphatically responded that there could be no fleet operations in the Bay of Bengal, owing to the lack of destroyers to escort the battleships of the Eastern Fleet. Chiang, for his part, wrote to Roosevelt that unless naval operations were undertaken, the Japanese would 'concentrate rapidly against our armies in the North' and imperil them. Without the naval operation, the best course would be to put off any offensive into Burma.[27]

Plans for Burma were picked up in mid-January 1943 at the Anglo-American conference in Casablanca. The conference was convened to arrive at definite decisions on grand strategy for the year. American and British joint planners submitted separate plans for Burma. The Americans emphatically called for Operation Anakim, 'with a view to keeping China in the war, keeping pressure on the Japanese in this area'. The British felt that the operations 'certainly required in 1943' were recapturing Akyab, establishing bridgeheads in the Chindwin Valley, and covering the construction of a road from Ledo via Myitkyina to Lungling in Yunnan. While plans for Anakim should be made for the winter of 1943–44, they were not sure if the requisite naval and amphibious forces could be found. Diversion of these to Anakim 'cannot but react adversely on the early defeat of Germany'.[28]

The Americans felt that the British were exaggerating the problem of resources. General Marshall came down heavily on them: 'unless Operation ANAKIM could be undertaken, he [Marshall] felt that a situation might arise in the Pacific at any time that would necessitate the United States regretfully withdrawing from the commitments in the European theatre'. The carrot accompanying the stick was an American commitment to make up any deficiency in landing craft and naval forces. It was eventually agreed that all plans and preparations should be made to mount Anakim by 15 November 1943, though the actual decision to attack would be taken in the summer of 1943.[29]

In the wake of Casablanca, a high-powered Anglo-American military delegation was sent to secure Chiang's assent for Anakim. En route, the delegation stopped in Delhi to sort out the details of Anakim as well as other operations before the monsoon set in. Stilwell reported that his plans for concentrating twenty-six Chinese divisions in Yunnan by March were well behind schedule. In consequence, no sizeable operations could be conducted in north Burma until after the monsoon. Wavell, too, expressed his inability to carry out anything serious before then. Everyone agreed that large-scale naval operations were impossible before the end of the year. It was decided, therefore, that the whole of Burma should be occupied in one campaigning season, from 1 November 1943 to 15 May 1944. In the meantime, logistical preparations should proceed apace and minor operations, including the capture of Akyab, should be attempted. The delegation then left for Chongqing, where they managed to get Chiang's formal acceptance for Operation Anakim – on the understanding that adequate naval forces would be available for operations in the Bay of Bengal and that the American airlift to, and aircraft for, China would be increased.

Although Wavell had swallowed the idea of Anakim, he strained at the requirements of the plan. The Americans in the delegation thought that his outline plan really consisted of 'several pages of well written paragraphs, telling why the mission could not be accomplished'.[30] No sooner had Chiang come on board than Wavell's qualms about Anakim deepened. Detailed studies by his staff suggested that the naval dimensions of the operation would be far more onerous than they had assumed. Even with a number of Allied aircraft carriers, the Japanese land-based air force would be able to inflict substantial damage on an expeditionary force. In mid-February 1943, Wavell wrote to the chiefs that Anakim was a gamble involving great risks and difficulties. While continuing to plan for it, they should recognize that Japanese strength and counter-preparations in Burma might make the operation too hazardous.

Wavell now felt that it might be altogether better to avoid a major offensive on Burma. For one thing, the Allies could not hope to surprise the Japanese by an attack there: 'this is an obvious move and must be expected by the enemy'. For another, they could 'only progress very slowly and at considerable cost'. Instead, Wavell felt that they should undertake an offensive to capture the Sunda Straits between Sumatra and Java. This would catch the Japanese off-guard and threaten their control of Singapore and the Dutch East Indies.

Such an operation, he argued, would be 'no more formidable than the capture of Burma'. The problem, of course, was in reneging on the plan agreed with the Chinese:

> it will be necessary to conceal our intentions from the Chinese who are naturally anxious to see the reconquest of Burma . . . we can continue preparations and discussions with the Chinese on an offensive into Burma . . . We shall in fact make a limited offensive into Upper Burma, with the object of confirming the Japanese of our intentions to attack in Burma.[31]

Anakim, in short, should be abandoned. Wavell, however, reckoned without the resources for this ambitious new plan – as well as without the providers of these resources, the Americans. His willingness to drop the idea of retaking Burma did not, however, stem solely from the difficulties of Anakim. It was also influenced by the unfolding debacle in Arakan.

The advance on the Arakan was originally envisioned by Wavell as part of a two-pronged offensive. Alongside the occupation of Kalewa and Sittaung, he aimed at retaking upper Arakan and capturing Akyab. Akyab was not only one of two serviceable ports in the eastern Bay of Bengal – Chittagong was the other – but was important as an airbase to strike into Rangoon. In September 1942, Wavell set afoot preparations for a seaborne expedition in early December to wrest control of Akyab. By mid-November, however, it became clear that the amphibious offensive was stillborn: neither shipping nor troops, nor yet the necessary aircraft, were made available. Wavell was forced to modify his plans. He decided to advance by land from Chittagong down the Arakan coast and secure the Mayu Peninsula, whence an attack on Akyab could be launched at a manageable distance. He knew that such an advance could not surprise the enemy, but hoped that if it proceeded speedily the Japanese would find it difficult to reinforce Akyab in time.[32]

In planning the operation, however, Wavell grossly underestimated the Japanese. This was partly because of his conviction that the Japanese had overstretched themselves in occupying Burma. Philip Mason, secretary of the chiefs of staff committee in Delhi, found

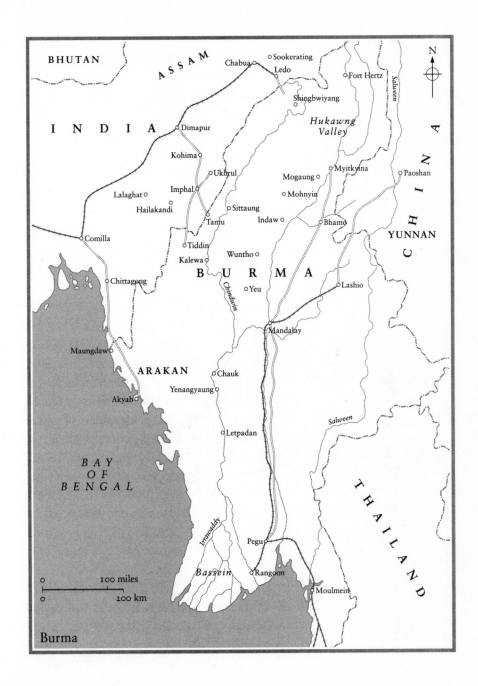

Burma

Wavell gazing at a map of Burma on a sultry evening in June 1942. 'Think how stretched *they* must be,' said Wavell. 'This is the moment to hit the Japs if only we could! If I had one division in India fit to fight I'd go for them now!'[33] When his planning staff pointed out the logistical difficulties of an early attack on Burma, Wavell told them off for having 'considered our own difficulties almost exclusively and not those of the enemy', and proceeded to issue planning instructions himself.[34] In mid-September, Wavell told his staff that he had 'a hunch ... that we may find Japanese opposition very much lower than we expect in Burma if we can only act with boldness and determination ... The Jap has never fought defensively and may not be much good at it.' He claimed to have had 'a similar hunch before the Sidi Barrani operations two years ago ... My hunch came off then.'[35] This was a curious comparison. Sidi Barrani had been the opening engagement with the Italians in North Africa. In Burma, by contrast, the Japanese had booted out the British-Indian forces barely months ago – as they had elsewhere in South-East Asia. Moreover, when the tide had turned against him in North Africa, Wavell had been rather circumspect in taking on Rommel's Afrika Korps. His assessment of the Japanese evidently had racial undertones as well.

The magnitude of Wavell's underestimation of the Japanese becomes clearer when we look at the condition of the Indian army. As early as mid-January 1942, the director of staff duties at GHQ India candidly wrote: 'The fighting value of Indian troops ... has fallen very, very far below the standard of Sidi Barrani and Keren.' Wavell himself admitted to Churchill that his troops had to be trained anew in jungle warfare. Later that summer, he also wrote to all commanding officers that the fighting power of the Indian army could be revived 'only by *real hard intensive training* such as we have not yet undertaken'.[36] To be sure, some disparate efforts were made to pass on the 'lessons' of Malaya and Burma to units in India. A new edition of the training pamphlet *Jungle Warfare* was circulated in early September. Tactical courses for fighting in the jungle were belatedly placed on the curricula of regimental training centres and officer training schools. Some formations, like the 17th, 20th and 23rd Indian Divisions, began seriously considering the problems of jungle warfare. Yet across the Indian army progress was patchy, to put it mildly.[37] In any case, the Arakan offensive began before these ideas could gain traction among the troops.

Troops stationed in eastern India were also laid low by a malaria outbreak in the autumn of 1942 – the worst in years. Both combat and logistical units faced considerable attrition due to disease. Several units reported 75–100 per cent of troops as sick with malaria. Over 20,000 sick soldiers had to be evacuated from the Eastern Army owing to lack of hospital beds. These losses further diluted the capabilities of the Indian army during the offensive on Arakan.[38]

The Eastern Army commander, Lieutenant General Noel Irwin, had one division, the 14th Indian, with which to advance overland and take all of the Mayu Peninsula. On reaching Foul Point, his forces would assault Akyab across the channel. Noel unwisely chose to keep the 15th Corps commander, General Slim, out of the operational picture. This was problematic, not least because the divisional commander, Major General Wilfrid Lloyd, eventually ended up with nine brigades – thrice the size of a normal division and closer to that of a corps.

The advance on Arakan began on 21 September 1942. Only by early December was Lloyd ready to strike at the Japanese outposts stretching from Maungdaw to Buthidaung. By the end of the month, both these places were under his control – the two Japanese battalions having withdrawn before the attack went in. An advance group from the 47th Indian Infantry Brigade occupied the village of Indin and a patrol reached the objective of Foul Point. And there Lloyd paused and waited for his administrative tail to catch up.

The 14th Division's sauntering advance and leisurely halt allowed the Japanese to reinforce their defensive positions in Donbaik and Rathedaung, and so neutralize the numerical superiority enjoyed by the Indian forces. At Donbaik, the Japanese laid down on a carefully chosen terrain a well-constructed, mutually supporting and brilliantly camouflaged complex of bunkers. Here, for fifty days, they staved off attack after massed attack, inflicting heavy casualties on the battalions of the 14th Division. The Indian units repeatedly attempted costly frontal assaults: the notions of outflanking, infiltration and encirclement remained beyond their tactical and operational horizons. Tanks were used in a piecemeal fashion without the faintest attempt at all-arms attacks. The situation was much the same in Rathedaung. None of this was surprising, given that the Indian army was hardly trained to fight this way.

In early February 1943, over four months into the campaign, Irwin asked Wavell 'to what extent we would be advised to continue to incur casualties if you are prepared to accept the unpalatable conclusion ... that "AKYAB" is too remote for this spring season'. Lloyd, in turn, informed Irwin that he wished to go on the defensive. Wavell, however, insisted on dealing 'a strong blow on the Mayu Peninsula'. 'I should like to finish up this campaigning season', he told Irwin, 'with a real success which will show both our own troops and the Jap that we can and mean to be top dog.'[39] Irwin blamed his subordinate commanders but proved incapable of shaping the battle. The bloody stalemate was demoralizing the troops. And fresh reinforcements proved too raw and untrained to take on the tenacious Japanese.

On 7 March, the Japanese launched their counter-offensive. Their use of infiltration on a wide front and the establishment of roadblocks to prevent a retreat should have been familiar to the Indian forces – but were not. The result was a replay in miniature of the fiascos in Malaya and Burma. Towards the end of the month, Lloyd ordered one of his brigades to withdraw in order to avoid encirclement. This was contrary to orders from Wavell, so Lloyd was sacked and replaced by Major General Cyril Lomax. The new divisional commander, too, strived to impose order on the fast deteriorating situation. Eventually, he pulled back his forces to defend the Maungdaw–Buthidaung road. But the division's situation remained parlous. Morale was at an all-time low; malaria sapped the strength of the troops; and desertions became a regular occurrence.[40]

As Lomax struggled to cope, Slim was belatedly brought into the fray. After examining the situation, he wrote a perceptive letter to Irwin:

> The British troops are tired and they are 'browned off' with operations in Arakan as a whole. Their health is deteriorating ... The Indian

troops . . . are tired too, but with them the fault is in the inferior quality in physique, training and spirit of the men, especially the drafts that have joined in Arakan.[41]

Indeed, when the Japanese attacked the defences covering Maungdaw and Buthidaung on 24 April, a well-prepared plan to trap the Japanese spearhead collapsed like a house of cards, owing to failures by two tired and demoralized battalions. By 15 May, the Indian army evacuated the port of Maungdaw and beat a hasty and confused retreat from Buthidaung. The Japanese decision to halt at that line let off the British and Indian units without further casualties. The first attempt to take the fight to the Japanese had ended in a humiliating defeat.

Even as the Arakan offensive was in meltdown, Wavell was pedalling back from Operation Anakim. By early April 1943, he was complaining to the chiefs that the actual allotment of shipping to India fell far short of the monthly requirements agreed for Anakim. The target date of 15 November, he declared, was already impossible to meet. Wavell was right: the decision at Casablanca to press ahead with Anakim had been taken on a misconception of the amount of shipping that would be available over the next six months. And the chiefs recognized that they had erred.

Later that month Wavell travelled to London to confer with the chiefs of staff. After some days of discussion, it was agreed that Anakim could not be attempted in the dry season of 1943–44. Apart from operational and logistical problems, it was felt that launching Anakim would commit British forces to a major operation that was not essential for the ultimate defeat of Japan. Only minor land operations should be undertaken from Assam in the coming campaign season.[42] The challenge, of course, was to convince the Americans. Opinion in Washington was divided. President Roosevelt seemed ready to drop the idea: '"Anakim out". Keep China going by air', he had scribbled in a note. But the joint chiefs wanted to take 'vigorous steps' to launch Anakim.[43]

In early May, Churchill and the chiefs of staff travelled to Washington for the 'Trident' Conference. The prime minister had never been enthusiastic about an overland invasion of Burma – an undertaking that he likened to munching a porcupine quill by quill. Examining the chiefs' latest proposal, he employed a marine metaphor: 'Going into swampy jungles to fight the Japanese is like going into the water to fight a shark. It is better to entice him into a trap or catch him on a hook and then demolish him with axes after hauling him out on to dry land.'[44] Churchill favoured a landing at some unexpected point in the crescent stretching from Moulmein to Timor. This slotted smoothly into place with Wavell's thinking about alternatives to Anakim.

At the conference, the British delegation expressed their inability to take on Operation Anakim. The reconquest of Burma, however desirable, was not 'indispensable from the military point of view'. Even if Anakim were successful, the Burma Road was unlikely to be open until mid-1945. After considering alternatives such as Sumatra, the joint planners recommended concentrating Allied efforts on increasing the airlift to China and operations in northern Burma. Wavell and the British chiefs of staff sought to whittle down the latter, but Stilwell insisted that abandoning Anakim would devastate Chinese morale. Roosevelt eventually came round to the view that operations should be undertaken to clear the Japanese from north Burma and open a road from Ledo to Yunnan.

The planners then came up with an outline of land operations that fell into three groups. First, a British-Chinese offensive to open the Burma Road by a three-pronged attack: three Chinese divisions advancing from Ledo to Myitkyina; ten Chinese divisions from Yunnan to a line from Myitkyina to Bhamo to Lashio; and three British-Indian divisions from Imphal to Mandalay. Second, simultaneous operations to establish airbases on the Arakan coast. Third, following the above, to capture Rangoon by overland advances from Prome and Bassein and from the north through Mandalay. The British were deeply sceptical. Wavell believed that such an operation could not be mounted in time; and if it were launched, British forces could not be maintained during the monsoon in Mandalay. The outcome, he insisted, 'would be that we should sacrifice large quantities of men and would achieve nothing'.[45] In fact, these plans would be the basis of the successful British campaign in Burma the following year – if under very different circumstances. The finally agreed resolution at the Trident Conference dropped the third phase entailing the capture of Rangoon.

In the course of the conference, news was received of the debacle in Arakan with the loss of Buthidaung and Maungdaw. The Indian army and its commander came under considerable flak. Churchill was rigid with reproach, describing the campaign as among the most disappointing and discreditable of the war. Although Wavell tried to outline the constraints under which the operations were undertaken, the prime minister was convinced that the Indian army and the India Command needed to be shaken up. Linlithgow had already suggested to Amery that the commander-in-chief should be freed from operational responsibilities: they were detracting from his other roles in India. Amery had agreed and recommended to Churchill the creation of a separate supreme commander for South-East Asia operations and the establishment of India Command as a base for organizing, training and supporting the forces. Churchill had also discussed this with Wavell, who observed that the supreme commander should be British, with an American deputy.[46] Wavell considered himself the 'obvious choice' for the appointment – though he felt that Churchill was disinclined to give him the job.[47]

In the wake of the Arakan fiasco, the prime minister decided to go ahead with the creation of a South-East Asia Command (SEAC). For some months past, Churchill had also been looking for a replacement for Linlithgow, who was due to step down as viceroy. The prime minister decided to kick Wavell upstairs. The decision to appoint the general as viceroy was a sharp departure from the past practice of keeping political and military roles in India resolutely apart. Some old India hands, such as the former viceroy Lord Halifax, felt that Wavell was 'a bad choice, tantamount to saying: "We don't care a d--n about the political side."'[48] Yet, this was precisely why Wavell commended himself to Churchill as a wartime viceroy of India. At Amery's recommendation, Churchill reluctantly agreed to reappoint General Auchinleck as commander-in-chief of India. But he was clear that Auchinleck would not be given command of SEAC. Not only was Churchill disappointed with Auchinleck's performance in North Africa, but he believed that the latter's cautious approach 'would rightly excite the deepest suspicion in the United States that we are only playing and dawdling with the war in this theatre'.[49]

Churchill's assessment was not wholly off-beam, though Auchinleck's caution came in handy to him in dealing with the Americans. By the time the next Allied conference was held in mid-August 1943, Auchinleck had been in harness for some six weeks. Prior to the conference, the new commander-in-chief had informed London that the lines of communication to Assam could not adequately be improved in time to support both the increased airlift to China and the proposed ground offensive into northern Burma. Further, the levels of shipping required to support the amphibious attacks on the Arakan coast would heavily impede the conduct of Allied operations in the Mediterranean. This enabled Churchill once again to pull out his pet idea of a strike on Sumatra – and thence Singapore – as an alternative to operations in Burma.

At the conference in Quebec, the Americans were insistent on sticking to the earlier agreement. They maintained that reopening the Burma Road, and indeed the eventual recapture of the whole of Burma, were imperative. Churchill's suggestion of Sumatra was shot down by Roosevelt. The president argued that the Japanese could be defeated only by an advance across the Pacific towards Formosa (Taiwan) and an advance from Burma into China proper. Ultimately, it was agreed that northern Burma should receive priority for the coming campaign season, while the target of an amphibious strike was left open.[50]

In any event, the Americans felt that the British were reluctant to use their resources in India to retake Burma and reopen the road to China. The British seemed far more interested in harbouring their strength for a strike at Singapore.[51] Their desire to establish SEAC under a British supreme commander was seen as a move in the same direction: to recover the prestige of the British Empire. As Stilwell's political adviser, John Davies, trenchantly noted in October 1943: 'We have chosen to bring a third-class island kingdom back to its anachronistic position as a first-class empire. We are rejecting the opportunity to move boldly forward with the historical tide.'[52]

SEAC was soon dubbed 'Save England's Asiatic Colonies'. Stilwell's staff sang: 'The Limeys make policy, Yank fights the Jap, / And one gets its Empire and one takes the rap.'[53] Davies pointed out in December that by participating in SEAC operations, 'we become involved in the politically explosive colonial problems . . . we compromise ourselves not only with the colonial peoples of Asia but also the free peoples of Asia, including the Chinese'. It would, therefore, be best to restrict involvement in SEAC: 'after the recapture of North Burma there comes a parting of ways. The British will wish to throw their main weight southward for the repossession of colonial empire.'[54]

As supreme commander of SEAC, Churchill nominated one of his favourites: Admiral Louis Mountbatten. As a naval commander and military planner, Mountbatten was something of a train wreck. His principal credentials for the new job were his royal pedigree and his acceptability to the Americans. Soon after arriving in Delhi, Mountbatten paid a visit to Chiang Kai-shek; his first task was to effect a reconciliation between the Generalissimo and his American chief of staff. Chiang and Stilwell periodically fell out, though on this occasion Chiang was determined to get Stilwell sacked. Mountbatten's charm and persuasive powers prevailed: Stilwell stayed put. The admiral hit it off with Chiang and his wife. 'He is a most arresting person,' wrote Mountbatten, 'far the most impressive Chinese I have ever seen.' As for Soong Mei-ling, 'She has a beautiful figure and the most lovely legs and feet imaginable.'[55] Mountbatten briefed Chiang about the decisions arrived at at Quebec and secured his agreement to place Chinese forces in Burma under Mountbatten's overall command with Stilwell as his deputy.

Mountbatten had his own ideas about the best way to implement the decisions of Quebec. On 1 November, he informed the combined chiefs of staff that the best objective for the amphibious operation would be the Andaman Islands.[56] Affirming his amphibious orientation, Mountbatten shifted his headquarters from India to Ceylon, though the botanical gardens of Kandy were rather removed from the island's coastline. Much discussion ensued between SEAC, New Delhi, London and Washington on whether the land operations in north Burma (Operation Tarzan) should be coupled with an amphibious operation for the capture of the Andamans (Operation Buccaneer) or one aimed at Akyab (Operation Bullfrog). Stilwell was soon disenchanted with the supreme commander: 'The Glamour Boy is just that. He doesn't wear well and I begin to wonder if he knows his stuff. Enormous staff, endless walla-walla, but damned little fighting.'[57]

The next Allied conference was held in Cairo in November 1943. Chiang Kai-shek was invited for the first time: as an equal partner. Since the combined chiefs had not yet made up their mind about the amphibious leg of the offensive, Mountbatten presented the plans for Tarzan. Chiang repeated his long-held views on the need to control the Bay of Bengal alongside a thrust into Burma from the north. The Chinese also claimed that Tarzan was insufficiently ambitious: it should encompass the reoccupation of all of Burma, though their forces would not operate south of Lashio. The Allied chiefs explained to Chiang that Tarzan was the first step towards capturing the entire country. Roosevelt, too, assured him that a considerable amphibious operation would be undertaken in the next few months. Chiang changed his mind thrice and left the conference without according his approval to Tarzan. Mountbatten pursued him to Ramgarh and persuaded him to come aboard – on the understanding that Operation Buccaneer would be launched in the spring of 1944.[58]

By the time the Allies met next, in Tehran, in late November 1943, no agreement had been reached on Buccaneer. Churchill felt that it was best postponed until the Allied landings on Western Europe had been successfully completed. After some consideration, Roosevelt sent a laconic message to Churchill: 'Buccaneer is off'. He also cabled Chiang asking if he would be willing to go ahead with Tarzan despite their inability to stage a major amphibious operation in the Bay of Bengal. 'Britain is not sincere about advancing into Burma', noted Chiang. Their attitude was 'suffocating our economy'.[59]

Chiang sent a convoluted reply, suggesting he might be willing – provided the Americans loaned China a billion dollars in gold. Even as Mountbatten toyed with various options for a smaller-scale amphibious operation, Chiang sent another message that he was not willing to play ball without a major naval show. By mid-January, Mountbatten realized that it was too late to put into motion any amphibious operation for that year. So the supreme commander issued a directive rescinding all previous orders for operations in 1944.

The only operations that would now be undertaken were an overland advance on Arakan, a limited probe from Imphal–Tamu, an advance on the northern front to cover the construction of the Ledo road, and operations by Long Range Patrol groups.[60] Stilwell and the American chiefs made one more attempt to persuade the British to launch a serious offensive on Myitkyina. Roosevelt agreed and a telegram was sent to Churchill. But the prime minister refused to consent.[61]

And so the Allies remained deadlocked on Burma. The impasse would be eventually overcome when the Japanese launched their own offensive on India on 7 March 1944.

14

War Economy

While the Allied statesmen and commanders were debating strategy, India began gearing up its economy for the enormous demands of war. Until early 1942, the Indian economy was hardly operating in wartime mode – the government's attempts at mobilizing it were commensurate with neither the requirements of war nor the latent resources of the country. Nor yet did the government tap into the entrepreneurial energies of the Indian business classes. Indeed, it took rather a narrow view of the kinds of industries that needed to be supported and nurtured. Thus a number of industries were prevented from being set up owing to concerns that they might not deliver the goods quickly, that imports of machinery would eat into shipping, or that they might undercut existing British producers.

Although Indian business was sympathetic to the Allies, and yearned to make the best of the war, it felt rebuffed by the government. The only crumb of comfort held out to the business community was the appointment in mid-1941 of a director of the Tata Group, Homi Mody, as supply member of the viceroy's Executive Council. Then, too, the government's unwillingness to associate Indian industry in managing the war economy, or even in exercises at stock-taking such as the Roger Supply Mission of 1940, rankled deeply. The authorities' attempts to arm-twist certain industries aggravated their concerns. In July 1941, for instance, GHQ India demanded the use of the Defence of India Act to take control of the entire textile industry, and so ensure the necessary quantum of production for military requirements. While the Supply Department protested against such a drastic move, it agreed that steps must be taken to ensure that government orders were accepted and delivered. The industry responded by collectively rallying against the government. Although a compromise was worked out, by appointing an advisory committee with representatives from the mill-owners' association,[1] the government's ham-handed methods grated on Indian businessmen.

Relations between business and government took another hit following the Japanese advance into Burma. At the end of January 1942, the India Office cabled New Delhi about the 'great military importance [of] "scorched earth" policy in territory invaded by enemy'. Military installations and telegraph networks, harbours and railway bridges, oil stocks and refineries, key industries and power stations: all must be denied to the enemy.[2] Given the concentration of industrial plant in and around Calcutta, the government began actively considering options in the event of a Japanese thrust into eastern India. While priority was accorded to physically removing key plants and materials to distant locations, the viceroy and his advisers were alert to the limitations of any such effort during a crisis. 'In the last resort', wrote Linlithgow's private secretary, 'we must be prepared to deny the use of valuable plant and materials. A junior officer of the Royal Engineers has been deputed to prepare for demolitions.'[3]

When the word got around, Indian business howled in protest. At its annual session of March 1942, the Federation of Indian Chambers of Commerce and Industry (FICCI) denounced the adoption of a scorched-earth or 'denial' policy. G. D. Birla trenchantly observed that

> we cannot be sure what the position of the enemy in respect of India will be, but supposing in a time of panic we just destroy all the good work that we have done in half a century and if after a few months or few weeks we find ourselves able to push back the enemy into the sea, we would realize that just in a mood of panic we have destroyed all the good work that we have done in a generation.[4]

Eventually, while some industrial plant was relocated to other parts of India the government did not destroy anything in haste.

Political developments, however, imposed additional strains on the relationship between Indian business and government. After the failure of the Cripps Mission, leading businessmen urged the government not to go into a sulk. As the Congress mulled the Quit India resolution, Purshottamdas Thakurdas, J. R. D. Tata and Birla, among others, wrote a joint letter to the viceroy:

> We are all businessmen and, therefore, need hardly point out that our interest lies in peace, harmony, goodwill and order throughout the country. We are also nationalists but we may add that our nationalism is not of a narrow type . . . We submit that the need of the hour is not strong action, but a proper and sympathetic understanding and tactful handling of a grave situation. We feel that in the midst of war political freedom to India could be granted.[5]

The outbreak of the Quit India revolt resulted in the upheaval that the industrialists feared. Yet the FICCI came out in support of Gandhi and deplored the repression unleashed by the government. Some industrialists, such as the textile magnate Kasturbhai Lalbhai of Ahmedabad, quietly encouraged their workers to go on a prolonged strike.[6]

Indian business's support for the Congress led to the airing of some strange ideas in London. Stafford Cripps urged the war cabinet to consider funding a programme of social and economic reform in India. 'The conditions of the Indian workers, who are today responsible for the output of munitions etc.', he wrote, 'is certainly appallingly bad compared to those of the other countries.' The 'main obstructions' to the improvement of their lot were the Indian capitalists, 'many of whom are the financial backers of Congress. They are not as a rule actual members of Congress but they in fact give Congress its financial backing.' If the British government could come out in support of workers and peasants by immediate action, 'the struggle in India would no longer be between Indian and British upon the nationalist basis, but between the classes in India upon an economic basis. There would thus be a good opportunity to rally the mass of Indian Opinion to our side.'[7]

The Conservatives in the cabinet, especially Churchill, were intrigued by the suggestion from the socialist.[8] But Amery was 'quite clear' that such a programme would have 'no effect'. The Indian government warned that the capitalists would describe any such move as an act of 'death-bed repentance' and the funds given as 'conscience money' to make up the 'organised loots' of the past.[9] Although Cripps persisted for some months, his plan proved a non-starter.

The long-standing political stalemate, however, limited popular support for the war and constrained the government's ability to mobilize the economy. The problems were evident during Linlithgow's last months in office. Yet the viceroy remained impervious to the need to take any serious steps on the political front. With the Congress leadership securely behind bars, neither Delhi nor London showed any interest in breaking the logjam.

At the end of 1942, Gandhi informed Linlithgow that he intended to go on a hunger strike. The government had blamed him for recent violence and expected him to condemn it. 'Convince me of my error or errors', he wrote, 'and I shall make ample amends.' Linlithgow politely replied that he could not but regard Gandhi as the leader of the Congress and expect him to dissociate himself from the Quit India resolution. Gandhi disagreed, insisting that the government had 'goaded the people to the point of madness' and unleashed 'leonine' violence on them. His fast would begin on 9 February 1943 and end three weeks later.[10]

The viceroy and the war cabinet contemplated three options: keep Gandhi in prison until he died; release him when in immediate danger of death; or adopt 'cat and mouse' tactics of releasing him at the first sign of danger. The war cabinet initially left it to Linlithgow to make the call. The viceroy conducted a poll among his provincial governors: five out of eleven preferred the first option. His Executive Council, however, unanimously favoured releasing Gandhi for the period of the fast – on the understanding that he would be taken back into custody when the fast ended.[11] Just as Linlithgow was leaning towards this option, Churchill convinced the war cabinet not to release Gandhi unless there was imminent danger of his death. 'This, our hour of triumph everywhere in the world, was not the time to crawl before a miserable little old man who had always been our enemy.'[12]

Linlithgow staved off prime ministerial pressure and took the position urged by his Executive Council. But Gandhi refused to go on a fast if released from prison. The fast began on 10 February and Linlithgow now toughened his stance. The outpouring of popular sentiment; a resolution of the central legislature; the resignation of three Indian members of the Executive Council: none could persuade or force the viceroy to release Gandhi. After eleven days, Gandhi's health was precarious. Although the government allowed doctors to attend to him, Gandhi refused intravenous feeding. On the thirteenth day, he sipped a bit of water. It was only on 2 March, however, that he ended his fast. Even thereafter, Linlithgow rebuffed calls from various quarters to release Gandhi.

When Wavell was appointed viceroy in October 1943, Indian politics stood in suspended animation. The new viceroy's attempt to raise the topic of politics was snubbed by the prime minister. Wavell therefore focused on restoring the relations between his government and the business community to an even keel. Notwithstanding the tension between government and business, Japan's entry into the war acted as a catalyst for the Indian economy. For one thing, the enormous requirements of turning India into a major Allied base ensured that the government could not do business as usual. For another, the United States began to take a keen interest in the war economy of India.

In late 1941, the Roosevelt administration had designated India as a direct recipient of Lend-Lease, and in early March 1942, the United States sent a technical mission to assess the needs of Indian industry in supporting the war effort. Led by Henry Grady, a former assistant secretary of state, the mission stayed in India for five weeks and produced its report towards the end of May. The report stated that

> India is of great strategic importance to the cause of the United Nations [i.e. the Allies] . . . because India can be utilised as a base for an offensive against the Japanese in Burma, because India and Burma are essential links in the efforts of the United Nations to supply China with war materials, and, finally, because India possesses great natural resources which . . . must be fully developed for the benefit of the United Nations.[13]

The remainder of the report was at once a sweeping survey of Indian industry and a sharp indictment of the Indian government. 'The Government of India and the industries of India, with few exceptions', the report noted, 'were not organized on a war basis.' No single official or group of officials was charged with co-ordinating the entire industrial war effort. A large number of industrial plants were 'mere jobbing shops'. The seriously congested railways plied goods with 'little regard for their importance or ultimate use'. Despite a shortage of electric power, no attempt was being made to reduce consumption for non-essential purposes. There was no method for prioritizing projects and allocating resources. Prices were rising but there was no mechanism for their control. The lack of co-ordination and inefficiency in the war economy were epitomized in a ship repair plant in Bombay which produced shoe-nails for the army and railway switch gear, while 'more than 100 ships waited in the harbor for major and minor repairs'.[14]

The report made specific recommendations to jump-start all major industries: transportation and communication, petroleum and minerals, iron and steel, shipping and armaments, motor vehicles and machine tools. The mission insisted that Indian workers had the mechanical aptitude to become 'skilled craftsmen after a short period of training'. In conclusion, the report emphasized 'India's great potentialities for industrial production because of its vast natural and human resources'.[15]

The Grady Mission's recommendations and plan came with a price tag of $212 million. The US joint chiefs felt, however, that the programme would throw an enormous burden on American shipping, machine tools and raw materials. Economic concerns were overlaid with strategic ones. The Anglophobe Admiral King reacted to the mission's conclusion that 'the value . . . of an India strengthened by a program of this magnitude will be very great' by scribbling on the margins: 'especially to England after the war'.[16]

The Indian government did not take kindly to the tenor of the report. All the same, the viceroy accepted the force of its arguments about the need to rationalize war industry and production. The problems were two-fold. First, the government clung to its traditional ideology of non-intervention in the economy. In practice, it was already intervening in many ways, although officials were concerned about 'our inability to step in and effectively take over inefficient plants'. Second, and more importantly, the government was concerned about the 'state of political opinion'. The nub of the matter was that the government was unsure, given the prevailing political deadlock, how the people would respond to any attempt to regiment economic life. The problem of war production was as much political as economic.

Still, the demands of the war impelled the government towards greater mobilization of the economy by adopting measures akin to those suggested by the Roger and Grady missions. From early 1942, the Indian economy began moving into a higher gear. GDP in real terms expanded during the war years by 10.6 per cent. In fact, in 1943–44 it expanded by 12.3 per cent before contracting a bit over the next two years. The growth in output was comparable to countries like the Soviet Union and Britain.[17]

The state played an important role in spurring industrial production, especially after 1941. The various government departments and bodies dealing with war supplies – the Department of War Supply, the War Supply Board, the Defence Council of Supply, the Stores Department, the Directorate of Contracts – began co-ordinating

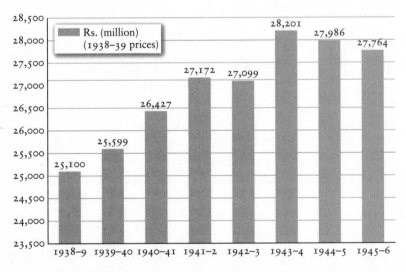

Source: S. Sivasubramonian, *National Income of India in the Twentieth Century* (New Delhi: Oxford University Press, 2000), Table 6.10

Figure 2. Real GDP of India, 1938–45

their activities and reducing duplication of effort. An Industrial Planning Organization was set up under the Department of Supply and staffed by experts from various sectors. The department also established links with industry through a plethora of advisory committees and panels that drew on technical expertise and experience. The government began encouraging industrial production by a variety of means. Key industries were provided with raw materials at controlled prices and information asymmetries were reduced by ensuring close contact between requisitioners and suppliers. Types and sizes of stores procured by the government were minimized to achieve standardization. Regular inspections were held to provide technical assistance and ensure quality control.

The government also helped industrialists to start new ventures or expand existing ones by providing capital assistance and the promise of protection for those ventures whose post-war prospects seemed uncertain. Capital assistance took the form of factories that were erected partly at government cost: finishing mills, clothing units, tyre retreading and repair, footwear manufacturers, including the famous Bata Shoe factory near Calcutta. Nearly 160 private factories – many of them undertaking heavy engineering – were expanded thanks to government finance.[18] In effect, the government was adopting a policy of import-substituting industrialization – one that would be continued in independent India.

The ordnance factories run by the government turned out impressive quantities of arms and ammunition during the war years: 1.73 million small arms and 980 million rounds of ammunition; 8.73 million artillery shells; 4.78 million mortar bombs, grenades and mines; and (starting supply from scratch) 6,250 armoured vehicles.[19] The government's procurement programme led to a large increase in industrial output. The basic industries received a much-needed spurt. The production during the war of steel ingots expanded by 34.4 per cent; of finished steel by 30.7 per cent; of sulphuric acid by 45.5 per cent; and of cement by 42.2 per cent.[20] Increases in quantity were accompanied by improvements in quality. For instance, the Tata Iron and Steel Company in Jamshedpur undertook research into the production of special alloys such as ferro-tungsten and ferro-vanadium. In consequence, they were able to develop and supply special alloy steel products for requirements ranging from rail wagon axles to bul-let-proof armour plates.[21] These developments in turn enabled the growth of another vital industry: machine tools.

Prior to the war there was no established machine-tool industry in India – a problem that was noted by the Chatfield committee, among others. Even simple machine tools like lathes and ordinary milling machines were imported, mainly from Britain and Germany. The shortage of engineering craftsmen was a major handicap in setting up a local machine-tool industry – and the predominance of imports did little to rectify this situation. At the outbreak of war, fewer than 100 basic machine tools were being produced in India – by larger engi-neering workshops for their own consumption. Only after the fall of France in 1940 did the government wake up to the importance of machine tools for India's industrial war effort.

The following year, a machine-tool control order was passed, whereby a licence was required for the importation, production and sale of machine tools. A machine-tool controller began liaising with industry to encourage local manufacture of up to 60 per cent of India's requirements. Five Indian firms were identified as promising entrants into the field and provided with American and British equip-ment. Among these was Kirloskars – an Indian company that had been producing steel furniture but wanted to branch out into machine tools for a while. The Great Depression, however, had put paid to their plans. With the government's support, the Kirloskar brothers were able to break into this industry, and after independence Kirlos-kars would grow into a big conglomerate.[22] The government helped firms like Kirloskars with planning and costing, standardization and rationalization of production. And it took over bulk ordering of machine tools and their distribution to users. By 1942–43, over a hundred licensed firms in India were manufacturing machine tools of various types, from drills to special machines for munition produc-tion. By 1944–45, the annual production of graded machine tools had shot up to 4,200.[23]

The performance of the manufacturing sector was impressive. Real output (net value added) in manufacturing expanded during the war by 61.6 per cent. Yet productivity (net value added per worker in real terms) increased by a mere 1.63 per cent. The increased output was

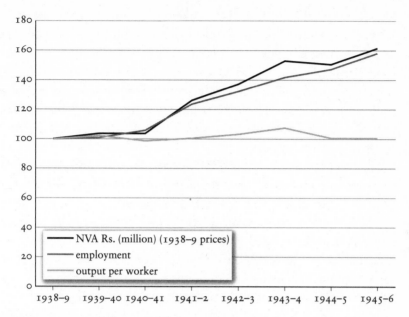

Source: S. Sivasubramonian, *National Income of India in the Twentieth Century* (New Delhi: Oxford University Press, 2000), Table 4.27

Figure 3. Net value added in manufacturing industries

essentially achieved by adding 1.1 million men and women to the industrial workforce. Labour productivity of the economy as a whole lagged much behind. Output per worker increased during the war by 3.3 per cent: even during the peak year of 1943–44 it touched only 7.3 per cent.[24] Put differently, the expansion of the Indian economy was due more to the greater use of manpower than higher investment or better machinery. The increased production of textiles in Ahmedabad, to take but one example, was not due to an increase in the number of mills. Production capacity was enhanced by increasing the size of the workforce and by introducing a three-shift system to use the machines more intensively. The number of people working night shifts went up over fourfold during the war.[25]

Irrespective of the drivers of production, business as a whole did rather well during the war. Aggregate paid-up capital of joint-stock companies in India had already risen by 17.6 per cent in 1942–43 – and this was before industrial output really began accelerating.[26] Big business registered spectacular gains. The net profit earned by Sir

Shri Ram's Delhi Cloth Mills in 1945 was almost seven times that of 1939. The operating profit margin – how much it made for each rupee of sale – of the company went from 12.4 per cent in 1938 to 18.4 per cent in 1945.[27] In fact, DCM's figures for the last year of the war understate the profits as demand had declined by then. The operating profit margin of the Kasturbhai group of mills rose from 1.19 per cent in 1939 to a peak of 38.79 per cent in 1943, before coming down to 18.12 per cent in 1945.[28]

Big business was not the only one to flourish, however. Smaller entrepreneurs too found several new avenues during the war. And nor were they necessarily British- or Indian-owned. Søren Kristian Toubro and Henning Holck-Larsen were young engineers from Denmark working in India for a Danish firm. Just before war broke out, they quit their jobs and decided to form their own venture for supplying capital goods and machinery to Indian companies. Hitler's occupation of Denmark in 1940 put paid to their plans. Responding to the growing wartime demand for dairy equipment in India, they set up a small workshop in Bombay that began producing butter-churners and unsophisticated pasteurizers. Thereafter, they were pulled into a diverse set of activities, including supplying anti-magnetic cable devices to protect merchant ships, and establishing a small chemical plant to service the Tata industries.

Along with two Jewish refugees from Germany, the Danish engineers floated a company with a paid-up capital of Rs. 120,000. Apart from almost monopolizing the production of celluloid umbrella handles, the company also provided automatic chargers and containers for mortars. In June 1943, the partners launched a new company: a floating workshop to service ships in the crowded Bombay docks. Starting with a share capital of Rs. 300,000, the company showed profits of Rs. 55,000 in the first six months of its existence. Towards the end of the war, the Danish engineers realized their original ambition to supply capital equipment. They struck a deal with the American company Caterpillar, which not only allowed them to market tractors in India but also gave them a sizeable stock of wartime earth-moving equipment imported by the US army.[29] In independent India, Larsen & Toubro would rise to become a leading engineering, construction and manufacturing group.

During the war, employment in all factories increased by 59 per cent over the 1939 level. The number of factories, however, increased only by 40 per cent. Government-owned factories rose by a massive 245 per cent and accounted for about 17 per cent of the industrial workforce. At the same time, employment in private factories increased by about 35 per cent. In contrast to countries like Britain, though, the composition of the labour force did not change much. In 1939, women and children accounted for 19.8 per cent of the total workers in factories, mines and plantations. In 1944, they comprised 17.7 per cent of the workforce.[30]

Indian labour also became more organized. The number of registered trade unions and their total membership almost doubled in these years.[31] As businesses began raking in profits, the workers were better positioned to bargain collectively for their wages and other demands. The number of stoppages – strikes and other disruptions – increased during the war years. Two-thirds and more of these stoppages were due to demands for better wages, bonuses and dearness allowances or for fewer working hours. Interestingly, while the number of strikes rose, the man-days of production lost showed a significant downward trend. The two anomalous years are easily accounted for: in 1940 there was a general strike in the cotton mills of Bombay; in 1942 there was considerable disruption owing to the wave of panic that washed over the country.

Industrial Disputes during the War

Year	Number of stoppages	Workers involved	Man-days lost	Wage and related	Others	Wage related (%)
1939	406	409,189	4,992,795	320	86	79
1940	322	452,539	7,577,281	275	47	85
1941	359	291,054	3,330,503	297	62	83
1942	694	772,653	5,779,965	508	186	73
1943	716	525,088	2,342,287	464	252	65
1944	658	550,015	3,447,306	540	118	82
1945	820	747,530	4,054,499	673	147	82

Source: *Indian Labour Yearbook 1946* (Delhi: Government of India, 1948), Table 32.

The drop in man-days lost was partly due to the elaborate machinery of industrial dispute resolution evolved and used by the government – especially after the appointment of B. R. Ambedkar as labour member of the viceroy's Executive Council in mid-1942. But it was also partly due to the fact that from 1942, the Communist Party of India, which exercised growing influence over the labour movement, switched its stance and supported the war effort.

The CPI asked the workers to focus on increasing productivity and downplay disputes with the management. 'Win freedom and bread' was the slogan they offered. Striking at work was described as a 'betrayal' of the working classes. Important labour unions followed suit. As Gangadhar Chitnis, general secretary of Bombay's Girni Kamgar Union, observed: 'Let the international struggle be over, then we can go on with our own struggle.'[32] The Bombay communist leader, Lalji Pendse, put it more graphically: if labour did not help the war effort, the British might lose and then the workers 'would no longer be able to ventilate their grievances as the invaders would shoot them'.[33] Indeed, overtly political strikes occurred on a large scale only during the Quit India revolt of 1942, when labour in several parts of the country went on strike for up to three months, protesting against the government's crackdown.[34]

The bottlenecks in industrial production came not from labour but from three other supply-side constraints. In the first place, there was a serious problem with the Indian railways. The war placed a significant burden on the railways by requiring them to transport unprecedented levels of personnel and goods. While the number of passengers carried during the six years of war increased by 75 per cent, the number of passenger-miles more than doubled. While in 1938–39 each passenger was transported over 35 miles on average, the figure increased to nearly 41 miles by the end of the war. Similarly, the tonnage of goods transported by rail increased by 32 per cent.

The burden on the railways rose sharply from early 1942. The Japanese advances resulted in the closure of shipping lanes along the eastern coast of India. Thenceforth, all important supplies had to be moved across India from the west by rail. Military preparations to

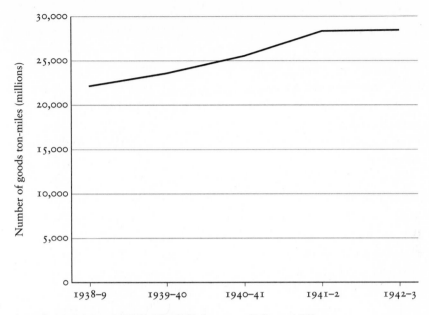

Source: *Statistics Relating to India's War Effort* (Delhi: Government of India, 1947), Table 33

Figure 4. Freight rail traffic, 1938/9–1942/3

meet the Japanese threat and to prepare India as a major base for the Allied effort added a crushing load on to the railways. Until the end of April 1943, for instance, the railways had to carry almost 5.5 million tons of freight simply for airfield construction. In early 1944, the Indian government estimated that the shortfall in rail transport for civilian requirements amounted to 22 per cent of the traffic carried in 1942–43. They may have understated the problem by assuming that all steel and cement output was only for military purposes.[35]

The inability to meet civilian, including industrial, needs stemmed from several sources. First, between September 1939 and December 1941, India had sent to the Middle East and North Africa some 1,500 miles of tracks, 206 locomotives and 8,000 wagons – all of which amounted to at least a tenth of its railway equipment. Two railway workshops had also been handed over to the military for munition production. Not surprisingly, by mid-1942 Wavell was demanding new locomotives and wagons to meet India's war demands. This shortfall was compounded by a second problem. The 41,000-mile rail network in India was made up of four different gauges: a broad-gauge, a metre-gauge, and two narrow gauges. About 48 per cent of the network, connecting the most economically important parts of India, was broad-gauge. This – as well as the other gauges used in India – differed from the standard gauge used in the railways of Britain, Canada, the United States and most of Europe. In consequence, India's attempts to import railway equipment faced a double problem of different specifications as well as high global demand.[36]

Between July 1942 and September 1943, orders were placed in the United States, Canada and Britain for 595 broad-gauge and 605 metre-gauge locomotives as well as 25,649 broad-gauge and 29,480 metre-gauge wagons. By end of 1943, only four broad-gauge and five metre-gauge locomotives had reached India. In April 1944, the Indian government hoped that 185 broad-gauge locomotives would be shipped by the following month. But in practice the entire order was not expected to be completed, if at all, before August 1945. By this time, however, the demands on the railways had increased even further. Apart from the existing order, India wanted another 361 broad-gauge locomotives and 24,700 wagons to meet the military load and to enable 'civil traffic to be restored to a level essential for the maintenance of the economy'. Even if freight were restored to pre-war levels, New Delhi argued, it would require no fewer than an additional 196 broad-gauge locomotives and 14,300 wagons.[37]

The problem of the railways was also exacerbated by the second supply-side bottleneck in the Indian economy: coal. Almost 80 per cent of all coal – and 100 per cent of high-grade coal – was mined in Bengal and Bihar, and from early 1942 there was a substantial decline in coal production in eastern India. The proximity of the coal belt to the eastern theatre of war, as well as nervousness about a Japanese attack, led to a considerable exodus of labour from the collieries. When calm was restored, there was an increasing demand for labour in the military works – construction of airfields and supply bases – that got underway. Coalfield workers found this work both more congenial and more remunerative. The upshot was a mounting

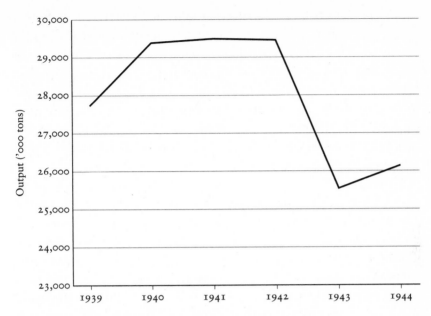

Source: *Statistics Relating to India's War Effort* (Delhi: Government of India, 1947), Table 12

Figure 5. Coal production, 1939–44

scarcity of labour to mine the coalfields and a substantial drop in output.

By the end of 1943, the situation became so critical that the government had to take steps to ensure that other industries, including the military, did not wean away the labourers. Wages for the coalminers were increased, and government contractors were forbidden from recruiting in districts that traditionally supplied workers to the coalfields. In January 1944, the government even raised its own 1,000-strong labour force to work the mines. Perhaps the most striking decision was to allow women to work underground.[38]

The declining production resulted in a shortfall of coal for the railways throughout India. By mid-1943, stocks which should have been maintained at forty-five to seventy-five days of supply had fallen to an average of seventeen days of supply. This naturally limited the operations of the railways. The relationship between coal and the railways ran the other way too. Over 40 per cent of the total tonnage transported by the railways was in fact coal. From the collieries of eastern

India, coal had to be transported to other industrial hubs in north, west and southern India. Apart from the steel industry, which was located near the coalfields of eastern India, coal had to be transported by rail to textile and munition factories in Calcutta and Cawnpore, Bombay and Ahmedabad, Madras and Lahore. From early 1942, railway allotment for the transportation of coal for industrial purposes sharply dropped. Although the Indian government moved to take full control of coal production and distribution, it was caught in the mutually reinforcing problems of coal and railways.

Throughout 1942 and early 1943, the coalfields of Bengal and Bihar had much trouble getting their desired allocation of 2,800–3,000 railway wagons a day. At most, they received only 2,300–2,500 wagons a day. By the end of 1943, when coal output had dropped, more wagons were available but the railways' own stock of coal was running low. More importantly, many factories engaged in war production were subsisting on a day-to-day basis and had to periodically stop work. A complete breakdown was only avoided by cutting back on passenger trains by as much as 40 per cent.[39] Even in August 1944, GHQ India was worried that the 'coal situation as yet shows no appreciable improvement':

> Unless more coal is raised the whole community of India will suffer; it is suffering already; the war effort of India is impeded ... The three greatest consumers of coal in India are the railways, the steel industry and the textile industries. None of them today are getting sufficient coal for their needs, not to mention the innumerable other consumers.[40]

The combined problem of rail and coal placed unprecedented pressures on the Indian forests. Already, the demands of the war were bearing down heavily upon the Forest Department, which was called upon to provide materials for an extraordinary range of military and industrial needs – from ammunition boxes to rifles and textile mill shuttles to electricity transmission poles. The Japanese occupation of Burma dealt a double blow. The demands of war, especially for construction, surged even as imports of teak from Burma ceased.

On top of this came the rising requirements of the railways,

especially for sleepers. The Forest Department was forced to improvise. The vast demand from the railways was met not only from the
deciduous forests, but more and more from evergreen rainforests by
felling hitherto unused timber. At the same time – as with coal – the
growing burdens on the rail network implied a reduced ability to
transport this timber. Further, the drop of production and supply of
coal led many industries to turn to firewood – charcoal – for power.
Some 18,000 tons of charcoal were required every month just for
charcoal-gas. Unsurprisingly, there were shortages. As A. K. Chettiar
observed, from 1942 buses in the city of Madras had begun running
on charcoal-gas and yet 'people were paying the fare and pushing the
buses'.[41]

As a consequence, millions of tons of wood from Indian forests
were felled and turned into grist for the war machine. By 1942–43,
the production of timber alone stood at 863,000 tons – a threefold
increase from 1940–41. By the end of the war, annual production of
timber touched a million tons. The Forest Department and the Forest
Research Institute struggled to ensure that their basic principles of
conservation were not entirely abandoned. Besides, they looked on
at the 'widespread devastation of forest lands which lay outside the
jurisdiction of the Department'. Environmental destruction was also
accelerated by the 'Grow More Food' campaigns launched by the
government to increase the number of acres under crops. Swamps
and grass areas in wastelands were leased out for cultivation during
the war. The pioneer farmers were even provided with weapons for
protection against animals to allow them to push ahead in unculti-
vated areas. The Forest Department was forced to release considerable
areas of scrub-land from its reserves. The cumulative impact of these
policies was immensely destructive.[42]

The rail-coal problem was also directly related to the third major
supply constraint on the Indian economy: food. Here too the problems were mutually reinforcing. On the one hand, the decline in coal
production was due to the labour force moving to find better sources
of income. And the decision to look for better-paid employment in
far-away places essentially arose from the increasing scarcity of food
and its rising price. The decline in coal production, on the other hand,
imposed constraints on the railways – the principal mode of

transporting food-grains in India. In fact, there was no aggregate problem of decline in food production during the war. The production of all cereals – rice, wheat, millet, barley – went from 46.5 million tons in 1938–39 to 55.3 million tons in 1943–44, and dropped slightly to 52.3 million tons in 1944–45. Military procurement of food, for troops as well as workers, never exceeded more than 1.1 per cent of total production in any year. Food exports as a proportion of production were also negligible.[43]

The reason food became a constraint lay partly in the problem of distribution between surplus and deficit regions – a problem that was bound up with that of the railways. More important, however, was the manner in which the government was mobilizing finances for the war.

Following the onset of war in Europe, the old question of who would pay for India's military – especially external – commitments had reared its head again. The financial proposals accompanying the Chatfield plan were overtaken by the burgeoning demands of the war. India not only was called on to raise and send formations for overseas service but had to mobilize the economy to provide for the war effort. In this context the problem of 'joint liabilities' to be shared by the Indian and British governments became more acute and urgent. The two governments negotiated the terms for a fresh financial settlement that was concluded in February 1940.

Under the terms of this settlement, India was to bear a fixed annual sum representing the peacetime costs of the army in India; the costs of such measures deemed to have been undertaken by India in its own interests; and a one-off payment of Rs. 10 million towards the cost of maintaining Indian troops overseas. Britain would shoulder the costs of the Chatfield measures for the modernization of the Indian army; the entire cost of additional forces raised by India for service outside India – but only after they were actually sent abroad; and the cost of military stores supplied by India for all British forces in the Middle East.[44]

Two unforeseen developments during the war sent the sums involved for both governments soaring. After the fall of France in 1940, India's contribution to the war in the Middle East and North

Africa rapidly increased. And then Japan entered the war. Between the financial years 1939–40 and 1940–41, India's financial commitment only doubled, while Britain's shot up from £40 million to £145 million. In 1941–42, India paid £200 million and Britain £230 million. In the next two years, India's share, at £297 million and £343 million respectively, exceeded Britain's at £283 million and £330 million.[45]

Whatever the fluctuation in expenditure, the fact was that Britain was not paying in real time for the bulk of its share. The supplies for the Middle East, for instance, were procured by the Indian government at its own cost. The British government would credit an equivalent amount in sterling – at a fixed exchange rate – to a government of India account in London. So Britain's share of the joint expenditure primarily accumulated as sterling balances in London. Further, the wartime decline in British exports to India – due to both problems of shipping and the absorption of Britain's industrial output for its own war effort – led to a steady increase in India's sterling

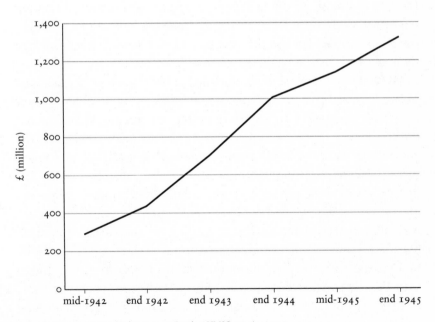

Source: R. S. Sayers, *Financial Policy 1939–45* (London: HMSO, 1956), p. 259

Figure 6. Sterling balances of India, 1942–5

balances. Some of these sterling balances were used to repatriate India's sterling debt, amounting to some £360 million, and so end India's contractual obligations to British bond-holders and annuitants.[46] This led to a remarkable transformation by 1943 in India's longstanding relationship with Britain – from a debtor to a creditor country. The economic rationale of the Indian empire, if ever there was one, evaporated in the white heat of war. Even so, India's sterling balances continued to pile up, reaching a whopping £1,321 million by the end of 1945.

The accumulation of sterling balances amounted to the gaining by India of a substantial claim on Britain's real resources after the war. If India were not paid back by British exports during the war, it would have to be once the war ended. As the significance of the growing sterling balances dawned on the British government, there were increasing calls for a revision of the financial settlement. The chancellor of the exchequer told the war cabinet that the burden on Britain was simply too onerous. The right principle was that of reciprocal aid: 'we should supply without charge whatever costs sterling, and India should supply without charge whatever costs rupees. We should not abandon that principle, even if it cannot be fully implemented at the present time.' For the time being, India's share of expenditure in the settlement had to be increased.[47]

The Indian government was appalled at the suggestion. Linlithgow warned Amery that if the current arrangement were altered, 'very gravest consequences would be quite certain to ensue'. Apart from the predictable protests of the nationalists, even those 'sections of the commercial and well-to-do public which are disposed to be sympathetic now will certainly be alienated'.[48] Amery too advised the British government not to rock the boat. 'Even to-day', he wrote, 'the agreement has worked out much more unfavourably to India than was ever contemplated at the beginning of the war.'[49] Churchill harangued the cabinet at great length about 'the monstrous idea that we should spend millions upon millions in the defence of India, then be told to clear out, and on top of it all owe India vast sums incurred on her behalf'. Although the prime minister stuck to his misapprehension about sterling balances, he was prepared to let the agreement stand – on the understanding that the question could be revisited at a later date.[50]

Influential voices in Britain, however, continued to hold that Britain was being altogether too generous to India. *The Economist* quipped in March 1943 that 'it will surely go down in the Imperial record that Britain gave twice and gave quickly'.[51] Insinuations were also made that Indian supplies were being provided at unconscionably high prices. The following year, no less a personage than John Maynard Keynes published an article in *The Economist* calling for a revision of the 1940 settlement. Keynes advanced a particularly ingenious argument that an increase in India's financial liability would not result in any increase in the real burden on the Indian people. Leading Indian capitalists were already concerned about the mutterings in Whitehall about the sterling balances. They feared that after the war Britain might disavow the balances on the principle of reciprocal aid, or whittle down their rupee value by depreciating sterling. Thakurdas, Birla and others responded ferociously to Keynes's essay, calling it 'cynical and fallacious'. They argued that it 'amounted to a pure and simple repudiation of England's debt to India', and that Britain would not contemplate such a move with any of the Dominions.[52]

Such concerns apart, the immediate problem for India was – to borrow Keynes's famous phrase – how to pay for the war. After all, the real burden of a war cannot be postponed: goods and supplies required by the fighting forces can only be provided through accumulated stocks and current production. The aggregate annual outlay of the Indian government during these years increased by almost forty times, to Rs. 40,000 million. The challenge for the Indian government was to finance these requirements.

There are only three ways of financing a war: to tax, borrow or print money. The Indian government had to resort to all of them in about equal measure. It had recourse both to indirect and to direct taxes. Prior to the war, indirect taxes – customs and excise duties – had been the main source of revenue for the government; the structure of taxation, in the jargon, was rather 'regressive'.[53] During the war, imports plummeted by almost 60 per cent from the pre-war level, due

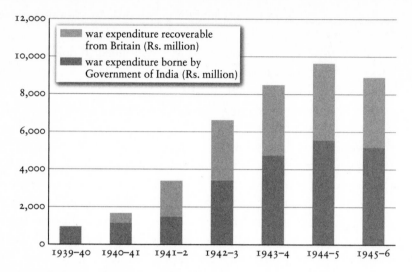

Source: R. N. Poduval, *Finance of the Government of India since 1935*
(Delhi: Premier Publishing, 1951), Table VII

Figure 7. Indian war expenditure, 1939/40–1945/6

to prioritization and disruption of shipping as well as the need to conserve precious foreign exchange for essential war goods. As a consequence, customs duties also fell sharply. Although the government increased the rates, the yield of customs duties continued to fall until 1945–46. The decline in customs revenues led the government to increase excise duties on articles of consumption – both by increasing the rates and by subjecting more items to the levy. Even so, the total yield of indirect taxes continued on a downward slope.[54]

To increase its revenues, the government had to rely more on direct taxes. Indeed, income taxes came to be the mainstay of the government's revenues during the war years. The war thus induced a fundamental change in the structure of taxation from a regressive system to a progressive one. As a proportion of total tax revenue, income tax rose by over threefold. The basic rates of income tax and super tax were left unchanged and increases were obtained by means of surcharges. The highest rate of income tax (including surcharges) during the war touched 30 per cent, while super tax – an additional levy on the very wealthy – went up to a maximum of 66 per cent. The

Tax Yield (Rs. million)

Year	Corporate Tax	Other Income Tax	Total Income Tax	Total Tax Revenue*	Total Revenue#	Income Tax as Proportion of Tax Revenue (%)
1938–39	20.4	152.4	172.8	754.0	844.7	22.9
1939–40	23.8	169.9	193.7	834.6	945.7	23.2
1940–41	41.4	217.9	259.3	813.0	1,076.5	31.9
1941–42	116.6	324.0	440.6	1,053.1	1,345.6	41.8
1942–43	314.0	543.6	857.6	1,357.9	1,770.9	63.2
1943–44	512.8	778.7	1,291.5	1,906.5	2,499.6	67.7
1944–45	836.5	1,076.5	1,913.0	2,804.6	3,357.0	68.2
1945–46	840.6	944.9	1,785.5	3,108.9	3,611.8	57.4
Total 1939–40 to 1945–46	2,685.7	4,055.5	6,741.2	11,878.6	14,607.1	

* Including provincial shares; # Including non-tax revenue such as railways, post and telegraph, salt, etc.

Source: N. C. Sinha and P. N. Khera, Indian War Economy: Supply, Industry and Finance (New Delhi: Combined Inter-Services Historical Section, India & Pakistan, 1962), Table 4.

exemption limit for income tax remained Rs. 2,000, except for 1942–43 when it was temporarily lowered to Rs. 1,500 in order to widen the tax net. Other steps were also taken to increase tax collection, such as the introduction of a pay-as-you-earn system from 1944–45. Corporate tax increased from 6.25 per cent in 1938–39 to 18.75 per cent in 1944–45. From 1940–41, a tax of 50 per cent was imposed on any 'excess profits' earned by businesses over their standard profits earned in the previous years. From 1941–42, this excess profits tax was increased to 66.66 per cent.[55]

Altogether, total revenues from tax and non-tax sources amounted to only 36.6 per cent of the total war expenditure of the Indian government. This was partly because the population base for income tax was meagre: it rose from 286,000 people in 1938–39 to 428,500 in 1945–46. This reflected the fact that India was a country with low per capita income and that the tax bureaucracy was weak. Further, while income tax rates in wartime India became comparable to countries like Britain, corporate tax rates – including the excess profits tax – were considerably lower. Indian business saw the war years as an opportunity to recover from the losses of the previous decade and so resisted further increases in the excess profits tax. And the government was too dependent on industry to apply the squeeze.

To plug the gap, the government resorted to borrowing from the public, and the government's rupee debt increased sharply. Throughout the war, the government was the main borrower in the money markets. From 1943, businesses had to obtain the government's sanction for any new capital issue – sanction that was denied to companies that were not producing essential goods. In consequence, the government was also able to borrow cheaply. The government bonds were floated at 3 per cent interest. The period of maturity of the first tranche in 1940 was six years; thereafter it steadily lengthened to fourteen and twenty-five years in the 1945 issues. Rupee counterparts were also issued for the sterling debt repatriated. Further, the government sought to mobilize small savings. A slew of post-office savings bank schemes as well as national savings certificates and defence savings certificates were offered.[56]

Subscriptions to Government Loans (Rs. million)

Year	Bonds	Small Savings	Total
1940–41	1,125.0	−265.5	859.5
1941–42	743.6	−132.4	611.2
1942–43	1,037.6	−28.0	1,009.6
1943–44	3,155.6	257.1	3,412.7
1944–45	2,222.6	418.1	2,640.7
1945–46	3,292.4	633.5	3,925.9
Total	11,576.8	882.8	12,459.6

Source: N. C. Sinha and P. N. Khera, *Indian War Economy: Supply, Industry and Finance* (New Delhi: Combined Inter-Services Historical Section, India & Pakistan, 1962), Table 9.

Borrowing accounted for 31.2 per cent of the total war outlay of the government. Why did the government not do better given its monopoly in the financial markets? In the first place, the small savings schemes did dismally until 1943–44. In the waves of panic following the fall of France and the Japanese advance towards eastern India, there had been heavy *withdrawals* from post offices across the country. This was triggered by a lack of confidence in the ability of the Raj to hold its own. Only after the military situation began looking up did the small saving offerings find increasing numbers of takers.

In the second place, the government was unwilling to offer a coupon of more than 3 per cent on its bonds. It felt that increasing the interest rates on bonds would be fatal, as it might lead to speculation about a continuous rise in the rates. As the governor of the Reserve Bank of India (RBI) put it, 'the cheap money policy on which the present war is being financed is therefore of vital importance'.[57] Although the subscription rate increased after 1942–43, it did not reach the expected levels. Fluctuations in the yield of the government's regular 3.5 per cent rupee paper suggest that depending on the progress of the war the market's willingness to sponsor the cheap money policy also changed. (Yield is inversely proportional to price, so an increase in yield means a drop in the trading price of the bond. In other words, investors want a higher rate of interest on government

345

borrowings.) The fall of Singapore led to such a sharp fall in the price of securities that in March 1942, the government ordered the fixing of a minimum price for its bonds.[58]

Current Yield of the Government of India's 3.5% Rupee Bond

Date	Yield (%)
Jun-39	3.68
Oct-39	4.38
Apr-40	3.68
Jun-40	4.07
Dec-40	3.72
Jun-41	3.65
Dec-41	3.80
Mar-42	4.17
Jul-42	3.85
Sep-42	3.72
Jun-43	3.70
Dec-43	3.58
Dec-44	3.51
Jun-45	3.44

Source: Calculated from Abhik Ray, *The Evolution of the State Bank of India, Volume 3, 1921–1955* (New Delhi: Sage, 2003), pp. 244, 247, 252, 256–8.

The most important reason for the government's inability to borrow adequately – as indeed its inability to gather sufficient tax – was politics. Given the political gridlock and uncertainty, public support for the war effort was muted. As Amery noted in late 1943:

> The fact cannot be ignored that, of all the united nations none has felt less moral incentive to co-operate in the prosecution of war than India. The Indian war effort . . . is pretty frankly a mercenary undertaking so far as the vast majority of Indians are concerned . . . we have to reckon all the time with strong forces which if not positively pro-Japanese, are certainly anti-British, or at best are indifferent.[59]

In any event, the government filled the remaining gap of 32.2 per cent of the overall war expenditure by cranking the printing presses. This amount was not much short of the share of expenditure incurred by India on behalf of London. Here the sterling balances came in handy. The government asked the RBI to treat sterling balances in London as assets against which it was entitled to print rupee notes of about two and a half times their sterling value.[60] The expansion in currency naturally resulted in galloping inflation and the over-heating of the economy.

Wartime Inflation

Year	General Index of Wholesale Prices	Notes in Circulation (Rs. million)
1938–39	NA	1,743.9
1939–40	125.6	1,981.3
1940–41	114.8	2,280.3
1941–42	137.0	2,874.8
1942–43	171.0	5,134.4
1943–44	236.5	7,771.7
1944–45	244.2	9,686.9
Aug 1945	244.1	11,387.0

Source: *Statistics Relating to India's War Effort* (Delhi: Government of India, 1947), Tables 46, 47.

Although the RBI had an Indian at the helm from mid-1943, it felt legally bound by the Reserve Bank of India Act to issue currency against sterling assets. In public, Governor Chintaman Deshmukh gamely insisted that inflationary financing was unavoidable: 'There is only one country in which the whole of the amount disbursed can be withdrawn by Government by means of taxation and borrowing, and that is, Utopia.'[61] Other Indians associated with the RBI were not to so coy. Manilal Nanavati, a deputy governor until October 1941, wrote to the finance member of the viceroy's Executive Council: 'the expansion of currency against purchases by His Majesty's Government . . . Is this not an abuse of the Reserve Bank Act that the Bank should be used to finance these purchases?'[62] The Indian directors on the board of the RBI, too, were deeply concerned about the spiralling inflation. Purshottamdas Thakurdas suggested that the government should make its borrowing more attractive by offering high interest for short periods and by making the bonds tax free if necessary. Kasturbhai Lalbhai tabled a resolution in May 1944 suggesting a limit on currency expansion.[63]

Indian economists also weighed in with their views in public. C. N. Vakil, a professor at the Bombay School of Economics, published a pamphlet in January 1943, *The Falling Rupee*. This was the first serious attempt at bringing to public notice the problems of war finance. In an excoriating critique of the government's approach, Vakil argued that British demands of India must be met by payment in durable assets; by payment in gold; by the British government raising rupee loans in India; and by the liquidation of British assets in India. A series of pamphlets were published in the following months, including two by G. D. Birla, advocating similar ideas.

In April 1943, Vakil rallied a group of twenty leading Indian economists to issue a joint statement. The economists stated that the inflation in India was 'a deficit-induced, fiat money inflation. It is the most disastrous type of inflation.' Calling for 'immediate and drastic measures to check inflation', they outlined a series of measures to soak up the excessive liquidity in the economy: steeper progression in rates of income tax; absorption of all profits above a limit by taxes or enforced special loans; and a Keynesian 'comprehensive scheme of compulsory savings'.[64] The government took no heed. However, when the Gandhian economist J. C. Kumarappa published articles attacking government policy and quoting extensively from Vakil, he was immediately sentenced to two years' imprisonment.[65]

The war-induced inflation benefited certain sections of Indian society.[66] Big business, especially the industrialists, obviously made huge windfalls from the booming prices. The urban middle classes did not do well, however. A survey of middle-class families in Bombay – those with pre-war incomes between Rs. 50 and 300 – found that their aggregate income had increased by 45 per cent, but this was insufficient to compensate for the rise in the cost of living.

The families were forced to change their patterns of consumption. While the consumption of food-grains – rice, wheat, pulses – did not change much, the intake of other items reduced considerably: clarified butter by 42 per cent, potatoes by 37 per cent, sugar by 28 per cent, milk by 18 per cent and meat by 15 per cent. Despite these cutbacks, the families spent 99 per cent more on food items than before the war. Aggregate expenditure on food rose to 51 per cent of income, as opposed to 37 per cent before the war.[67] The position of those on the lower rungs of urban society could be precarious. The wife of a soldier wrote from the town of Sargodha in Punjab:

> everything is very dear. For 6 months I have been feeling uneasy . . . At present I am in great difficulty . . . The creditors are troubling me and I have mortgaged all my ornaments. I am in a crisis . . . Your children have been starving continuously for 3 days. My plight is very bad.[68]

The pattern in rural India was not dissimilar. Large peasant-proprietors gained from the surge in prices for agricultural commodities. Very like big business, the combined result of soaring profits and restricted consumption for these groups was an increase in savings and in potential post-war investment. The effect on other sections of rural society was mixed. In the wake of the Great Depression, which had immiserated large sections of agrarian India, the war years came as a balm. Rural families that had been pushed into debt during the previous decade now found that the increasing demand as well as rising prices for their produce enabled them to pay off their debt. An inquiry into the villages of the Ludhiana district of Punjab found that even poor cultivators were partially able to shake off the manacles of debt. If nothing else, 'a rise in the mortgage value of land . . . made it possible for them to redeem a part of their land simply by changing the mortgagee'. The wages of labourers working on the farms rose over fourfold during the war. Yet even in the Punjab, the most prosperous agrarian province of India, the rise in income trailed the overall rise in prices.[69] As the father of a Punjabi soldier wrote in early 1943, 'every domestic requirement has become scarce and expensive, particularly articles of food and clothing. Their prices have quadrupled.'[70]

In most other parts of rural and urban India, the numbers of those skirting the edge of subsistence was much larger. The soaring inflation thus led to deprivation and hunger in many parts, and to star-vation and famine in some. The famine in Bengal of 1943–44, which resulted in perhaps 3 million deaths owing to starvation and disease, was the extreme manifestation of the problems triggered by inflation. It is also the best studied.[71] As Amartya Sen has famously argued, the famine was caused not by a shortage in the availability of food in the province but by the drastic reduction in the 'entitlements' – the over-all ability to obtain food – of the Bengali people. This, in turn, was primarily due to the war-induced inflation.[72]

Other factors, such as the 'denial' policy that destroyed the boats – in case these might be useful to the invading Japanese – and livelihoods of fishing communities, the panic hoarding by producers and traders, the inefficiency of the local government in procuring and distributing food-grains to various districts, and the unwillingness of the govern-ment to initiate a famine works programme to increase the purchasing power of the destitute, grimly exacerbated the problem. Irrespective of the causes, the consequences could have been mitigated by chan-nelling large quantities of food through a public distribution system. Shipping of imports was constrained by the competing demands of war. More importantly, Churchill was cruelly callous in his consider-ation of Wavell's requests for imports of food-grains into India. 'I hate Indians', he told Amery. 'They are a beastly people with a beastly religion.' Even when overall demands on British shipping dropped, Churchill held that 'We cannot afford to send ships merely as a ges-ture of goodwill.'[73]

The calamity of Bengal has engendered an understandable desire to find the guilty men. Yet, however appalling Churchill's attitude and devastating the consequences for Bengal, the taproot of the prob-lem was the inflationary financing of the war. Indeed, deprivation and hunger stalked large parts of India from late 1942. 'Dearness has surpassed all limits and is worrying me too much', wrote the father of a soldier from Gonda in the United Provinces:

> Adults can bear sufferings and can live without food for some time, but infants can't survive for even an hour. I am helpless to make both ends meet ... Death is better than this life. I am tired of this state of

affairs and sometimes I think of putting an end to my life. We are experiencing days of Judgment and the people will starve to death, if these conditions continue.[74]

The mother of another soldier wrote from Ranipet in Madras Province: 'Our food problem still shows no sign of improvement. You see my son, I have to purchase the foodstuff at very high prices, to manage other daily necessities, pay the tuition fees for the children, pay the medical bill and meet with many other items.'[75]

A wife wrote from Hyderabad State:

I am too helpless to make both ends meet. Dearness is increasing day by day. Prices have risen double, treble and quadruple even in some cases . . . You are always asking me to send a photo of mine and children; but it would cost me at least five rupees nowadays and where will I get so much . . . Please increase my allotment, otherwise we are really going to starve.

Of a train journey from Cochin to Bombay, another wrote:

we could see hundreds of men, women and children of all ages on the sides of the roads and crying for alms. The sight of those naked and half-naked wretches reduced to skeletons was too strong even for the most strong-hearted persons. They were begging from all indiscriminately and even soldiers of other nationalities took pity on them and gave them alms. These wretches had left their villages and were moving towards towns in crowds.[76]

A visitor to Poona similarly noted that 'People are in a terrible condition there. Every living person looks like a skeleton. No flesh on their bones and the youth have no sign of youth on their faces. They seemed to be over 50.'[77]

The problem was not just the price but also the availability of essential commodities for civilian consumption, owing to myriad problems of procurement, storage and distribution. As an elderly villager in the United Provinces observed, 'scarcity and dearth is ranging throughout the land . . . even at these [high] rates, very little is available for most of the time. Many people return empty handed from the shops. Many go to different parts of the country to get rice but from there also come back disappointed.'[78] The brother of an Indian officer from the Central Provinces complained that

> all corn is being collected forcibly by the Govt. authorities. They do not care whether you have got enough for you and your servants or not. They snatch away all except Jawari [millet] and spare us as much as they like. Up till now such a tyranny has never been experienced under British rule as going on now.[79]

Just when Indian factories were clothing armies across Asia and beyond, the Indian people were faced with an acute shortage.

> There is no other dress for the girls except the one they are wearing and that too is worn out. The price of cloth has risen 6 times ... We have never seen such times in our life ... we can bear all other difficulties but we cannot bear to see the girls wearing torn garments.[80]

By early 1942, the Indian government was alert to the problem of inflation. The provincial governments were told that 'Inflation is at present a greater danger to India than either the Germans or the Japanese.'[81] Nevertheless, its response proved largely ineffective. Although wartime powers allowed the central government to control prices, the authority to do so in the initial stages was devolved to the provinces. Moreover, it was restricted to a few essential consumer goods. When New Delhi did wake up to the magnitude of the problem it remained focused on curbing the prices of wheat and cloth.[82] The government not only lacked the requisite statistics but was apparently impervious to basic economic considerations such as relative costs of various items in a consumption basket as well as the regional disparity in prices. The subsequent expansion of controls to other commodities happened without any overall conception of price controls. Rationing too was adopted in a half-baked manner. The mechanism of control that came into being would go on to play a central role in the planned economy of independent India.[83] But during the war it did not appreciably check the soaring rate of inflation.

Some provinces did better than others in responding to the problems of hunger and deprivation. The Madras government began operating 'Famine Camps' in the Bellary district – one of the famine-prone 'dry districts' of the province – as early as March 1942. These camps provided work for villagers of the district. The numbers engaged in these works rose steadily in the subsequent months. Interestingly, there was an 'unusual preponderance of women' in the camps. The Madras government also opened weavers' relief centres. The government paid 'an advance of Rs. 2 per loom to the distressed weavers to enable them to convert their looms so as to weave cloth of [military] uniform texture and of other types to be produced in relief centres'.[84] A year later, the famine camps in Bellary were supporting 180,000 people. Similar camps were operating in Anantapur and Kurnool, assisting another 100,000. By November 1943, as the harvest looked promising in most parts of Madras Province, these camps began to be wound down.[85] Yet food remained a serious problem in the province and the government there had to operate relief camps and fair-price shops in various places throughout the war. The Malabar district was particularly hard hit in 1943. 'Dear brother,' wrote a man from Malabar, 'as regards news out here, death and death everywhere. Starvation and epidemics sweep away daily a good number. You will be astonished to see that ¼ of our neighbours have left for the better world – when you come back with anxiety to see them.'[86]

The Bombay government too was alert to early signs of trouble. The Bijapur district in the southern part of the province (today's Karnataka) was declared as afflicted by famine in December 1942. Even as measures were being initiated, the commissioner of the southern districts reported that the situation in the neighbouring districts of the Dharwad and Belgaum was also 'very grave': 'Unless stocks are received immediately, the position will undoubtedly become most serious and it will become increasingly difficult elsewhere to preserve law and order . . . all districts of the Karnatak are now faced with the problem of how to tackle Mass Hunger on a menacing scale.'[87] The Bombay government initially sought to regulate trade and distribution throughout the province in order to stabilize prices. But it quickly found that it did not have the capacity to do this. The upshot was the widening of the black market and a rise in profiteering. The government was forced to attempt other measures, such as rationing and a basic plan of allotments, to ensure that the province did not tip over into famine.[88]

Outside Bengal, the part of India worst hit by inflation-led famine was the princely state of Travancore. In 1942, there was a shortage of food-grains there owing to the cessation of imports from Burma – a major source of rice for all of south India. This initial shortfall led, as in Bengal,[89] to an exclusive focus on estimating the 'real shortage' based on 'requirements' and 'availability' and to a neglect of other factors that shrank the ability of the people to procure food. The deeper problems were widespread, including the loss of employment owing to the decline of the local export-based coir industry during the war. And, of course, there was the scourge of inflation.[90]

Travancore had an ostensibly progressive and competent government led by the diwan, Sir C. P. Ramaswami Iyer. But its handling of the famine was no better than that of the Bengal government. As the government fumbled along from expedient to expedient, the effect on the population was devastating. A soldier's relative wrote from Travancore:

> For days together I couldn't even see a grain of rice. Of course Govt. is supplying us rice after three days. It is only a very nominal quantity. The quality too is hopelessly bad. To tell the truth, many of us are dying of starvation. A sack of rice costs Rs. 65/- in Cochin.[91]

Outsiders travelling through Travancore were shocked: 'I shuddered to see men, women and children with no flesh on their bodies and all skeletons just as if they were half dead.'[92] As the shadow of famine lengthened in the state, the government was unable to appreciate the fundamental problem of insufficient purchasing power. Even after food stocks were built up and rationing introduced in the latter part of 1943, ration-card holders were taking in only 40 per cent of their allotment.[93]

In desperation, people began migrating out of the state to nearby parts of Madras Province. A resident of the relatively prosperous Chettinad district noted that:

> Great distress has been caused by the severe famine in Travancore, from whence so many families have migrated to big towns like Madras, Karaikudy, Tanjore and Chettynad [sic]. They are coming day by day in overwhelming numbers begging for alms. They present a pathetic sight.

All of them have got no flesh on their bodies, in fact they can be called living skeletons . . . they do not accept money. They want only food.[94]

The largest such exodus took place to Malabar in 1943. Around 15,000 Travancoreans travelled 300 miles by rail and foot to Malabar, where they cleared upland jungles – designated 'wastelands' by the government – for cultivation. About a fifth of them succumbed to cerebral malaria and other diseases, while the rest straggled home two years later. All told, famine and disease in Travancore exacted a mighty toll on the people. Between 1941 and 1944, the number of 'excess deaths' – above the normal rate of fifteen per thousand of population – was almost twenty-two per thousand.[95]

By 1944, the cumulative and mutually reinforcing problems of railway capacity, coal production and food became increasingly evident to the Indian government. An inquiry into the problems of war production led by Lieutenant General Thomas Hutton observed that

> The blunt fact is that India's resources are very limited and have been overstrained. She cannot now feed her population, nor can she get the coal required out of her mines, nor move it if she could. Her existing war industries are not working to capacity and existing contracts are not being fulfilled. Her capacity for executing military works has already been mortgaged for 1943–44 and nearly 80% for 1944–45.

The inquiry's conclusion was equally stark. 'India has now by and large reached the peak of her war effort. The country can subscribe no further real resources. An endeavour to extract more in one direction generally involves a diminution in another. The plight of the civil population is serious and inflation has assumed dangerous proportions.' At best, by adopting 'remedial measures in respect of transport, coal, food and on anti-inflationary measures it may be possible to maintain India's war effort at its present level for a time'.[96]

The government was seriously worried by the prospect of a collapse of the home front owing to the combined pressures of war and political stalemate. The deadlock, however, could only be eased once the situation on the war front began to change.

15

Around the Mediterranean

On 1 July 1942, Cairo was humming with rumours about Rommel's imminent entry into the city. As in Calcutta six months before, women, children and the elderly were streaming out in all modes of transport. Trains bloated with passengers puffed and wheezed their way out of Cairo to Upper Egypt, Sudan and Palestine. As the people fled, the city was cloaked in smoke. Bits of burnt paper twisted in the breeze as a fountain of soot rose from the courtyard of the Middle East Command's headquarters. The British civilian and military staff were hastily consigning thousands of confidential documents to improvised incinerators. Days after 'Ash Wednesday', street vendors of Cairo sold peanuts in paper cones made of half-burnt British secret documents.[1] General Francis Tuker was sent up the Nile to reconnoitre positions for a retreat southwards along the river: 'it looked as though it would be inevitable that we should soon be driven on to Alexandria and Cairo and those positions would in the end be needed. It was a most trying atmosphere.'[2]

The 'flap', as it came to be known, occurred in the absence of the commander-in-chief. General Auchinleck, having taken charge of the Eighth Army, was in the Western Desert where his troops were squaring up against the Axis forces at El Alamein. The Alamein Line ran 38 miles south from an eponymous railway station on the Mediterranean coast to the Qattara Depression, an immense stretch of sand dunes and salt marshes impassable to tanks and hence incapable of being flanked. The terrain on which the defences were organized was broken up by sharp ridges, sand banks and hillocks. The Alamein Line, however, was no more than a series of scattered 'boxes' sited on commanding positions – the most important of these being the ridges of Ruweisat and Alam Halfa.

Auchinleck's plan was to block Rommel's advance in this 38-mile funnel and use his own mobile forces – organized as 'battle groups' with infantry and artillery – to punch at the enemy's flanks and rear. Rommel had crossed the Egyptian frontier on 23 June and four days later had taken Mersa Matruh in an audacious attack. On 30 June Rommel circled his wagons ahead of the British defences at Alamein. As his forces stood less than a hundred miles from Alexandria, Mussolini flew to Derna in anticipation of a triumphal entry into Cairo.

The 10th Indian Division, which had been garrisoning Matruh, had been cut off by the attacking Axis forces. The division decided to abandon the coastal road and fight its way back to Alamein through the desert. The breakout proved successful, but the division was in such disarray that it had to be sent all the way back to the Nile Delta for reorganization and re-equipping. Meanwhile, other Indian units were deployed for the defence of Alamein.

The northern sector of the Alamein Line was held by the 30th Corps, while the 13th Corps was deployed in the southern sector. No sooner had the two corps taken up their positions than the Axis forces fell upon them. Rommel's attack on 1 July was hastily improvised and mounted. His confidence buoyed by the battle at Matruh, he dispensed with such formalities as proper reconnaissance – he hoped to catch the Eighth Army on the hop and give it the *coup de grâce*. As the 15th and 21st Panzer divisions advanced towards the Ruweisat ridge, held by a division of the 30th Corps, they came under fire from an unanticipated corner.

The 18th Indian Infantry Brigade was deployed in a box at Deir el Shein to the north-west of the Ruweisat ridge. A large depression in the desert, Deir el Shein was a good position for all-round defence. It carried the added advantage of being more or less invisible to the enemy – unless he came right up to its rim. Not surprisingly, it was overlooked by the Axis forces as they advanced on Ruweisat. Once under fire, though, the Panzers realized that bypassing the Deir el Shein box could render the British positions at the northern edge of

Ruweisat untenable. When the Panzers decided to attack in full strength, the minor element of surprise afforded by its position was the only thing that counted in the brigade's favour.

The 18th Brigade's unenviable position underscored the problems that continued to plague Indian units in the Middle East, as well as the Eighth Army. Formed in October 1940 in India, the brigade was originally assigned to the 8th Indian Infantry Division. About a year later, it was despatched for independent policing duties at Abadan in Iran. Subsequently, the brigade found itself in Erbil in Iraq. In early June 1942, as the Middle East Command cast about for additional formations, the brigade was moved by air from Iraq to Palestine. When its transport did not arrive in a week, one battalion – the 2/3rd Gurkhas – was sent by road to Egypt; the remaining battalions – 4/11th Sikh and 2/5th Essex – arrived by train. The units that moved by rail came under attack from German aircraft and took a few casualties. On the morning of 27 June, they were brusquely dropped off at Alamein. The brigade commander, with his headquarters and artillery, had set out by road and had lost his way. So the senior battalion commander took charge and was ordered by the corps commander to Deir el Shein.[3]

The brigade reached Deir el Shein in the small hours of 29 June and immediately started digging in. 'Time was against us from the start', noted the new brigade commander.[4] The box was a little over 2 miles long by a mile wide. Tired and cramped from the long journey, the brigade worked round the clock over the next two days to dig defences, wire the perimeter and sow mines. Since the brigade had no compressors to bore through the stony ground, emplacements could not be properly prepared. Nor did it have a suitable stock of mines: three different types were sent to it and many were without fuses.[5] The box, therefore, had several gaps which could not adequately be sealed with mines. Still more problematic was the lack of artillery. 'Guns did not exist when we first arrived', an officer recalled, 'but there were rumours of some coming from various sources.' Eventually, on the evening of 30 June, an assortment of artillery tricked in. However, the eighteen 25-pounders, sixteen 6-pounders and twenty 2-pounders reached the brigade too late to be dug in.[6]

Such was the parlous state of the 18th Brigade on the morning of 1

July 1942 when it sighted a column of dust moving towards Deir el Shein. At 1000 hours Axis artillery began pounding a part of the perimeter held by the Essex battalion. This was a baptism by fire for the battalion. Indeed, with the exception of the Sikh battalion, which was originally from the 7th Indian Brigade, none of the troops had any experience of desert warfare. After an hour of shelling and probing, the Axis forces resorted to a familiar ruse. Two British prisoners of war walked forward under a white flag and relayed a message from the Germans: surrender or prepare to be slaughtered. After gleaning some useful information on the enemy's strength, the officers were sent back with a reply: 'stick it up and be damned'.[7]

By early afternoon, the Afrika Korps had laid down a heavy barrage and began probing and thrusting against the Indian defences. As the German sappers sought to blow a crater on the perimeter, they came under heavy fire from the Essex troops. But the battalion was short of ammunition and could not lay down a steady field of fire. Around forty German tanks rammed their way through and went straight for the brigade headquarters. The seven Matildas that had arrived the previous night were swiftly snuffed out. The Panzers then pounced on the Essex position, forcing its surrender, before moving on to the Sikhs.

Meantime, the corps commander had ordered the 1st Armoured Division to assist the defenders of Deir el Shein. The 18th Brigade was informed that the tanks were on their way. None turned up. The armoured division's assets were widely scattered and by the time its commander had scrambled to put a force together, it was too late. 'The effect of this disappointment', the brigade commander observed, 'cannot have done other than lower the morale of the whole garrison, particularly the Indian troops.'[8] The brigade nevertheless hung on by its fingernails – taking a toll of eighteen German tanks – until it was overrun at 1930 hours. Just about a third of the brigade managed to break out of the battle.

The outcome was never in doubt. Tired and inexperienced, unprepared and ill-supported, the 18th Brigade was no match for the two veteran Panzer divisions; it did not survive this encounter and was never reconstituted. Yet its tenacious resistance had blunted Rommel's offensive and bought invaluable breathing space for the

Eighth Army to organize for the defence of the Alamein Line. As Niall Barr rightly argues, 'the resistance of the 18th Indian Brigade had stemmed the tide'.[9]

Having taken Deir el Shein, it seemed evident that Rommel would swing at the South African Division blocking the Alamein railway station and coastal road to Alexandria. Axis radio addressed a message to the 'Ladies of Alexandria', asking them to make appropriate arrangements for the reception of the victors. Auchinleck was not amused. That night he decided on a diversionary counter-attack. The 13th Corps was ordered to wheel north and hit the flank and rear of the Germans, while the 30th Corps checked their advance towards the north and east.[10] On the afternoon of 2 July, the 13th Corps began its attack with the New Zealand and the 5th Indian Divisions. The Indian division was, in fact, under the command of the 30th Corps – its allotment to the 13th Corps for the offensive was characteristic of the game of Chinese checkers played in the Eighth Army. Amply supported from the air, the advance initially made good headway. By 5 July, the 13th Corps stood at touching distance from Deir el Shein. There they came up against a series of strongpoints prepared and held by the enemy and soon the corps' advance juddered to a halt.

Auchinleck was unwilling to hand the initiative to Rommel. So he ordered the 30th Corps to open a new offensive in the coastal area. This was the first of a series of jabs at the Axis forces that he attempted in the weeks ahead, but to little avail. The 5th Indian Division played its part in some significant operations. On the night of 14 July, the division's 5th Indian Infantry Brigade, along with the New Zealanders, attacked in the centre – in front of the Ruweisat ridge. The Indian brigade captured Point 64, a tactically important feature overlooking Deir el Shein and areas to its north; the New Zealanders took a position to the west of Point 64, but were overrun by Axis tanks on the afternoon of 16 July, leaving the 5th Indian Brigade dangerously exposed. Throughout the day, Stukas dived in to bomb the defences and artillery fire poured in. Even as the brigade was reinforced by armour, artillery and anti-tank guns, the Panzers counter-attacked. However, this time the Panzers were stopped in their tracks and forced to report that they could go no further. When the tanks returned after dusk, they ran into an ambush laid by the 4/6th Rajputana Rifles. The brigade netted a haul of twenty-four tanks, six armoured cars, eighteen anti-tank guns, six 88mm guns and one self-propelled gun.[11]

Be that as it may, tactical defensive victories could not compensate for the Eighth Army's overall operational weaknesses: the reliance on a line of boxes to hold territory; the farming out of divisions as brigade groups; the inability to conceive systematically of all-arms doctrine and tactics; the sheer fatigue and weariness of the troops; above all, Auchinleck's inability to articulate his thinking to his senior commanders and to ensure that it percolated down the chain. By the end of July 1942, Auchinleck placed on hold his plans for destroying the Afrika Korps in front of Alamein and decided to stay on the defensive, awaiting reinforcements that were on their way.

Political leaders on both sides were fed up of the stalemate. Having waited in vain for three weeks, Mussolini flew back from Libya in a foul mood. On 3 August, Churchill arrived in Cairo. Auchinleck's insipid briefing did not inspire much confidence in the prime minister. Convinced that the Eighth Army was a 'baffled and somewhat unhinged organization', Churchill decided that it needed new leadership.[12] Auchinleck was divested of his duties – both as commander of the Eighth Army and the Middle East. However, he declined to accept Churchill's offer of commanding the newly created Persia and Iraq Force (Paiforce). So, for the second time in as many years, a sacked commander-in-chief was sent from the Middle East to India.

After toying with a few options, Churchill appointed General Harold Alexander as the commander-in-chief of Middle East Command. Lieutenant General Bernard Montgomery – not Churchill's first choice – took over as commander of the Eighth Army. Montgomery was – and remains – a polarizing figure, evoking devotion and detestation in about equal measure. Critics point to his prima donna style and his resolute refusal to give any credit to Auchinleck. They underline the enormous material advantage enjoyed by the Eighth Army under his command. They also rightly identify his strength at the set-piece battle and his weakness at the pursuit. All said, however, Montgomery had qualities that set him apart from his predecessors. For one thing, he was completely self-confident and self-contained – impervious to the views of others but also preter-naturally calm during crises. For another, he realized that the Eighth Army was much less than the sum of its parts and that his main task was infusing a sense of identity and purpose that it had hitherto lacked. Finally, Montgomery was acutely alert to the character of the troops he commanded: their limited training, the vagaries of morale and their unwillingness to be led by their noses into battle.[13] Having spent three years in India between the wars, including a stint as instructor in the Staff College in Quetta, Montgomery – very like Wavell – understood the Indian army and its officer corps. At the same time, he shared at least some of the prejudices of senior British officers towards the 'sepoy' generals and their troops.

When Montgomery took command the Eighth Army was in the grip of a crisis of morale following the long retreat to Alamein. His approach and style came as a tonic to the demoralized force. He welded the Eighth Army together by banishing the invidious system of hiving off brigades from divisions. He communicated his aims clearly and forthrightly. He ensured that 'formations and units were not given tasks which were likely to end in failure' owing to the 'low standard of training'. And he trained his divisions hard, focusing on toughening the troops with battle inoculation exercises, developing combined-arms battle drills and training under conditions as close as possible to actual combat. The effect of all this was perceptible. As the military censor noted:

> the fact that the G.O.C-in-C., 8 Army, took the whole army into his confidence right down to the last man and stated exactly what he hoped to do and how he was going to do it, the belief that the plan was good, and the knowledge that the tools at their disposal were more numerous and effective than they have ever been, brought the spirit of the troops to a new high level and intensified their assurance and grim determination.[14]

Montgomery's role in the resuscitation of the Eighth Army is well established; less clear, however, is his impact on the Indian troops under his command. Unfortunately, few letters from Indian soldiers of the Eighth Army have survived. Nor do the surviving fragments of military censor reports from this period throw much light on the state of their morale. Then again, the Indian units could not have been immune to the Eighth Army's malaise. The fall of Tobruk had shaken the confidence of the Indian troops. Writing of the subsequent withdrawal, the official historian of the 5th Indian Division noted that its troops were among those 'who had struggled in the bewilderment and butchery ... who had fought a rear-guard action day after day ... who had seen battalions decimated, brigades over-run, head-quarters captured, armoured forces destroyed, transport hurrying towards Egypt'.[15]

Statistical evidence also suggests that the Indian soldiers' morale – like that of British and Dominion troops – plummeted steeply during the withdrawal from Gazala to Alamein. There is a sharp rise in the percentage of those counted as 'missing' during this period. Barring a small fraction of those who might have been genuinely lost, the overwhelming number of those classified as missing were soldiers taken as prisoners of war. Put differently, the numbers 'missing' are a good proxy for the numbers surrendering to the enemy. To be sure, rates of surrender cannot automatically be read as an indicator of morale. Under the mobile conditions of desert warfare, infantry forces with limited anti-tank weaponry or armoured support could not hold their own for long when surrounded by enemy tanks. This was particularly true of the Indian units in the Eighth Army, which were plagued by deep deficiencies in their equipment.

Even so, the rates of missing/surrendered are astonishingly high during the long withdrawal from Gazala to Alamein: 95 per cent of the total casualties counted among Indian units in this period were those that had gone missing or who had surrendered. (The figures for British and Dominion troops were 86 and 81 per cent resepectively.) By contrast, during the advance to Cyrenaica from November 1941 to February 1942, missing/surrendered accounted for only 23 per cent of the total casulties in Indian units. (The figures for British and Dominion units were 35 and 53 per cent.) Equally telling are the numbers of dead and wounded. Although two-and-a-half times more Indian troops fought during the withdrawal than in the advance, the numbers of killed or wounded in the former were only 20 per cent of those in the latter. Clearly, the problem of plunging morale in the Eighth Army afflicted the Indian forces as well.

Casualty Figures of Indian Troops in North Africa

	Nov 1941 to Jan 1942	27 May 1942 to 24 Jul 1942
Strength engaged	19,000	48,000
Killed and wounded	1,000	600
Missing	300	13,000
Total casualties	1,300	13,600
% Killed and wounded	5%	1%
% Missing to total casualties	23%	95%

Source: Jonathan Fennell, *Combat and Morale in the North African Campaign: The Eighth Army and the Path to El Alamein* (Cambridge: Cambridge University Press, 2011), p. 42.

What about the restoration of morale after Montgomery took over? The 5th Indian Division's historian wrote: 'A new spirit went abroad through the Eighth Army. Hope sprang high. Fresh divisions and American tanks began to arrive. Morale rose all round.' Yet the advent of Montgomery did not have an altogether salutary impact on the Indian troops. The lacklustre record of Auchinleck – the senior-most Indian army officer – as well as the Indian formations that had been plucked out of the Middle East cast a long shadow on Indian forces in North Africa. Francis Tuker felt that their performance had been 'so disastrous and had so shattered the prestige of the I.A. [Indian Army] that it can never recover in this war . . . The name of Indian tps [troops] and Indian Divs stank in the nostrils of GHQ M.E.C. and they showed it too.' General Alexander was not alone in looking askance at the Indian forces. Montgomery held them in no higher esteem. As Tuker wrote to General Alan Hartley, the deputy commander-in-chief of India, 'Monty has not much use for the I.A. and used to say so: only thinks it now.'[16] This could not have done much for the morale and self-esteem of the Indian units in the Eighth Army.

As Rommel squared up for another offensive, Montgomery made his moves deliberately. The 5th Indian Division's historian noted that 'there had been no hurry, no lack of co-ordination, no want of proper co-operation, such as had characterized many of the recent engagements'.[17] The anticipated attack came late on the night of 30 August. Rommel threw the whole of the Afrika Korps as well as the Italian armoured divisions in a southerly swing on the Alam Halfa ridge. By contrast, the attacks on the northern and central sections of the Alamein Line were no more than mild jabs. On the Ruweisat ridge, held by the 5th Indian Division, a German parachute battalion over-ran a forward company, but were soon dislodged by a counter-attack with infantry and tanks. By the evening of 5 September, Rommel's main offensive ran into the sand. For a heavy price of men, armour and vehicles, Rommel had gained little more than 5 miles in the desert. More importantly, he had lost the opportunity to destroy the Eighth Army before it was swelled by fresh reinforcements of troops and tanks. Montgomery forbore from further counter-attacks, choosing to bide his time before launching a major offensive.

Among the troops rotated out from the battle front was the worn-down 5th Indian Division, replaced by the 4th Indian Division. This division had been the most experienced infantry formation in North Africa and its dismantling in March 1942 was a sad commentary on the state of the Eighth Army under Auchinleck. The divisional commander, General Tuker, had requested that the division be reinforced by 4,000 troops from India and pulled out to 'train on certain new lines as a result of its experience of last winter's fighting'. Tuker had wanted the division to train as a whole and return to the front line in May 1942.[18] In the teeth of his protests, however, the division was parcelled out in brigade groups.

The 7th Brigade had been sent to Cyprus in March. The rest of the division prepared to move in April to the Nile Delta for re-equipping and retraining. Tuker prepared detailed training instructions for the division to operate as a mobile formation alongside armoured forces. In the meantime, the 5th Brigade with the field artillery regiment was sent to Palestine. The 11th Brigade with the divisional headquarters landed in the combined training area without a single 2-pounder anti-tank gun. In May, this brigade was sent to Sollum and thence to Tobruk; half the divisional headquarters deployed near Cairo, and the other half – with the divisional commander – was despatched to conduct reconnaissance of defences in Cyprus. So frustrated was Tuker with the state of his division that he contemplated resigning in August. The Middle East Command, however, assured him that the division would be re-formed. As the battle of Alam Halfa raged on, the 4th Division waited in the wings.[19]

On 6 September, Tuker was asked to stand ready to replace the 5th Division. The 5th Brigade of his division had for some weeks been operating under the command of the 5th Division. Thus, when the 4th Division reached the Ruweisat ridge it was almost complete. Apart from the 5th and 7th Brigades, the division was allotted another vagrant, free-floating Indian formation: the 161st Indian Infantry Brigade. The division's highly trained field artillery regiment, however, failed to fetch up for several months. Tuker expected Rommel's next attack to be concentrated on the Ruweisat ridge. 'It's great news', he wrote to General Hartley.[20]

Tuker believed that the newly positioned 4th Division 'must be the pivot on which our [counter]attack revolves'. After taking over Ruweisat on 9 September, he 'worked the men like niggers to get the defence built up'. Apart from a few forays, though, the division was mostly battling the weather:

> a terrific sandstorm. Quite foul. My caravan is full of dust. The enemy has been getting pretty touchy lately on our front. I think he expects us to attack him. We've been fairly offensive. The Sussex got into a Hun post and killed the whole issue on night 5/6 Oct. I was v. glad . . . A bit of ferocity is good for all of us and I hope the rest of the Div will be equally ferocious and savage.[21]

Montgomery's offensive was set for 23 October. Contrary to Tuker's expectations, however, the Allied attack did not turn on Ruweisat. Montgomery's main thrusts were aimed along the northern and southern ends of the Alamein Line. The 4th Division was tasked with launching only a diversionary raid in front of Ruweisat.

From the outset, Tuker was clear that 'we've got to restore the name of the Ind Divs out here'. The army commander's low opinion of Indian troops was not lost on them. 'I've told my chaps', he wrote to Hartley the night before the battle, 'they're to fight as if 4 div had no name at all and was starting now to make it. I've absolute faith in them.'[22] The raid led by the 1/2nd Gurkhas went well: '30 casualties out of the Coy [Company] but damaged the Boche pretty considerably in some very close fighting ... our wounded are in tremendous form. Morale v. high.'[23]

Tuker restively followed the fight to his north and south, longing for a piece of the action. 'There are tanks on my front to-night,' he observed on 25 October, 'I hope they attack. They don't know what I've got waiting for them.' As the Axis forces seemed to stymie the offensive, he felt that Montgomery 'must give me the means to jump in. This is the strongest part of his [Rommel's] front but I know we can break it and so prick out most of his army.' The 'scrappy fighting' the following day left Tuker depressed: 'I think I shall resign if I don't get a crack at the Boche this time. The Div is feeling as savage as tigers. It is really hard to restrain units from going in and "crowning him" as they put it.'[24]

In the event, the 4th Division did nothing more onerous than supporting the offensive elsewhere by putting on 'a complete dummy attack with MT [Mechanical Transport] movement, barrage and so on, and various local frills (some rather funny)' and bringing down 'a tornado of enemy defensive fire'. Worse, the 5th Indian Brigade was torn off from the division and incorporated into the Eighth Army reserve. The Corps headquarters unctuously claimed that the brigade was recognized as the best in the Middle East. 'Damned hard on us to do this', wrote Tuker, 'I've only just got the Div going.'[25]

The 5th Indian Brigade did however participate in a significant action against the Axis anti-tank screen in the north, which opened the way for British armour to break out. Although proud of the brigade's performance, Tuker was distressed at being stripped of other assets like light artillery. 'I do not think Monty intends to use us', he wrote on 4 November. 'He doesn't like the I.A.' That night Rommel began his retreat. As the curtain fell on the battle of Alamein, the 4th Division was divested of its motor vehicles and tasked, with the Greek and Free French forces, to clear the battlefield of debris.[26]

Tuker felt that 'without doubt 8 Army treated us shockingly'. Months after the battle of Alamein, he wrote that 'though we knew what Monty thought of us, we never lost hope. We trained like hell and got on with the job.'[27] This seems an accurate description of the

4th Indian Division's feelings. As an Indian lieutenant wrote home after Alamein:

> I'd love to tell you that we played a great and gallant part in the recent offensive but the truth is that Indian troops have played a very minor part in the campaign. The laurels go to the Tommy, I'm afraid. However Indians will before this war is over have an opportunity for action. And then we will once again prove to an admiring world that on God's earth there is no fighter in courage, perseverance and endurance who can be even remotely compared with us.[28]

The division got its chance a couple of months later. But not before Tuker had complained to his corps commander. The latter took up the matter with Montgomery. '[T]his is an experienced Division', he wrote, 'imbued with a fine fighting spirit and in my opinion it would be a tragedy if this fine Division was not given a further opportunity of representing India.'[29] In March 1943, the 4th Indian Division was ordered to Medenine in Tunisia, near the Mareth Line where the retreating Axis forces had decided to stand and fight. Tuker was stunned to find that the two remaining brigades of his division – the 7th and 11th – were to be parcelled out between two of the Eighth Army's corps. Only a vigorous protest with the corps commander and a meeting with Montgomery himself prevented the division from being dismantled.

By the time these contretemps were resolved, Rommel had pulled further back to a line along the Wadi Akarit. This was an excellent defensive position, bounded by an impassable salt marsh at one end and the sea at the other: 'A series of transverse crests merge in a labyrinthine tangle of pinnacles, escarpments, counter-escarpments, deep fjord-like chimneys and corridors.'[30] The Eighth Army made contact with the enemy on the morning of 30 March. Montgomery had initially hoped quickly to tackle the Akarit defences with the leading division of the 10th Corps. Reconnaissance suggested, however, that the enemy was well dug in and capable of inflicting substantial damage. Accordingly, Montgomery ordered the 30th Corps – comprising the 4th Indian Division, the 51st Division and a Guards brigade – to force the enemy defences and secure a bridgehead. The 10th Corps would then break out towards the north and destroy the Axis forces in the area.

Tuker felt that the plan was misguided. Not only was the main ridge held by the enemy a formidable position, but it was overlooked by an even sharper ridge – the Zouai Hill to its west. Tuker offered to take the latter position with his units and also suggested bringing a third division into the attack. In the event, it was decided that the 50th and the 51st Divisions would launch the main set-piece offensive at 0430 hours on 6 April. Before the main attack went in, the 4th Division would strike the Zouai Hill. In contrast to the Eighth Army's firepower-heavy approach, Tuker's plan relied on stealth, surprise and small-unit tactics. The attack went in after dusk on 5 April. The 7th Indian Infantry Brigade's war diary noted:

> We are now creeping forward into the foothills where we know the enemy's FDL [forward defensive lines] are, suddenly an Italian sentry challenges, immediately a yell of 'pugaroo' goes up and the Gurkhas charge. A fiendish uproar takes place ... Some [Italians] fight as the clatter of exploding grenades and tommy guns shows. Others run screaming away from their positions.[31]

By first light, the 4th Division had punched a 5-mile-deep hole in the enemy line and taken over two thousand prisoners. More importantly, it was able to establish contact with the 50th Division on its flank. And the divisional engineers set about preparing a crossing over the enemy's anti-tank ditch. Yet the 10th Corps' breakout never really materialized. The Axis anti-tank guns and the terrain combined to slow down its advance. This gave the defenders enough time to disengage, pull back and live to fight subsequent battles in North Africa.

The battle of Wadi Akarit may have proved operationally abortive, but it showcased the qualities of the Indian division: its standard of training, excellent small-unit leadership and, above all, its flexibility in adapting from fighting in the desert to mountain warfare.[32] These qualities were evident in subsequent engagements, too. An Indian captain of the Rajputana Rifles wrote an unusually vivid account of a battle to his father in Calcutta:

> Well here we are again back in a great area, after some of the bloodiest fighting that I have seen for a long time. It was hand to hand fighting

from hill top to hill top and our Jawans [soldiers] were magnificent . . .
One of the Coys [companies] got on to their objective where there was
severe fighting, in which they were counter attacked four times with the
result that they ran out of ammn. [ammunition], instead of calling it a
day they threw stones at the adv. Germans, who as soon as they realised
the jawans had no ammns., stood about 30x off and threw grenades at
them. They killed poor [missing] and thirty of his men. But these were
Rajputs. My M. Guns [machine guns] came into action and sprayed the
adv. Germans with death. The Rajput Coy seeing this charged with the
sword and after 20 mins. the hill was ours again. We took 20 German
prisoners and buried 300 of them. One of their senior NCOs (with Iron
Cross) was babbling with fright when I brought him in.[33]

These qualities would stand the Indian units in good stead as the
Allies moved on from North Africa to Italy.

The Middle East military censor noted that the morale of the division could not be higher: 'Tails up is hardly a fitting description.' A
soldier of the Rajputana Rifles wrote to his brother: 'You must have
heard on radio that the Indian troops are doing very well. They have
earned a very good name in breaking the Mareth Line and round
about; they have kept up the old tradition. We are now very happy
though we have to undergo great physical strain.' Another wrote of
life at the front:

my palatial abode now is slit trench surrounded by barren hills. It is a
very exciting and adventurous life that we are having. Artillery duel is
the most impressive, a rolling rumbling noise and the ground shaking
and the whole horizon lit up with smoke and light from the flash of
guns. Enemy guns firing and our guns replying with double rigour. All
this is very intoxicating and imagine me still sleeping and carrying on
as usual . . . I think the recruitment slogan 'join the army and see the
world' is quite right.[34]

In striking contrast to the situation some months back, Indian casualties were raring to get back to their units. As an Indian doctor noted,
'After applying "Morphia", I asked some of them "How are you
now". In reply they said, *Thik hai sahib, mujhe* firing line *par bhejd-
ijie*" ["I am fine Sir, please send me back to the front"].'[35]

Success also infused a competitive spirit among the units. As stories of the *khukri*-waving Gurkhas got abroad, the commanding officer of a Punjab battalion wrote:

> We are all rather browned off with this terrific 'Gurka' advertisement which is going on; they forget our lads and regiments like Raj Rif have been out here for 3 years and taken part in the Eritrea show as well. There is no glamour about the old Punjabi but he is the back bone of the Indian Army and has been unobtrusively magnificent in all the momentous desert fighting, taking success and defeat with equal calmness. I cannot express my admiration for the Punjabis, Sikhs and Dogras – they are all splendid.[36]

The campaign in North Africa came to an end with the fall of Tunis and Bizerte. The tide was finally turning in favour of the Allies. An Indian captain was among the 26,000 troops that took part in a victory parade in Tunis:

> It was a very impressive show. There were 500 planes flying very low over us as we marched the streets of Tunis – and the people of Tunis lining both sides of the road were cheering madly when the Indian troops marches past them ... men and women alike were yelling at the top of their voices – 'Bravo! Bravo! Indian Soldiers' – we were marching to a bagpipe played by an Indian soldier – a Punjabi.

The impact of the victory in North Africa on the home front was considerable. Coming in the wake of the series of reverses against the Japanese, the 4th Division's performance was praised in extravagant terms. The brother-in-law of a Tamil soldier was hailed by a poor lady and given a large quantity of sweets.

> I was amazed at her strange behaviour and exuberant joy and asked her for an explanation. And she told me that her son happens to be one of the heroes that have killed lakhs of Germans and conquered a Kingdom for the emperor and that she had come to know that I too had a brother-in-law fighting with that famous Army, and therefore she wanted me to share her joy and celebrate the occasion with her.[37]

After over two continuous years in operations, the Indian units now had ample opportunities for rest and recreation. 'With the end of the battle there is no excitement here', wrote a young Indian officer:

> At the moment we are completely relaxing on the beaches of the Medi-terranean, under a big palm-grove. All sorts of Tamashas [shows], Indian films and other recreations are being conducted for the troops. Nearly the whole day is spent on the beach, in playing and bathing and in the evening either cinema or some other show is on. The troops enjoy it.[38]

Yet they also knew that a lot more fighting lay ahead of them. As another officer put it,

> what does the African Campaign matter, whilst there is still the whole of Europe and the East after that? . . . We are fed up with rest out here and wish to return back among bombs and shells. We are quite used to them now and life seems incomplete without them. You will be surprised to read it, but all officers and O.R.s have the same impulse in them.[39]

As the Allied conquest of North Africa proceeded apace, plans for an invasion of Sicily were being drawn up. The Indian army played a very minor role in the landings on Sicily and the mainland. A few Indian battalions were deployed on beachhead duties, and a battalion of the Jodhpur Sardar Light Infantry worked with the Americans at Salerno. Not until the end of September 1943 did the first Indian for-mation go into action in Italy.

Indian soldiers were overwhelmed by the jaw-dropping beauty of the country. Sicily, wrote a soldier of a Z-Craft company, 'is the Kashmir of Europe. Wherever you go you will find groves of date palms and innumerable vineyards . . . We get for one shilling one bottle of wine and for 1 penny 2 lbs. of almonds. Where will you get things so cheap?' The people were 'very sympathetic and kind-hearted' to the Indians. 'They call us often "DESERT FOXES" and say that we are the fittest soldiers to break the stony head of Hitler.' Equally important, 'The people here display no colour prejudice. The coloured are better loved than the white.'

Indian soldiers also struck up relationships with the Sicilians. A captain in an engineer unit saw an Italian farmer struggling to thresh a massive heap of harvested wheat. 'My men took pity on him and led by their curiosity joined him in the work. They were busy throughout the day and expect to finish it soon. He seems to be very grateful to me. Our relations with local inhabitants are cordial and they are very social.' Sex was evidently part of the Sicilian experience. 'I am passing some of the happiest hours of my life in a beautiful European island', wrote an infantryman. 'We are free from every sort of restriction and shall never forget this liberty throughout our lives.'[40]

For all its bewitching beauty, Italy proved an extraordinarily difficult country to invade – especially from the south. Initially the going seemed rather good. As an Indian officer noted,

> The occupation of Sicily in such a short time and with such low casualties was not even dreamt of by its planners . . . What followed soon after came as a surprise to all i.e. fall of Mussolini, crumbling of Fascism like a house of cards over-night, and the unconditional surrender of Italy.

Another officer conceded that 'it's a bit tough going in the hills and valleys all covered with thick greenery'. Yet it was 'definitely better than the western desert, I don't mind fighting – and now the Ities are also helping us to fight the Jerries out from their own homes'. Rome, he believed, was not very far: 'now don't you envy me – spending my X'mas in Rome?'[41]

But the Germans proved tenacious defenders, contesting every mile of the country in a protracted and bitter campaign. In September, the 8th Indian Division landed at Taranto, fighting its way up successive lines of German river defences: Trigno, Sangro and Moro. In early February 1944, the 4th Indian Division was placed under the US Fifth Army to capture the town of Cassino and the surrounding hills. The Allied troops launched three bloody and costly attacks in the next six weeks. In the third offensive, the 4th Indian Division came close to capturing Castle Hill, thanks to the magnificent effort of the 1/9th Gurkhas in reaching Hangman's Hill. But a determined German counter-attack restored the stalemate. By the time the final battle took place in May, the 4th Indian Division had been sent back to the Adriatic sector. But the 8th Indian Division arrived in time for the attack on

11 May on the German defences south of Cassino. After a few days of bitter fighting the 8th Indian and the 4th British Divisions knocked a hole in the Germans' Gustav Line. The road to Rome was now open.

After the fall of Rome on 4 June 1944, the 8th Indian Division continued to pursue the Germans until it was relieved at Perugia by the 10th Indian Division. The latter, in turn, had been replaced in the Adriatic sector by the 4th Indian Division. This division began advancing towards Florence on 30 June. By mid-August all three Indian divisions had reached Florence, whence they joined the attack on the German defences along the Gothic Line. The next month, the 4th Indian Division was redeployed to intervene in the civil war in Greece. But the 8th and 10th Divisions stayed on in Italy for the final offensives across the Senio River in April 1945. The 10th Indian Division and the 43rd Gurkha Lorried Brigade pushed the Germans across the Idice River – the last crossing before the Po River. And soon the war in Italy was at an end.

Although three Indian divisions – totalling over 50,000 troops – took part in the Italian campaign, their overall operational contribution is difficult to judge. For one thing, they never amounted to more than a sixth of the Allied forces in Italy. For another, the Indian divisions did not operate under a single corps, let alone one commanded by an officer of the Indian army. Indeed, the absence of an Indian corps and a British-Indian corps commander rankled deeply with senior Indian army officers, many of whom saw it as another marker of the differential treatment meted out to their forces. More irksome was the fact that Indian units were constantly shuttled from one formation and front to another.

Nevertheless, it is clear that the Indian divisions deployed in Italy attained high levels of training and operational flexibility. For a start, Indian army officers played a central role in the setting up of a Mountain Warfare Training Centre in Lebanon in early 1943. Their pre-war experience of fighting on India's north-west frontier came in handy in training troops for conventional mountain warfare in Italy. In October 1943, the centre offered mountain warfare training teams – comprising mostly of Indians – to General Alexander. Senior British officers observed that 'they accomplished very useful results in subjects in which both officers and men had had little or no previous training'. Individual formations also placed considerable emphasis on training. The 4th Division under General Tuker was quick off the blocks, producing a 'Mountain Warfare Training Instruction' booklet in early 1943. The document stressed the importance in mountains of physical fitness and tactical awareness, junior leadership and specialist training, mobility and surprise, concentration of forces and all-arms co-operation. Not surprisingly, the division was converted into a mountain division later that year.[42]

The 8th Indian Division under Major General Dudley Russell had been part of the Paiforce in the Middle East. In the run up to their deployment in Italy, the division prepared seriously. As one officer commented: 'We have been extremely busy all summer . . . training circulars, almost daily demonstrations, lectures, little memos, about this and that.'[43] The division also attended courses at the Combined Training Centre in Kabrit and the Mountain Warfare Training Centre in Lebanon. The 10th Division underwent a similar programme of training and preparation prior to deployment in Italy. In fact, the 8th and 10th Divisions conducted a joint exercise in Palestine in the summer of 1943.

Once the campaign was underway, a series of military training pamphlets, *Army in India Training Manuals* (AITMs) began to be issued. Units and formations wrote up their own notes on lessons learnt for wider circulation. Learning from Italy also fed back into the units and formations in India, especially those deployed on the Burma front. The experience of opposed river crossings and operating in a geographically diverse country was deemed particularly useful. Thus, AITM no. 27, issued to units in Burma in early 1945, had a section titled 'Notes by a Corps Commander in Italy', followed by another section 'What the Brigadier Said'.[44] By the time, the Italian campaign ended, the Indian army's transmission-belt of tactical learning was working perfectly. The real challenge, however, lay in its operational performance in the east.

16

Preparation

The dismal failure of the first Arakan offensive drove home the need for far-reaching changes to enhance the Indian army's fighting power. In the wake of the mauling, the Indian government and the India Command initiated a series of reforms. The army's organization and doctrine, tactics and training were revised in the light of the experience of fighting the Japanese. Attempts were also made to rejuvenate the health and morale of the soldiers. A massive logistical effort was undertaken to support and sustain the forces on the eastern frontiers and beyond. These seemingly mundane administrative changes may lack the glamour of grand strategy, but they are central to understanding how a debilitated India eventually delivered a knockout blow to the apparently invincible Japanese forces.

Wavell was well aware that the Arakan campaign had sent severe shock waves through the army. Months of effort and fighting in only a small part of Burma had led to nothing but humiliation. Worse still, it had fostered a false notion about Japanese fighting skill and nurtured a myth about their invincibility. In consequence, Wavell believed, the army sought to shield itself from the enemy and shrank from taking the fight to him. Restoring their offensive spirit necessitated the demolition of the myth of Japanese invincibility. Japanese successes, Wavell held, stemmed primarily from their superior organization and training for operating in the terrain of Malaya and Burma. The Indian army units, by contrast, were hastily formed, partially equipped and trained to fight in the deserts of the Middle East. The army in India, therefore, had to be reorganized, re-equipped and retrained before any further operations against the Japanese could be risked.[1]

The need for organizational changes to the Indian army was recognized even before the Arakan campaign flopped. In the summer of 1942, Wavell convened a conference in Delhi of commanders of formations and units as well as staff officers of all ranks. The conference examined the lessons learnt from the recent defeats and sought to apply them to the organization and equipment of the Indian army. A central problem, the conference quickly realized, was that the standard Indian division was too mechanized and too dependent on roads for its movement. The Japanese had exploited this to the hilt by brilliant use of roadblocks. When compelled to fight off the main roads and in the jungle country, the absence of animal transport had left Indian divisions at a distinct disadvantage.[2]

This was an ironic conclusion; for until a couple of years before, the central problem of the Indian army was its lack of mechanization. The battles in the east, however, had shown that 'modern' warfare did not automatically mean mechanized warfare. The Burma campaign necessitated a hybrid organization as well as a range of operational concepts and tactical skills. Thus, following the Delhi conference, Wavell decided to introduce a new type of formation: the Indian light division. This formation would be given only a light scale of motor vehicles – mainly jeeps and smaller four-wheel drive lorries – and would depend largely on pack mule transport companies. The structure of the light division would also differ from that of the standard infantry division, even if the number of troops remained roughly similar. It would comprise a divisional headquarters – with a support battalion, equipped with troop carriers and medium machine guns, intended to function as 'shock troops' – and only two brigades. Each of the brigades, however, would have three infantry battalions and a reconnaissance battalion. The latter would consist of two jeep companies and two mounted ('lorried') infantry companies. The divisional artillery would include two fully kitted-out mountain regiments, one mechanized field regiment and a mixed light anti-aircraft and anti-tank regiment.

So designed, the light division was expected to combine maximum mobility on and off the roads with firepower – a combination that was essential to blunt Japanese attempts at encirclement. The 17th and 39th Divisions were selected for conversion to the new model.

Simultaneously, the levels of mechanization of the 7th, 20th and 23rd Divisions were curtailed and some animal transport injected into them. These mixed formations came to be known as 'animal and mechanical transport' (A&MT) divisions. Subsequently, the 26th Division was also converted into an A&MT division. The remaining Indian divisions – the 14th, 19th, 25th and 34th – as well as the three British divisions in India (the 2nd, 5th and 70th) were left intact.

In mid-1943, further organizational changes were introduced drawing on the experience of the botched Arakan operation. There would now be three types of divisions: A&MT with higher scale motor vehicles (the 19th and 25th Indian Divisions); A&MT with lower scale motor vehicles (the 5th, 7th and 20th Indian Divisions)*; and the light divisions (the 17th and 39th). The infantry battalions in both types of A&MT divisions would be divested of all vehicles except the minimum required for carrying essential fighting equipment – effectively anything less mobile than a four-wheel drive 15-cwt truck. The fighting strength of the infantry battalions in the light divisions was increased by about 160 men, which added a platoon to each of the four rifle companies. The mobility of these units was enhanced by allowing them thirty-one jeeps – increased from ten.[3]

Initially, these changes did not go down very well with the army. Units that were de-mechanized reported 'disappointment at the withdrawal of vehicles and the equipment and the relegation to roles less technical and less attractive'. A lorried Indian infantry battalion that was shorn of its vehicles and sent into a frontier defence role noted that the men had 'accepted the change philosophically' and 'morale remains good but by no means as enthusiastic as it was a month ago'.[4] Some Indian officers – particularly KCIOs – also resented being transferred out of mechanized units to infantry battalions; a move that they perceived as discriminatory.[5] While these concerns were ironed out, GHQ India had more trouble coping with the multiple divisional structures and requirements. Indeed, the operations of 1944 would point to the need for further streamlining of the structure of the Indian divisions.

* The 5th Indian Division had come back to India from the Middle East.

Divesting the infantry divisions of motor vehicles was easy; not so their replacement with animal transport. At the outbreak of war, the Royal Indian Army Service Corps (RIASC) had thirty-six companies of mules and four of camels. The bulk of these were deployed in the Middle East and North Africa. From mid-1942, the RIASC went on an accelerated drive for expansion, and by 1944 it counted no fewer than 102 animal transport companies – an overwhelming majority of which were deployed in the India–Burma theatre. The expansion was, however, hampered by a host of problems. The most important was the lack of trained personnel to work the animals. Finding suitable animals, too, proved tricky. Prior to the war, mules were imported from Argentina and bred in remount depots. This was no longer possible. Although the breeds available in the domestic market were inferior, the RIASC was forced to make do with them. To augment animal transport, the army imported donkeys from South Africa. The RIASC also raised an experimental pack bullock transport company. So successful was this attempt that twenty-six such companies were created by 1944. The bullock companies were used in the rear areas, so freeing up the mule companies for deployment with the forward formations. The success with bullocks led to the raising of buffalo companies for similar roles.[6]

The most spectacular unit, however, was the 'Experimental Elephant Transport Company'. This was formed from the elephants that had escaped from Burma as well as those loaned by civilian firms in Assam. The RIASC soon realized that the elephants were not economical for use as transport. While they were capable of lugging huge loads, they also required enormous quantities of fodder. In consequence, they were used for engineering works instead: moving timber, building bridges over streams and log roads over swampy areas. After a brief tug of war, the elephant company was handed over to the Corps of Engineers.

This period also saw a major expansion in the Long Range Penetration (LRP) special forces groups under the command of General Orde Wingate. Even as the first 'Chindit' expedition was underway with the 77th Indian Infantry Brigade, Wavell had raised another LRP force: the 111th Indian Infantry Brigade. The hype and publicity generated by the Chindit expedition made Wingate rather more expansive in his plans. Following the Quebec Conference of 1943, where he sat at Churchill's elbow, Wingate was allowed to form six LRP brigades. Much against the wishes of the India Command and Slim, the 70th British Division was broken up to accommodate Wingate's grandiose designs. The meagre combat outcomes would be entirely disproportionate to the investment.

In tandem with the organizational changes, the India Command began addressing other weaknesses that had been cast into harsh relief by the fight against the Japanese. On 16 May 1943, Wavell told the chief the of general staff in Delhi that they must quickly assimilate the lessons of Arakan. Towards this end, he set up a committee 'to examine and report on the present standard of readiness for war of British and Indian infantry battalions in India, and to make recommendations for their improvement'. The Infantry Committee, chaired by the deputy chief of the general staff, Major General Roland Richardson, along with four more two-star and two one-star officers, convened at the end of May. The committee's diagnoses and recommendations led to series of significant and far-reaching reforms.[7]

The nub of the problem, the committee argued, was the hasty and excessive expansion of the army in India. In particular, infantry units had been raised in a lackadaisical fashion. The adage that 'any man can be an infantry man' had long been outdated. The India Command had been oblivious to the fact that infantry had become a technical arm needing special skills. The low status and pay of the infantry had immediately to be redressed. Indian infantry battalions should also be given first claim in the selection of officer cadets and recruits.

Second, the practice of milking existing units to raise new ones had resulted in a haemorrhage of experienced officers, VCOs and NCOs and so blunted the combat capabilities of the Indian battalions. The committee identified the absence of pre-war regular officers with five to eight years' service as a serious handicap. It had led to a sharp slackening in the standards of leadership and discipline, tactics and morale. At least three such officers, the committee insisted, were required in every fighting unit to teach the trade to the Indian and British ECOs as well as the troops.

Third, the standard of basic fighting skills, fitness and discipline of the newly joined recruits in battalions was alarmingly low. The committee cuttingly observed that the recruits that had fought in Arakan were no more than a 'mob of partially trained village youth'. This stemmed from the fact that the regimental training centres were over-burdened and underprepared to impart quality training to recruits. Some of these centres catered for up to fifteen battalions of a regiment. What was more, battalions of every regiment were organized and equipped differently and were deployed variously for desert and jungle warfare. The centres were chronically short of experienced training officers and NCOs: the front-line battalions being rightly chary of sparing their best. In consequence, the recruits churned out by the regimental centres were 'jack of all trades and master of none'.

The committee recommended increasing the training period of recruits to eleven months. Nine of these would be spent picking up basic infantry skills at regimental centres, while the last two months would involve specialized jungle warfare training in a designated 'training division'. Two training divisions would be established and would also enable the training of all British and African infantry soldiers that arrived in India. The absence of a formalized and functional training regime, the committee observed, was 'the most urgent problem facing us, and one which requires prompt and energetic action'.[8]

The implementation of the Infantry Committee's incisive and far-reaching recommendations was left to Auchinleck, who took over as commander-in-chief the following month. With his long association with and insight into the Indian army, Auchinleck was perfectly cut out for the job. By the time Mountbatten was appointed supreme commander of SEAC, Auchinleck had ensured that experienced Indian army officers were running the show. Eastern Command was renamed the Fourteenth Army and General Slim was appointed as the army commander. Commanders who had fought in North and East Africa as well as the Middle East were brought into the Burma theatre. For instance, Frank Messervy and Peter Rees – both with chequered records – were given another crack at commanding front-line formations: the 7th and 19th Indian Divisions respectively. Major General Temple Gurdon was appointed director of military training and tasked with overseeing the reform of training and army doctrine. Major General Reginald Savory, who had commanded the 23rd Indian Division, took over as Inspector of Infantry. 'I spent most of my time', Savory recalled, 'not only visiting the training establishments, but also infantry units throughout India. I also made regular trips to the front, so as to acquaint myself with the conditions at the time and apply the lessons learnt.'[9]

Indeed, training was Auchinleck's top priority. As he wrote to the CIGS in mid-September, 'I hope that all divisions will be trained and ready by the end of this year [1943]. I can assure you that I shall not allow any formation to go into battle until it is adequately trained.'[10] The 14th and 39th Indian Divisions were identified as training divisions, plucked out of their operational areas and located in the suitable terrain of Chhindwara and Saharanpur in central India.

The course for new soldiers and officers was divided into two parts. The first month was spent in a 'base camp' where they learnt the basic skills of operating in the jungle: movement in day and night, elementary navigation, minor tactics, field craft, and preparation of slit trenches. During the next month, the men moved into the jungle with their training companies and practised more advanced techniques: patrolling, infiltration, concealment, construction of larger defensive positions, personal hygiene and weapon maintenance. The course ended with a three-day jungle exercise involving 'enemy' troops.[11] Thereafter, the soldiers were sent to reinforcement camps where they continued to train until they were called up by their units.

Formations, too, began to take training seriously. Messervy, for instance, circulated a series of operational notes in his division outlining weaknesses observed during exercises, especially in patrolling, concealment and preparation of defences. The commander of the 20th Indian Division, Major General Douglas Gracey, was another proponent of continuous training and feedback. The battle-hardened 5th Indian Division reached India in the summer of 1943 after its stint in the Middle East. The entire division, including its commander, Major General Harold Briggs, attended lectures and trained for jungle warfare and animal management. The training instructions were clear:

'This division has now to train for operations of a character different to which it has been accustomed and to train quickly.'[12]

The revamped training system was not as smooth as it sounds. Both the training divisions were dogged by the shortage of experienced officers. Most of the trainers themselves had only a hazy idea of the realities of fighting in the jungle. In fact, many of them had to undergo a crash course in jungle warfare before they could pretend to teach others. The unfamiliarity with the terrain also lent an air of artificiality to the efforts of the training divisions. To come up to speed on jungle craft and lore, the training divisions resorted to an interesting expedient. They sought the services of India's best-known big-game hunter: Jim Corbett. The sixty-eight-year-old 'Carpet Sahib' was a legendary figure in the hills of Kumaon and beyond. The author of best-selling books – especially *Man-eaters of Kumaon* and *The Man-eating Leopard of Rudraprayag* – had been associated with the army earlier. During the Great War, he had raised a Kumaoni labour levy of 500 men and commanded them on the Western Front. With the onset of the Second World War, he had served on the district Soldiers' Board, helping out with recruitment. Now, with the honorary rank of a lieutenant colonel, Corbett became an instructor in jungle craft.

Corbett spent time with both the training divisions and travelled to other formations across India as well. His principal contribution was to allay concerns among the troops that the jungle was an alien environment – as much an enemy as the Japanese. Using slides, illustrations and short films, Corbett lectured on a range of themes relating to survival in the jungle: animal and human tracking; edible and inedible plants; brewing tea with herbs and wild honey; identifying snakes and bird calls. The troops were evidently taken by the genial old man and his tales of the jungle. As one of his students put it, he seemed a cross between 'a magician and a master-detective'. *Man-eaters of Kumaon* became required reading in the training divisions. It was also translated into Roman Urdu by GHQ India, so that officers could read it out to soldiers.[13]

That said, racy accounts of *shikar* (hunting) would have scarcely sufficed to prepare the troops to fight the Japanese. Rather more important were the training instructions and pamphlets, memoranda and circulars that flowed among formations and units. Yet this profusion of paper carried the risk of confusing as much as clarifying. As the Infantry Committee had noted,

> many doctrines exist, all of them fundamentally different and all of them being put into effect in different parts of India. They would stress the urgent need for GHQ to control the Pandits, who produce such doctrines, so that the training of the recruit and the trained soldier can follow one accepted doctrine.[14]

In order to streamline the doctrine, the fourth edition of *The Jungle Book* was published in September 1943. This training pamphlet was considerably revised to take into account the lessons of all operations against the Japanese, including the recent ones in Arakan.[15]

An updated edition of *Instructors' Handbook on Fieldcraft and Battle Drill* was issued, along with *Battle Drill for Thick Jungle*. Both these pamphlets helped convert doctrinal principles into tactical practice. Simultaneously, units and formations were being educated about the tactics adopted by the Japanese and ways of countering them. The operation in Donbaik, for example, had underscored the defensive strength of the Japanese bunker system. After a careful examination of this experience, various training outfits organized lecture-demonstrations of techniques to be adopted in attacking the bunkers. Training companies would carry out in slow motion the various phases of the attack and the operation would be dissected in the subsequent discussion. The use of light tanks in a 'bunker busting' role was also carefully examined. The evolving doctrine realized the mistakes made earlier – use of tanks in small numbers and lack of all-arms training – and sought to rectify them. Similar efforts were made to disseminate doctrine on dealing with Japanese offensive tactics: infiltration, encirclement and the use of roadblocks. The solution lit upon by the Indian army was the use of 'boxes': compact and strong all-round defensive positions, which if necessary could be supplied by air. Ironically, the idea of a 'box' had been discredited in the Western Desert, particularly after the first battle of Alamein. In the Burma campaign, though, it would prove rather more successful.[16]

*

Fighting an experienced opponent in the jungle called for not only intense training but a high level of physical fitness. By 1943, though, the physical standards of recruits to the Indian army had sharply plummeted. Given the widespread scarcity of food across most parts of India – including famine in some – it is hardly surprising that recruits were malnourished and afflicted with nutritional diseases such as anaemia. Special feeding was required to bring them up to the minimum acceptable operational standard. Indeed, the availability of good quality food was a major incentive for joining the army.

In the initial months of the war, the army rigidly adhered to the physical standards laid down in the *Recruiting Regulations* of 1939. The men recruited during this period were not prone to malnutrition. They needed no more than the normal peacetime scale of rations to fight well in the Middle East. With the surge in expansion from 1941, the army realized that recruits of the peacetime standards were unavailable in adequate numbers. So physical standards had to be relaxed. Even these standards proved difficult to maintain, leading to a further lowering of them in June 1942.

By early 1944, the army was forced to reduce the standards still more. Only the infantry saw a slight upward revision in standards – owing to the recommendations of the Infantry Committee. Yet recruiting officers were given leeway to take in men who weighed 5 lbs below the new scale – provided they felt that the recruit could gain this weight by eating army rations for three months. In practice, recruiting officers took in men who were underweight by 10–20 lbs.[17] Importantly, the drop in physical standards applied as much to the martial classes as to the newer social groups entering the army. In fact, the fall in standards of the martial classes was steeper. Since these groups remained the cutting edge of fighting formations, the India Command's nutritional anxieties multiplied.

The declining physical standard of the recruits necessitated revisions to the army's scale of rations. At the outbreak of war, the peacetime scale of daily rations provided by the RIASC amounted to 3,385 calories. Units could supplement this by purchasing additional rations, for which they were given a monthly allowance of Rs. 0.6 per soldier. Rampant inflation, however, rendered this pittance entirely worthless. In early 1942, the cash allowance was raised to Rs. 2 per

Physical Standards for Recruitment of Infantry

Year	Sikh		Punjabi Muslim		Mabrattas		Madras	
	Height	*Weight*	*Height*	*Weight*	*Height*	*Weight*	*Height*	*Weight*
1939	5ft 6in	122 lbs	5ft 6in	120 lbs	5ft 4in	115 lbs	5ft 4in	115 lbs
1941	5ft 4in	115 lbs	5ft 4in	115 lbs	5ft 2in	110 lbs	5ft 2in	110 lbs
1942	5ft	105 lbs	5ft	105 lbs	5ft	105 lbs	5ft	105 lbs
1944	5ft 2in	110 lbs	5ft 2in	110 lbs	5ft 2in	110 lbs	5ft 1in	105 lbs

Source: B. L. Raina (ed.), *Preventive Medicine (Nutrition, Malaria Control and Prevention of Diseases)* (Delhi: Combined Inter-Services, Historical Section, India & Pakistan, 1961), Appendix II.

soldier per month. In September 1942, it was further increased to Rs. 3. By this time, units were also struggling to source food from local markets.[18]

Alongside these measures, the India Command began nutritional testing of troops to arrive at a more scientific scale of rations. As elsewhere, the availability of trained personnel proved problematic. In January 1943, a nutritional section was established in the medical services directorate of GHQ India. This set-up turned out to be inadequate for conducting field surveys and advising units on nutrition. Hence, the director of the Nutrition Research Laboratories in Coonoor, Dr W. R. Aykroyd, was roped in as an honorary consultant and his team supported the efforts of the army.

Preliminary investigations in 1942 had shown that the vitamin A and C content of Indian rations was well below the generally accepted estimates of optimum requirements. A more detailed study of a pioneer engineer unit in September 1942 had not only confirmed these findings but found that the scale of rations was deficient in practically all nutrients and calories. Clearly, Indian troops were subsisting on a very narrow margin of nutritional adequacy. In January 1943, the medical services director recommended placing all Indian troops on the higher, field-service scale of rations (3,950 calories per day). British troops in India had already been upgraded to this scale in October 1942. The India Command demurred. For one thing, the RIASC was not yet ready to procure and supply to all Indian units on this scale. For another, the additional financial burden was believed to be too onerous. After six months of discussion, the India Command decided to do away with the additional cash allowance and introduce an enhanced daily scale of rations for non-operational areas.[19]

Reality did not match the ration scale, however. Troops deployed on the Burma frontier consumed on average about 3,550 calories per day. A study by the newly formed Indian Operational Research Section observed: 'Compared with a 20 year old Englishman of similar weight (a low standard for a mature man is some 10 lbs heavier), the average weight of the Indian troops fell short by 14 to 23 lbs.' The energy value of food consumed by them was almost 500 calories short of the minimum prescribed. Their food was deficient in all varieties of vitamins. There was a 'serious shortage of meat'. Each man got 14 grams of animal protein – a third of the figure accepted as 'the absolute minimum daily requirement'. The report grimly concluded that the 'men cannot be expected to maintain maximal output of work on the energy available in the diet supplied'.[20]

And yet the India Command proved itself unable to upgrade the ration scale. Part of the reason was differences among nutritional experts on the methods of testing. Many believed that simple clinical investigation by stripping men to the waist and examining for signs of deficiency would suffice. Experts were divided over the utility of biochemical and other clinical aid in surveying troops. By 1944, however, a consensus developed on methods of survey – mainly owing to the influence of practices pioneered in the United States (by the Fatigue Laboratory at Harvard) and Britain. It was agreed that four different types of data had to be collected: nutritional measurement of ration scale; analysis of food actually consumed; medical examination of soldiers; and biochemical testing of blood and urine samples.

On this basis, studies were conducted from mid-1944 to early 1945 in two recruiting centres to ascertain the effects of army diet on the recruit's physical condition. The sample of recruits was divided into two groups: one received only the basic ration (3,950 calories) and the other received an additional 16 fl oz of milk every day (4,250 calories). The investigations revealed that the average wartime recruit gained 5–10 lbs within four months of enlisting. Thereafter, he continued to gain weight at a slower rate. The extra milk did not make any difference in the average weight gained. A further study examined the response of recruits to meat and milk in rations. One group was placed on the basic diet. A second was given 12 oz of meat instead of the normal 2 ozs. And a third group was given 48 fl oz of fresh milk instead of any meat. The results showed that while all three diets increased the weight of the recruits, those on the meat diet gained the most and those on the milk diet the least. Analysing the detailed results, the investigators concluded that the advantage of the meat diet lay not in its greater calorific value, nor yet in the higher proportion of animal protein, but in the inherent nutritional quality of meat that seemed to stimulate the general metabolism.[21]

In the wake of these surveys, GHQ India decided that the daily ration scale in field service or training should provide a minimum of 4,200 calories, including 100 grams of protein. Animal protein supplied daily to the Indian soldier increased from 14 grams in 1943 to 32 in 1945. In practice, though, they got only 23–26 grams a day.[22] Part of the problem was the difficulty encountered in the supply lines leading up to the Burma frontier.

Equally constraining were dietary restrictions observed by Indian troops. Muslims would not touch pork and ate only *halal* meat; Hindus ofter forswore beef and the meat of female animals; Sikhs took only non-*halal* meat; and certain groups like Jats were strictly vegetarian. Soldiers of all backgrounds regarded even certified meat with considerable suspicion.[23]

Culture compounded the problem in other ways too. The Indian soldiers' methods of cooking tended to dilute the nutritional content of their diet. Vegetables were boiled in water and clarified butter (*ghee*) for two or more hours; rice was cooked with excessive water. The Paxton cooker provided to Indian units was typically used for storing rations or utensils – the cooks preferring to light up a traditional brick-and-mud stove, which coughed up enormous quantities of smoke as well as reducing the quality of the food.

Then there was the long-standing tradition in the Indian army – mirroring wider societal practice – of giving soldiers two meals a day: one just before noon and the other in the evening. With the enhanced ration scales, it became clear that the soldiers' digestive systems could not cope with 2,000 calories at one go. When the Fourteenth Army sought to change this routine in 1943, there was considerable objection from the Indian units. As the senior VCO of one battalion said: '*Hazur, aisa to hamare* unit *mein kabhi nahin hua*' ['Sir, this has never happened in our unit']. Commanding officers, too, tended to see this as 'a shattering of old-time tradition'.[24]

By 1944, however, a new regime was enforced. Soldiers started their day at around 5 a.m. with sweet milky tea, supplemented with sugar-coated fried biscuits or *chapattis*. Between 10.30 and 11.30 a.m. they took rice or *chapattis* with a vegetable curry. Tea was brewed again at 2.30 p.m. And around 6 p.m. they had their main meal of the day: *chapattis* or rice with vegetable curry supplemented by eggs, fish or meat and fruit. Efforts were made to educate troops to avoid wasting food on the plate. Copies of a booklet *Food and Fitness* were issued to all units to make them conscious of nutrition and health.[25]

A directorate of food inspection was created within GHQ India in 1944. To improve the standard of cooked food, the idea of creating an Indian army catering corps – along the lines of that of the British army – was examined but not implemented.[26] The supply corps was already overwhelmed by the magnitude of its tasks. The mere management of multiple ration scales – forty-three on the last count – for Allied troops in India taxed its resources. As the official historian of the supply corps noted in dismay: 'there were strange items such as anhydrous lanoline (wool fat issuable on medical recommendation), *burghal* (a kind of dal [lentil] admissible to transjordanian troops), mealie meal (in South African rations) and so on which the Indian clerk and issuer had never heard of'. Indian ration scales, too, had their own peculiarities – not least the allowance on medical advice of opium to addicts.[27]

Even so, the supply corps mounted a superb effort to keep up with the burgeoning demands. The army's systems of procurement, holding and distribution were radically overhauled and modernized. In 1939, the Indian army had only one, small supply depot in Lahore. From late 1942, a series of depots linked to transportation hubs were constructed in Karachi, Benares, Bilaspur, Panagarh near Calcutta, Avadi near Madras, and Waltair near Vizag. These depots had massive storage sheds linked by an internal rail network. By 1944, their total capacity stood at 328,000 tons. The supply corps also obtained and produced dehydrated food and meat as well as other nutritional substitutes such as multivitamin tablets. A cold storage network was created from scratch to provide fresh beef to British and African soldiers. Four types of ration packs of varying bulk and calorie content were created for troops out on patrol and other operations. Methods of supplying forward forces by air were learnt, practised and perfected.[28] The supply corps did not manage to fully bridge the nutritional gap, but its valiant efforts ensured that the Indian soldiers that fought the Japanese in 1944 were not the emaciated men of the earlier campaigns.

Nutrition was only one aspect of the wider problem of military health. Of equal concern was the vulnerability of Indian troops to disease. As Slim noted, 'We had to stop men going sick, or, if they went sick, from staying sick.'[29] Especially dangerous in the India–Burma theatre was malaria. In 1942, 83,000 soldiers had been admitted to hospitals in the Eastern Command with malaria; many more were not, owing to the shortage of beds.[30] One of the reasons for the Arakan debacle had been the epidemic scale in which malaria had struck troops of the Eastern Army command. The Infantry Committee observed that malaria accounted for 90 per cent of the casualties in the Arakan campaign.[31] What's more, troops had lost confidence in the utility of preventive measures against malaria and were refusing to co-operate with malaria control efforts. The army began a major drive to educate the troops – using lectures, pamphlets and circulars – about the nature of the problem and methods of controlling it. Notwithstanding these efforts, it was realized that the confidence of troops in anti-malaria measures could only be restored by securing a substantial drop in malaria rates.[32]

The Indian Medical Service (IMS), a hybrid civil-military entity, had a considerable track record in malaria research. It was an officer of the IMS, Ronald Ross, who had first demonstrated that malaria was transmitted by mosquitoes.[33] During the Second World War, however, the IMS was in grave crisis. The requirement of catering to public health as well as the military had stretched the service to breaking point. As a senior Indian doctor colourfully put it in late 1943, the IMS had 'produced twins, both males – lusty rascals – vigorously kicking . . . One of them is destined to wear the Sam Browne and the other the Hippocratic Toga. But they must part company immediately and begin to lead independent lives straightaway.'[34]

The somnolent Malaria Institute of India was revivified in 1942, when the Rockefeller Foundation offered to donate the equipment of its malaria research unit in Coonoor. The offer was at once generous and timely. The institute accepted it with alacrity and embarked on a renewed programme of malaria research. The director of the institute, Lieutenant Colonel Gordon Covell, was appointed consultant malariologist to GHQ India. Covell travelled extensively across India, inspecting units and formations. He also travelled to Australia,

New Guinea and the United States to understand their methods and medicines for combating malaria.[35]

In the summer of 1943, Covell outlined a series of preventive measures to be adopted by units and soldiers. First, and most important, was the selection of sites for deploying troops. 'In a malarious country', he wrote, 'no site should be selected within half a mile of local habitations, unless it is the only one available.' Second, adult mosquitoes had to be killed by spraying pyrethrum insecticide. Third, personal protection measures such as the use of mosquito nets at night, full-sleeved shirts at dawn and dusk, and anti-mosquito cream – a non-greasy version was made available – had to be regularly enforced. Fourth, small doses of mepacrine should be taken as a prophylactic drug. Covell argued that this would only work if mepacrine was classed not as a medicine but as a ration. Drawing on French and Italian campaigns in Macedonia and Abyssinia, he concluded that both personal protection and suppressive treatment could only work 'where a very high degree of anti-malarial discipline is maintained. Experience has shown that such discipline cannot be brought to the requisite degree [of] protection unless officers commanding units are made aware that if it breaks down they are likely to be deprived of their commands.'[36]

As Fourteenth Army Commander, Slim took this advice seriously.

> Good doctors are no use without good discipline. More than half the battle against disease is fought, not by the doctors, but by regimental officers. It is they who see that the daily dose of mepacrine is taken, that shorts are never worn, that shirts are put on and sleeves turned down before sunset.

Slim began organizing surprise checks of whole units, every man being examined. 'If the overall result was less than 95 per cent positive I sacked the commanding officer. I only had to sack three; by then the rest had got my meaning.'[37] Special anti-malaria units were created to carry out other activities such as spraying and installation of drainages. In 1944, pyrethrum insecticide was supplanted by DDT. The Malaria Institute had first received DDT towards the end of 1943. To be used against mosquitoes, DDT had to be turned into a solution in kerosene or xylene-triton. Both these solvents were hard to come by in India and expensive as well. Several experiments were conducted to find a cheap alternative. The Council of Scientific and Industrial Research suggested turpentine; GHQ India could only spare toluene. Eventually, they settled on a medium kerosene extract as a solvent. Experiments carried out on the efficacy of DDT underscored its problematic environmental effects: 'amount [of DDT] which did not completely kill the vegetation in the area was found to be insufficient for adequate control of mosquitoes in the area'. When sprayed on water, it 'killed a large number of small fish'. The India Command was undeterred by such considerations, though it did abandon the idea of aerial spraying of DDT within India after a few trials over Delhi.[38]

The cumulative effect of these measures was a steady decline in the incidence of malaria among the troops of the Fourteenth Army. Allowing for seasonal variation – mid-November to mid-March was the period when transmission of malaria was always low – the results are striking. From a high point of almost 3,300 men per day in July 1943, the numbers afflicted daily dropped to 1,700 in July 1944 and reached 370 in June 1945.

Equally important were the organizational innovations that enabled the rapid recovery of those laid low by malaria and other diseases.[39] The Infantry Committee had noted that on average the men who had contracted malaria took between three and eight months to return to their units. This deprived battalions of their experienced personnel for unacceptably long periods. In consequence, the committee had recommended the creation of special medical organizations directly behind the front line.[40] Slim sanctioned the raising of Malaria Forward Treatment Units (MFTU). These were effectively field hospitals, located a few miles behind the front and capable of treating 600 men at a time. Apart from reducing transit and treatment time, the MFTUs also discouraged men from malingering in the hope of getting away from their battalions for lengthy periods.[41]

Another innovation was the establishment of Corps Medical Centres – combined units that pooled all Allied medical resources to enable forward treatment of battle casualties. These centres, usually made up of MFTUs and Casualty Clearing Stations, included mobile surgical units. The latter were made possible by blood transfusion units that had been raised in 1942. At this point, blood transfusion services were scarce in India. Barring Bombay, Madras and Calcutta none of the cities and towns had a blood bank. Over the following year, the army transfusion units were equipped and trained in Calcutta and Dehra Dun. By December 1943, an elaborate transfusion service organization was operating from the base transfusion unit in Dehra Dun to field ambulances on the Assam and Arakan fronts. Despite the shortage of refrigeration, the Fourteenth Army created small blood banks at various places and prepared wet plasma. Blood donation propaganda also proceeded apace: civilian donors were awarded a badge of white metal with a bronze star of India.[42] The availability of such facilities near the front lines not only helped reduce the casualty turnaround times, but also bolstered the morale of the men.

Indeed, in focusing on the training and health of troops, the India Command aimed as much at improving morale as operational efficacy. An intangible yet indispensable element of fighting power, morale was affected by several factors: training and equipment, health and welfare, leadership and command. And with the Indian army in 1943, yet another issue was seen as crucial in shaping morale: susceptibility to the propaganda of the INA.

The India Command's concern on this score was accentuated during the Arakan campaign. An Indian platoon was reported to have walked over to the Japanese positions, holding aloft propaganda leaflets dropped on them. Delhi had already been worried by the scale of recruitment for the INA and the strength of Japanese propaganda. Using information from Indian officers who had escaped from Malaya, GHQ India groped its way towards discerning the links between the changing size and composition of the army and enrolment in the INA.[43]

Equally concerning was the apparently sophisticated network being used by the Japanese to suborn the loyalties of the Indian soldier. An espionage school had been set up in Penang for training Indian nationals as agents, who would then be inserted into India.[44] Products of this school were active in Arakan. Among their Japanese handlers was Maruyama Daisaburo, who had lived in India through the 1930s. In 1937, Maruyama had joined Gandhi's ashram in Wardha for a couple of years, engaging himself in various pursuits, including the study of English and Hindi with the Mahatma's private secretary, Mahadev Desai. In 1940, he was expelled from India on suspicion of espionage for the Japanese. On returning to Tokyo, Maruyama had grown close to Rash Behari Bose and thence to the Indian Independence League as well as the INA. His activities north of Akyab were closely shadowed by the Indian intelligence service.[45]

The India Command remained oblivious, though, to the importance of the operational context in which the defections to the INA occurred – a point that was underlined again by the incident in Arakan. In consequence, the army leadership felt that the Indian soldier must be inoculated against enemy propaganda. Doctrine had to be fortified by indoctrination.

London regarded the problem with rather more alarm. In early May 1943, Amery circulated a note to his colleagues drawing their attention to these attempts at subverting the loyalty of the Indian army. The expansion of the army and its increasing political awareness; the sky-rocketing inflation; continuing political uncertainty; 'excellent propaganda' by the Japanese exploiting these concerns – all contributed to the problem. Amery was careful to point out that Japanese attempts had so far met with 'limited success', but he feared the 'possible dangers'. In particular, Amery insisted that 'It would be dangerous to contemplate any further expansion of the Indian Army, and wise to concentrate on keeping establishments up to standard and, so far as possible, weeding out unstable elements and replacing them by more reliable.'[46]

Churchill pounced on Amery's note. The prime minister was displeased both with the morale of the Indian army – including the defections to the INA – and its operational performance in the Arakan. He argued that not only should further expansion of the army be curbed, but its current size should be substantially reduced to improve quality.[47] Amery was more responsive to military realities. The chiefs of staff in London also felt that any discussion on trimming the Indian army should take place only after full consideration of the matter. At Churchill's insistence, the note was taken up by the war cabinet. At a meeting chaired by Attlee, Amery pointed out that the target of expansion had already been scaled down, from seventeen to fifteen infantry divisions and three to two armoured divisions. The war cabinet agreed that the new target of fifteen infantry and two armoured divisions should be completed – but not exceeded. To improve the troops' morale, the possibility of an increase in pay should also be explored.[48]

Wavell went along with this decision; so did Auchinleck. Churchill, however, deemed it inadequate. He wanted to reduce the Indian army by a quarter and use the money saved to hike the salary of the troops.[49] Churchill held that the British could stay on in India only if the army were 'healthy'. And the health of the army depended on the martial classes. Amery wrote to Linlithgow that Churchill 'has got into one of his fits of panic and talks about a drastic reduction of any army that might shoot us in the back'.[50] Unaware of the fact that his beloved martial classes had joined the INA in droves, Churchill insisted that both economy and efficiency demanded a steep reduction in the Indian army. In the event, Auchinleck wrote a long letter highlighting the impossibility of a large reduction in size or of replacing non-martial classes with the martial ones. If anything, a change in the composition of the army at this stage would do more harm – both economically and politically.[51]

Nevertheless, the new commander-in-chief was concerned about his troops' vulnerability to Japanese propaganda. Under Wavell, GHQ India had taken some steps to counter the INA's influence. Forward Interrogation Centres had been set up in Assam and Bengal for preliminary interrogation and classification of personnel returning from Japanese-occupied territories. Those suspected of being Japanese agents were sent on to a combined civilian and military interrogation centre in Delhi. Within the GHQ, another civilian-military unit – known as GSI(b)(i) – was created to sift intelligence reports and initiate measures against the Japanese intelligence unit overseeing the INA. To head this most secret of units, Wavell had chosen an Indian officer from the most reliable of the Raj's allies: princely India. Lieutenant Colonel Himmatsinhji hailed from the royal family of Nawanagar in western India. A nephew of the great Ranji and brother of Duleepsinhji, he had played first-class cricket, had fought in the Great War, and had a brief diplomatic career too. In March 1943, Himmatsinhji was also appointed as the GHQ's liaison officer to visit formations and units in connection with the INA and related matters.[52]

Soon after Auchinleck took over as commander-in-chief, Subhas Bose landed in Singapore. The Raj had been closely monitoring Bose's broadcasts from Germany and realized that his presence in Japanese-occupied territory would give a fillip to the INA's propaganda and recruitment. So, Auchinleck decided to expand the counter-propaganda efforts within the Indian army. A small group of hand-picked British officers was summoned to the cantonment town of Sabathu near Simla and briefed by the director of military intelligence. The plan was to form counter-propaganda cells within each combat unit, consisting of a few British officers, VCOs and NCOs. These cells would act as a conduit for the flow of information and propaganda against the Japanese and the INA (designated as Japanese-Inspired Fifth Columnists or JIFs) aimed at the ICOs as well as Indian soldiers. The assembled officers would serve as 'patrol officers', moving around units and formations, supporting the cells and providing them with materials for their own propaganda.

Among those chosen was Major John Heard – an Emergency Commissioned Officer with a Royal Engineers regiment in India. A civilian engineer trained at King's College London, Heard had been living in India since the early 1930s. As an air-conditioning salesman for an American firm, he had travelled extensively across the country. Before signing up as an ECO, Heard had indulged his amateur interest in military matters by joining the Delhi Light Horse – a British-only auxiliary force – and later the Bombay ARP.[53]

Heard was initially puzzled at being picked for the counter-propaganda outfit. But his meeting with the commander-in-chief made it clear that GHQ knew its job. Was it true, asked Auchinleck, that he had lived in India for thirteen years and visited a large number of Native States? 'I had been promoting Air Conditioning', replied Heard, 'and Princes were the only people in India who could afford it.' After a few questions on his experience in India, Auchinleck asked Heard to 'try this job for a month' and then decide if he wanted to stay on. Other British officers, too, were uneasy about the assignment. Some felt that their job was soldiering and were 'damned if they were going to act as moral spies'. Others thought that the enterprise smacked of a communist cell. Eventually, they reconciled themselves to the job on the assumption that it might actually benefit the ordinary Indian soldier.[54]

The officers were then given extensive briefings by Himmatsinhji and his team about Japanese recruitment tactics and training outfits, the organization and leadership of the IIL and the INA, the mistreatment of prisoners of war and brutality against those who refused to join them, and the resistance of many Indian officers and other ranks. The Indian soldier had to be informed about the 'traitors' and warned that he should 'expect to be the object of severe propaganda directed against him perhaps by a member of his own caste, even his own village'.[55] But this would have to be done artfully. To begin with, the counter-propaganda cell in the units would be called the 'Josh' – spirit, enthusiasm or pep – group. They would use a host of informal techniques to disseminate propaganda, including casual chats, entertainment programmes and visits to specially designed 'information rooms'. The content of the propaganda would range from conveniently potted histories of Japanese expansionism and Indian nationalism – Bose being held up as a renegade – to stories about Japanese atrocities and heroism of Indian prisoners.

The apostles of Josh quickly fanned out to spread the gospel in various formations – especially those on the front lines. Cells sprang up in units; battalions buzzed with talk of 'Japs' and 'JIFs'. Local talent was pressed into service for propaganda decked up as entertainment. Units staged skits with such titles as 'The Capture of an Indian Village by Japanese Troops'. Around a hundred recruits took to the parade-ground stage with 'a vivid representation of mass murder of civilians, robbery, violation of women and temples, and other examples of Japanese atrocities'. The finale was the liberation of the village by Indian troops.

These staples of propaganda were circulated by a weekly Josh newsletter aimed at the leaders of cells. Apart from tales of atrocities, the newsletter also gave information on ostensible Japanese 'reverses' and their impending defeat. Another standard theme was the apparently growing camaraderie between Indian and British soldiers: 'British troops are eating Indian food and liking it'; RAF soldiers have 'adopted orphans' in Bengal; and so on. Each edition of the newsletter also carried a specially designed cartoon depicting a Japanese-looking rat – the rodent being deeply disliked in the Indian countryside for damaging crops and food. Josh leaders were told to cut out these cartoons and put them up in the information rooms. Six months into production, the newsletter also carried pieces in Roman Urdu, which could be read out to the troops.[56]

India Command supplemented these efforts by producing a thirty-seven-page pamphlet *Against Japan*. This widely circulated pamphlet detailed Japan's 'planned aggression from 1830 to present'. It emphasized the debasing effect of the Japanese religion: Shintoism – 'not Buddhism' as believed by the Hindus. And it gave graphic examples of Japanese atrocities in occupied areas.[57] From the outset, counter-propaganda was dovetailed with the director of military training's efforts to cultivate an 'offensive spirit against the Japs'.[58] Training divisions and other formations sought to cultivate a deep hatred of the Japanese among the Indian troops. The object of fighting, they were told, was not to seize ground or capture the enemy, but to kill him like vermin. For instance, a training instruction of the 5th Indian Division stated: 'The JAP is a fanatic and therefore a menace until he is dead! . . . It will be our fanatical aim to KILL JAPS. Hunt him and kill him like any other wild beast! He is NOT a superman.'[59]

How successful were these efforts at counter-propaganda and indoctrination? By mid-1944, the India Command felt that the Josh groups were 'generally satisfactory'.[60] To be sure, there were no further defections to the INA either in Arakan or elsewhere in the Burma theatre. But this was mainly because of the improved battle performance of the Indian army against the Japanese. Even at the end of the war the Indian soldiers' attitudes towards the INA would be considerably removed from the ideas peddled by the Josh groups. More difficult to judge is the success of the efforts to instil hatred for the Japanese soldier. The Burma campaign in 1944–45 was marked by considerable levels of brutality. As an Indian officer, Gian Singh, put it in his poem 'Kohima':

> No prisoners we took, no mercy we gave
> Their crimes against comrades we never forgave.

This suggests that indoctrination did work to some extent. Yet the fierceness of the battles also stemmed from an interactive escalation at the tactical level. In particular, Japanese soldiers' unwillingness to surrender even in the direst of situations left the Indians with little option but to take out every man standing.[61]

Alongside the attempts to improve the quality of men and their morale ran a mammoth logistical effort. At the end of September 1943, the British chiefs of staff directed that India be prepared as a base by October 1944 for 20 divisions (Indian, British and African), 154 squadrons of RAF and some naval forces, as well as American and Chinese troops in the India–Burma–China theatre. Towards this end, the India Command organized a massive military and civilian labour force of over 1 million workers. These men and women were employed in constructing various installations required by the India Base and for a range of other activities, such as unloading, stacking and sorting supplies, and cleaning, repairing and maintaining military installations.[62]

Labour was recruited through both civilian and military channels. Civilian contractors engaged by the India Command brought in their own workers. The Indian army had its Pioneer and Auxiliary Pioneer companies, which were expanded. In addition, India Command was allowed – from early 1942 – to raise a Civil Pioneer Force.[63] The unskilled component of this force was largely raised from the margins of Indian society, especially the depressed classes and the tribal groups. The eponymous Munda Labour Battalion, for instance, was drawn from a single tribe, the Mundas, in central India. In raising this battalion, the authorities relied heavily on the services of the most prominent Munda leader, Jaipal Singh.[64] Born in 1903 to a family of Christian converts, Jaipal Singh had been educated in a missionary school in Ranchi before going up to Oxford. A gifted sportsman as well as student, he took a Blue in hockey and captained the Indian hockey team that went on to win Olympic gold in 1928. A year before the war broke out, Jaipal Singh had formed the Adivasi Mahasabha – a political outfit aimed at advancing the interests of the tribes. The demands of the war offered an unprecedented opportunity that he was quick to seize. Jaipal Singh soon emerged as an articulate spokesman of tribal rights. After the war, he would go on to secure special provisions for the tribes in the Constituent Assembly of India.

The recruitment of the depressed classes was similarly facilitated by their stalwart leader, B. R. Ambedkar. In July 1942, Ambedkar was appointed labour member of the viceroy's Executive Council. Although his main responsibility was to address the problems of organized labour and ensure its continued support for the war effort,[65] Ambedkar sensed an opportunity to promote the interests of the so-called 'untouchables'. At his urging, the army raised six regiments from these castes and inducted them in larger numbers to the labour units as well. Ambedkar also petitioned the government to expand affirmative action for these castes. On 29 October 1942, he submitted a memorandum demanding a fixed percentage of employment in government services for them and financial aid for promoting their education. The government accepted these recommendations. In August 1943, the depressed classes were granted an 8.3 per cent reservation of government jobs – the figure was later raised to 12.5 per cent.[66] These measures would subsequently be enshrined in the constitution of independent India – a document that would be drafted by a team led by Ambedkar.

The southern princely states of Travancore, Cochin and Pudukottai also provided labour battalions. These units typically had thirty-two 'gangs' of twenty-five men under the command of a British officer. The governor of Assam raised a Civil Porter Corps from his province and the hill town of Darjeeling to service the Fourteenth Army. The India Tea Association raised and supplied labour for use in north-east Assam and in rear installations close to the tea gardens.[67] All in all, upwards of 1.5 million Indians were drawn as labour into the vortex of the war effort.

The top priority for India Command was the construction of airfields. This had begun soon after the fall of Rangoon in March 1942. At the time, India had just sixteen all-weather airfields – only one of which was in Assam. By October 1942, a programme was underway for the construction of 215 new airfields. Each of these would require an all-weather runway at least 1,600 yards long and 200 yards wide. Constructing a concrete runway of these dimensions called for 4,000 tons of cement and 40,000 tons of crushed stone. Materials were also required for taxiways and parking aprons, rail and road access, workshops and hangars, fuel storage and accommodation. In many places, even basic facilities such as water and electricity were unavailable. The logistics of the programme were further complicated by the fact that the location of the airfields frequently involved a trade-off between operational requirements and availability of rail and road connectivity.[68]

Airfield construction was the largest and costliest works programme in the Indian war economy. It was also the most successful. By the end of 1944, the target of 215 was well within sight. The statistics of work completed in the airfields by then was impressive: 310 miles of runways, 960 miles of all-weather taxi tracks, 2,200 miles of roads, 72 million square feet of aprons and hardstandings, 20 million square feet of technical accommodation, 3 million square feet of hangars, almost 4.5 million gallons of fuel storage, and electricity generation of 64,100 kW.[69]

Apart from airfields, India Command also began building reserve base depots to hold and supply ordnance, rations, fuel and other stores. Until early 1942 there was only one such base – in Lahore, to support troops deployed on the north-west frontier. In the wake of the Japanese attacks, a second reserve base depot began to be set up in Benares and a reserve ordnance depot at Jamalpur. Both locations were sufficiently removed from air threats while also being linked by rail to the rest of India, including to the Bengal & Assam Railway (B&AR) that served east Bengal and Assam. Although lower in priority to airfields, the construction of the bases proceeded apace. By January 1943, depot accommodation in India increased from a mere 2.5 million square feet to 13 million – with another 11 million square feet under construction. Following the Casablanca Conference, the network of reserve bases was further expanded to support (the eventually shelved) Operation Anakim. Two new reserve bases were built, in Panagarh near Calcutta and Avadi near Madras. The Panagarh base had 570,000 square feet of covered storage, serviced by an 85-mile internal railway. And Avadi had 450,000 square feet of covered storage with internal railway of 107 miles. Both bases were initially designed to hold thirty days' worth of stocks. This was quickly scaled up to forty-five days and eventually doubled to ninety days' stocks – a quantity considerably higher than that held in the other theatres. Five smaller bases were also created in other parts of India, including two near the port of Vizag on the eastern seaboard.[70]

The stocking of the base depots as well as their ability to support the fighting formations was crucially dependent on the state of transport infrastructure: especially the ports and railways. Both of these were riddled with shortcomings and inefficiencies. Following the Japanese occupation of Burma, the Bay of Bengal was closed to shipping. Ports on the east coast – Calcutta, Chittagong, Vizag, Madras – were evacuated and seaborne traffic diverted to the western ports of Bombay, Karachi and Cochin. The magnitude of the dislocation can be gauged from the fact that Calcutta alone had handled an annual traffic of 8.25 million tons. Compounding the problem was the large influx of refugees from South-East Asia and the arrival of military reinforcements. In May 1942, Bombay handled over 220 ships a day, up from the pre-war daily average of 25.[71]

In November 1942, a joint Anglo-American shipping mission visited India and made a series of recommendations to improve the capacity of the western ports: the provision of additional lighterage and lighter frontage to receive the traffic; new equipment, especially cranes; and the construction of more berths. These recommendations were reinforced by an expert committee led by Guy Cooper, the chairman of Burmah-Shell in Bombay, which sought to improve the turnaround time of ocean tankers in the major ports. This led to a series of steps to enhance the capacity of the western ports, including the procurement under Lend-Lease of American mobile cranes. As the threat from the Japanese navy receded, the eastern ports recommenced their operations. From mid-1943, as operational requirements for Assam and Burma came to the fore, they bore the brunt of the shipping traffic. Calcutta was particularly prominent. In July 1943, it was handling just over 117,000 tons of imports. The next month it had to cope with 254,000 tons.[72]

The resultant problems in Calcutta port were a major source of friction between American and Indian authorities. The American logisticians believed that the inefficiency of the port stemmed from its management by the civilian Port Commission. They felt that the port must be under a military director to supervise and rationalize operations and that the dock labour must be militarized. Equally galling to them was the fact that they controlled nothing other than two African-American port companies and their equipment. As an American official complained, 'the British were following a peace time routine which they were not particularly interested in disturbing to meet the American demand for speed'.[73]

The Indian government was unwilling to countenance the American recommendations. Placing the port under military control would, they feared, draw public ire and result in avoidable political tension. So the Americans had little choice but to adopt innovative practices to increase efficiency. They began to bypass the contractors and directly recruit local labour. These men were paid daily wages based not on the number of hours worked but on the amount of tonnage unloaded. American supervisors and their Indian 'gangs' also developed a degree of camaraderie that came in handy. Yet the congestion caused by British heavy-lift cargo continued to hamper American operations at the port.

Matters came to a head after a Japanese air raid on Calcutta on 5 December 1943. In the following days, almost two-thirds of the labour force failed to turn up at the port. The Americans were aghast. President Roosevelt wrote bluntly to Churchill in early 1944:

> Congestions begin in Calcutta itself where many vessels are seriously delayed ... I urge that all lines of communication, from Calcutta inclusive, into Assam be placed at once under full military control and that officers of outstanding competence who will tolerate neither failure nor delay be assigned to this work. The United States stands ready to assist in furnishing personnel should you desire this.[74]

Wavell was peeved at the pressure from the highest American quarters, but eventually agreed to appoint a British civilian as director of Calcutta port. The Americans inducted two experienced port battalions of four companies each – equipped with modern port and heavy-lift machinery such as automatic and floating cranes, tractors and forklifts. American equipment as well as techniques were adopted by the Indians to remarkable effect. By mid-1944, Calcutta became one of the most efficient Allied ports in the world. At the end of 1943, uncleared cargo lying in the port was 96,000 tons. By the end of June 1944 the figure was reduced to 32,000 tons and by the end of October to 11,000 tons. During the same ten-month period, Calcutta had handled 2.25 million tons of cargo.[75]

The efforts to improve the ports were, however, dealt a huge blow in April 1944. Just after 4 p.m. on 14 April, the city of Bombay was rocked by an enormous explosion. Within an hour came a second and even more devastating flast. The governor of Bombay reported 'great columns of smoke in the air weaving patterns of incredible beauty . . . a dumb city watched from hilltop and terrace long sheets of angry flame'.[76]

The explosions had occurred on SS *Fort Stikine* in Victoria Dock, Bombay port. The ship was carrying nearly 1,400 tons of explosives and ammunition. Besides this, it was laden with other materials, mainly cotton and timber. A minor fire on board had touched off this combustible cargo with disastrous consequences. Some 900 people were killed or injured. Seventeen nearby ships were destroyed, with losses totalling 50,000 tons of shipping. Several other vessels sustained varying degrees of damage. The Victoria and adjacent docks were put out of action. In the resulting fire, over 36,000 tons of foodgrains were also lost. A commission of inquiry constituted by the Indian government submitted a damning indictment of the port authorities and various official agencies. As the secretary of state for India observed, 'its findings contain much material which will provide useful ammunition for critics of British administration in India'.[77] The potential critics were, of course, not just the Indians but also the Americans.

The Indian government had, in fact, swung rapidly into action. Labour at the docks was cajoled to return to work within days of the explosions. The task of reconstruction was handed to the army. Working with the Port Trust, the army undertook a massive effort to clear wreckage and debris, reconstruct and repair the damaged docks, and restore and improve the rail network and water supply. By 1 October 1944, Bombay port was fully functional again.

Other Indian ports too witnessed an impressive expansion of capacity owing to new construction and equipment, procedures and drills. The management of the Vizag and Chittagong ports was also militarized along the lines suggested by the Americans. By the end of the war, the annual capacity of Indian ports rose to 25 million tons from the pre-war capacity of 19.75 million.[78]

The rail network linking the ports and reserve bases to the Burma front was initially unequal to the demands of the war. Built in 1902 to cater for the needs of local tea and jute cultivators, the Bengal & Assam Railway was a peculiar system. For one thing, over two-thirds of the 3,300-mile line was built on metre-gauge as opposed to the broad-gauge adopted in most other parts of India. This necessitated the unloading and reloading of materiel at stations to the west of the Brahmaputra River. For another, the railway crossed the enormous, un-bridged river by rail ferries. From the eastern bank of the river ran two branch lines: the northern to Assam and the southern to east Bengal. By 1942, however, many of the river steamers and barges that plied the waters of the Brahmaputra had been transferred to Iraq and Iran.[79] In addition, the entire system operated on single track – there were few passing stations and loops to ply two-way traffic. And finally, the signal and telegraph systems were primitive and considerably slowed down the traffic. In May 1942, the northern line of the B&AR could carry only 600 tons of freight a day. The capacity dropped to 500 tons later in the year owing to both the rains and the disruptions caused by rebels during the Quit India campaign.[80]

In early 1943, the army needed 900 tons of supplies to be delivered daily at Dimapur, near the Assam–Burma border, both to sustain the 4th Corps units and to build up thirty days' reserve stock. In consequence, two newly formed Indian army railway operating groups were deployed to augment the manpower of the B&AR. Steps were also taken to enhance the capacity of the rail lines and the ferry service. Twenty-nine new stations and fifty-six crossing loops were constructed to enable two-way traffic. The northern branch line was improved to the point where it could sustain a daily traffic of fourteen supply trains, each of fifty to sixty wagons – both ways. Trans-shipment facilities between the broad-gauge and metre-gauge systems were also improved to cope with 160 vehicles and 3,000 tons of stores and fuel every day.[81]

Nevertheless, these improvements continued to fall short of those required. First, the demands of men and materials for construction along the rail line reduced the amount of military supplies that could be transported. The trade-off between short-term and long-term considerations was not easy to achieve. Second, the logistical requirement proved to be a moving target. By the end of June 1943, the B&AR's capacity had increased from 600 to 1,720 tons a day. Yet the Trident Conference, held the previous month, had approved a series of plans that increased the daily demand for Assam alone to 4,300 tons. Auchinleck estimated that by undertaking further improvements to the line and by curbing civilian requirements the capacity to Assam could be enhanced to 3,400 tons a day by early November 1943. Even this figure proved impossible to achieve – not least because the main railway lines servicing Calcutta were breached by a major flood of the Damodar River. In mid-August, ahead of the Quebec Conference, Auchinleck reported that the build up in Assam by March 1944 would fall short by 128,000 tons.[82]

The Americans tartly concluded that Auchinleck was

overwhelmed with the magnitude of his problem in moving the insignificant amount of 3,400 tons a day over the Assam L. of C. [Lines of Communication]. He listens too much to the no-can-do boys at G.H.Q. [India], particularly the QMG's [Quarter-Master General's] office, who are probably influenced by Indians who actually run the works.[83]

The Americans were particularly concerned because their promises of supplies to China over the Himalayan Hump were not being met. At Quebec, the American chiefs of staff offered some US Army railway units for use on the B&AR. In subsequent discussions, Auchinleck welcomed the offer provided the units worked under the existing central control of the Indian railways. Then too, owing to concerns about political repercussions, he wanted the Americans to come in only at the end of the 1943–44 operational season. When US General Brehon 'Bill' Somervell visited Delhi in October 1943, he was told that the Assam line was carrying only 3,200 tons per day: this could go up to 4,400 tons in October 1944. Somervell felt that unless the capacity were increased to 4,800 tons per day by April 1944, American promises to Chiang Kai-shek could not be kept. The

Americans were also irritated by the India Command's reluctance to accept their railway units. Eventually, they found an ally in the SEAC commander. Mountbatten insisted that the Indian government must accept the American offer, if only in a limited section of the B&AR line for starters. Auchinleck protested that American methods would not work in India, but eventually gave in.[84]

Towards the end of January 1944, the 705th Railway Grand Division – containing five operating battalions and one workshop battalion – arrived in India. Negotiations for the takeover of a crucial 800-mile section of the metre-gauge line were concluded the following month. Somervell insisted that 'We cannot undertake to work under British management.'[85] Consequently, an arrangement was worked out whereby the entire line remained under the general manager of the B&AR but complete operational autonomy was given to the Americans. From 1 March 1944, the American units began to work their section of the line.

The Americans brought with them a blast of energy as well as innovative operational methods. For instance, they found that the average tonnage carried in the 10-ton metre-gauge wagons was 7.3 tons. By contrast, the Americans resorted to the practice of 'volume loading' wagons. This ensured that the 10-ton cars could carry almost double their average load. The Americans also introduced an 'economy scheme' in which the length of freight trains was increased from a maximum of sixty wagons to a hundred – by using two engines if necessary. This not only increased the tonnage being carried but also reduced the density of traffic. The performance of the B&AR was also enhanced by reducing the number of stops and adhering strictly to train schedules – even at the cost of inconveniencing the local populace. The bottleneck at the rail ferries was broken by using two engines on each ferry: as one pulled cargo wagons off the ferry, the other pushed cargo heading in the other direction. Equally impressive were the changes introduced in the workshops that serviced the railway. American equipment as well as practices of shop-floor and inventory management drastically increased the efficiency of the workshops: twenty-five locomotives could be completely overhauled every month – up from the earlier record of seven. The upshot of the

Traffic on the Bengal & Assam Railway

Date	Tons per Day	Quebec Target
February 1944	3,443	3,400
March 1944	3,631	3,400
April 1944	4,697	3,400
May 1944	4,945	4,667
June 1944	4,973	4,667
July 1944	5,420	4,667
August 1944	6,296	
September 1944	6,537	
October 1944	6,766	

Source: James M. Ehrman, 'Ways of War and the American Experience in the China-Burma-India Theater, 1942–1945', PhD thesis, Kansas State University, 2006, p. 285, Table 9.

all this was a transformation of the logistical picture. By May 1944, the supply shortages in Assam and Bengal were brought under control. From the following month, despite the monsoon, the B&AR proved capable of moving more supplies than requested by British and American forces.[86] This dramatic turnaround occurred not a day too soon. For the Japanese were already on the move.

17

Back to Burma

The Arakan offensive of early 1943 had forced the India Command to undertake far-reaching changes in organization, tactics and logistics. By the end of the year, these preparations were well under way. And Arakan was yet again chosen as the proving ground for the Commonwealth forces. For one thing, the planned amphibious operation to capture Akyab entailed operations in the Arakan. Although the amphibious component would be shelved in January 1944, the Fourteenth Army was prepared for a land attack. For another, the formations in Assam were not yet ready. Nor indeed was the larger strategic plan for Burma as yet clear. By default, then, SEAC went on the offensive in the Arakan.

As earlier, in the opening phase the plan was to capture the small port of Maungdaw. Thereafter, the Japanese defences along the 10-mile road connecting Maungdaw with Buthidaung – held by the experienced 55th Division – would be attacked. The operation would be carried out by the 15th Indian Corps, made up of three battle-hardened divisions of the Indian army: the 5th and the 7th, with the 26th in reserve. These troops were supported by a massive, unprecedented quantity of medium artillery, Lee-Grant tanks and other supporting units. RAF fighters and dive-bombers were earmarked as close air support for the ground offensive.

The 15th Corps had begun to be inducted into the Arakan from the late summer of 1943. This gave the troops adequate time to get acquainted with the jungle as well as each other. Units and formations kept up with a gruelling regime of realistic training. As Slim noted, 'Our training grew more ambitious until we were staging inter-divisional exercises over wide ranges of country under tough conditions. Units lived for weeks on end in the jungle and learnt its ways. We hoped we had finally dispelled the fatal idea that the Japanese had something we had not.'[1]

Following Slim's promotion to Fourteenth Army commander, Lieutenant General Philip Christison took command of the 15th Corps on 1 November 1943. Thereafter, the forward units began creeping south towards the string of Japanese outposts. By mid-November contact was made with the Japanese, but the 7th Division came up against stern resistance. The Japanese defences were organized in bunkers sited atop razor-back ridges. Set-piece attacks on such positions rapidly came unstuck – even when supported by RAF dive-bombers. The divisional commander, Frank Messervy, swiftly switched tactics. He ordered his units to eschew frontal attacks and instead resort to infiltration, bypassing and envelopment through the gaps between the Japanese positions. When his troops were behind the Japanese positions, these could be systematically ground down. 'We will undoubtedly have a Neapolitan sandwich of British-Japs-British', he observed, 'but it will be one made by ourselves, and with the initiative in our hands, it will soon be transformed to British-British-Jap.'[2]

On the night of 30 November, the 15th Corps began a major offensive against the Japanese defences along the Mayu Ridge. Although the going was rough, the emphasis on infiltration and encirclement proved timely. In several tactical actions, Indian and British units managed to surprise the Japanese. Two weeks on, the 7th Division stood athwart the main Japanese defences screening Buthidaung. Meanwhile, the 5th Division was advancing along the coastal plain towards Maungdaw. Here too Japanese bunkers proved a tough target for conventional assaults. Patrols of the division began to infiltrate the gaps between these defended localities, forestalling mutual support and reinforcements by the Japanese. While costly frontal attacks could not always be avoided, the new tactics usually compelled the Japanese to pull back without a fight. As a newsletter of the 5th Division noted, 'The only way to deal with the Jap def posns [defensive positions] is by INFILTRATION. Recent experience has shown that the Jap has produced nothing new in def [defensive] tactics.'[3]

Infiltration was easier said than done. The problems were amply highlighted by the 5th Division's own attempt to push through the main Japanese defences along the Maungdaw–Buthidaung line. Breaking through this line entailed the clearing of a formidable defensive fortress at Razabil – a self-contained warren of mutually supporting bunkers set on a ring of jungle-covered hillocks. On 26 January 1944, the 161st Indian Infantry Brigade began its assault on Razabil. As the divisional historian laconically remarks, the operation was 'at once the most ambitious conception and most complete failure'.[4]

The attack opened with a spectacular bombing of the enemy's positions by dive-bombers and medium guns. The ground attack, led by 4/7th Rajput and supported by a squadron of medium tanks, initially made headway. As the tanks sought to suppress the defenders by fire, the assaulting infantry moved up to the Japanese bunkers. Co-ordination between tanks and infantry proved less than perfect, however. By the time the tanks lifted their fire the Rajputs were several yards short of the enemy defences. The Japanese bunkers erupted into action. Machine-gun fire and mortars rained down on the Indians from entirely unexpected directions, including the reverse slopes of the hills. Tanks were unable to move much in this terrain and the attack proved abortive. Successive attempts over the next three days failed to dislodge the Japanese from Razabil. Faced with mounting casualties, the operation was called off on 30 January.

Razabil provided a costly reminder of the need to avoid frontal assaults wherever possible. But it also showed that the alternative of infiltration was not easily adopted in all contexts. The 15th Corps did not, however, have the luxury of time to mull these lessons. For the Japanese counter-offensive was not long in coming.

The commander of the Japanese Fifteenth Army in northern Burma, Lieutenant General Mutaguchi Renya, had been raring to take the fight to India. An extreme nationalist and militarist, Mutaguchi had commanded a division that captured Singapore in 1942. His record, however, stretched right back to the start of Japan's Asian war, and it gave Mutaguchi a messianic sense of his own role in the manifest destiny of his country. As he confided to his diary in late 1943:

I started off the Marco Polo Incident which broadened out into the China Incident and then expanded until it turned into the great East Asian War. If I push into India now, by my own efforts and can exercise a decisive influence on the Great East Asian War, I, who was the remote cause of the outbreak of this great war, will have justified myself in the eyes of our nation.[5]

Mutaguchi's colleagues and subordinates, however, had deep reservations about his plan. As one of them brusquely told him, 'It would no doubt satisfy you to go to Imphal and die there. But Japan might be overthrown in the process.'[6] It took several months of operational planning and war-gaming before they reluctantly came around. The strategic assumption underpinning Mutaguchi's plan was not wholly off-beam. The operations in the Arakan earlier that year had shown up the Indian army as a friable force. A rapid thrust into India could not only deal a decisive blow to the enemy, but also enlarge and secure the perimeter of the Co-Prosperity Sphere. They could then credibly threaten to knock out India and China, and so convince the Americans to come to terms with Japan.

Mutaguchi's efforts to persuade his superiors, especially Premier Tojo and the emperor, were supported from an unexpected quarter. By late 1943, Subhas Bose's efforts to raise a second INA were rapidly progressing. His force of 40,000 men and women was impressive – at least on paper, and he urged the Japanese to mount an advance into India with the INA in the vanguard. The mere appearance of his troops, Bose argued, would catalyse a major uprising in Bengal and other parts of India. The only requirement of 'ultimate success', he claimed, was that 'action within the country must synchronize with the action from without'.[7] In the context of the Quit India upheaval and the Bengal famine, Bose's plan seemed plausible.

The Allied operations in the Arakan tilted the balance in favour of Mutaguchi's plans, and on 7 January 1944 Tokyo gave him the go-ahead: 'For the defence of Burma, the Commander-in-Chief Southern Army shall destroy the enemy on that front at the appropriate juncture and occupy and secure a strategic zone in North-East India in the area of Imphal.'[8] Mutaguchi's main offensive, codenamed Operation U-Go, was directed towards the Imphal Plain in Assam.

His plan was 'to secure that area in order to establish permanent occupation'.[9]

The Japanese counter-attack in the Arakan was intended as a subsidiary thrust. On the night of 3 February, they launched Operation Ha-Go. The attack was aimed at stopping and destroying the 5th and 7th Indian Divisions along the Mayu Ridge. The Japanese hoped to repeat the pattern of operations hitherto employed with great aplomb: a speedy advance along several columns to infiltrate, surround and attack the isolated enemy positions. The Indian formations were expected to attempt a withdrawal – whereupon the Japanese would use roadblocks and ambushes to destroy them piecemeal.

The attack initially worked to plan. Four battalions of the Japanese 55th Infantry Group, supported by artillery, tore through the defended localities and gaps of the 114th Indian Infantry Brigade. By 0900 hours on the morning of 4 February, the Japanese, supported by their fighters and bombers, stood a dozen miles north of Buthidaung poised to cross the river and move south. Thereafter the 7th Division's position grew progressively precarious. A determined counter-attack by the 89th Indian Infantry Brigade failed to stem the tide. On the morning of 6 February, Japanese troops overran the divisional headquarters, though Messervy and his staff managed to elude the dragnet.

Despite deploying the army reserve, the 26th Division, Christison and Slim were unable to prevent the total encirclement of the 7th Division. Instead of withdrawing, however, the division operated according to the new doctrine: adopting all-round defensive 'boxes' and switching to half-rations. Once the Japanese offensive resumed, the Fourteenth Army mounted a valiant logistical effort to get supplies to the 'boxes'. The animal transport companies brought up replenishments in the face of Japanese machine-gun fire. The rudimentary air supply units were also pressed into service. After air superiority over the Japanese was regained, the volume of air drops was steadily increased. In five weeks Allied transport aircraft flew over 700 sorties, dropping rations, ammunition and other supplies into the 'boxes'.[10] The air drops were a new experience for most men on the ground as well. Young Indian soldiers became 'wildly excited and rushed about clapping their hands at the sight of small parachutes, opening in mid-air, gently gliding down with the more breakable type of packages'. The boom-and-thud of Japanese guns served as a reminder of the war, however.[11]

The Japanese threw their main effort at a hastily prepared position covering the Corps Administrative Base at Sinzweya. Although the 'Admin Box' was well stocked with supplies, it was manned by an assortment of non-combatant troops from supply and administrative units. The flat terrain ringed by hills also favoured the attacker. The corps commander ordered Brigadier Geoffrey Evans of the 9th Indian Infantry Brigade to take charge of the area: 'Put it into a state of defence and hold it at all costs.' Evans's order to his subordinates was equally terse: 'Your job is to stay put and keep the Japanese out.'[12] Bolstered by a battalion of Gurkhas, some companies of the West Yorkshires as well as two tank squadrons, the defenders gave a good account of themselves in the 'Battle of the Box'. Notwithstanding repeated and intense attacks by the Japanese resulting in mounting casualties and exhaustion, the 7th Division stood its ground. As a senior officer put it: 'We've learned now to fight where we stand and NOT to be frightened by the bogey of infiltration.'[13]

Even as the Japanese hurled themselves at these 'boxes', the 26th Division advanced into the Kalapanzin Valley, recaptured lost positions, and moved south to relieve the pressure on the 7th Division. Meanwhile, on the western side of the Mayu Ridge, the 5th Division launched a ferocious assault, destroying the Japanese forces almost entirely. As the 15th Corps began closing its maw, the beleaguered Japanese launched ever more desperate attacks on the box defences. The 2/13th Frontier Force was among the battalions that endured successive waves of Japanese assault. As one officer wrote:

Crouching in our shallow fox-holes, it was an eerie feeling hearing the first boom of a mortar discharge, seeing the trace of a thin line of light as ignition commenced, and wondering over which exact spot the delicate red stars would break out. Then down underneath where they had been blossoming would thunder the shattering crump of heavy Jap mortar shells. The night would be lit up by the criss-cross of clouds of tracer bullets being poured on us from all sides. Hand-grenades bursting amongst our positions showed how close, in some cases, the enemy were able to creep up unseen. In grim silence, every man, including clerks and followers, pumped back his answering fire ... The crescendo of noise would increase to a roar as the assaults came close in, to die away as each attack was broken off.[14]

Eventually, having lost as many as 5,000 men, the Japanese commander ordered a general retreat on 24 February.

Ten days later, the 15th Corps was yet again on the offensive in the Arakan. The retreating Japanese staged a stunning recovery and put up staunch resistance. Yet the momentum was now with the other side. By the end of March 1944, the 7th Division had captured Buthidaung. More impressive was the 5th Division's demonstration of operational flexibility. On 9 March, the division launched another operation to seize Razabil. Unlike the earlier attempts, the division now resorted to brigade-level infiltration and envelopment. Even as the 123rd Indian Infantry Brigade feigned a frontal attack, the 161st Brigade penetrated unopposed through the Japanese positions at night and reached the rear of Razabil by first light. The fortress was then taken by the 123rd Brigade, leaving the 161st to capture another important section of the Japanese line.[15]

The night before Razabil fell, the Japanese launched their main offensive towards Imphal. Mutaguchi had planned a four-pronged attack. The 33rd Division would smash the 17th Indian Division in the Chin Hills and head south along the Tiddim Road towards Imphal. A brigade-sized all-arms force – the Yamamoto Group – would advance through the Kabaw Valley, roll-up the 20th Indian Division and attack the airfields at Palel on the edge of the Imphal Plain. The 15th Division would cut west through the Naga Hills and sever the road link between Imphal and Dimapur before turning south on Imphal. Lastly, the 31st Division would also advance through the Naga Hills, capture the hill town of Kohima and help mop-up Imphal and Dimapur.

Apart from these three infantry divisions, Mutaguchi had the 1st INA Division – in all about 100,000 troops. Yet he was weaker than his adversary both numerically and logistically. Most importantly, he had no hope of gaining air superiority – a crucial determinant of

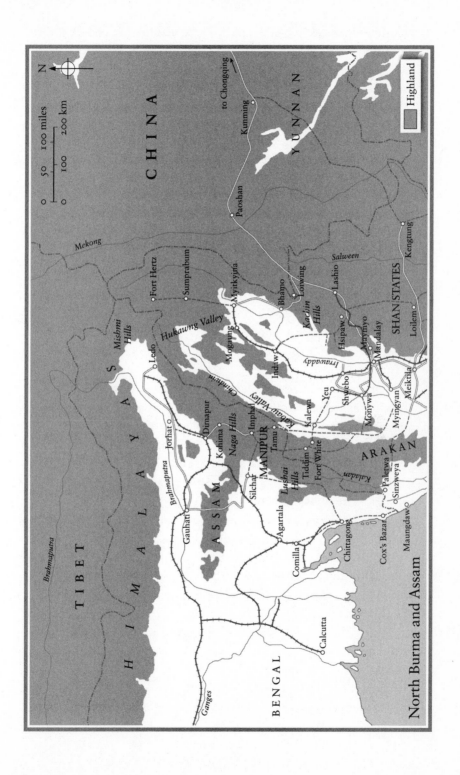

North Burma and Assam

Japanese victories in Burma in 1942. Mutaguchi hoped to surmount these handicaps by bold and aggressive planning as well as surprise and speed in execution. Indeed, he expected the campaign to end in three weeks.

The Fourteenth Army, however, was broadly aware of the Japanese intentions – thanks to documents captured by their patrols and intelligence provided by the locals. Both the commander of the 4th Corps, Lieutenant General Geoffrey Scoones, and Slim felt that in the event of a Japanese attack, the forward divisions should be pulled back to the Imphal Plain. Although a withdrawal might impair morale ahead of crucial battles, the logistical advantages of concentrating on the defence of Imphal were considerable. As Slim put it: 'I was tired of fighting the Japanese when they had a good line of communications behind them and I had an execrable one. This time I would reverse the procedure.'[16] Apart from the three Indian divisions of the 4th Corps – the 17th, 20th and 23rd – Slim planned to move in, if necessary, reserves from other fronts by airlift. This force, backed by ample guns, tanks and air power, would pummel the Japanese on the plain of Imphal.

Operation U-Go began on the night of 7–8 March 1944. The 33rd Division achieved tactical surprise and nearly managed to envelop and attack the 17th Indian Division. Part of the reason for this initial success was the delay in the division's planned withdrawal along the Tiddim Road towards Imphal. Once the division regained its poise, the practised Japanese tactics of infiltration and encirclement failed to work. The divisional commander's orders were short and snappy: 'Forget those bloody Japs and keep your eye on the ball.'[17] His troops managed both to blast the roadblocks hastily erected by the enemy and to effectively delay the pursuing Japanese. Throughout the 160-mile withdrawal to Imphal, the division's fighting power was sustained by rations and ammunition supplied by air. On 4 April, the 17th Division reached the Imphal Plain. Despite sustaining heavy casualties, the division was ready for operations after a brief rest and reorganization.

Meanwhile, the central front of the 4th Corps was reinforced by airlifting the 5th Indian Division from the Arakan. This was one of the most experienced Indian divisions: it had fought in North and East

Africa and served in Cyprus and Iraq before moving to the Burma front. Yet the division had had no training as an airborne force. Initially the plan was to move the troops, vehicles and animals by barge, road and rail over some 800 miles. The Japanese offensive towards Imphal threw the plan off kilter. The Air Transport Command and the US Army Air Force were called in to convert the planned eight-day trek into an aerial hop of less than two hours. Troops were pulled out of battle and sent on a long and dusty journey to the airfield. Even mules were taken by rafts and trucks to reach the zone in time. Within three days the first units were emplaning. The operation was hurriedly improvised. As the divisional logistics officer wrote:

> To stand on the airfield was reminiscent of standing on the kerb in Piccadilly or Oxford St. in pre-war days calling for a taxi ... Every few moments a plane was landing or taking off – everything was very informal and within a matter of minutes wounded were unloaded from planes, mules, jeeps and personnel were loaded, planes refuelled, the doors closed, and the plane was off on another journey.

The Indian troops were awestruck at these encounters with aircraft:

> Once on board they [Indian troops] passed the time gazing at the panorama below, excitedly pointing out features which, by their size or shape, attracted their attention. Some, completely unperturbed, discussed the battles they had just left and the prospect of the battles to which they were flying. One or two even slept.[18]

By the end of March, two brigades of the 5th Indian Division were deployed near Imphal to halt the Japanese 15th Division's march across the Naga Hills via Ukhrul. Although the leading units of the 5th Division managed to slow the advance, the Japanese switched direction and cut the Imphal–Dimapur road at Kangpokpi. Thereafter, they took control of key features overlooking the headquarters of the 4th Corps on the plain of Imphal.

The 20th Indian Division was struck by the vanguard of the Yamamoto Group on 12 March. The opening attack was blunted by the Indian units. Having tasted success, the divisional commander, Major General Douglas Gracey, was loath to withdraw. He wrote to the corps commander:

Our morale is sky high, as we have beaten the enemy and given him a real bloody nose everywhere. Everyone is prepared to hang on where they are now like grim death. It is their Verdun. It will be most shattering to morale if they are now asked to assist in the Imphal Plain and they will feel someone has let them down.[19]

In the event, the division pulled back to prepared positions overlooking the Imphal–Sittaung road. While doing so, it also tore up the supply depot at Moreh. Even the 200 head of cattle held in the depot were put to the knife. Thus the Japanese were the denied the 'Churchill rations' on which they had hoped to survive.

The most serious threat to the Fourteenth Army, however, came from the Japanese 31st Division. Slim had miscalculated his adversary's capability. Kohima was nestled in a series of formidable, trackless ridges running at over 7,000 feet, and Slim reasonably assumed that Mutaguchi would throw only a brigade at the town. As the scale of the offensive on Kohima became clear, the Allies scrambled to organize an effective defence. The 33rd Indian Corps was pulled out of reserve in India and tasked with reopening the Imphal–Kohima road and linking up with the 4th Corps. In the meantime, a motley garrison force of 2,500 men was cobbled together for the defence of the town.

On 4 April, the Japanese began attacking. Two days later, they cut the water supply, so forcing the garrison to rely on air supplies of water as well as rations and ammunition. By this time, formations of the 33rd Corps – now headquartered at Jorhat – began to operate on the Dimapur–Imphal road. The 33rd Corps was not particularly well suited for the task at hand: its training and preparation were for combined operations. For instance, its leading division – the 2nd British – was heavily mechanized and despite two months of training in jungle warfare was largely unprepared for fighting in Assam. Nevertheless, the division managed to clear the Japanese roadblocks and relieve the Kohima garrison on 18 April.[20]

The battle for Kohima continued for over six weeks. The Japanese defences on the hills overlooking the town proved extremely difficult to crack. The tactics of large-scale infiltration and encirclement adopted in Razabil were difficult to pull off in Kohima, and the 33rd

Corps was forced to rely on a succession of heavy set-piece attacks backed by massive artillery fire and air power. In the event, the Japanese 31st Division's strength began to sap, owing to problems of supply and reinforcements. Conversely, the 33rd Corps' fighting power was augmented by the arrival in mid-May of the battle-hardened 7th Indian Division from Arakan. Once the Indian formations started pushing back the weakened Japanese posts, they also managed to outflank the enemy and snip his lines of supply. From the first week of June, the Japanese began slipping away. The Kohima they left behind, noted Slim, was 'a cross between Delville Wood on the Somme and Keren; the whole place is a mass of splintered trees, shell craters, a honeycomb of trenches and dugouts, spread over precipitous, broken hills, 5000 ft high'.[21]

In retrospect, it is evident that the Japanese offensive on the Imphal Plain began to lose steam from the end of March. By early April, the 4th Corps had concentrated its troops – now amounting to four divisions – on the various approaches leading to Imphal. The Japanese pressed in on the defenders from three sides and managed to cut off the only remaining land route connecting Imphal to India. Contrary to their hopes, though, the isolated 4th Corps did not retreat in panic but stood its ground and fought. As in the Arakan, the defenders cut back their rations and were continually replenished by air. Over 400 British and American planes were employed to sustain the 155,000 men and 11,000 animals in Imphal. From mid-April to the end of June 1944, Allied aircraft flew in 19,000 reinforcements, 13,000 tons of cargo and 835,000 gallons of petrol. They also evacuated 13,000 casualties and 43,000 civilians to India.[22] As in the Admin Box, the availability of blood transfusion facilities in Dimapur meant that surgery could be performed on casualties within a few hours. Only the cases deemed most severe were sent back to the base hospitals. The creation of a new Corps Medical Centre proved particularly useful as this was an integrated medical and surgical unit serviced by its own airfield.[23]

The Japanese wore themselves out in a string of costly assaults. The Indian formations, for their part, relied heavily on their superiority in artillery, armour and air power to whittle down the attacks.

Co-operation between infantry and tanks gave a distinct edge to the Indian units, especially when they launched counter-offensives along the axes leading out of Imphal. Lieutenant Harpratap Singh's tank troop, for instance, supported the advance of a Gurkha battalion on the Tiddim Road. When the Japanese sprang a well-concealed ambush on the Gurkhas, Harpratap's tanks trained their fire on the bunker as well as the snipers hidden in the foliage. The Gurkhas had two men injured at the end of the encounter, while fifteen Japanese were found dead.[24] Even the units that lacked combat experience demonstrated tactical discipline – a good indicator of their level of training. A company of the 3rd Madras Regiment – a non-martial class infantry unit – was defending a rear area installation that was attacked by a Japanese platoon at the dead of night. The Japanese were unsure of the disposition of the defenders and sought to jitter them by random fire and shouting. 'We did not open fire as we could not see them', reported Captain Sethuram. 'Since we were in bunkers and trenches, their fire did not cause us any harm and as we kept quiet the Japs who came within 100 yards of us moved away.'[25]

The fight against the Japanese was brutal by any standards. As a British officer who had also fought in Europe observed, 'I would go through the whole campaign in Europe again rather than that 7 days in Sangshak [near Imphal]. The tempo and fierceness of fighting did not compare.'[26] Part of the reason for the ferocity of the fight was both sides' belief that the other would give no quarter. The Indians were struck by the brutal methods adopted by the Japanese. During the Battle of the Box, for example, the Japanese briefly captured a field hospital:

> the prisoners were dragged out of the medical inspection room and mown down by automatic weapons fired from a carrier. Others were bayoneted in their beds. A party of twenty who were told, 'come and get treatment', were taken to a dried-up watercourse by a Japanese officer and then shot.[27]

Such behaviour hardened the attitude of the Indian soldier who wrote home that the 'Japs are most uncultured and cruel . . . They have got beastly characteristics. Such a nation should be totally destroyed for the good of the world.'[28]

Equally striking to the Indian soldiers was the unwillingness of the Japanese to surrender even in thoroughly hopeless situations. After a fierce battle on the Imphal–Ukhrul road, Subedar Abdur Rauf of the 13th Frontier Force exclaimed: 'The Japs were like mad men. Their behaviour looked like that – one of them was clinging to one of our mortars with a tight hold whom I had to shoot down.'[29] Havildar Baggi Ram of the same unit found a famished, starving and sick Japanese soldier eating grass from his mess tin. Asked to surrender, he wounded himself with a grenade. When Baggi Ram moved towards him, the Japanese soldier lobbed another grenade. The Indian was nimble enough to dodge it, and proceeded to bayonet the dying man.[30] Viewing the battle from on high, Slim found that

we can kill the first 50%, of a Jap formation comparatively easily, because they attack and counter-attack thus giving us the opportunity. It is the second 50%, and especially the last 25%, who cause us our losses and who hold us up. They dig in and have to be literally prized out and killed individually in the bitterest kind of fighting imaginable.[31]

Unsurprisingly the campaign dragged on despite the onset of the monsoon. Even in early June Mutaguchi was goading his divisional commanders to renew their offensive on Imphal. By the end of the month, the Japanese formations had been drained of up to 70 per cent of their strength and were verging on starvation. On 4 July, the Imperial General Headquarters called off Operation U-Go. Four days later, Mutaguchi ordered the remnants of his army to fall back along the Tiddim Road towards Tamu. The Japanese had suffered their most ignominious land defeat of the war.

The Fourteenth Army's operational, logistical and material superiority had tilted the scales of battle in its favour. An important, if overlooked, contribution was made by its local allies: the Nagas, Kukis, Chin and other hill tribes. The Japanese came into the hills professing racial affinity and friendship. 'We are brothers and sisters', they declared in English, 'we belong to the race of small bodied people, the British are well built, they are not our brothers and so we need to help one another.' Dining with the village elders, the commander of the 31st Division, Major General Sato, said: 'I eat and drink what you eat and drink, we are brothers and sisters.' The Japanese promise to build schools, as well as their willingness to pay for food and supplies – albeit in their own currency – went down well with much of the local population. Within a couple of weeks, though, the veneer of politeness was dropped. The Japanese began to compel the people to off-load their stocks of meat and grain – often at gunpoint. Rape may not have been official policy, but it was not random either. Soon, the Nagas were deeply enraged. The Japanese, a Naga recalled, 'were very cruel to us. They killed our pigs and chicken and they ate our grain. They killed people and they frequently took men away to carry their loads.'[32]

Not surprisingly, the hill peoples turned against the occupiers. Not only did they mislead the Japanese forces about British numbers and dispositions, but they actively assisted the Fourteenth Army in its operations. As military intelligence observed in mid-1944, 'The quantity and quality of operational information received from the local inhabitants has been a major factor in our success to date. A high percentage of successful airstrikes have been the direct result of local information.'[33]

The battles of 1944 also brought the Indian army face to face with a new enemy: the Indian National Army. The Japanese had propped up the INA not for its operational capabilities but for its propaganda value. Best placed to assess Bose's military pretensions, the Japanese sought to avoid deploying the INA in combat. Thus the Bose Brigade of the INA was deployed in the Chin Hills – a relatively inactive sector. Then, too, the men under the command of Lieutenant Colonel Shahnawaz Khan were used to repair lines of communication and fetch supplies for the Japanese troops. When Shahnawaz complained to Bose, the Japanese promised him and his men a combat role but had no intention of fulfilling that promise. Nor could the INA's field espionage and propaganda units suborn the loyalty of Indian troops as they had done in 1942.[34] The fundamental difference, of course, was the operational context. With the Indian army gaining the upper hand over the Japanese, the INA's propaganda had little impact. As the former governor of Burma, Reginald Dorman-Smith, quipped: 'Poor old Netaji [Bose], he still slaughters the 7th Indian Division nightly over the radio and is most pained that their imminent surrender never takes place.'[35]

Following the launch of the U-Go offensive, Bose plonked himself in Mutaguchi's headquarters in Maymyo, proffering gratuitous strategic advice and demanding a combat role for his men. On 30 April 1944, the INA's 1st Division was allowed to attack the Palel airbase near Imphal. The Japanese had relented owing to their impression that the defenders were on the brink of defeat and might surrender to the INA. The raid on the airfield was assigned to a 300-strong group led by Major Pritam Singh. The strike force took the Indians initially by surprise, but was swiftly beaten back.

In mid-May, the Bose Brigade was redeployed to Kohima. Its most successful act was to plant an Indian flag in the town – even as the battle was going against the Japanese. In the subsequent offensives launched by the Fourteenth Army, the INA suffered heavily alongside the Japanese. Casualties also mounted during the withdrawal of July 1944 – an order that was made without any pretence of consultation with Bose. Numbers are difficult to ascertain, but it appears that of the 9,000 INA soldiers deployed in the campaign of 1944, about 1,000 were killed or wounded, between 2,000 and 3,000 died due to sickness and starvation, and some 700 men, including officers, surrendered.[36] The British continued to regard Bose as a political threat, but as a fighting force the INA was no match for the Indian army.

Imphal and Kohima have rightly been described by their official historian as the decisive battles of the war in South-East Asia. Yet, even as these battles were being fought to their deadly denouement, the Allies continued to debate the course ahead. In early June 1944, the combined chiefs of staff instructed Mountbatten to plan the campaign for 1944–45 with a view to preserving the air link to China and to eventually developing overland communication with China. Within this remit, he was asked to press advantages against the enemy. Meeting Mountbatten a month later, Slim said that a full-scale offensive could be launched on 1 November – provided he had at his disposal all the forces available to him for the battle of Imphal. As Slim would write later,

A year ago I would not have looked at the proposal. Even now it was not so much our advantage in the air, in armour, in greater mobility in the open, which gave me confidence to go on with my plan, but the spirit of my troops, my trust in their experienced commanders and in the high fighting value and hardihood of them all.[37]

Mountbatten and his staff developed two plans that could fit well with the combined chiefs' directive and the operational situation. The first, 'Capital', was for an advance to the general line Pakokku–Mandalay–Lashio in order to deny the Japanese access to northern Burma. The second, 'Dracula', was for the capture of Rangoon by an amphibious and airborne operation and for movement northwards to secure the Pegu area. Both the plans committed SEAC to the recapture of all of Burma. Churchill, as ever, was unenthusiastic about getting back into Burma. He was willing to support 'Dracula' as the least bad option, but would not contemplate movement northwards from Rangoon. It would be better, he felt, to swing eastwards after taking Rangoon. The British chiefs agreed that 'Capital' would be 'a slow and costly process that we are most unwilling to contemplate'. Operations in northern Burma should be the minimum necessary to pin down the Japanese, while 'Dracula' was undertaken.[38]

Commanders in SEAC, however, insisted that the Japanese had been decisively defeated and had lost heavily in men and material. The Fourteenth Army was pursuing them to the Chindwin and making excellent progress. It would be unwise to limit the extent or scope of the pursuit, else the Japanese would have the time to regroup and go on the offensive. On 13 September 1944, Mountbatten cabled the British chiefs that he was most anxious to carry out both the operations. To stop pursuing a beaten enemy not only would be misunderstood by the Americans, but would be most damaging to the excellent morale of the Fourteenth Army. Three days later, the combined chiefs sent a directive to Mountbatten, with the approval of Churchill and Roosevelt, stating that his objective was the 'recapture of all Burma at the earliest date'. Approval was granted for the stages of Operation Capital necessary to secure the overland link to China. Operation Dracula should be launched by 15 March 1945 and certainly before the monsoon set in.

In thinking through these operations, British military planners assessed that the India Base would be almost three-quarters complete by the end of 1944 and would be able fully to meet all operational requirements by March/April 1945. The improvements in communication to Assam and eastern Bengal had produced very satisfactory results. The overall capacity of the Assam rail and river line of communication had reached 6,470 tons a day and was expected to touch 9,400 tons a day. This was about 2,000 tons more than the target set the previous year.[39] The laying of fuel pipelines had also helped ease the load. By late 1944, an American-built 6-inch pipeline from Calcutta to Tinsukia in Assam (750 miles) was operational. As was a British-Indian 6-inch pipeline from Bombay to Bhusaval in central India (300 miles) and a 4-inch pipeline from Chandranathpur to Manipur Road. And the construction of more pipelines was underway. In 1944, an average of 75,000 tons of petroleum products were being moved every month over the Assam lines of communication. It was expected that by June 1945, the figure would stand at 200,000 tons.[40] Beyond the Imphal Plain, the Fourteenth Army planned for logistical support by constructing an all-weather two-way road down the Kabaw Valley to Kalewa. This would be supplemented by airlifts from the airfields in Imphal.

The organization of the army in India had been changed several times to meet the requirements of fighting the Japanese in the jungle. By early 1944, there were no fewer than five different types of infantry divisions under SEAC: the Indian light division, the Indian (A&MT) division, with higher or lower scales of motor transport; the 36th Indian Division comprising two brigades of four battalions each organized for amphibious operations; and the 2nd British Division, also geared for an amphibious role. However, the operations of early 1944 underscored the difficulty and wastefulness of sustaining such differently set up infantry divisions. So, in May 1944, GHQ India and SEAC drew up an organization for a standard infantry division that would at once be capable of fighting in the jungle, of being moved by air and of conducting amphibious operations. The new division would consist of three brigades of three battalions each, a reconnaissance and a machine-gun battalion. The divisional artillery would include two field regiments, one mountain and one anti-tank regiment. Mechanical transport would be reduced. In addition to first-line mules – as in the A&MT divisions – three animal transport companies would be provided to each division.[41]

SEAC also reviewed the problems faced in providing air support and air supply during the recent campaign. In order to improve ground-air co-operation, two RAF groups were recast as mobile groups, each with a main headquarters designed to combine with the headquarters of the appropriate army formation fighting ahead of it. The formation of such flexible land-air headquarters would prove very useful as the Fourteenth Army moved on the offensive. Changes were also made to improve the air supply systems. Special staff sections dealing with air supply were established down the chain of command to ensure better co-ordination during the coming offensive campaign.

The Fourteenth Army also continued to hone its combat skills by learning and passing on the lessons of the recent campaigns as well as by realistic training. Three types of reports were prepared by the Fourteenth Army: a weekly summary of operations with lessons learnt; detailed reports on recent operations; and periodic liaison letters. The main conduit for transmission of learning from the front to other units remained the *Army in India Training Manuals*. The July 1944 AITM discussed at length the preliminary lessons of fighting in the Arakan and Assam. The September 1944 AITM expanded on these and also underlined the importance of co-operation in combined-arms and joint land-air operations. The divisions that had fought in 1944 prepared their own pamphlets pointing out the lessons learnt. 'Our doctrine has proved to be sound', noted the 20th Indian Division's *Battle Instruction for Jungle Fighting*, 'but we have learnt many lessons.' The Fourteenth Army also began to prepare for the change in character and tempo of operations once they sloped down to the plains of central Burma. In early October, divisional commanders and other senior officers attended a training exercise at the new Tactical Training Centre in Dehra Dun. Over three days they deliberated on how an Indian infantry division should conduct pursuit and offensive operations, including in open terrain.[42]

Captain Gul Hassan Khan was sent to a jungle warfare school

at Sevoke in north Bengal. 'It was by far the toughest thing I have ever been through', recalled the man who would later lead the Pakistan army.

> Instead of training for the jungle it would have been beneficial for those who were destined to enter hell! It started in a novel fashion too – we had to walk to the school from the nearest railway station, thirteen miles away, lugging the kit we had been instructed to bring with us. We were kept on the hop day and night and it was dangerous business because live bullets were flying around ... A British officer, my basha-mate, remarked: 'If my grandmother were to see me here, she would burst into tears!'[43]

Slim's assessment was correct: his troops were ready to attack in November.

The 4th Corps' leading division crossed the Chindwin at Sittaung on 19 November 1944. The other two divisions crept up the Kabaw Valley. The 19th Indian Division, led by Major General Peter Rees, discovered that the razor-back, thickly forested but trackless hills were mostly undefended. Despite its lack of combat experience the division passed through the area swiftly and stealthily, covering 140 miles in four weeks. By this time, the 20th Division of the 33rd Corps was also advancing beyond the Chindwin. On 24 December, the 33rd Corps captured Pynigaing in the face of stern Japanese resistance. Kaduma fell six days later. By the end of 1944, the corps was on the Shwebo Plain.

Within days, it became apparent that the Japanese did not intended to hold the Shwebo Plain but to pull back and fight the main battle behind the Irrawaddy River. The Irrawaddy was a formidable natural obstacle for the Fourteenth Army. An opposed river crossing was a costly operation at the best of times. With its logistical tail stretching all the way back to Dimapur, the Fourteenth Army could attempt a crossing only at its own peril. Forced by the Japanese to improvise, Slim came up with a striking and bold plan.

Operation Extended Capital had two principal components. In the first, the 33rd Corps would capture the Shwebo–Monywa area and then proceed to create a series of bridgeheads on the Irrawaddy near Mandalay. The idea was to get the Japanese to commit their reserves to repulse the attack by 33rd Corps. Second, the 4th Corps would move from the left front of the Fourteenth Army, behind the 33rd Corps, and head south towards the Kabaw and Myittha valleys, and eventually appear at Pakokku. Crossing the Irrawaddy, the 4th Corps would then attack Meiktila – the principal administrative, logistics and communications hub for the Japanese in central Burma. Once Meiktila was taken, the 33rd Corps would smash south from Mandalay and destroy the Japanese forces.[44]

Extended Capital was implemented like clockwork. The Fourteenth Army's superiority in material and morale was evident throughout. The fact that the troops could switch so effectively from jungle warfare to fighting on the plains was testimony to their high standard of training and operational readiness. Logistical support for the troops operated at a high pitch of professionalism. The medical support available to the advancing forces would have been unimaginable even eighteen months earlier. Take the mobile neuro-surgical units that followed the fighting formations. Captain J. H. Hovell was with one such unit attached to a brigade – with Gurkha, Sikh and British battalions – that was moving towards the Irrawaddy.

> We marched every day for thirteen days, we were supplied throughout by air drops & the food throughout was excellent. We were with an A.D.S. [Advanced Dressing Station] & altogether had over a hundred mules to carry our equipment and patients, for we had to bring our patients with us on account of roving Japs. In fact we moved with the brigade. We halted and set up theatre three times, twice under a Burmese Basha and once in Nulla . . . The unit has moved further forward so we now get our heads within a few hours of injury & we are working very hard too. All night sessions sometimes . . . Our theatre is a large tent lit by our own power plant . . . Our results so far have been good.[45]

The malaria discipline of the Fourteenth Army was excellent too. When the novelist and RAF officer H. E. Bates flew into Burma, his new room-mate struck up a conversation:

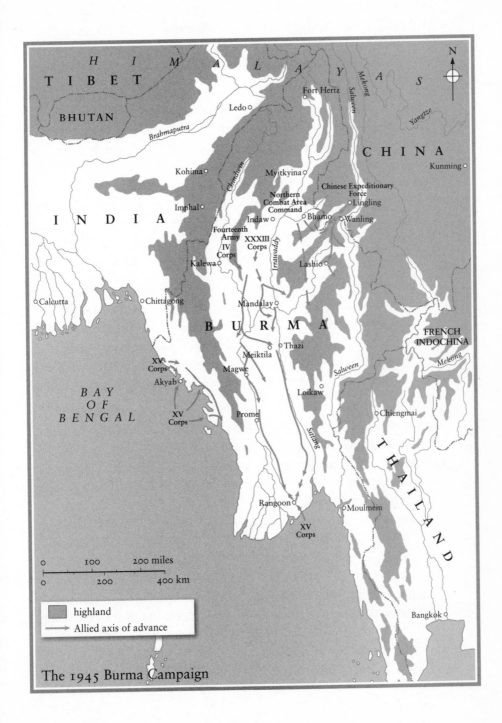

The 1945 Burma Campaign

'I hope you brought your mepacrine, old boy? Terribly important. You need the proper dosage every day. I never miss.'

'Mepacrine? What's it for?'

'Good grief, old boy, you don't know? Malaria, of course. You must take it. Absolutely essential.'[46]

On 22 January 1945, the 20th Indian Division, supported by an RAF group, took the town of Monywa and began moving towards the Irrawaddy. Further north, the 2nd British Division was engaging an important Japanese bridgehead on the river. The 19th Division was near the Irrawaddy some 60 miles north of Mandalay. The Japanese, for their part, were preparing to 'crush the enemy driving towards the Irrawaddy River'.[47] The attacks on the Japanese positions on the west bank of the river saw the latter at their tenacious best. An officer serving with the 11th Sikhs recalled the tempo of the battles:

> First came four squadrons of [Allied] Mitchell bombers, uprooting whole trees with their 1000lb bombs. Three squadrons of Thunderbolt and one of Hurricanes followed, sending up showers of earth and dust lit by the lightning flashes of explosions – all bang on target . . . even they had failed to dislodge the deepest bunkered Japs, who had to be winkled out almost one by one in a final infantry assault.[48]

Although the 33rd Corps managed to surprise the Japanese by its choice of some landing points, the latter hit back at the bridgeheads with everything they had. By a seemingly unending sequence of counter-attacks, the Japanese managed to prevent the corps from breaking out of its bridgeheads until the end of February 1945 – but only at an enormous price.

Meanwhile, the 4th Corps was conducting its looping advance towards the Irrawaddy. In order to fully exploit the opportunities offered by the terrain of central Burma, the 4th Corps' main striking formation, the 17th Indian Division, was hastily reorganized and re-equipped with completely mechanical transport. This was yet another indication of the growing confidence and flexibility of the Fourteenth Army. The drive towards Meiktila succeeded beyond the expectations of anyone in the chain of command. By 3 March, the town had fallen with heavy losses for the Japanese. When the latter regrouped for a ferocious counter-attack on the town, Slim finally had the chance to bring to bear his superiority in armour and air power. When the Japanese eventually pulled out of the Meiktila area, their fighting power was seriously sapped. Around the same time, three Japanese divisions fell back from Mandalay after a desperate but failed bid to block the advance of the 33rd Corps.

The race for Rangoon began immediately. As Slim reorganized his forces for the 300-mile advance to Rangoon, he realized that 'this dash to Rangoon by a mechanized force, confined to one road, thrusting against time through superior numbers, was a most hazardous and possibly rather un-British operation ... Whatever the risks, we were winning. We had kicked over the ant-hill; the ants were running about in confusion. Now was the time to stamp on them.'[49] The Fourteenth Army met with some serious resistance at the mouth of the Sittang Valley, yet the Japanese were unable to curb its momentum. As the 17th Division stood ready to take the town of Pegu just north of Rangoon, weather came to the assistance of the defenders.

The early onset of the monsoon slowed the advance of the Allied formations. But it was only a short reprieve for the Japanese. For one thing, the Allied high command decided to launch Operation Dracula – the amphibious assault towards Rangoon. For another, the Japanese decided to use the rain-induced lull in fighting to reorganize their defences in southern Burma. On 3 May 1945, the 26th Indian Division entered Rangoon.

The advancing Indian formations also rolled up the INA units all the way to Rangoon. In early March, Subhas Bose was dismayed to learn that five officers of the INA's 2nd Division had deserted to the Fourteenth Army. In mid-April, an INA battalion was decimated a few miles south of Taungdwingyi. By the end of the month, Bose read the writing on the wall: the battle for Burma was almost at an end. He decided to pull out his best units to Thailand and Malaya, leaving behind a small garrison force to maintain order in Rangoon. It was these units that handed control of the city to the 26th Indian Division. Having organized a dignified retreat Bose relocated to Malaya. He was in Penang on the night of 11 August when he learnt of the Japanese decision to surrender. A week later a Japanese plane carrying Bose crashed in Formosa.[50]

Rangoon resounded with roars and cheers on 14 August 1945. The British and Indian soldiers went

> wild with joy on hearing the news of the unconditional surrender of the Japanese. Supported by the same black-bereted Indian tankmen who fought alongside them on the drive to Rangoon, Indian and British troops . . . went round the streets of the city shouting and waving with joy . . . Army clerks, cooks, sweepers and barbers – all those who never are in the limelight and who rarely get honours and awards – were equally enthusiastic.

Subedar Major Ganpat Singh captured the emotions of the Indian soldiers: 'we rejoice at news because our people at home will get more of the necessities of life. It would also mean that we could return to our homes and rest which we need badly.' Subedar Latif Khan echoed this view: 'it will mean better days at home'.[51]

The more perceptive British officers realized that much had changed on the battlefields of Burma. As Colonel John Masters, now a staff officer in the 19th Indian Division, observed:

> As the tanks burst away down the road to Rangoon . . . [they] took possession of the empire *we* had built . . . Twenty races, a dozen religions, a score of languages passed in those trucks and tanks. When my great-great-grandfather first went to India there had been as many nations: now there was one – India . . . It was all summed up in the voice of an Indian colonel of artillery. The Indian Army had not been allowed to possess any field artillery from the time of the Mutiny until just before the Second World War. Now the Indian, bending close to an English colonel over the map, straightened and said with a smile, 'O.K., George. Thanks. I've got it. We'll take over all tasks at 1800. What about a beer?'[52]

18

Post-war

India's war may have begun without any serious planning. By the time it ended, however, there was a host of plans for post-war India. Economists and businessmen, intellectuals and bureaucrats, politicians and ideologues – all were taken up with the idea of planning. And the Indian soldier too. Even before the war had ended, men in uniform were looking ahead to promises of peace. A Marathi storeman in the Middle East wrote home asking who, if anyone, was planning in India. 'Through daily newspapers I came to know that every country is thinking and planning for the soldiers' future.' He had heard of the Beveridge Report, but

> for our Indian soldiers' future, what is going on and what will be done or who is planning? ... if there is anything of such kind in India, please let me know, I think something might be done and something might be going on there, if not something will be done, but who is going to say so?[1]

Planning for post-war reconstruction was undertaken in several quarters. The blueprints varied considerably in approach and content, but they all bore the watermark of war-time experiences. The best known of these was the 'Bombay Plan' – the first part of which was published in 1944. The plan was the product of the collective deliberations of a group of leading Indian businessmen: Purshottamdas Thakurdas, J. R. D. Tata, G. D. Birla, Lala Shri Ram and Kasturbhai Lalbhai. The details of the plan owed much to three senior executives of the Tata group: John Mathai, Ardeshir Dalal and Ardeshir Shroff, who in turn were assisted by a socialist intellectual, Minoo Masani.

The impetus for the plan came from two wartime developments. First, despite the friction between business and the Indian government, the war had effectively led to a form of import-substituting industrialization. The Indian capitalists not only looked forward to continued support from the government, but felt that they could do a lot better under a national government that would treat them as partners in the development of the country.[2] Second, they were concerned about the burgeoning sterling balances accumulated by India in London – IOUs given by the British government to India in exchange for wartime supplies. By the end of the war, India's sterling balances stood at an eye-watering £1.3 billion. Indian businessmen feared that Britain might unilaterally write these off or reduce its obligations by depreciating sterling. Whatever remained might be used by the government and by British businesses in India to place orders on firms in Britain. In short, India and Indian business would gain nothing out of the enormous economic sacrifices made during the war. By proposing a plan, the industrialists hoped both to position themselves vis-à-vis a post-war government and to forestall any adverse attempt at drawing down the sterling balances.

The Bombay Plan advanced a fifteen-year scheme for economic development that would unfold over three stages. The objective of the plan was to raise the per capita income of India to such a level that 'after meeting minimum requirements, every individual will be left with enough resources for enjoyment of life'. More specifically, per capita income would be doubled in fifteen years from $22 to $45. This in turn would require a tripling of the national income over the same period. The minimum standard of living was defined as a daily diet of 2,800 calories, 30 yards of cloth for clothing and 20–40 square feet of shelter for every person. These objectives would be attained by increasing industrial output by 500 per cent, services by 200 per cent and agriculture by 130 per cent. In the light of wartime experience, it is not surprising that the Bombay Plan laid maximum emphasis on the development of capital goods industry and infrastructure. The total capital outlay envisaged by the plan was to the tune of $27.6 billion. The single largest source of this would be the sterling balances, worth $3 billion.[3]

The plan drew criticism from all corners. The liberal economist

B. R. Shenoy questioned the financial assumptions of the plan and warned of the dangers of inflation latent within it. The Marxist Left denounced it as a plan for Indian fascism. The British establishment was mostly disdainful of the pretensions of the Indian industrialists. For all the scorn heaped upon it, however, the Bombay Plan would be influential in the early years of independent India. At the time, though, it mainly goaded others to come out with their own plans.

The unorthodox Marxist M. N. Roy published a 'People's Plan' that aimed to satisfy the pressing basic needs of the Indian people within ten years. The plan emphasized agricultural reform, arguing that the people's needs could not be met unless agriculture became a paying proposition in India. Nationalization of land and writing down of agricultural debts were the first steps to be taken. Roy's also differed from the Bombay Plan in his emphasis on the production of consumer goods – as opposed to capital goods. 'It is indeed a little pathetic, and may even prove to be considerably harmful,' he claimed, 'to start with half-filled bellies and half-clad bodies thinking in terms of automobiles and aeroplanes.' Better to focus on textiles and leather, sugar and paper, drugs and chemicals, tobacco and furniture. While private enterprise would not be entirely banned, it would have to work under the close stewardship of the state.[4]

The economist and follower of Gandhi S. N. Agarwal published *The Gandhian Plan for Economic Development of India* towards the end of 1944. The aims of the plan in raising living standards were broadly in line with the Bombay and People's plans. But Agarwal rejected these plans as imitative of Western thought. India needed an indigenous plan firmly rooted in its realities. In line with Gandhi's own thinking, Agarwal underlined the need to revive village community life. 'The attainment of increased productivity with the help of efficient and labour-saving machines is not and should not be our goal.' The emphasis was as much on moral economy as the real economy. All land would be nationalized and a system of village tenure introduced. Large industries would be gradually brought under government control, and 'decentralized to the maximum possible extent'.[5]

Not to be outdone, the Raj produced its own plan documents. In fact, the government had appointed a Reconstruction Committee as far back as 1941 – even as William Beveridge was getting down to work in Britain. The committee, however, was somnolent throughout the years of Linlithgow's viceroyalty. Part of the problem was the absence of statistical data for serious planning. More importantly, Linlithgow did not deem the exercise of much significance. Things began to change after Wavell took over in October 1943. Among his foremost concerns was to improve ties between the government and business. Wavell had no qualms in reaching out to Indian industrialists. In fact, it was Birla who proposed to him the idea of appointing a special member for reconstruction. Four months after the publication of the Bombay Plan, Wavell created a new Planning and Development Department and appointed Ardeshir Dalal as planning member of his Executive Council. A few months later the viceroy asked the authors of the Bombay Plan, along with other industrialists, to visit Britain and the United States to study their plans for post-war industrialization.[6] Unsurprisingly, the documents put out by the planning department echoed many of the ideas voiced by Indian industrialists.[7]

In the closing stages of the war, India also participated in planning for the post-war international order. India's involvement in these initiatives at once underlined its wartime contribution and its perceived post-war importance. The country was not a party to the preliminary discussions on the successor to the League of Nations – especially those at Dumbarton Oaks in late 1944 between the United States, Britain, the Soviet Union and China.[8] Yet it was among the Allied countries invited to the conference at San Francisco that convened from April to June 1945. As with its pre-war membership of the League of Nations, India's presence at the founding of the United Nations was anomalous: it was the only colonial entity in a group of sovereign states that were shaping the international order.

The government of India nominated a trio of knighted nonnationalists – led by Sir Ramaswamy Mudaliar, supply member of the Executive Council – to represent India at San Francisco. The Congress was predictably outraged. Gandhi, having been released from prison some months previously, led the charge. Speaking to the press prior to the conference, Gandhi harked back to the view that he had taken when Churchill had denied the Atlantic Charter to India. Thus he insisted that the 'Exploitation and domination of one nation over another can have no place in a world striving to put an end to all wars.' Complete independence for India was an essential first step towards peace. This would demonstrate to all colonized peoples that their 'freedom is very near and that in no case will they henceforth be exploited'. Gandhi demanded that 'the camouflage of Indian representation through Indians nominated by British imperialism should be dropped. Such representation will be worse than no representation. Either India at San Francisco is represented by an elected representative or represented not at all.'[9]

The government went ahead regardless. The Indian delegation was active in the discussions on the various articles of the United Nations Charter, especially those dealing with the composition of the Security Council and the voting procedures used by it. Mudaliar questioned the wisdom of handing the permanent members a veto, but agreed that an imperfect Security Council was better than none at all. The delegation also sought to advance India's claims for non-permanent membership of the Security Council. They argued that countries should be nominated – not elected – by the General Assembly based on a set of criteria, including size of population and armed forces, and industrial and economic capabilities. The Indians also suggested that in addition to six non-permanent members, the Security Council should have six observers that would partake of its deliberations but not vote. Neither of these suggestions was taken up, however. Be that as it may, India was one of the founding signatories to the United Nations Charter.

During the conference, the question of India's independence served as a platform that brought together diverse groups and personalities that pressed the new organization to grant independence to India, as well as justice and equality for all colonial subjects.[10] Prominent among these was Vijayalakshmi Pandit, the sister of Jawaharlal Nehru and seasoned member of the Congress. In a flurry of public speeches in San Francisco, Pandit lambasted the British government for speaking with a forked-tongue – freedom for the world and servitude for India – and urged the United States to give full effect to the Atlantic Charter. Much to the discomfort of Anglo-American officials, Pandit also circulated a memo to all conference attendees: 'The recognition of India's independence now will be a proclamation and an assurance to the whole world that the statesmen of the United Nations, assembled in this solemn conclave in San Francisco, have in truth and in honour heralded the dawn of a new and a better day for an all but crucified humanity.'[11]

Less politically charged was India's participation in the Bretton Woods Conference of July 1944. This conference sought to mould the post-war international monetary and financial order.[12] As in San Francisco, India was the only non-independent country at the conference. The Indian delegation at Bretton Woods was led by Jeremy Raisman, finance member of the Executive Council, and included C. D. Deshmukh, governor of the Reserve Bank of India, Ardeshir Shroff, and Sir Shanmukham Chetty, who went on to become independent India's first finance minister. The Indian delegation's efforts at Bretton Woods were driven by four main considerations.

In the first place, India wanted to expand the remit of the proposed International Monetary Fund (IMF) to include economic development. The Indian case, Deshmukh later explained,

> rested on the proposition that poverty and plenty are infectious and that if the operation of an international body like that projected [at Bretton Woods] was not to grow lopsided, it was necessary to pay special attention to the development of countries like India with resources awaiting development. Our appeal was to enlightened self-interest.[13]

The Indian delegation also emphasized the need to ensure balanced international trade for underdeveloped countries. Merely increasing the volume of raw material exports and manufactured imports would not suffice. The industrial needs of countries like India had to be taken into account. The delegation tabled two amendments to the articles of the Fund reflecting these concerns. While its call for the inclusion of development was not taken on board, the point about balanced trade was incorporated.

The second, and most important, objective was to ensure an equitable settlement of the sterling balances. As the largest holder of sterling balances, India proposed an amendment to the articles, calling for the settlement of 'abnormal indebtedness arising out of the

war'. When British and American delegates opposed it, Shroff argued
that 'we never intended the International Monetary Fund . . . to take
over straightaway in one lump sum the entire accumulated credit balances during the war'. They only sought 'multilateral convertibility
for a reasonable portion of these accumulated balances'. Indeed, the
Indian delegation was aiming at no more than a gold and dollar over-
draft against a part of the balances, which could be deployed for
India's development plans while Britain rebuilt its capacity for exports
to India. By refusing to accept India's point, Shroff quipped, 'You are
placing us in a situation which I compare to the position of a man
with a $1 million balance in the bank but not enough sufficient cash
to pay his taxi fare.'[14]

The British opposition to this move was not surprising. Their delegation was led by John Maynard Keynes, who had been in any event
been uneasy over the piling up of sterling balances. To his credit,
however, Keynes did not stick to his earlier position. He expressed

> Britain's gratitude to those Allies, particularly our Indian friends who
> put their resources at our disposal without stint and themselves suf-
> fered from privation as a result. Our effort would have been gravely,
> perhaps critically, embarrassed if they had held back from helping us
> so wholeheartedly and on so great a scale.

This was a gracious acknowledgement of India's contribution to the
war. But Keynes went on to insist that the sterling balances were 'a
matter between those directly concerned'. He would accord no role to
the IMF in the matter; nor would he offer any assurance to India on
the convertibility of sterling into dollars or gold. Keynes stated, however, that Britain would 'settle honourably what was honourably and
generously given'.[15] This assurance helped allay, to some extent, the
deep misgivings in India about its sterling balances.

The third aim of the delegation was to ensure a satisfactory quota
for India in the Fund. The initial allocation suggested by the Americans in March 1944 was just $300 million – half of that for China.
The Indian government bridled at this proposal: 'India's international
liabilities both actual and potential are likely to be considerably more
important than those of China . . . Indian public opinion is likely to
be extremely sensitive on the size of the quota and any attempt to put

India below China would . . . gravely imperil the acceptability of the scheme.' In consequence, the quota for India announced at the conference was raised to $400 million, while China's was reduced to $550 million. The Indian delegation remained dissatisfied. As Raisman argued, 'It is not only a question of India's size, nor alone of her population, but that on purely economic criteria India is an important part of the world and will be an even more important part in the years to come.'[16] India could do no more than register its reservation. Keynes had had a hand in increasing India's quota to $400 million. But when the Indians wanted more, 'Keynes, who received them, lying on his couch [he was unwell] . . . railed them on their ingratitude and urged with much force that they now had an excellent case to present at home . . . All this was without much visible effect.'[17]

This was because the question of quotas was linked to the final objective of the Indian delegation: a permanent seat on the Executive Board of the IMF. The board was conceived as having five executive directors. And India ranked sixth in the quota allotted to it by the Fund. Despite its best efforts, the delegation was unable to persuade the others to increase the number of permanent seats to six. Although disappointed on many counts, the Indian government signed up to the articles in December 1945, so making India a founder member of both the IMF and the World Bank. In the event, the Soviet Union's decision to pull out of the IMF enabled India to secure a permanent seat on the Executive Board. Yet Shroff and Chetty felt that they could have done much better – especially on sterling balances – if their delegation had been led by an Indian.[18]

India's post-war development and international role depended crucially on politics. After being shut in the green room for almost three years, politics returned to centre stage following the surrender of Germany in May 1945. Towards the end of June 1945, Wavell convened a political conference in Simla. Twenty-two Indian leaders of all persuasions were invited. The viceroy sought their co-operation in reconstituting his Executive Council. He proposed 'parity' between the 'Caste Hindus' and the Muslims in nominating representatives to the Council. Although the Congress was not pleased with the idea of parity, it saw the measure as a step towards the formation of an interim government at the centre. The Congress agreed to join an Executive Council consisting of five 'Caste Hindus', five Muslims and two 'minor minorities'.[19]

Wavell was prepared to concede the Muslim League's demand that the Congress should not nominate any Muslim representative. Jinnah wanted more. He insisted on Hindu–Muslim parity in the Executive Council. Moreover, he claimed that all the Muslim members should be nominated by the Muslim League. In doing so, Jinnah sought to drive home two points. First, the Hindus and the Muslims were two nations, and hence entitled to equal representation in an interim arrangement. Second, Jinnah should be the 'sole spokesman' for the Muslims of India.

This was a bold, not to say extraordinary, claim. For at the time of the conference, the Muslim League was out of office in all the Muslim-majority provinces with the sole exception of Sindh. However, the Congress's political exit after the Quit India movement had enabled the Muslim League to make deep inroads into Punjab and Bengal. And Jinnah knew that despite appearances he was playing a strong hand. Wavell stuck to his initial formula, but suggested that of the five Muslim members the League could nominate four. The fifth would be nominated by the Punjab Unionist Party, which ran the provincial government in Punjab. Faced with Jinnah's persistent opposition, the viceroy decided to call off the conference. The aborted conference proved a victory for the Muslim League. The party had shown that it was a critical player at the all-India level and held a veto on any move towards a transfer of power.

In the aftermath of the Simla conference, Wavell announced elections. These would serve two purposes: to form governments in the provinces and to create a central legislature that would work towards a fresh constitutional structure for India.

By the time elections were held, a Labour Party government led by Clement Attlee had come to power in Britain. Leaders of the new government were sympathetic to Indian demands for self-rule, but they were also keenly aware of Britain's weakened imperial position following the Second World War. The Attlee government wished to rid itself of the incubus of governing India and to restructure the imperial system for the exigencies of the post-war international order.

As far as the subcontinent was concerned, its policies were mainly shaped by strategic considerations. The large standing army and the vast reservoir of potential military manpower; the well-developed strategic infrastructure; the rich natural resources and industrial potential; India's importance in securing sea lines of communication in the Indian Ocean, and in defending the Middle East and the Far East – all of these mandated both preserving Indian unity and ensuring India's continued presence in the Commonwealth.[20]

Developments in India, however, cast a shadow on these aspirations and affected the negotiations on the transfer of power. Indeed, the high politics of negotiations comprised only one strand of a complex story. It is easy to focus exclusively on the minutiae of the negotiations – not least because they are so well documented. But it is erroneous to assume that these were insulated from the wider currents swirling in Indian society in the aftermath of the war.

For a start, the army's recruitment drive had relied on highly inflationary rhetoric about the country's post-war prospects: from large transportation companies to vocation training for industrial jobs, from new irrigation canals to co-operative savings banks – all were promised.[21] This naturally raised equally high hopes among the soldiers. Coupled with a less than satisfactorily organized demobilization process, this set the stage for the emergence of widespread disturbances in the Indian armed forces in the aftermath of the war.[22]

More importantly, the experience of war had raised the political and social awareness of Indian soldiers and officers. As one Indian air force officer put it, 'I am sure the Indians who are fighting now in this war will be the real reformers of India. I am not a politician but . . . you can be sure of one thing, definitely India must be reformed on the lines of modern thought.'[23] Even groups within the 'martial classes' that were deemed thoroughly apolitical came out of the war with expanded horizons. As a Pashtun soldier who had fought in North Africa and Italy told the British official Malcolm Darling: 'We suffered in the war but you didn't . . . we bore with this that we might be free.'[24]

Then there was the inevitable post-war economic slump. The contraction of government demand after the war left considerable idle capacity in industries and many workers without jobs. Those lucky to

444

retain their jobs found their salaries shrinking, as businesses and state enterprises took the opportunity to reduce the 'dearness allowance' paid during the war. Then, too, the inflation, black-marketeering and scarcity produced by the war persisted into the post-war years. In 1946, nearly half of India's population was subject to food rationing. This in turn led to protests by farmers against forcible requisitioning, and increased trading in black markets. All in all, these conditions frayed the social fabric of communities, especially in the bigger cities. And they set the context for popular mobilization of various kinds.

The first major movement was touched off by the British decision to prosecute three officers of the Indian National Army. During the campaigns of 1944–45, the Fourteenth Army had taken into custody a large number of INA soldiers as well as some officers. The British were determined to prosecute them as traitors. But they were dismayed at the attitude of Indian officers and soldiers towards the INA, including those who had fought against it. Colonel John Heard, the architect of the 'Josh' programme aimed at countering INA propaganda, received the 'biggest shock' when he reached Rangoon in 1945 and discussed with Indian officers and men the subject of the INA.

> Mainly the reaction was one of praise!! Hadn't the I.N.A. safeguarded Indian civilians from the Japs and the Burmese? Wasn't it a fact that the I.N.A. guarded the banks from looting and maintained order in the town until it could be handed over to the British and Indian Army? So they were misguided chaps, but . . . they were Indians and worth their salt after all.

Heard found that even soldiers with thirty years' service in the Indian army and unquestioned loyalty towards their British officers were 'not inclined to dismiss these I.N.A. as traitors though they were not willing to reclaim them as heroes'. In other, especially technical, units that contained a greater proportion of educated men from outside the 'martial classes', 'the reaction was even more definite with almost a sense of gratitude that at least somehow the idea of independence had been made into a reality even if it was only an army one'.[25] Military intelligence similarly found that 'throughout Burma Indian troops had an undisguised admiration for the I.N.A. . . . I did not meet any officer or I.O.R. [Indian Other Ranks] who did not sympathise with the I.N.A.'[26]

Back in India too the soldiers of the INA were widely admired. Even those who believed that they had been wrong in joining forces with the Japanese tended to feel that they were true patriots. Once it became clear that soldiers and officers of the INA were likely to face prosecution, there was widespread demand for their release. The Congress leadership was quick to tap into this wave of protest. A national defence fund was instituted, and some of the best Indian lawyers offered to act as defence counsel for INA men put on trial. But Congress leaders were also concerned that the future Indian army should not be divided by factions originating in the war.

The British initially resisted the campaign to release the INA soldiers. They were particularly keen to prosecute an estimated 7,000 men who had flogged and tortured fellow Indian soldiers who had refused to join the INA. They were also concerned that the INA issue should not aggravate communal tensions. The INA had attracted a substantial number of Sikhs. Some Muslim soldiers from the northwest now looked upon Subhas Bose and his followers as traitors. But in November 1945, the authorities decided that given the support for the INA among both the armed forces and the populace, the safest option was to release all the INA men except those officers who were specifically accused of brutality against fellow soldiers. Much to their chagrin, the released INA men were received rapturously, garlanded and feted everywhere as heroes.[27]

The decision to prosecute some officers was taken on two considerations. There was an undoubted desire for retribution. More importantly, British officials, including the viceroy, feared that the Congress would use the INA to spearhead another revolt. On 5 November 1945, the military trial against Captain Shahnawaz Khan, Captain P. K. Sehgal, and Lieutenant G. S. Dhillon commenced in Delhi's Red Fort. They were accused of torturing and executing INA soldiers who had tried to switch sides yet again and rejoin the British forces towards the end of the war.

Jawaharlal Nehru, Bhulabhai Desai and Tej Bahadur Sapru were among the defence lawyers. The arguments between the prosecution and defence continued for several days. Court transcripts were published every day and eagerly consumed by the Indian public. The unwitting decision to try together a Muslim, a Hindu and a Sikh officer added to the symbolic import of the proceedings. Unsurprisingly, the trial led to a countrywide wave of protest. The government's intelligence agencies reported that seldom had a matter attracted so much public attention and sympathy. They also noted that the sentiment cut across communal barriers.

An 'INA week' was celebrated starting 5 November 1945; 12 November was observed as 'INA day'. The campaign attracted a wide range of people who attended protest meetings, donated money to the INA relief fund, and shut down shops and other commercial outfits. The protests turned violent following an incident where the police fired on a group of protestors on 7 November. Three weeks later rioting occurred in various parts of the country, starting with Subhas Bose's hometown, Calcutta. Students, taxi drivers and tramway workers clashed with the police. Thirty-three were killed and nearly two hundred injured in the clashes that went on for three days. Anti-government riots also erupted in Allahabad, Banaras, Karachi, Patna and Rawalpindi, among other towns.

The popular reaction against the INA trials was strengthened by the growing food crisis of 1946 and the resulting deep cut in rations. Another contributing factor was increasing public disapproval (especially in urban areas) of the use of the Indian army in South-East Asia. These troops occupied Vietnam and Indonesia after the end of the war. The ostensible aim was to repatriate Japanese troops, and to release internees and prisoners of war from camps established by the Japanese army. In both cases the British also deemed it in their interest to restore French and Dutch rule. Confronted with nationalist opposition, the British not only employed their own forces, but co-opted tens of thousands of Indian troops to control the situation. In the Indonesian city of Surabaya, the 20th Indian Division fought its largest set-piece battle since the end of the war. Large parts of the city were reduced to rubble; some 15,000 people were killed.[28]

The three INA officers were eventually convicted, but only of the lesser charge of rebellion against the king emperor. The sentences passed were never imposed. All three were later released from jail and given dishonourable discharges from the Indian army. But the trials and the protests had driven a further nail into the Raj's coffin. Not only were the British increasingly unsure about the political reliability of the Indian army, but they also realized that the army could no longer be taken for granted as the strategic reserve of the Empire.

During the INA trials, the British were exceedingly worried that popular feeling might percolate into the ranks of the armed forces. Members of the Royal Indian Air Force (RIAF) and some army personnel had openly donated money to the INA fund and attended protest meetings in uniform. The real blow, however, was delivered by the Royal Indian Navy (RIN) mutiny of February 1946.

The mutiny started on 18 February in Bombay.[29] The naval ratings on HMIS *Talwar* protested against the poor quality of food and racial discrimination by British officers. The protest spread rapidly to Castle and Fort barracks on shore, and to twenty-two ships in Bombay harbour. By the following evening, a Naval Central Strike Committee was elected. The mutineers marched out in a procession through Bombay, holding aloft a portrait of Subhas Bose. Their ships also raised the flags of the Congress, Muslim League and the Communist Party. By this time, the news of the strike had reached the naval ratings in Karachi. In response, the ratings from HMIS *Himalaya*, *Bahadur* and *chanak* unanimously resolved to mutiny. The programme of protests would involve complete abstention from work, processions through Karachi, shouting of slogans denouncing the British and calling on the Congress and the Muslim League to unite.

The demands advanced by the Naval Central Strike Committee combined service grievances with wider national concerns. The latter included the release of INA personnel and other political prisoners; withdrawal of Indian troops from Indonesia; and the acceptance of only Indian officers as superiors. Ratings in striking naval establishments outside Bombay echoed these themes.[30] The strike spread to other naval establishments around the country. At its height, 78 ships, 20 shore establishments and 20,000 ratings were involved in the mutiny. The revolt at various locations was co-ordinated by signal communication equipment on board HMIS *Talwar*.

The RIN mutiny also influenced Indian army and air force

personnel. There were instances of 'collective insubordination' among supply and transport companies of the army in Bombay. The 17th Maratha Light Infantry, which arrived in Bombay from Malaya on 22 February, also experienced a case of 'collective insubordination'. About 250 Indian soldiers of the Signal Training Centre in Jubbulpore (Central Provinces) 'broke barracks on 27th February and paraded the town shouting slogans'. The airmen in various RIAF bases refused to eat or come on duty, placing '"demands" for settlement of alleged grievances such as the rate of demobilization, gratuity, deferred pay, leave with pay etc. . . . [and in] sympathy with other mutineers and a protest against the official attitude adopted towards the R.I.N.' Military intelligence noted that in general 'there is amongst many [soldiers] an undoubtedly strong sympathy for the R.I.N. ratings'.[31]

The ratings' hesitation in opting for a full-blown mutiny enabled the British to pin them down to their locations. Subsequently, owing both to British threats of force and to assurances from Patel and Jinnah, the ratings in Bombay surrendered on 23 February. Others followed suit. The most significant feature of this short uprising was the massive outpouring of public support for the mutineers. The city of Bombay went on strike on 22 February in solidarity. The public transport network was brought to a halt, trains were burnt, roadblocks were created and commercial establishments were shut down. An army battalion was inducted to control the situation. Three days later Bombay was quiet, but 228 civilians had died and 1,046 had been injured. Similar strikes occurred in Karachi and Madras on 23 and 25 February. Smaller strikes took place in other parts of the country.

The RIN mutiny had a significant impact on both the British and Indian leadership. To the former it demonstrated that the Indian armed forces were no longer entirely under control. The ratings were not only influenced by the INA trials, but had shown considerable political consciousness. Leaders of the Congress realized that any mass uprising would inevitably carry the risk of not being amenable to centralized direction and control. Besides, they were eager not to encourage indiscipline in the armed forces. Patel told the agitating sailors that the 'armed forces were being taken over by Indians as free India's defence forces, and they did not want to start off with indiscipline'.[32] The promise held out by the INA protests and RIN mutiny of communal solidarity also proved to be short-lived. As the elections approached, the competitive mobilization by both Congress and the Muslim League gave an edge to inter-communal relations.

The outcome of the elections in 1946 was a major turning point. The Congress, as expected, won the bulk of non-Muslim seats in the provinces and for the central legislature. The Muslim League had presented the elections to the Muslim electorate as virtually a referendum on 'Pakistan'. It reaped major rewards. In contrast to its poor showing in the elections of 1937, the League now proved to be a force to reckon with.

The party's main achievement lay not in the number of seats won, but in the fact that it managed both to widen its appeal and to overcome the regional barriers that had blocked the emergence of a strong Muslim party. The League's performance in provinces like Madras and Bombay was striking. These areas could in no conceivable scheme form part of Pakistan; but the Muslim electorate did respond overwhelmingly to the call. In other provinces, too, Jinnah had succeeded in making the League an important force by careful power-broking with local politicians and grandees. In any event, the Muslim League's performance gave substantial ballast to its political position and to the demand for Pakistan.

In retrospect, the elections of 1946 were significant because they reflected and contributed to the communal polarization. In so doing, they cleared the path for Pakistan and set the stage for the carnage accompanying Partition.

To try to stave off the former, a cabinet mission was sent to India in late March 1946 to create a constitutional package for a united India and to plan for the transfer of power.[33] The mission consisted of three senior members of the Labour government: Lord Pethick-Lawrence (secretary of state for India), Stafford Cripps (president of the board of trade), and A. V. Alexander (first lord of the Admiralty). They spent three months in India, holding a number of meetings with the leaders of the Congress and the Muslim League. Neither party was able to advance suggestions that met the other side's approval.

The discussions, however, made it clear that Jinnah was averse to a Pakistan that involved partitioning Punjab and Bengal, both of which had substantial non-Muslim minorities. Jinnah's stance reflected two considerations. The idea of partitioning Punjab and Bengal was unlikely to go down well with his supporters in both these provinces. Further, Jinnah himself attached great importance to the presence of substantial non-Muslim minorities within the boundaries of Pakistan. This would ensure that India would agree in turn to provisions for safeguarding the rights of Muslims in the Hindu-majority provinces. In fact, this idea of reciprocal safeguards (or 'hostage theory' as it came to be called) had been a recurring theme in the Muslim League's mobilization campaigns in provinces such as United Provinces since the passage of the Lahore Resolution of 1940.[34]

Following another ineffective round of negotiations with the two main parties in Simla, the Cabinet Mission declared its own plan for a united India on 16 May 1946. Partition, on the basis of either a large or a small Pakistan, was rejected. The mission laid out a three-tier structure for the future Indian Union. At the top-most tier, the central government would deal only with foreign affairs, defence and communications, and would have the powers to raise finances for these subjects. All other subjects would rest with the provinces. The idea of parity at the centre was dropped. But a decision on any major communal issue in the central legislature would require a majority of each community as well as an overall majority.

The Constituent Assembly would be elected by the provincial assemblies. The latter formed the lowest tier of the structure. The provinces would be free to form groups, and each group could determine the provincial subjects to be taken in common. These groups formed the middle tier of the structure. Members of the Constituent Assembly would divide up into three sections. Section A would consist of Bombay, Madras, Bihar, Central Provinces and Orissa. Section B of Punjab, North-West Frontier Province and Sindh. Section C of Bengal and Assam. Each section would draw up provincial constitutions for the provinces included in that section. Each section could also decide whether any group constitution was required.

Any province could by a majority vote of its assembly call for a reconsideration of the Union and group constitutions periodically after ten years. Any province could elect to come out of any group in which it had been placed after the first general elections under the new constitution. Till such time as the constitutions were framed, an interim government having the support of the major political parties would be set up immediately.

The Congress and the Muslim League claimed to accept the plan. But in fact their 'acceptance' was based on their own interpretations of what the plan promised and how it would work. Anxious to secure an agreement, however weak, the Cabinet Mission played along with both sides. Eventually, after the mission left for London, its plan would quickly unravel.

Historians continue to debate why the Muslim League went along with the plan. It has been argued that Jinnah's acceptance of the plan demonstrates that he did not want a separate state.[35] But it is equally plausible that Jinnah went along with the plan because the alternative would have been a sovereign but truncated Pakistan with partitioned Punjab and Bengal. Further, Jinnah appears to have considered the plan as a preliminary step towards an independent Pakistan with all of Punjab and Bengal. The Muslim League's acceptance statement claimed that the provision of compulsory grouping laid the foundation of Pakistan and that the right of secession of groups was provided in the plan by implication. Indeed, members of the Muslim League had written to Jinnah that 'we work the Plan up to the Group stage and then create a situation to force the hands of the Hindus and the British to concede Pakistan of our conception'.[36]

The Congress, for its part, insisted from the beginning that the procedure of sections and grouping could not be mandatory. The Congress's major concern was that North-West Frontier Province and Assam (both of which had Congress governments) would be compelled to accept constitutions that would be drawn up by sections B and C, dominated by the Muslim League. The leaders of both these provinces had made it clear that this would be totally unacceptable to them. The Muslim League's acceptance statement reinforced these concerns. On 25 June 1946, the Congress sent a cleverly worded letter of 'acceptance'. It claimed that in the first instance, the provinces could choose whether or not to belong to the section in which they were placed. However, the Congress did not make its acceptance of the plan conditional upon the Cabinet Mission's acceptance of this interpretation.

The Muslim League was right in claiming that the sectional procedure had to be followed; but wrong in insisting that grouping was compulsory and that the groups could secede subsequently. The Congress was right in claiming that grouping was not mandatory; but wrong in insisting that the provinces could opt out of the sectional procedure for provincial constitution-making. Each side's interpretation unnerved the other. The fundamental problem was the lack of trust between the Congress and the Muslim League.

Owing to the Congress's open proclamation of its interpretation, Jinnah withdrew the League's acceptance towards the end of July 1946. The League now insisted that it would settle for nothing less that the immediate establishment of an independent and fully sovereign Pakistan. It observed 16 August as Direct Action Day. Three days later nearly 4,000 residents of Calcutta were dead and over 10,000 injured. The violence quickly spread from Bengal to Bihar and to Garhmukhteshwar in United Provinces. The resulting communal polarization made some form of partition almost inevitable.

Throughout 1946, urban India was rocked by an almost continuous series of strikes. The year witnessed 1,629 industrial disputes involving almost 2 million workers.[37] An all-India railway strike was narrowly averted in the summer. There were a number of police strikes in places as far apart as Dhaka and Delhi, Malabar and the Andamans. A great majority of these strikes were due to rising inflation and deepening cuts in rations. Rural India was not quiescent either. There were several organized militant peasant movements, mainly involving sharecroppers and poor peasants.[38] Interestingly, many of these movements sprang up in the regions of India that were most affected by war-induced inflation and scarcity, hunger and deprivation. Thus the Varli tribal agricultural labourers in the Bombay province mobilized against the demands of the landowners and money-lenders for forced labour.

In eastern India, the communists had fanned out into the countryside during the war years. Their popularity owed much to their response to the Bengal famine of 1943. In contrast to the ineffective relief operations organized by the government and by groups such as the Hindu Mahasabha, the communists responded with vigour. They organized meetings criticizing the government's food policy and simultaneously undertook extensive relief work in central and northern parts of Bengal. In consequence, they gained a major following among the poor peasants and sharecroppers. This enabled them to create a sound platform for the 'Tebhaga' movement aimed at securing the sharecroppers' long-standing demand for a two-thirds share of their produce as opposed to the customary share of half.[39]

In September 1946, the communists helped kickoff the Tebhaga campaign. Soon the movement spread out to several districts all over Bengal. The sharecroppers' agitation was at its most intense in the northern districts. The peasants harvested their crop and stored it in their own storehouses. They then asked the landlords to collect their share of a third. In eastern, central and western Bengal, the peasants declared Tebhaga *ilaka* or liberated areas. Here they set up parallel administrative and legal structures. The rapid spread of the movement from February 1947 invited a tough response from the government. The peasants put up strong resistance but ultimately the communists decided to pull back.

Another popular uprising occurred in October 1946 at Punnapra-Vayalar in the state of Travancore. In 1946, the government of Travancore state started making moves towards a declaration of independence from the Union. As a first step, an undemocratic constitution was imposed on the state. This development coincided with serious food scarcity and a lockout in the coir industry. The workers joined forces with agricultural labourers and other occupational groups, and attacked a police check-post at Punnapra. In the face of massive government retaliation, resulting in nearly 270 deaths, the movement died out.

The urban unrest and rural revolts of the post-war period did not amount to a mass revolutionary movement. Even so, they did leave a significant imprint on the course of events. They reinforced the British government's assumption that it would be extremely difficult to continue governing India. At the same time, they contributed to the Congress leadership's belief that the country was teetering on the brink of anarchy and hence a swift transfer of power was desirable.

Epilogue: Last Post

'Whatever the present position of India might be,' wrote Jawaharlal Nehru, 'she is potentially a Great Power.' Barely three days earlier, on 2 September 1946, Nehru had been sworn in as the vice-president of the viceroy's Executive Council – effectively prime minister – in a Congress-led interim government. Now, he was telling the Ministry of External Affairs why India must aim to be elected as a non-permanent member of the United Nations Security Council. 'Undoubtedly,' continued Nehru, 'she [India] will have to play a very great part in security problems of Asia and Indian Ocean, more especially of the Middle East and South-East Asia. Indeed, India is the pivot round which these problems will have to be considered ... India is the centre of security in Asia.'

While Nehru was not opposed to having countries of the Middle East or South-East Asia in the Security Council, he insisted that 'it is India that counts in the security and defence of both these regions far more than any other country'. It was obvious therefore that 'India, by virtue of her geographical and strategic position, resources and latent power, should be a member of the Security Council.'[1] The mandarins and strategists of the Raj would have applauded. The Raj might be on its way out, but India would continue to work its own empire – especially the spheres of influence constructed so carefully over a century and a half and defended at so high a cost in the recent war.

Yet Nehru was not merely embracing the strategic mantle of the Raj. He was clear that India would no longer remain an appendage of the British imperial system – nor indeed of any other great power. 'India should adopt', he wrote in the same note, an independent attitude with no marked alignment with any group. We should make it clear that we stand not only for Indian interests but, more especially, for the interests of peace and freedom everywhere and that we are not going to be dragged in the wake of power politics so far as we can help it. It is fitting especially now that there has been a change in the Government of India that India should play a much more independent role in foreign affairs.[2]

Here was an adumbration of the idea of 'non-alignment' that would come to be closely associated with Nehru's India. Yet India's policy of non-alignment mattered in world politics only because of India's potential value as an ally – one that had been amply demonstrated during the Second World War.

Even as Nehru sought to position India as a major regional power in Asia, the Indian army was undergoing rapid retrenchment. Soon after the war ended, GHQ India expected the army to shrink from 2.5 million men to 700,000 by the end of 1946. This entailed, in the first instance, a major exercise in repatriating soldiers from various theatres back to India. Between the Japanese surrender and the end of April 1946 some 600,000 men and officers were demobilized at an average rate of 70,000 to 80,000 a month, and around 2,000 units were disbanded. If demobilization was slower than anticipated, it was not only due to the massive logistical challenges of bringing troops home. Rather, it also reflected the continuing military demands on India. In April 1946, the Indian army still had two brigades in Middle East; four divisions in Burma; three divisions in Malaya; four divisions in Indonesia; one division in Borneo and Siam; a brigade in Hong Kong; and two brigades in Japan. Over the next few months, repatriation and demobilization gathered pace. By October 1946, the Indian army had 800,000 men and officers. By April 1947, it stood close to 500,000 strong.[3] So, as independence approached, India's ability to project military power in Asia was increasingly circumscribed.

The larger, unspoken assumption in Nehru's strategic vision was, of course, the unity of India. Yet securing this was no longer easy. The interim government proved as unworkable as the rest of the Cabinet Mission's plan. The Muslim League decided to join the government six weeks later, but continued to boycott the Constituent Assembly. Far from working as a coalition, the two parties were constantly at loggerheads with each other. Instead of acting as a bridge between the two sides, the interim government accentuated the gulf between them.

Faced with the continued impasse and with the rapidly increasing communal violence and other unrest in the country, Wavell advocated a breakdown plan for a phased British withdrawal from India. As a consequence, an alarmed British government decided to recall him. On 20 February 1947, Prime Minister Attlee announced Lord Mountbatten's appointment as viceroy. In deference to the latter's wishes, Attlee also announced that the British would withdraw from India no later than June 1948.

Developments at the provincial level imparted further momentum for the move towards partition. The Muslim League's agitation in Punjab forced the resignation of the Unionist-led coalition on 2 March 1947.[4] Now the Shiromani Akali Dal made it clear that the Sikhs would press for the partition of the Punjab. The province was soon engulfed in a spiral of violence and retaliation that would assume the form of ethnic cleansing as partition neared.

By this time, influential sections of the Bengal Congress had begun advocating partition of the province. The 'Great Calcutta Killings' and the subsequent violence had marked a critical turning point. More importantly, the upper-caste Hindu *Bhadralok* saw partition as a means to do away with the dominance of Muslims in provincial politics and to secure their own primacy. Further, the Muslim League had managed to mobilize the support of the province's largely Muslim peasantry against the landlords and money-lenders. This too threatened to undercut the *Bhadralok* rentiers, and gave impetus to their calls for partition. Some Bengal Congress leaders, such as Sarat Chandra Bose and Kiran Shankar Roy, reached an agreement with Muslim League leaders H. S. Suhrawardy and Abul Hashim on a united independent Bengal. Although Jinnah approved of it, the idea failed to take-off, owing to opposition from the Provincial Congress Committee and the Congress High Command.[5]

When Mountbatten arrived in India in late March 1947, he still hoped to reach an agreement on the basis of the Cabinet Mission plan. After several rounds of meetings with Indian leaders, it became clear that partition was the most realistic option. And it had to be done quickly. The Congress leadership, too, had reached the conclusion that a partition of Punjab and Bengal was inevitable. The mounting violence showed that the Muslim League could not be forced to remain within India against its wishes. The experience of the interim government reinforced this point. Concerns about the growing violence and anarchy led the Congress to revive its demand for an immediate grant of full powers to the interim government while the constitution was being drawn up. Towards this end, the Congress agreed to accept Dominion status as a device for the interim transfer of power.

After tortuous and prolonged negotiations, Mountbatten presented the Indian leaders with the Partition Plan on 2 June 1947. In effect, the plan called for the splitting of Punjab and Bengal, and for plebiscites in the North-West Frontier Province and in the Muslim-majority Sylhet district of Assam. The Congress agreed to the plan. Jinnah accepted it very reluctantly, for it left him with the truncated Pakistan that he had wanted to avoid. Mountbatten also declared that the British would now quit India on 15 August 1947, nine months ahead of the original schedule. A boundary commission, led by the British lawyer Cyril Radcliffe, began its work with barely a month to go before partition. In the event, the boundaries drawn up by the commission would be unveiled only on 17 August, after the new Dominions had come into existence. But in anticipation rival communal groups – Hindus, Sikhs and Muslims – had taken up arms and had begun creating facts on the ground. The bloodbath of Partition was well underway.

The staggering violence and ethnic cleansing that eventually accompanied Partition was unanticipated by the Congress, the Muslim League or the British. Almost a million people may have perished in those months – and many more millions were displaced. The human cost of Partition continues to tax the explanatory powers of historians and social scientists. It is perhaps not surprising that in recent years there has been a turn towards recovering the subjective experience of the violence and trauma of Partition, especially for women, by recourse to literature and memory.

Yet the rapid and enormous escalation of communal violence during Partition cannot be understood without taking into account the impact of the Second World War. In the first place, wartime economic mobilization had led to urbanization at an unprecedented scale and pace. There was an enormous increase in the number of towns and cities with a population of over 100,000. Urban areas with a population of between 100,000 and 400,000 rose from eleven in 1941 to seventeen in 1943 and to twenty-three in 1944. Those between 400,000 and 1 million increased from four in 1941 to nine in 1943 and to thirteen in 1944. Those with over a million shot up from seven in 1939 to nine in 1941 and to seventeen in 1944.[6] Accelerated urbanization unmoored people not just from their homes but from traditional ties of sociability. The weak social fabric of these huge urban concentrations was further frayed by the post-war economic slump and competitive political mobilization.

Secondly, the war had led to overt militarization of a large chunk of the population. The manifold expansion of the Indian armed forces provided military training and combat experience to hundreds of thousands of men. On demobilization, they joined in droves the self-defence units and volunteer outfits of all communities that were mushrooming in post-war India. To these outfits, the former soldiers brought their professional skills in the organized application of force and the ability to impart basic training to other recruits. Those with combat experience were not only inured to the idea of killing people but capable of improvising in rapidly changing and violent circumstances. Nor were the skills that they had picked up during the war restricted to using force. The organizational techniques learnt in the military enabled them to construct safe-havens for their communities and ensure safe passage through hostile territory. Reporting from Lyallpur in the Punjab during Partition, Ian Morrison of *The Times* noted the 'orderly and well organized' movement of 200,000 Sikhs out of the town:

> The Sikhs moved in blocks of 40,000 to 60,000 and cover about 20 miles a day. It is an unforgettable sight to see one of these columns on the move. The organization is mainly entrusted to ex-servicemen and soldiers on leave who have been caught by the disturbances. Men on

horseback, armed with spears and swords, provide guards in front, behind, and on the flanks. There is a regular system of bugle calls. At night a halt is called near some village where water is available, watch fires are lit, and pickets are posted.

Indeed, during Partition, the districts that had higher numbers of men with combat experience saw significantly higher levels of ethnic cleansing.[7]

By contrast, the capacity of the state to halt the violence had considerably diminished. Not only were the armed forces wracked with a host of troubles, but they too were being partitioned between the new states of India and Pakistan. The partition of the Indian army would be completed only several months after August 1947. In a further ironic twist, the armies of India and Pakistan were soon confronting each other as a rash of crises broke out over the princely states of Junagadh, Hyderabad and, above all, Kashmir.[8] Officers and men, companies and battalions, regiments and formations that had fought together in the Second World War were now ranged on opposite sides. Field Marshal Auchinleck was forced to look on from his titular perch of 'Supreme Commander India and Pakistan' as senior British officers directed the armies of both sides: among others, Frank Messervy and Douglas Gracey in Pakistan; Dudley Russell and Francis Tuker in India.

The legacy of the Second World War coloured the first India–Pakistan war over Kashmir in other ways too. For instance, the crucial airlift of Indian troops to Srinagar on 27 October, which stopped the Pakistani raiders in their tracks, owed a great deal to the techniques and capabilities honed during the battles of Imphal and Kohima. Both armies fought using American as well as British weapons and equipment, and when the United States imposed an informal embargo on supplying arms and spares to India and Pakistan, both countries were forced to use their shares of the sterling balances to import military equipment from Britain.[9] Nevertheless, India was the principal beneficiary of the wartime expansion in ordnance factories and strategic infrastructure – most of which had occurred outside the areas that became Pakistan – for Allied operations against Japan. Not surprisingly, Pakistan sought to offset its military weakness by seeking an ostensibly anti-communist military alliance with the United States.

By the time the First Kashmir War ended in December 1948, India and Pakistan were locked in a rivalry that persists to this day. Interestingly, one of the few acts of co-operation between them was the formation of a combined historical section to write the official history of the Indian army during the Second World War. Yet this was a history that neither country wanted much to recall. The nation-states of India and Pakistan needed new histories for self-legitimization. And so they sought to gloss over the war years of common mobilization and sacrifice. Commemoration of the Second World War was conspicuously absent in post-colonial South Asia: even the war cemetery in Kohima is maintained by the Commonwealth War Graves Commission. This perhaps explains why, as a fresh cadet in the Officers Training Academy, I was unable to recognize the significance of Meiktila and Jessami, Kohima and Keren, Sangro and Cassino.

Modern South Asia remains a product of the Second World War. The Partition of India might have been inconceivable without the stances and policies adopted by the Raj, the Congress and the Muslim League during the war. Equally important was the sundering of India's links with its eastern neighbours. The 'Great Crescent' stretching from Bengal to Singapore via Burma, Thailand and Malaya, was shattered by the devastation of Burma in war and by Britain's unwillingness to invest in its reconstruction in peace.[10] As Burma embarked on a prolonged period of introversion and international isolation, India's geographical and economic, cultural and strategic links with South-East Asia were broken. The cumulative impact of these developments, against the backdrop of the emergent Cold War, put paid to Nehru's vision of India as a regional hegemon that could don the mantle of the Raj. India's strategic horizons narrowed to its immediate borders and it proved incapable of exerting any real influence in the Persian Gulf, East Africa or South-East Asia. Instead, India had to fall back on claims to solidarity with, and leadership of, the still-colonized countries – and subsequently the Third World and non-aligned nations.

Not all the consequences of India's war were deleterious. Popular mobilization during the war led to a widening of the political horizons of the Indian peoples. Ideas of freedom and democracy, social and individual rights seeped into the discourse – not just of the elite but also of the marginalized. This underpinned the subsequent decision of the Indian Constituent Assembly to adopt a universal adult franchise and provide for economic and social as well as political rights. The war also left a deep economic imprint on independent India. Progressive taxation and public distribution systems were among its lasting legacies. Wartime measures and ideas also enabled the post-war state to play a prominent role in planned economic development – by import-substituting industrialization, by focusing on basic and heavy industries, by a range of controls on the economy, and by deficit financing. If India is today regarded as a major 'emerging economy', it is worth remembering that the roots of this transformation stretch all the way back to the Second World War.

Perhaps the most pressing reason to recall India's Second World War is geopolitical. Today India stands again at the centre of an Asia whose eastern end is unsettled by the rise of a new great power and whose western end is in the throes of ideologically driven turmoil. To be sure, the situation now is very different from that of the early 1940s. Yet India is seen as a key player in ensuring a balanced regional order in East Asia. And India's own dependence on oil, as well as the presence of a large diaspora, impels it towards a more active role in stabilizing the Middle East. Yet if India is to revert to its older role as the 'pivot' of Asian security, it will first have to aim at the economic and strategic integration of the subcontinent: both to its west with Pakistan and Afghanistan and to its east with Bangladesh and Burma. Only then can the rise of India – prefigured in the Second World War – be fully realized.

Notes

ABBREVIATIONS

AAC   Asian and African Collections, British Library, London

CWMG   *Collected Works of Mahatma Gandhi* (New Delhi: Government of India, 1958–94), 100 vols.

FRUS   *Foreign Relations of the United States*

IAR   *Indian Annual Review*

IWM   Imperial War Museum, London

LHCMA   Liddell Hart Centre for Military Archives, King's College London

NAI   National Archives of India, New Delhi

NCW   Sisir K. Bose and Sugata Bose (eds.), *Netaji: Collected Works Volume 11: Azad Hind, Writings and Speeches 1941–43* (Calcutta: Netaji Research Bureau and New Delhi: Permanent Black, 2002)

NMML   Nehru Memorial Museum and Library, New Delhi

SWJN   S. Gopal (gen. ed.), *Selected Works of Jawaharlal Nehru* (New Delhi: Orient Longman, 1972–82), 15 vols.

TF   *Towards Freedom: Documents on the Movement for Independence in India* (New Delhi: Oxford University Press, 1985–2010), 11 vols.

TNA   The National Archives, London

TP   N. Mansergh et al. (eds.), *Constitutional Relations between Britain and India: The Transfer of Power, 1942–47* (London: HMSO, 1970–83), 12 vols.

WCP   War Cabinet Papers

PROLOGUE

1. *IAR*, July–December 1939, vol. 2, p. 21.
2. Honourable mention must be made of books and articles by Daniel Marston, T. R. Moreman, Alan Jeffreys, Anirudh Deshpande, Kaushik Roy, Tarak Barkawi and Indivar Kamtekar.
3. Robert J. Blyth, *The Empire of the Raj: India, Eastern Africa and the Middle East, 1858–1947* (London: Palgrave Macmillan, 2003); James Onley, 'The Raj Reconsidered: British India's Informal Empire and Spheres of Influence in Asia and Africa', *Asian Affairs*, vol. 40, no. 1 (2009), pp. 44–62.
4. Cited in Blyth, *Empire of the Raj*, p. 8.
5. Karl Joseph Schmidt, 'India's Role in the League of Nations, 1919–39', PhD thesis, Florida State University, 1994.

1. POLITICS OF WAR

1. Thomas R. Metcalf, *Imperial Connections: India in the Indian Ocean Arena 1860–1920* (Berkeley: University of California Press, 2007); Sugata Bose, *A Hundred Horizons: The Indian Ocean in the Age of Global Empire* (Cambridge, Mass.: Harvard University Press, 2009).
2. Sunil S. Amrith, *Crossing the Bay of Bengal: The Furies of Nature and the Fortunes of Migrants* (Cambridge, Mass.: Harvard University Press, 2013).
3. Fortnightly Report by Secretary of State for India, 12 September 1939, WCP, NMML.
4. Quarterly Review, May–31 July 1939, Linlithgow Papers, Acc. No. 2324, NAI.
5. Statement to press, 5 September 1939, *CWMG*, vol. 70, pp. 161–2.
6. Mahadev Desai to G. D. Birla, 10 September 1939, *TF*, 1939, part 1, pp. 299–300.
7. Rajmohan Gandhi, *Rajaji: A Life* (New Delhi: Penguin, 1997), p. 203; Sugata Bose, *His Majesty's Opponent: Subhas Chandra Bose and India's Struggle Against Empire* (Cambridge, Mass.: Belknap Press, 2011), p. 171; Rajendra Prasad, *Autobiography* (New Delhi: Penguin, 2010, originally published in 1946), p. 473.
8. Text of Resolution, 14 September 1939, *CWMG*, vol. 70, pp. 409–13.
9. Gandhi's statement, 15 September 1939, *CWMG*, vol. 70, p. 177.

10. Linlithgow to H. J. Twynam, 9 September 1939, Linlithgow Papers, Acc. No. 2174, NAI.
11. Erskine to Linlithgow, 3 September 1939, cited in Sarvepalli Gopal, *Jawaharlal Nehru: A Biography*, vol. 1 (London: Jonathan Cape, 1975), p. 250.
12. Linlithgow to Zetland, 12 September 1939, Linlithgow Papers, Acc. No. 2156, NAI.
13. Ibid.
14. *IAR*, July–December 1939, vol. 2, p. 19.
15. Cited in Ian Copland, *The Princes of India in the Endgame of Empire 1917–1947* (Cambridge: Cambridge University Press, 1999), p. 181.
16. Fortnightly Report by Secretary of State for India, 12 September 1939, WCP, NMML.
17. Figures are from Fortnightly Reports by Secretary of State for India, 17 October 1939 and 17 February 1940, WCP, NMML and Copland, *Princes of India*, p. 185.
18. Dhananjay Keer, *Dr. Ambedkar: Life and Mission* (Mumbai: Popular Prakashan, 1954, reprtd 2009), pp. 325–6.
19. Linlithgow to Zetland, 7 October 1939, Linlithgow Papers, Acc. No. 2156, NAI.
20. Savarkar's statement of 9 October 1939; Savarkar to Tatyarao, 6 September 1939; Jayakar to Ganpat Rai, 12 September 1939, *TF*, 1939, part 2, pp. 1900, 1889–90.
21. Linlithgow to Zetland, 7 October 1939, Linlithgow Papers, Acc. No. 2156, NAI; Savarkar's statement of 9 October 1939, *TF*, 1939, part 2, p. 1900.
22. Cited in Gowher Rizvi, *Linlithgow and India: A Study of British Policy and the Political Impasse in India, 1936–1943* (London: Royal Historical Society, 1978), p. 84.
23. Cited in ibid., p. 110.
24. Ayesha Jalal, *The Sole Spokesman: Jinnah, the Muslim League and the Demand for Pakistan* (Cambridge: Cambridge University Press, 1985), pp. 47–8.
25. Note of an interview between the viceroy and Jinnah, 4 November 1939, Linlithgow Papers, Acc. No. 2306, NAI.
26. Note of an interview between the viceroy and Jinnah, 5 October 1939, cited in Rizvi, *Linlithgow and India*, p. 110.
27. Fazlul Haq to Linlithgow, 13 October 1939, Linlithgow Papers, Acc. No. 2306, NAI.

28. Linlithgow to Zetland, 10 October 1939, Linlithgow Papers, Acc. No. 2335, NAI.

29. Article by Chhotu Ram, *Leader*, 27 September 1939, *TF*, 1939, part 1, pp. 342–4.

30. Linlithgow to Zetland, 25 September 1939, Linlithgow Papers, Acc. No. 2335, NAI.

31. War Cabinet, 27 September 1939, CAB 65/1/29, TNA.

32. Sarvepalli Gopal, 'Churchill and India', in idem, *Imperialists, Nationalists, Democrats: The Collected Essays* (Ranikhet: Permanent Black, 2013), p. 139.

33. Cited in Gandhi, *Rajaji*, p. 206.

34. *CWMG*, vol. 70, pp. 413–14.

35. Viceroy's declaration, 17 October 1939, *TF*, 1939, part 1, pp. 394–8.

36. Gandhi's statement to the press, 18 October 1939, *CWMG*, vol. 70, p. 267; Nehru's statements, 18 October 1939, *SWJN*, vol. 10, pp. 191, 193.

37. Cited in Gandhi, *Rajaji*, p. 205.

38. Congress Working Committee Resolution, 22 October 1939, *CWMG*, vol. 70, pp. 419–20.

39. Gandhi's statements of 10 October 1939, *CWMG*, vol. 70, p. 246.

40. Intelligence Bureau report 'Communism in India – A Survey of Recent Developments', *TF*, 1939, part 2, p. 1722.

41. Victor Kiernan, 'The Communist Party of India and the Second World War', in Prakash Karat (ed.), *Across Time and Continents* (New Delhi: LeftWord, 2003), p. 210.

42. Editorial in *New Age*, 4 September 1939, *TF*, 1939, part 1, pp. 348–52.

43. Intelligence Bureau report 'Communism in India – A Survey of Recent Developments', *TF*, 1939, part 2, pp. 1724–5.

44. The best study on Roy is Kris Manjapra, *M. N. Roy: Marxism and Colonial Cosmopolitanism* (New Delhi: Routledge, 2010).

45. Roy to Central Executive Committee Members, 8 October 1939, M. N. Roy Papers, NMML.

46. Article by G. Adhikari in *National Front*, 23 April 1939, *TF*, 1939, part 2, pp. 1579–80; Narayan's statement, 21 May 1939, *TF*, 1939, part 2, pp. 1610–11; Article by P. C. Joshi in *National Front*, 18 June 1939, *TF*, 1939, part 2, pp. 1634–5.

47. Memorandum by Zetland, 23 October 1939, CAB 67/2/3, TNA.

48. War Cabinet, 25 October 1939, CAB 65/1/60, TNA; War Cabinet, 4 November 1939, CAB 65/2/70, TNA.

49. Memoranda by Zetland, 23 October 1939, TNA; 4 November 1939, CAB 67/2/3, TNA.
50. Cited in Jalal, *Sole Spokesman*, p. 48.
51. Cited in Rizvi, *Linlithgow and India*, p. 90.
52. 19 November 1939, *CWMG*, vol. 70, pp. 362–3.
53. Congress Working Committee Resolution, 22 November 1939, *CWMG*, vol. 70, pp. 370–73.
54. Cited in Gopal, *Nehru*, p. 258.
55. Jinnah's statement, 9 December 1939, *TF*, 1939, part 2, pp. 1827–8.
56. Jinnah's statement of 6 December 1939, *TF*, 1939, part 2, 1826.
57. Cited in Keer, *Ambedkar*, p. 330.
58. Cited in Gandhi, *Rajaji*, p. 207.
59. Statement of 15 January 1940, *CWMG*, vol. 71, pp. 109–10
60. Telegram to Zetland, 18 December 1939, Linlithgow Papers, Acc. No. 2335, NAI.
61. Viceroy's speech, 10 January 1940, Linlithgow Papers, Acc. No. 2329, NAI.
62. Memorandum by Zetland, 21 September 1939, CAB 66/2/5, TNA.
63. Chiefs of Staff appreciation, 11 October 1939, CAB 66/2/33, TNA.
64. Memorandum by Zetland, 31 January 1940, CAB 67/4/37, TNA.
65. The next three paragraphs draw on War Cabinet, 2 February 1940, CAB 65/5/30, TNA.
66. Gandhi to Linlithgow, 14 January 1940, *CWMG*, vol. 71, p. 107.
67. Statement to the press, 6 February 1940, *CWMG*, vol. 71, pp. 186–8.
68. Gopal, *Nehru*, p. 261.
69. Discussion at Congress Working Committee, 15 March 1940, *CWMG*, vol. 71, pp. 337–40.
70. Gandhi's speech, 20 March 1940, *CWMG*, vol. 71, pp. 357–8.
71. Bose's presidential address, 19 March 1940, *TF*, 1940, part 1, pp. 267–70.
72. Statement of 7 March 1940, *TF*, 1940, part 1, pp. 287–91.
73. Linlithgow to Zetland, 6 February 1940, Linlithgow Papers, Acc. No. 2162, NAI.
74. Jalal, *Sole Spokesman*, pp. 50–57.
75. Linlithgow to Zetland, 8 March 1940, Linlithgow Papers, Acc. No. 2335, NAI.
76. Linlithgow to Zetland, 5 April 1940, Linlithgow Papers, Acc. No. 2162, NAI.

77. Linlithgow to Zetland, 6 April 1940, Linlithgow Papers, Acc. No. 2162, NAI.
78. Cited in Rizvi, *Linlithgow and India*, p. 118.
79. Memorandum by Zetland, 11 March 1940, CAB 67/5/23, TNA.
80. Report for April 1940, WCP, NMML.
81. Memorandum by Zetland, 9 April 1940, CAB 67/5/46, TNA.

2. DEFENCE OF INDIA

1. David Omissi, *The Sepoy and the Raj: The Indian Army 1860–1940* (Basingstoke: Macmillan, 1994), p. 199.
2. The Army in India Committee Majority Report, 1912, L/MIL/17/5/1751, AAC. 'Army in India' was the official term used after 1895 to describe the entire military establishment in India, including British troops. The term 'Indian Army' was applied to units comprising Indian soldiers, while 'British Army in India' referred to units of the British Army deployed in India.
3. Alan Warren, *Waziristan, the Faqir of Ipi and the Indian Army: The North West Frontier Revolt of 1936–37* (Oxford: Oxford University Press, 2000); T. R. Moreman, *The Army in India and the Development of Frontier Warfare 1849–1947* (Basingstoke: Macmillan, 1998).
4. Bisheshwar Prasad, *Defence of India: Policy and Plans* (Delhi: Combined Inter-Services Historical Section, 1963), pp. 22–61.
5. Cited in Keith Jeffery, '"An English Barrack in the Oriental Seas"? India in the Aftermath of the First World War', *Modern Asian Studies*, vol. 15, no. 3 (1981), p. 372.
6. B. R. Tomlinson, *The Political Economy of the Raj 1914–1947: The Economics of Decolonization in India* (London: Macmillan, 1979).
7. Cited in John Gallagher and Anil Seal, 'Britain and India between the Wars', *Modern Asian Studies*, vol. 15, no. 3 (1981), p. 399.
8. G. Balachandran, *John Bullion's Empire: Britain's Gold Problem and India between the Wars* (London: Curzon Press, 1996).
9. Dietmar Rothermund, *India in the Great Depression, 1929–1939* (New Delhi: Manohar, 1992).
10. Srinath Raghavan, 'Liberal Thought and Colonial Military Institutions in India', in Kanti Bajpai et al. (eds.), *India's Grand Strategy: History, Theory, Cases* (New Delhi: Routledge, 2012).

11. Cited in Anirudh Deshpande, *British Military Policy in India, 1900–1945: Colonial Constraints and Declining Power* (New Delhi: Manohar, 2005), p. 136.

12. Michael Howard, *The Continental Commitment: The Dilemma of British Defence Policy in the Era of the Two World Wars* (Harmondsworth: Penguin, 1974), pp. 97–106; Arthur J. Marder, *Old Friends, New Enemies: The Royal Navy and the Imperial Japanese Navy, Strategic Illusions, 1936–1941* (Oxford: Clarendon Press, 1981).

13. Report of the Expert Committee on the Defence of India, 1938–39, L/MIL/5/886, AAC.

14. Cited in Elisabeth Mariko Leake, 'British India versus the British Empire: The Indian Army and an Impasse in Imperial Defence, c. 1919–1939', *Modern Asian Studies*, vol. 48, no. 1 (2014), p. 317.

15. The Defence Problems of India – Report by the Sub-Committee, May 1938, L/MIL/5/886, AAC.

16. John Connell, *Auchinleck: A Biography of Field-Marshal Sir Claude Auchinleck* (London: Cassell, 1959), pp. 68–9; Lord Chatfield, *It Might Happen Again* (London: Heinemann, 1947), pp. 148–9.

17. Fortnightly Report by Secretary of State for India, 12 September 1939, WCP, NMML.

18. Government of India (Defence Department) to Secretary of State for India, 6 September 1939, CAB 67/1/6, TNA.

19. Memorandum by Foreign Office, 6 December 1939, CAB 66/3/50, TNA.

20. Milan Hauner, 'The Soviet Threat to Afghanistan and India, 1938–40', *Modern Asian Studies*, vol. 15, no. 2 (1981), pp. 293–6.

21. Joint Memorandum by Secretary of State for India and Foreign Secretary, 7 September 1939, CAB 67/1/14, TNA.

22. Fortnightly Report by Secretary of State for India, 16 January 1940, WCP, NMML; G. N. Molesworth, *Curfew on Olympus* (London: Asia Publishing House, 1965), p. 149.

23. Memorandum by Zetland, 21 September 1939, CAB 66/2/5, TNA.

24. Appreciation by Chiefs of Staff, 9 October 1939, CAB 66/2/24, TNA; Draft telegram to India, 11 October 1939, CAB 66/2/33, TNA; Review of Strategic Situation by Chiefs of Staff, 2 November 1939, CAB 66/3/3, TNA.

25. Memorandum by Foreign Office, 6 December 1939, CAB 66/3/50, TNA.

26. Memorandum by Chiefs of Staff, 8 March 1940, CAB 66/6/21, TNA.

27. War Cabinet, 5 April 1940, CAB 65/6/27, TNA.

28. Report by Secretary of State for India for May 1940, WCP, NMML.

29. Report by Secretary of State for India for June 1940, WCP, NMML.
30. Cited in Prasad, *Defence of India*, pp. 66-71.
31. Ibid.
32. Ibid., pp. 72-4.
33. Government of India (Defence Department) to Secretary of State for India, 18 May 1940, CAB 67/6/37, TNA.
34. Report by Chiefs of Staff, 29 May 1940, CAB 67/6/37, TNA.
35. Government of India (Defence Department) to Secretary of State for India, 25 June 1940, CAB 66/10/22, TNA.
36. Appreciation by Chiefs of Staff, 9 October 1939, CAB 66/2/24, TNA.
37. Memorandum by Foreign Office, 6 December 1939, CAB 66/3/50, TNA; Report by Chiefs of Staff, 5 December 1939, CAB 66/3/48, TNA.
38. Report by Minister for Defence Coordination, 13 January 1940, CAB 66/4/48, TNA.
39. Report by Chiefs of Staff, 17 October 1939, CAB 66/2/35, TNA.
40. Ian Kershaw, *Fateful Choices: Ten Decisions that Changed the World 1940-41* (London: Allen Lane, 2007), ch. 1.
41. Report by Chiefs of Staff, 28 April 1940, CAB 66/7/18, TNA; Reports for May and June 1940, WCP, NMML.
42. Report by Chiefs of Staff, 5 December 1939, CAB 66/3/48, TNA.
43. Review of Strategic Situation by Chiefs of Staff, 2 November 1939, CAB 66/3/3, TNA.
44. Memorandum by Chiefs of Staff, 18 March 1940, CAB 66/6/32, TNA; Report by Secretary of State for India for April 1940, WCP, NMML.

3. COMPETING OFFERS

1. Report by Secretary of State for India for June 1940, WCP, NMML.
2. 'Panic', 4 June 1940, *CWMG*, vol. 72, p. 135.
3. Gandhi's interview, 22 April 1940, *CWMG*, vol. 72, p. 11.
4. Rajendra Prasad, *Autobiography* (New Delhi: Penguin, 2010, originally published in 1946), p. 479.
5. Nehru to Azad, 16 May 1940, *SWJN*, vol. 11, p. 34.
6. Nehru to Prasad, 15 May 1940, *SWJN*, vol. 11, p. 31.
7. Sarvepalli Gopal, *Jawaharlal Nehru: A Biography*, vol. 1 (London: Jonathan Cape, 1975), p. 264.
8. Cited in Rajmohan Gandhi, *Rajaji: A Life* (New Delhi: Penguin, 1997), p. 219.
9. Cited in Rajmohan Gandhi, *Patel: A Life* (Ahmedabad: Navjivan Publishing House, n.d.), p. 293.

10. Rajagopalachari's draft resolution, 3 July 1940, *CWMG*, vol. 72, p. 466
11. Discussions at Congress Working Committee, 3–7 July 1940, *CWMG*, vol. 72, pp. 235–6, 245–6.
12. Congress Working Committee resolution, 7 July 1940, *CWMG*, vol. 72, p. 467.
13. Gopal, *Nehru*, p. 265.
14. Nehru's article, 21 July 1940, *SWJN*, vol. 11, p. 84.
15. Nehru note, n.d., *SWJN*, vol. 11, pp. 28–9.
16. Cited in Sarvepalli Gopal, 'All Souls and India', in idem, *Imperialists, Nationalists, Democrats: The Collected Essays* (Ranikhet: Permanent Black, 2013), p. 78.
17. Amery's statement, 23 May 1940, *TF*, 1940, part 1, pp. 166–7.
18. Gopal, *Nehru*, p. 264.
19. Amery to Linlithgow, 2 June 1940, War Cabinet, 20 July 1940, CAB 66/10/2, TNA.
20. Linlithgow to Amery, 10 June 1940, War Cabinet, 20 July 1940, CAB 66/10/2, TNA.
21. Amery to Linlithgow, 17 June 1940, War Cabinet, 20 July 1940, CAB 66/10/2, TNA.
22. Gandhi to Linlithgow, 30 June 1940, *CWMG*, vol. 72, pp. 212–15.
23. Ayesha Jalal, *The Sole Spokesman: Jinnah, the Muslim League and the Demand for Pakistan* (Cambridge: Cambridge University Press, 1985), p. 62.
24. Memorandum by Amery, 6 July 1940, War Cabinet, CAB 67/7/23, TNA.
25. These exchanges can be followed in War Cabinet, 30 July 1940, CAB 66/10/3, TNA.
26. These exchanges are available in War Cabinet, 20 July 1940, CAB 66/10/2, TNA.
27. War Cabinet, 25 July 1940, CAB 65/8/24, TNA.
28. Viceroy's statement, 8 August 1940, *TF*, 1940, part 1, pp. 173–4.
29. Gowher Rizvi, *Linlithgow and India: A Study of British Policy and the Political Impasse in India, 1936–1943* (London: Royal Historical Society, 1978), p. 159.
30. Nehru's article and remarks to press, 10 August & 27 August 1940, *SWJN*, vol. 11, pp. 101–14, 128.
31. Gandhi, *Patel*, p. 295.
32. Gandhi, *Rajaji*, p. 222.
33. Nehru's remarks to press, 10 August & 27 August 1940, *SWJN*, vol. 11, p. 129.

34. Congress Working Committee Resolution, 22 August 1940, *TF*, 1940, part 1, pp. 185–6.

35. All-India Congress Committee Resolution, 15 September 1940, *CWMG*, vol. 73, pp. 1–3.

36. Statement, 18 September 1940, *CWMG*, vol. 73, p. 31.

37. Gandhi, *Patel*, p. 295.

38. Rajagopalachari to Gandhi, 23 September 1940, *CWMG*, vol. 73, pp. 56–7.

39. Gandhi, *Rajaji*, p. 222.

40. Muslim League Working Committee Resolution, 2 September 1940, *TF*, 1940, part 1, pp. 187–9.

41. Muslim League Working Committee Resolution, 28 September 1940, *TF*, 1940, part 1, pp. 191–2.

42. Statement, 15 January 1940; Hindu Mahasabha Working Committee Resolution, 19 May 1940, *TF*, 1940, part 1, pp. 111, 165.

43. Savarkar to Linlithgow, 19 August 1940, *TF*, 1940, part 1, pp. 180–83.

44. Savarkar to Linlithgow, 22 October 1940, *TF*, 1940, part 1, pp. 25–6.

45. War Cabinet, 16 October 1940, CAB 65/9/34, TNA.

46. Ambedkar to Linlithgow, 18 August 1940; Independent Labour Party statement, 4 September 1940, *TF*, 1940, part 1, pp. 180, 189.

47. Exchanges between Linlithgow and Gandhi, 30 September & 6 October 1940, *CWMG*, vol. 73, pp. 71–3, 450–51.

48. Statement of 15 October 1940, *CWMG*, vol. 73, pp. 102–7.

49. Resolution of Bombay Provincial League of Radical Congressmen, 4 August 1940, *TF*, 1940, part 1, pp. 32–3.

50. Roy's circular letter, 17 August 1940, *TF*, 1940, part 1, pp. 34–5.

51. Nehru to Roy, 23 September & 23 October 1940, *SWJN*, vol. 11, pp. 237–8, 249–50.

52. Rizvi, *Linlithgow and India*, pp. 162–3.

53. War Cabinet, 21 November 1940, CAB 65/10/13, TNA.

54. Rizvi, *Linlithgow and India*, p. 166.

55. Linlithgow to Haig, 19 June 1941, Linlithgow Papers, Acc. No. 2237, NAI.

56. Linlithgow to Amery, 3 June 1941, L/PO/105, AAC.

57. Draft of Churchill's unsent letter to Linlithgow, 30 May 1941, L/PO/105, AAC.

58. War Cabinet, 9 June 1941, CAB 65/18/37, TNA.

59. Ambedkar to Amery, 1 August 1941, *TF*, 1940, part 1, p. 47.

60. Linlithgow to Haig, 19 June 1941, Linlithgow Papers, Acc. No. 2237, NAI.

61. Jalal, *Sole Spokesman*, pp. 67–9.

62. Reports of March and November 1941, WCP, NMML.

63. War Cabinet, 17 November 1941, CAB 65/20/8, TNA.

4. MOBILIZING INDIA

1. Figures from Appendix I to Sri Nandan Prasad, *Expansion of the Armed Forces and Defence Organization, 1939–1945* (New Delhi, Ministry of Defence, Government of India, 2012), pp. 398–9.

2. Government of India (Defence Department) to Secretary of State for India, 18 May 1940, CAB 67/6/37, TNA.

3. Ibid.

4. Memorandum by Secretary of State for India, 23 May 1940, CAB 67/6/37, TNA.

5. Memorandum by Chiefs of Staff, 25 July 1940, CAB 66/10/22, TNA.

6. Prasad, *Expansion of the Armed Forces*, pp. 61–2.

7. Bisheshwar Prasad, *Defence of India: Policy and Plans* (Delhi: Combined Inter-Services Historical Section, 1963), pp. 87–90.

8. Prasad, *Expansion of the Armed Forces*, pp. 63–5.

9. Memorandum by Secretary of State for India, 30 January 1942, CAB 66/21/34, TNA.

10. Milan Hauner, *India in Axis Strategy: Germany, Japan, and Indian Nationalists in the Second World War* (Stuttgart: Klett-Cotta, 1981), pp. 167–72.

11. Government of India (Defence Department) to Secretary of State for India, 5 May 1941, WO 106/3740, TNA.

12. This paragraph and the next draw on Memorandum by Secretary of State for India, 30 January 1942, CAB 66/21/34, TNA; Prasad, *Expansion of the Armed Forces*, pp. 66–70.

13. Secretary of State for India to Government of India, 20 April 1944, WO 193/119, TNA.

14. Prasad, *Expansion of the Armed Forces*, p. 73.

15. Minute by P. J. Griffiths, 20 November 1939, WO 193/114, TNA.

16. Memorandum by Secretary of State for India, 29 June 1940, WCP, NMML.

17. Prasad, *Expansion of the Armed Forces*, pp. 60–61.

18. Muspratt to Dill, June 1941, WO 193/119, TNA.

19. Government of India (Defence Department) to Secretary of State for India, 1 September 1941, WO 106/3740, TNA.

20. Memorandum by Wavell, 11 September 1941, WO 106/3740, TNA.

21. Memorandum by Secretary of State for India, 30 January 1942, CAB 66/21/34, TNA.

22. Cited in Prasad, *Expansion of the Armed Forces*, pp. 69–70.

23. Kaushik Roy, 'Expansion and Deployment of the Indian Army during World War II: 1939–45', *Journal of the Society for Army Historical Research*, vol. 88 (2010), p. 256.

24. Prasad, *Expansion of the Armed Forces*, p. 76.

25. David Omissi, *The Sepoy and the Raj: The Indian Army 1860–1940* (Basingstoke: Macmillan, 1994), pp. 10–34; Thomas Metcalf, *Ideologies of the Raj* (Cambridge: Cambridge University Press, 1994); Douglas M. Peers, 'The Martial Races and the Indian Army in the Victorian Era', in Daniel Marston and Chandar Sundaram (eds.), *A Military History of India and South Asia: From the East India Company to the Nuclear Era* (Westport, Conn.: Praeger, 2007), pp. 34–52.

26. Cited in Anirudh Deshpande, *British Military Policy in India, 1900–1945: Colonial Constraints and Declining Power* (New Delhi: Manohar, 2005), p. 147.

27. Rajit Mazumder, *The Indian Army and the Making of Punjab* (New Delhi: Permanent Black, 2003); Tan Tai Yong, *The Garrison State: The Military, Government and Society in Colonial Punjab, 1849–1947* (London: Sage, 2005).

28. Omissi, *Sepoy and the Raj*, pp. 38–41.

29. Calculated from Bisheshwar Prasad (ed.), *Recruiting for the Defence Services in India* (Delhi: Combined Inter-Services Historical Section, 1950), Appendix H, pp. 140–42.

30. Calculated from ibid.

31. Prasad, *Expansion of the Armed Forces*, pp. 84–5.

32. Note by Adjutant General, 2 November 1942, L/WS/1/1680, AAC.

33. Steven Wilkinson, *Army and Nation: The Military and Indian Democracy since Independence* (Cambridge, Mass.: Harvard University Press, 2015), pp. 75–6.

34. Molesworth to Jenkins, September 1943, L/WS/1/1680, AAC.

35. Fortnightly Censor Summary, 21 April to 5 May 1943, L/P&J/12/655, AAC.

36. Fortnightly Censor Summary, 2 June to 15 June 1943, L/P&J/12/655, AAC.

37. Fortnightly Censor Summary, 30 June to 13 July 1943, L/P&J/12/655, AAC.

38. Fortnightly Censor Summary, 14 July to 27 July 1943, L/P&J/12/655, AAC.
39. Fortnightly Censor Summary, 21 April to 5 May 1943, L/P&J/12/655, AAC.
40. Fortnightly Censor Summary, 14 July to 27 July 1943, L/P&J/12/655, AAC.
41. Deshpande, *British Military Policy in India*, p. 157.
42. Cited in Namrata Narain, 'Co-option and Control: Role of the Colonial Army in India, 1918–1947', PhD thesis, Cambridge University, 1993, pp. 123–4.
43. Information Summaries from Chief Censor, 1942, 39-W/2, NAI.
44. Prasad, *Expansion of the Armed Forces*, pp. 89–90.
45. Deshpande, *British Military Policy in India*, pp. 154–7.
46. Prasad (ed.), *Recruiting for the Defence Services*, Appendix R; Narain, 'Co-option and Control', pp. 137–8.
47. Stephen Cohen, *The Indian Army: Its Contribution to the Development of a Nation*, rev. edn (New Delhi: Oxford University Press, 2001), p. 180.
48. Craik to Linlithgow, 15 November 1940, in Lionel Carter (ed.), *Punjab Politics 1940–43: Strains of War* (New Delhi: Manohar, 2005), p. 199.
49. Cited in Prasad, *Expansion of the Armed Forces*, p. 91.
50. Cited in Weekly Intelligence Summary, 8 January 1943, L/WS/1/1433, AAC.
51. General Office of the Commander-in-Chief Central Command to Chief of the General Staff, 31 March 1943, L/WS/1/1576, AAC.
52. Cited in Indivar Kamtekar, 'A Different War Dance: State and Class in India, 1939–1945', *Past & Present*, no. 176 (2002), p. 190.
53. Prasad, *Expansion of the Armed Forces*, p. 91.
54. Weekly Intelligence Summary, 13 February 1942, L/WS/1/1433, AAC.
55. Weekly Intelligence Summary, 9 July 1943, L/WS/1/1433, AAC.
56. Weekly Intelligence Summary, 28 August 1942, L/WS/1/1433, AAC.
57. Cited in Narain, 'Co-option and Control', p. 142.
58. 17th Dogra Regimental Centre to Chief of General Staff, 28 March 1943, L/WS/1/1576, AAC.
59. Cited in Tan, *Garrison State*, pp. 286–8.
60. Glancy to Linlithgow, 4 March 1942, in Carter (ed.), *Punjab Politics 1940–43*, p. 294.
61. Calculated from Prasad (ed.), *Recruiting for the Defence Services*, Appendix H.

62. Fortnightly Censor Summary, 16 June to 29 June 1943, L/P&J/12/655, AAC.

63. Resolutions on Esher Committee, CID 119-D, CAB 6/4, TNA.

64. Jinnah's speech on 6 March 1924, in M. Rafique Afzal (ed.), *Selected Speeches and Statements of the Quaid-i-Azam Mohammad Ali Jinnah 1911–34 and 1947–48* (Lahore: Research Society of Pakistan, 1966), pp. 122–8.

65. Omissi, *Sepoy and the Raj*, pp. 168–78; Deshpande, *British Military Policy in India*, pp. 91–8.

66. Speech on 8 March 1928, in K. M. Panikkar and A. Pershad (eds.), *The Voice of Freedom: Selected Speeches of Pandit Motilal Nehru* (Bombay: Asia Publishing House, n.d.), pp. 345–9.

67. Chandar Sundaram, 'Grudging Concessions: The Officer Corps and its Indianization, 1817–1940', in Daniel Marston and Chandar Sundaram (eds.), *A Military History of India and South Asia: From the East India Company to the Nuclear Era* (Westport, Conn.: Praeger, 2007), pp. 98–100.

68. Cited in Narain, 'Co-option and Control', pp. 219–20.

69. Cassels to Linlithgow, 29 June 1940, L/PO/55, AAC.

70. K. V. Krishna Rao, *In the Service of the Nation: Reminiscences* (New Delhi: Viking, 2001), p. 6.

71. J. F. R. Jacob, *An Odyssey in War and Peace: An Autobiography* (New Delhi: Roli Books, 2011), p. 6.

72. Prasad, *Expansion of the Armed Forces*, pp. 75, 101–2.

73. Fortnightly Censor Summary, 13 January to 26 January 1943, L/P&J/12/654, AAC.

74. Cited in Christopher Bayly and Tim Harper, *Forgotten Armies: The Fall of British Asia, 1941–1945* (London: Allen Lane, 2004), p. 74.

75. Rao, *In the Service of the Nation*, pp. 5–6.

76. S. Sivasubramonian, *The National Income of India in the Twentieth Century* (New Delhi: Oxford University Press, 2000), Table 6.10.

77. Dietmar Rothermund, *India in the Great Depression 1929–1939* (New Delhi: Manohar, 1992).

78. A large body of writing is judiciously synthesized in Tirthankar Roy, *The Economic History of India 1857–1947*, 3rd edn (New Delhi: Oxford University Press, 2011), pp. 183–212.

79. Sivasubramonian, *National Income of India*, Table 6.9.

80. Alfred Martin Wainwright, 'The Role of South Asia in British Strategic Policy, 1939–50', PhD thesis, University of Wisconsin–Madison, 1989, pp. 36–40.

81. Report of the Modernization Committee, 1938, L/MIL/17/5/1801, AAC.

82. Report of the Expert Committee on the Defence of India, 1938–9, L/MIL/5/886, AAC.

83. P. C. Jain, *India Builds Her War Economy* (Allahabad: Kitab Mahal, 1943), pp. 4–5; Dwijendra Tripathi, *The Dynamics of a Tradition: Kasturbhai Lalbhai and His Entrepreneurship* (New Delhi: Manohar, 1981), p. 79.

84. P. S. Lokanathan, *India's Post-War Reconstruction and Its International Aspects* (New Delhi: Indian Council of World Affairs, 1946), pp. 6–8 (esp. table on p. 7).

85. Arun Joshi, *Lala Shri Ram: A Study in Entrepreneurship and Management* (New Delhi: Orient Longman, 1975), p. 301.

86. Note of Meeting, 10 July 1940, H. P. Mody Papers, NMML.

87. Medha M. Kudaisya, *The Life and Times of G. D. Birla* (New Delhi: Oxford University Press, 2003), pp. 197–8.

88. Speech at Town Hall Meeting, 10 July 1940, Part I, File No. 139, Purshottamdas Thakurdas Papers, NMML.

89. Shri Ram to Thakurdas, 6 July 1940, Part I, File No. 139, Purshottamdas Thakurdas Papers, NMML.

90. Draft statement, 21 June 1940, Part I, File No. 139, Purshottamdas Thakurdas Papers, NMML.

91. N. C. Sinha and P. N. Khera, *Indian War Economy: Supply, Industry and Finance* (New Delhi: Combined Inter-Services Historical Section, India & Pakistan, 1962), pp. 33–7, 164–85.

92. Note of 20 November 1941, cited in J. H. Voigt, *India in the Second World War* (New Delhi: Arnold-Heinemann, 1987), p. 74.

93. G. D. Khanolakara, *Walchand Hirachand: Man, His Times and Achievements* (Bombay: Walchand & Co., 1969), pp. 376–401 (quote on p. 384).

94. Dwijendra Tripathi and Makrand Mehta, *Business Houses in Western India: A Study in Entrepreneurial Response, 1850–1956* (New Delhi: Manohar, 1990), pp. 162–3.

95. See Walchand's correspondence with Auchinleck in April–May 1941, Subject File 67, Walchand Hirachand Papers, NMML.

96. The next three paragraphs draw on Khanolakara, *Walchand Hirachand*, pp. 355–75; Subject Files 45 and 47, Walchand Hirachand Papers, NMML.

97. Edgar Snow, *People on Our Side* (New York: World Publishing Company, 1944), p. 56.

5. INTO AFRICA

1. Victoria Schofield, *Wavell: Soldier & Statesman* (London: John Murray, 2006), p. 145.
2. Michael Howard, *The Mediterranean Strategy in the Second World War* (London: Weidenfeld & Nicolson, 1968).
3. Douglas Porch, *Hitler's Mediterranean Gamble: The North African and Mediterranean Campaigns in World War II* (London: Weidenfeld & Nicolson, 2004), pp. 38–40.
4. Harold E. Raugh, Jr, *Wavell in the Middle East, 1939–1941: A Study in Generalship* (Norman: University of Oklahoma Press, 2013), pp. 74–5.
5. Schofield, *Wavell*, p. 150.
6. Porch, *Hitler's Mediterranean Gamble*, p. 45.
7. Raugh, *Wavell in the Middle East*, p. 85; Schofield, *Wavell*, p. 154; Porch, *Hitler's Mediterranean Gamble*, p. 46.
8. P. C. Bharucha, *The North African Campaign, 1940–43* (New Delhi: Ministry of Defence, Government of India, 2012), p. 37.
9. Tim Moreman, 'From the Desert Sands to the Burmese Jungle', in Kaushik Roy (ed.), *The Indian Army in the Two World Wars* (Leiden: Brill, 2012), p. 227.
10. Geoffrey Evans, *The Desert and the Jungle* (London: William Kimber, 1959), p. 17.
11. Middle East Censor Reports, June–July 1940, L/WS/1/1172, AAC.
12. Namrata Narain, 'Co-option and Control: Role of the Colonial Army in India, 1918–1947', PhD thesis, Cambridge University, 1993, p. 258.
13. Bharucha, *North African Campaign*, p. 80.
14. Ravi Inder Singh Sidhu, *As Told by Them: Personal Narratives of Indian Soldiers who Fought during World War II* (New Delhi: Quills Ink Publishing, 2014), p. 16.
15. Schofield, *Wavell*, pp. 155, 157.
16. J. G. Elliott, *A Roll of Honour: The Story of the Indian Army, 1939–1945* (Delhi: Army Publishers, 1965), pp. 29–30.
17. Porch, *Hitler's Mediterranean Gamble*, pp. 117–18; Bharucha, *North African Campaign*, pp. 84–6.
18. Compton Mackenzie, *Eastern Epic Volume I: Defence, September 1939–March 1943* (London: Chatto & Windus, 1951), pp. 37–40.
19. Bharucha, *North African Campaign*, p. 99.
20. Raugh, *Wavell in the Middle East*, p. 104.
21. Schofield, *Wavell*, p. 172.

22. Raugh, *Wavell in the Middle East*, pp. 88–9, 171.
23. J. N. Chaudhuri, *An Autobiography* (New Delhi: Vikas Publishing House, 1978), p. 118.
24. Sidhu, *As Told by Them*, pp. 23–4.
25. Chaudhuri, *Autobiography*, p. 120.
26. Gerard Douds, ' "Matters of Honour": Indian Troops in the North African and Italian Theatres', in Paul Addison and Angus Calder (eds.), *Time to Kill: The Soldier's Experience of War in the West, 1939–1945* (London: Pimlico, 1997), p. 119.
27. Letter of 6 October 1940, in Ashali Varma, *The Victoria Cross: A Love Story* (Delhi: Pearson, 2013), p. 12.
28. Sidhu, *As Told by Them*, p. 25.
29. Bisheshwar Prasad, *East African Campaign 1940–41* (New Delhi: Ministry of Defence, Government of India, 2012), pp. 30–31.
30. Chaudhuri, *Autobiography*, p. 120.
31. William Slim, *Unofficial History* (London: Cassell, 1959), p. 130.
32. Letter of 16 November 1940, Varma, *Victoria Cross*, pp. 18–19.
33. Slim, *Unofficial History*; Prasad, *East African Campaign*, pp. 34–5.
34. Raugh, *Wavell in the Middle East*, pp. 173–4.
35. Wavell's despatch on Operations in East Africa, November 1940–July 1941, 21 May 1942. Accessed online at http://www.ibiblio.org/hyperwar/UN/UK/LondonGazette/37645.
36. Prasad, *East African Campaign*, pp. 37–9.
37. Elliott, *Roll of Honour*, pp. 44–6.
38. Letter of 10 February 1941, Varma, *Victoria Cross*, pp. 31–2.
39. Wavell's despatch 'Operations in East Africa, November 1940–July 1941', 21 May 1942. Accessed online at http://www.ibiblio.org/hyperwar/UN/UK/LondonGazette/37645.
40. Schofield, *Wavell*, p. 173.
41. Mackenzie, *Eastern Epic*, pp. 53–4.
42. Sidhu, *As Told by Them*, p. 37.
43. Report by Platt, 11 September 1941, in Wavell's despatch on Operations in East Africa, November 1940–July 1941.
44. Prasad, *East African Campaign*, p. 59.
45. Elliott, *Roll of Honour*, pp. 51–2.
46. Prasad, *East African Campaign*, pp. 63–71.
47. Account of the Eritrean campaign 1941, p. 32, 67/31/1, G. R. Stevens Papers, IWM.
48. Report by Platt, 11 September 1941, in Wavell's despatch on Operations in East Africa, November 1940–July 1941.

49. Alan Jeffreys, 'Training the Indian Army, 1939–1945', in Alan Jeffreys and Patrick Rose (eds.), *The Indian Army, 1939–47: Experience and Development* (Farnham: Ashgate, 2012), p. 80.
50. Prasad, *East African Campaign*, p. 87.
51. Report by Platt, 11 September 1941, in Wavell's despatch on Operations in East Africa, November 1940–July 1941.
52. Mackenzie, *Eastern Epic*, pp. 59–61.
53. Letter of 10 April 1941, Varma, *Victoria Cross*, p. 35.
54. Sidhu, *As Told by Them*, p. 28.
55. Letter of 14 May 1941, Varma, *Victoria Cross*, p. 37.
56. Sidhu, *As Told by Them*, p. 30.
57. Wavell's despatch on Operations in East Africa, November 1940–July 1941.
58. Jeffreys, 'Training the Indian Army', p. 81.
59. Sidhu, *As Told by Them*, pp. 38–9.

6. THE OIL CAMPAIGNS

1. Daniel Yergin, *The Prize: The Epic Quest for Oil, Money and Power* (New York: Simon and Schuster, 1991).
2. Robert Lyman, *First Victory: Britain's Forgotten Struggle in the Middle East, 1941* (London: Constable, 2006), pp. 3–4.
3. Chiefs of Staff Paper, 9 October 1940, WO 106/3077, TNA.
4. Milan Hauner, *India in Axis Strategy: Germany, Japan, and Indian Nationalists in the Second World War* (Stuttgart: Klett-Cotta, 1981), pp. 195–6. On German attitudes towards the Islamic countries, see also David Motadel, *Islam and Nazi Germany's War* (Cambridge, Mass.: Harvard University Press, 2014), esp. pp. 38–132.
5. Dharm Pal, *Campaign in Western Asia* (New Delhi: Ministry of Defence, Government of India, 2012), pp. 32–47.
6. John Connell, *Auchinleck: A Biography of Field-Marshal Sir Claude Auchinleck* (London: Cassell, 1959), pp. 193–4.
7. Pal, *Campaign in Western Asia*, pp. 49–50.
8. Connell, *Auchinleck*, pp. 187–9.
9. This paragraph and the next draw on Pal, *Campaign in Western Asia*, pp. 51–4.
10. Lyman, *First Victory*, pp. 49–50.
11. Connell, *Auchinleck*, pp. 200–201; Pal, *Campaign in Western Asia*, p. 63.
12. Compton Mackenzie, *Eastern Epic Volume I: Defence, September 1939–March 1943* (London: Chatto & Windus, 1951), p. 91.

13. Connell, *Auchinleck*, pp. 203–5.
14. Satyen Basu, *A Doctor in the Army* (Calcutta: privately published, 1960), pp. 22–3.
15. Pal, *Campaign in Western Asia*, p. 70; Connell, *Auchinleck*, pp. 205–6.
16. Lyman, *First Victory*, p. 63.
17. Connell, *Auchinleck*, p. 208.
18. Pal, *Campaign in Western Asia*, pp. 71–2; Connell, *Auchinleck*, pp. 208–9.
19. Geoffrey Warner, *Iraq and Syria 1941* (London: Purnell, 1974), p. 96.
20. Ibid., pp. 98–9.
21. Hauner, *India in Axis Strategy*, pp. 199–203.
22. John Connell, *Wavell: Supreme Commander 1941–1943* (London: Collins, 1969), pp. 435–7; Victoria Schofield, *Wavell: Soldier & Statesman* (London: John Murray, 2006), p. 196.
23. Connell, *Auchinleck*, pp. 221–2.
24. Winston Churchill, *The Second World War Volume III: The Grand Alliance* (London: Penguin Classics, 2005), pp. 230–31.
25. Connell, *Auchinleck*, pp. 227–30; Pal, *Campaign in Western Asia*, pp. 106–7.
26. Connell, *Auchinleck*, p. 196; Lyman, *First Victory*, pp. 98–9.
27. Basu, *Doctor in the Army*, p. 34.
28. Conclusions, 1 July 1940, CAB/95/1, TNA.
29. Report by Chiefs of Staff, 1 November 1940, CAB/66/13/1, TNA.
30. Connell, *Wavell*, p. 241.
31. Lyman, *First Victory*, pp. 154–61.
32. Warner, *Iraq and Syria 1941*, p. 125.
33. Lyman, *First Victory*, pp. 164–5.
34. Minute to Chiefs of Staff, 8 May 1941, PREM 3/422/6, TNA; Churchill to Wavell, 9 May 1941, PREM 3/309/4, TNA.
35. Wavell to Dill, 17 May 1941, PREM 3/309/4, TNA.
36. Harold E. Raugh, Jr, *Wavell in the Middle East, 1939–1941: A Study in Generalship* (Norman: University of Oklahoma Press, 2013), p. 219.
37. Connell, *Wavell*, p. 462.
38. Mackenzie, *Eastern Epic*, pp. 106–16.
39. Pal, *Campaign in Western Asia*, pp. 213–17.
40. William Slim, *Unofficial History* (London: Cassell, 1959), p. 153.
41. John Masters, *The Road Past Mandalay* (London: Cassell, 2002), p. 45.
42. Basu, *Doctor in the Army*, pp. 37–8.
43. Masters, *Road Past Mandalay*, p. 15.

44. Basu, *Doctor in the Army*, p. 42; Slim, *Unofficial History*, p. 170.
45. Pal, *Campaign in Western Asia*, p. 121.
46. Gavin Hambly, 'The Pahlavi Autocracy: Riza Shah, 1921–41', in P. Avery et al. (eds.), *The Cambridge History of Iran: Volume 7, From Nadir Shah to the Islamic Republic* (Cambridge: Cambridge University Press, 1991), pp. 213–43.
47. Richard Stewart, *Sunrise at Abadan: The British and Soviet Invasion of Iran, 1941* (New York: Praeger, 1988), p. 40.
48. Report by Chiefs of Staff, 23 February 1940, CAB/66/5/46, TNA.
49. Lyman, *First Victory*, p. 253.
50. Stewart, *Sunrise at Abadan*, p. 55.
51. Pal, *Campaign in Western Asia*, pp. 300–302.
52. Lyman, *First Victory*, pp. 257–8.
53. Pal, *Campaign in Western Asia*, pp. 301–5.
54. Lyman, *First Victory*, p. 262.
55. Stewart, *Sunrise at Abadan*, pp. 71–4.
56. Pal, *Campaign in Western Asia*, pp. 306–10.
57. Slim, *Unofficial History*, pp. 181–2.
58. Pal, *Campaign in Western Asia*, p. 353.

7. FOX HUNTING

1. Gerhard Schreiber et al., *Germany and the Second World War*, vol. 3: *The Mediterranean, South-East Europe, and North Africa* (Oxford: Clarendon Press, 1995), pp. 654–6.
2. Douglas Porch, *Hitler's Mediterranean Gamble: The North African and Mediterranean Campaigns in World War II* (London: Weidenfeld & Nicolson, 2004), pp. 122–8.
3. For the argument that Tripoli could have been captured, see Harold E. Raugh, Jr, *Wavell in the Middle East, 1939–1941: A Study in Generalship* (Norman: University of Oklahoma Press, 2013), pp. 120–26.
4. Ralph Bennett, *Ultra and Mediterranean Strategy, 1941–1945* (London: Hamish Hamilton, 1989), pp. 15–30.
5. Schreiber et al., *Germany in the Second World War*, vol. 3, p. 676.
6. Raugh, *Wavell in the Middle East*, pp. 192–5.
7. Compton Mackenzie, *Eastern Epic Volume I: Defence, September 1939–March 1943* (London: Chatto & Windus, 1951), p. 72.
8. P. C. Bharucha, *The North African Campaign, 1940–43* (New Delhi: Ministry of Defence, Government of India, 2012), pp. 157–8.
9. Ibid., pp. 150–51.

10. Mackenzie, *Eastern Epic*, pp. 72–4.
11. J. G. Elliott, *A Roll of Honour: The Story of the Indian Army, 1939–1945* (Delhi: Army Publishers, 1965), p. 104.
12. Bharucha, *North African Campaign*, p. 155.
13. Porch, *Hitler's Mediterranean Gamble*, p. 230.
14. Raugh, *Wavell in the Middle East*, pp. 206–7.
15. Bharucha, *North African Campaign*, p. 167.
16. Mackenzie, *Eastern Epic*, pp. 141–4.
17. Bharucha, *North African Campaign*, pp. 177–9.
18. Elliott, *Roll of Honour*, pp. 106–7.
19. Raugh, *Wavell in the Middle East*, pp. 235–7; Williamson Murray and Allan R. Millett, *A War to be Won: Fighting the Second World War* (Cambridge, Mass.: Harvard University Press, 2001), p. 267; Bharucha, *North African Campaign*, p. 184.
20. Niall Barr, *Pendulum of War: The Three Battles of El Alamein* (London: Pimlico, 2005), pp. 58–60.
21. Winston Churchill, *The Second World War Volume III: The Grand Alliance* (London: Penguin Classics, 2005), p. 308.
22. Porch, *Hitler's Mediterranean Gamble*, pp. 243–4.
23. Tim Moreman, 'From the Desert Sands to the Burmese Jungle', in Kaushik Roy (ed.), *The Indian Army in the Two World Wars* (Leiden: Brill, 2012), p. 232.
24. Bharucha, *North African Campaign*, p. 204.
25. Porch, *Hitler's Mediterranean Gamble*, p. 250.
26. Bharucha, *North African Campaign*, p. 228.
27. Elliott, *Roll of Honour*, pp. 110–13.
28. Bharucha, *North African Campaign*, p. 240.
29. Mackenzie, *Eastern Epic*, pp. 162–4.
30. Elliott, *Roll of Honour*, pp. 115–16.
31. Bharucha, *North African Campaign*, p. 275.
32. Ibid. p. 294, Appendix R.
33. Connell, *Auchinleck*, pp. 423–31.
34. Mackenzie, *Eastern Epic*, pp. 291–5.
35. Bharucha, *North African Campaign*, pp. 308–9.
36. Elliott, *Roll of Honour*, pp. 184–5.
37. Bharucha, *North African Campaign*, p. 352.
38. Barr, *Pendulum of War*, p. 13.
39. A. S. Naravane, *A Soldier's Life in War and Peace* (New Delhi: A. P. H. Publishing, 2004), p. 69.
40. Ibid., pp. 74–5.

41. Ibid., p. 77.
42. Bharucha, *North African Campaign*, pp. 364–6, 372.
43. Ibid, p. 395.
44. Basu, *Doctor in the Army*, p. 88.

8. COLLAPSING DOMINOES

1. John Connell, *Wavell: Supreme Commander 1941–1943* (London: Collins, 1969), pp. 45, 41.
2. Joyce Chapman Lebra, *Japan's Greater East Asia Co-Prosperity Sphere in World War II: Selected Readings and Documents* (Kuala Lumpur: Oxford University Press, 1975), pp. 71–2.
3. Michael A. Barnhart, *Japan Prepares for Total War: The Search for Economic Security, 1919–1941* (Ithaca: Cornell University Press, 1988).
4. The best account is Herbert Bix, *Hirohito and the Making of Modern Japan* (New York: HarperCollins, 2000), pp. 367–437.
5. Figures computed from data in C. N. Vakil and D. N. Maluste, *Commercial Relations between India and Japan* (Calcutta: Longmans Green & Co., 1937), pp. 92, 100.
6. Ibid., pp. 146–9, 177–91.
7. Eri Hotta, *Pan-Asianism and Japan's War 1931–1945* (London: Palgrave Macmillan, 2007); Rustom Bharucha, *Another Asia: Rabindranath Tagore & Okakura Tenshin* (New Delhi: Oxford University Press, 2009). See also Cemil Aydin, *The Politics of Anti-Westernism in Asia: Visions of World Order in Pan-Islamic and Pan-Asian Thought* (New York: Columbia University Press, 2007).
8. Cited in J. H. Voigt, *India in the Second World War* (New Delhi: Arnold-Heinemann, 1987), p. 84.
9. S. Woodburn Kirby, *The War Against Japan Volume I: The Loss of Singapore* (London: HMSO, 1957), pp. 33–6, 45–6.
10. Paul Haggie, *Britannia at Bay: The Defence of the British Empire against Japan 1931–1941* (Oxford: Clarendon Press, 1981), pp. 180, 184, 191, 203.
11. Bisheshwar Prasad, *Defence of India: Policy and Plans* (Delhi: Combined Inter-Services Historical Section, 1963), p. 142.
12. Ibid., p. 148.
13. John Connell, *Auchinleck: A Biography of Field-Marshal Sir Claude Auchinleck* (London: Cassell, 1959), p. 186
14. Woodburn Kirby, *Loss of Singapore*, pp. 17, 34

15. Winston Churchill, *The Second World War Volume III: The Grand Alliance* (London: Penguin Classics, 2005), p. 157.

16. K. D. Bhargava and K. N. V. Shastri, *Campaigns in South-East Asia 1941–42* (New Delhi: Ministry of Defence, Government of India, 2012), p. 13.

17. Philip Snow, *The Fall of Hong Kong* (London: Yale University Press, 2003), p. 14.

18. Lionel Carter (ed.), *Punjab Politics 1940–43: Strains of War* (New Delhi: Manohar, 2005), *passim*.

19. Chandar Sundaram, 'Seditious Letters and Steel Helmets', in Kaushik Roy (ed.), *War and Society in Colonial India* (New Delhi: Oxford University Press, 2006), pp. 142–5, 265–7.

20. Bhargava and Shastri, *Campaigns in South-East Asia*, pp. 25–67; Snow, *Fall of Hong Kong*, pp. 68–9.

21. Robert Lyman, *The Generals: From Defeat to Victory, Leadership in Asia 1941–45* (London: Constable, 2008), pp. 21–33.

22. Brian P. Farrell, *The Defence and Fall of Singapore 1940–1942* (Stroud: Tempus, 2005), pp. 87–8.

23. Ong Chit Chung, *Operation Matador: World War II – Britain's Attempt to Foil the Japanese Invasion of Malaya and Singapore* (Singapore: Times Academic Press, 1997). For a shorter, perceptive analysis, see Louis Allen, *Singapore 1941–1942* (London: Frank Cass, 1993), pp. 92–100.

24. Cited in Lyman, *The Generals*, p. 61.

25. Farrell, *Defence and Fall*, p. 115; T. R. Moreman, *The Jungle, the Japanese and the British Commonwealth Armies at War 1941–45: Fighting Methods, Doctrine and Training for Jungle Warfare* (London: Frank Cass, 2005), pp. 20–21.

26. Farrell, *Defence and Fall*, pp. 117–18.

27. John Baptist Crasta, *Eaten by the Japanese: The Memoir of an Unknown Indian Prisoner of War* (New York: Invisible Man Press, 2011), Kindle location 226–7.

28. Moreman, *The Jungle*, pp. 12–19.

29. Allen, *Singapore*, pp. 112–13.

30. Tsuji Masanobu, *Japan's Greatest Victory, Britain's Worst Defeat* (New York: Sarpendon Press, 1993), p. 77.

31. Bhargava and Shastri, *Campaigns in South-East Asia*, pp. 121–38.

32. Tsuji, *Japan's Greatest Victory*, pp. 89–91.

33. Mohan Singh, *Soldiers' Contribution to Indian Independence: The Epic of the Indian National Army* (New Delhi: Army Educational Stores, 1974), pp. 60–61.

34. Bhargava and Shastri, *Campaigns in South-East Asia*, pp. 150–51.
35. Farrell, *Defence and Fall*, p. 159; Bhargava and Shastri, *Campaigns in South-East Asia*, p. 167.
36. Bhargava and Shastri, *Campaigns in South-East Asia*, pp. 179–80.
37. Crasta, *Eaten by the Japanese*, Kindle location 260.
38. Moreman, *The Jungle*, p. 31.
39. Ravi Inder Singh Sidhu, *As Told by Them: Personal Narratives of Indian Soldiers who Fought during World War II* (New Delhi: Quills Ink Publishing, 2014), pp. 118–19.
40. Farrell, *Defence and Fall*, p. 202; Connell, *Wavell*, pp. 84–5.
41. Arthur Percival, *The War in Malaya* (London: Eyre and Spottiswoode, 1949), p. 228.
42. Bisheshwar Prasad, *The Retreat from Burma 1941– 42* (New Delhi: Ministry of Defence, Government of India, 2014), p. 31.
43. Frank McLynn, *The Burma Campaign: Disaster into Triumph 1942–45* (London: Vintage, 2011), p. 20.
44. Connell, *Wavell*, pp. 52–7.
45. Prasad, *Retreat from Burma*, pp. 46–51.
46. Moreman, *The Jungle*, pp. 36–7.
47. Louis Allen, *Burma: The Longest War* (London: J. M. Dent & Sons, 1984), p. 27.
48. Prasad, *Retreat from Burma*, pp. 100–101.
49. Moreman, *The Jungle*, p. 38.
50. Allen, *Burma*, pp. 33–4.
51. McLynn, *Burma Campaign*, p. 25.
52. Daniel Marston, *Phoenix from the Ashes: The Indian Army in the Burma Campaign* (Westport, Conn.: Praeger, 2002), pp. 63–5.
53. M. Attiqur Rahman, *Back to the Pavilion* (Karachi: Oxford University Press, 2005).
54. Prasad, *Retreat from Burma*, pp. 149–52.
55. Connell, *Wavell*, pp. 201–2.
56. Allen, *Burma*, pp. 48–9.
57. McLynn, *Burma Campaign*, p. 27.
58. Prasad, *Retreat from Burma*, pp. 238–41.
59. Connell, *Wavell*, pp. 56, 62–4.
60. Christopher Thorne, *Allies of a Kind: The United States, Britain and the War Against Japan, 1941–1945* (New York: Oxford University Press, 1978), p. 187.
61. Theodore H. White (ed.), *The Stilwell Papers* (New York: Shocken Books, 1972), pp. 54–7.

62. Jay Taylor, *The Generalissimo: Chiang Kai-shek and the Struggle for Modern China* (Cambridge, Mass.: Belknap Press, 2009), pp. 196-9.

63. Charles F. Romanus and Riley Sunderland, *United States Army in World War II, China–Burma–India Theater: Stilwell's Mission to China* (Washington, DC: Center of Military History, United States Army, 1987, orig. pub. 1953), pp. 86, 94-6.

64. William Slim, *Defeat into Victory* (Dehra Dun: Natraj Publishers, 2014; first publ. 1956), pp. 39-40.

65. Rana Mitter, *China's War with Japan 1937-1945: The Struggle for Survival* (London: Allen Lane, 2013), pp. 256-7.

66. Prasad, *Retreat from Burma*, p. 260.

67. White (ed.), *Stilwell Papers*, p. 88 (emphasis in original).

68. Moreman, *The Jungle*, p. 44 (emphasis in original document).

69. Sunil Amrith, *Crossing the Bay of Bengal: The Furies of Nature and the Fortunes of Migrants* (Cambridge, Mass.: Harvard University Press, 2013), pp. 181-92.

70. Hugh Tinker, 'A Forgotten Long March: The Indian Exodus from Burma, 1942', *Journal of Southeast Asian Studies*, vol. 6, no. 1 (March 1975), pp. 1-15.

71. J. H. Williams, *Elephant Bill* (London: Penguin Books, 1950), pp. 156-7.

72. On the longer history, see Thomas R. Trautmann, *Elephants and Kings: An Environmental History* (Chicago: University of Chicago Press, 2015).

73. Slim, *Defeat into Victory*, pp. 109-10.

9. COILS OF WAR

1. 19 September 1940, *SWJN*, vol. 11, p. 141.

2. Nehru to Sampurnanand, 14 December 1941; interview, 17 December 1941, *SWJN*, vol. 12, pp. 15-16, 33.

3. *CWMG*, vol. 75, pp. 188-91, 197-8, 224-5; *SWJN*, vol. 12, pp. 45-5.

4. Nehru to Gandhi, 5 January 1942, *SWJN*, vol. 12, pp. 73-4; Speech at All-India Congress Committee, 15 January 1942, *CWMG*, vol. 75, pp. 219-29; Rajmohan Gandhi, *Rajaji: A Life* (New Delhi: Penguin, 1997), p. 229.

5. Cited in Sarvepalli Gopal, *Jawaharlal Nehru: A Biography*, vol. 1 (London: Jonathan Cape, 1975), p. 276.

6. Nehru to Jagannath, 6 March 1942, *SWJN*, vol. 12, pp. 150, 168-77.

7. This paragraph and the next draw on Gary R. Hess, *America Encounters India, 1941-1947* (Baltimore: Johns Hopkins Press, 1971), pp.

2–4; Kenton J. Clymer, *Quest for Freedom: The United States and India's Independence* (New York: Columbia University Press, 2005), pp. 4–8. Also see Sujit Mukherjee, *Passage to America: The Reception of Rabindranath Tagore in the United States 1912–1941* (Calcutta: Bookland, 1964).

8. Mrinalini Sinha, *Specters of Mother India: The Global Restructuring of an Empire* (Durham, NC: Duke University Press, 2007).

9. Nico Slate, *Colored Cosmopolitanism: The Shared Struggle for Freedom in the United States and India* (Cambridge, Mass.: Harvard University Press, 2012); Gerald Horne, *The End of Empires: African Americans and India* (Philadelphia: Temple University Press, 2008); Asha Sharma, *An American in Khadi* (New Delhi: Penguin, 2000).

10. Dennis Kux, *India and the United States: Estranged Democracies 1941–1991* (Washington, DC: National Defense University Press, 1992), p. 3.

11. Clymer, *Quest for Freedom*, pp. 14–19.

12. Hess, *America Encounters India*, pp. 18–21.

13. British Aide Memoire, 17 April 1941; Hull to Halifax, 28 May 1941; Press release, 21 July 1941, *FRUS*, 1941, vol. 3, pp. 170–74.

14. Memorandum on 'India and the Lend Lease Act', 14 May 1941, File no. 2, Roosevelt Library Papers, NMML.

15. Memorandum by Berle, 5 May 1941, *FRUS*, 1941, vol. 3, pp. 176–7.

16. Sarvepalli Gopal, 'Drinking Tea with Treason: Halifax in India', in idem, *Imperialists, Nationalists, Democrats: The Collected Essays* (Ranikhet: Permanent Black, 2013), pp. 77–95.

17. Memorandum by Hull, 7 May 1941, *FRUS*, 1941, vol. 3, p. 178.

18. Winant to Hull, 1 August 1941, *FRUS*, 1941, vol. 3, pp. 178–9.

19. Berle to Welles, 5 August 1941; Welles to Hull, 6 August 1941, *FRUS*, 1941, vol. 3, pp. 179–81.

20. William Roger Louis, *Imperialism at Bay: The United States and the Decolonization of the British Empire, 1941–1945* (Oxford: Oxford University Press, 1978).

21. Dhananjay Keer, *Veer Savarkar* (Mumbai: Popular Prakashan, 2012), p. 297.

22. Erez Manela, *The Wilsonian Moment: Self-Determination and the International Origins of Anticolonial Nationalism* (New York: Oxford University Press, 2007).

23. Report for August 1941, WCP, NMML.

24. Christopher Thorne, *Allies of a Kind: The United States, Britain, and the War Against Japan, 1941–1945* (New York: Oxford University Press, 1978), p. 61.

25. Indian reactions to the Atlantic Charter can be sampled in *TF*, 1941, part 1, pp. 60–75.

26. Interview to Evelyn Wrench, December 1941, *CWMG*, vol. 81, p. 348.

27. Clymer, *Quest for Freedom*, p. 35.

28. Winant to Hull, 4 November 1941, *FRUS*, 1941, vol. 3, pp. 181–2.

29. Memorandum by Murray, 7 November 1941; Welles to Hull, 15 November 1941, *FRUS*, 1941, vol. 3, pp. 184–7.

30. Clymer, *Quest for Freedom*, p. 44.

31. Winston Churchill, *The Second World War Volume IV: The Hinge of Fate* (London: Penguin Classics, 2005), p. 185; Churchill to Attlee, 7 January 1942, in *TP*, vol. 1, p. 14.

32. J. H. Voigt, *India in the Second World War* (New Delhi: Arnold-Heinemann, 1987), pp. 98–9.

33. These negotiations can be followed in *FRUS*, 1941, vol. 3, pp. 192–9.

34. Voigt, *India in the Second World War*, p. 99.

35. Cited in memorandum by Murray, 24 April 1942, *FRUS*, 1942, vol. 1, p. 640.

36. Memorandum of conversation by Berle, 23 January 1942, *FRUS*, 1942, vol. 1, pp. 593–5.

37. Memoranda of conversations by Berle, 23 January and 28 January 1942, Memorandum to President, 29 January 1942, *FRUS*, 1942, vol. 1, pp. 595–9.

38. Memorandum by Berle, 17 February 1942, *FRUS*, 1942, vol. 1, pp. 602–4.

39. Clymer, *Quest for Freedom*, p. 41; Hess, *America Encounters India*, p. 35.

40. Long to Welles, 25 February 1942, *FRUS*, 1942, vol. 1, p. 606.

41. Pearl Buck to Eleanor Roosevelt, 7 March 1942; President to Eleanor Roosevelt, 11 March 1942, File no. 12, Roosevelt Library Papers, NMML.

42. Clymer, *Quest for Freedom*, p. 45.

43. Roosevelt to Churchill (draft), 25 February 1942, in Warren Kimball (ed.), *Churchill and Roosevelt: The Complete Correspondence* (Princeton: Princeton University Press, 1984), vol. 1, pp. 400–401.

44. Message to Winant, 25 February 1942, *FRUS*, 1942, vol. 1, p. 604.

45. The best account is Rana Mitter, *China's War with Japan, 1937–1945: The Struggle for Survival* (London: Allen Lane, 2013).

46. Clark Kerr to Eden, 24 January 1942; Linlithgow to Clark Kerr, 26 January 1942; Linlithgow to Amery, 1 February 1942, *TP*, vol. 1, pp. 76, 78–9, 102–3.

47. Churchill to Linlithgow, 3 February 1942; Churchill to Chiang, 3 February 1942; Linlithgow to Amery, 5 February 1942; Churchill to Linlithgow, 5 February 1942, *TP*, vol. 1, pp. 113–14, 119–21.

48. Linlithgow to Amery, 9 February, 16 February & 20 February 1942, *TP*, vol. 1, pp. 136–7, 185, 214.

49. Linlithgow to Amery, 10 February & 20 February 1942, *TP*, vol. 1, pp. 143, 213.

50. Linlithgow to Governor of Burma, 16 February 1942, Linlithgow Papers, NAI.

51. *SWJN*, vol. 11, pp. 515–20.

52. Speech, 11 February 1942, *SWJN*, vol. 12, pp. 467–9.

53. Mitter, *China's War*, p. 247; *TP*, vol. 1, p. 213.

54. Nehru to Chiang, 13 February 1942, *SWJN*, vol. 12, pp. 470–71.

55. Churchill to Chiang and Eden to Churchill, 12 February 1942, *TP*, vol. 1, p. 153.

56. Cited in Mitter, *China's War*, p. 247.

57. Discussion with Chiang Kai-shek and wife, *CWMG*, vol. 75, pp. 333–4.

58. Cited in Mitter, *China's War*, p. 248. Also see, Jay Taylor, *The Generalissimo: Chiang Kai-shek and the Struggle for Modern China* (Cambridge, Mass.: Belknap Press, 2009), pp. 194–5.

59. Rajmohan Gandhi, *Patel: A Life* (Ahmedabad: Navjivan Publishing House, n.d.), p. 303; Gandhi to Patel, 25 February 1942, *CWMG*, vol. 75, p. 359.

60. T. V. Soong to Roosevelt, 25 February 1942, *FRUS*, 1942, vol. 1, pp. 604–6.

61. Matthews to Hull, 26 February 1942, *FRUS*, 1942, vol. 1, p. 608.

62. War Cabinet 131 (41), 19 December 1941, CAB 65/20/24, TNA.

63. Churchill to Attlee, 7 January 1942, *TP*, vol. 1, p. 14.

64. Linlithgow to Churchill, 21 January 1942; Amery to Churchill, 21 January 1942, *TP*, vol. 1, pp. 53–4.

65. Attlee to Amery, 24 January 1942, *TP*, vol. 1, p. 75.

66. Memorandum by Attlee, 2 February 1942, *TP*, vol. 1, pp. 110–12.

67. Amery to Linlithgow, 9 and 11 February 1942; Linlithgow to Amery, 12 February 1942, *TP*, vol. 1, pp. 137–9, 151–2.

68. R. J. Moore, *Churchill, Cripps and India, 1939–1945* (Oxford: Clarendon Press, 1979), pp. 63–8.

69. Churchill to Roosevelt, 4 March 1942, *FRUS*, 1942, vol. 1, p. 612.

70. Amery to Linlithgow, 5 March 1942; Churchill to Roosevelt, 7 March 1942, *TP*, vol. 1, pp. 324, 363.

71. Moore, *Churchill, Cripps and India*, pp. 70–74.
72. Amery to Linlithgow, 10 March 1942, *TP*, vol. 1, pp. 396–7, 404.
73. *FRUS*, 1942, vol. 1, pp. 613, 617.
74. *FRUS*, 1942, vol. 1, pp. 615–17.

10. DECLARATIONS FOR INDIA

1. Extract from BBC Weekly News Review for India, 14 March 1942, in Peter Davison (ed.), *Orwell and Politics* (London: Penguin, 2001), pp. 150–51.
2. My account draws mainly on R. J. Moore, *Churchill, Cripps and India, 1939–1945* (Oxford: Clarendon Press, 1979); Peter Clarke, *The Cripps Version: The Life of Sir Stafford Cripps, 1889–1952* (London: Penguin, 2003), pp. 276–322; Sarvepalli Gopal, *Jawaharlal Nehru: A Biography*, vol. 1 (London: Jonathan Cape, 1975), pp. 279–87; *TP*, vol. 1; *FRUS*, 1942, vol. 1.
3. Cited in Louis Fischer, *A Week with Gandhi* (New York: Duell, Sloan & Pearce, 1943), p. 12.
4. Interview, 12 April 1942, *SWJN*, vol. 12, p. 214.
5. Entries of 10–11 April 1942, John Barnes and David Nicholson (eds.), *The Empire at Bay: The Leo Amery Diaries 1929–1945* (London: Hutchinson, 1988), p. 794.
6. Ram Manohar Lohia, *The Mystery of Sir Stafford Cripps* (Bombay: Padma Publications, 1942), pp. 1–38.
7. Diary, 3 April 1942, in Davison, *Orwell and Politics*, p. 154.
8. Mulk Raj Anand, *Letters on India* (London: George Routledge, 1942), pp. 8–15.
9. Susheila Nasta, 'Negotiating a "New World Order": Mulk Raj Anand as Public Intellectual at the Heart of Empire', in Rehana Ahmed and Sumita Mukherjee (eds.), *South Asian Resistances in Britain, 1858–1947* (London: Continuum Books, 2012).
10. 'The British Crisis', in Davison, *Orwell and Politics*, p. 163.
11. *Tribune*, 19 March 1943, in Davison, *Orwell and Politics*, pp. 173–5.
12. 17 August 1942, Davison, *Orwell and Politics*, pp. 171–2.
13. Diary, 18 April 1942, in ibid., p. 160.
14. Diary, 18 April 1942, in ibid., p. 158.
15. Johnson to Roosevelt, 11 April 1942, *FRUS*, 1942, vol. 1, pp. 631–2.
16. Roosevelt to Churchill, 11 April 1942; Churchill to Roosevelt, 12 April 1942, *FRUS*, 1942, vol. 1, pp. 633–5.

17. Auriol Weigold, *Churchill, Roosevelt and India: Propaganda during World War II* (New Delhi: Routledge, 2009), p. 112.

18. Clarke, *Cripps Version*, p. 343.

19. Memorandum by Alling, 13 May 1942, *FRUS*, 1942, vol. 1, pp. 651–3.

20. Spry's note and report, *TP*, vol. 2, pp. 89–92, 473.

21. Moore, *Churchill, Cripps and India*, p. 131

22. Reginald Coupland, *The Cripps Mission* (London: Oxford University Press, 1942), p. 77 (emphasis in original).

23. Cited in Weigold, *Churchill, Roosevelt and India*, p. 141.

24. Nehru to Roosevelt, *SWJN*, vol. 12, pp. 212–13.

25. Kenton J. Clymer, *Quest for Freedom: The United States and India's Independence* (New York: Columbia University Press, 2005), p. 82.

26. Auriol Weigold, 'Cripps' Offer and the Nationalist Response: Constructing Propaganda in the United States', *South Asia*, vol. 23, no. 2 (2000), pp. 69–70.

27. Fischer, *Week with Gandhi*, pp. 12–16, 89–90.

28. Weigold, 'Cripps' Offer', pp. 67–8.

29. Edgar Snow, *People on Our Side* (Cleveland, Ohio: World Publishing Company, 1944), pp. 29–30, 41, 48–49.

30. Louis Fischer, 'Why Cripps Failed', *The Nation*, 19 and 26 September 1942.

31. Clarke, *Cripps Version*, pp. 353–4.

32. Edgar Snow, 'Must Britain Give up India?' *Saturday Evening Post*, 12 September 1942.

33. Halifax to Eden, 16 September 1942, *TP*, vol. 2, pp. 969–70.

34. Gandhi to Roosevelt, 1 July 1942, File No. 12, Roosevelt Library Papers, NMML.

35. Fischer telegram and letter to Roosevelt, 5 and 7 August 1942, File No. 12, Roosevelt Library Papers, NMML.

36. Chiang to Roosevelt, 25 July 1942; Welles to Roosevelt and Roosevelt to Churchill, 29 July 1942, *FRUS*, 1942, vol. 1, pp. 695–700.

37. Churchill to Roosevelt, *TP*, vol. 2, p. 533.

38. Memorandum by Hull, 15 August 1942, File No. 12, Roosevelt Library Papers, NMML.

39. Milan Hauner, *India in Axis Strategy: Germany, Japan, and Indian Nationalists in the Second World War* (Stuttgart: Klett-Cotta, 1981), pp. 238–9.

40. Jan Kuhlmann, *Netaji in Europe* (New Delhi: Rupa, 2012), p. 19.

41. Report of an interview by Alberto Quaroni, 2 April 1941, *NCW*, vol. 11, pp. 34-5.

42. Romain Hayes, *Bose in Nazi Germany* (New Delhi: Random House India, 2011), pp. 29-30.

43. Secret memorandum, 9 April 1941, *NCW*, vol. 11, pp. 38-49.

44. Memorandum of conversation between Bose and Ribbentrop, 12 April 1941, in T. R. Sareen (ed.), *Subhas Chandra Bose and Nazi Germany* (New Delhi: Mounto Publishing, 1996), pp. 89-99.

45. Supplementary memorandum, 3 May 1941, *NCW*, vol. 11, pp. 50-51.

46. Hauner, *India in Axis Strategy*, pp. 253-4; Kuhlmann, *Netaji in Europe*, p. 53.

47. Draft of Declaration, May 1941, *NCW*, vol. 11, pp. 57-58; Message to comrades in India, May 1941, *NCW*, vol. 11, p. 53.

48. Hayes, *Bose in Nazi Germany*, p. 54; Kuhlmann, *Netaji in Europe*, pp. 54-5.

49. Report of conversation, 17 July 1941, *NCW*, vol. 11, pp. 60-61.

50. Bose to Ribbentrop, 15 August 1941, *NCW*, vol. 11, pp. 63-5 (emphasis in original).

51. Kuhlmann, *Netaji in Europe*, pp. 84-5; Hayes, *Bose in Nazi Germany*, pp. 63, 68.

52. Memorandum of conversation between Bose and Ribbentrop, 29 November 1941, in Sareen (ed.), *Bose and Nazi Germany*, pp. 163-7.

53. Hayes, *Bose in Nazi Germany*, pp. 93-5.

54. Kuhlmann, *Netaji in Europe*, pp. 92-4.

55. Hauner, *India in Axis Strategy*, pp. 435-6.

56. William J. West (ed.), *Orwell: The Lost Writings* (New York: Arbor House, 1985), p. 33.

57. Broadcasts of 25 March and 31 March 1942, *NCW*, vol. 11, pp. 80-86.

58. Broadcast of 17 June 1942, *NCW*, vol. 11, p. 120.

59. Leonard Gordon, *Brothers Against the Raj: A Biography of Indian Nationalists Sarat & Subhas Chandra Bose* (New Delhi: Rupa, 1990), p. 477.

60. Hauner, *India in Axis Strategy*, p. 438.

61. Broadcast of 6 April 1942, *NCW*, vol. 11, pp. 87-8.

62. Hauner, *India in Axis Strategy*, p. 477.

63. Kuhlmann, *Netaji in Europe*, p. 111.

64. Hayes, *Bose in Nazi Germany*, pp. 106-7; Hauner, *India in Axis Strategy*, pp. 479-80; Kuhlmann, *Netaji in Europe*, pp. 112-14.

65. Sugata Bose, *His Majesty's Opponent: Subhas Chandra Bose and India's Struggle Against Empire* (Cambridge, Mass.: Belknap Press, 2011), p. 218.

66. German record of conversation, 30 May 1942, *NCW*, vol. 11, pp. 102–8.

67. Bose to Ribbentrop, 23 July 1942, in Sareen (ed.), *Bose and Nazi Germany*, p. 289.

11. RUMOUR AND REVOLT

1. See the superb treatment by Indivar Kamtekar, 'The Shiver of 1942', in Kaushik Roy (ed.), *War and Society in Colonial India* (New Delhi: Oxford University Press, 2006), pp. 330–57. An earlier, more tentative exploration of these links is in Arun Chandra Bhuyan, *The Quit India Movement: The Second World War and Indian Nationalism*, 2nd edn (Guwahati: Lawyer's Book Stall, 1993).

2. Cited in *CWMG*, vol. 72, pp. 223, 134.

3. Fortnightly reports from Bihar and United Provinces in April 1941, 18/4/41 – Poll (I), Political Section, Home Dept, NAI.

4. Srimanjari, *Through War and Famine: Bengal 1939–45* (New Delhi: Orient Black Swan, 2009), p. 52.

5. Fortnightly report from Assam in second half of August 1941, 18/8/41 – Poll (I), Political Section, Home Dept, NAI.

6. The propaganda work can be followed in the fortnightly reports from various provinces in 1941.

7. Fortnightly reports for second half of May 1941, 18/5/41 – Poll (I), Political Section, Home Dept, NAI.

8. Fortnightly report from Bengal for first half of March 1942, 18/3/42 – Poll (I), Political Section, Home Dept, NAI.

9. From various fortnightly reports for 1942. Also see, Kamtekar 'Shiver of 1942', pp. 332–3.

10. Weekly Intelligence Summaries, 13 and 20 February 1942, L/WS/1/1433, AAC.

11. Fortnightly reports from United Provinces and Bihar for March 1942, 18/3/42 – Poll (I), Political Section, Home Dept, NAI.

12. Weekly Intelligence Summaries, 6 March, 22 May, 5 June, 24 July 1942, L/WS/1/1433, AAC; Fortnightly reports for January and May 1942, NAI.

13. Fortnightly reports from Bihar and Bengal for March–June 1942, Poll (I), Political Section, Home Dept, NAI.

14. Srimanjari, *Through War and Famine*, p. 64.

15. Marc Bloch, *Réflexions d'un historien sur les fausses nouvelles de la guerre* (Paris: Allia, 1999).

16. Fortnightly reports from Bombay and Bihar for January and April 1942, Poll (I), Political Section, Home Dept, NAI; Weekly Intelligence Summaries, 20 February and 6 March 1942, L/WS/1/1433, AAC.

17. Fortnightly reports from Bengal for March 1942, 18/3/42 – Poll (I), Political Section, Home Dept, NAI.

18. Fortnightly reports from Bengal and Bihar for January and March 1942, Poll (I), Political Section, Home Dept, NAI; Weekly Intelligence Summaries, 20 February and 13 March 1942, L/WS/1/1433, AAC.

19. Fortnightly reports for Bombay, Bengal and United Provinces, January–March 1942, Poll (I), Political Section, Home Dept, NAI; Weekly Intelligence Summaries, 13 March and 3 April 1942, L/WS/1/1433, AAC.

20. Fortnightly report for Bihar, April 1942, 18/4/42 – Poll (I), Political Section, Home Dept, NAI.

21. Fortnightly reports, March 1942, Poll (I), Political Section, Home Dept, NAI; Weekly Intelligence Summary, 13 March 1942, L/WS/1/1433, AAC.

22. Fortnightly reports, March–April 1942, Poll (I), Political Section, Home Dept, NAI.

23. Fortnightly reports for Bengal and Bihar, January–April 1942, Poll (I), Political Section, Home Dept, NAI; Weekly Intelligence Summary, 20 February 1942, L/WS/1/1433, AAC; Monthly Intelligence Summary, 4 May 1942, L/WS/1/317, AAC.

24. The amount of paperwork generated by ARP was equally impressive. See, for instance, 25-F (1939), 49(5)-W/43, 49(5)-W/44, NAI.

25. Fortnightly reports for Assam and United Provinces, April and June 1941, Poll (I), Political Section, Home Dept, NAI.

26. Srimanjari, *Through War and Famine*, p. 52.

27. Fortnightly reports, May 1941, Poll (I), Political Section, Home Dept, NAI.

28. A. K. Chettiar, 'Chennai Nagaram, 1942', *Kumari Malar*, 1 April 1943, p. 115; Srimanjari, *Through War and Famine*, pp. 53–4.

29. Weekly Intelligence Summary, 15 May 1942, L/WS/1/1433, AAC.

30. Pudhumaipithan, 'Patapatappu'.

31. Srimanjari, *Through War and Famine*, p. 59.

32. Figures from Kamtekar, 'Shiver of 1942', pp. 338–9.

33. Fortnightly report from Bengal, February and April 1941, Poll (I), Political Section, Home Dept, NAI.

34. Fortnightly reports from Bombay and Bihar, February and March 1942, Poll (I), Political Section, Home Dept, NAI.

35. Fortnightly report from Bengal, 18/1/42, Poll (I), Political Section, Home Dept, NAI.

36. Srimanjari, *Through War and Famine*, pp. 55–7, 61–3.

37. Benoy Kumar Sarkar, *The Political Philosophies Since 1905, Vol. 2: The Epoch of Neo-Democracy and Neo-Socialism* (Lahore: Motilal Banarsidass, 1942), pp. 67–70.

38. Fortnightly reports from Bombay, January–June 1942, Poll (I), Political Section, Home Dept, NAI; Weekly Intelligence Summaries, February–March 1942, L/WS/1/1433, AAC.

39. Weekly Intelligence Summary, 3 April 1942, L/WS/1/1433, AAC.

40. Fortnightly reports from Madras, April 1942, 18/4/42 – Poll (I), Political Section, Home Dept, NAI.

41. Fortnightly reports from Bihar and Bombay, February–May 1942, Poll (I), Political Section, Home Dept, NAI; Weekly Intelligence Summaries, February 1942, L/WS/1/1433, AAC.

42. Fortnightly reports from Madras, January–February 1942, Poll (I), Political Section, Home Dept, NAI.

43. Gul Hassan Khan, *Memoirs of Lt. Gen. Gul Hassan Khan* (Karachi: Oxford University Press, 1993), **p. 12.**

44. Fortnightly reports from Madras, April 1942, 18/4/42 – Poll (I), Political Section, Home Dept, NAI.

45. O. Pulla Reddy, *Autumn Leaves* (Bombay, 1978), p. 70, cited in Kamtekar, 'Shiver of 1942', pp. 343–4.

46. Pudhumaipithan, 'Patapatappu'; Chettiar, 'Chennai Nagaram, 1942', p. 111.

47. Weekly Intelligence Summary, 10 April 1942, L/WS/1/1433, AAC.

48. Personal communication from Keshava Guha.

49. Chettiar, 'Chennai Nagaram, 1942', p. 116.

50. 'Question Box', 26 April 1942, *CWMG*, vol. 82, pp. 217–18.

51. Interview to journalist, before 25 July 1942, *CWMG*, vol. 83, pp. 134–5.

52. 28 July 1942, *CWMG*, vol. 83, p. 145.

53. Note on letter from Horace Alexander, 3 August 1942, *CWMG*, vol. 83, pp. 165–6.

54. Speech at All-India Congress Committee Meeting, 8 August 1942, *CWMG*, vol. 83, pp. 196–7.

55. J. H. Voigt, *India in the Second World War* (New Delhi: Arnold-Heinemann, 1987), pp. 157–8.

56. Cited in Gyanendra Pandey, 'The Revolt of August 1942 in Eastern UP and Bihar', in idem (ed.), *The Indian Nation in 1942* (Calcutta: K. P. Bagchi, 1988), p. 155.

57. Francis Hutchins, *Spontaneous Revolution: The Quit India Movement* (Delhi: Manohar, 1971), pp. 337-9.

58. Cited in *CWMG*, vol. 83, p. 172 n. 3.

59. War Cabinet Conclusions, 13 July 1942, CAB 65/27/7, TNA.

60. Srinath Raghavan, 'Protecting the Raj: The Army in India and Internal Security, c. 1919–1939', *Small Wars and Insurgencies*, vol. 16, no. 3 (2005), pp. 253–79.

61. Fortnightly Censor Summary, 27 January to 9 February 1943, L/P&J/12/654, AAC.

62. Weekly Intelligence Summary, 28 August 1942, L/WS/1/1433, AAC.

63. Weekly Intelligence Summaries, 21 August and 16 October 1942, L/WS/1/1433, AAC.

64. Weekly Intelligence Summary, 9 October 1942, L/WS/1/1433, AAC.

65. Cited in Voigt, *India in the Second World War*, p. 167.

12. INDIAN NATIONAL ARMIES

1. Jan Kuhlmann, *Netaji in Europe* (New Delhi: Rupa, 2012), p. 119.

2. Milan Hauner, *India in Axis Strategy: Germany, Japan, and Indian Nationalists in the Second World War* (Stuttgart: Klett-Cotta, 1981), p. 254. Also see, Mukund R. Vyas, *Passage Through a Turbulent Era: Historical Reminiscences of the Fateful Years 1937–1947* (Bombay: Indo-Foreign Publications, 1983), p. 306.

3. Hauner, *India in Axis Strategy*, p. 256; Kuhlmann, *Netaji in Europe*, p. 51.

4. Romain Hayes, *Bose in Nazi Germany* (New Delhi: Random House India, 2011), pp. 41-2.

5. Hauner, *India in Axis Strategy*, pp. 366–7; Hayes, *Bose in Nazi Germany*, pp. 59–60.

6. Kuhlmann, *Netaji in Europe*, p. 121.

7. Rudolf Hartog, *The Sign of the Tiger: Subhas Chandra Bose and his Indian Legion in Germany, 1941–45* (New Delhi: Rupa, 2001), pp. 49–52; Martin Bamber, *For Free India: Indian Soldiers in Germany and Italy during the Second World War* (Netherlands: Oskam-Neeven Publishers, 2010), p. 39.

8. Hayes, *Bose in Nazi Germany*, p. 76.

9. Kulhmann, *Netaji in Europe*, p. 122.

10. Hartog, *Sign of the Tiger*, p. 61.

11. Bamber, *For Free India*, p. 51.

12. Intelligence reports in WO 311/41, TNA; Hayes, *Bose in Nazi Germany*, pp. 193–4.

13. Hartog, *Sign of the Tiger*, pp. 55–6; Bamber, *For Free India*, pp. 51–2.

14. Swami Agehananda Bharati, *The Ochre Robe* (London: Allen & Unwin, 1961), pp. 25–85.

15. Hartog, *Sign of the Tiger*, p. 79.

16. Iwaichi Fujiwara, *F Kikan: Japanese Army Intelligence Operations in Southeast Asia during World War II* (Hong Kong: Heinemann Educational Books, 1983), pp. 27–32.

17. Joyce Chapman Lebra, *The Indian National Army and Japan* (Singapore: Institute of Southeast Asian Studies, 2008, originally published 1971), pp. 18–25.

18. Appendix B, CSDIC (I) Report No. 1007, WO 208/833, TNA.

19. Mohan Singh to Fujiwara, 31 December 1941; Note on role of Fujiwara Kikan volunteers, T. R. Sareen (ed.), *Select Documents on the Indian National Army* (Delhi: Agam Prakashan, 1988), pp. 4–7, 24–33.

20. Fujiwara, *F Kikan*, pp. 180–87.

21. Memorandum by the Secretary of State for India, 20 October 1945, *TP*, vol. 6, p. 369.

22. Pradeep Barua, *Gentlemen of the Raj: The Indian Army Officer Corps, 1817–1949* (Westport, Conn.: Praeger, 2003), p. 116; Apurba Kundu, *Militarism in India: The Army and Civil Society in Consensus* (London: I. B. Tauris, 1998), p. 54.

23. Memorandum by the Secretary of State for India, 30 January 1942, CAB 66/21/34, TNA.

24. Weekly Intelligence Summary, 8 May 1942, L/WS/1/1433, AAC.

25. Note by an Indian ECO, n.d. (*c.* 1 April 1943), L/WS/1/1576, AAC.

26. Extracts from a letter from a KCIO to Director of Military Intelligence, 13 March 1943, L/WS/1/1576, AAC.

27. Weekly Intelligence Summary, 22 May 1942, L/WS/1/1433, AAC.

28. A. O. Mitha, *Unlikely Beginnings: A Soldier's Life* (Karachi: Oxford University Press, 2003), p. 54.

29. 'Without a Shot in Anger', TS Memoir, P. W. Kingsford Papers, IWM. See also Ralph Russell, *Findings, Keepings: Life, Communism and Everything* (London: Shola Books, 2001).

30. Chandar Sundaram, 'Seditious Letters and Steel Helmets: Disaffection among Indian Troops in Singapore and Hong Kong, 1940–41, and the Formation of the Indian Army', in Kaushik Roy (ed.), *War and*

Society in Colonial India (New Delhi: Oxford University Press, 2006), pp. 134, 138; Tarak Barkawi, 'Culture and Combat in the Colonies: The Indian Army in the Second World War', *Journal of Contemporary History*, vol. 41, no. 2 (2006), pp. 333–4; Kaushik Roy, 'Military Loyalty in the Colonial Context: A Case Study of the Indian Army during World War II', *Journal of Military History*, vol. 73, no. 2 (April 2009), p. 509.

31. Military Censor Summary, 19 August to 25 August 1942, L/P&J/12/654, AAC.

32. Note by an Indian ECO, n.d. (*c.* 1 April 1943), L/WS/1/1576, AAC.

33. Ibid.

34. Namrata Narain, 'Co-option and Control: Role of the Colonial Army in India, 1918–1947', PhD thesis, Cambridge University, 1993, p. 223.

35. Weekly Intelligence Summary, 22 May 1942, L/WS/1/1433; Extracts from a letter from a KCIO to Director of Military Intelligence, 13 March 1943, L/WS/1/1576, AAC.

36. Sundaram, 'Seditious Letters', pp. 135–6, 139.

37. Barkawi, 'Culture and Combat', p. 340.

38. Mohan Singh, *Soldiers' Contribution to Indian Independence: The Epic of the Indian National Army* (New Delhi: Army Educational Stores, 1974), p. 97.

39. Christopher Bayly and Tim Harper, *Forgotten Armies: The Fall of British Asia, 1941–1945* (London: Allen Lane, 2004), p. 147; Narain, 'Co-option and Control', p. 227.

40. G. J. Douds, 'The Men who Never Were: Indian POWs in the Second World War', *South Asia*, vol. 27, no. 2 (2004), pp. 196–7.

41. Gajendra Singh, *The Testimonies of Indian Soldiers and the Two World Wars* (London: Bloomsbury, 2014), p. 163; Narain, 'Co-option and Control', p. 228.

42. Roy, 'Military Loyalty', pp. 512–13.

43. Singh, *Testimonies of Indian Soldiers*, pp. 176–7; Narain, 'Co-option and Control', p. 226.

44. Douds, 'Indian POWs', pp. 201–6.

45. T. R. Sareen, *Indian Revolutionaries, Japan and British Imperialism* (New Delhi: Anmol Publications, 1993), pp. 1–56.

46. Lebra, *The Indian National Army and Japan*, p. 52.

47. Fujiwara, *F Kikan*, pp. 238–46.

48. Sugata Bose, *His Majesty's Opponent: Subhas Chandra Bose and India's Struggle Against Empire* (Cambridge, Mass.: Belknap Press, 2011), p. 243.

49. Shah Nawaz Khan, *My Memories of INA and its Netaji* (Delhi: Rajkamal Publications, 1946), *passim*.

50. Sunil Amrith, *Crossing the Bay of Bengal: The Furies of Nature and the Fortunes of Migrants* (Cambridge, Mass.: Harvard University Press, 2013).

51. Joyce Chapman Lebra, *Women Against the Raj: The Rani of Jhansi Regiment* (Singapore: Institute of Southeast Asian Studies, 2008).

52. Lebra, *The Indian National Army and Japan*, pp. 123–4; Bose, *His Majesty's Opponent*, pp. 251–2.

53. South-East Asia Translation and Interrogation Centre, Bulletin No. 232, Item 2137, WO 203/6312, TNA.

54. Bose, *His Majesty's Opponent*, p. 260.

13. ALLIES AT WAR

1. Frank Moraes, *Witness to an Era: India 1920 to the Present Day* (Delhi: Vikas Publishing House, 1973), pp. 110–11.

2. Fortnightly Censor Summary, 25 August to 7 September 1943, L/P&J/12/655, AAC.

3. Weekly Intelligence Summary, 16 July 1943, L/WS/1/1433, AAC.

4. Untitled TS Memoir, Virginia K. Franklin Papers, IWM.

5. Nayantara Pothen, *Glittering Decades: New Delhi in Love and War* (New Delhi: Penguin, 2012), pp. 68–9.

6. Nico Slate, *Colored Cosmopolitanism: The Shared Struggle for Freedom in the United States and India* (Cambridge, Mass.: Harvard University Press, 2012), pp. 152–5.

7. Gerald Horne, *The End of Empires: African Americans and India* (Philadelphia: Temple University Press, 2008), p. 163.

8. Charles F. Romanus and Riley Sunderland, *United States Army in World War II, China–Burma–India Theater: Stilwell's Mission to China* (Washington, DC: Center of Military History, United States Army, 1987, orig. pub. 1953), p. 151.

9. Barbara Tuchman, *Sand Against the Wind: Stilwell and the American Experience in China, 1911–45* (New York: Macmillan, 1970), p. 301.

10. http://cbi-theater-5.home.comcast.net/~cbi-theater-5/ramgarh/ramgarh.html.

11. Romanus and Sunderland, *Stilwell's Mission*, pp. 212–19.

12. Tuchman, *Sand Against the Wind*, pp. 328, 331.

13. Exchanges between Delhi and London over Chinese troops in Ramgarh can be followed in WO 106/3547, TNA.

14. Theodore H. White (ed.), *The Stilwell Papers* (New York: Shocken Books, 1972), pp. 161, 163.
15. Linlithgow to Amery, 25 February 1943, cited in Christopher Thorne, *Allies of a Kind: The United States, Britain, and the War Against Japan, 1941–1945* (New York: Oxford University Press, 1978), p. 310.
16. Wavell to Chiefs of Staff, 3 June 1943; Minutes of Chiefs of Staff Meeting, 23 July 1943, WO 106/3547, TNA.
17. Jay Taylor, *The Generalissimo: Chiang Kai-shek and the Struggle for Modern China* (Cambridge, Mass.: Belknap Press, 2009), pp. 211–16.
18. Romanus and Sunderland, *Stilwell's Mission*, pp. 177–83.
19. Memorandum by Davies in Gauss to Secretary of State, 12 August 1942, *FRUS*, China 1942, p. 129.
20. John Connell, *Wavell: Supreme Commander 1941–1943* (London: Collins, 1969), pp. 236–9.
21. S. Woodburn Kirby, *The War Against Japan Volume II: India's Most Dangerous Hour* (London: HMSO, 1958), pp. 235–6.
22. Romanus and Sunderland, *Stilwell's Mission*, pp. 226–8; Woodburn Kirby, *India's Most Dangerous Hour*, pp. 291–2.
23. Woodburn Kirby, *India's Most Dangerous Hour*, p. 294.
24. White (ed.), *Stilwell Papers*, p. 171.
25. Romanus and Sunderland, *Stilwell's Mission*, pp. 247–9.
26. Philip Mason, *A Shaft of Sunlight: Memories of a Varied Life* (London: Andre Deutsch, 1978), p. 168.
27. Romanus and Sunderland, *Stilwell's Mission*, pp. 258–60; Woodburn Kirby, *India's Most Dangerous Hour*, pp. 295–7.
28. Michael Howard, *Grand Strategy Volume IV: August 1942–September 1943* (London: HMSO, 1970), pp. 248–9.
29. Romanus and Sunderland, *Stilwell's Mission*, pp. 270–71.
30. Tuchman, *Sand Against the Wind*, p. 356.
31. Woodburn Kirby, *India's Most Dangerous Hour*, pp. 362–3.
32. N. N. Madan, *The Arakan Operations 1942–45* (New Delhi: Ministry of Defence, Government of India, 2012), pp. 20–21.
33. Philip Mason, *A Matter of Honour* (London: Jonathan Cape, 1974), pp. 493–4.
34. Madan, *The Arakan Operations*, p. 18.
35. Connell, *Wavell*, p. 239.
36. T. R. Moreman, *The Jungle, the Japanese and the British Commonwealth Armies at War 1941–45: Fighting Methods, Doctrine and Training for Jungle Warfare* (London: Frank Cass, 2005), pp. 46, 51 (emphasis in original).

37. Daniel Marston, *Phoenix from the Ashes: The Indian Army in the Burma Campaign* (Westport, Conn.: Praeger, 2002), pp. 81-3.

38. Moreman, *The Jungle*, p. 63.

39. Louis Allen, *Burma: The Longest War* (London: J. M. Dent & Sons, 1984), pp. 100-101.

40. Woodburn Kirby, *India's Most Dangerous Hour*, p. 348; Madan, *The Arakan Operations*, pp. 66-71.

41. Allen, *Burma*, p. 113.

42. Woodburn Kirby, *India's Most Dangerous Hour*, pp. 368-9.

43. Howard, *Grand Strategy*, pp. 397-404.

44. Winston Churchill, *The Second World War Volume IV: The Hinge of Fate* (London: Penguin Classics, 2005), p. 702.

45. Howard, *Grand Strategy*, p. 445.

46. Woodburn Kirby, *India's Most Dangerous Hour*, pp. 370-71.

47. Penderel Moon (ed.), *Wavell: The Viceroy's Journal* (Oxford: Oxford University Press, 1973), p. 5.

48. Victoria Schofield, *Wavell: Soldier & Statesman* (London: John Murray, 2006), p. 295.

49. Thorne, *Allies of a Kind*, p. 298.

50. Howard, *Grand Strategy*, pp. 573-4; Woodburn Kirby, *India's Most Dangerous Hour*, pp. 419-22.

51. Romanus and Sunderland, *Stilwell's Mission*, p. 359.

52. Memorandum by Davies, 21 October 1943, cited in J. H. Voigt, *India in the Second World War* (New Delhi: Arnold-Heinemann, 1987), p. 222; Merrell to Secretary of State, 23 October 1943, *FRUS*, China 1943, pp. 879-80.

53. Thorne, *Allies of a Kind*, p. 337.

54. Memorandum by Davies, December 1943, *FRUS*, China 1943, pp. 188-9.

55. Philip Ziegler, *Mountbatten: The Official Biography* (Glasgow: William Collins, 1985), p. 245.

56. S. Woodburn Kirby, *The War Against Japan Volume III: The Decisive Battles* (London: HMSO, 1961), pp. 14-15.

57. White (ed.), *Stilwell Papers*, pp. 277-8.

58. Charles F. Romanus and Riley Sunderland, *United States Army in World War II, China–Burma–India Theater: Stilwell's Command Problems* (Washington, DC: Center of Military History, United States Army, 1985, orig. pub. 1956), pp. 57-70.

59. Rana Mitter, *China's War with Japan, 1937–1945: The Struggle for Survival* (London: Allen Lane, 2013), p. 314.

60. Woodburn Kirby, *Decisive Battles*, pp. 58-66.
61. Tuchman, *Sand Against the Wind*, p. 431.

14. WAR ECONOMY

1. D. R. Mankekar, *Homi Mody: A Many Splendoured Life* (Bombay: Popular Prakashan, 1968), pp. 156-7, 163-5.
2. Secretary of State for India to Secretary, Defence Department, 30 January 1942, ECO/36/42, NAI.
3. Note on Preparations for War in Eastern India by E. M. Jenkins, 2 March 1942, ECO/41/42, NAI.
4. Medha M. Kudaisya, *The Life and Times of G. D. Birla* (New Delhi: Oxford University Press, 2003), p. 221 n. 87.
5. Letter of 4 August 1942, cited in Frank Moraes, *Sir Purshotamdas Thakurdas* (Bombay: Asia Publishing House, 1967), pp. 219-22.
6. Dwijendra Tripathi, *The Dynamics of a Tradition: Kasturbhai Lalbhai and His Entrepreneurship* (New Delhi: Manohar, 1981), p. 86.
7. Note by Cripps, 2 September 1942, *TP*, vol. 2, pp. 882-4.
8. Churchill to Cripps and Amery, 20 September 1942, *TP*, vol. 2, p. 999.
9. Amery to Cripps, 2 October 1942; Mudaliar to Linlithgow, 2 October 1942, *TP*, vol. 3, pp. 69-71.
10. Louis Fischer, *The Life of Mahatma Gandhi* (London: HarperCollins, 1997; first published 1951) pp. 482-4.
11. Memorandum by Secretary of State for India, 6 February 1943, CAB 66/34/7, TNA.
12. Amery to Linlithgow, *TP*, vol. 3, pp. 631-2.
13. Report of the American Technical Mission to India, WO 32/10269, TNA.
14. Ibid.
15. Ibid.
16. James M. Ehrman, 'Ways of War and the American Experience in the China-Burma-India Theater, 1942-1945', PhD thesis, Kansas State University, 2006, p. 49.
17. Cf. Mark Harrison (ed.), *The Economics of World War II: Six Great Powers in International Comparison* (Cambridge: Cambridge University Press, 1998).
18. S. C. Aggarwal, *History of the Supply Department (1939-1946)* (Delhi: Government of India, 1947), pp. 127-9.
19. *Statistics Relating to India's War Effort* (Delhi: Government of India, 1947), Table 9.

20. *Statistics Relating to India's War Effort*, Table 15.
21. Tata Iron and Steel Company, *Annual Report 1942–43*, Tata Archives, Jamshedpur.
22. Dwijendra Tripathi and Makrand Mehta, *Business Houses in Western India: A Study in Entrepreneurial Response, 1850–1956* (New Delhi: Manohar, 1990), pp. 140–41.
23. Aggarwal, *History of the Supply Department*, pp. 198–201; N. C. Sinha and P. N. Khera, *Indian War Economy: Supply, Industry and Finance* (New Delhi: Combined Inter-Services Historical Section, India & Pakistan, 1962), p. 269.
24. Calculated from S. Sivasubramonian, *The National Income of India in the Twentieth Century* (New Delhi: Oxford University Press, 2000), Tables 2.10, 6.10.
25. Jan Breman, *The Making and Unmaking of an Industrial Working Class: Sliding down the Labour Hierarchy in Ahmedabad, India* (New Delhi: Oxford University Press, 2004), p. 79.
26. Calculated from S. Subramanian and P. W. R. Homfray, *Recent Social and Economic Trends in India* (Delhi: Government of India, 1946), Table 17. Aggregate data for the rest of the war years is unavailable.
27. Calculated from Arun Joshi, *Lala Shri Ram: A Study in Entrepreneurship and Management* (New Delhi: Orient Longman, 1975), p. 300, Table 44.
28. Tripathi, *Kasturbhai Lalbhai*, p. 87, Table V.2.
29. Tripathi and Mehta, *Business Houses in Western India*, pp. 170–77.
30. Calculated from *Indian Labour Yearbook 1946* (Delhi: Government of India, 1948), pp. 3, 262, Table 74.
31. Ibid., p. 114, Table 23.
32. Neera Adarkar and Meena Menon, *One Hundred Years One Hundred Voices: The Millworkers of Girangaon, An Oral History* (Calcutta: Seagull Books, 2004), pp. 177–8.
33. Fortnightly report from Bombay, 16 July 1942, NAI.
34. See fortnightly reports from United Provinces, Bihar, Bombay and Madras for July–November 1942, NAI.
35. Avinash Celestine, 'State Power and the Collapse of a Colonial War Economy: India 1939–45', MA thesis, London School of Economics, 2007, pp. 28–32.
36. S. Woodburn Kirby, *The War Against Japan: Volume III The Decisive Battles* (London: HMSO, 1961), p. 20.
37. Monthly Report by Secretary of State for India, April 1944, WCP, NMML.

38. Bishwa Mohan Prasad, *Second World War and Indian Industry 1939–45: A Case Study of the Coal Industry in Bengal and Bihar* (Delhi: Anamika Prakashan, 1992), pp. 232–3.

39. Woodburn Kirby, *Decisive Battles*, p. 11; Prasad, *Coal Industry*, pp. 132–3; Supply Department note on Rationalization of the Jute Mill Industry, 26 June 1942, ECO/89/42, NAI.

40. Speech by Principal Administrative Officer to Defence Consultative Committee, 5 August 1944, Lindsell 3/3, Lindsell Papers, LHCMA.

41. A. K. Chettiar, 'Chennai Nagaram, 1942', *Kumari Malar*, 1 April 1943, p. 112.

42. E. P. Stebbing, *The Forests of India Volume IV: Being the History from 1925 to 1947 of the Forests now in Burma, India and Pakistan* (Oxford: Oxford University Press, 1962), pp. 145–63 (quote on p. 150).

43. Celestine, 'State Power and Collapse of a Colonial War Economy', pp. 25–6.

44. Letters exchanged on financial agreement, February 1940, in Sinha and Khera, *Indian War Economy*, Appendix 24.

45. R. S. Sayers, *Financial Policy 1939–45* (London: HMSO, 1956), p. 254.

46. For details, see S. L. N. Simha, *The Reserve Bank of India Volume 1: 1935–1951* (Bombay: Reserve Bank of India, 1970), pp. 377–404.

47. Memorandum by Kingsley Wood, 30 July 1942, *TP*, vol. 2, pp. 504–8.

48. Linlithgow to Amery, 31 July 1942, *TP*, vol. 2, p. 510.

49. Amery to Wood, 7 August 1942, *TP*, vol. 2, p. 613.

50. Amery to Linlithgow, 16 September 1942, *TP*, vol. 2, p. 975.

51. Cited in Sayers, *Financial Policy*, p. 272.

52. Moraes, *Purshotamdas Thakurdas*, pp. 232–4; Aditya Mukherjee, 'Indo-British Finance: The Controversy over India's Sterling Balances, 1939–1947', *Studies in History*, vol. 6, no. 2 (1990), pp. 238–42.

53. Dharma Kumar, 'The Fiscal System', in idem (ed.), *The Cambridge Economic History of India Volume II: c. 1757–2003* (New Delhi: Orient Longman, 2004), pp. 927–30.

54. R. N. Poduval, *Finance of the Government of India since 1935* (Delhi: Premier Publishing, 1951), pp. 60–70.

55. Sinha and Khera, *Indian War Economy*, pp. 355–67.

56. Poduval, *Finance of the Government of India*, pp. 107–12.

57. Cited in Simha, *Reserve Bank of India*, p. 297.

58. Abhik Ray, *The Evolution of the State Bank of India, Volume 3 1921–1955* (New Delhi: Sage, 2003), p. 249.

59. Memorandum by Secretary of State for India, 11 August 1943, L/WS/1/581, AAC.

60. D. R. Gadgil and N. V. Sovani, *War and Indian Economic Policy* (Poona: Gokhale Institute, 1943), p. 6.

61. Speech in Bombay, September 1943, 1ˢᵗ Instalment, C. D. Deshmukh Papers, NMML.

62. Nanavati to Raisman, 5 March 1943, Subject File 27, Manilal Nanavati Papers, NMML.

63. Simha, *Reserve Bank of India*, pp. 295, 303–5.

64. C. N. Vakil, *The Financial Burden of the War on India* (Bombay, July 1943), Appendix I; idem, *War against Inflation: The Story of the Falling Rupee 1943–77* (Delhi: Macmillan, 1978).

65. Venu Madhav Govindu, *The Web of Freedom: J. C. Kumarappa and Gandhi's Struggle for Economic Freedom* (New Delhi: Oxford University Press, forthcoming), ch. 10.

66. See the excellent analysis in Indivar Kamtekar, 'A Different War Dance: State and Class in India, 1939–1945', *Past & Present*, no. 176 (2002), especially pp. 201–10.

67. J. J. Anjaria et al., *War and the Middle Class: An Inquiry into the Effects of Wartime Inflation on Middle Class Families in Bombay City* (Bombay: Padma, 1946).

68. Fortnightly Censor Summary, 8 September to 21 September 1943, L/P&J/12/655, AAC.

69. Ram Swarup Nakra, *Punjab Villages During the War: An Enquiry into Twenty Villages in the Ludhiana District* (Delhi: The Board of Economic Enquiry, Punjab, 1946), pp. 10, 17, 32, Table 4.

70. Fortnightly Censor Summary, 21 April to 5 May 1943, L/P&J/12/655, AAC.

71. In particular, see Paul Greenough, *Prosperity and Misery in Modern Bengal: The Famine of 1943–44* (New York: Oxford University Press, 1982); Janam Mukherjee, *Hungry Bengal: War, Famine, Riots and the End of Empire* (New Delhi: HarperCollins, 2015).

72. Amartya Sen, *Poverty and Famines: An Essay on Entitlement and Deprivation* (New York: Oxford University Press, 1981), especially ch. 6.

73. Cited in Madhusree Mukerjee, *Churchill's Secret War: The British Empire and the Ravaging of India During World War II* (New Delhi: Tranquebar, 2010), p. 80; Cormac Ó Gráda, *Eating People is Wrong and Other Essays on Famine, Its Past and Its Future* (Princeton: Princeton University Press, 2015), pp. 38–91.

74. Fortnightly Censor Summary, 19 May to 1 June 1943, L/P&J/12/655, AAC.

75. Fortnightly Censor Summary, 2 June to 15 June 1943, L/P&J/12/655, AAC.

76. Fortnightly Censor Summary, 21 April to 5 May 1943, L/P&J/12/655, AAC.

77. Fortnightly Censor Summary, 8 September to 21 September 1943, L/P&J/12/655, AAC.

78. Fortnightly Censor Summary, 14 July to 27 July 1943, L/P&J/12/655, AAC.

79. Fortnightly Censor Summary, 14 July to 27 July 1943, L/P&J/12/655, AAC.

80. Fortnightly Censor Summary, 2 June to 15 June 1943, L/P&J/12/655, AAC.

81. Secretary, Civil Defence Department to All Provincial Governments, 8 February 1943, 49(5)-W/43, NAI.

82. Gadgil and Sovani, *War and Indian Economic Policy*, pp. 77–84.

83. S. Bhoothalingam, *Reflections on an Era: Memoirs of a Civil Servant* (Delhi: Affiliated East-West Press, 1993), pp. 19–25.

84. Fortnightly reports from Madras, for May 1942, NAI.

85. Fortnightly reports from Madras, for April, May, June, November 1943, NAI.

86. Fortnightly Censor Summary, 25 August to 7 September 1943, L/P&J/12/655, AAC.

87. Cited in Fortnightly reports from Madras for June 1943, NAI.

88. Fortnightly reports from Bombay for 1944, NAI.

89. Cf. Sen, *Poverty and Famines*, p. 80.

90. K. G. Sivaswamy et al., *Food Famine and Nutritional Diseases in Travancore (1943–44)* (Coimbatore: Servindia Kerala Relief Centre, 1945).

91. Fortnightly Censor Summary, 16 June to 29 June 1943, L/P&J/12/655, AAC.

92. Fortnightly Censor Summary, 21 April to 5 May 1943, L/P&J/12/655, AAC.

93. Sivaswamy et al., *Food Famina and Nutritional Diseases in Travancore*, p. 159.

94. Fortnightly Censor Summary, 2 June to 15 June 1943, L/P&J/12/655, AAC.

95. Sivaswamy et al., *Food Famina and Nutritional Diseases in Travancore*, pp. i–ii, 145–50.

96. 'The Limitations on India's War Effort', L/WS/1/581, AAC.

15. AROUND THE MEDITERRANEAN

1. Niall Barr, *Pendulum of War: The Three Battles of El Alamein* (London: Pimlico, 2005), p. 69.

2. Note by Major General F. S. Tuker, n.d. (*c.* early 1943), 71/21/1/3, Tuker Papers, IWM.

3. P. C. Bharucha, *The North African Campaign, 1940–43* (New Delhi: Ministry of Defence, Government of India, 2012), p. 547.

4. Barr, *Pendulum of War*, p. 76.

5. Compton Mackenzie, *Eastern Epic Volume I: Defence September 1939–March 1943* (London: Chatto & Windus, 1951), p. 581.

6. Bharucha, *North African Campaign*, p. 548.

7. Ibid., p. 549.

8. Barr, *Pendulum of War*, p. 79.

9. Mackenzie, *Eastern Epic*, pp. 581–2; Barr, *Pendulum of War*, p. 80.

10. John Connell, *Auchinleck: A Biography of Field-Marshal Sir Claude Auchinleck* (London: Cassell, 1959), pp. 633–4.

11. Barr, *Pendulum of War*, pp. 144–6.

12. Douglas Porch, *Hitler's Mediterranean Gamble: The North African and Mediterranean Campaigns in World War II* (London: Weidenfeld & Nicolson, 2004), pp. 288–9.

13. Biographies of Montgomery are numerous. For a perceptive brief assessment, see Michael Howard, *The Causes of Wars* (London: Unwin, 1983), pp. 247–62.

14. Jonathan Fennell, *Combat and Morale in the North African Campaign: The Eighth Army and the Path to El Alamein* (Cambridge: Cambridge University Press, 2011), pp. 231–7, 26.

15. Antony Brett-James, *Ball of Fire: The Fifth Indian Division in the Second World War* (Aldershot: Gale & Polden, 1951), ch. 17. Accessed online at http://www.ourstory.info/library/4-ww2/Ball/fire10.html.

16. Notes by Major General F. S. Tuker for the Records of the 4th Indian Division, 31 August 1943; Letter from Tuker, 22 October 1942, 71/21/1/3, Tuker Papers, IWM.

17. Brett-James, *Ball of Fire*, ch. 17.

18. Tuker to Hartley, 27 August 1942, 71/21/1/6, Tuker Papers, IWM.

19. Notes by Major General F. S. Tuker for the History of the 4th Indian Division, December 1943, 71/21/1/6, Tuker Papers, IWM.

20. Letter to Hartley, 6 September 1942, 71/21/1/6, Tuker Papers, IWM.

21. Tuker to Hartley, 24 September & 16 October 1942, 71/21/1/6, Tuker Papers, IWM.

22. Tuker to Hartley, 27 August & 22 October 1942, 71/21/1/6, Tuker Papers, IWM.

23. Tuker to Hartley, 24 October (12 noon), 71/21/1/6, Tuker Papers, IWM.

24. Tuker to Hartley, 25 & 26 October 1942, 71/21/1/6, Tuker Papers, IWM.

25. Tuker to Hartley, 30 October & 2 November 1942, 71/21/1/6, Tuker Papers, IWM.

26. Tuker to Hartley, 4 & 11 November 1942, 71/21/1/6, Tuker Papers, IWM.

27. Notes by Major General F. S. Tuker for the History of the 4th Indian Division, 31 August 1943, 71/21/1/6, Tuker Papers, IWM.

28. Fortnightly Censor Summary, 20 December 1942 to 4 January 1943, L/P&J/12/654, AAC.

29. Cited in Mackenzie, *Eastern Epic*, p. 604.

30. G. R. Stevens, 4th *Indian Division* (Toronto: M Laren and Son, 1948), p. 217.

31. Cited in Chris Mann, 'The Battle of Wadi Akarit, 6 April 1943', in Alan Jeffreys and Patrick Rose (eds.), *The Indian Army, 1939–47: Experience and Development* (Farnham: Ashgate, 2012), p. 97.

32. Ibid., pp. 105–7.

33. Letter of 23 April 1943, reproduced in Fortnightly Censor Summary, 21 April to 5 May 1943, L/P&J/12/655, AAC.

34. Fortnightly Censor Summary, 24 March to 6 April 1943, L/P&J/12/655, AAC.

35. Fortnightly Censor Summary, 21 April to 5 May 1943, L/P&J/12/655, AAC.

36. Ibid.

37. Fortnightly Censor Summary, 19 May to 1 June 1943, L/P&J/12/655, AAC.

38. Ibid.

39. Fortnightly Censor Summary, 16 June to 29 June 1943, L/P&J/12/655, AAC.

40. Fortnightly Censor Summary, 11 August to 23 August 1943, L/P&J/12/655, AAC.

41. Fortnightly Censor Summary, 22 September to 5 October 1943, L/P&J/12/655, AAC.

42. Alan Jeffreys, 'Indian Army Training for the Italian Campaign and Lessons Learnt', in Andrew L. Hargreaves et al. (eds.), *Allied Fighting*

Effectiveness in North Africa and Italy, 1942–1945 (Leiden: Brill, 2014), pp. 105–6.

43. Fortnightly Censor Summary, 8 September to 21 September 1943, L/P&J/12/655, AAC.
44. Jeffreys, 'Indian Army Training for the Italian Campaign', p. 117.

16. PREPARATION

1. S. Woodburn Kirby, *The War Against Japan Volume II: India's Most Dangerous Hour* (London: HMSO, 1958), p. 385.
2. Ibid., pp. 242–3.
3. The exchanges on these changes can be followed in L/WS/1/616, AAC. For a useful summary, see, S. Woodburn Kirby, *The War Against Japan: Volume III Decisive Battles* (London: HMSO, 1961), Appendix 6.
4. Weekly Intelligence Summary, 7 April 1943, L/WS/1/1433, AAC.
5. Letter from an Indian Major in 42nd Cavalry to Colonel Cariappa, 29 November 1943, Group I, Part I, Cariappa Collections, NAI.
6. V. J. Moharir, *History of the Army Service Corps (1939–1946)* (New Delhi: Sterling Publishers, 1979), pp. 86–8, 91–2, Appendix B on p. 115.
7. Report of the Infantry Committee, 1–14 June 1943, L/WS/1/1371, AAC.
8. Ibid.
9. Alan Jeffreys, 'Training the Indian Army, 1939–1945', in Alan Jeffreys and Patrick Rose (eds.), *The Indian Army, 1939–47: Experience and Development* (Farnham: Ashgate, 2012), pp. 82–3.
10. Auchinleck to Brooke, 18 September 1943, WO 106/4659, TNA.
11. Details of the training regime under the 14th Division are from Major General A. C. Curtis Papers, IWM.
12. Daniel Marston, *Phoenix from the Ashes: The Indian Army in the Burma Campaign* (Westport, Conn.: Praeger, 2002), pp. 99–102; Jeffreys, 'Training the Indian Army', p. 84.
13. Martin Booth, *Carpet Sahib: A Life of Jim Corbett* (London: Constable, 1986), pp. 224–6; Alan Jeffreys, 'The Officer Corps and the Training of the Indian Army', in Kaushik Roy (ed.), *The Indian Army in the Two World Wars* (Leiden: Brill, 2012), p. 298.
14. Report of the Infantry Committee, 1–14 June 1943, L/WS/1/1371, AAC.
15. *Military Training Pamphlet No. 9 (India): The Jungle Book* (Delhi: General Staff India, 1943).

16. T. R. Moreman, *The Jungle, the Japanese and the British Common-wealth Armies at War 1941–45: Fighting Methods, Doctrine and Training for Jungle Warfare* (London: Frank Cass, 2005), pp. 98–102.

17. B. L. Raina (ed.), *Preventive Medicine (Nutrition, Malaria Control and Prevention of Diseases)* (Delhi: Combined Inter-Services Historical Section, India & Pakistan, 1961), p. 14.

18. Ibid., pp. 53–4.

19. Ibid., p. 55.

20. Extracts from No. 1 Indian Operational Research Section Report, 12 November 1943, WO 203/269, TNA.

21. Results of these surveys were published by A. M. Thomson, O. P. Verma and C. K. Dilwali in *Indian Journal of Medical Research*, vols. 34 (1946) and 35 (1947).

22. Raina, *Preventive Medicine*, pp. 20–22.

23. Report on Nutritional Status of Indian Troops – Fourteenth Army, by Canadian Nutritional Research Team, 31 May 1945, WO 203/269.

24. A Medical Officer, 'Feeding the Indian Soldier', *Journal of the United Services Institution of India*, vol. 74, no. 314 (January 1944), pp. 90–92.

25. Raina, *Preventive Medicine*, pp. 6, 79.

26. Cf. Lizzie Collingham, *The Taste of War: World War Two and the Battle for Food* (London: Allen Lane, 2011). This otherwise excellent book misleadingly claims that a catering corps was created in the Indian army.

27. Moharir, *Army Service Corps*, p. 45.

28. Ibid., pp. 20–49; Raina, *Preventive Medicine*, pp. 61–3, 92–6, 139–41.

29. William Slim, *Defeat into Victory* (Dehra Dun: Natraj Publishers, 2014; first published 1956), p. 178.

30. Mark Harrison, *Medicine & Victory: British Military Medicine in the Second World War* (Oxford: Oxford University Press, 2004), pp. 194–5.

31. Report of the Infantry Committee, 1–14 June 1943, L/WS/1/1371, AAC.

32. Raina, *Preventive Medicine* p. 278.

33. David Arnold, *Science, Technology and Medicine in Colonial India* (Cambridge: Cambridge University Press, 2000).

34. Note on Indian Medical Service by Lieutenant Colonel G. B. S. Chawla, Part II, Group XXII, Part II, Cariappa Papers, NAI.

35. Raina, *Preventive Medicine*, pp. 362–3.

36. G. Covell, 'Malaria and War', *Journal of the United Services Institution of India*, vol. 73, no. 312 (July 1943), pp. 303–6.

37. Slim, *Defeat into Victory*, p. 180.

38. Raina, *Preventive Medicine*, pp. 369–70.

39. Harrison, *Medicine & Victory*, p. 186.

40. Report of the Infantry Committee, 1–14 June 1943, L/WS/1/1371, AAC.

41. Harrison, *Medicine & Victory*, p. 197.

42. B. L. Raina (ed.), *Medicine, Surgery and Pathology* (Delhi: Combined Inter-Services Historical Section, India & Pakistan, 1955), pp. 621–51.

43. These discussions are available in L/WS/1/1576, AAC.

44. For a detailed account of these activities, see Azharudin Mohammed Dali, 'The Fifth Column in British India: Japan and the INA's Secret War, 1941–1945', PhD thesis, London University, 2007, pp. 142–236.

45. Weekly Intelligence Summary, 24 December 1942, L/WS/1/1433, AAC.

46. Note to War Cabinet, 10 May 1943, CAB 66/36/47, TNA.

47. Churchill to Amery, 10 May 1943, L/WS/1/707, AAC.

48. War Cabinet Conclusions, 20 May 1943, CAB 65/34/26, TNA.

49. Churchill to Amery, 20 June 1943, L/WS/1/707, AAC.

50. Amery to Linlithgow, 21 June 1943, *TP*, vol. 4, p. 25.

51. Auchinleck's note, 22 August 1943, L/WS/1/707, AAC.

52. Chief of General Staff to Army Commanders, 18 March 1943, L/WS/1/1576, AAC.

53. 'Traitors or Heroes' TS memoir, Heard 20, J. A. E. Heard Papers, LHCMA.

54. Ibid., pp. 33–4.

55. Ibid., pp. 39–41.

56. The full set of Josh newsletters is available in Heard Papers, LHCMA.

57. *Against Japan* (Delhi: General Staff India, 1944).

58. 'Traitors or Heroes', p. 37, Heard Papers, LHCMA.

59. Moreman, *The Jungle*, p. 103.

60. GHQ India to Army Commands, 12 May 1944, L/WS/1/1576, AAC.

61. Tarak Barkawi, 'Peoples, Homelands, and Wars? Ethnicity, the Military, and Battle among British Imperial Forces in the War against Japan', *Comparative Studies in Society and History*, vol. 46, no. 1 (2004), pp. 151–6 (quote on p. 152). While mostly persuasive, Barkawi's argument conflates counter-propaganda and indoctrination.

62. 'The India Base', January 1945, WO 203/5626, TNA.

63. Ordinance No. X of 1942, 7 March 1942, WO 203/1323, TNA.

64. Fortnightly reports from Bihar, January–April 1942, NAI.

65. On Ambedkar's activities as labour member, see Vasant Moon (ed.), *Dr. Babasaheb Ambedkar: Writings and Speeches*, vol. 10 (Mumbai: Government of Maharashtra, 2003).

66. K. N. Kadam (ed.), *Dr. B. R. Ambedkar: The Emancipator of the Oppressed* (Bombay: Popular Prakashan, 1993), p. 162; Dhananjay Keer, *Dr. Ambedkar: Life and Mission* (Mumbai: Popular Prakashan, 1954, reprtd 2009), pp. 361–2.

67. Appreciation for the Employment of Labour in India, n.d. (*c.* early 1945), WO 203/791, TNA.

68. Graham Dunlop, *Military Economics, Culture and Logistics in the Burma Campaign* (London: Pickering & Chatto, 2009), p. 55; S. Verma and V. K. Anand, *The Corps of Indian Engineers 1939–1947* (Delhi: Ministry of Defence, Government of India, 1974), pp. 110–12.

69. 'The India Base', January 1945, WO 203/5626, TNA.

70. Dunlop, *Military Economics,* pp. 56–8; Moharir, *Army Service Corps,* pp. 30–32.

71. *History of the War Transport Department, July 1942 to October 1945* (New Delhi: Government of India, 1946), p. 6.

72. Ibid., pp. 7–9.

73. James M. Ehrman, 'Ways of War and the American Experience in the China-Burma-India Theater, 1942–1945', PhD thesis, Kansas State University, 2006, pp. 209–10.

74. Ibid., pp. 219–20.

75. 'The India Base', January 1945, WO 203/5626, TNA.

76. Fortnightly Report, 15 April 1944, NAI.

77. Memorandum on the Explosions in Bombay Docks, 9 September 1944, CAB 66/55/11, TNA.

78. *History of the War Transport Department,* pp. 10–13.

79. Hilary St George Saunders, *Valiant Voyaging: A Short History of the British India Steam Navigation Company in the Second World War 1939–1945* (London: Faber and Faber, 1948), pp. 44–5.

80. Woodburn Kirby, *Decisive Battles,* pp. 21–3.

81. Dunlop, *Military Economics,* p. 82.

82. Woodburn Kirby, *Decisive Battles,* pp. 25–6.

83. Ehrman, 'Ways of War', pp. 240–41.

84. Woodburn Kirby, *Decisive Battles,* pp. 31–2; Ehrman, 'Ways of War', pp. 243–6.

85. Ehrman, 'Ways of War', p. 250.

86. Ibid., pp. 265–78.

17. BACK TO BURMA

1. William Slim, *Defeat into Victory* (Dehra Dun: Natraj Publishers, 2014; first published 1956), p. 146.
2. 7th Division Commander's Operational Note No. 6, 15 November 1943, Messervy Papers, LHCMA.
3. Newsletter of 3 January 1944, cited in T. R. Moreman, *The Jungle, the Japanese and the British Commonwealth Armies at War 1941–45: Fighting Methods, Doctrine and Training for Jungle Warfare* (London: Frank Cass, 2005), p. 113.
4. Antony Brett-James, *Ball of Fire: The Fifth Indian Division in the Second World War* (Aldershot: Gale & Polden, 1951), ch. 20. Accessed online at http://www.ourstory.info/library/4-ww2/Ball/fire11.html.
5. Louis Allen, *Burma: The Longest War* (London: J. M. Dent & Sons, 1984), p. 154.
6. Ibid., p. 158.
7. K. K. Ghosh, *The Indian National Army: Second Front of the Indian Independence Movement* (Meerut: Meenakshi, 1969), p. 171.
8. Allen, *Burma*, p. 167.
9. 'The Japanese Account of their Operations in Burma', December 1945, Gracey 6/13, Gracey Papers, LHCMA.
10. V. J. Moharir, *History of the Army Service Corps (1939–1946)* (New Delhi: Sterling Publishers, 1979), pp. 365–72; Raymond Callahan, *Burma 1942–1945* (Newark, Del.: University of Deleware Press, 1979), p. 133.
11. 'Unofficial History of 2/13th F.F. Rifles from January 1942 to November 1946', Gibson 1/4, Gibson Papers, LHCMA.
12. Allen, *Burma*, pp. 180–81.
13. Moreman, *The Jungle*, p. 120.
14. 'Unofficial History of 2/13th F.F. Rifles', Gibson 1/4, Gibson Papers, LHCMA.
15. S. Woodburn Kirby, *The War Against Japan: Volume III Decisive Battles* (London: HMSO, 1961), pp. 155–9.
16. Slim, *Defeat into Victory*, p. 291.
17. Allen, *Burma*, p. 198.
18. 'Move of the 5th Indian Division by Air', end of May 1944, Mace Papers, LHCMA.
19. Gracey to Scoones, 26 March 1944, Gracey Papers, LHCMA.
20. For a detailed and vivid account, see Fergal Keane, *Road of Bones: The Epic Siege of Kohima* (London: HarperPress, 2011).
21. Slim to Smyth, 3 June 1944, cited in Moreman, *The Jungle*, p. 140.

22. Snelling to Rear HQ 11 Army Group, SEA, 10 August 1944, WO 203/1976, TNA.

23. Mark Harrison, *Medicine & Victory: British Military Medicine in the Second World War* (Oxford: Oxford University Press, 2004), pp. 215–18.

24. Indian Army Observer Report of 4 June 1944, Series 2, PRS Mani Collection, University of Technology, Sydney.

25. Indian Army Observer Report of 3 May 1944, ibid.

26. Tarak Barkawi, 'Peoples, Homelands, and Wars? Ethnicity, the Military, and Battle among British Imperial Forces in the War against Japan', *Comparative Studies in Society and History*, vol. 46, no. 1 (2004), p. 150.

27. Allen, *Burma*, p. 183.

28. Barkawi, 'Peoples, Homelands, and Wars', pp. 152, 159.

29. Indian Army Observer Report of 26 June 1944, Series 2, PRS Mani Collection, University of Technology, Sydney.

30. Indian Army Observer Report of 21 July 1944, Series 2, PRS Mani Collection, University of Technology, Sydney.

31. Moreman, *The Jungle*, p. 140.

32. Robert Lyman, *Japan's Last Bid for Victory: The Invasion of India 1944* (Barnsley: Praetorian Press, 2011), pp. 112–14.

33. Christoper Bayly and Tim Harper, *Forgotten Wars: The End of Britain's Asian Empire* (London: Allen Lane, 2007), p. 386.

34. Chandar Sundaram, 'A Paper Tiger: The Indian National Army in Battle, 1944–45', *War & Society*, vol. 13, no. 1 (1995), pp. 42–7.

35. Bayly and Harper, *Forgotten Wars*, p. 374.

36. Sundaram, 'Paper Tiger', p. 49; Sugata Bose, *His Majesty's Opponent: Subhas Chandra Bose and India's Struggle Against Empire* (Cambridge, Mass.: Belknap Press, 2011), p. 282.

37. Slim, *Defeat into Victory*, p. 382.

38. S. Woodburn Kirby, *The War Against Japan: Volume IV The Reconquest of Burma* (London: HMSO, 1965), p. 7.

39. Graham Dunlop, *Military Economics, Culture and Logistics in the Burma Campaign* (London: Pickering & Chatto, 2009), ch. 7.

40. 'The India Base', January 1945, WO 203/5626, TNA.

41. Woodburn Kirby, *Reconquest of Burma*, pp. 25–6.

42. Alan Jeffreys, *The British Army in the Far East 1941–45* (London: Ospreys, 2013), p. 20.

43. Gul Hassan Khan, *Memoirs of Lt. Gen. Gul Hassan Khan* (Karachi: Oxford University Press, 1993), p. 25.

44. Woodburn Kirby, *Reconquest of Burma*, pp. 165–6.
45. Letter to Major R. Shaw, 22 February 1945, J. H. Hovell Papers, IWM.
46. H. E. Bates, *An Autobiography* (London: Methuen, 2006), pp. 451–2.
47. 'The Japanese Account of their Operations in Burma', December 1945, Gracey 6/13, Gracey Papers, LHCMA.
48. Robin Schlaefli, *Emergency Sahib: Of Queen's, Sikhs and The Dagger Division* (London: R J Leach, 1992), cited in Moreman, *The Jungle*, p. 186.
49. Slim, *Defeat into Victory*, p. 472.
50. Bose, *His Majesty's Opponent*, pp. 290–306.
51. Army Observer Report, 14 August 1945, Series 4, PRS Mani Collection, University of Technology, Sydney.
52. John Masters, *The Road Past Mandalay* (London: Cassell, 2002), pp. 312–13.

18. POST-WAR

1. Fortnightly Censor Summary, 22 September to 5 October 1943, L/P&J/12/655, AAC.
2. Medha Kudaisya, '"The Promise of Partnership": Indian Business, the State and the Bombay Plan of 1944', *Business History Review*, vol. 88 (2014), pp. 97–131.
3. Aditya Balasubramanian, 'From *Swarajya* to *Swatantra*: Economic Liberalism in India, 1943–70', BA thesis, Harvard University, 2012, pp. 23–40.
4. D. S. Nag, *A Study of Economic Plans for India* (Bombay: Hind Kitabs, 1949), pp. 44–8.
5. Cited in Raghabendra Chattopadhyaya, 'The Idea of Planning in India, 1930–1951', PhD thesis, Australian National University, 1985, pp. 174–80.
6. Tata to Commerce Member, 26 April 1944, in Arvind Mambro (ed.), *Letters: J. R. D. Tata* (New Delhi: Rupa, 2004), pp. 99–100.
7. Chattopadhyaya, 'The Idea of Planning in India', pp. 186–9; Benjamin Zachariah, *Developing India: An Intellectual and Social History c. 1930–1950* (New Delhi: Oxford University Press, 2005), pp. 99–109.
8. The best account is Robert Hildebrand, *Dumbarton Oaks: The Origins of the United Nations and the Search for Postwar Security* (Chapel Hill, NC: University of North Carolina Press, 1990).
9. Statement to the Press, 17 April 1945, *CWMG*, vol. 86, pp. 188–90.

10. Marika Sherwood, 'India at the Founding of the United Nations', *International Studies*, vol. 33, no. 4 (1996), pp. 408–12.

11. Manu Bhagavan, *The Peacemakers: India and the Quest for One World* (New Delhi: HarperCollins, 2012), p. 54.

12. For excellent new accounts, see Benn Steil, *The Battle of Bretton Woods: John Maynard Keynes, Harry Dexter White, and the Making of a New World Order* (Princeton: Princeton University Press, 2013); Eric Helleiner, *Forgotten Foundations of Bretton Woods: International Development and the Making of the Postwar Order* (Ithaca, NY: Cornell University Press, 2014).

13. Talk on the Bretton Woods Meetings, 3 October 1944, Subject File 43 (5), First Instalment, C. D. Deshmukh Papers, NMML.

14. Kurt Schuler and Andrew Rosenberg (eds.), *The Bretton Woods Transcripts* (New York: Center for Financial Stability, 2012), Kindle locations 1504–23, 1523–43.

15. Anand Chandavarkar, *Keynes and India: A Study in Economics and Biography* (London: Macmillan, 1989), p. 125.

16. S. L. N. Simha, *The Reserve Bank of India Volume 1: 1935–1951* (Bombay: Reserve Bank of India, 1970), pp. 431–3. Also see, C. D. Deshmukh, *The Course of My Life* (New Delhi: Orient Longman, 1974), p. 128.

17. Robert Skidelsky, *John Maynard Keynes, Volume III: Fighting for Freedom, 1937–1946* (New York: Viking, 2001), pp. 351–2.

18. Bakhtiar K. Dadbhoy, *Barons of Banking: Glimpses of Indian Banking History* (New Delhi: Random House India, 2013), p. 224.

19. For details, see *TP*, vol. 5; Penderel Moon (ed.), *Wavell: The Viceroy's Journal* (Oxford: Oxford University Press, 1973).

20. John Darwin, *Britain and Decolonisation: The Retreat from Empire in the Post-War World* (Basingstoke: Palgrave Macmillan, 1988), pp. 67–166; Anita Inder Singh, *The Limits of British Influence: South Asia and the Anglo-American Relationship, 1947–56* (New York: St. Martin's Press, 1993), pp. 16–21; R. J. Moore, *Escape from Empire: The Attlee Government and the Indian Problem* (Oxford: Clarendon Press, 1983), pp. 61–5.

21. Sanjoy Bhattacharya and Benjamin Zachariah, '"A Great Destiny": The British Colonial State and the Advertisement of Post-War Reconstruction in India, 1942–45', *South Asia Research*, vol. 19, no. 1 (1999), pp. 71–100.

22. Anirudh Deshpande, 'Hopes and Disillusionment: Recruitment, Demobilization and the Emergence of Discontent in the Indian Armed

Forces after the Second World War', *Indian Economic and Social History Review*, vol. 33 (1996), pp. 175–207.

23. Fortnightly Censor Summary, 2 June to 15 June 1943, L/P&J/12/655, AAC.

24. Malcolm Darling, *At Freedom's Door* (Oxford: Oxford University Press, 1949), p. 17.

25. 'Traitors or Heroes', TS memoir, f. 58, J. A. E. Heard Papers, LHCMA.

26. Report from Deputy Director of Public Relations, enclosed in Richard O'Connor to Auchinleck, 29 November 1945, Mace Papers, LHCMA.

27. My account draws on Daniel Marston, *The Indian Army and the End of the Raj* (Cambridge: Cambridge University Press, 2014), pp. 116–50.

28. Christopher Bayly and Tim Harper, *Forgotten Wars: The End of Britain's Asian Empire* (London: Allen Lane, 2007).

29. My account draws on Biswanath Bose, *RIN Mutiny, 1946* (Delhi: Northern Book Centre, 1988); Sumit Sarkar, *Modern India 1885–1947* (Delhi: Macmillan, 1983), pp. 363–6.

30. Anirudh Deshpande, 'Sailors and Crowds: Popular Protests in Karachi, 1946', *Indian Economic and Social History Review*, vol. 26 (1989), pp. 1–28.

31. Extracts from India Command Fortnightly Security Intelligence Summary, 1 and 15 March 1946, Tuker Papers, IWM.

32. S. M. Nanda, *The Man Who Bombed Karachi* (New Delhi: Harper-Collins, 2004), p. 54.

33. For details, see *TP*, vol. 6. Also see Anita Inder Singh, *The Origins of the Partition of India, 1936–1947* (New Delhi: Oxford University Press, 1987); Ayesha Jalal, *The Sole Spokesman: Jinnah, the Muslim League and the Demand for Pakistan* (Cambridge: Cambridge University Press, 1985).

34. Cf. Venkat Dhulipala, *Creating a New Medina: State Power, Islam and the Quest for Pakistan in Late Colonial North India* (Cambridge: Cambridge University Press, 2014).

35. Jalal, *Sole Spokesman*.

36. Cited in Moore, *Escape from Empire*, p. 183.

37. *Indian Labour Yearbook 1946* (Delhi: Government of India, 1948), p. 125.

38. See the excellent survey in Sekhar Bandyopadhyay, *From Plassey to Partition: A History of Modern India* (Hyderabad: Orient Longman, 2004).

39. Asok Majumdar, *Peasant Protest in Indian Politics: Tebhaga Movement in Bengal 1946–1950* (Delhi: South Asia Books, 1993); D. N.

Dhanagare, 'Peasant Protest and Politics: The Tebhaga Movement in Bengal (India), 1946–47', *Journal of Peasant Studies*, vol. 3, no. 3 (1976).

EPILOGUE

1. Note, 5 September 1946, *SWJN*, second series, vol. 1, pp. 438–42.
2. Ibid., p. 441.
3. Daniel Marston, *The Indian Army and the End of the Raj* (Cambridge: Cambridge University Press, 2014), pp. 242–7.
4. Ian Talbot, *Khizr Tiwana: The Punjab Unionist Party and the Partition of India* (Karachi: Oxford University Press, 2002).
5. Joya Chatterji, *Bengal Divided: Hindu Communalism and Partition 1932–1947* (Cambridge: Cambridge University Press, 1995).
6. Figures from P. S. Lokanathan, *India's Post-War Reconstruction and Its International Aspects* (New Delhi: Indian Council of World Affairs, 1946), p. 20.
7. Saumitra Jha and Steven Wilkinson, 'Does Combat Experience Foster Organizational Skill? Evidence from Ethnic Cleansing during the Partition of South Asia', *American Political Science Review*, vol. 106, no. 4 (2012), pp. 883–907 (Morrison quote on p. 905).
8. Srinath Raghavan, *War and Peace in Modern India* (London: Palgrave Macmillan, 2010).
9. On the use of the sterling balances, see Alfred Martin Wainwright, 'The Role of South Asia in British Strategic Policy, 1939–50', PhD thesis, University of Wisconsin–Madison, 1989, pp. 469–86.
10. Cf. Christopher Bayly and Tim Harper, *Forgotten Wars: The End of Britain's Asian Empire* (London: Allen Lane, 2007).

Index

Page references in *italic* indicate figures, tables and maps. These are also listed in full after the Contents.

SRINATH RAGHAVAN is a senior fellow at the Centre for Policy Research. The author of *1971: A Global History of the Creation of Bangladesh*, he lives in New Delhi, India.